CAMBRIDGE LIBRARY COLLECTION

Books of enduring scholarly value

Literary Studies

This series provides a high-quality selection of early printings of literary works, textual editions, anthologies and literary criticism which are of lasting scholarly interest. Ranging from Old English to Shakespeare to early twentieth-century work from around the world, these books offer a valuable resource for scholars in reception history, textual editing, and literary studies.

A Late Eighth-Century Latin–Anglo-Saxon Glossary

Prior to his 1890 publication of the Corpus Christi Latin–Old English MS, also reissued in this series, Jan Hendrik Hessels (1836–1926) had begun transcribing this equally important text, of which his edition was published in 1906. (He explains the delay by referring to 'work of another nature': his monumental edition of the archive of the Dutch Church in London (1887–1897), also now available in the Cambridge Library Collection.) Hessels again provides a thorough introduction, including a detailed physical description of the manuscript alongside its history, provenance, and a wealth of other information. The work contains extracts from various texts and treatises, and Hessels' cross-references to other glossaries demonstrate the importance of the Leiden MS for gloss-literature, and will be of use to philologists, scholars of Old English and medieval Latin, and historians of the medieval period.

T0381863

Cambridge University Press has long been a pioneer in the reissuing of out-of-print titles from its own backlist, producing digital reprints of books that are still sought after by scholars and students but could not be reprinted economically using traditional technology. The Cambridge Library Collection extends this activity to a wider range of books which are still of importance to researchers and professionals, either for the source material they contain, or as landmarks in the history of their academic discipline.

Drawing from the world-renowned collections in the Cambridge University Library, and guided by the advice of experts in each subject area, Cambridge University Press is using state-of-the-art scanning machines in its own Printing House to capture the content of each book selected for inclusion. The files are processed to give a consistently clear, crisp image, and the books finished to the high quality standard for which the Press is recognised around the world. The latest print-on-demand technology ensures that the books will remain available indefinitely, and that orders for single or multiple copies can quickly be supplied.

The Cambridge Library Collection will bring back to life books of enduring scholarly value (including out-of-copyright works originally issued by other publishers) across a wide range of disciplines in the humanities and social sciences and in science and technology.

A Late Eighth-Century Latin–Anglo-Saxon Glossary

Preserved in the Library of the Leiden University

Edited by Jan Hendrik Hessels

CAMBRIDGE
UNIVERSITY PRESS

CAMBRIDGE UNIVERSITY PRESS

Cambridge, New York, Melbourne, Madrid, Cape Town,
Singapore, São Paolo, Delhi, Tokyo, Mexico City

Published in the United States of America by Cambridge University Press, New York

www.cambridge.org
Information on this title: www.cambridge.org/9781108029094

This edition first published 1906
This digitally printed version 2011

ISBN 978-1-108-02909-4 Paperback

A

LATIN-ANGLO-SAXON GLOSSARY

CAMBRIDGE UNIVERSITY PRESS WAREHOUSE,
C. F. CLAY, MANAGER.
London: FETTER LANE, E.C.
Glasgow: 50, WELLINGTON STREET.

Leipzig: F. A. BROCKHAUS.
New York: G. P. PUTNAM'S SONS.
Bombay and Calcutta: MACMILLAN AND CO.,

A
LATE EIGHTH-CENTURY
LATIN-ANGLO-SAXON GLOSSARY

PRESERVED IN THE LIBRARY OF

THE LEIDEN UNIVERSITY

(MS. VOSS. Q° LAT. N°. 69)

EDITED BY

JOHN HENRY HESSELS, M.A.,

ST JOHN'S COLLEGE, CAMBRIDGE.

CAMBRIDGE:
AT THE UNIVERSITY PRESS
1906

TABLE OF CONTENTS.

PAGE

INTRODUCTION . . . . vii—lvii

Prefatory remarks (§§ 1, 2).

Plan of the present edition (§§ 3, 3ᵃ).

Description of the MS.; *its contents* (§§ 4—6).

Age, handwriting and place of origin of the MS. (§§ 7—7ʲ).

The whereabouts of, and other details connected with the MS. after leaving St. Gallen (§§ 8—10).

Further description of the MS. (§§ 11—23).

Number of *leaves* (§ 11); *ruling* and *number of lines* (§ 12); its *scribes* (§ 13).

Contractions (§ 14); *different forms* of letters (§ 15); *ligatures* (§ 16); *Capitals* (§ 17); *Greek* letters (§ 18); *Illustration* (§ 19); *Numerals* (§ 20); *Punctuation* (§ 21); *Signs of reference* (§ 22).

Corrections (§ 23[a]); *division* of words, syllables, glosses (§ 23[b]); *insertions* (§ 23[c]); *marking* words or glosses by strokes and an insulated V (§ 23[d]); *omissions* (§ 23[e]); *signatures* (§ 23[f]); *signs* (§ 23[g]); *spots* (§ 23[h]); *strokes* (§ 23[i]); *transposition* (§ 23[k]); *uncertain words* (§ 23[l]); *underlining* (§ 23[m]); *vacant spaces* (§ 23[n]); *wrong letters* (§ 23[o]).

BIBLIOGRAPHY OF THE GLOSSARY, pp. xxxvii—lvii.

A. *Headings* or *Titles* of the Chapters, pp. xxxvii—xli.

B. *Sources* from whence the lemmata (and some of the interpretations) are excerpted.—*Books* and *MSS.* used and consulted in tracing the lemmata to their sources.—*Abbreviations* employed in the references, quotations, &c. (chiefly in the Latin Index), pp. xli—lvii.

TEXT OF THE GLOSSARY . . . . 1—50

INDEXES

I. *Latin* Index . . . . 51—217

II. Index of *Latin Numerals* expressed by Roman Signs . 217, 218

III. *Greek* Index . . . . 218—221

IV. *Hebrew* Index 221

V. *Germanic*, but chiefly *A.-S.* Index . . . . . . 222—239

CORRIGENDA, ADDENDA . . . . 239—241

PHOTOGRAPHIC PLATE REPRESENTING FOL. 26, AND (THE GREATEST PART OF) FOL. 27[aa] . . . . *At end*

INTRODUCTION.

§ 1. In the preface to my edition of the *Corpus Glossary*, published in 1890* by the Syndics of the Cambridge University Press, I stated, on pp. XL, XLIV etc., that already in 1885 I had made a transcript of the kindred Glossary preserved in a MS. of the Leiden University Library (Voss. Q°. Lat. No. 69), with the view of publishing it as a companion volume to the Corpus Glossary. But the editing of the latter had caused me such difficulties and labour that I shrunk from immediately taking the Leiden Glossary in hand, especially as work of another nature left me little time for a task which would not be easy and would require the editor's undivided attention.

§ 2. Meantime much valuable material on glosses continued to be published in the *Archiv für Latein. Lexicographie*, in the great works of Steinmeyer and Sievers (*Althochdeutsche Glossen*), Goetz (*Corpus Glossariorum Latinorum*) &c. So that, when Prof. Henry Jackson, who takes a keen interest in studies of this kind, expressed to me, in June 1902, his wish to see the Leiden Glossary published, and the Syndics of the University Press, after carefully considering my suggestions for the edition, consented to bear the expense involved in the publication of a book of this abstruse nature, which is not likely to be remunerative, I felt sufficiently encouraged to undertake the editing. On my application, Dr S. de Vries, the Leiden University Librarian, kindly sent the MS. again to Cambridge to enable me to collate it with my transcript, which I had been unable to do in 1885, because the MS. had unexpectedly to be returned, after Dr du Rieu, the late Librarian, had left it with me for a long time.

Plan of the present edition.

§ 3. The present edition is an exact reproduction, as far as type could make it, of the Latin-Anglo-Saxon Glossary preserved on the pages 20—36 (see below § 6) of the above-mentioned Leiden MS., the notes at the foot of the pages recording nothing but the graphic peculiarities and scribal alterations and emendations noticed in the MS.

* An Eighth-Century Latin-Anglo-Saxon Glossary, preserved in the Library of Corpus Christi College, Cambridge (MS. No. 144), edited by J. H. Hessels. Cambridge, at the University Press, 1890. 8°.

After this *text* follows (on p. 51) the *First Index* (*Latin*), which is, in reality, a complete repetition of every one of the Glosses in *alphabetical* order, and embodies all *editorial* emendations, corrections, elucidations of, or suggestions for emending, the Glosses. The system adopted for the compilation of this Index, may be seen from the first three or four articles: (*a*) under *a* are given the words in which *a* represents some other letter, or combination of letters, or from which *a* is omitted. So also under *b*, *c* and all the other letters of the alphabet. In this way I have endeavoured to compile for this Glossary tables similar to those printed on pp. XXI to XXXIX (§§ 39—60) of my Introduction to the *Corpus Glossary**. (β) the second *a*, or *preposition*, records all the places where it may be found in the text. (γ) the *lemmata* are printed in *Clarendon* or *black* type, ex. gr. **aabita** (3rd article of the Index); the figures after this lemma and the Glossator's *interpretation* or *gloss* on the lemma, refer to the *text* (see p. 5[a]; *Chapter* II, *gloss* 87); then follows, between ( ), the source from whence the lemma has been extracted, with a short quotation † from this source showing the *lemma* in its context. After this follow editorial observations wherever necessary.

The *Second Index* (p. 217) records the *Latin Numerals* expressed by the Glossator in *Roman signs*; the *Third Index* (p. 218) registers the *Greek* words *quoted* or *referred to* in the I. or *Latin* Index. These Greek words are printed exactly as they are quoted. The *Fourth Index* (p. 221) registers the *Hebrew* words also *quoted* or *referred to* in the I. or *Latin* Index; while the *Fifth Index* (p. 222) is a register of all the *Anglo-Saxon* or other *Germanic* words which either occur in the Glossary (and then printed in *Clarendon* or *black* type) itself, or have been quoted from other Glossaries or other works in the I. or *Latin* Index by way of explanation or elucidation.

§ 3[a]. The affinity, which, in many instances, suggests identity of sources, between certain parts of the Leiden Glossary, and the *Corpus*, *Epinal*, and (First) *Erfurt* Glossaries has been pointed out in the I. (*Latin*) Index under the various glosses; the *identity* of Glosses being indicated

* Here and there I have, no doubt, suggested spellings or emendations, which would not agree with the spellings of the post-classical MSS. with which our Glossary must be classed. For instance, under *e* I print (li. 34) manichei (manich*ae*i), which means, not that the latter spelling is to be substituted for the former, but that the classical form has *ae*; see also under *h* (*h*arena) &c. Again, under *f* I give a collection of words which have *f* for *ph* (= φ), not as a novelty, but as a help for studies of this kind.

† Without these quotations it would not always be easy to realise the meaning of certain expressions or the grammatical forms of words. Ex. gr. in Ch. xv. 40 *oraculum* is explained by two accusatives; the quotation in the Lat. Index (p. 159[b]) from Ezech. shows that this is done because *oraculum* is used there in the accus. On the other hand the Glossator turned the gen. *electri* of Ezech. I. 4 into *electrum*.

by the symbol=*. When there is merely *similarity* the word conf. (cf.) is used. These references will show the importance of the present Glossary for the gloss-literature, especially for the study of the Corp., Ep. and Erf. Glossaries.

Description of the MS.; its contents &c.

§ 4. The Leiden Manuscript, in its present condition, consists of 52 small folio vellum leaves, besides 2 blank paper leaves (numbered 50 and 51, and bound between the vellum leaves 49 and 52), all consecutively numbered 1 to 54, by a modern hand, and divided into 8 quires or gatherings $a^6bcdefgh^8$; which would have made 62 leaves, if the last three leaves of quire *c*, the last four of quire *g*, and the first of quire *h* had not been cut away.

§ 5. These 52 leaves are bound in a simple, comparatively modern, red paper binding, measuring, including the margins of the binding, $10\frac{1}{4}$ inches or 261 mm. in height, and (slightly more than) $6\frac{1}{2}$ inches or 168 mm. in breadth. Without reckoning the binding, the vellum leaves measure $9\frac{7}{8}$ inches or 250 mm. in height (except the first 6 leaves which are a little shorter, and measure $9\frac{5}{8}$ inches or 246 mm.), and $6\frac{5}{16}$ inches or 161 mm. in breadth.

§ 6. *Contents*† of the MS.: Fol. 1ª—4ª line 3 (*the Sibylline prophecies*) INCIPIT‡ PRÆFATIO IN LIBRO SIBILLĘ; Fol. 4ª li. 4—4ª li. 27 (*a prayer*) [T]IBI igitur xpiste cum patre spirituque sancto gloria; Fol. 4ª li. 28—4ᵇ li. 29 (*a sermon*) [A]UDITE itaque karissimi fratres et filii; Fol. 4ᵇ li. 30—6ª li. 1 HVCVSQ. ATHANASIVS (*on an image*: hycona *of Christ*) [E]A TEMPESTATE apud eandem ciuitatem; 6ª li. 2—li. 17 (*another fragment of*

* That the affinity or similarity does not, in all cases, amount to identity, is, perhaps, owing to alterations or modifications on the part of one or more of the Glossators or copyists. Even the Leiden MS. does, perhaps, not always represent that original Glossary from which also parts of the Corpus, Epinal and Erfurt are derived, though, for its greatest part, it stands on an earlier stage than the latter three. We meet, here and there, with lemmata in the present Glossary, the corruption of which makes it clear that the Corp., Ep. and Erf. Glossaries could not have been copied from it, though they all point to the same source. For instance, the corrupt *amopaga* of Leiden xxxv. 130 appears correctly as *ariopagita* in Ep. and Ef., and partly corrupt as *aripagita* in Cp. Again, Leiden xxxv. 93 has *moluerunt* for *inoleuerant*, whereas Cp. and Ef. have *ioluerunt*, and Ep. *ioluerunt*, corrected from *ioloerunt*.

† See also *Catal. Bibliothecae Univers. Lugd.-Batavae* (Aº 1716, p. 382); Steinmeyer (*Althochd. Glossen*, IV. 481 sqq.; Paul v. Winterfeld in *Neues Archiv der Gesellsch. f. ält. d. Geschichtsk.* XXV. 379 sqq.). A facsimile of its Fol. 45ª (which is unconnected with our Glossary) is given in Vol. I. p. 256 of *Sitzungsber. der philos.-philol. und hist. Cl. der k. bayr. Akad. der Wissensch. zu München*, 1898, as appendix to a treatise by Karl Rück, *Die Naturalis Historia des Plinius im Mittelalter*.

‡ All the headings of the Chapters are in rustic capitals.

a sermon) [C]ETERA quę secuntur; 6^{a} li. 17—6^{b} li. 30 (*Fragment of the story of the linen cloth sent by Christ to King Abgar; also the letter of King Abgar to Christ, and the letter of Christ to King Abgar*) INCIPIT TRACTATVS EX LIBRO SIRORVM TRANSLATVS IN LATINVM A DOMNO SMIRA ARCHIATRALI DE QVODAM LINTEO DIVINITVS TRANSFORMATO; QVI IN HAC SOLLEMPNITATE OPTIME CONGRVIT. [R]EDEMPTOR igitur et saluator noster; 7^{a} *blank*; 7^{ba} [here the pages begin to be divided into 2 columns, and the headings of the Chapters written in rustic capitals, mixed, here and there, with uncials]—7^{bb} li. 25 INCIPIT OPVS FVRTVNATI IN LAVDEM SANCTAE MARIAE (cf. Mon. Germ. Auct. antiq. IV. 371); 7^{bb} li. 26—8^{ba} li. 16 HAEC EST PRAEFATIO DE IHESV XPISTO DOMINO INTER VESPASIANVM ET TITVM QVOMODO VINDICAVERVNT XPISTVM; 8^{ba} li. 17—9^{ab} li. 9 (*Poems*) VERSVS DE ASIA ET DE VNIVERSI MVNDI ROTA (cf. Pertz in *Abhandl. der Berl. Akad.*, 1845, 253 sqq.); 9^{ab} li. 9—9^{ba} li. 26 DE SEX ĘTATIBVS MVNDI (cf. E. Dümmler, in *Zeitschr. für deutsch. Alt.* XXII. 423); 9^{ba} li. 27—35, and 9^{bb} li. 1—25 blank; 9^{bb} li. 26—10^{ab} li. 16 INCIPIT UERSVS DE ADUENTV DOMINI (cf. Duméril, *Poésies inédites*, 280); 10^{ab} li. 17—10^{ba} li. 13 ITEM VERSUS DE IHESU DOMINO XPISTO; 10^{ba} li. 14—35, and 10^{bb} li. 1—12 blank; 10^{bb} li. 13—12^{ba} li. 25 ITEM UERSVS DE IHESU CHRISTO DOMINO (*Mon. Germ.*, Poetae Lat. II. 252); 12^{ba} DE BONE (sic) SACERDOTE (*Mon. Germ.*, Poetae Lat. I. 79); 13^{ab} De* malo sacerdote (*ibid.* I. 81); 13^{ba} De diuite et paupero Lazaro (E. Dümmler, in *Zeitschr. f. d. Alt.* XXIII. 271; P. v. Winterfeld, *l.c.* p. 392 sqq.); 13^{bb} Incipit ymnus ad gallicantum *and other hymns of Prudentius till* Hymnus in honore Quirini, ending 17^{bb}; 18^{a} Versus Damasi episcopi Vrbis Romae (De S. Paulo ap.; see Migne, *P.L.* XIII. 379); 18^{ba} (no heading) Continet hęc ara reliquis beati gregorii pape; Ephitafium sancti Gregorii Pape urbis Romae; 18^{bb} Item eiusdem sancti Gregorii Pape; In icona Sancti Petri hii duo sunt uersi; In Basilica sancti Pauli apostoli Romae; In uelo quodam Chintilane rege Rome dictum est (Riese, 494); Ephitafium papae Damasi quod sibi edidit ipse (Migne XIII. 408); 19^{aa} Ephitafium beatae Monnice genetricis Sancti Agustini (Riese, 670); 19^{ab} Uersus in avla ecclesie in aqvis palatio (*Mon. G.*, Poetae Lat. I. 432); 19^{ba} Oratio Eugenii Tolletane sedis episcopi; Rex deus inmensi quo constat machina mundi &c. (Migne, *P. L.* LXXXVII. 359).

Foll. 20^{aa}—36^{aa} *the present Glossary* (see further below, §§ 11, 12 &c.).

Foll. 36^{ab}—46^{ab}† *Extracts from various authors and treatises* (for which see Steinmeyer, *l.c.*, p. 482 sq.); Fol. 46^{ba}—47^{bb} (in a hand of the end of the 9th cent.) Letter to Alcuin on Quadragesima (Dilectissimo

* The headings of the Chapters are still all in rustic capitals, though no longer printed here in capitals.

† Foll. 39^{b}, second col. to 46^{a} second col., contain the excerpts from Pliny's *Nat. Hist.*, published by Karl Rück in *Sitzungsberichte* mentioned above, p. ix, note †.

magistro nobisque cum amore nominando Albino abbati &c.; cf. Jaffé, *Bibl.* VI. 403); Fol. 48[a]—48[b] (in a hand of the XIth cent.) *fragment* (leaf 1 of quire *h* has been cut away) *of a poem on the martyrdom of S. Fides* (Dümmler, in *Neues Arch. für ältere d. Geschichtsk.*, X. 336 sq.; Winterfeld, *ibid.* XXIII. 741 sq.); Fol. 49[a]—49[b] (in a hand of the XIth cent.) *interpretations of Latin words*; Foll. 50 and 51 blank paper leaves; Fol. 52[a] Fragment of a vellum leaf, on the recto of which is written *a Charter of the Monastery of St. Gallen of* A.D. 1262*; Fol. 53[a] to end of Fol. 53[b] (in a hand of the XII. or XIII. cent.) *The seven wonders of the world*; Fol. 54[a], by a first hand, *a Catalogue of the Abbats of St. Gallen till Vdalricus* (A.D. 1277), and continued, by another hand, till "Franciscus *superstes*" Anno MDXXI° (see *S. Galler Mitteil.* XI. 135 sq.; Holder-Egger in *Mon. Germ.*, SS. XIII. 326 sqq.); Fol. 54[b], in a hand of the 16th cent., five lines recording: *Censuales monasterij S. Galli in Turgoew, Madach* &c.

§ 7. *Age, handwriting* and *place of origin of the MS.* The accompanying facsimile (which represents the verso of Fol. 26† in natural size, and exhibits the *two hands* that wrote the Glossary; see below § 13) shows that it was written (from Fol. 7 to the end of Fol. 46 recto) at a time when the Roman cursive, the Lombardic and the Merovingian minuscules, after having done duty, side by side, for a long period, were all merging, or had already merged into one kind of writing which is now called *insular* (*West-Frankish*).

§ 7[a]. This insular writing, chiefly formed by natives (Scottish or Irish monks) of the British Isles, who flocked to the monasteries of West-Frankland (Salzburg, Fulda, Würzburg, St. Gallen, Lorsch &c.), shows, besides the chief characteristics‡ of the three minuscules which it supplanted, also some traces§ of the Hiberno-Saxon handwritings of the

* On the verso, a hand of the 16th cent. has written "An. Christi 343," and another hand of the same cent. "Von der geburt Christi biss vff S. Othmarij ist 720 Jar. Von Sant Othmarii biss vff Abt Francisci todt ist 809 Jar. So man die zwo zalen zu samen thut bringt sij 1529 Jar vnd ist recht."

† The photographer having, in the course of his work, accidentally taken also a portion of the first column of Fol. 27, though reduced in size, it was not obliterated from the plate, since it will, no doubt, be found as helpful in judging of the writing of the MS. as the full-sized page.

‡ To point out these characteristics would require a number of special types, which it was not considered advisable to procure for this work. They may be seen, still in their unmixed condition, in *The Palaeographical Society*, Ser. II. pl. 51—53 (*Roman cursive*, 7th cent.), pl. 32 (*Rom. cursive*, late 7th cent.), 59 (*Rom. curs.*, 7th or 8th cent.), 11 (*Merovingian*, 7th cent.), 8 and 9 (*Lombardic*, 8th cent.). Plate 4 of Chroust's 5th part gives a more or less stately Merovingian bookhand of the beginning of the 8th cent., and the capital A[s] seen on this plate closely resemble those of our MS.

§ These traces especially enable us to distinguish this writing from a similar hand employed, about the same time, in Upper Italy (Bobbio).

8th cent., especially in its contractions (see below § 14) and punctuation (see below § 21). After a comparatively brief career, however, it was, towards the latter end of the 8th, and the early years of the 9th cent., superseded, in its turn, by the Caroline minuscule*, which, however, preserved several of the peculiarities of the writing which it replaced.

§ 7[b]. On examining the handwritings of the first 25 years of the 9th cent., figured in *The Palaeographical Society*, Ser. I. pl. 185 (a modified and rounded Lombardic minuscule of c. A.D. 800), pl. 45 (c. A.D. 804—820), pl. 122 (A.D. 821), pl. 123 (A.D. 823); and in Chroust's *Monumenta Palaeogr.*, Pt. V pl. 5 (A.D. 800), pl. 6 (c. A.D. 800—825), Pt. VII pl. 4 (c. A.D. 802—804), Pt. I pl. 1 and 2 (A.D. 818), pl. 3 (c. A.D. 822), Pt. II pl. 1 (after A.D. 823), it will be found that all these writings, though still showing many peculiarities of the writing of the Leiden Glossary, exhibit the Caroline minuscule either fully developed, or very nearly so. And as this development may be observed, even in its best form, as early as A.D. 781 (cf. Steffens, *Latein. Paläogr.*, pl. 35, and pl. 43 representing a Carol. min. of the beginning of the 9th cent.), it follows that we must go back to a period before A.D. 800 to fix the approximate date of the present Glossary.

§ 7[c]. Plate 35 of *The Palaeogr. Society*, Ser. II, exhibits a *late 8th century* hand, in the transitional style between Merovingian and Caroline, but it has already more of the latter than of the former. Decisive, however, for fixing the approximate date of the Glossary, are pl. 31 of Steffens' *Latein. Paläogr.*, which exhibits an attestation of Gundohinus, written, A.D. 754, in half cursive minuscules; pl. 32 a St. Gallen charter dated A.D. 757; pl. 33 showing (*a*) a document of Winithar of St. Gallen circa A.D. 761; (*b*) the Lord's Prayer in German, end of the 8th cent.; (*c*) a St. Gallen Charter of A.D. 782; pl. 40 a St Gallen Charter of A.D. 798 (792);—pl. 184 of *The Palaeogr. Soc.*, Ser. I, giving a page of a *Lex Salica* MS. written at St Gallen, in A.D. 794, in Lombardic minuscules mixed with several of the characteristics of the writing of the present Glossary;—three facsimiles in Vol. II of the *Scriptt. Rerum Merov.* (*Monum. Germ. Hist.*, 4° coll.), taken from Cod. Lugd. Voss. quarto, No. 5, and Cod. Vatic. bibl. Christ. reg. No. 713, both ascribed to VIII/IXth cent., showing the very same hand as the Glossary;—Chroust's Pt. XI pl. 5 A.D. 795, 796, in the Monastery of Lorsch; *ibid.* pl. 6 and 7 the Rado Bible, ca. A.D. 790—808 in North. France; Pt. VII, pl. 3[c] Alcuin Letters, A.D. 798 or soon after, by a scribe who accompanied Bishop Arns of Salzburg on his travels to Rome.

§ 7[d]. Among all these writings, dating from A.D. 754 to 800, especially among those executed at *St. Gallen*, the Leiden Glossary takes a natural

* Except in legal documents.

place, whereas among the handwritings of the beginning of the 9th century, it looks a comparative stranger. Hence we have, as far as I can see, no choice but to ascribe the Glossary to the *latter end*, say the *last decade, of the 8th century*, and regard *St. Gallen* as the place where it was written. It is difficult to say whether the writer was an Irishman or a South German; several glosses are interpreted by O.H.G. words, but the scribe may have found them in the MS. which he copied*.

§ 7[c]. Other circumstances point to *St. Gallen* as the birthplace of the MS., and to its being, moreover, a copy from some earlier Glossary, which, in its turn, may be supposed to have been preserved, if not actually written or compiled, in the Monastery there. First of all, several of the Leiden glosses occur likewise in glossaries still preserved at St. Gallen, with occasionally slight modifications only. For instance, Hattemer (*Denkmahle des Mittelalters*, I. 237) records from a St. Gallen MS. (1395, 9th cent.) "*murenula* (De prologo Job), piscis similis anguillae marinae sed grossior, i.e. lantprida," which reads in Leiden: "*murenula*, piscis similis anguile marinus sed grossior." On the same page Hattemer quotes from the same MS. (from Job) "*Clarea*, lapides modici, i.e. chisilinga"; the Leiden MS. has "*Glarea*, lapides modici." The same St. Gallen MS. has (De libro Tobiae) "*Brancicæ*, cheuun"; the Leiden MS. *Brantie*, chyun.

§ 7[f]. The similarity of the Leiden Glosses to those of the St. Gallen MS. 299 (Hattemer, *l.c.* p. 238 sqq.) is still more pronounced. From Hester the latter has (on p. 241) *tenta*, giteid; *aeri*, hasye; *iacinthinis*, idest suidur haye; *lectuli aurei*, berianbed gildi bilegid i.e. tragabetti mit goldo bilegit; *purpura*, uilucbæsu; *coccus*, uurumbæsu cornvurma; *rubeum*, yretebæsu; the Leiden MS.: *tenda*, trabus gezelt; *aeri*, haue; *iacyntini*, syitor heuuin; *lecti aurei*, berian beed deauratum; *purpura*, uuylocbaso; *coccus*, uuyrmbaso; *rubeum*, uuretbaso.

§ 7[g]. These similarities and identities † suggest that there was, or had been, at St. Gallen, a Glossary or several Glossaries (perhaps all Latin-Latin), still in the first stage of their existence, that is, arranged under

* The above remarks regarding *the age* &c. of the MS., refer exclusively to the handwriting of the leaves 7 to 46 which include the Glossary (see above § 6). But the writing of the first 6 leaves, which form a quire by themselves (see above §§ 4 and 6), differs entirely from that of the rest of the MS. volume, though it points to the same time and the same locality. As neither the contents (described above § 6) nor the writing of these leaves come within the scope of this work, I need not say more than that the writing is also insular West-Frankish, similar to that figured on Chroust's pl. 3[b] Pt. VII (Alcuin Letters, A.D. 798), except that it has not the open *a*, though it shows the uncial *N* at the commencement of a word in the body of a sentence.

† Many more of the same kind could be quoted from MSS. preserved in other Swiss Libraries (Basel, Bern, Einsiedeln, Engelberg, and at Carlsruhe, Erfurt, Munich &c.), all described and published by Steinmeyer and Sievers.

the titles of the books from which, in an unalphabetical order, the difficult and out-of-the-way words with their interpretations had been excerpted, and that from this Glossary, or these Glossaries, various other Glossaries were compiled, perhaps by different persons of different nationalities; some of the compilers omitting all such lemmata with their interpretations which they considered unsuitable to their purpose, others substituting vernacular (O.H.G., A.S., or other dialects) interpretations for the Latin ones*.

§ 7[h]. At the end of the MS., moreover, there are three documents relating to the St. Gallen monastery, although these documents, being of a much later date than the other portions of the MS., may have been added to it at any time during or after the 13th century.

§ 7[i]. Further it seems probable that the Leiden MS., before it came into the possession of Isaac Vossius, was in the Library of St. Gallen, and that there it became known to Melch Goldast, who had worked in that Library, and resided for a long time in Switzerland. In his *Paraeneticorum Veterum* Pars I, published in 1604 (Insulae, 4°), he refers to various glosses occurring in the Leiden Glossary, as, p. 81 Glossae anonymae: *Sarabaite* &c. (II. 161); p. 88 Interpretatio sermonum de Regulis: *suggectionem* (sic!) &c. (II. 167); p. 93 Gloss. vet.: *Carus*, nomen hominis auari (!) &c. (XLIII. 19); p. 100 Glossae in Histor. Eccles.: *exitiali* &c. (IV. 29); p. 100 in Cassianum: *letheo* &c. (XXXIV. 2); p. 114 Gloss. vett.: *grauitas* &c. (II. 83); p. 118 Gloss. in Histor. Eccles.: *affecit* &c. (IV. 118); p. 123 Glossae vett. in Esdram: *cratera* &c. (XXIII. 7); p. 123 in Clementem: *climacteras* &c. (XXXVIII. 25); p. 126 Gloss. vett. in Esdram: *memores salis* &c. (XXIII. 12); p. 131 Gloss. vet.: *Kyrieleison* &c. (II. 98); p. 136 Gloss. vett. in Lib. Rotarum: *faria* &c. (XXVII. 2); p. 235 Interpretatio sermonum de Regul.: *regula* &c. (II. 146); p. 241 id.: *acidiosus* &c. (II. 9); p. 423 Gloss. vett.: *talpa* &c. (XLVII. 79); p. 430 Glossae in Dialogorum Gregorii: *fledomum* &c. (XXXIX. 6); and three others which cannot be traced, as p. 39: Gloss. vett.: *nocentia*, culpa, reatus; Eædem: *noxia*, sententia, noxa (see II. 117); p. 85: *alternandis*, alternis vicibus (see XL. 5 alternandis, inuicem).

* In this way we may, perhaps, explain why, for instance, some glossaries have glosses to all, or nearly all, the parts of the Bible, whereas others (ex. gr. the Cambridge MS. Kk. 4. 6, wholly Latin-Latin; the Leiden MS. Voss. 69, partly Latin-Latin, partly Latin-A. Sax.) begin at Paralipomenon; or, why in some of these kindred glossaries, the lemmata extracted from some books of the Bible, are all, or nearly all, the same in the various MSS., but have Latin interpretations in some cases, and Germanic (in different dialects) interpretations in others. A MS., which seems to have been copied from a source similar to that of Leiden, but has none of the A. S. Glosses, is in the Ambrosian Library at Milan (Cod. Ambrosian. M 79 sup. Saec. XII. fol. 124—); a specimen of it is published by Goetz, *Corp. Glossar. Lat.* v. pp. 425—431. Another is mentioned by Glogger as being in the Bern Town Library (2° 258).

The whereabouts of, and other details connected with, the MS. *after leaving St. Gallen.*

§ 8. Isaac Vossius is known to have gone in 1641 on a tour through France, Italy, Switzerland &c., and to have returned to Leiden, after an absence of about five years, with great treasures of MSS., and it is possible that among them was the MS. now known as Voss. Lat. 69, which contains the present Glossary.

§ 8[a]. In 1649, on the invitation of Queen Christina, Vossius went to Stockholm to teach her Greek, and to collect a royal library, for which purpose he sold her his father's library for twenty thousand florins, reserving to himself its superintendence. He withdrew from Sweden in 1652, and Catteau-Calleville (*Histoire de Christine*, 1815, I. 330), without adducing any evidence, accuses him of having carried off "rich but scandalous spoils" from the royal library.

§ 8[b]. In 1655, when Vossius may be supposed to have been in possession of the Leiden MS., Franc. Junius, jun., published at Amsterdam his *Observationes in Willerami Abbatis Francicam Paraphrasin Cantici Canticorum* (8°). In this work he often alludes to Glossaria A, B, C, D, without, apparently, making any mention of Vossius or of a Glossarium E, or any other Glossaria marked with letters of the alphabet.

But ten years later he published (Dordrecht, 1665, 4°) his *Quatuor D. N. Jesu Christi Euangeliorum Versiones perantiquae duae...*, and in the *Gothicum Glossarium*, which he added to this work, makes references to, or extracts from 13 Glossaria marked A to N, which he says, on fol. 12[a] (***4) of his preface, were all *copied* from, or forming part of, the Library "propinqui mei Vossii" *.

§ 8[c]. In 1670 Vossius came to reside in England, was presented by King Charles II to a vacant prebend in the royal Chapel of Windsor in 1673, and died 21 February 1689 in London.

He bequeathed his Library to the two children (Gerard Jan, Councillor of Flanders, at Middelburg, and his sister Aafje) of his brother Matthæus, who first negociated † with the Oxford University, but declined the latter's offer, and, by the intervention of Van Beverningh, one of the Curators of the Leiden University, offered the library to this Institution for the same price (33,000 Guilders = £3000) that Oxford had offered.

The Leiden Academy effected the purchase, and 34 boxes (five of

* In the text he mentions more Glossaries, ex. gr. Gloss. R (pp. 80, 102, 190).

† See *R. Bentleii et doct. vir. Epistolae*, ed. F. T. Friedeman (1825), p. 152 sqq.

which contained the manuscripts) were delivered to Van Citters, the Dutch Ambassador at London, from whence they were taken by a Dutch man-of-war to Texel, and thence to Leiden, where the whole arrived in October 1690*.

§ 9. The copies or *apographa* made by Junius (see above § 8[b]), were all in the Bodleian Library† in 1694‡ when Frid. Rostgaard made a copy of them, which in Erasm. Nyerup's time was preserved in the Royal Library at Copenhagen (see pp. xxv, xxvi of his *Symbolae ad Literaturam Teut. ant. ex Codd. manu exaratis, qui Hauniæ asservantur*, Hauniae, 1787, 4°). In 1697 they are described as *Juniana* 116, 117 on p. 255 of the *Catal. Mstorum Angliae et Hiberniae* (Oxon. fol.), and again in 1705 on p. 324 of Humphr. Wanleii *Librorum Vett. Septentrionalium qui in Angliae Bibliothecis extant...Catal.* (Oxon., fol°. = Vol. II. of Geo. Hickesii *Linguarum Vett. Septentrionalium Thesaurus*).

§ 9[a]. From Frid. Rostgaard's transcript an (inexperienced) amanuensis made again a copy which came into the possession of Barth. Chr. Sandvig, and with the help of this and Rostgaard's copy, Erasm. Nyerup published, in 1787, on coll. 360–382 of his above-quoted *Symbolae*, a large number of glosses contained in the Leiden Glossary, but not always in the same order, omitting many, and sometimes substituting other words for those of the Leiden MS. For instance, of the present edition he prints of Chapter I the nos. 13, 17, 20, 22, 30, 65, 81, 92, 101, 127, 128, 90; of Ch. II, nos. 6, 14, 12, 7, 13, 33, 43, 151, 119, 152, 5, 58, 69, 72, 100, 101, 98, 99, 110, 113, 156, 97, 95, 129, 149, 175; of Ch. III, nos. 6, 7, 8; then again II. 15, 80, 161; III. 11, 12, 17, 34, 41, 19, 35, 40, 48, 37, 38, 44, 52, 53, 54 in the order given here.

§ 10. L. Bethmann appears to have been the first who published, in 1845, extracts from Voss. Lat. 69 itself, in Moriz Haupt's *Zeitschr. für deutsches Alterthum*, Bd. v, pp. 194—198, confining himself to the Germanic glosses. In 1869, in Bd. XIV, p. 191 of the same *Zeitschr.*, Ernst Martin

* For the above details and further particulars of the purchase of Vossius' library, see P. C. Molhuysen, *Geschied. der Universiteits-Bibliotheek te Leiden* (Leiden, 1905), p. 28 sq.; Tydeman in *Mnemosyne*, 1825, pt. 15, pp. 259—290. Also Van der Aa, *Biograph. Woordenb.; Diction. of National Biography; Reliq. Hearn.* I. 205, 206 (ed. 1857); Evelyn, *Diary*, III. 306, 308.

† Junius died 19 Nov. 1677, and bequeathed his MSS. to the Bodleian Library.

‡ One of them, marked E, of which Junius said in 1665 "itidem descripsimus ex membranis ejusdem Vossii," is an extract from the present Glossary (Voss. Lat. 69), as appears from the extracts which Junius published in his "*Glossarium Gothicum*" (see above § 8[b]).

corrected a few of Bethmann's readings, and published some glosses omitted by the latter.

§ 10[a]. Of later editors of extracts El. Steinmeyer and Ed. Sievers should be mentioned, who, in their monumental work *Die althochdeutschen Glossen* (Berlin, 1879 &c.), beginning on p. 460 of Vol. I, give all the Germanic glosses under the specific titles of the books of the Bible under which they appear in the Leiden Glossary and numerous other kindred Glossaries. In their second volume they continue the same plan with respect to all the Ecclesiastical and other authors whose works have been glossed by Germanic interpretations in the Leiden and other Glossaries; cf. their Vol. I, pp. 460, 470, 475, 481, 488, 496, 525, 549, 561, 589, 640, 656, 666, 676, 678, 708, 738; II, pp. 41, 154, 244, 334, 341, 356, 596, 597, 746. See also Steinmeyer in *Zeitschr. f. d. Alterth.* Vol. XXXIII, p. 248.

§ 10[b]. Geo. Goetz published copious extracts from the present Glossary in the 5th Vol. (pp. 410—425) of his great *Corpus Glossariorum Latinorum* (8°, Lipsiae, 1894).

A complete edition of the Leiden Glossary was published in 1901 at Augsburg by P. Placidus Glogger, O.S.B., under the title: *Das Leidener Glossar Cod. Voss. lat.* 4° 69. 1. Teil: *Text der Handschrift.* Programm des kgl. human. Gymnasiums St. Stephan in Augsburg zum Schlusse des Schuljahres 1900/01 *.

* I only became aware of this publication after a good part of my own text was in type, and nearly all my preparations for it had been completed. In April 1903 I accidentally found Glogger's name and edition mentioned in a list of Scholars who had used the MS., pasted in the MS. by the authorities of the Leiden Library. As I saw no notice of it in any of the German bibliographical Catalogues accessible to me, I wrote to Dr Glogger himself, and it then came out that he had forwarded a copy to me on 17 Oct. 1902, but addressed to 'Corpus Christi College,' where I do not reside, and the Librarian of that College, to whom it had been delivered, had, inadvertently, not sent it on to me.

Glogger generously offered to destroy his own edition rather than do anything which seemed to interfere with mine. But, though regretting that he had not informed me of his plan in the first instance, I requested him to go on with his work, as, in my opinion, there could be no harm in publishing two separate editions, in two different countries, of this interesting and difficult Glossary.

As Glogger sent me, in September 1903, the second part of his work, containing his explanations of the text, I have been able to use it with great advantage to my own. Under the circumstances I am naturally prevented from criticising his edition, but I have no hesitation in saying that it is excellent in every respect: and it is to be hoped that, in the proposed third part of his work, he will deal with all the material still to be found in a number of kindred Glossaries and other sources, but not touched by me or my predecessors, and yet so necessary for the further elucidation of the present most important Glossary.

Further description of the MS.; number of leaves; ruling and *number of lines;* its *scribes; contractions.*

§ 11. The Glossary, as stated above (§ 6), is written on the leaves 20*—36, beginning on the recto of leaf 20, and ending at the end of the first column of the recto of leaf 36; and each page being divided into two columns, the Glossary occupies 16 leaves and one column of a 17th, or 32 pages and one column of the 33rd page, or 65 columns in all.

§ 12. *Ruling* and *number of lines.* The division of the pages into two columns has been effected by the drawing of three pairs of perpendicular blind lines on one side (either on the *recto*, or on the *verso*) of each vellum leaf with a hard point, namely one pair of lines (a space of about 5 or 6 mm. between them) on the left-hand side, another pair in the centre, and a third pair on the right-hand side of the leaf. The impression made by the drawing of these lines on one side (recto or verso) of the vellum leaves, served to mark off the other side (verso or recto) in a similar manner.

§ 12^{a}. Within the columns formed by these 3 pairs of *perpendicular* lines, are drawn, in a similar way, *horizontal* blind lines for the writing, namely 35 on the leaves 20—27 (recto and verso), and the verso † of leaf 30, and 36 ‡ to the columns of leaves 28 and 29 (recto and verso), the

* If, in the numbering of the leaves, account had been taken of the three leaves cut away after quire *c*, the leaf on which the Glossary begins would have been numbered 23. In other words, the Glossary begins on the first leaf of quire *d*, and ends on the first leaf of quire *f*.

† This page is ruled for 36 lines as on the recto of the leaf.

‡ Apart from the usual 35 and 36 lines to each column, the scribe wrote occasionally one or more words, which he was unable to bring within, at the foot of, the column, as: one word below col. 21^{bb}; six words below col. 22^{aa}; four syllables below col. 23^{ba} (preceded by L, see below § 22); one word below col. 25^{ab} (preceded by L); two (a gloss) below col. 26^{ab}; four glosses (a whole line) below the two columns of leaf 26 verso; one word below col. 31^{bb}; two below col. 34^{aa} (preceded by L); two below col. 35^{ab}; one line above col. 35^{ba}, and two words above col. 25^{bb} (preceded by Γ, see below § 22).

On the other hand, in several places lines are left blank, but quite irregularly. From the first Chapter, where the glosses are arranged alphabetically according to the first letter of each gloss, it would seem that the original plan was to leave a vacant space between each letter of the alphabet. But the plan was not strictly carried out, as there is no blank left between the A and B, nor between the C and D, and after O it was abandoned altogether. Hence we only find the following blank lines: on Fol. 20^{aa}, the lines 19—21 (between the B and C Glosses); Fol. 20^{ab} the lines 23 (between the E and F), and 28 and 29 (between the F and G); Fol. 20^{ba} li. 6, 18 and 23 (between the I and L, N and O and O and P); 21^{aa} one li. between Chapter I and II; 23^{ab} the lines 27—35 between Ch. IV and V; 23^{bb} lines 11—15 between Ch. VII and VIII; 24^{ab} lines recto of leaf 30, the leaves 31 to 35 (recto and verso), and the last column* (leaf 36[aa]).

As a space of about 20 mm. is left between each of the three pairs of bounding lines, and the two margins on each page take up about 27 mm. of the width of the page, a width of about 60 mm. is left for each column. The length of each column, as set off by the horizontal blind lines, is about 196 mm., giving a space of about 5½ mm. between each horizontal line. Hence the *writing* occupies about 196 mm. of the length, and about 120 mm. of the width of a page.

At the commencement the scribe appears to have made, here and there, attempts to separate the interpretation from the lemma by a more or less well-regulated space, and to subdivide, in this way, each column into two, so as to bring four columns on a page. But after fol. 23 verso these attempts cease.

§ 13. Two *scribes* appear to have been at work: one who began the Glossary on Fol. 20[aa], continued it till the end of Fol. 23[ba] (VI. 31 inequiperabilis†) in one universal style of writing and size of letters, and with the same colour of ink. The next column (Fol. 23[bb]) is evidently written by another (second) scribe. But the first hand begins again on Fol. 24[aa] in his usual style, and with the same colour of ink, though occasionally writing somewhat finer letters, and continued till Fol. 26[aa] li. 5, when (beginning with Ch. XVI) he proceeds, with slightly blacker ink and heavier writing, till Fol. 26[ba] li. 15, when he stopped at the word "Oriona," and the second hand again begins with the word "ebirdhring," and continues till li. 28 of the same column (26[ba]), when the first hand resumes till the end of Fol. 26[bb]. On Fol. 27[aa] the *second* hand resumes and continues till Fol. 27[ba] li. 21 (porcis). At the word "Symphonia" in the same line 21, the first hand commences again and continues till Fol. 28[ba] li. 27 (repetitur), when the *second* hand resumes and continues till 28[bb] li. 6 (explicatur). At li. 7 of Fol. 28[bb] the *first* hand resumes and continues till Fol. 33[bb] li. 14 (auctorale); then the *second* hand begins again at li. 15 (Item incipiunt verba) till 34[aa] li. 26 (Neutricis nouis).

23—26 between Ch. X and XI; 24[bb], 26[aa], 27[bb], 28[bb], 32[ba], 34[ab], 35[bb] one line each between the Ch. XII and XIII, XV and XVI, XXVII and XXVIII, XXVIII and XXIX, XXXV and XXXVI, XLII and XLIII, XLVII and XLVIII respectively; 25[ab] three li. between Ch. XIII and XIV; 25[ba] four lines between Ch. XIV and XV; 26[ab] two li. between Ch. XVI and XVII; 32[ba] two li. at end of col. between Ch. XXXVI and XXXVII; 34[ba] one li. between the head-line and the first gloss of Ch. XLIV; 36[aa] at end of col. before the scribe's final line 'Sicut inueni &c.'

* Here one line is left blank between the last line of the text, and the scribe's explanation of his work (Sicut inueni &c.).

† The references refer to the present edition.

The first hand resumes at li. 27 (sutrinator), and continues till the end of Fol. 36[aa], where the Glossary ends.

§ 13[a]. If this analysis of the scribal work is correct, it may be tabulated as follows:

First hand:

20[aa] (Commencement of Glossary) till end of 23[ba] (VI. 31 inequiperabilis).

24[aa] (VIII. 14 Blena) till 26[aa] li. 5 (XV. 48 leuem facere).

26[aa] li. 6 (XVI Incipit) till 26[ba] li. 15 (XIX. 17 Oriona*).

26[ba] li. 29 (XIX. 31 Rinocerus*) till end of Fol. 26[bb] XXI. 5 (eorum*).

27[ba] li. 21 (XXV. 7 Symphonia) till 28[ba] li. 27 (XXVIII. 72 repetitur).

28[bb] li. 7 (XXVIII. 79 Epexergasia) till 33[bb] li. 14 (XXXIX. 73 auctorale).

34[aa] li. 27 (XLII. 6 Sutrinator) till end of Fol. 36[aa] (end of Glossary).

Second hand:

23[bb] li. 1 (VII De Paral.) till end of 23[bb] (VIII. 13 incedit).

26[ba] li. 15 (XIX. 17 ebirdhring*) till 26[ba] li. 28 (XIX. 30 sterelis*).

27[aa] li. 1 (XXI. 5 significantes) till 27[ba] li. 21 (XXV. 6 porcis).

28[ba] li. 28 (XXVIII. 72 quando) till 28[bb] li. 6 (XXVIII. 78 explicatur).

33[bb] li. 15 (XL tit. Item) till 34[aa] li. 26 (XLII. 5 nouis)†.

§ 14. *Contractions*‡ (i.e. the omission of one or more letters from a word or syllable) are indicated in the MS. by

(A) a horizontal (sometimes waved) stroke.

* See Facsimile.

† Some parts of the writing ascribed above to the *first* hand, might be attributed to *a third*, some even to *a fourth* hand, as, here and there, we observe words or whole lines in much finer and thinner writing than that which the first hand usually produces. And with the heading of Ch. XXIX., the ink begins to be blacker till the end of gloss N°. 35. But it is impossible to speak with certainty on these points. This much is certain that the writing of the *second* scribe, though not differing, in its chief characteristics, from that of the *first*, is yet finer and more *angular*; the up-strokes of his *b*, *d*, *l* are taller and often reach the line above them; the down-strokes of his *f*, *p* &c. longer, and his *ſ* (long *s*) is usually taller than that of the first hand, and has occasionally no tack on its left side. His work may further and chiefly be distinguished from that of the first scribe by its having no other mark of *punctuation* than a mere point (.) between words and at the end of glosses or lines, whereas the first scribe has a more elaborate system of punctuation (see below § 21).

‡ This general term includes all suspensions, abbreviations or other curtailments of words or syllables. Horizontal or perpendicular strokes often represent one or two letters omitted in, or at the end of a syllable or word; in many cases only the beginning

(*a*) above *vowels*.

above a the stroke = (1) *m*: I. 2 (quoda*m*) &c. (2) *ne*: XXV tit. (Johan*ne*). (3) *ostr*: XXVIII. 51 (n*ostr*a). (4) *ine*: I. 19, 22, II. 107 (lat*ine*). (5) *an* and *t*: XVI. 23, XXI. 18 (s*a*n*ct*a).

„ e = (1) *m*: I. 12 (eiusde*m*), 95 (exe*m*pli) &c. (2) *st*: I. 111 (e*st*; pote*st*) &c. (3) *ss*: II. 188 (e*ss*e; above final e). (4) *s*: XLIII. 30 (festiuitate*s*, not -tate*m*, the lemma being plural).

„ i = (1) *m*: II. 189, XII. 42 &c. (eni*m*); XXVIII. 4 (exti*m*plo) &c. (2) *citur*: XXX. 20 (di*citur*). (3) *iscop*: XLI. 2 (chorep*iscop*i). (4) *an* and *t*: IV. 86 (s*anct*ificatus). (5) *e*: XXX. 20 (d*e*i; but perhaps here for dic*endi*), 29; XXXV. 17, 147 (dei).

„ o = (1) *m*: I. 25 (co*m*mess-), 94 (o*m*nia), II. 33 (co*m*mune), 39 (co*m*missum, co*m*mendatum) &c.* (2) *and*: XXXVI. 1 (qu*and*o). (3) *niam*: XXXVIII. 57 (quo*niam*). (4) *men*: XLIII. 29 (no*men*). (5) *ae*: IV. 27 (sinagog*ae*). (6) *iscop*: XL. 1 (ep*iscop*os). (7) *u*: XXXII. 3 (d*u*o †).

„ u = (1) *m*: I. 2 (ludu*m*) &c. (2) *er*: I. 90 (diu*er*sa); XXVIII. 24, 25, 30, 37 (u*er*ba; u*er*borum) &c. (3) *tem*: XVI. 27; XXXI. 2, 3; XXXIII. 8; XLIV. 1 (au*tem*). (4) *it*: I. 125 (iudicau*it*). (5) *itas*: XXX. 266 (ciu*itas*).

(*b*) above *consonants*.

„ B = (1) *A*: XL. tit. UERB*A*. (2) = *RIS*: XLII. tit (LIB*RIS*).

„ c = (1) *on*: I. 19 (c*on*silium), 25 (c*on*uiuia) &c. (2) = *it*: XIII. 57 (cresc*it*); XXXIII. 8 (fac*it*) &c. (3) = *ut*: XII. 9; XIII. 59 (sic*ut*). (4) = *itur*: XV. 22 (dic*itur*). (5) = *undum*: XLIV. 11 (sec*undum*).

„ uncial ð = *E*, *UN* and *U*: XXXIII. tit. (S*E*C*UN*D*U*M).

„ g = *rece*: I. 31 (g*rece*). Sometimes the stroke is over an *r*

of a word is given, a stroke over the last letter, or the last two or three letters, representing the omitted remainder.

All the contractions are expanded by italics in the present edition. It should be pointed out that the present paragraphs 14—16 cannot adequately express the palaeographic features of the MS. But what has been said above (p. xi, note ‡) about the *special types* required for palaeographic discussions, the reader will indulgently bear in mind with regard to the types necessary for showing the *contractions*, *peculiar forms* of the letters, *ligatures* &c. mentioned here. A good many of them, however, can be seen in the photographic plate added to this work.

* For *com-* perhaps *con-* was intended, as the scribe wrote conmanipularius in I. 30, and an original comparatio is actually corrected into conparatio (see note to Ch. XXVIII. 48).

† Here dō may be the sign for a weight.

following the g = (1) *ece* : I. 6, 19, 22 &c. (gr*ece*). (2) *ecos* : XLIV. 18 (gr*ecos*)*.

above g = *o* : XXX. tit. (prolog*o*).

„ m = (1) *en* : I. 111 (nom*en*; tam*en*; frum*en*torum) &c. (2) *nes* : XXIX. 66; XXXIX. 52 (om*nes*). (3) *ni* : XXI. 12 (homi*ni*bus). (4) *inis* : XXXV. 164 (hom*inis*). (5) *ensis* : XXII. 13 (m*ensis*). (6) *ore* : XXVII. 33 (temp*ore*). (7) *gram* and *aton* : XXXV. 147 (tetra*gram*m*aton*). (8) *an* and *tu* : IV. 14; X. 1 (s*an*c*tu*m). (9) uncertain : XLIV. 11 (om̄), 29 (dnm̄s).

„ n = (1) *on* : VIII. 19; XXXIV. 19 &c. (n*on*). (2) *em* : XV. 38 (oration*em*). (3) *omi* and *u* : XXI. 17 (d*omi*n*u*s). (4) *i* and *icat* : X. 11 (sign*i*f*icat*). (5) *ant* : XLIV. 11 (design*ant*). (6) *icu* : XXXIII. 13, 16 (d*icu*nt). (7) *ame* : XXXVII. 12 (t*ame*n). (8) *a* : XLIII. 4 (pan*a*).

„ nn = *ome* : IV. 93 (n*ome*n).

„ p = (1) *re* : I. 44 (p*re*terita), 52 (p*re*sto); XXVIII. 21 (p*re*dicentia †). (2) *it* : XV. tit.; XIX. tit. &c. (incip*it*). (3) *ni* and *otens* : XXI. 17 (om*ni*p*otens*). (4) *iritu* : II. 7 (sp*iritu*s). (5) *ores* : XXVII. 27 (script*ores*). (6) *iunt* : XL. tit. (incip*iunt*). (7) *er* : XXXVIII. 13 (prop*er*ter ‡).

„ q = (1) *uas* : XXXI. 19, 29, 30 (siliq*uas*). (2) *ue* : XXXIV. 44 (q*ue*stio). (3) *uae* : XXXIII. 27, 30 (siliq*uae*).

„ r = (1) *es* : I. 22 (audito*res*), 104 (p*res*biterorum). (2) *as* : VII. 3 (ligatur*as*; conpositur*as*). (3) *unt* : XIII. 43 (uider*unt*; manser*unt*) &c. (4) *int* : VIII. 2 (coacuer*int*). (5) *tius* : XXII. 13 (mar*tius*). (6) *icitu* : II. 161; III. 61; VIII. 12 (d*icitu*r). (7) *citu* : II. 118; XIII. 25 (di*citu*r).

„ s = *unt* : VIII. 2; X. 8, 14, 18 (s*unt*); XXXVIII. 42 (pres*unt*).

„ t = (1) *er* : I. 4 (int*er*dum), 51 (uiolent*er*) &c. (2) *em* : XV. 36; XLIII. *tit.*; XLIV *tit.* (it*em*). (3) *est* : XIX. 28 (pot*est*). (4) *as* : XIII. 26; XLII. 3 (ciuit*as*). (5) *es* : XXII. 9 (sequent*es*) &c. (6) *is* : XIII. 13 (uest*is*). (7) *ae* : IV. 98 (collect*ae* §). (8) *u* and *em* : XXXIII. 13 (*au*t*em*). (9) *uose* : II. 172 (presumpt*uose*). (10) *a* and *ine* : I. 31, 80, 114 &c. (l*a*t*ine*). (11) *un* : XXXIII. 5 (s*un*t). (12) *ici* : XXXI. 22 (d*ici*t). (13) *at* : XLVII. 89 (habit*at*).

„ x = *it* : X. 1 (porrex*it*); XII. 4 (sedux*it*) &c.

* This expansion, not *graece* &c., is suggested by greco (II. 188), grecos (II. 189) &c. written in full in the MS.

† Here is a dot above the stroke as a mark for insertion, the *p* being added above the line.

‡ The scribe, in this case, misread the *pp* with stroke above (for proprium) of his example (see below, A[c] *pp*, and *ppt*).

§ The mark of contraction above the *t* is more like an open cursive *a*.

(*c*) over *two* or *more letters.*

accip (ip*) = accipi*t*, XXXVII. 9.—accipit (it) = accipi*un*t, XVI. 27.—AGUST(UST) = AGUSTI*NI*, XXXVII. tit.—apost (post) = apost*olos*, X. 11.

baln (ln) = baln*eu*m, XXXIX. 14.—baptsm (apts) = bapt*i*sm*ate*, X. 3.

cal (ca) = cal*lidus*, XLVI. 23.—ciuit (it) = ciuit*atis*, XXXV. 256.—ciuit (uit) = ciuit*as*, XIII. 26; XXIII. 17; = ciuit*ates*, XI. 7; = ciuit*atis*, XLIII. 17.

diac (ac) = diac*onus*, XXXIX. 22.—dicr (cr) = dic*itu*r, XXXIX. 28.—dicunt (nt) = dicunt*ur*, XIII. 6.—dicut (ut) = dicu*n*t*ur*, XI. 5.—dimin (in) = dimin*itiuum*, XIX. 60; XXXV. 56.—dimini (mini) = diminit*iuum*, XVII. 10.—dint (in) = di*cu*nt, XXVIII. 55.—dne (ne) = d*omi*ne, II. 98.—dni (ni) = d*omi*ni, XXI. 18.—dns (ns) = d*ominus*, XXI. 17.—drag (ag) = drag*mas*, XXXII. 8, 11; = drag*ma*, XXXIII. 4; = drag*mis*, XXXIII. 6.—dragm (gm) = dragm*as*, XXXII. 7, 9.

ee = e*ss*e II. 67 (prode*ss*e).—en (en) = en*s*, XLI. 9 (lucen*s*).—episc (isc) = episc*opi*, XXXIX. 56.

facit (it) = faci*un*t, XXXV. 42.—femin (in) = femin*ino*, XXXV. 144.—forn (rn) = forn*icationis*, IV. 72.

gen (en) = gen*us*, XXXVII. 4.—grec (ec) = grec*um*, XLIV. 11.

homib (mi) = homi*ni*bus, XXI. 12.—homin (in) = homin*es*, XLIII. 6.

incp (cp) = inc*i*pi*t*, VI. *tit.*; XIV. *tit.*—istor (tor) = istor*iae*, IV. *tit.*

lat (at) = lat*ine*, I. 19, 22; II. 107; XXXVIII. 16; = lat*ino*, II. 161.

nauigat (at) = nauigat*ione*, XXXVIII. 44.

ordinat (at) = ordinat*ionem*, XXXIX. 22.

plur (ur) = plur*ale*, XLIII. 17.—pote (te) = pote*st*, XXXV. 192.—pp (pp) = p*ro*p*ter*, XXI. 16; = p*ro*p*rium*, XXXVIII. 11, 12, 14; XXXIX. 10, 26.—ppt (pp and t), XXXIX. 9 (p*ro*p*ter* or p*ro*p*rium*t*er*).—prbri (rbr) = pr*es*b*ite*ri, XXXIX, 22.—prolog (og) = prolog*o*, XXX. *tit.*

qs (qs) = q*ua*s*i*, XXXIX. 48.—qund (nd) = qu*a*nd*o*, XLVII. 28.—quo (uo) = qu*an*d*o*, XXVII. 4; XXVIII. 32; = quo*niam*, XXVIII. 47.

sacer (er) = sacer*dos*, XLVI. 8.—sci (ci) = s*an*c*t*i, XXXVII. *tit.*—scribs (ibs) = scribs*it*, XLIII. 25, 27.—script (pt) = script*ores*, XXVII. 27.—serm (serm) = serm*onum*, II. *tit.*—signs (gn) = sign*ificans*, XXVIII. 39.—siliq (iliq, through the *l*) = siliq*uas*, XXXIII. 8.—siliq (iq) = siliq*uas*, XXXIII. 29.—sinagog (og) = sinagog*ae*, IV. 27.—sold (through the ld) = sol*i*d*orum*, XXXII. 6; = sol*i*d*i*, XXXIII. 21.—superumeral (ral) = superumeral*e*, V. 9.

temp (mp) = temp*ore*, XXVII. 33.

uerb (erb) = uerb*orum*, I. *tit.*—ungent (gent) = ungent*orum*, X. 3.—unt (nt) = unt*ias*, XXXVII. 9; XXXIX. 36.

xpiana (pi) = xp*isti*ana = Christ-, IV. 84†; xp*isti*anorum (= Christ-), XXX. 35.—xpianiam (pi) = xp*isti*aniam (wrongly for Christianam), X. 5.—xpo (xpo) = xp*isto*, X. 5.—xps (ps) = xp*istus*, X. 1.

* The letters over which the stroke is written are here printed between ( )

† The same word occurs again, XXXV. 293, but without the sign for contraction.

(*d*) drawn through the up-strokes of the tall letters *b*, *d*, *l*.

through b = (1) *is*: II. 98 (nob*is*); XIX. 28 (uerb*is*) &c.—(2) *er*: I. 36 (gub*er*nationibus); XXII. 14 (decemb*er*).—(3) *rem*: XXII. 11 (mulieb*rem*).—(4) *itum*: XVII. 7 (amb*itum*, or amb*ulationem*?).—(5) *es* and *itero*: I. 104 (pr*es*b*itero*rum).—(6) *es*, *i* and *er*: II. 130 (pr*es*b*i*t*er*).—(7) *es* and *iter*: XLI. 1 (Pr*es*b*iter*i).—(8) *et*: XXIII. 20; XXXIII. 1, 4 (hab*et*).—(9) *ent*: XXXIX. 7 (hab*ent*).

" bb = *atem*: II. 161 (abb*atem*).

" d = (1) *ius*: II. 86 (med*ius*).—(2) *us*: I. 67 (intollerand*us*).—(3) *is*: IV. 78 (turgid*is*); XXII. 7 (uirid*is*).—(4) *est*: VIII. 13, 16, 19 &c.; XV. 13; XXVIII. 58, 61 (id*est*).—(5) (with : following) = *est*: I. 36; XV. 45; XVII. 20 (id*est*).—(6) (with . following) = *est*: V. 11; XI. 5; XIII. 25; XXVIII. 21; XXXIX. 42; XLII. 25 (id*est*).—(7) *e*: XXVIII. 18 (ind*e*).—(8) *uo*: I. 76, 101, 109, 111; II. 146 &c. (q*uo*d).—(9) *ica*: XXIII. 17 (mod*ica*).—(10) *entes*: XXII. 16 (descend*entes*).—(11) *es*: XIX. 50 (laud*es*); XXXIX. 7 (ped*es*).—(12) *otes*: XXVII. 7 (sacerd*otes*).—(13) *os*: XXXI. 5, 7; XXXII. 5, 28 (solid*os*).—(14) *un* and *u*: XXXIX. 68 (sec*u*n*d*u*m).—(15) *e*, *un*, and *u*: XIII. 25 (sec*u*n*d*u*m).—(16) *itu*: XXIII. 1 (incend*itu*r).—(17) *st*: XXVIII. 44 (ide*st*).—(18) *unt*: XXXIX. 7 (mand*unt*).—(19) *ae*: XXXIX. 34 (calid*ae*); XLIII. 17 (kalend*ae*).—(20) *era*: XXXIII. 1 (pond*era*).

" dd = d*auid*: X. 24; XXIII. 17.

" l = (1) *ue*: I. 4, 19, 27, 28 &c. (*ue*l)*.—(2) *e*: I. 4, 28, 30 &c. (uel); XXII. 5 (gezelt); V. 9 (superumeral*e*); XXXVII. 5 (simil*e*).—(3) *is*: II. 128 (disperabil*is*; inreuocabil*is*) &c.—(4) *o*: X. 2 (apostoli).—(5) *em*: XXIII. 17 (hierusal*em*).—(6) *ogi*: I. 5 (anal*ogi*o).—(7) *a* and *ine*: I. 80, 114 &c. (l*atine*).—(8) *esi*: IV. 37 (eccl*esi*ę).—(9) *es*: XIII. 15 (diurnal*es*).—(10) *ia*: XV. 36 (al*ia*).—(11) *i* and *ua*: XXXIII. 26 (sil*iqua*).—(12) (uncertain): XL. 6 (crinicul-funicul).

(*e*) drawn through the down-stroke of

p = *er*: I. 49 (sup*er*), 73 (yp*er*beretheus), 84 (p*er*uadere), 94 and 109 (p*er*).

p (curving round in front of) = *ro*: I. 61 (p*ro*cacitas), 85 (p*ro*scribantur) &c.

q = (1) *ui*: XIX. 23 (q*ui*; loq*ui*tur) &c.—(2) *ua*: XXVIII. 67 (q*ua*ndo).

" (waving stroke) = (1) *uae*: I. 112 (q*uae*, nom. plur. neut.); XLIII. 51 (q*uae*, nom. plur. fem.).—(2) *ui*: XVII. 19 (q*ui*a).—(3) *uo*: XLIV. 16, 26 (q*uo*d).

" (slanting stroke) = (1) *ui*: II. 104 and XIV. 36 (q*ui*bus); IV. 99 (q*ui*dem); XIII. 43 (aliq*ui*) &c.—(2) *uam*: XIV. 9 (q*uam*uis).

* In two cases (I. 22; II. 151) the *l* has, besides the stroke, two dots (:) on its left and one on its right.

(*f*) a horizontal (waved) stroke attached to the right-hand side of:

q (1) with a dot *underneath* the stroke = *uae*: I. 49 (q*uae*, nom. plur. neut.).—(2) with a dot *above* the stroke = *uae*: XI. 16 (nom. sing. fem.).

„ two strokes attached in the same way (written like <) = *uia*: X. 21 (q*uia*).

(B) a *perpendicular* somewhat curved, or twisted stroke.

(*a*) *above a letter.*

above c = *an* and *tu*: II. 7; XXVII. 19; XXXV. 50 (s*anctus*).—i = *citu*: II. 35, 188 (di*citur*).—n = (1) *omi*: XXVIII. 33; XXIX. 63 (d*omi*ne). —(2) *omi* and *u*: II. 7 (d*om*in*um*).—*p* = (1) *iritu*: II. 7 (sp*iritus*). —(2) *is*: XXXV. 293 (xp*is*tiana).—r = *icitu*: III. 62; XXII. 4; XXVIII. 62: XXXV. 144 (d*icitu*r).

(*b*) *above the line*

between do = *e*: I. 109; XXX. 29 (deo).—between ds = *eu*: I. 39; XXVIII. 52, 53 (d*eu*s).

(*c*) above an *i* lengthened below the line after *e* = *us*: VIII. 8 (ei*us*).

(*d*) drawn through a horizontal stroke attached to the final stroke of

m+ = *us*: I. 36 (dom*us*), 38 (protulim*us*) &c.; in XXVIII. 40 (congregam*us*) it is like the contraction for *us* in col. 1, li. 22 of the facsimile.

n+ = *us*: I. 72 (Machomen*us*); II. 89 (inportun*us*); III. 18 (mun*us*cula); in XIX. 24 (asin*us*) the contraction is -8, as may be seen in col. 1, li. 22 of the facsimile.

(*e*) drawn through the lengthened right, sloping stroke of

r+ = *um*: I. 23 (catafrigar*um*), 49 (columnar*um*) &c.

(C) by a mark resembling *a comma* above, or on the right side of,

e = *us*: XXXIX. 48 (ei*us*).—i = *us*: XXII. 4; XXIII. 1; XXXI. 24 (ei*us*).—m = (1) *u*: I. 109 (religam*u*r); (2) *us*: XXII. 13 (prim*us*).—n = *us*: XXXVIII. 28 (cacodemon*us*), XLIV. 13 (Isemerin*us*), 14 (Exemerin*us*).—p = (1) *ost*: I. 39, XLIII. 43 (p*ost*); (2) *ri*: XXVIII. 33* (prop*ri*a; prop*ri*).—t = (1) *ur*: I. 39 (habet*ur*), 47 (experiunt*ur*), 49 (ponunt*ur*), 59 (informat*ur*), 70 (mancipant*ur*, capiant*ur*); III. 19 (cludit*ur*)†; XIX.

* Here the mark may be for *i*, for which see below under G.

† The mark is on the left side of the stroke for *t* when this forms a ligature with a preceding *n*; otherwise it is above the *t*.

23 (loqui*tur*); XXII. 16 (dat*ur*que; perficiant*ur*).—(2) *us*: XXI. 1 (exercit*us*).

(D) by a mark resembling a semicolon (;) on the right side of

b = *us*: I. 25 (meretrib*us*), 36 (gubernationib*us*), &c.* It occurs also after B (= *US*): I. tit. (CANONIB*US*). This mark is occasionally more like a colon (:), as XI. 15 (forib*us*). Sometimes it has the form 3 : II. 104 (quib*us*cumque).

p = *us*: XIII. 43, XXXIX. 33 (corp*us*); XXXV. 7 (top*us*); XXXIX. 19 (temp*us*).

q = *ue*: I. 106 (q*ue*rellam); II. 104 (quibuscumq*ue*), 134 (atq*ue*); III. 41 (laq*ue*aria); XIX. 53 (aq*ue*).

(E) by *dots.*

: (1) after *d* with horizontal stroke through its up-stroke = *est*: I. 36 (id*est*); (2) after i = *dest*: XII. 3 (i*dest*).

. after i = *dest*: XI. 15; XII. 24, 41, 42 &c. (i*dest*)†.

. on both sides of i = *dest*: XXI. 20; XXII. 7, 9, 12, 13; XXXI. 17, 23, 24 (i*dest*).

÷ = *est*: XXXIII. 11.

·Ꝣ = *Grece*, XXXI. 32, 33, 34‡.

(F) by ᴄ (a small arc of a small circle).

(1) above i (which is drawn out below *e*) = *us*: XXI. 5 (ei*us*); (2) above p (p̔) = *er*: XXVII. 7 (Lup*er*ci), 9 (Lup*er*calia), 11 (Lup*er*cal).

(G) by a small letter written above another letter.

i (like a perpendicular stroke) (1) above p = *ri*: XXVIII. 43 (prop*ri*ores); XXIX. 39, and XXX. 26 (prop*ri*um); (2) above q = *u*: I. 39; II. 149; XVI. 26 &c. (q*u*i); XV. 9 (q*u*ibus).

o (1) above q = *u*: XXVIII. 33 (q*u*o), 44 (q*u*oties); (2) in one and the same word above q = *u*, and above m = *do*: XXXIII. 5 (q*u*omo*do*); (3) above u = *and*: XXVII. 4 (qu*and*o).

Special contractions.

ꜧ (curved perpendicular stroke over the loop of the h) IV. 98 (usually for *autem*; but here it is uncertain, and may mean *hoc est*).

ɔ (this sign, which resembles c turned round upside down does not appear

* In one case this contraction has been expanded by *er*; see XXXV. 72.

† Occasionally the *i* seems to have been written between two dots, but the dot on the left was, perhaps, meant as a mark of punctuation.

‡ The dot on the left may be meant as a mark of punctuation.

before Ch. XXVIII; in the previous Chapters *con* is always expressed by c̄) = *con*: XXVIII. 20 (*con*tinuatio), 31 (*con*geminat), 45 (*con*iunctio; *con*cluduntur), 67 (*con*uerso); XXIX. 21 (*con*silium), 60 (*con*cup-), 64 (*con*templ-), 68 (*con*pos-); XXX. 9 (*con*textum), 13 (*con*templ-), 18 (*con*flictus), 26 (*con*flictus; in this case there is a dot above the sign), 31 (*con*sintagmata; here *con* stands wrongly for eius &c.).

ę = æ, I. 2, 68 &c.

s (following *q*, perhaps meant for *s*) = *ui*, XXXV. 195 (q*ui*squilea).

ⱶ (= enim). It may be that we have this contraction in XXXV. 1; see the note *ibid.*

§ 15. *Different forms* of some of the letters.

a, three varieties: (1) open at the top, resembling (in a few cases *u*, but mostly) two *c*s; (2) the form ᴀ; (3) formed somewhat like *c*, and written above the line, usually on a perpendicular stroke which connects it with a following *m*, *n* (see facs. li. 21), *r*, (long) *s* or *t*.

c (1) our present ordinary form; (2) having the form of two *c*s, one written on the top of the other, linking on with its top-bow to a following *t*.

d, always our ordinary form; in one case (VIII. 7 domus) it has the uncial form ᴅ, and might be read as capital, though it is smaller than the initial of Domatis, which is also uncial.

e (1) our present ordinary form, occasionally linked on, with its tongue, to a following *f*, *n* or *r*; (2) formed like an epsilon, and mostly, though not always, appearing in ligature with a following *c*, *m*, *n*, *p*, *r*, *s*, *t*, *x*.

g. Besides the ordinary form which may be seen in the facsimile, *g* has occasionally an extra curl to its base, as I. 133 (angor); XXVIII. 63 (congregatio).

i (1) the present ordinary form, but without a dot on its top; it is often linked on to *f* or *l*, more especially to the cross-bar of a preceding or following *t*, or to the *L* form of t; see facs. li. 10, 11.—(2) lengthened and drawn out below the line (like ꝭ), and linked on to a preceding *c*, *f* (the two having nearly the form of ʙ), *l*, *r*, *t*; (3) resembling a comma, and linked on, below the line, to the final stroke of *m*, *n* or *t*; occasionally to the bow of *h* or to the tongue of *e*, or below the bow of *b*, as in XXVIII. 28 (inridebit).

o (1) the ordinary form; (2) resembling the delta, and appearing, mostly, in ligature with the right-hand bar of a preceding *r*, though it is also found separate, after *d*, *m* or *t*. It twice commences a word (XXXV. 66, oma; XXXIX. 57 oroccerum).

p, always the now usual form, except in VII. 7 (*carpenta*, written by the second hand), where it is in ligature with a preceding *r*, and has the peculiar form in which it often occurs in ligature in the Roman cursive writing, as early as the 6th century, for which see pl. 2, A.D. 572, of *The Palaeographical Society*, Series I, li. 6 (e *p*ollicetur), 15 (inter*p*osita); pl. 68, li. 10 (per*p*etuis); also li. 1 (reci*p*isti), 3 (mane*p*olos; re*p*onendi), 4 (*ap*ponet), 7 (*ap*eri). The same form occurs again XXXV. 166 (turpes), in ligature with the preceding *r*, and again XXXV. 293, after, and linked on, by its top, with *x*. Another, slightly different form of Roman cursive p appears in the last line of the Glossary (the advertisement of the scribe ne rep-); this resembles the *p* of "sponsione" in li. 15 of pl. 2 of *The Palaeogr. Society*, First Ser.

r (1) the now ordinary form. In two instances (XIII. 7 discernuntur, and XIII. 15 diurnales) the *r* reminds us of earlier A.S. writing, and might be misread as *n*, though in both cases it differs sufficiently from the following *n* to guide a careful reader. In XXVIII. 88 (formȩ), however, we have an *n* corrected into *r*, and XXXV. 295 has catha*n*os for catha*r*os; (2) somewhat like the numeral 2, always after *o*, also after the capital O, and then written larger, as in IV. 51; (3) the right-hand stroke lengthened and slightly bent, to link on with a following ᴀ, *e* (*e* or ϵ), *i*, *m*, *n*, *o*, (long) *ſ**; (4) left-hand stroke lengthened below the line, and the top bending down to combine with a following *t* or *e*, and so resembling a long ſ (an *r* of this kind appears XIV. 22, in fatores, but so misshapen that it seems more *i* corrected into *r*).

s, long ſ, which is nearly always ſ, except occasionally in the handwriting of the second scribe. It is frequently linked on, by a rounded top, to a following *t*.

t, (1) with a flat top, is found in three varieties: (*a*) its cross-bar is curled round† (like *c*), or (*b*) ends in a mere down-stroke (like *i*) on its left-hand side; (*c*) when final, the right-hand end of its cross-bar is curled upward towards the left.—(2) having the shape of an epsilon, and linked on to a following lengthened *i*, or to *r*, or forming with following *ri*, one ligature (tri).—(3) resembling a slightly twisted *l*, and combining with a following *r* or *i*. This *t* is mostly written on the final stroke of *n* drawn out towards the right‡. Its form is smaller when combined with a preceding epsilon-shaped *e*.

v is never found in the text, except by way of correction: ex. gr. II. 62, where it is written above the line to be inserted in place of an omitted *u*; III. 27, where it is written above an *e*, which it is to replace. For other

* The same appears also I. 19 (gr*e*ce) as final *r*. For a somewhat similar *r*, lending itself to receive the contraction for *um*, see above § 14 B[e].

† This curl and stroke are occasionally disconnected from the cross-bar, and might be read as a separate *c* or *i*, as I. 8 (allectat), 50 (mittent); II. 187 (ueterem); III. 1 (ueternorum).

‡ See Facsim. li. 8, 11. In I. 117 (contra) its shape is ϱ.

instances, see IV. 5; XV. 33; XXVIII. 53, 54; XXX. 73; XXXIV. 10, XXXV. 179; XXXVIII. 27. For a sign resembling this *v* see below § 23 *d.*

w; Anglo-Saxon w is written as uu. Its old form ƿ appears misread as *p* in uuld-paexhsue (for uuld-w-).

y has nearly always a dot on its top, as in facs. col. 1 li. 18, col. 2 li. 11.

z may be seen in facs. col. 1 li. 17.

§ 16. *Ligatures* or *combinations* of two or more letters are numerous; ex. gr.

æ (=ae), appears in this form only three times: XLIII. 41 (suæ ald), XLVII. 90 (snægl), and CÆLO* in the title of Ch. XLIV. In one place (XXX. 37) the ligature consists of the left-hand stroke of an open *a*, and an ordinary *e*. Otherwise the diphthong ae is represented often by e, see I. 24 (sepulture), 120 (subnixe &c.); II. 88 (materie), but mostly by ę; I. 2 (tabulę), 68 (quę) &c.; so also AE by Ę (title to Ch. IV). *Combined* appear mostly: ci; cr; ct; cti; &c; ect; em; en; ent; enti; ep; er; eri; es; est; esti; et; ex; fe; fi; fit; i; j; ici; it; li; lj; LX (Roman numerals); mi; ni; nt; nti; or; ra; rei; ret; rg; ri; rm; rn; ro; rs; rt; st (two forms); str; tj (three forms); tri; tro.

§ 17. *Capitals.* The titles of the Chapters are all written in *rustic* capitals, indiscriminately mixed with *uncials.*

Every lemma has either a capital or an uncial as initial. In the few instances where this is not the case (ex. gr. Ch. II. 139, 144; III. 13–16), we may suppose the scribe to have been unaware of beginning a new gloss.

The capital initial of the first lemma of the Chapters I—IV, XXIII, XXVI, XXX, XXXI, XXXVII–XXXIX, XLIV†–XLVII, is somewhat larger than the initials used for the other lemmata, and more or less ornamental, in the style of the Capitals in the St. Gallen MS. of the Lex Salica (A.D. 794), figured on pl. 184 of *The Palaeogr. Society*, 1st Series.

In the first two Chapters (which are arranged alphabetically according to the first letter of the lemmata) some attempts have been made to commence each new letter of the alphabet with a larger or more distinctive initial. Ex. gr. the initial of the first lemma of the D glosses (I. 35 Dogma) is a capital (D), but the initials following are uncials (ð).

§ 18. *Greek letters.* There are a good many Greek words in the Glossary, but all written in Latin characters. Greek letters, however,

* This ligature is really minuscule, but written larger than usual; it is here printed as capital.

† In Ch. XLIV. the glosses 24 and 28 have also ornamental capitals.

c 2

appear in IV. 101 (πο, in porsutas), and a whole Greek word XVIII. 1 (CYNXPONON). And as such we must also describe the *xp* in "Christus" and its derivatives, see above § 14 A *c*.

§ 19. *Illustration.* See *Signs*, below § 23 *g*.

§ 20. *Numerals* (for which see below, *Index of Latin numerals*, p. 217) are usually placed between two dots.

§ 21. The *Punctuation* of the MS. has everywhere been strictly adhered to. It has been pointed out above (§ 13[a], note †) that the *second* hand employed no other mark of punctuation than a point (.).

The *first* scribe, however, used a more elaborate system of punctuation. There are first the three ordinary marks (. ; :) to divide words from each other or to indicate the end of lines &c.

The point (.) is sometimes written level with the line; sometimes raised to the centre of the word preceding it.

The semicolon (;) and colon (:) can, in many cases, hardly be distinguished from each other, as the , of ; is often so small that it looks almost like a point (.), while the lower point of the colon is very often more like a comma (,).

Besides these three marks of punctuation we occasionally find .: (see I. 13), or :· (I. 87), or ⁝ (I. 125), or :; (II. 131), or ;: (II. 132), apparently without any special meaning.

§ 22. *Signs of reference.* When there was, as frequently happened, no room for the whole gloss on the line where it had been commenced, the scribe wrote the remaining words or syllables either on the line *above* or *below* the proper line, prefixing ┌ to the words or syllables written *above*, └ to those written *below* the line. In one case (XX. 12) the ┌ is followed by a colon (:). In XII. 9, there being no further room in the line after "habens", the scribe wrote :· after it, added "aliquando de ęrę" two lines higher up in the space left vacant after gloss 7, prefixing : to these words, and wrote the remainder of the gloss (mento sicut et olla) on the next line after gloss 8, dividing these additions to the lines of glosses 7 and 8 and the mark (⁝) of reference by the hook ┌.

In I. 91, 92, the reading of the MS., in strict accordance with these signs, leads to two wrong glosses; see the note to these glosses on p. 2.

For a further use of these signs see above, p. xviii, note ‡.

§ 23. A few more features of the MS. have to be dealt with, most of which have already been pointed out in the foot-notes to the text. They will, however, give a better idea of the MS. when classified under such headings as *corrections* (§ 23[a]), *division* of words, syllables and glosses

(§ 23^{b}), *insertions* (§ 23^{c}), *marking* words (§ 23^{d}), *omissions* (§ 23^{e}), *signatures* (§ 23^{f}), *signs* (§ 23^{g}), *spots* (§ 23^{h}), *strokes* (§ 23^{i}), *transposition* (§ 23^{k}), *uncertain* words (§ 23^{l}), *underlining* (§ 23^{m}), &c.

§ 23^{a}. *Corrections* seem all to have been made by the scribes themselves, and not afterwards by some *corrector*. They are indicated or effected by (A) writing the letter to be substituted *above* the one to be replaced; see I. 103; II. 9, 155, 164; III. 27; IV. 6, 106; VIII. 18 &c.—(B) *altering* one letter into another, which was sometimes done distinctly, as II. 71; IV. 2, 52, 65; sometimes indistinctly, as I. 115; II. 29; III. 43.—(C) *erasing* one or more letters and leaving a blank space instead, as II. 134. In some cases the erased letter or letters or parts of them may still be discerned, I. 39; II. 36, 112; VI. 7; in other cases the original letter or letters are entirely effaced, II. 45; III. 63; IV. 89.—(D) *erasing* one or more letters, and writing the required letter or sign on the erasure, II. 39; XIII. 41; XIV. 11 &c. Occasionally the wrong letters have been erased without the correct letters being substituted, II. 10; XVI. 6.—(E) marking a letter or stroke to be erased by (*a*) a dot: XXXII. 8, 11 (both these cases are doubtful); (stroke to be erased) II. 176; XXXI. 27; XLIV. 8.—(*b*) two dots (one above and one below, or one on each side of the letter, or both underneath the letter): XVI. 22; XXVIII. 48; XXX. 33; XXXI. 8; XXXII. 4; XXXIV. 10*; XXXV. 179; XXXVIII. 24; XXXIX. 1, 5; XLIV. 11; XLVIII. 47.—(*c*) three dots: IV. 55; VI. 7; XIV. 3; XVI. 29; XXVIII. 49; XLVII. 22.—(*d*) four dots: XXVIII. 20; XXX. 35; XLIII. 13.—(*e*) five or six dots, XXX. 73.—(F) marking a letter to be erased by (*a*) one dot, and writing the letter to be substituted above the line, XXVIII. 69; XXXV. 14; XXXVII. 6; XLVII. 82; (with the correct letter below the line) XLVIII. 35.—(*b*) two dots: XXXV. 27.—(*c*) three dots: XLVII. 22.—(*d*) :, as in XXVI. 5.—(*e*) ÷ above a wrong word, referring to a similar sign above the correct word written in the margin within lines forming a square, XXVIII. 77.—(*f*) a dot underneath the letter to be erased, and another dot on the right-hand side of the letter to be substituted written above the line, XXXVIII. 37.

§ 23^{b}. The *division* between words, syllables and glosses is often very defective, in spite, or perhaps on account of the rather elaborate system of punctuation described above in § 21. For instance, in I. 15 the MS. has 'ame mo ria' for 'a memoria'; I. 36 it has 'par ro chiis,' and so on. It was not considered necessary to follow the MS. in this respect, except in a few cases where the gloss is obscure.

As regards the individual glosses, at the outset the scribe seems to have intended to reserve one line to each lemma and its gloss, however

* In this case the correcting letter is written above the line between two dots, but the wrong letter (a) is not marked for erasure.

short these might be, and to write, wherever practicable, words or syllables which could not be brought into their proper line, either above or below it, as I. 12 &c. Somewhat lengthy glosses, as I. 36, 90, 95, 100, 115, 127 occupy two lines, the second line slightly indented. But the scribe seems soon to have realised that, in this way, he would leave a good deal of vacant space, and so, at and after III. 42, 43 he commenced a second gloss wherever there was any vacant space left in the line after the first, adhering to his former plan of writing any words or syllables that could not be brought into the line either above or below it*.

§ 23[c]. *Insertion* is indicated by writing (1) the omitted and to be inserted letter, or letters, above the line over or between the letter or letters where the insertion is to be made, II. 19, 56, 62, 173, 180; III. 34, 43, 48; IV. 1, 77, 93 &c.—(2) the letter to be inserted above the line with a dot underneath, or on its left-hand side, II. 29.—(3) the letter to be inserted above the line with a dot on its left, and another dot after the letter where the insertion is to be made, II. 71.—(4) the letter, or letters to be inserted, above the line between two dots, IV. 91; XLIV. 1.—(5) a word to be inserted above the line between three dots, II. 182. In XXX. 52, 95, 96 some Latin words are written over Greek words to explain or translate the latter.—(6) an omitted syllable (p̄ = p*re*) above the line, with a dot above the stroke, XXVIII. 21.—(7) the letter to be inserted *below* the line (attached to *h*), XXX. 46.—(8) a word to be inserted above the line with a mark of reference (·|·) before it, and a similar mark after the word after which it is to be inserted, XXII. 12.—(9) a word to be inserted on the left of the lemma within lines forming a square, with a mark of reference (÷) above the word, referring to a similar mark written above the place where the insertion is to come, XXX. 7.

§ 23[d]. *Marking* words or glosses. With a few exceptions† all the

* To prevent confusion the individual glosses have here been numbered. The first instances of two glosses being written in one line are II. 138, 139 and 143, 144, but they seem attributable to inadvertence or ignorance on the part of the scribe, as in both cases the second gloss does not begin with a capital, which seems to show that the scribe was not aware of having begun a second gloss. At II. 112 we meet with two lemmata in one line, without a gloss; but the scribe left some space between the two words, probably intending to write the glosses afterwards. III. 13—16 are three glosses written together, but perhaps by mistake, as the scribe does not seem to have understood them.

† The exceptions are: III. 34 (briudid), 38 (haeslin), 44 (su), 48 (uastrung), 53 (floda), 57 (pox); IV. 66 (borgenti), 71 (gaesuopę), 77 (tunderi), 83 (mixin); V. 2 (lomum), 5 (poccas); VII. 4 (dunnę); XIX. 16 (hreod), 17 (ebirdhring), 19 (fezra), 26 (haubit loh), 36 (haefuc), 38 (chelor), 41 (osifelti), 54 (ẏmaeti gold), 59 (uuldpaexhsue); XX. 3 (chyun), XXII. 5 (gezelt), &c. None of these words are marked.

*Germanic** glosses are marked in our MS. either by a *horizontal* (sometimes waving) *stroke* above them, or by an insulated v, also written above one or more letters of such glosses.

As it was found impracticable to print either the strokes or the v above the words, their presence in the MS. has been pointed out in the footnotes. But it is necessary here to discuss the possible meaning of the latter mark.

The *strokes* occur III. 11, 15 (here wrongly over a Latin word), 35, 37, 63–66; IV. 24, 74–76, 99 (here wrongly over a Latin word); V. 11, 15, 19, 22, 30; (VIII. 15); XVI. 28; XIX. 29, 35, 59, 63; XXIX. 11; XLVII. 31; XLVIII. 28, 54, 61, and are obviously intended to draw special attention to the words over which they are written.

The v occurs first of all XII. 18, and thenceforward (excepting the few cases just mentioned, where strokes are employed) regularly above Germanic words: XIII. 24, 34, 35, 40, 50; XV. 4; XVII. 11; XVIII. 2; XIX. 35 (see photogr., 1st col. li. 32), 43 (ib., li. at foot), 60 (ib., 2nd col. li. 15), 61 (ib., li. 16); XXI. 20 (ib., add. col., li. 17); XXII. 3 (ib., li. 22); XXIV. 3; XXVII. 25; XXXIV. 3; XXXV. 3, 6, 35, 54, 55, 59, 66, 69, 73–75, 122, 157, 158, 165, 175, 176, 203, 288; XXXVI. 7, 10, 14; XXXVII. 7; XXXIX. 6, 12, 20, 27, 30, 37; XLII. 6, 27; XLVI. 18 (here a stroke above the a was corrected into v); XLVII. 36 (v written sideways with top towards the left).

In none of these cases does the v differ from the v described above (§ 15), which latter is never used in the *text* of the Glossary, but only above the line, by way of correction, whenever *u* had been omitted; hence it was clearly intended for v (= *u*). There seems, therefore, no reason against accepting the v above the Germanic words likewise as v (= *u*).

It is true, in *four* instances (XIII. 41; XLII. 2; XLIII. 38; XLVII. 19), the mark looks more like y; in one case (XXII. 8; see photogr., add. col., li. 26) we could hardly read anything but y; in two cases (XLVII. 33, 65) it may be said to resemble x; in one case (XIX. 43; see photogr., last word of li. added at foot) it is v·; in another (XXVI. 6) y:; and in two instances (XLII. 4 and XLVI. 42) it is more y with a dot above it. But these deviations seem to be nothing but the result of the scribe having accidentally drawn down the right-hand stroke of the v a little more than was strictly necessary†.

* There are, apparently, no Germanic glosses in the first two Chapters; toscia (II. 101), which has been regarded as such, is most likely a late Latin word, for which see the Index.

† In most cases the real y has a dot above it, as: Kyrieleison (II. 98); Typo (II. 179); Myrtus (XIII. 48); Synicias (XV. 2); and (by second hand) uuylocbaso (XXII. 16); uuyrmbaso (XXII. 18). Occasionally it has no dot, as: hymnum (II. 85); crypta (XVI. 3). But wherever we examine it, it was clearly formed by first writing the v, and then *adding* the down-stroke to it. The scribe, therefore, knew when he had to write y not v.

It is impossible to say whether the scribe added the v above the line immediately after having written the word to be marked, or whether in all cases it was added afterwards either by the scribe himself or by a corrector. In most cases the v looks, in duction and colour of ink, exactly like the letters over which it stands, but here and there it looks finer than most of the other v[s], and also finer than the word over which it stands, whence we may infer that, in these cases, some corrector added the v.

As this marking of the Germanic glosses commenced with the horizontal stroke, and the v was adopted afterwards, it seems not unreasonable to say that it originated with our scribe, and that he did not merely follow the MS. from which he copied. If so, the v must have been intended to be v (=u), and only became, in a few instances, more like y or x by accident.

If the MS which our scribe followed had, say ſ (for *saxonice*), above the Germanic glosses, he might have misread this for y; but then we should find the latter character more frequently, or perhaps some other mark for the misunderstood ſ in our MS. The corruption might even go back to an earlier MS. than that copied by our scribe. None of these guesses, however, will sufficiently explain the regularity and uniformity of the v in our MS.

Hence it seems more reasonable to assume that the mark v really means v and is the initial of the word "*vernacule*," which would be most appropriate to our case.

In one instance (xxxi. 4), indeed, the v is found above a Latin word (*uncias**); in another (xxx. 6) over the word *sax*. The former may be due to inadvertence of the scribe, or to some other unexplained cause; and as to *sax* its meaning is supposed to be *saxonice*, and if this be the case, it would not be inappropriately marked by our scribe with v (= vernacule).

§ 23[e]. *Omissions* may be noticed occasionally as: (1) of *interpretations*, i. 14, 18, 23, 26, 42, 43, 72, 75, 79, 83, 99 &c. It is possible that in such cases the original Glossator had excerpted the lemmata from his sources with the intention of adding the interpretations later on.—(2) of one or more *letters*, i. 25 meretribus (for meretr*ic*ibus); ii. 100 (uestmenta for uest*i*menta).

§ 23[f]. *Signatures* to the quires do not appear in the MS., though it is possible that they have been cut away by the binder.

§ 23[g]. Two *Signs* for weights occur in Ch. xxxii. 2, see Latin *Index* (*C. apud latinus* &c.); another in xxxii. 4 (see ibid. *Obolus*) and another xxxii. 5 (see ibid. *uncia*); a sign for a shepherd's crook occurs in Ch. xlv.

* Glogger suggests that this may refer to an original A.S. *ynce*, or to O.H.G. *unza*.

18 (see ibid. *pedum*). Other signs, the meaning of which is not certain, are (1) three *dots* above *i*, III. 18; (2) two *dots* above an open *a*, IV. 77 (as the a is much like two cc, the scribe, perhaps, indicated that the dotted tops had to be erased); (3) † in the margin (to indicate something wrong), XII. 13, also by the side of a line left blank, XIII. 53; (4) ·|· above the line, as mark of *division* (?), XIV. 9 (see also above § 23 *b*).

§ 23h. *Spot*, in the vellum, and hence a blank left by the scribe, II. 91.—Accidental (ink) spot, IV. 75.

§ 23i. *Strokes*. Besides the strokes employed to indicate *contractions* (see above § 14), we find

A. *Perpendicular* strokes, (1) meaningless (?), or perhaps the top of a wrongly commenced *b*, *d*, *l* or other letter, I. 126 and XXX. 87 (above *u*); II. 11 and 167; XXXV. 33 (above *p*); X. 22 and XXVIII. 38; XXXV. 44 (above *r*); XIII. 36 (above *o*); XXXV. 227 (above *t*).—(2) as mark of transposition, XV. 14 (perhaps here = *i* ?).—(3) to separate two glosses (?), II. 144. B. *Horizontal* strokes. (1) to mark A.S. (or supposed A.S.) words (see above § 23 *d*).—(2) to mark a Greek word, XVIII. 1.

§ 23k. *Transposition* is indicated by writing above the words to be transposed (1) three *dots* (:·), IV. 105; XXVIII. 68; XXXVI. 3.—(2) the mark ÷, XXXV. 195; XL. 17.

§ 23l. *Uncertain* words, letters or signs, or expansion of contractions, XII. 27; XIII. 42; XXX. 85, 95; XXXII. 5, 7; XXXIII. 5; XXXV. 1, 236, 297.

§ 23m. *Underlining* both lemma and interpretation (meaningless ?), XLVII. 57, 82.

§ 23n. *Vacant spaces* left, II. 112; XIX. 13, 17, 18.

§ 23o. *Wrong letters*, III. 36.

It is hoped that the text of the Glossary is free from serious blemishes, especially as I was able to compare my readings of the MS. with Dr Glogger's carefully prepared edition (see above p. xvii, note).

That my critical Indexes will be free from errors and shortcomings is more than I can expect. But those who use the work will, I trust, pardon them on account of the hundreds of difficult, obscure and intricate points that had to be ascertained, examined and solved. There remain certain obscure points, ex. gr. amatorie, ars *philophie* (?). What is meant by the latter word?—antesignato, signatore *suspectum*. What word or what meaning is hidden in *suspectum*?—arcticos, here the sentence after *antarticus* does not seem to be quite correct.

In view of all that has been published during the last fifty years on Glosses, I felt that a mere reproduction of the text and a mere Index to the Latin and Germanic words, which seemed to be the only feasible plan for the Corpus Glossary, would not be of much use with respect to the present one, especially as it indicates the sources of a great many of the Glosses, and affords, therefore, a firmer basis for editorial researches and emendations. The Syndics of the University Press readily agreed with my views, and it is hoped that the result may be considered fairly satisfactory.

In tracing the glosses to their sources I have derived much help from the eminent labours of Goetz, Steinmeyer, Glogger, Schlutter (various articles in the *Archiv für Lat. Lexic.*; *Anglia*; *Journ. of Engl. Philol.* &c. &c.). But I may be excused for saying that, in spite of this advantage, I had to read most of the sources myself again, in the endeavour to find, if possible, those words which they had been unable to trace. I read *Rufinus* five or six times, as the Glossary contains six collections of words excerpted from him (see next page). The *Canones*, the *Regula S. Benedicti*, *St Jerome's Liber de Viris illustribus* and other sources I read three or four times, because the glosses from these sources either appear alphabetically, and, therefore, no longer in the order of their source, or have become misplaced by the scribes. Cassiodorus' Comment. on the Psalms I read two or three times, apart from the time I spent in tracing the words of Ch. XXVIII to him, as the Glossary does not ascribe them to him, but to the Liber Antonii, though only seventeen of them are excerpted from this last source.

To discover, if possible, the source of the words glossed in Ch. VI I spared no efforts, and as several of them had a poetical look about them, I read Dracontius, Prudentius and other Latin poets, but in vain. They have now been traced to Gildas (see below p. xxxviii).

Space does not allow me to point out either the importance of various glosses for lexicographical and other purposes, or the special features of this Glossary in connection with other Glossaries. Such further remarks I reserve for another work which I am preparing for the London Philological Society, and which will deal with the Corpus, Epinal and Erfurt Glossaries in combination with the present Glossary.

To conclude, I discharge a pleasant duty in thanking the Syndics of the University Press for bearing the expenses involved in the publication of this edition; the Reader of the same Press for his unremitting attention to the correctness of the work; Prof. John E. B. Mayor and Mr Alex. Souter (of Mansfield College, Oxford), for reading the proof-sheets and helping me with corrections and observations; Mr Israel Abrahams, Mr H. T. Francis, Prof. Henry Jackson, Mr F. J. H. Jenkinson, Mr H. L. Pass, Dr W. Aldis Wright, the Rev. the Master of St. John's College, for help in various ways; and the Council of Trinity College for the loan of one of their copies of the Augsburg edition of

c. 1470 of *St Jerome's Liber de Viris illustribus* (see below p. xlix). Prof. W. W. Skeat has not only read all the proof-sheets, but assisted me in the A.S. portion of the work by copious notes, observations and corrections with the utmost readiness and generosity. His notes, corrections &c. appear with respect to some words in the I. (*Latin*) Index, with respect to others in the V. (*Germanic*) Index in a more or less abridged form, for which I alone am responsible.

BIBLIOGRAPHY OF THE GLOSSARY.

A. *Table of Contents*, that is: **Headings** or **Titles** of the Chapters in the Glossary.

B. **Sources** from whence the *lemmata* (and some of the interpretations) are excerpted.—*Books* and *MSS.* used and consulted in tracing the lemmata to their sources.—*Abbreviations* employed in the references, quotations &c. (chiefly in the Latin Index).

A. The Glossary is divided into 48 Chapters with the following Headings or Titles:

I. Glosae Verborum de Canonibus . . . . . p. 1—3[b]

For further information on the chapters see below (B) *Sources*, art. *Can. Canon.*, &c. &c.

II. Interpretatio Sermonum de Regulis (see below *Bened.*) p. 3[b]—7[a]

It is uncertain whether this plural form means that other *Regulae* besides that of S. Benedict have been excerpted.

III. Verba de Sancti Martyni Storia (see below *Sulpicius* Severus), glosses 1 to 52 . . . . p. 7[a]—8[a]

[Vita S. Antonii, auctore S. Athanasio, Evagrio interprete (see below *Vita* S. Antonii), glosses 52—66] . . . . . . p. 8[a]

This Source is not indicated in the Glossary in any way, unless, perhaps, by the word *Antoni* (Gloss 52), see I. Index (*Latin*), sub v. *Antoni.*

IV. Liber Ecclesiasticae istoriae (120 glosses) . . p. 8[a]—10[a]
V. De Ecclesiastica Storia (32 glosses) . . . . p. 10[a]—10[b]
XXXV. De Eusebio (306 glosses) . . . . . p. 33[a]—38[b]

These three chapters consist of *five* or *six* collections of glosses to the nine Books of Rufinus' Latin translation of Eusebius' Ecclesiastical History and to the Books x and xi which Rufinus added of his own to Eusebius. The Chapters iv and v are evidently two independent collections, the one being the first 111 glosses of Chapter iv, for the most part arranged (*unalphabetically*) in the order in which the lemmata occur in Rufinus' text. The second (*alphabetically* arranged, and, therefore, no longer following the order of Rufinus' text) extends (as far as the A and B glosses) from gloss 112 to the end (gloss 120) of Chapter iv, and (for the C to T glosses) till the end of the *fifth* Chapter. This arrangement, therefore, shows that the heading to Ch. v (*De Ecclesiastica Storia*) is out of place, and should have come before the 112th gloss of Ch. iv.

In Ch. xxxv. we have *three* (perhaps *four*) independent collections, in which the lemmata are arranged, not alphabetically, but, with a few exceptions, in the order in which they occur in Rufinus' text. The *first*, which deals with his *eleven Books*, extends from gloss 1 to 73. The *second* (which likewise deals with the eleven Books) extends from gloss 88 to gloss 247. The *third* seems to have been split up (perhaps in the process of copying) into two portions, one (glosses 300 to 306) dealing with Rufinus' Books i to iv, the other (glosses 248 to 299) with his Books v to xi.

A *fourth* collection may be traced in the glosses 74 to 87, the lemmata of which are extracted from Rufinus' Books i, iii, iv, vii, viii, x, xi, ix.

It is to be remarked that in the *first*, *second*, and *fourth* collections of Ch. xxxv the glosses to Rufinus' *ninth* Book follow, not after those to the eighth, but after those to the *tenth* and *eleventh* Book.

VI. Incipit breuis exsolutio (= Gildas, *De Excidio Britanniae Lib.*) p. 10[b]

All efforts to identify the glosses of this chapter had hitherto been unsuccessful, till Glogger recognised them by Schlutter's reference (see *The Journal of English and Germanic Philology*, Vol. v, p. 466) to a line in Gildas. As he kindly pointed this out to me on 1 Jan., 1906 (after my text and Latin Index had been printed), the references of all the words identified are given in the *Addenda*. Only three or four remain to be traced.

The heading, *breuis exsolutio*, is, apparently, not derived from Gildas' work, and is, perhaps, to be attributed to the Glossator.

VII. De Paralipomenon (i and ii = Chronicc. i and ii). The lemmata of Chapters vii to xxv are (with few exceptions, specially pointed out) excerpted from the Vulgate . . . . p. 10[b]—11[a]

VIII. De Salamone (= Liber Proverbiorum) . . . p. 11[a]—11[b]

IX. De Eclesiasten (= Ecclesiastes) . . . . p. 11[b]

X. In Cantico Canticorum (= Canticum Canticor.) . . p. 11[b]—12[a]

XI. De Sapientia (= Liber Sapientiae) . . . . p. 12[b]

XII. De Ecclesiastico (= Ecclesiasticus) . . . p. 12[b]—13[b]

XIII. In Libro Isaie prophete (Isaias) . . . . p. 13[b]—15[a]

XIV. Incipit in Hieremia (Glosses 1—31, 34—36 = Jeremias; Glosses 32 and 33 = Threni, id est Lamentationes) . . p. 15[a]—16[a]

XV. Incipit in Hiezechiel (Glosses 1—31 and 37—48 = *Ezechiel*; Glosses 32—36 = *Osee*[1], though quoted in the Glossary as from Ezechiel; but the heading 'Item Alia,' found after No. 36 may have been meant as title to these five Glosses) . . . . . . p. 16[a]—17[a]

XVI. Incipit in Danielem . . . . p. 17[a]—17[b]

XVII. De Johel uel de Prophetis minoribus (lemmata extracted from *Joel*, *Amos*, *Jonas*, *Michaeas*, *Nahum*, *Habacuc*, *Sophonias*, *Zacharias*, *Malachias*) . . . . p. 17[b]—18[a]

XVIII. De Ose specialiter (Repetition of xv. 32—36, except No. 35 which is here omitted) . . . . p. 18[a]

XIX. Incipit in Job . . . . p. 18[a]—19[b]

XX. Incipit in Tobia . . . . p. 19[b]

XXI. Incipit in Judith . . . . p. 19[a]—20[a]

[1] See also Ch. xviii.

XXII. De Ester . . . . p. 20^a—20^b

XXIII. Incipit in Esdra (= 1 Esdras; 2 Esdras or Liber Nehemiae) p. 21^a

XXIV. Incipit in Matheum . . . . p. 21^a—21^b

XXV. De Marco et Luca et Johanne . . . . . p. 21^b

XXVI. In Libro Officiorum (= S. Isidori *De Ecclesiasticis Officiis Libri duo*) . . . . p. 22^a

XXVII. In Libro Rotarum (= S. Isidori *Liber de Natura Rerum*; see below, Ch. XLIV) . . . . p. 22^a—22^b

XXVIII. In Libro Antonii (the *first* part, i.e. Glosses 1—17 and 22 and 23 = *Vita* Beati Antonii Abbatis; the *second* part, i.e. Glosses 18—21, 24—88 = Magni Aurelii *Cassiodori* in Psalterium Expositio). p. 22^b—25^b

N.B. It is to be observed that the *second* portion of this chapter consists mostly of *extracts* (*lemmata* as well as *interpretations*) from *Cassiodorus*. For inst. XXVIII. 20 (*diapsalma* &c.) occurs, word for word, in Cassiodore. The differences between the Glossary and Cassiodore's text have been pointed out in the Latin Index.

XXIX. Incipit Uerborum interpretatio (= S. Eus. *Hieronymi* Commentt. in Evangelium Matthaei) . . . . . . p. 25^b—27^a

N.B. Gloss No. 71 (p. 27^a) is from the *Catalogus S. Hieron.*, and should have come in Chapt. XXX.

XXX. De Ca[ta]logo Hieronimi (= S. Eus. *Hieronymi* Liber, or Catalogus, de Viris illustribus) . . . . . . p. 27^a—29^a

{XXXI. De Ponderibus incipit . . . . . p. 29^a—30^a
{XXXII. De Ponderibus . . . . p. 30^b—31^a

For these two chapters no text on Weights &c. could be found entirely agreeing with the extracts and explanations of the Glossary. Hence no suggestions as regards the Glosses have been made. For instance XXXI. 3 the nom. *libra* must be wrong, but whether the Glossator meant *libras* or some other form cannot be determined.

XXXIII. De Ponderibus secundum Eucherium . . . p. 31^a—32^a

See below, *Eucherius*. (The Glosses 17, 18, and 21 to 31 do not seem to occur in the editions of Eucherius now known to us.)

XXXIV. De Cassiano (= Johannes *Cassianus*) . . . p. 32^a—33^a

See also below, Chapter XLVIII.

XXXV. De Eusebio (see above under Chapters IV and V) p. 33^a—38^b

XXXVI. De Orosio (= Pauli *Orosii* Historiae adversum paganos) p. 38^b—39^a

XXXVII. De Sancti Agustini (= either De libris Sermonum S. *Augustini*, which is the title given by two MSS., or = De Sermonibus Sancti *Augustini*) . . . . p. 39^a—39^b

For some of the words in this chapter special references to other works of S. Augustine have been given.

XXXVIII. De Clemente (= 1 *S. Clementis* Romani Recognitiones, Rufino Aquileiensi Presb. interprete; 2 Epistola prima *Clementis* ad Jacobum fratrem Domini) . . . . p. 39^b—40^b

XXXIX. De Dialogorum. [The Glosses 1—44, 46, 47, 48 (?), 54 (?), 72 (?) = *S. Gregorii* Magni Dialogorum libri quatuor; Glosses 45, 49—52 = *S. Gregorii* Magni Liber Regulae pastoralis, partes IV.; Glosses 53, 54 (?), 55—71, 72 (?), 73 are excerpted from the *Canones*, see above, Chapter I, and below, Ch. XLI]. . . . p. 40[b]—42[b]

XL. Item incipiunt Uerba . . . . p. 42[b]—43[a]

Nearly all the lemmata in this chapter have also been traced to Gildas (see above the note to Ch. VI), and the references will be found in the *Addenda*.

XLI. Item de nominibus diuersis . . . . . p. 43[a]—43[b]

The Glosses 1—6 are excerpted from the *Cănones*, in continuation to Nos. 53—73 of Ch. XXXIX (see also above Ch. I). The Glosses 7—16 are ten names of precious stones, excerpted, it seems, from *Apoc.* xxi. 19, 20, as the lemmata all follow there in the same order as in the present Glossary. They are also mentioned, though in a different order, in *Exod.* xxviii. 17—20 and xxix. 10—13, and *Ezek.* xxviii. 13. They all occur in the Cp., Ep. and Ef.[1] Glossaries (except that Nos. 7 and 8 are wanting in Cp., and 8 also in Ep. and Ef.[1]), and in Ep. and Ef.[1] (which have, in spite of their later date, in certain parts, a more primitive alphabetical arrangement than Corpus), in the same order under their respective initial letters, as here.

Certain parts of the explanations of the names of these stones appear in the present Glossary under different stones than in the Cp., Ep. and Ef.[1] Glossaries, as is indicated in the I. Index (*Latin*).

The Glosses 17—21 are probably all from Sulpicius Severus' *Dialogi* (where No. 17 occurs) or *Vita S. Martini* (where No. 19 is found); but Nos. 18, 20 and 21 have not yet been traced.

XLII. Incipit ex diuersis libris . . . . . . p. 43[b]—44[a]

The Glosses 1, 3, 5, 10, 12, 15—19 occur in the *Dialogi* of Sulp. Severus. No. 4 is found in the same author's *Vita S. Martini.*

Glosses 2, 6—9, 11, 13, 14, 20, 22 have not yet been traced; 21, 23—27 occur in the *Vita S. Eugeniae Virginis et Martyris* (Migne's *Patr. Lat.* Vol. LXXIII, col. 605 sqq., and id. Vol. XXI, col. 1105 sqq.).

XLIII. Item de diuersis nominibus (On divers *nouns*) = Donati *Ars Grammatica* (Henr. Keil, *Grammatici Latini*, Vol. IV, Lipsiae, 1864, p. 367 sqq.) . . . . p. 44[a]—45[a]

Some of the lemmata do not occur in the text of *Donatus* as known to us, but have been excerpted from other grammatical works specially referred to in the I. (*Latin*) Index.

XLIV. Item alia; de Caelo = S. Isidori *de natura Rerum* (see also above Ch. XXVII) in Vol. VII of Areval's ed. of Isidore's *Opera*, Romae, 1803. Reprinted in Vol. LXXXIII of Migne's *Patr. Lat.*; to this last ed. most of the references are made . . . . . . p. 45[a]—46[b]

XLV. Uerba de multis (= Ars *Phocae* de nomine et verbo, in Henr. Keil's *Grammatici Latini*, Vol. V, Lipsiae, 1868, pp. 405 sqq.) p. 46[b]—47[a]

XLVI. Item alia [Glosses 1—39 = Ars *Phocae*, like Ch. XLV. For the Glosses 40—43, see the I. (*Latin*) Index]. . . . p. 47[a]—47[b]

XLVII. Item alia . . . . p. 47[b]—49[b]

None of the 103 Glosses comprised in this Ch. have as yet been traced to any source with certainty. But perhaps the following are excerpted from Aldhelm;

Nos. 6 (*cirris* = A. p. 66, 8), 13 (*perna* = A. p. 251), 15 (*tappula*, tip- = A. p. 254), 56 (*ciconia* = A. p. 257), 87 (*castorius*; see A. p. 264), 93 (*scrufa* = A. p. 266). If this be right, possibly other lemmata might be traced to him. It will be seen from the I. (*Latin*) Index that they all occur in the Cp. and Ef.[1] Glossaries, and most of them also in the Ep. Glossary.

XLVIII. Item de Cassiano (see above, Chapter XXXIV) p. 49^b—50^b

B. **Sources** from whence the *lemmata* (and some of the *interpretations*) are excerpted.—*Books* and *MSS.* used and consulted in tracing the lemmata to their sources.—*Abbreviations* employed in the references, quotations, &c. (chiefly in the Latin Index).

Acta SS. = Acta Sanctorum. Fol. Antv., Paris., Brux. 1643—.

Aelfr. = *Alfric* (q.v.).

Afric. = Africani; see *Can.*

Agustini; see *Augustinus.*

Alfr. Vocab. = Archb. *Alfric's Vocabulary* in Wright-Wülcker's Anglo-Saxon and Old Engl. Vocabularies, col. 104 sqq.

Aldh. = Aldhelmus (S. Aldhelmi *Opera*, ed. J. A. Giles. 8° Oxon. 1844).

Alia (heading of Chapter XLVI) = *Ars Phocae* (q.v.).

Alia (heading of Chapter XLVII), refers to various unknown sources; and is, therefore, always followed by (= ?) in the Latin Index.

Alia: de Caelo (heading of Chapter XLIV) = *Liber Rotarum* (q.v.) = Isidori (q.v.) *Liber de natura rerum.*

Amos (one of the Minor Prophets, for which see Chapter XVII).

Ancyr. = Ancyrani; see *Can.*

Anglia. Zeitschr. für Englische Philologie, 8°. Halle. 1878—.

Antioch. = Antiocheni; see *Can.*

Anton.; Antoni Vita; *or* Lib. Anton.; *or* Antoni Storia = S. Antonii Vita.

A. *Vita b. Antonii* Abbatis, auctore Sancto Athanasio, episcopo Alexandrino, interprete Evagrio presbytero Antiocheno [Migne's *Patrologia Lat.*, vol. LXXIII (*Vitae Patrum*), col. 126 sqq.].

B [Fol. 159^a of] D. Athanasii Archiep. Alexandrini...*opera omnia.* Fol. Coloniæ. 1548.

C [p. 77^A of Append. to] *Liber de Passione D. N. Jesu Christi*, &c., ed. Wolfg. Lazius; Basil. 1552.

D. Athanasii *Opp.*, Paris. 1572.

E. [p. 35 sq.] Herib. Rosweydi *Vitae Patrum*, fol. Antw. 1615.

F. [tom. II. Jan., p. 126^b] Acta Sanctorum (1643).

G. Athanasii Opp., ed. Monach. Ord. S. Ben. e Congr. S. Mauri, Paris. 1698.

H. Cambridge Univ. Library MS. (pressmark Mm. 4. 28), fol. 3^a to 21^b.

Apoc. = Apocalypse.

Apostt. = Apostolorum; see *Can.*

Arch. f. L. L.; *or* Arch. f. Lat. Lex.; or Archiv = *Archiv für Latein. Lexicographie und Grammatik*, herausgeg. von Eduard Wölfflin. 8° Leipz. 1884—.

Ars Phocae in *Grammatici Latini* ex recens. Henr. Keilii, 8° Lips. 1868, vol. v, p. 405 sqq.

A.S. = Anglo-Saxon.

Athanasius (S.), Episc. Alex., *Vita B. Antonii*; see *Anton.*

Aug. = *Augustinus* (q.v.).

Augsburg edition (C) of the Catalogus *S. Hieronymi* (q.v.).

Augustinus (S.), Sermones, in Migne's *Patrol. Latina*, vols. XXXVIII and XXXIX (S. Augustini *Opera*, tom. v, ptes 1 & 2).—For some of the words special references to other works of S. Augustine have been given (see *sationis*).

B = text B = Utrecht edition of the Catalogus *S. Hieronymi* (q.v.).

Bened. reg. = *S. Benedicti* Regula.

(A) Benedicti *Regula Monachorum*. Rec. Ed. Woelfflin. 8° Lipsiae (Teubner), 1895. All references are to the chapters and lines of this edition, with the corresponding chapters and lines of the Cassino edition (B) between [ ]. Wherever reference is made to C, D &c. these works are specially mentioned by their titles.

(B) *Regulae* S. Benedicti Traditio Codicum MSS. Casinensium... cura et studio Monachorum in archicoenobio Casinensi degentium. Fol. Montiscasini. 1900.

(C) *Regula* S. Patris Benedicti...rec. a P. Edmundo Schmidt. 8° Ratisbonae, 1880 [Lib. II of *Vita et Regula SS. P. Benedicti una cum* (Lib. III) *expositione Regulae a Hildemaro tradita*, 8° Ratisbonae. 1880].

(D) Migne's *Patrologia Lat.* tom. LXVI: S. Benedicti *opera omnia* [col. 205 sqq. S. Benedicti *Regula*, cum Comm.].

(E) *Regula* S. P. Benedicti...rec. a P. Edm. Schmidt. 8° Ratisb. 1892.

(F) Die Benediktinerregel (MS. 916), herausgeg. von Paul Piper (Bd 162 of Jos. Kürschner's *Deutsche National-Litteratur*, 1898).

(G) *Textgeschichte der Regula S. Benedicti*, von Ludwig Traube [Band XXI, Abth. III of *Abhandlungen der hist. Classe der Kön. Bayer. Akademie der Wissenschaften*, 4° Munchen. 1898]. Cf. also Keronis Monachi S. Galli *Interpretatio Vocabulorum Barbaricorum in Regula S. Benedicti* [in Tom. II fol. 69 of M. H. Goldasti *Rerum Alamannicarum Scriptores*, Fol. Francof. 1661]; Arn. Schröer, *Die Winteney-version der Regula S. Benedicti*, Latein. u. Englisch, 8° Halle a. S. 1888. H. Logeman, The Rule of S. Benet, Lat. & A.S. interlin. version, 8° Lond. (E.E.T.S.), 1888, &c., &c.

Blume = Blume (F.), K. Lachmann und A. Rudorff, *Die Schriften der Römischen Feldmesser*, herausg. und erläutert. 2 Bde, 8°, Berlin, 1848 (Also quoted under the title *Gromatici veteres*).

Bonif. = (Pope) Bonifacius, see below *Can.*, *Canon.*

Bosw. T.; *or* Bosworth T. = Bosworth (Jos.) and T. Northcote Toller, An Anglo-Saxon Dictionary; IV parts, 4°, Oxford, 1882—1892.

Breu. exsol. = Breuis exsolutio (heading of Chapter VI), which Glogger, guided by a quotation made by Schlutter (in vol. V of *Journ. of Engl. and Germ. Philol.*), discovered to be a collection of words extràcted from Gildas' *De excidio Britanniae* (for which see the *Addenda*, at the end of this volume).

Brit. Mus. MS. (pressmark 28. h. 7; Cotton, Vesp. B. VI fol. 106^b); see *Eucherius*.

Brüll (Ad.), Trachten der Jüden im nachbiblischen Alterthume. 8° Frankf. o. M. 1873.

Bülbring (Karl D.), Altengl. Elementarbuch. 8° Heidelb. 1902.

C = text C = Augsburg edition of the Catalogus *S. Hieronymi* (q.v.).

Cacciari (Petr. Thom.), *Eccles. Hist. Eusebii Pamph.* libri novem Ruffino interpr.; see below, *Rufinus* (edition C).

Calch. = Calchedonensis; see *Can.*

Cambr. MS.; or Cambridge MS.; or Cambridge Un Libr. MS. (= one of the XIIth cent., Pressmark Kk. 4. 6) contains (1) on foll. 41—44, a wholly Latin-Latin (without any Germanic interpretations) Glossary to the Old Testament, from Genes. to Job. It is akin to our Leiden Glossary, as is evident from the Glosses from Paralip. (Chapt. VII) to Job (Ch. XIX, gloss 38), which occur on fol. 43^b to 44^b, and to which references are made in the I. or Latin Index. (2) on ff. 166^b—176^b Sancti Hieronymi (q.v.) Catalogus virorum illustrium. This latter work is also found in another Cambridge MS. referred to, which belongs to the XVth cent., and bears the Pressmark Dd. 7. 2. It is, however, imperfect, and the Greek words are not written in. Another Cambridge Univ. Library MS. of the XIIth cent. (Pressmark Mm. 4. 28) contains, on foll. 3^a to 21^b, Vita S. Antonii...ab Athanasio...transl. ab Evagrio.

Can.; Canon. = Canones.—Can. *Apostt.* (= Canones Apostolòrum); Can. Conc. *Afric.* (= Canones Concilii Africani); Can. Conc. *Ancyr.* (= C. C. Ancyrani); Can. Conc. *Antioch.* (= C. C. Antiocheni); Can. Conc. *Calch.* or *Chalc.* (= C. C. Calchedonensis); Can. Conc. *Carth.* or *Carthag.* (= C. C. Carthaginensis); Can. Conc. *Constant.* (= C. C. Constantinopolitani); Can. Conc. *Gangr.* (= C. C. Gangrensis); Can. Conc. *Laod.* (= C. C. Laodiceni); Can. Conc. *Neocaes.* (= C. C. Neocaesariensis); Can. Conc. *Nic.*, or *Nicaen.* (= C. C. Nicaeni); Can. Conc. *Sard.* or *Sardic.* (= C. C. Sardicensis).

(A) The Canons and Decrees of the Popes, transl. into Latin, and collected by Dionysius Exiguus (circa A.D. 514—523), published in (pp. 97—274) *Bibliotheca Juris Canonici Veteris...Ex antiquis Codd. MSS. Bibliothecæ* Christ. Iustelli..., *cum versionibus Latinis...*, *opera et studio* Gul. Voelli...et Henr. Iustelli...Fol. Lut. Paris. 1661.

The (first vol. of this) work contains (on pp. 1—96):

1. Codex *Canonum Ecclesiæ Universæ* a Concilio Calchedonensi, et Justiniano Imp. confirmatus, Græce et Latine, cum notis Chr. Iustelli: (*a*) A.D. 314 Concilii *Ancyrani* Canones XXV; (*b*) A.D. 314 Conc. *Neocæsariensis* Can. XIV; (*c*) A.D. 325 Conc. *Nicæni* oecumenici I Can. XX; (*d*) A.D. 325 Conc. *Gangrensis* Can. XX; (*e*) A.D. 341 Conc. *Antiocheni* Can. XXV; (*f*) A.D. 364 Conc. *Laodiceni* Can. LIX; (*g*) A.D. 381 Conc. *Constantinopolitani* oecumenici II Can. VII; (*h*) A.D. 431 Conc. *Ephesini* oecumenici III Can. VIII; (*i*) A.D. 451 Conc. *Calchedonensis* oecumenici IV Can. XXIX.

2. Codex *Canonum Ecclesiasticorum* Dionysii Exigui, sive Codex *Canonum Vetus Ecclesiæ Romanæ*, ab Hadriano Papa I Carolo Magno Romæ quondam oblatus...Cui accesserunt antiquiora *Pontificum Romanorum decreta*, ab eodem Dionysio collecta, pp. 97—274.

This Collection was used by our Glossator, and contains, besides *Dionysius*' second redaction of his Latin interpretation of the above Canons [excluding *h*] pertaining to the Greek Church, also (*a*) Dionysius' *Preface*; *tituli* Canonum &c. (pp. 97—111); (*b*) *sine dat.*, Regulæ (50) Eccles. *SS. Apostolorum*, prolatæ per Clementem Ecclesiæ Romanæ Pont., pp. 112—116; (*c*) A.D. 343 Canones Synodi *Sardicensis* XXI, pp. 137—141; (*d*) A.D. 419 Synodus apud *Carthaginem Africanorum*, quæ constituit canones CXXXVIII (Praef.; *Professio fidei Nicæni Concilij*, and Cann. I—CXXXVIII), pp. 141—174.—(*e*) *Epistola Synodica S. Cyrilli* et *Concilii Alexandrini contra Nestorium* (a Dionysio Exiguo in Latinum sermonem translata), pp. 175—180.—(*f*) Collectio *Decretorum Pontificum Romanorum*, authore Dionysio Exiguo, pp. 181—248. [This Collection contains Decrees of the Pontiffs: (1) *Siricius*, A.D. 385, pp. 190—194; (2) *Innocentius*, A.D. 404, pp. 194—211; (3) *Zozimus*, A.D. 417, pp. 211—212; (4) *Bonifacius*, A.D. 419, pp. 213—215; (5) *Cœlestinus*, A.D. 429, pp. 215—222; (6) *Leo* I., A.D. 444, pp. 222—239; (7) *Gelasius*, A.D. 492, pp. 239—245; (8) *Anastasius*, A.D. 498, pp. 245—248].—(*g*) Collectio II. *Decretum Pontificum Romanorum* ab Hilario ad Gregorium II., pp. 249—274. This (second) Collection contains Decrees of: (1) *Hilarius*, A.D. 461, pp. 249—253; (2) *Simplicius*, A.D. 467, p. 254; (3) *Felix*, A.D. 483, pp. 255—257; (4) *Symmachus*, A.D. 497, pp. 257—267; (5) *Hormisda*, A.D. 514, pp. 267—272; (6) *Gregorius* jun., A.D. 715, pp. 272—274.

The whole Collection has been reprinted in Migne's *Patr. Lat.* Tom. LXVII.

(B) *Collectio Canonum S. Isidoro Hispal. ascripta* (contain. (*a*) Excerpta Canonum; (*b*) Graecorum Concilia; (*c*) Africæ Concilia; (*d*) Galliæ Concilia; (*e*) Concilia Hispaniæ; (*f*) Epistolae Decretales), in S. Isidori Hispalensis episcopi *Opera Omnia*, tom. VIII [Migne's *Patrologia Latina*, vol. LXXXIV].

(C) Maassen (Dr Friedr.), *Geschichte der Quellen und der Literatur des canonischen Rechts im Abendlande bis zum Ausgange des Mit-*

telalters. Erster Band, 8° Gratz, 1870. [As *Appendix*, pp. 903 sqq.. (1) Caecilian's Version der Canonen von Nicaea; (2) Die gallisch-spanische Version der Canonen von Nicaea; (3) Die gallische Version der Canonen von Nicaea; (4) Das Fragment der freisinger Handschrift, der nicaenischen Canonen, c. 15—19; (5) Unknown version of the 13th and 20th Canon of Nicenum in a MS. of Saint Germain; (6) Die isidorische Version der Canonen von Nicaea, Ancyra, Neocaesarea, Gangra in ihrer ältesten Gestalt; (7) Canonen von Ancyra, Neocaesarea, Gangra und Antiochien in der gallischen Version; (8) A Canon not found among the known Canons of Antiochia (in a MS. of Saint Germain); (9) Die Canonen von Constantinopel in eigenthümlicher Version; (10) Die Canonen von Chalcedon in eigenthümlicher Version; (11) Die Canonen von Ephesus in eigenthümlicher Version, &c. &c.].

(D) *Sacrorum Conciliorum Nova, et amplissima Collectio, in qua praeter ea quae* Phil. Labbeus, et Gabr. Cossartius, et Nicolaus Coleti *in lucem edidere ea omnia insuper suis in locis optime disposita exhibentur quae* Joannes Dominicus Mansi...evulgavit. Editio novissima ab eodem Patre Mansi...curata. Fol. Florentiae, 1759.

(E) El. Steinmeyer u. Ed. Sievers, *Althochd. Glossen*, Berlin, 1882, 8°, II, pp. 82—152.

(F) Turner (C. Hamilton), *Ecclesiae Occidentalis Monumenta Juris antiquissima*, Fasciculi I pars prior (Canones Apostolorum, &c.), pars 2ª (Nicaeni Concilii Praefat. Capitula Symbolum Canones). 4°, Oxon. 1899, 1904.

Cant. = Canticum Canticorum, in the Vulg.

Carth.; or Carthag. = Carthaginensis; see *Can.*

Cass.; *or* Cassian.; *or* De Cass.; *or* De Cass. Inst. = De Cassiano (heading of Chapters XXXIV and XLVIII) = Johannes Cassianus, *Institutionum* libri XII, ex recens. Michael. Petschenig (vol. XVII of the Vienna *Corpus Scriptt. Eccles. Latin.*, Vindob. 1888).—Nest. = Joh. Cassianus, De Incarnatione Domini *Contra Nestorium*, libri VII, ex recens. Mich. Petschenig (ibid.).—Conl. = Joh. Cassianus, *Conlationes*, ed. Mich. Petschenig (vol. XIII, pars 2, ibid.).

Cass. Psalm.; or Cass. in Psalm. = Magni Aurelii Cassiodori *in Psalterium Expositio* (vol. LXX of Migne's *Patr. Lat.*).—Cassiod. Hist. Eccl. = M. Aur. Cassiodori *Historia Eccles.* vocata *tripartita* (ibid. vol. LXIX).

Cat.; Catal.; Cat. Hier.; Cat. Hieron. = Catalogus Hieronymi = S. *Hieronymi* (q.v.) *Catalogus* or Liber de Viris illustribus.

Cent. Dict. = The Century Dictionary...of the English Language, ed. Will. Dwight Whitney, 6 vols., New York, 1889—91, fol.

Chalc. = Chalchedonensis, see *Can.*

Chron. I & II (also ent. Paralipomenon), in the Vulg.

Clem.; *or* Clem. Recognitt.; *or* Clem. Rom. Recognitt. = De Clemente (heading of Chapter XXXVIII) = S. Clementis Romani *Recognitiones*, Rufino Aquileiensi Presb. interprete, ed. E. G. Gersdorf, 8° Lips. 1838 (reprinted Migne, *Patr. Gr.* I, col. 1201 sqq.).—Epistola prima Clementis ad Jacobum Fratrem Domini, in Migne's *Patr. Lat.* CXXX col. 19 sqq.

Conc. = Concilii; see *Can.*

Conl. = (Cassiani) Conlationes; see *Cass.*

Constant. = Constantinopolitani; see *Can.*

Cormac's Glossary, in W. Stokes' (q.v.) *Three Irish Glossaries.*

Corpus Glossary; see *Hessels.*

Cotgrave (Randle), A Dictionarie of the French and English tongues. Fol. Lond. 1611.

Cp.; *or* Cp. Gloss.; *or* Cp. Glossary; *or* Corp. Gl.; *or* Corpus; *or* Corpus Gl. = *Corpus Glossary*, ed. J. H. Hessels (q.v.).

Cp. Int. = The Interpraetatio or First Part of the *Corpus Glossary*; see *Hessels.*

Cyprianus De op. et eleem. (in the Vienna *Corp. Scriptt. Eccl. Latin.* III, 1).

D. = Dutch or Deutsches.

Dan. = Daniel (heading of Chapter XVI); see (besides the edd. of the Vulgate) Migne's *Patr. Lat.* vol. XXVIII.

Decr.; *or* Decret. = Decretum *or* Decreta (Decr. Bonif.—Decret. Caelest. —Decret. Gelas.—Decr. Hil. (Hilar.)—Decr. Horm.—Decret. Innoc. —Decret. Leon.—Decr. Siricii—Decret. Symm.—Decret. Zosimi); see above *Can.*, *Canon.*

Def. fid. Chalc. (Calch.) = Definitio fidei Chalcedonensis, ap. Mans. (q.v.) VII, 752[a].

Def. fidei Conc. Nic. = Definitio fidei Concilii Nicaeni (for which see Chapter CXXXVII of the *Can. Conc. Carth.*); see above *Can.*; *Canon.*

Defin. = Definitio; see *Vetus Defin.*

De Vit, Gloss. = Glossarium (in Aeg. Forcellini Totius Latinitatis Lexicon, ed. Vinc. De-Vit, vol. VI, p. 461).

Dial. = Sulpicii Severi *Dialogi*; see *Mart.* (= S. Martini Storia). See also *Greg. Dial.*

Dief. = Diefenbach (Laur.), Glossarium Latino-German. mediae et infimae aetatis. 4° Francof. 1857.

Diez (Friedr.), Etym. Wörterb. der Romanischen Sprachen. 5[e] Ausg. 8° Bonn, 1887.

Dion. praef., *or* Dionys. Praef. = The Preface of *Dionysius Exiguus*, to his Latin translation of the Canones; see above *Can.*; *Canon.*

div. = diversis; see *Ex* diuersis libris.

Don. Ars = Donati Ars Grammatica (in Grammatici Latini, ex recens. Henr. Keilii, vol. IV, p. 353 sqq.).

Dracont. = Dracontii Carmina omnia (in Migne's *Patr. Lat.* vol. LX, col. 595 sqq.).

Du. = Dutch.

Du C.; *or* Du Cange = Glossarium mediae et infimae Latinitatis conditum a Car. Dufresne Dom. Du Cange, ed. G. A. L. Henschel, 7 vols., 4° Paris, 1840—1850 (Edit. nova, a Leop. Favre, 10 vols., 4° Niort, 1883—1887).

E. = English.

E = text E = Cambridge University Library MS. (pressmark Kk. 4. 6) containing the *Catalogus* S. Hieronymi (q.v.).

Eccl. Ist.; *or* Eccl. Istor.; *or* Eccles. Istor. = Ecclesiastica Istoria (heading of Chapter IV).—Eccl. Stor. = Ecclesiastica Storia (heading of Chapter V); see *Eusebius*.

Eccles. = Ecclesiasticus (Vulgate ed.).

Eclesiast. = Ecclesiastes (Vulgate ed.).

Ef.[1] (= Glossary Erfurt[1]); Ef.[2] (= Glossary Erfurt[2]); both published by Georg. Goetz (Corpus Glossariorum Latinorum, vol. 5), the first (as Glossarium Amplonianum primum) on pp. 337—401; the second (as Glossarium Amplonianum secundum) on pp. 259—337. See Goetz' Preface (ibid.), p. xxvi.

Egilsson (Sveinbjörn), Lexicon Poëticum antiquae Linguae Septentrionalis. 8° Hafniae, 1860.

Engl. Dial. Dict. = The English Dialect Dictionary, ed. Jos. Wright, 6 vols., Lond. 1898—1905, 4°.

Ennius. Ennianae Poesis Reliquiae, recens. Joan. Vahlen. 8° Lips. 1854.

Ep. = The Epinal Glossary, Lat. and Old Eng., Fol. Lond. 1883 (Philol., and Early Engl. Text Societies).—Ep. —, means that the word is wanting in the Epin. Glossary.

Ep. S. Cyr. Alex. = Epistola Synodica S. Cyrilli; see above *Can.*; *Canon.*

Esdr.; *or* Esdra = Esdras (in Vulgate ed.).

Esther (in Vulgate ed.).

Etym. Magnum = Etymologicon Magnum, ed. Thom. Gaisford. Fol. Oxon. 1848.

Euch. de Pond. = (A) in Chapters De Ponderibus et De Mensuris, p. 158 sqq. S. Eucherii Lugdun. *Instructionum* libri duo, ed. Carol. Wotke (vol. XXXI of the Vienna *Corpus Scriptt. Eccles. Lat.*, 1891); (B) MS. Brit. Mus. 28. h. 7; Cotton, Vesp. B. VI, fol. 106^{b}.

Eucher. Instr.; *or* Eucher. Instructt.; *or* Eucherii Instructt.; *or* Eucherius = S. Eucherii *Instructt.* (as above).

Eugeniae (Vita S.), quoted as *Ex diversis libris* (heading to Ch. XLII); published in Migne's *Patr. Lat.* vol. LXXIII, col. 605 sqq.

Eus.; *or* Euseb. = Eusebius Pamphili (Eccles. Historia) = *Rufinus* (q.v.).

Evagrius, Presbyt. Antioch.; see *Anton.*

Ex div. libris (heading of Ch. XLII), partly = Sulp. Sev. *Dialogi*; partly = Sulp. Sev. *Vita S. Martini*, partly = *Vita S. Eugeniae Virg.*

Exod. = Exodus, in the Vulg.

Exsol. = Exsolutio; see *Breu. Exsolutio.*

Ezech.; *or* Ezek. = Ezechiel = Hiezechiel (heading of Ch. XV), in Vulgate ed.

Facundi Def. = Facundi Hermian. Ep. Pro defensione trium Capitulorum Concilii Chalcedonensis libri XII (in Migne's *Patr. Lat.* LXVII, col. 527 sqq.).

Fann. [Prisc.] = Q. Rhemnii Fannii Palaemonis De ponderibus et mensuris carmina (ad calc. Lucae Paeti de mensuris et ponderibus Romanis et Graecis...libri quinque, 4° Venet. 1573).

Florio (John), A worlde of wordes, or...dictionarie in Italian and English, 4° London, 1598.

Forcell.; *or* Forcellini; *or* Forcellini-De-Vit Lex. = Aeg. Forcellini Totius Latinitatis Lexicon, ed. Vinc. De-Vit, 6 vols. fol. Prati, 1875—. Id., Onomasticon, ed. Vinc. De-Vit, 4 vols. (A—O), fol. Prati, 1859—.

Franck; *or* Franck, Woordenb. = Franck (Joh.), Etymologisch Woordenboek der Nederlandsche Taal. 8° 'sGravenhage, 1892.

G. = German.

Gaisford (Thom.), see *Etym. Magnum.*

Gallée (Johan Hendr.), Old Saxon texts (with facsimiles). 8° Leiden, 1894.

Gangr. = Gangrensis; see *Can.*

Gebhardt (Oscar von), editor of Sophronius' Greek translation of St Jerome's Catal. de viris illustribus; see *Hier.*

Gen.; *or* Genes. = Genesis.

Georg.; *or* Georges' Wörterb.; *or* Georges Wrtb. = Georges (Karl Ernst), Latein.-Deutsches Handwörterbuch, 7th ed., 2 vols. 8° Leipz. 1879.

Germania. Vierteljahrsschrift für deutsche Alterthumskunde. Herausg. von Fr. Pfeiffer, K. Bartsch, Otto Behaghel. Jahrg. I—XXXVII, 8° Stuttg., Wien, 1856—1892.

Gesenius (Will.), Hebrew and Chaldee Lexicon, transl. by Sam. P. Tregelles. 4° Lond. 1853.

Gildas Sapiens, *De Excidio Britanniae*, recens. Jos. Stevenson, Londin. 1838, 8°. Also in Migne's *Patr. Lat.* (1848), vol. LXIX, col. 327 sqq., and (ed. Th. Mommsen) in Monum. Germ. (*Chron. Min.* vol. III).

Glogger (P. Plac.), O.S.B., Das Leidener Glossar (Cod. Voss. lat. 4° 69). 2 parts. 8° Augsb. 1901—3.

Gloss. Werth. = Werden Fragments of Glossaries, published by J. H. Gallée (q.v.), p. 330 sqq.

Goetz; *or* Goetz' Corp. Gl. Lat. = Corpus Glossariorum Latinorum a Gust. Loewe incohatum...ed. Georg. Goetz, 7 vols. (2—7 published). 8° Lips. 1888—1901. The 6th and 7th vols. contain elaborate indices to the Corpus.

Graff (E. G.), Althochdeutscher Sprachschatz, 6 vols. 4° Berl. 1834—1842.

Greg. Dial. = S. Gregorii Magni *Dialogorum* libri quatuor (in Migne's *Patr. Lat.* LXXVII, col. 149 sqq.).

Greg. Reg. Past. = S. Gregorii Magni Liber *regulae pastoralis,* partes IV (in Migne's *Patr. Lat.* LXXVII, col. 14 sqq.).

Grimm (Jacob & Wilh.), Deutsches Wörterbuch, vols. I— , 8° Leipz. 1854—.

—— (Jacob), Gesch. der deutschen Sprache, 3e Aufl., 2 vols. 8° Leipz. 1868.

—— Deutsche Mythologie, 4te Ausg. Besorgt von E. H. Meyer, 3 Bde. 8° Berlin, 1875.

Habac. = Habacuc (in Vulg. ed.).

Hagen (Herm.), Ars Anonyma Bernensis (pp. 62—142, Supplementum contin. Anecdota Helvetica, ex recens. H. Hageni in Grammatici Latini, ex recens. Henr. Keilii).—Id Commentum Einsidlense in Donati Artem minorem (ibid. pp. 202—274).

Hattemer (Heinr.), Denkmahle des Mittelalters. 3 vols. 8° St Gallen, 1844—49.

Helmreich (G.); Heraeus (Wilh.), contributors to the *Archiv f. Lat. Lex.*

Hessels (John Henry), An Eighth-Century Latin-Anglo-Saxon Glossary (Corpus Christi College, Cambridge, MS. No. 144). 8° Cambridge (Univ. Press), 1890.

Heyse (Theod.), Biblia Sacra Latina Vet. Testamenti Hieronymo interprete. 8° Lips. 1873.

Hier.; *or* Hierem. = *Hieremia* (heading of Chapter XIV), or Jeremia, in Vulg. ed.—Hier. Threni (in Vulg. ed.).

Hier.; *or* Hieron. = S. Eus. *Hieronymus.*

I. Hieronymi *Catalogus* or *Liber de Viris illustribus.*

A. For general references and quotations regarding this work, Migne's edition has been used (*Patrol. Lat.* XXIII = S. Hieronymi *Opera,* vol. II, p. 602 sqq.).

Further references are made to

B = Liber de Viris illustribus [Utrecht, Ketelaer & De Leempt, c. 1473, 26 leaves, small fol. Copy in the Cambridge University Library, AB. 9. 38]. *Without Gennadius.*

C = Liber de Viris illustribus, Augsburg, G. Zainer, c. 1470, *with Gennadius* 38 leaves (1—38), fol. [The vol. contains various other tracts. The Library of Trinity College, Cambridge, possesses two copies of this edition.]

D. Hieronymus Liber de Viris illustribus..., herausg. von Ernest Cushing Richardson [Bd. XIV, Heft 1 of *Texte und Untersuch. zur Geschichte der Altchristlichen Literatur,* herausgeg. von Oscar v. Gebhardt und Adolf Harnack. *The Latin text.*—Bd. XIV, Heft 1b Hieronymus de Viris illustribus in Griechischer Uebersetzung (der sogenannte Sophronius) herausg. von Oscar von Gebhardt.—Bd. XIII, Heft 3 Die Griechische Uebersetzung der Viri Inlustres des Hieronymus, von Geo. Wentzel].

E. A manuscript of the 12th century, in the Cambridge University Library (pressmark Kk. 4. 6), containing among other works (for which see the Cat. of MSS. preserved in that Library) also the *Catalogus* of St Jerome. This MS. is mentioned by E. C. Richardson, but not, it would seem, used for his edition.

F. Another MS. of the xvth cent., likewise in the Cambridge Univ. Libr. (pressmark Dd. 7. 2).

II.

For references to the other works of St Jerome the vols. of Migne's ed. (*Patr. Lat.* XXII—XXX) have been used. It is to be noted that Hier. Comm. in Matth. (= Uerborum Interpretatio, heading of Ch. XXIX of Glossary) = S. Eus. Hieronymi Commentt. in Evangelium Matthaei (vol. XXVI of Migne's *Patr. Lat.*).—Hieron. Exposit. Interlin. libri Iob (vol. XXIII ibid.).—Hieron. Comm. in lib. Iob (vol. XXVI ibid.).—Id. translation of Bk. of Iob (vol. XXVIII ibid.).—Hieron. Praef. = his Praefationes to the various books of the Bible (in the Vulgate, q.v.).—Cf. Goelzer (Henri) *Étude de la Latinité de St. Jérome*, 8° Paris, 1884.—Paucker (C.) *de Latinitate B. Hieronymi Observatt.* 8° Berol. 1880.

Hiezech. = Hiezechiel; see *Ezech.*

Hil. = Hilarius; see above *Can.*

Hildebrand (Geo. Friedr.), Glossarium Latinum biblioth. Paris. antiq. saec. IX. 8° Goett. 1854.

Holder (Alfr.), Alt-Celtischer Sprachschatz, 2 vols. 8° Leipz. 1896—1904.

Holthausen (Ferd.), on Glosses (in *Anglia*, &c.).

Horm. = Hormisda; see *Can.*

Innoc. = Innocentius (Decret. Innoc.); see *Can.*, *Canon.*

Inst. = Institutiones; see Cass. = *Cassianus.*

Int. = Interpraetatio; see *Cp.*

Isai. = Isaiah (in the Vulgate).

Isid. = S. Isidorus.—Isid. Diff.; *or* de diff. Verbb. = S. Isid. Liber de differentiis Verborum (in Isidore's *Opera*, ed. Faust. Arevalo, tom. V, pp. 1—76; Migne, *Patr. Lat.* LXXXIII, coll. 9—70).—Isid. de natura rerum, or Liber de nat. rer. (Arev., tom. VII, pp. 1—62; Migne's *Patr. Lat.* LXXXIII, col. 957 sqq.). In the Glossary this treatise is entitled *Liber Rotarum*, on which see Areval I. 659.—Isid. Offic.; *or* de Offic. Eccles. = S. Isid. de Ecclesiasticis Officiis libri duo (Arev. tom. VI, pp. 363—471; Migne, LXXXIII, coll. 737—826).—Isid. Etym. = S. Isidori Etymologiae, libri XX (Arev. tomm. III & IV; Migne, LXXII).—Isid. Lib. Gloss. = Liber Glossarum, ex variis Glossariis, quae sub Isidori nomine circumferuntur, collectus (Arev. tom. VII, p. 443 sqq.; Migne, LXXXIII, col. 1331 sqq.).—Isid. contra Judaeos (in Napier's Old English Glosses, p. 205).—Isid. Epp (Arev. VI, p. 557 sqq.; Migne, LXXXIII, col. 893 sqq.).

Ist.; *or* Istor. = Istoria; see *Eccl. Ist.*

Jer. = Jeremia = *Hieremia* (q.v.).

Jerome; Jerome's *Catalogus;* see *Hieronymus.*

Joann. = Joannes = Johannes, q.v.

Job (heading of Ch. XIX), in Vulg.

Joel (heading of Ch. XVII), in Vulg.

Joh. (= Johannes, heading of Ch. XXV), in Vulg.

Jon. = Jonas (heading of Ch. XVII), in Vulg.

Journal of Germanic Philology, ed. by Gust. E. Karsten, &c., vols. 1—5. 8° Bloomington, 1897—. (Vol. V ent. The Journ. of English and Germanic Philol., ed. by Albert S. Cook and Gust. E. Karsten.)

Jud. = Judith (heading of Ch. XXI), in Vulg.

Keil (Henr.), Grammatici Latini ex recens. Henr. Keilii, 7 vols. (cum Supplem., ed. Herm. Hagen). 8° Lips. 1857—1880.

Kern (Hendr.), Notes on the Salic Law (in *Lex Salica,* ed. J. H. Hessels, 4° Lond. 1880).

Kluge (or Kluge, Wrtb.; or Et. Wört.; or Dict.) = Kluge (Friedr.), Etymologisches Wörterbuch der deutschen Sprache, 6e Aufl. 8° Strassburg, 1899.—Kluge, Leseb. (or A. S. Leseb.; Ang. Les.) = Angelsächsisches Lesebuch, 3e Aufl. 8° Halle, 1902.—Kluge (Friedr.), Vorgeschichte der altgerman. Dialekte (in vol. I of Herm. Paul's Grundriss der German. Philol., 8° Strassb. 1901).—Kluge (Friedr.) & F. Lutz, English Etymology. 8° Strassb. 1898.

Körting (Gustav), Latein.-romanisches Wörterbuch, 2e Ausg. 8° Paderb. 1901.

Landgraf (Gust.), contributor to the *Archiv f. Lat. Lexic.* (vol. IX).

Laod. = Laodiceni; see *Can.*

Lazius (Wolfg.); see Vita S. *Anton.*

Lchdm = Leechdom (quoted by Bosw. T.) = Leechdoms, Wortcunning...of Early England, ed. by Cockayne (Master of the Rolls' series, 3 vols.).

Leo (Pope), see *Can.*

Leutsch (Ernst Ludw. von), see *Paroemiogr.*

Lew. and Sh.; *or* Lewis & Sh. = Lewis (Charlt. T.) and (Charles) Short, Latin Dict. 8° Oxf. 1879.

Lib. Anton. (Liber Antonii) = S. Antonii Vita; see *Anton.*

Liber de illustribus viris, see *Hieronymus.*

Lib. Rot. = Liber Rotarum (heading of Chapter XXVII) = S. Isidori (q.v.) *Liber de natura rerum.*

Liddell & Sc. = Liddell (Henry Geo.) and (Rob.) Scott, Greek-Engl. Lexicon, 7th ed. 4° Oxf. 1883.

Löfstedt (Einar), on Glosses, in *Archiv* für Lat. Lexicogr. (vol. XIV).

Loewe (Gust.), Prodromus corporis glossariorum Latinorum. 8° Lips. 1876.

Lomm. = Lommatzsch; see *Rufinus* (Origen.).

Luc. = Lucas, in the Vulg.

Lutz (F.), see *Kluge.*

Maassen (Friedr.), Geschichte der Quellen...des Canonischen Rechts... Bd. I. 8° Gratz, 1871.

Mai (Angelo, Card.), Spicilegium Romanum, 10 vols. 8° Romae, 1839—44.

Malach. (heading of Ch. XVII) = Malachias, in the Vulg.

Man.; *or* Mans. = Mansi (Joann. Domin.) Sacrorum Conciliorum...collectio. Fol. Florent. 1759—

Ms. Sangerm. (Saint-Germain MS. quoted by Sabatier, q.v.).

Marc. = the Gospel of Mark, in the Vulg.

Mart. = S. Martinus = S. Martini (Martyni) Storia.

A. Sulpicii Severi Libri qui supersunt, recensuit et commentario critico instruxit Carolus Halm. 8° Vindob. 1866 [In vol. I of *Corpus Scriptorum Ecclesiasticorum Latinorum.* Editum consilio et impensis Academiae Litterarum Caesareae Vindobonensis, 8° Vindob. 1866. —(*a*) *Vita Sancti Martini* episcopi et confessoris, pp. 107—137.—(*b*) *Epistulae* III., pp. 138—151.—(*c*) *Dialogi* III., pp. 152—216].

B. *Vita B. Martini* Sabariensis, episcopi Turonensis, a Sulpitio Seuero Rhetore Latine conscripta [pp. 1—48 of vol. II of *Liber de Passione* D. N. Jesu Christi, carmine hexametro, incerto autore ad Donatum Episcopum scriptus. Abdiae Babyl. episcopi...de historia certaminis apostolici, libri x &c., ed. Wolfgangus Lazius. Fol. Basil. 1552].

C. Steinmeyer & Sievers, *Althochd. Glossen*, II, pp. 746—760.—Cf. *Ueber die Weltchronik des sogenannten Severus Sulpitius* und Südgallische Annalen des fünften Jahrhunderts, von Dr Oswald Holder-Egger. 8° Göttingen, 1875.

Math.; Matth. = Matheum (heading of Ch. XXIV) = the Gospel of Matthew, in the Vulg. See also *Hier. in Matth.*

Mich. = Michaeas (one of the Minor Prophets, quoted, without name, in Ch. XVII), in the Vulg.

Migne = Migne's *Patr. Graec.*, or Migne's *Patr. Lat.*

Münst. Gloss. see *Gallée* (J. H.), Old Saxon texts p. 332 sqq.

Mus. M. = Museum Manuscript = British Museum Manuscript; see *Brit. Mus. MS.*

Nahum (one of the Minor Prophets, quoted, without name, in Ch. XVII), in the Vulg.

Napier, Gl.; *or* Napier, OEG. = Napier (Arth. S.), *Old English Glosses.* Oxford (Anecdota Oxoniensia) 1900. 4°.

Nennius; Nennius Vindicatus...von Heinr. Zimmer. 8° Berlin, 1893.

Neocaes. = Neocaesariensis; see *Can.*

Nest. = Contra Nestorium (see *Cassianus*).

Nic. or Nicaen. = Nicaeni; see *Can.*

Nomin. = nominibus = De diversis nominibus = Donati Ars Gramm. (q.v.).

Non. = Nonius Marcellus, De compendiosa doctrina libros xx,...ed. W. M. Lindsay (Bibl. Teub.). 8° Lips. 1903—

Num. = the Book of Numbers, in the Vulg.

Nyerup (Erasmus), Symbolae ad literaturam Teutonicam antiquiorem. 4° Hauniae, 1787.

OHG. = Old High German.

Origen. = Origenes; see *Rufinus* (Origen.).

Oros. = Pauli Orosii Historiarum adversum paganos libri VII, ed. Car. Zangemeister, Vindobonae, 1882, 8° [vol. v of Corpus Scriptt. Eccles. Lat., Acad. Vindobonensis].

Ose; *or* Osee (heading of Ch. XVIII), see, besides the Praef. Hier. in XII Proph. in the editions of the Vulg., also Migne's vol. XXVIII col. 1016A.

Oxf. D., *or* Dict. = A New Engl. Dict. on histor. principles, ed. James A. H. Murray, Henry Bradley &c. Fol. Oxf. 1889.

Paral. = Paralipomenon (also entit. Chron. I & II), in the Vulg.

Paroemiographi Gotting. = Paroemiographi Graeci, edd. Leutsch & Schneidewin, 2 vols. 8° Gött. 1839.

Patr. Lat. = (Migne's) Patrologia Latina.

Paul (Herm.), Grundriss; see *Kluge*.

Phocas = Ars Phocae; see *Ars*.

Piper (Paul), Nachträge zur älteren deutschen Litteratur. 8° Stuttg. 1893.

P.L. = (Migne's) Patrol. Lat.

Pond.; Ponder.; ponder. = Ponderibus (in the headings of the Chapters XXXI and XXXII, the sources of which are not known). Some references are made to *Blume* (q.v.); cf. also Lucae *Paeti* de mensuris et ponderibus Romanis et Graecis...libri quinque, 4° Venet. 1573 (ad calc. Q. Rhemnii Fannii Palaemonis de ponderibus et mensuris carmina, which is identical with *Carmina de ponderibus et mensuris*, published by Steph. Ladisl. Endlicher, as *Prisciani* Gramm. de laude Imperatoris Anastasii et de Ponderibus et Mensuris, 8° Vindob. 1828). —De Ponderibus, Nummis et Mensuris libri v, Auct. Jac. Capello, 2 pts., 4° Francof. 1606, 7.—*De pond. Euch.* = De ponderibus secundum Eucherium; see *Eucherius*.

Postgate (John P.), Corpus poetarum Latinorum. 8° Lond. 1893— .

Praef. Hieron. = Praefatio Hieronymi (besides his prefaces to the various books of the Bible, in the Vulg., see also Migne's Patr. Lat. XXIX).

Praef. in Ps. = Praefatio *Cassiodori* (q.v.) in Psalterium.

Probi Catholica (vol. IV p. 1 sqq. of Grammatici Latini, ed. Henr. Keilius).

prooem. = prooemium, see *Ruf.*

Prompt. Parv.; Promptorium Parvulorum sive clericorum, ed. Alb. Way, 3 vols. 4° Lond. 1843—65.

Ps. = Psalterium = Cassiodori (q.v.) Comment. in Psalterium.

Reg. = I & II Regum, in the Vulg.

Reg.; *or* Regula; see *Benedicti* regula.

Rhenanus' edd. of *Rufinus* (q.v.).

Rhys (John), Celtic Britain (First ed.), 8° Lond. 1882; (Third ed.) 8° Lond. 1904.

Rich.; *or* Richardson = Richardson (Ern. Cushing) his text of the Catalogus S. *Hieronymi* (q.v.).

Rosweydus (Herib.); see Vita S. *Antonii.*

Rot.; see *Lib. Rot.*

Rufin. (Origen.) = Origenis Opera omnia, ed. Car. Henr. Edu. Lommatzsch, 25 vols. Berol. 1831 &c.

Ruf. = Rufinus, presbyt. Aquil. (his translation into Latin of Eusebius' *Ecclesiastica Historia*, in IX Books, with a Xth and XIth of his own added). Ruf. *prooem.* (= *prooemium*, or his general preface)—Ruf. II *prooem.* (= preface to his 2nd chapter).—Ruf. Ep. ad Chrom. (= his preface to Chromatius, prefixed to the editions of the Eccles. Hist.).

A. D. Eusebii Pamphili Caesareae Palestinae Episcopi *Ecclesiasticae historiae* libri IX [Rufino presbyt. Aquil. interprete]...Ruffini ...*Ecclesiasticae historiae* libri II, ed. Beatus Rhenanus. Antverpiae, 1548, small 8°.

B. Eusebii Pamphili Caes. libri nouem, Ruffino interprete. Ruffini ...libri duo, ed. Beatus Rhenanus [pp. 1 to 260 of: *Autores historiae Ecclesiasticae*, Basileae, 1535, fol.].

C. *Ecclesiasticae Historiae* Eusebii Pamphili libri novem Ruffino... interprete, ac duo ipsius Ruffini libri, studio F. Petri Thomae Cacciari, 2 ptes; acced. Dissertat. de vita, fide, ac Eusebiana ipsa Ruffini Translatione. 4° Romae, 1740, 41.

D. Steinmeyer & Sievers, *Althochd. Glossen*, II, pp. 596—607.

E. Eusebius *Werke*, Zweiter Band. *Die Kirchengeschichte*, bearbeitet...von Ed. Schwartz. *Die Lateinische Uebersetzung des Rufinus*, bearbeitet...von Theod. Mommsen; *erste Hälfte* = Band IX. 1 of *Die Griechischen Christlichen Schriftsteller der ersten drei Jahrhunderte.* 8° Leipzig, 1903.

The references in the Lat. Index are all to the edition A; the editions B and C are specially named, where reference is made to them. Cacciari's edition (C) would have been used as the primary one, if it had been accessible to me at the outset. Only after I had read edition A four or five times, and made all my references to it, did I learn that a copy of this apparently rare work (which is neither in the Cambridge University Library, nor in the British Museum) was in the possession of the Rev. Prof. John E. B. Mayor, who kindly lent it to me for further reference.

It was, for various reasons, not practicable to use Mommsen's edition, or to verify the references to the Rhenanus ed. of 1548 with his text. Firstly, Mommsen's edition as yet does not go further than Rufinus' fifth Book, so that, in any case, the work of verification would have remained incomplete. Secondly, the arrangement and pagination of edition A differ so widely from that of Mommsen's that a verification of all the references would have been too great a labour. Those who use the present work are, therefore, requested to make these verifications themselves if they require them. The differences between Mommsen's text and that of the earlier edition do not seem to be very material.

Sab.; *or* Sabat. = Bibliorum Sacrorum Latinae versiones antiquae, seu Vetus Italica...Op. Petri *Sabatier*, 3 tomm. fol. Remis, 1743.

Salam. = De Salamone (heading of Ch. VIII) = Liber Proverbiorum, in the Vulg.

S. Aug. (see Sanctus *Augustinus*); S. Hier. (see S. *Hieronymus*); S. Isidorus (see S. *Isidorus*); St Jerome; St Jerome's Catalogus (see *Hieronymus*).

S. Mart. Stor.; *or* S. Martyni Storia; see *Mart.*

Sangerm.; see *Ms. Sangerm.*

Sap. = Sapientia (heading of Ch. XI), in the Vulg.

Sard.; *or* Sardic. = Sardicensis; see *Can.*

Schade = Schade (Oskar), Altdeutsches Wörterbuch, 2[e] Aufl. 8° Halle, 1872—82.

Schlutter (Otto B.), Articles on Glosses in *Journal* (q.v.) *of German Philol.*; *Anglia* (q.v.); *Arch.* (q.v.) *f. Latein. Lexicogr.*

Schmeller (Joh. Andr.), Bayerisches Wörterbuch, 4 vols. 8° Stuttg. 1827—37.

Schmidt (Edm.), Regula S. Benedicti; see *Bened.* reg.

Schneidewin (Friedr. Wilh.), see *Paroemiogr.*

Sept. = Septuagint.

Serm. = Sermones, see *Augustinus* (S.).

Sermones de Regulis (heading of Ch. II); see *Bened.* reg.

Servius Comm. in artem Donati (vol. IV p. 403 sqq. of Grammatici Latini, ed. Henr. Keilius).

Sev. = Severus (Sulpicius); see *Mart.*

Siev.; *or* Sievers; *or* Sievers, *Gr.*; or Sievers, *A. S. Gramm.* = Sievers (Ed.), *An Old English Grammar*, transl. and edited by Alb. S. Cook, 3rd ed. 8° Boston and London, 1903.

Skeat (Rev. Prof. W. W.). An etymol. dictionary of the Engl. language, 3rd ed., 4° Oxf. 1898.—A concise etymol. dictionary of the English language, new ed. 8° Oxf. 1901.—The Vision of William concerning Piers the Plowman, 2 vols. 8° Oxf. 1886.—The Complete Works of Geoffrey Chaucer, 8 vols. 8° Oxf. 1894—97.—Principles of Engl. Etymol., 2nd ed., Ser. I. 8° Oxf. 1892.

Sonny (Adolf), contributor to *Archiv f. Lat. Lexicogr.*

Sophon. = Sophonias, one of the minor prophets excerpted by the Glossator (under Chapter XVII), in the Vulg.

Sophron. = Sophronius, translator of St Jerome's Cat. de Viris illustribus into Greek; see *Hier.*

Souter (Alex.), A Study of Ambrosiaster. 8° Cambr. 1905.—*De codicibus manuscriptis Augustini* in *Sitzungsber. der philos. hist. Klasse der Wiener Akad.*, Bd. 149 (p. 1 sqq.), Wien, 1905.

SS. = Sanctorum, see *Acta* Sanctorum.

Steinm.; *or* Steinm. A.H.G.; *or* Steinm. Ahd. Gl. = Steinmeyer (Elias) und Eduard Sievers, Die althochdeutschen Glossen, gesammelt und bearbeitet. 4 vols. 8° Berlin, 1879—98.

Stephanus (Henr.), Thesaurus Graecae Linguae, edd. C. B. Hase, &c. 8 vols. fol. Paris, 1831—65.

Stokes (Whitley), Three Irish Glossaries. 8° London, 1862.

Stor. = Storia; see *Eccl. Stor.*

Suidae Lexicon, Cambridge (Lud. Kuster, 1705) and Oxford (Thom. Gaisford, 1834) editt. of.—Reprint of the Oxf. ed. by God. Bernhardy, Halis, 1843—53.

Sulp. Sev. = Sulpicius Severus (*Dial.*; or *Vit.* or *Vit. S. Mart.*; or *Epist.*); see *Mart.*

Symm. = (Pope) Symmachus, see above *Can.*, *Canon.*

Thalhofer (Valent.), Erklär. der Psalmen, 7e Aufl. 8° Regensb. 1904.

Thes. L. Lat.; *or* Thes. Ling. Lat.; *or* Thesaur. L. Lat. = Thesaurus Linguae Latinae, edit. auctoritate...Academiarum...Berolin., Gotting. &c. 4° Lips. 1900— .

Thesaurus Graecae Linguae; see Henr. *Stephanus.*

Thren. = Threni; see *Hieremia.*

Tobias, in the Vulg.

Tommaseo (Nicc.), Dizionario della lingua italiana. 4° Torino, 1861.

Traube (Ludw.), Textgeschichte der Reg. Benedicti, 1898 (see *Benedicti* regula).

Utrecht ed. (B) of the *Catalogus* Hieronymi (q.v.).

Vahlen (Johann); see *Ennius.*

Uerba (heading of Chapter XL; the sources of which have not yet been ascertained).

Uerba de multis (heading of Ch. XLV) = *Ars* (q.v.) Phocae.

Uerba de S. Martyni Storia; see *Sulp. Sev.*

Uerb. Int.; Uerb. Interpr. = Uerborum Interpretatio (heading of Ch. XXIX) = *Hieronymi* (q.v.) Comm. in Matth. [In certain cases this heading refers to St Jerome's Cat. or Liber de Vir. illustr.]

Verdam (J.), Middelnederl. Woordenboek. 8° 'sGravenhage. 1882— .

Verg.; Vergilius, see *Virgilius.*

Vers. ant. Sab., see *Sabatier.*

Vet. Defin. fid. Chalc. *or* Vetus Defin. fidei Conc. Chalc. (in Mansi's Sacrorum Conciliorum Collectio).

Vienna Corpus Scriptt. Eccles. Latinorum. 8° Vindobonae, 1866— .

Virg. Ecl.; Virg. Geo.; Virg. Aen. = P. Vergili Maronis Eclog., Georg., and Aen., ed. John Conington, 3 vols. 8° London, 1881—1884.

Vit. S. Ant.; Vit. S. Anton.; Vita S. Anton.; Vita S. Antonii; Antoni Vita; Antoni Storia; *or* Liber Antonii; see *Anton.*

Vit.; *or* Vita S. Eugen.; see *Euchen.*

Vita S. Martini; see *Mart.*

Vulg. = Vulgata, or Vulgate = Biblia Sacra Vulgatae editionis, 4° Antwerp (Joan. Bapt. Verdussen, 1715).

Wace (Henry), The Apocrypha, 2 vols. (Speaker's Commentary). 8° Lond. 1888.

Werd. or Werden Gloss.; or Werden fragm.; or Gloss. Werth.; see *Gallée* (J. H.), Old Saxon texts.

Windisch (Ernst), Irische Texte mit Wörterbuch. 8° Leipz. 1880— .

Wölfflin, or Woelfflin (Eduard), Editor of, and contributor to *Archiv f. Lat. Lexicogr.*

Wordsw. and White = Wordsworth (John) & (Henry Jul.) White, Novum Testamentum...Latine secundum editionem S. Hieronymi. 4° Oxon. 1898.

Wotke (Karl), Editor of *Eucherius* in the *Vienna* Corpus.

Wright W. = Wright-Wülcker = Wright (Thom.) & Rich. Paul Wülcker, *Anglo-Saxon and Old Engl. Vocabularies*, 2 vols. 8° Lond. 1884.

Wrt. Voc.; see *Wright-Wülcker.*

Wrtb. = Wörterbuch.

Wuelcker, Vocab.; see *Wright* (Thom.) & (R. P.) *Wülcker.*

W. W. = *Wright-Wülcker* (q.v.).

Zachar. = Zacharias, in the Vulg.

Zeitschr. f. d. (D.) A. (or Alt. or Alterth.) = Zeitschrift für deutsches Alterthum, herausg. von Moriz Haupt. 8° Leipz. 1841— .

Zimmer (Heinr.); see *Nennius.*

Zycha (Joseph.), Editor of vol. XXVIII (Augustinus) of the *Vienna* Corpus Scriptt. Eccl. Latin.

Fol. 20^{aa}

[I] GLO SAE* UERB*ORUM* DE CANONIB*US*;

1 Aleator ludor cupiditatis.
2 Alea . lud*um* tabulę a quod*am* mago.
3 Anathema . abhominatio.
4 Alias . alibi . u*e*l int*er*du*m* *uel* no*n*nu*m*qua*m*.
5 Ambone anal*ogio*
6 Absida*m* . gr*ece* . sedem episcopalem.
7 Alligare insinuare . mittere.
8 Allectat : expectat :
9 Adeptus : consecutus . indeptus :
10 Admittere : exequere :
11 Adnisus : conatus :
12 Aemulu*m* : eiusde*m* rei studiosu*m* quasi imitatore*m*
13 Autenticu*m* : auctorale. :
14 Arcimandritis† :
15 Aboleri : a memoria tolli :
16 Barbari : feroces . inmites . atroces :
17 Byrrus : cuculla breuis :
17[a] NOTE§
18 Barbarus§
19 Conciliu*m* : gr*ece* . lat*ine* : *con*siliu*m* : conuentus : *uel* concentus . coetus :
20 Catezizatur : inbuitur :
21 Conpetentes : appetentes :
22 Caticumini : gr*ece* : lat*ine* : instructi : *uel* auditor*es* :
23 Catafrigar*um* :
24 Cymiteria : sepulture :
25 Co*m*messationes : luxosa . *con*uiuia cu*m* meretrib*us*
26 Conductores :
27 Conibentes : consentientes : *uel* *con*spirantes ;
28 Coetus : *con*uentus : u*e*l *con*gregacio : *uel* socius :
29 Concinnant : consonant :
30 Collega : conmanipularius : uel *con*scius :
31 Catholicus : gr*ece* . lat*ine* . uniuersalis :

Fol. 20^{ab}

32 Coniuratio : consensio : conuentio
33 Conspiratio : consensio
34 Carperetur : consumeretur
35 Dogma : doctrina : *ue*l difinitio :
36 Diocesis : parrochiis : id*est* adiaciens dom*us* uel : gub*er*nationib*us* :
37 Delirantes . mente . deficientes :
38 Depromsimus : protulim*us*
39 Diuus : imperator¶ . q*ui* po*st* morte*m* ut de*us* habet*ur*
40 Defensores : custodes : presides :
41 Diaconico : ministerio :
42 Decisio :
43 Deuocari
44 Dissimulat . conticiscit : p*re*terita neglegit
45 Emergit : surgit . uel . exuperat :
46 Essentia . substantia.
47 Experiunt*ur* . explicantur . uel cognoscant.

* MS. leaves space for one letter between O and S.

† The second *r* is blurred, and not clear.

§ The words numbered 17[a] and 18 are written (Note or Nolk? *in capitals*; Barbarus, *in somewhat larger characters than the other glosses*) in a vacant space left between the B and C glosses, in faint ink, but apparently by the same hand as the rest of the Glossary.

¶ Between the *m* and *p* a letter (apparently ꝑ, for *pro*) has been erased.

48 Extorris : ui . expulsus . quasi exterris :
49 Epistilia : gr*ece* . q*uae* sup*er* capitella colu*m*nar*um* ponunt*ur*
50 Emancipent : manu*m* mittent.
51 Exempta : uiolent*er* sublata :
52 Exhibere : accersire : adesse : *uel* p*re*sto esse.
53 Funestis : mortiferis . u*el* scelestis :
54 Foenus usura . u*el* lucr*um*
55 Fauor : plausus
56 Foro : otio :
57 Genuinu*m* decus : naturale u*el* intimu*m* :
58 Gesta municipalia : *uel* publica :
59 Inoleuit : increuit informat*ur*
60 Immolatio : mactatio :
61 Inprobitas ; p*ro*cacitas :
62 Idonea : apta utilis habilis ;
Fol. 20[ba]
63 Inhibere : detineri : morare :
64 Insigne : nobile : clare.
65 In pulpito : in gradu . ubi lectores legunt ;
66 Intimare : suggerere :
67 Insolens : inportunus ; inpotens : intollerand*us*
68 Liberalitas : donatio quę a diuite . fit :
69 Lasciuientes : feruentes :
70 Mancipant*ur** ; manu . capiant*ur*
71 Modeste : moderate : u*el* recte :
72 Machomen*us*
73 Mensis . ẏp*er*beretheus
74 Massa diocesiu*m* :
75 Matricis :
76 Manumissio : eo q*uo*d manu . mitterent*ur*
77 Negotia ecclesiastica . actu*m* rei alicuius :
78 Nauiter : ualde :
79 Obtentu
80 Omousion : gr*ece* . l*atine* . una substantia patris . et filii :
81 Orariu*m* : mappa*m* . *uel* linteamen
82 Opera*m* dare : benigne facere : *uel* . co*n*ciliare :
83 Parrochia :
84 P*er*uadere : aliena*m* re*m* . manifeste p*re*sumere. :
85 P*ro*scribant*ur* : porro . u*el* pala*m* scribant*ur* :
86 Prorsus . plane : p*ro*cul dubio : uere :
87 Presul : iudex .:· *uel* . p*re*sidens . u*el* defensor :
88 Paruipendens : p*ro* nihilo habens : *uel* ducens :
89 Prosequant*ur* : comitant*ur* :
90 Philacteria : scriptura diu*er*sa : quę p*ro*pt*er* infirmos habent*ur* . u*el* carmina ;
91 Ptochiis in dispensationib*us* paup*er*um : *uel* negotia†
92 Pragmatica forma : principalia i*m*peria :†
93 Primate*m* : dioceseos ;
Fol. 20[bb]
94 Passim ; p*ro*miscue : publice . uulgo : *uel* . p*er* o*m*nia
95 Portentuose : monstruose : ex*em*pli . causa . cum sex digitis nati ;
96 Promulgantes : p*ro*ponentes :
97 Preces dictare :
98 Predia : possessiones :
99 Papa :
100 P*ro*consolaris : in uice consulis : quia suffecti erunt consulib*us* :

* Goetz, Corpus v. 411, 13 has manicipantur; but MS. as above.

† Goetz, Corpus v. 411, 34, 35 prints the glosses 91 and 92 thus: (34) Ptochiis indispensationibus pauperum uel negotia imperia; (35) Pragmatica forma principalia. And Nyerup has negotia after principalia. But the MS. has distinctly:

(91) P. in d. paup*erum* ł
(92) Pragmatica forma : principalia | negotia
(93) Primatem : dioceseos : | imperia

and hence we must here read as above; see, however, below, Ch. xxxix. 58, 63.

101 Procuratores : q*uo*d uice curatoris fungant*ur* :
102 Prosequor : deducor :
103 Primicirius :*
104 Presbiteras . uxores : pr*esbiter*-*orum* quas antea
105 Pubertas :
106 Querimonia*m* : q*ue*rella*m* graue*m* :
107 Ruris : uille :
108 Redigerit : reuocauit :
109 Religio : q*uo*d p*er* ea*m* uni d*eo* religam*ur* :
110 Resipiscant : amissa*m* . recipiant sapientia*m*
111 Sicera : e*st* omnis potio . que extra uinu*m* inebriare pote*st* . cuius licet nom*en* hebreu*m* sit= tam*en* latinum sonat . p*ro* eo q*uo*d ex suco frum*en*tor*um* . et pomor*um* : conficitur :
112 Stipendiis† q*uae* militib*us* dant*ur* :
113 Sacrilego : p*ro*fano :
114 Sÿnodus : gr*ece* : l*atine* comitatus : *ue*l coetus
115 Sescopla§ : semi dupla : u*e*l semi . tripla u*e*l sedecim p*ro* uno :
116 Seditio : rixa . tumultus
117 Secus . contra . difinita . alit*er* . p*ro*pe.
118 Simbulu*m* : gr*ece* . l*atine* . signu*m* . *uel* . cognitio :
119 Scismatici : dissensatores : seperatores
120 Subnixe . subposite : subiecte :
121 Secta . heresis : insecutio :

Fol. 21[aa]

122 Sanctiones : iudicationes : *ue*l difiniciones :
123 Scolasticus :
124 Stipulatio : testatio :
125 Sanxit : iussit : tribuit . iudicau*it* . difiniuit :
126 Spectacula : ubi o*m*nia publicis¶ uisib*us* p*re*bet*ur* inspectio
127 Striones : qui muebri indum*en*to gestus inpudicar*um* feminar*um* exprimebant
128 Secretale*m* . penetrabiliore*m* : occultiore*m* .
129 Suspicio : coniectura : *ue*l . argum*en*tu*m* :
130 Sexus : natura :
131 Sinceritas : integritas :
132 Satagim*us* : delibam*us* . *ue*l cogitam*us* :
133 Scrupulu*m* : axietas : angor : molestia :

[II] INTERPRETATIO SERM*ONUM* : DE REGULIS :

1 Adtonitis : intentis :
2 Anachorita : gr*ece* . heremita :
3 Angarizanti : cogenti : u*e*l conpellenti :
4 Abba : syr*um* . pater : genitor :
5 Antiphona : uox . recip*ro*ca :
6 Analogiu*m* : lectoriu*m* ligneu*m* . in quo legunt*ur* libri ;
7 Alleluia : laudate d*ominu*m : siue pat*er* : filius : sp*iritu*s s*anctus*.
8 Apostatare ; retrorsu*m* ire ;
9 Acidiosus|| : ociosus : instabilis . tristis : uagus ;
10 Ad missas . ad nitas‡ :
11 Absurdu*m* : inconueniens ; turpe*m*** : indignu*m* ;
12 Anxius : angustiosus :
13 Biblioteca : reconditoriu*m* librorum.
14 Bracile : zona
15 Bĭberes : potiones :
16 Aptet : congruet ; implet :
17 Angariati : portati ;

* MS. Primicerius, with *i* above the *e*.

† A letter (e) erased between the ii of stipendiis.

§ MS. apparently sescopla ; but perhaps *o* was badly altered into *u*.

¶ MS. has a perpendicular stroke over the *u*.

|| MS. Acediosus, with *i* above the *e*.

‡ Two letters erased between ad and nitas.

** MS. has perpendicular stroke over the *p*.

18 Aditu*m* : introitum ;
19 Adhibenda*; prestanda ;
20 Alim*en*tis : cibis ;
Fol. 21[ab]
21 Adsignato : tradito ; *uel* deputato :
22 Acco*m*modent*ur* ; prestant*ur* :
23 Adolatur : plandus ; adsentatur :
24 Causetur, murmuret*ur* :
25 Contuentes : conspicientes ; con :
26 Conte*m*pto : p*er*tinax : durus ; sup*er*b*us*
27 Crapula : ingluuies : *ue*l uomitum ;
28 Continuanda : iugit*er* . se*m*p*er* . p*er*petuo :
29 Conlationes : conlocutiones † : conferentes§ :
30 Condatur : reponatur
31 Congruus aptus.
32 Contentus ; patiens ; sufficiens ;
33 Cenobita : gr*ece* : in co*m*mune : uiuens
34 Catholicus : uniuersalis ;
35 Candela : a candendo : dic*itur*
36 Contuma ¶ contradictor ;
37 Canonicas : regulares horas ;
38 Cocula*m* :
39 Co*m*missu*m* : co*m*mendatu*m* : ||
40 Deificu*m* lum*en* . diuinu*m* : lum*en* :
41 Desidiosus : ignauus : pigrus :
42 Degradauerit : deposuerit ;
43 Diocesim ; gub*er*nationem ;
44 Discretio ; seperatio . diuisa ;
45 Desidia ‡ ignauia ;
46 Desidens : negligens ; u*e*l otiu*m* cupiens :
47 Digessimus : congrecauim*us* ; ordinauim*us*
48 Diru*m* : asperu*m* : durum :
49 Dissimulat : preterita neglegit :
50 Discussio : examinatio ;
51 Digesti : dispositi : excocti :
52 Deuteronomii : secunda : lex :
53 Decani : a decim nominantur :
54 Demum ; postea :
55 Deliberatio :
Fol. 21[ba]
56 Exhibita** : adtributa : p*r*estita :
57 Excesserit : oblitus fuerit : culpauerit ;
58 Eulogias . salutationes ;
59 Expedit : p*r*odest : co*m*modum est :
60 Excessus : extulit se ;
61 Excedere . abire . effugire ;
62 Examine . ivdicio †† . discussione.
63 Efficaciter . uelotiter§§ :
64 Edace*m* : commedente*m* ;
65 Excussu*m* : obliuione*m* : u*e*l derelictu*m* :
66 Explicantur.
67 Expedire : p*r*ode*sse* : u*e*l co*m*modare :
68 Expenso : expleto :
69 Eptaticu*m* ; septe*m* . libroru*m* : u*e*l septenariu*m*.
70 Exigerit : poposcerit : u*e*l petierit
71 Extollit . abstrahit¶¶ :
72 Experim*en*to : p*r*obam*en*to :
73 Emulatione : zeli :
74 Feria :
75 Fom*en*ta : nutrim*en*ta :
76 Fortuitu : subito :
77 Facile : citius : uelotiter ;

* *h* added above the line, between the *d* and *i*.

† The letter following the *l* seems to be *u* altered to *o*.

§ MS. conferentęs, but above the ę is a small slanting perpendicular stroke (=*i*), with a dot, as mark for insertion, underneath ; hence leg. conferentięs ; the word required is, apparently, *conferentiae* or *conferentias*.

¶ One or two letters erased after the *a* ; traces of *x* are still visible.

|| The first : on an erasure.

‡ Several letters erased between the lemma and the interpret.

** The *h* added above the line, between *x* and *i*.

†† *v* added above the line between *i* and *d*.

§§ The *i* lengthened by a stroke below the line.

¶¶ The *h* added above the second *a* with . on its left side, and after the second *a*. The *r* is a correction of *c*.

78 Fungi . administrare ;
79 Feruentissimo ; ardentissimo :
80 Girouagum ; circu*m* uacantiu*m* ;
81 Gradu suo : honore priuato :
82 Gestantes : portantes.
83 Grauitas : modestia :
84 Heremita : remota.
85 Hymnu*m* ; laude*m* ;
86 Himina : med*ius* sextarius : cyatos. III.
87 Aabita* : dicta : constituta :
88 Instrum*en*ta : peritię : utensilia : *ue*l materie :
89 Inprob*us* ; ingratus p*ro*cax . inportun*us*
90 Indigeries : ingluuies ;
Fol. 21[bb]
91 Inconpententib*us*† : n*on* aptis . inc*on*gruis.
92 Inbicilles : infirmi . flebiles :
93 Inlecebris : inlicitis sollitationib*us* :
94 Inrogatis.
95 In§ scamnis . in subselliis§ :
96 Inprobitas : p*ro*cacitas : inportunitas :
97 Kalende : uocationes :
98 Kẏrieleison : d*omi*ne . miserere . nob*is* ;
99 Laetania ; rogatio : postulatio
100 Lectisternia : uestm*en*ta¶ lecti : u*e*l . ordo lector*um*.
101 Lena : toscia :
102 Literis co*m*me*n*datitiis ,
103 Licet : qua*m*uis :
104 Libet : q*u*ib*us*cumq*ue* :
105 Loquacitate . uerbositate :
106 Leguminum : omne gen*us* fauor*um* :
107 Monachus : gr*ece* . singularis lat*ine* ;
108 Merito : iuste :
109 Modulatis : suauit*er*|| cantatis :
110 Missas ; amissas . u*e*l finite :
111 Morbida : languida.
112 Matta‡ . Mappula.
113 Morosa . diuturna : *ue*l longa :
114 Maturitas.
115 Munuscula : parua : dona
116 Materia : origo : u*e*l initio :
117 Noxa : culpa . crim*en* :
118 Non detegere . n*on* publicare n*on* manifestare
119 Nonnos : patres :
120 Norma ; regula :
121 Non p*ro*dicus ; n*on* sup*er*fluus.
122 Nimius . sup*er*fluus.
123 Non expedit : n*on* conuenit.
124 Moderate : te*m*perate :
125 Magnopere : forti animo : *ue*l maiore opere
Fol. 22[aa]
126 Officina :
127 Obiurgetur ; increpetur : culpet*ur* :
128 Obstinatus ; disperabil*is* u*e*l . inreuocabil*is*.
129 Ortodoxis : recte gloriosis ;
130 Pr*es*b*iter*
131 Pentecosten : ;
132 Plane : sane : certe ; :
133 Procaciter : sup*er*be :

* The initial capital is distinctly A; but the place where the word appears suggests Habita.

† Owing to some spot in the vellum the scribe left a blank for about four or five letters between In and con-

§ These four words are written in one line in the MS., and in subselliis may be an interpretation to in scamnis. But it is also possible that we have here two lemmata, to which interpretations are wanting, as in scamnis appears in IX. 10, and in subselliis in XI. 6 of the *Regula*.

¶ So in MS.

|| Goetz, Corpus v. 413, 69, prints succuit, and suggests suauiter in his Index. But the MS. has distinctly suauiter, not succuit.

‡ MS. leaves a vacant space for about seven letters between Matta and Mappula.

134 Passim : huc* atq*ue** illuc : u*e*l : leuit*er* :
135 Psalm*us* : cantus :
136 Priuatis ; alienatis . seperatis :
137 Prodicus : dissipator : substantię
138 Penso ; censo † ; 139 p*re*latus . p*re*positus †.
140 Pedules .
141 Prouide : caute : iuste :
142 Quantitas . mensura :
143 Quippia*m* . modis : 144 remota§ . ablata
145 Reculicet . reculcet ; reu
146 Regula dicta . eo q*uo*d recte ducit ;
147 Ratiociniis . unde ratio conp*ro*bet*ur* ;
148 Recreare :
149 Responsoria : q*ui* ab uno incipit*ur* et ab aliis respondit*ur*
150 Rubor ; uerecundia :
151 Sinaxis : solemnitas uesp*er*tinor*um* : *uel* . collectio coadunatio
152 Senpectas : sapientes : u*e*l seniores pectore.
153 Scrupolositas : dubietas : *uel* . anxietas . u*e*l animi molestia :
154 Scapulare :
155 Suspendatur : separetur¶ : [*Here follow the words* Sarabaita : rennuita, *but crossed through.*]
156 Stirpator : desertator :
157 sin alias . sin alit*er* :
158 Si quo minus : alioquin ;
159 Subrogetur ; submittit*ur* : *uel* . ministret*ur* :
160 Sagatitas . inuestigatio : uelocitas :
161 Sarabaite ; lingua egẏptiaca : in lat*ino* d*icitur* rennuite : qui refutant . abb*atem* habere ;

Fol. 22[ab]

162 Subiectione : subditione :
163 Spernendo : despiciendo :
164 Suaderi‖ ; censeri : hortari :
165 Sane ; certe :
166 Sincera : integra ;
167 Suggessione*m* : supplicatione*m*‡ . indicatione*m* : suffragatione*m* :
168 Uilicationis ; prepositure :
169 Ubi et ubi ; ubicu*m*q*ue* :
170 Uerbotenus : sicut dico ;
171 Uerbigratione : sermotinatione :
172 Temere ; sine consilio : u*e*l p*re*su*m*pt*u*ose :
173 Tirannide*m*** ; crudelem : siue durit*er*.
174 Temperie*m* : moderatione :
175 Teterrimum ; nigerrimu*m* :
176 Te*m*perius †† ; temperam*en*to
177 Taxauim*us* ; designauim*us* :
178 Tirannides ; iniquas potestates ;
179 Tẏpo : inflatio cordis : uel : sup*er*bia :
180 Tueri p*ro*tegere . u*e*l custodire§§ :
181 Uiolentia : fortia :
182 Uerbi gratia : ut si forte . u*e*l u*er*bi¶¶ causa,
183 Uicib*us* ; unu*m* post unum :
184 Uti : que*m*admodu*m* sicuti :
185 Uerbera ; flagella :
186 Utatur ; fruatur :
187 Uetusta*m* : uetere*m* :

* An erasure between these two words.

† Here and in a great many following cases the MS. makes one entry of two glosses.

§ There is a stroke over the rem, and Goetz prints remmota. But the stroke differs from the usual sign for contraction. The scribe probably meant to separate the two glosses.

¶ MS. seperetur, with *a* above the second *e*.

‖ MS. suadere, with *i* above the second *e*.

‡ A perpendicular stroke above the first *p*.

** MS. Tirande*m*, with ni above the line between the *n* and *d*.

†† MS has—over the *u* with a dot above the stroke to mark it for erasure.

§§ The *i* is added above the line.

¶¶ Added above the line between three dots.

188 Coenobiu*m* . ex greco et latino conpositu*m* esse dic*itur* : e*st* enim habitaculu*m* plurimor*um* :

189 Monasterium : unius monachi e*st* habitatio mono eni*m* apud grecos solu*m* e*st* :

190 Parcitate : abstinentie :

191 P*ro*diderit ; manifestauerit :

192 Pusillanimes : inbicilles ;

193 Precipuis ; maximis ;

Fol. 22[ba]

[III] UERBA DE S*ANCTI* MARTYNI STOR*IA*

1 Ueternor*um* : ueter*um* :

2 Ambiensiu*m* : prouintie,

3 Quartane : XIIII lune :

4 Inficiabor ; contradico ;

5 Amiculo : amicto ;

6 Toronicum :: gen*us* ligni ;

7 Byrr*um* : cocula breuis.

8 Lacerna*m* ; p*ro*lixor cocula ;

9 Turnodo ;

10 Hispida : deforma nodis :

11 Anfibula ; oberlagu* :

12 Bigiricum ; breue*m* ;

13 Uulnusculum † ; 14 p*er* aggerem : Pro exercitu 15 appulli : huuitabar§ 16 reda : nom*en* uehiculi

17 Nitidula*m* : 18 senium Mun*us*cula : 19 h ¶ ereticum || Pessuli : quo cludit*ur* cornu :

20 Merocem ; nom*en* piscis,

21 Ad seduforu*m* : p*ro* similitudine*m* fori :

22 Bornacula ; gen*us* ignis ;

23 Non obsecundare : n*on* obedire :

24 Sacro tegmini : domini martini :

25 Agellum ; agrum ;

26 Bacula : uacca :

27 Fvribundus ‡ ; feruens ;

28 Nutabundus ; agitatus ;

29 Clade*m* ; inferens .

30 Appulli ; inuitabant ;

31 In pago ; in uico : conpetis

32 Patera : uas regia ;

33 In sirtim ; mare arenosa ;

34 Fatescit** : briudid :

35 Promontoriu*m* ; hog †† :

36 Uitaha§§ ; uiscera ;

Fol. 22[bb]

37 Abenis ; halsledir ¶¶

38 Toracina ; haeslin ;

39 Carricibus ; gen*us* ligni ;

40 Conclauia : porticos ;

41 Laq*ue*aria ; celu*m* ex lignis ;

42 Flagris : flagellis ; 43 Mautigia |||| ; gen*us* flagellis ‡‡

44 Soeue : su : 45 Fretus . *con*fidens ,

46 Apparabilis ; ministratio ;

47 Indecentius : inaptius .

48 Murmur : uastrung***. 49 Lugoria : exuberat

50 Neotricis ; noua fide : 51 Stigmata ; signa :

* MS. has over this word a horizontal waving stroke, which crosses through the top of the *b* and *l*; and from this stroke a perpendicular stroke comes down, which may be the top of a *b* or *l*, or some such letter, erroneously commenced by the scribe.

† The glosses 13—16 are written as two entries in the MS. But uulnusculum is a lemma without interpretation; likewise per agg- ; Pro ex- belongs, apparently, to reda; but app- and huuitabar, for (h)inuitabar, go together (cf. below no. 30).

§ MS. has waving stroke over *uuit.*

¶ MS. has a stroke through this separately written *h*, which belongs to ereticum.

|| MS. has three dots over the i.

‡ MS. Ferebundus with v above the first, and i above the second, e.

** The s written above the line between the e and c. †† MS. has stroke over the *og*.

§§ So in MS. for uitalia. ¶¶ MS. has a waving stroke over *lsle*.

|||| The first letter is apparently N; but an alteration has been made at the first stroke to make M; Mastigia is the word required.

‡‡ The e is written above the g. *** The n has been added above the line.

52 Antoni; 53 lacuna : floda :
54 Enrusa; dapulas; 55 Inuitiat; *con*tradicat
56 Ependiten; tonica; u*e*l cocula; *ue*l : omnis uestis : desup*er* aliis uestib*us* pendens :
57 Lurida : pox; 58 Memoria : sepulcr*um* :
59 Explosa : elisa : u*e*l exp*er*ta :
60 Sofismatu*m*; questionum;
61 Explosa; mortua; 62 Uiridariu*m*; a uirido : d*icitu*r.
63 Labefacare : agleddęgo :*
64 Ultro; citro : hidirandidir†
65 Arguta : ordancas§ : 66 Exenia : madmas¶

[IV] INCIPIT IN LIBR*UM* ECCLESIASTICĘ ISTOR*IAE*

1 Pannigericis|| : in laudibus :
2 Coagmentare; congregare‡ :
3 Ilix nom*en* ligni : 4 Ma*m*bre : homo : *ue*l. ciuitas :
5 Fates : p*ro*pheta : 6 Editus : ostiarivs** :
Editu*m*; te*m*plu*m*; 7 Curia : conuentus :
8 Co*mm*e*n*tatus; tractatus. 9 fastib*us* : libris :
10 Ogdoade. nouu*m* testam*en*tu*m* :
11 Tragoedia; luctus; ac cladis; 12 Uncus : lepra :
13 Fascib*us* : onorib*us* : 14 Asitu*m*; *sanctum* : 15 Plexus : truncatus.
16 Asiliu*m*; diuinu*m*; 17 Fadus. aliud nom*en* erodis :
18 Urban*us* : sapiens; 19 Sicarii : gladiatores;
20 Pungios : pullus; gladius; 21 Fas : diuinum :
Fol. 23^{aa}
22 Ius : humanu*m*; 23 Apollogeticus; excusans;
24 Callas; uarras††; 25 In edito; in excelso;
26 Adstipulatione; adiutorio;
27 Ariopagitis : princeps : sinagog*ae*;
28 Mulcatus; p*er*cussus; 29 Exitiali; mortali;
30 Dispicatis; diuisis; 31 P*re*statio§§; custodia;
32 Dependisset; sustinuisset; 33 Inuastu*m*. inuisu*m*;
34 Petulu*m*; lumina aurea;
35 Antelucanu*m* : ante calli cantus; 36 Meandr*um*. nom*en* montis.
37 Trallis; nom*en* eccl*esi*ę; 38 Facessat; lacessat;
39 Incessere : accusare; 40 duellis; bellum;
41 Pessimos darent; circu*m*darent;
42 Quatere : mouere : 43 Gnostici : scientes;
44 Amatorie; ars. philophie :
45 Parethris; ministeriis; 46 P*ro*cacia : adrogantia;
47 Stadiu*m* : ubi iocus agit*ur*; 48 Munerarius : munera accipiens :
49 Furtunata*m*; p*ro*speritate*m*;
50 Camer*um*; tectu*m*; 51 ORatorie : eloquentie;
52 Monarchia : regiminis culm*en* *ue*l pugnę¶¶.

* MS. has stroke over *gleddę*, crossing through the tops of the *l* and *dd*; also stroke over the final *o*. Some letters have been erased after the *o*.

† MS. has stroke over *idir*, crossing through the top of *d*, and another stroke over *ndidi*, crossing through the *dd*.

§ MS. has stroke over *rdanc*, crossing through the top of *d*.

¶ MS. has stroke over *adm*, crossing through the top of *d*.

|| The c added above the line. ‡ MS. congregitre, but *it* altered into *a*.

** MS. ostiarias, with v above the second a. †† MS. has stroke over the *rr*.

§§ MS. has P, with contraction for *re* above it, therefore P*re*statio; but Rufinus has per stationes.

¶¶ MS. punnę, with the lower part of g added under the first n so as to form one letter.

53 Psaltes; castus : 54 Metalla; uincula;
55 auspiciis*; auxiliis : 56 Encratiani; *con*tinentes;
57 Thesteas : indiscretas concubitas;
58 Oedipia : obscene; Dapes : car-
niu*m* infantiu*m*;
59 Puncto : pede : 60 Neruu*m* : uin-
culu*m* : 61 Muner*um* 62 nundinas :
63 Po*m*pa; fallatia; 64 Fiscu*m* :
tributu*m* :
65 Liciniosa†; questiosa; 66 Terebrantes; borgenti;
67 Meticulosi : pauidi; 68 Elogis;
uerbis :
69 Piaculu*m* : pollutio; 70 Fibras;
intestinas;
71 P*e*ripsima, gaesuopę; 72 P*ro*stipu-
lu*m*; locus forn*icationis* .
73 Litat; immolat; 74 Trogleis§;
hlędrę¶
75 Latriuncula; herst||; 76 Pusti;
brandas‡
77 Cäutere**; tunderi††; 78 Suppuratis; turgid*is* :
79 De triuio : de trib*us* uiis; 80 Spurca : inmunda;
81 Calones : saltantiu*m* t*ur*ba; 82 Codicib*us* liminib*us* :
83 Ruder : mixin; 84 uoti co*m*pos;
xp*ist*iana;
Fol. 23[ab]
85 Thecis : custodiis; 86 Iniciatus,
s*anct*ificatus;
87 Infensus; inoffensus; 88 purulenta; fetida;
89 Morbo re o§§; lep*ro*sitas : 90 Calles;
lapides,
91 Cem*en*ta : gluttina¶¶; 92 Pastoforia : gazofilatia;
93 Angiportos||||; n*omen* porti : 94 Co-
niculu*m*; a conando;
95 Fautorib*us* : consentientib*us* :
96 Stomatu*m* : op*us* uariatu*m*;
97 Thoraces; capud et pectus,
98 Comellas h uniuscuiusq*ue* int*er*-
p*re*tis translatio in unu*m* collect*ae* : et e regione posite;
99 Quadraplas die; hoc e*st* III horę‡‡
quę *con*crescunt in quarto
anno quando fit q*uide*m bissextus :
100 Bustus, tumulu*m* : u*e*l ab ustu*m*;
101 ΠOrsutas motatores;
102 Catacesseos : doctrinar*um*
103 Sinisascas : sociatrices : 104 Manius : demones,
105 Propositus*** uestis regie : propositura***;
106 Candentes††† : ardentes : 107 Scrip-
tione*m*; calcu*m*;
108 Excessu*m* : cauatu*m*; 109 Defecatior; purior;
110 Defecatu*m* : liquida*m*; 111 Pu-
r*um*; extersum;
112 Adigent; surgentes; 113 Apulisse; pulsasse;
114 A theologia; a diuina generatione;

* MS. Aauspiciis, but the A marked by three dots for erasure.

† The *c* is a correction from *t*.

§ The *l* seems a correction from some other letter.

¶ MS. has stroke over this word, which crosses through the tops of *hld*.

|| MS. has stroke over this word, and an inkspot above the *e*.

‡ MS. has stroke over *rand*.

** MS. has two dots over the a.

†† MS. tundri, with *e* above the line between the d and r.

§§ One or two letters are erased between the e and o; read: Morbo regio.

¶¶ The first t is added above the line, between two dots.

|||| The n has been added above the line.

‡‡ MS. has a stroke over orę.

*** MS. has three dots (marks of transposition) over the first o of Propositus; over the e of uestis; over the first e of regie, and over the t of propositura.

††† MS. condentes with a above the o.

115 Auspiciis . adiutoriis :
116 Acoluthos . accensores : 117 Ad coemetoria ad ecclesia
118 Afficit : ditauit; 119 Antesignato; signatore suspectu*m*;
120 Bibennem : securis bina*m* acie*m* habens,
Fol. 23[ba]

[V] ITEM DE ECCLESIASTICA STORIA:

1 Cẏati; mensu*m* minutu*m*; 2 Colomellas*; lomum
3 Conolas : quę contia uocant;
4 Canto : uectis; 5 Carbunculi : poccas;
6 De octoade : De octaua die .
7 Doriu*m* : indiculu*m* : 8 Auo·i· utj eza . septe*m*plici :
9 Ephod : sup*er*umeral*e*; 10 Exedre; parue dom*us*
11 Labru*m* . ambone*m* . id*est* haet†; 12 Labris : uentis nome*n*
13 Operiunt : co*n*spiciunt :
14 Oedippa : de odippo : 15 Pruriginem : bleci§
16 Podagra : tumor pedu*m* : 17 Paredu*m*; p*re*stigiu*m*
18 Parchredis : p*re*strigiis : 19 Publite : hamme¶
20 Quorsu*m*; quocu*m*q*ue*; 21 Editiones . thestisuir
22 Fibraru*m*; darmana‖; 23 Suppeditans : p*ro*ficiens,
24 Subrigeris : eleuaris; 25 Solaria : onores .
26 Subsaltare; sonare : 27 Siniscas; u*e*l seniscatas :
28 Simbulis; co*n*siliis co*n*pactis; 29 Simbulion : pactu*m*;
30 Sescuplum : dridehalpf‡ :
31 Sugillato : stranguillato; 32 Thoraces**, Imagines :

[VI] INC*IPIT* BREUIS. EXSOLUTIO:

1 Ne : uel : 2 Uiscide; uiscerade; 3 Eaten*us*; acten*us*
4 Uersus : contra; 5 Boriali : aquiloni :
6 Meliorata; ornata;
7 Ambrones†† : deuoratores§§; 8 Ast; statim :
9 Thiticu*m*; marinam; 10 Crusticis; bucellis¶¶;
11 Catasta*m*; lupa*m*; 12 Albri; uas apium;
13 For : euentus;, 14 Du*m* nomine : ciuitatis .
15 Perigamini : Me*m*brano : 16 Leonine : de leone;
17 Lanio; lacetur; 18 Nemphe, ministri nequa*m* :
19 Modoli; lateria; 20 Molosi; canes,
21 Conueniens; appellans; 22 Placoris : uolun : tatis
23 Raucos . crispantes, 24 Intentos; extensos;
25 Defetimur; renitimur. 26 P*er*ossus; abhominatus;
27 Panguit*ur*; pinguit*ur*; 28 Clustello; claustro;
29 Ollita : de ollitim; 30 Quoadquo; adusq*ue*; 31 inequiperabilis :
Fol. 23[bb]

[VII] DE PARALIPOMENON.

1 In nablis . In cimbal*is* quę p*er* pedes ponunt*ur*
2 Pro octaua . In nouissimo die azimor*um*
3 Commissuras . ligatur*as* : u*e*l co*n*positur*as*

* *e* corrected from *o*.
† MS. has waving stroke over *aet*.
§ MS. has stroke over *leci*.
¶ MS. has stroke over *amm*.
‖ MS. has stroke over *darma*, crossing through the top of the *d*.
‡ MS. has stroke over *dridehal*, crossing through the tops of the *dd* and *h*.
** MS. Toraces, with h added above the o.
†† MS. Aambrone, but *a* marked by three dots for erasure, and *s* added above *e*.
§§ An *a* has been erased over the *t*.
¶¶ MS. bulellis, but the first *l* corrected into *c*.

4 Lapides onichinos . dunnę .
5 Creacras . fuscinulas .
6 In mausilio . In monumento .
7 Carpenta carra .
8 Obtigit contigit
9 In fastu In dignitate .

[VIII] DE SALAMONE.

1 Panarethos . sapientia .
2 Coacuer*int* . uersę s*unt* in acaetum
3 Ne innataris . ne incu*m*beris . ne co*n*sidas .
4 Aucupes . aucellatores .
5 Uersipellis . peruersus .
6 Fornice*m* signu*m* uictorię
7 Domatis . dom*us* sine tecto . *u*el spinaru*m*
8 In aceruo mercurii . consuetudinem habebant ambulantes in uia ubi sepultus e*st* mercurius lapidem iactare in aceruum ipsius unusq*uis*q*ue* p*ro* honore ei*us* .
9 Lamuhel . agnom*en* salamonis . sicut ecclęsiastes ab actione .
10 Conflatorium . ubi ferru*m* *u*el argentu*m* conflatur .
11 Cinamu*m* . cortix dulcis .
12 Uaena . d*icitu*r p*er* qua*m* aqua currit
13 In sublime . id*est* anticristus . qui quasi feliciter incedit .

(*Fol.* 24^{aa})

14 Blena dicit*ur* : p*er* qua*m* aqua currit .
15 Flauescit : color olei : glitinot* :
16 Mala aurea in lectis argenteis; mila : id*est* poma de auro in circuitu lecto*rum* p*ro* orna*men*to;
17 Nit*rum*; in t*er*ra inuenit*ur* : instar atram*en*ti p*ro* sapone habe*tur* : si in acętu*m* mittit*ur* ad nihilu*m* soluit*ur* qui atr*um*q*ue* amarescit .
18 Ptisanas†; de ordeo fiunt grana . que decortica*ntur* in pilo u*e*l uase lapideo;
19 Si usq*ue* ad lacu*m* fuerit. id*est* si stagnu*m* faciat de sanguine n*on* satiabitur;
20 Offer . adduc qui n*on* satiant*ur*;
21 Co*m*mandit; manducat

[IX] DE ECLESIASTEN;

1 Lustrans; circu*m*iens§ et inluminans;
2 Cassa; uacua; 3 Contegnatio; tectio dom*us*;
4 Amictalu*m* . arbor nucum :
5 Capparis . erba bona ad co*m*messatione*m* nascit*ur* in montib*us*
6 Anacefaleos; recapitulatio :

[X] IN CANTICO CANTICOR*UM*

1 Oscule*tur* me; ista oscula quę execlesie porrex*it* xp*istus* qua*m* baptismi nitore mundata*m* et ornata*m* p*er* sp*iritu*m s*anctu*m odoris sui;
Gratia inuitat ut sponsa*m*; 2 Ubera; apostoli;
3 Odor ungent*orum*, donu*m* q*uo*d in bapt*ism*ate accipim*us* .
4 Uina; p*ro*phete; 5 Nom*en* tuu*m* : xp*isti*aniam a xp*ist*o et chrisma*m*
6 Unguentu*m*; exinanitum.
Chrisme uocabulu*m* dedictu*m* e*st* q*uo*d n*on* ante d*icitu*r chrisma qua*m* sup*er* homine*m* fuerit fusu*m*;
7 Aduliscentulę; ecclesię . u*e*l animę de numero gentiu*m*
8 Redimicula; s*unt* orname*n*ta ceruicis;
9 Nardu*m* spica unde faciunt unguenta;

* MS. has stroke through the bar of the second *t*, which looks like a hook (Γ) that remained after some word, written by the side of *glitinot*, had been erased.

† MS. Ptisinas, with *a* above the second *i*.

§ *u* corrected from *o*.

10 Cyprus : arbor e*st* similis salice
habens flores miri odoris et
butros . sicut erba pratear*um* .
11 Tigna tecta cedri natura arbor*um* cedri inputribili uigore
co*n*sistunt

Fol. 24^{ab}

quar*um* sucus u*er*mib*us* e*st* obuius ; sign*ificat* apost*olos* ;
12 Ficus p*ro*tulit grossos suos flore
ipsius . antequa*m* aperiant*ur**
sic dicunt*ur*
13 Ferculu*m* lectu*m* e*st* q*uo*d portari
potest ;
14 Amana : et liban*us* . sanir et hermon montes s*unt*
15 Emissiones tuę : munera delectabilia ;
16 Crocus herbe flos e*st* modice mire
odoris.
17 Fistola : arbor e*st* boni odoris n*on*
boni saporis ;
18 Murra et aloe . herbe s*unt* ;
19 Gutta . de arbore currit ; id*est*
balsamu*m* ;
20 Cassia . erba e*st* similis coste ;
21 Elatę palmar*um* ; folia palmar*um*
quę eleuent*ur* sursu*m* q*uia* n*on*
pendent deorsu*m* sicut aliar*um*
arbor*um* ;
22 Areola † d*icitu*r ubi aqua diriuat*ur*
in ortu*m* et stat in modico stagnello ipse d*icitu*r ereola p*ro*pt*er*
inrigatione*m* ubi crescunt aromata ; 23 Aminab : p*ro*priu*m*
nom*en* uiri :
24 Salamitis concubina d*aui*d que
ministrabat ei in senectute,
25 Uinum candidu*m* : piperatu*m* .
u*e*l mellatum ;
26 Mustu*m* facit*ur* de malis granatis .
id *est* malis punicis ;

[XI] DE SAPIENTIA :

1 Fascinatio : laudatio stulta ;
2 Subtatio§ : q*uo*d subito fit ;
3 Lanugo : et aluginatio . pene ide*m*
est ;
Squalor lanugo in carne ;
4 Torax . lurica manicas n*on*
habens et tunica sine manicis
sic d*icitu*r ;
5 Uitulamina . id*est* . filii a uitulis
dicu*ntur*, qui de adulterio nati ;
6 Supremu*m* : extremum :
7 Pentapolim ; u. ciuit*ates* quę arserunt :

Fol. 24^{ba}

8 Eletrix : electrix : 9 Abene ; corrigia frenor*um* :
10 Signu*m* . habentes ; serpente*m*
aeneu*m* :
11 In aqua ualebat ignis : fulgura
in pluuia ad impios missa ;
12 Malagma : multe herbe contrite in
una massa*m* uulner*um* ;
13 In carcere sine ferro . in mare
rubro ;
14 Poderis : uestis e*st* sacerdotum a
pedib*us* usq*ue* ad umbilicu*m*
p*er*tingens . et ibi stringebatur
cingulo in cuius subteriore parte
habebantur ¶ tintinnabula et
mala punica ; 15 In forib*us* iusti :
i*dest* loth ;
16 Bona*m* esca*m* . manna . q*uae* sol-
uebat*ur* a sole n*on* ab igne .

[XII] DE ECCLESIASTICO :

1 Euergetis : boni operis ; u*e*l factoris ;
2 Scandaligeris : scandalizaueris :

* The *n* is added above the line.

† MS. has a perpendicular stroke over the *r*, which is, perhaps, the top of a wrongly commenced *b*, *d* or other letter.

§ MS. has almost subttotio ; the word required is subitatio.

¶ The *n* has been added above the line.

3 Obductionis dilectiones . i*dest* mortis;
4 Inplanauit : sedux*it* inmisit :
5 Magnato; magno : 6 Acide;
triste :
7 Placore*m* : placationem;
8 Rusticatio; cultura te*r*re;
9 Cacabus; de testa e*st* duas manubrias habens . aliquando de ęręme*n*to sic*ut* et olla .
10 Ceruicatus; sup*er*b*us*; 11 Inpen-
diis; rebus;
12 Calculus; minutissima petra arenę;
13 Alacriter*; sine gratia . amariter;
14 Lorame*n*tu*m*; ligame*n*tu*m*; 15 Ce-
me*n*ta; petre molliores
16 Infrunite; infrenate;
17 Platanus; arbor e*st* boni odoris;
18 Aspaltum; spaldur† : 19 Calban*us*;
pigme*n*tu*m* album
20 Aromatizans; redolens;
21 Ungula et gutta : pigme*n*tu*m* de arborib*us*;
22 Storax . incensum; 23 N*on* trices;
n*on* tardes;
24 Dorix . i*dest* p*ro*priu*m* nome*n* fluminis;
25 In ormentu*m*; in ornamentum;
26 Aporia; abominatio; subitania§;
27 Tortura; torquemi*na*¶; 28 Solide;
fortiter

Fol. 24[bb]

29 Lingua te*r*tia; discordians lingua *ue*l rixosa
30 Colera; nausia; 31 Auocare, oc-
cupare;
32 Frugis; parcus; 33 De traiectione
de datione : id*est* malu*m*
34 Infrunita sine freno : *ue*l moderatione;
35 Equus emissarius : qui mittitur ad iume*n*ta :
36 Similagine*m*; genus tritici . 37 lor
funis;
38 Sophistice : conclusione *ue*l rep*re*hensione;
39 Plestia : abundantia *ue*l indegeries;
40 Cẏneris nablis . id*est* citharis longiores qua*m* psalteriu*m* . na*m* psalteriu*m* triangulu*m* fit . theodorus . dix*it*;
41 Lino crudo; i*dest* uiride non cocto ueste;
42 Uasa castroru*m* : arma exercitu*m* . i*dest* milicie cęli; d*icitu*r eni*m* q*uo*d bella futura possent p*re*-
uidere . in sole et luna; 43 Ago-
niare; certare;
44 Inpingaris : inpelleris;
45 Caupo; qui uinum p*er*miscet ad p*er*dendum;
46 Accommorante; conhabitantes;
47 Offusio; effusio; 48 Pululent;
crescunt|| in miraculis

[XIII] IN LIBRO ISAIE PROPHETE;

1 Cucumerariu*m* : hortus in quo cucumerus crescit . bona erba ad manducandum siue ad medici-
na*m*; 2 Tuguriu*m*; domuncula;
3 Uermiculus; a similitudine uermis;
4 Fissura; scissura; diuisura;
5 Co*m*molitus . exterminatus;
6 Lunulas; quas mulieres in collo habent de auro u*e*l argento : a similitudine lunę diminit*iue*
dicunt*ur*; 7 Discriminalia; unde discernunt*ur* crines de auro . *ue*l . argento *ue*l aere;
8 Periscelidas; armillas de tibiis;
9 Olfactoriola‡; turibula modica . de auro . u*e*l argento mulieres habent p*ro* odore :

* MS. has here † in the margin, to indicate, no doubt, that there is something amiss; the word should be *acriter*. After the *i* of sine one letter has been erased.

† MS. has v above the *a*.

§ MS. subitanea, with *i* above the *e*.

¶ MS. has torquem, with stroke over the *m*, to which is attached an *i* written below the line.

|| The *s* has been added above the line.

‡ Third *o* corrected from *a*.

10 Murenulas : catenulas ;
Fol. 25[aa]

11 Mutatoria : uestimenta ; alia meliora et mundiora

12 Teristra : subtilissima curtina ;

13 Fascia pectoralis , uest*is* circa pectus uoluit*ur* ;

14 La*m*bruscas ; malas uuas ;

15 Dece*m* iugera uinear*um* ; x . iugeres . *uel* . diurnal*es* .

16 Tabehel ; p*ro*priu*m* nom*en* uiri :
17 Par*um* . paruum ;

18 Sarculu*m* ; ferr*um* fossoriu*m* . duos dentes habens .

19 Sarient*ur* ; fodient*ur* : 20 Inniti . co*n*fisi . co*n*fidentes ;

21 Carcamis : nom*en* loci . uel . ciuitatis ;

22 Calanan ; similit*er* ; 23 Ganniret : quasi cum ira inrideret,

24 Pilosi : incubi . monstri ; i*dest* menae* ;

25 De radice colubri . nascit*ur* regulus : qui manducat aucellas ; id*est* basiliscus : sec*undum* historia*m* di*citu*r de colubri nasci ; 26 Gabaa : ciuit*as* saul*is*,

27 Flaccentia ; contracta ; 28 Sirene . mulieres marine

29 Mede : nom*en* loci : 30 In triuiis : in trib*us* uiis ;

31 Papiri ; unde faciunt cartas ;

32 Riui . agger*um* †, congregatio aquarum ;

33 Bige . equitu*m* : duor*um* exercitum ;

34 Tela*m* orditus : inuuerpan uuep§

35 Uiciam ; pisas agrestes ; i*dest* fugles¶ beane,

36 In serris ; serra d*icitu*r lignu*m* habens multas dentes quod|| boues trahent ;

37 Malus nauis : caput in arbore nauis a similitudine milui ;
38 Artum ; angustum ;

39 Migma : et mixtum : idem est ;

40 P*er*pendiculu*m* ; modica petra de plumbo qua licant in filo quando edificant parietes ; pundar‡

41 Paliurus ; erba quę crescit** in tectis†† domor*um* grossa folia habens fullae§§ ; 42 Epocentaurus ; equo ;
Onocentaurus asino mixtum ; most*er*¶¶.

43 Lamia : dea siluę d*icitu*r habens pedes similes caballi caput et manus totu*m* corp*us* pulcrę mulieris : et uider*unt* multi aliq*ui* manser*unt* cum ea ;

44 Fouit : cubat calefaciendo ;
Fol. 25[ab]

45 Apotecas|||| : cellaria . 46 Cataplasmarent : contritos inponerent ;

47 Plaustr*um* ; in similitudine*m* arce rotas habens intus : et ipse dentes habent quasi rostra d*icitu*r in quib*us* frangent spicas ;

48 Mẏrtus . modicus arbor boni odoris, se*mper* uiride .

49 Plastes ; figulus ;

50 Runtina ; pidugio : uitubil‡‡ ;

51 Calamum ; pigm*en*tum ex arbore ;

52 Lima ; qua limatur ferr*um* ; fiil***

53 Circino ; ferr*um* duplex unde pic-

* MS. has v above the *m*. † First *g* added above the line.

§ MS. has v above the second *u* of uuerpan, and above the second *u* of uuep.

¶ MS. has v above the *s*.

|| MS. has perpendicular stroke above the *o*, perhaps for *i*, or the stroke of a wrongly commenced *d*? ‡ MS. has v above the *n*. ** *cr* written on an erasure.

†† *tec* written on an erasure. §§ MS. has v (almost looking like y) above the *a*.

¶¶ MS. has most, with a somewhat lengthened bar through the *t*, and a stroke above it ; therefore most*er*, or most*um* ; perhaps for mo*n*str*um*.

|||| A stroke over the *t* has been erased. ‡‡ MS. has v above the second *i*.

*** There is, apparently, a perpendicular stroke over the second *i* of fiil, but it is the , belonging to the ; after arbore.

tores faciunt circulos; i*dest*
gaborind*;

†

54 Del et hnabot
55 Adcola† . et acola idem *sunt*;
56 Uellentib*us* tollentib*us* pilos
de genis :
57 Saliuncula : erba medicinalis habens spinas miri odoris, cresc*it*
in montib*us* :
58 In lecticis : a similitudine lecti
dicuntur .
59 Feretri; in quib*us* portant*ur*
filię nobilium sup*er* .IIII. equis
coop*er*tis desup*er* cortina sic*ut*
currus;
60 Dromedarię; castrati cameli : dromedarius unus; 61 Mure*m*;
soricem;

[XIV] INC*IPIT* IN HIEREMIA

1 Construpauer*unt*; *con*taminauer-
unt§
2 Nitr*um*; in terra inuenitur;
3 Uorith : erba e*st* . de ipsa panes¶
faciunt quos erbaticas appellant
et siccant illos : habentq*ue* p*ro*
sapore .
4 Pedica; tenticula; 5 Placentas;
dulces|| faciunt de simila . et
oleo; *ue*l adipe et melle; 6 resina
de arbore e*st* sic*ut* et pix . 7 lig-
nu*m* in pane : crucem . in carne;
8 Lu*m*bare; bragas modicas .

9 In unge‡ adamantino . q*uam*uis
modicu*m* sit sic*ut* ungula tam*en*
insolubile sic*ut* adamans petra
durissima;
Fol. 25[ba]
10 Mirice : arbor est : lat*ine* : tramaritius d*icitu*r;
11 P*er*dix : auis in deserto . alt*er* .
p*er*dit** alit*er* fouit oua
12 Domatib*us* porticib*us* u*e*l atriis
quę n*on* tegent;
13 Sinopide : petra rubea unde pingent;
14 Calati . canistri de uirgis fiunt angusti in p*ro*dis lati in ore;
15 Caeleuma; exortatio in naue;
16 Inclusor; qui ge*m*mas inclusit
auro;
17 Arreptitiu*m*; demoniosum; 18 Arua : t*er*ra††
19 Arugo; color sic*ut* pedes accipitris,
20 Scalpellu*m* : ferr*um* e*st* . q*uo*d
habent scriptores unde incidunt
cartas et pennas . acuent ex altera parte latu*m* sic*ut* graphium;
21 Torta panis; incisus panis;
22 In fatores : nom*en* loci; 23 Rata;
placita;
24 Stipulationis; p*ro*missionis;
25 Polite; mundate; 26 Lidii; gens .
27 Stratores; conpositores, 28 Ster-
nente*m* : allidente*m*
29 Ficarius : qui ficos collegit
30 Pedalis§§ : mensura in tela quando
uolunt incidere

* After this word one line is left blank, with † in the right-hand margin.

† The *la* corrected from some other letter (*n*?).

§ After this word, and after inuenitur of the next line, some words have been erased which had evidently been *added* in the first instance, as the ⌈, usually prefixed to such additions, is still visible after contam-.

¶ The *s* is surrounded by three dots.

|| The *l* is added above the line.

‡ MS. Inunge, with horizontal stroke between two dots above the line between the first *n* and *u*. As the text has *in ungue*, this stroke above the line seems to be meant as a mark of division.

** The *d* is written on an erasure.

†† The two words of N° 18 are written in the MS. as one word, so that the second stroke of the open *a* is connected with the back part of the bar of the *t*, but : was inserted to mark the division.

§§ MS. Pedales, with *i* above the second *e*.

31 Tyrones*; noui milites .
32 Croceis : erba bona ad medicinam .
33 Lacinias : extremas partes uestium .
34 Uitula*m* consternante*m* . lasciuiante*m* aut aeste p*ro* uermibus .
35 Thimiamateria ; turibula ;
36 Urceos : uasa erea in q*uibus* aqua*m* portant ;

[XV] INCIP*IT* IN HIEZECHIEL†;

1 Atramentariu*m* : uas atram*en*ti ;
2 Sẏnicias : uituperans : 3 Uas transmigrationis aut carru*m* aut uas alter*um* paruum ;
4 Litura; inpensa : lim§ u*e*l clam¶;
Fol. 25bb
5 Paxillus; fusticellus qui in stante*m* mittit*ur* . negil||
6 Struices; congregationes;
7 N*on* conpluta; sine pluuia, 8 Conplosi; plausu*m* feci :
9 Transtra ; tabula . quę iacent in transuersu nauis in q*uibus* sedent remigantes,
10 Ebor : arbor inputribilis nigro colore
11 Preteriola : domuncula micina in naue unius cubiti . in quibus abscondunt cibos suos;
12 Bibli : artifices qui faciunt trapezitas : *uel* p*ro*priu*m* nom*en* gentis ;
13 Pigmei : homines cubitales . id*est* unius cubiti
14 Hebenenos‡ : u*e*l eberenos‡ : de arbore hebore ;
15 Dan : p*ro*prium nomen gentis .
16 Mozel : mauritani : 17 Nundinis; mercatis .
18 Inuoluere; quando inuoluitur uestim*en*tum in corio, u*e*l in sago;
19 Gazar*um* ; diuitiar*um*; 20 Sabuli : arene ;
21 Foramina; ubi mittunt gemmas :
22 Speties ęris ∴ de eram*en*to dic*itur*;
23 Sẏeres; p*ro*priu*m* nom*en* loci;
24 Pollinctores; qui sepeliunt homines pro pecunia;
25 Hecthetas . 26 peribolus 27 arihellio;
28 Fornacula;
29 Thalamus; altior locus ubi sedet sponsa;
30 Cata mane; iuxta mane
31 Salinas; loca ubi sal inuenitur;
32 Sinchronon; unius te*m*poris :
33 Uinacia; q*uod*** remanet in uuis . qvando†† p*re*muntur
34 Foedi : foedera*m*ni ; 35 Teraphin; idolu*m* sic nominatur ; 36 Lappa; clitę ; IT*EM* AL*IA* ;
37 Electr*um* ; de auro : et argento§§ et ęrę
38 Conectura; auguria : 39 Exertu*m*; sollicitu*m* ;
40 Oraculu*m* ; oration*em* ; u*e*l locutionem ;
41 Lebes; caldarius . 42 Culine : fornacula :
Fol. 26aa
43 Puluillos : plumatios micinos duos coniunctos habent in sella;
44 P*ro*phana; deforma .
45 Iacincto : id*est* de pelle iacinctino;
46 Pusillumin*us* : paulomin*us*; 47 Limati; mundati :

* *y* corrected from *i*.

† MS. NIE-, but N corrected into H.

§ MS. has v above the *m*, and lim uel as one word limuł.

¶ MS. has v above the *a*.

|| MS. gil, with ne written above the line.

‡ MS. has a perpendicular stroke over the third *e* of Hebenenos, and over the third *e* of eberenos, probably as marks of transposition, as the text has (xxvii. 15) dentes eburneos et hebeninos.

** Written on an erasure.

†† MS. qando, with *v* above the line between the *q* and *a*.

§§ The *r* is a corrected letter.

48 Ad leuicandu*m*; leuem facerę;

[XVI] INCIP*IT* IN DANIELEM:

1 Pistrinu*m* : ubi panes : coquuntur;
2 Offa; morsus; 3 Crypta; spelunca pe*r*uia;
4 Ilicus; arbor e*st* : folia modica habens* fructusq*ue* sic*ut* glandi modici;
5 Lentiscus; arbor folia modica habens et fructus sine grana . i*dest* muras rubras; ursi :
6 Discofor m† : discum portante*m* .
7 Aruspices; qui aras inspiciunt;
8 Satrapa : princeps§ pe*r*sarum :
9 Malleolis; q*uo*dcu*m*q*ue* tunguit*ur* ad excitandu*m* igne*m*
10 Nappa : genus fomitis
11 Saraballa : crura hominu*m* uocant. apud caldeos :
12 Regina; uxor . nabuchodonosor p*ro* reuerentia
13 Efferatus . e*st* . a ferocitate d*icitu*r :
14 Ex latere regni : de adulterio regine;
15 Ab exitu sermonis : ab exordio sermonis;
16 Ditione : potestate;
17 Castrum : modica ciuitas; altiorib*us* muris
18 Trieres : i*dest* naues a trib*us* sessionibus,
19 Apethno . p*ro*prium nom*en* loci;
20 Smigmata; unguenta .
21 Aggere*m* : co*n*gregatione*m* de lignis; u*e*l lapidib*us*
22 Trinte artabę; xi¶ modios faciunt;
23 Agiografa : s*anct*a scriptura :
24 Iuge sacrificiu*m*; legale officiu*m* .
25 Arioli; qui in‖ ara coniectura*m* faciunt;
26 Magi : q*ui* magica*m* arte*m* faciunt siue philosophia*m*
27 Malefici; qui sanguine et uictimis

Fol. 26[ab]

et sepe contingunt corpora mortuor*um* consuetudo au*tem* et sermo co*m*munis : magos p*ro* meficiis accipi*unt* Magi uero apud chaldeos‡ philosophi habent*ur*
28 Cubitu*m*; elin**;
29 Chaldei†† suntquos uulgus mathematicos uocat§§
30 Aruspices; qui exta inspiciunt et ex his futura predicant;
31 Incantatores *sunt* : q*ui* re*m* . uerbis pe*r*agunt;
32 Auspices; qui aues inspiciunt;

[XVII] DE IOHEL . U*E*L DE P*RO*PHETIS¶¶ MINORIB*US*,

1 Area sitiens; siccans in tritura;
2 Ligones : ferr*um* fusoriu*m* : i*dest* tyrfahga;
3 Occu*m*bere; cadere . u*e*l mori;
4 Torris‖‖ : arrura quę de igne rapit*ur* :

* A letter or something else has been wiped away after habens.

† The *r* is a corrected letter. A letter (perhaps *o*) erased, the scribe, or corrector, omitting to write the required letter instead.

§ *cep* written on an erasure.

¶ MS. xiii, but the last two numerals are each marked for erasure, by a dot above and underneath.

‖ *in* added above the line.

‡ The *h* is added above the line.

** MS. has a waving stroke over *in*.

†† *Chald* is written on an erasure; above the *a* the stroke of *b* or *d*, or some such letter, is still visible, and the upper parts of the strokes of the present *l* and *d* are the remains of a former *l* or *d*.

§§ MS. uocant, but the *n* marked by three dots for erasure.

¶¶ After this word one letter has been erased.

‖‖ MS. Terris, but *e* altered to *o*.

5 Trulla : ferr*um* lat*um* unde parietes liment ;
6 Sacelli : sedes diminitiui ;
7 Niniue . tri*um* dier*um* it*er* inde ubi in t*er*ra*m* p*ro*iectus est una*m* die*m* p*er* amb*itum* ;
8 Nau*m* . helcesei pat*er* ipsius
9 Asolatis*; plane factis, 10 Geniculor*um* genuu*m* : diminit*iuum*
11 Hedera*m* : ibaei†; 12 Fulgorantes; aste quando fulgurant contra sole*m* ;
13 Concidisti : occidisti : 14 Subigens : co*n*fice macera
15 Pile : p*ro*priu*m* nome*n* ciuitatis .
16 Infusuria ; olearia uasa unde infundunt lucernas
17 Succidi : interfici ; 18 Tene latere*m* : fac latere*m* .
19 Herba fullonu*m* ; borit q*uia* inde faciunt sapore*m*
20 Myrteta, ubi multę sunt mirtę id*est* : arbores fructuos*ae* ;
21 Configent ; crucifigent, [XVIII] ⁝DE OSE⁝ spetialit*er* ;
1 CẎNXPONON§; unius te*m*poris :
2 lappa ; clate¶
3 Uinatia ; que remansit in uuis quando p*re*munt*ur* ;
4 Foedi ; foederaui ;||

Fol. 26[ba]

[XIX] INCIP*IT* IN IOB ;

1 Obelis ; uirgis ; 2 Asteriscis ; stellis ;
3 Obligus ; obscurus ; 4 Tinnulus ; sonans ;
5 Eschematismenos‡; id*est* : du*m* aliud loq*uitur* aliud agit
6 Comma ; breuis pars :
7 IDioma ; p*ro*prietas ; 8 Murenula : piscis . similis anguile marin*us* sed grossior ;
9 Untialib*us* ; longis .
10 Ridhmus ; dulcis sermo sine pedib*us*
11 In exaplois : ui . editiones *con*gregate ;
12 Theman : i*dest* p*ro*uintię :
13 Lumbire ;** 14 p*ro*sa : proemio : *uel* p*re*facionę
15 Tigris ; gen*us* leonis uario colore et uelocissim*us*
16 Carectu*m* ; hreod††;
17 Oriona : ebirdhring
18 Inquilini§§ ministri .
19 Pedica . fezra . ligam*en* .
20 Tẏmpanu*m* . in quattuor lignis extensa pell*is*
21 Glarea . lapides modici .
22 Coquiton . fluuius infernor*um*
23 Susurrat . q*ui* in aure*m* murmurans loq*uitur* .
24 Onager . asin*us* siluaticus .
25 Saba . prouintia .
26 Capitio . haubit loh,
27 Conpingebant*ur* . pinguiscebant,
28 Iubilo . lętitia quę n*on* pot*est* uerb*is* exponi .
29 Hibicu*m* . firgingata¶¶
30 T*er*ra salsuginis . t*er*ra sterelis .

* There is some mark (perhaps ∴) over the last *s*.

† MS. has **v** above the *a*.

§ MS. has a stroke over CẎNXPONO.

¶ MS. has **v** above the *a*.

|| This gloss has been added at the foot of the column.

‡ The last *e* is a correction from *o*.

** Here space is left for about five or six letters, probably for the interpretation.

†† The *h* added above the line.

§§ The third *i* of Inquilini is written over an erasure, and between Inq- and ministri space for about 6 or 8 letters is left, just as between Oriona and eb- in the preceding line.

¶¶ MS. has stroke over *gin* and another over *ta*. It divides firgin gata.

31 Rinocerus*; naricornu . in nari na*m*q*ue* cornu habet
32 Monocerus†; unicornis;
33 Arctur*um*; septentrio; 34 Adluuio; lauatio;
35 Herodion : ualchefuc§ : 36 Accipitres; haefuc;
37 Ueemoth ; bestia ignota;
38 Gurgustiu*m*; ehelor;
39 Leopardus; ex leone et pardo generatus;
40 olla¶ . de t*er*ra et de erame*n*to fit; 41 Incus : osifelti . 42 Torax : pectus : 43 Armilla; ermboeg‖;
Fol. 26^{bb}
44 Tęde; facule : de ligno pini . de quo pice*m* faciunt;
45 Adtonitos : adtentos; 46 Cassia; pigm*en*ta;
47 Aruina; pinguitudo;
48 Necromantia : diuinatio de mortis infantib*us*
49 Lacertos; pars brachii;
50 Carmina in nocte; laud*es* in tribulatione;
51 Fabula; poetar*um est* . gigantes t*er*ra*m* sustentare sub aquis;
52 Obsetricante; ministrante,
53 Gurgitum; modica congregatio‡ aq*ue* a pluuie :
54 Obrizum : ẏmaeti gold :
55 Concentu*m*; cantu*m*; 56 Molas : intimi dentes;
57 Plumescit : mutat; 58 Iunip*er* : arbor :
59 Cartillago : uuldpaexhsue . *uel* grost**;
60 Lagunculas†† . ex lagina dimin*i*-*tiuum* : croog§§;
61 Salices; salhas¶¶, 62 Uiri cordati‖‖; bono corde;
63 Ancillis : animalibus : figl‡‡;
64 Apostata; discessus a fide;
65 Sternutatio : nor; [XX] INCIP*IT* : IN TOBIA :

1 Mancipar*unt* : tradiderunt;
2 Nason : mons : 3 Brantie : chyun :
4 Accito; uocato; 5 Extricat***; ext*er*minat : foras mittit :
6 Extentera; inicium excoriandi†††:
7 Nutaret; dubitaret :
8 Taermę; aq*ue* calide . et balnea lapidea : sic nominantur;
9 De cassidie . pera pastoralis;
10 Infula : ornamenta :
11 Angor; adflictio; 12 Didascaliu*m* : magisteriale.

[XXI] INCIPIT IN IUDITH;

1 In expeditione : in preparatione exercit*us* :
2 Lucubraciuncula : unius noctis uigilantia .
3 Subal; nom*en* uiri unde oriatur

* *no* over an erasure which reaches to the next line.

† The top of first *o* is written on the lower part of the erasure begun on the preceding line.

§ The first *c* and left-hand part of the *h* are written on an erasure. MS. has **v** above the word, between the *l* and *c*.

¶ The words *olla* to *ermboeg* are added in one line at the foot of the page.

‖ MS. has **v**· above the *o*.

‡ The *r* seems an alteration from *t*.

** MS. has stroke over the right-hand part of the bar through the *t*.

†† The *g* is a correction from *n*.

§§ MS. has **v** above the line between the *r* and *o*.

¶¶ MS. has **v** over the first *a*.

‖‖ *c* corrected from *o*, and *or* written on an erasure.

‡‡ MS. has a stroke over the *g*.

*** *c* is an alteration from *i*.

††† *a* is a correction from *d*.

illa gens : 4 Arge : nom*en* montiu*m* :
5 Cu*m* coronis; circul*is* aureis . in
capitib*us* eor*um* .
Fol. 27[aa]
significantes uictoria*m* ei*us* *u*el
in choris cantantes .
6 Abra . ancilla . 7 Femur uirginis .
i*dest* dinę
8 Discriminauit . diuisit . 9 In contis . in lancis .
10 Sandalia . calciam*en*ta quę n*on*
habent desup*er* coriu*m* . 11 Restis . funis ex herb*is* .
12 Filii titan . filii solis q*ui* s*unt*
fortiores homin*ib*us
13 Ascopa . similis utri . 14 Cincinnos . crines .
15 Polenta . farina subtilissima .
16 Conopeu*m* . in similitudine retis
contextu*m* p*ropter* muscas et
culices . na*m* culix conix hebraice d*icitu*r .
17 Adonai . d*omin*us exercituum uel
om*ni*p*otens* .
18 S*anct*a do*min*i . primitias uel decimas de oleo et uino . 19 In
anathema . in obliuione .
In separatione : i*dest* a se *u*el
in dona ad te*m*plu*m* .
20 Labastes . in similitudine sculdre*
de ligno duas tales faciunt int*er*-
ponentes ficos ne citius putrescant .

[XXII] DE ESTER

1 Themate . conpositione *u*el ordine .
2 Tentoria . Tectura . 3 Aeri . haue† .
4 Eburneis . de ossib*us* elefantis .
ebur . os ei*us* d*icitu*r
5 Tenda . trab*us* gez*e*lt§
6 Iacẏntini . sẏitor heuuin . 7 Carbasini . color ge*m*me . i*dest*
uirid*is* . 8 Lecti aurei . berian¶
beed . deaurat*um*
9 Pedisequas . pedes sequent*es* .
i*dest* obsequentes .
10 Diadema . corona aurea .
11 Mundu*m* muliebre*m* . multo tempore debuerunt unguere uariis
pig*m*e*n*tis et indui uestib*us*
regalib*us* illud d*icitu*r mundu*m*
muliebr*em*
12 Urna i*dest* uas aureu*m* rotundu*m*
longu*m* aliq*ui*d subtilis in duo-
b*us* finib*us*|| clusu*m* undiq*ue*
exceptis foraminib*us* modicis in
laterib*us* habens . intus XII
ciatos modicos plu*m*beos haben-
Fol. 27[ab]
tes XII menses scribtos in eis
unde sortiunt*ur* quicu*m*q*ue*
primo exiit p*er* forame*n* uertente
uase sicut ante condixer*unt* .
13 Nisan . prim*us* m*ensis* i*dest*
mar*tius*
14 Tebetht i*dest* decemb*er* . 15 Scita
i*dest* monita .
16 Ueredarii dicunt*ur* a ueendo q*ui*
festinant*er* in eq*ui*s curr*unt* non
descend*entes* de eq*ui*s antequa*m*
liberant responsa sua habent
pennas in capite ut inde intel-
legat*ur* festinatio itineris . da-
t*ur*q*ue* eis se*m*p*er* equus paratus
n*on* manducant nisi sup*er* equos
antequa*m* p*er*ficiant*ur* . 17 Purpura . uuẏlocbaso‡.
18 Coccus . uuẏrmbaso : 19 Rubeu*m* .
uuretbaso .

* MS. has v above the *r*.

† MS. has v above the line between the *a* and *u*.

§ MS. has gezlt, with stroke through the l=*el*, as in uel.

¶ MS. has (not v, but more) Y above the *a*.

|| finibus is written above the line, with marks (·|·) of reference both after duobus and before finibus.

‡ The ẏ is a correction from v by the addition of a stroke below the line.

[XXIII] INCIP*IT* IN ESDRA

1 Exedra . serpens e*st* . si occidit*ur*
surgent de capite ei*us* plures
serpentes nisi cicius incend*i*-
tur
2 Filii faros . duo milia generationis
numerat q*ui* in captiuitate nati
s*unt* .
3 Latomi . q*ui* maiores lapides incidunt .
4 Cẏm*en*tarii . q*ui* minores dolant .
5 Lapide inpolito . ungebat . ne-
stane . n*on* exciso .
6 Stabur* nazannai . nom*en* fluminis .
7 Cratera . patena siue calix .
8 Recenser*unt* . leger*unt* . 9 Porta
stercoris . ubi st*er*cora p*ro*
10 Ualuas . modicus murus ante
port*am* .
11 Pagi . prouintię . 12 Memores sal*is* .
p*ro* cibo posuit sal . u*e*l doctrina*m* . 13 Nemias . alio nomine
atersatha .
14 In domate suo . in solario suo .
15 Collecta*m* . congregatione*m* . 16
Senatores . iudices .
17 Ciuitas d*aui*d . archis in hierusa-
l*em* mod*ica* ciuit*as* altior .
18 Contione*m* . contentione*m* tumultuosam .
19 Mulsu*m* . dulce . 20 Frondes d*ici*-
tur quando folia hab*et*†

[XXIV] INCIP*IT* IN MATHEUM§.

1 Fiole . in similitudine*m* calicis .
2 P*er*na . fossa .
3 Umecta . gebẏraec . ¶
4 Dimitte ea*m* . absolue eam .
Fol. 27^{ba}
5 Mocu*m* . quasi fabę albo colore
inueniunt*ur* in conca . 6 Publicani . q*ui* publicam rem faciunt .
non a peccando .
7 Stater . III . solidos . 8 Tributu*m* .
q*uo*d se*m*p*er* fit .
9 Censum . quod repente indicit*ur* .
10 Altilia . saginata de auib*us* tantu*m* d*icitu*r .
11 Nomisma . solidus . 12 Exolantes .
mundantes a colendo d*icitu*r .
13 Alabastru*m* . p*ro*prium nom*en*
lapidis et uas sic nominat*ur* de
illo lapide factu*m* . 14 Tẏrus .
insula .
15 Sidon . ciuitas . 16 Caminus . a
caumando d*icitu*r
17 Clibanus . desup*er* ap*er*tus . 18 Pretorium . domus iudicaturia .

[XXV] DE MARCO ET LUC*A* ET IOHANN*E*‖

1 Catinu*m* . discu*m* modicu*m* ligneu*m* *uel* lapideu*m*
2 Murratu*m* . amaru*m* . 3 Sirofenissa . de siriis qui in cananea
sunt .
4 Loculu*m* . portatoriu*m* de tabulis .
5 Scorpiones . in similitudine cancri . cauda longa . 6 De siliq*ui*s .
fructus arboris . colligit*ur* porcis . 7 Sẏmphonia de tibiis et
cornu ; 8 Byssus : in arbore nascit*ur* ad uestimentum :
9 Decurio : princeps sup*er* x homines ;
10 Salim : ciuitas : 11 Enchenia .
dedicationes ;
12 Institis : suithelon : 13 In pelue*m* :
uas rotundu*m* ligneu*m*‡ : 14
Lithostrotus ; co*n*positio lapidum** :
15 Hẏsopo : in similitudine*m* absinthi :

* *b* corrected from *l*.
† MS. babet, but first *b* corrected to *h*.
§ MS. has a long downstroke (like long *i*) added to the *U*, as if correcting *U* to *Y*.
¶ MS. has v over the *a*.
‖ *H* is a correction from some other letter (*A* ?).
‡ *g* corrected from *n*.
** MS. lapadum, but second *a* corrected to *i*.

[XXVI] IN LIBRO OFFICIOR*UM*;

1 Commolita : molata : 2 Casulas; domunculas :
3 Communitoriu*m* : munitionem;
4 Delibutus; unctus; 5 Folligantes* : uestis grossior†;
6 Pronuba :: herdusuepe§.
7 Simila : smetuma¶; 8 Mitras : haetas|| :
9 Decrepita; fracta; u*e*l uetorosa‡;
Fol. 27[bb]
10 Melodia; modulatio
11 Auguria; auspicia;
12 Follicantes; uestis grossior;
13 Uaruassi : de uana; dictu*m*;

[XXVII] IN LIBRO : ROTARUM;

1 Deliquiu*m* : defectio; 2 Faria; eloquia**;
3 Frugali : larga : *uel* lata;
4 Suprima; qu*ando* sol ad occasu*m* subprimit*ur* :
5 Scina†† : imitatio *uel* : grina;
6 Explosi; extincti : 7 Lup*er*ci : sacerd*otes* lup*er*cales :
8 Bruma : breuitas; 9 Lup*er*calia : ipsa sacra;
10 Zoziacu*m*; sideralem; 11 Lup*er*cal; te*m*plu*m* panos;
12 Uaporat; exurit; 13 Lustr*um* : inluminatio;
14 Anomala : dissimilia; 15 Mappa-n*us* apollo;
16 Hyadas : a tauri similitudine;
17 Genthliatici : gentiles;
18 Secunda : prospera§§. DEODE*M* Libro;
19 Feriatus; s*anctus* u*e*l requies : 20 Menstruu*m* : quando luna distruit*ur*. u*e*l instruit*ur*;
21 Eclipsis : defectio : 22 Fatescit : soluit *con*triuit.
23 Phoebe : sol :. 24 Hiebernis : hiemalibus;
25 Orion : eburdnung¶¶; 26 Atris : nigris. tetris.
27 Genthliatici : gentiles. u*e*l naturaliu*m* script*ores*
28 In georgicis; ubi de cultura agri cecinit :
Uia secta : iringesuuec;
29 Titania; solaria; 30 Moloncolia. humor. fellis;
31 Tethis; aquis; 32 Opago temp*or*ę : denso. u*e*l ęstiuo : 33 artofilax : custos aquilonis||||.

[XXVIII] IN LIBRO ANTONII;

1 Deficiet; fatiget; 2 In agillo; in agro;

* MS. has Folligantos, with one letter or : erased after the *i*; and *e* with :, (as marks of correction) written above the *o*.

† First *o* written on an erasure.

§ MS. has **v** : (or rather) **y** : above the *r*.

¶ MS. has **v** above the *et*.

|| MS. has **v** above the *et*.

‡ *toro* written on an erasure.

** *loqu* written on an erasure.

†† The *Sc* and *a* alone are distinct, but between these letters something has been erased, and after the *c* now follows a small thick stroke which appears to be meant for *i*; after this stroke follows what resembles a dot or a blot large enough to be taken as *i*; then, after a vacant space (sufficient for one letter), follows (next to the *a*) a letter which may be read as *n*, though it is blurred, and might also be read as *ri*. It is, therefore, possible to read sciiria, or scuria, or scina.

§§ *sp* on an erasure.

¶¶ MS. has **v** above the first *u*, and a horizontal stroke turned upwards to the left above the final *ng*.

|||| One letter (l, h or b) has been erased between the *o* and *n*.

3 Infestionib*us*; iniuriis; 4 Exti*m*plo; stati*m*;

5 Iufitiandi; negandi; 6 Frugali; larga *u*el lata;

7 Tifon; filius : saturni :

8 Sputacu*m*; sputu*m*;

Fol. 28[aa]

9 Saturnus; rex grecor*um*; 10 Luridam; luto sordida*m*

11 Diana; filia* iouis; 12 Stipan*tur*; conplen*tur*;

13 Ionan; filia uulcani : 14 Explosi : extincti;

15 Laodes; nom*en* regine; 16 Argula; acuta :

17 Inpolastis; inpugnastis† : u*e*l inpinguastis :

18 §Apo tu pt : saum : a tangendo e*st* ind*e* q*u*ida*m* psalmu*m* uolunt dici cognosce uero q*u*o*d* isti tantum p*ro* excellentia sui dican*tur* psalmi;

19 Sympsalma : uocu*m* adunata¶ copulatio;

20 Diapsalma ||uero : sermonu*m* rupta *con*tinuatio;

21 Prolezomena : id*est*. p*re*dicentia‡ :

22 Sophismatu*m*; questionu*m*; 23 Iouis : filius sat*ur*ni nouissim*us* :

24 Ypozeuxis; quando diuersa** u*er*ba singulis apta clausulis apponuntur;

25 Scema e*st* . figura dictionis in ordine u*er*bor*um* cum decore conposita;

26 Paradigma; narratio p*er* exe*m*pla ortans alique*m* aut deterrens;

27 Erotema; int*er*rogatio; 28 Metonymia . transnominatio ut e*st* qui habitat in cęlis inridebit††..

29 Exallege : p*er*motatio; 30 Epembabis; iteratio enumerationis studio . u*er*ba repetens,

31 Ausesis quę addenda queda*m* nomina p*er* me*m*bra singula rer*um* aucme*n*ta *con*geminat;

32 Climax gradatio qu*an*d*o* quib*us*da*m* gradib*us* se*m*p*er* accrescit§§;

33 Tropus e*st* dictio ab eo loco in quo p*ro*p*ri*a e*st* translata in eu*m* locu*m* in q*u*o p*ro*p*ri* n*on* e*st* ut e*st* exsurge d*omi*ne

34 Figura metopoea¶¶ que p*er*sonis se*m*p*er* cognoscit certissime applicari;

35 Nenias; m*en*datiu*m* : 36 Peusis; p*er*cunctatio ubi et int*er*rogatio fit et responsio;

37 Metabole : id*est* iteratio unius rei sub uarietate u*er*bor*um* . 38 P*er* figura*m* : yperbolen|||| . p*er* qua*m* solent aliqua in magnitudine*m* exaggerationis extendi .

* *li* are added above the line.

† The *g* is a correction from *n*.

§ The Glosses following till No. 88 are excerpted, not from the Vita S. Antonii, but from Cassiodori *Comment. in Psalterium* (except Nos. 22 and 23, which are taken from the Vita S. Antonii). As, however, the MS. makes no mention of this fact, and combines the two collections in one Chapter, it was considered advisable to number the glosses consecutively till the end of the Chapter.

¶ Something has been erased above the first *a*.

|| MS. Diaspsalma, but first *s* marked for erasure by four dots.

‡ p*re* ($\bar{p}$) is added above the line, with a dot above the stroke.

** MS. duiersa, corrected to diuersa, by lengthening the first stroke of *u* to *i*.

†† The .. after inridebit are written above the line, on the right-hand side of the *t*, and above it some letters (*eos*? see Ps. II. 4) have been erased.

§§ The *s* has been added above the line and before gradibus something has been erased.

¶¶ The second *o* added above the line.

|||| There is a perpendicular stroke above the *r*.

Fol. 28^{ab}

39 Allegoria* . id*est* inuersio aliud dicens aliud sig*nificans*† .

40 Silemsis; quoties casus discrepantes in una*m* significatione*m* congregam*us*;

41 Sinecdochen : a toto parte*m*;

42 Idea : cu*m* speciem rei future uelut oculis efferente motu*m* animi co*n*citam*us* :

43 Caracterismos quando aliq*uis* . aut p*er* forma*m* discribit*ur* . aut p*er* actus p*ro*priores indicatur;

44 Hypallage : ide*st* . p*er*mutatio q*u*oties in alium intellectu*m* u*er*ba quę dicta s*unt* transferunt*ur* :

45 Zeuma : id*est* . *con*iunctio quando multa pendentia aut uno u*er*bo aut una sententia *con*cludun*tur* .

46 Aetilogia : id*est* cause redditio quoties p*ro*misse§ rei ratio decora subiungit*ur*;

47 Parenthesin : id*est* . int*er*positione*m* : quo*niam* in sensu medio recipit u*er*ba quedam queda*m* ordine*m*¶ sententie uideant*ur* posse diuidere

48 Parabole : conparatio ||

49 Periscema icon‡ : quę latini *dicitur* imaginatio :

50 Catepenon : latini per laudem;

51 Hyp*er*thesis : id*est* sup*er*latio cu*m* aliqua*m* rem opinione omniu*m* nota sententia n*ostr*a** exsuperare contendim*us* :

52 Epizeusis : quę latine coniunctio *dicitur* ut e*st* dies diei . et d*eus* d*eus* meus :

53 Paraprosdocia . latine inopinatus exitus cu*m* aliud p*ro*ponitur aliud explicat*ur* . ut est d*eus* d*eus* mevs†† inpolluta uia eius.

54 Aposiopesis§§ : id*est* dictio cuivs¶¶ finis reticet*ur* .

55 Metaforan. latini p*er* translatione*m* di*cunt* cu*m* re*m* aliqua*m* sub breui p*re*conio quę sit ostendim*us* .

56 Auxesis : augm*en*tu*m* paulatim eni*m* ad superiora concrescit :
57 Figura e*st* sic*ut* nomine ipso dat*ur* . intellegi queda*m* conformatio dictionis a co*m*munione remota qua*m* ostentatione*m* et habitu*m* possum*us* nuncupare :

Fol. 28^{ba}

58 Apostropei : id*est* conu*er*sio quoties ad diuersas p*er*sonas crebro uerba *con*uertim*us*

59 Sÿncrisis : conparatio||||; 60 Enthi-
mema : interp*re*tat*ur* . mentis conceptio;

61 Amphibolia : id*est* dictio ambigua . dubiu*m* faciens pendere sententia*m* :

62 Tapynosin . que latine humiliatio *dicitur* quoties magnitudo mirabilis reb*us* humilissimus conparatur;

63 Sinatrismos *con*gregatio . quoties multa in unu*m* colliguntur :

64 Epitrocasmos; i*dest* dicti rotatio cum succincte ea quę s*unt* effusius dicenda p*er*stringit;

* The first *l* added above the line.

† *g* corrected from *n*.

§ *m* corrected from *n*.

¶ *d* corrected from *i*.

|| MS. comparatio, but the final stroke of *m* marked by two dots for erasure.

‡ MS. Periscemagicon, but the *g* marked by three dots for erasure.

** MS. has nā, therefore properly nam, but the text has nostra.

†† MS. meus, but the *u* is indistinct and may be some other letter, *v*, however, is written over it; above the *e* there is a stroke like that over the preceding two *ds ds*.

§§ The final *s* is a correction from some other letter (*n*?).

¶¶ The *v* has been added above the line.

|||| The *r* is a correction from some other letter (*i*?).

65 Epiphonima : id*est* adclamatio quę post narratas reb*us* breuiter cum exclamatione prorumpit :

66 Exaetasmos : i*dest* exquesitio .

67 Anastrophe . i*dest* p*er*u*er*sio q*uan*do p*ro*mim*us* ordine . *con*u*er*so sententia*m*

68 Anadiplosis* : congeminatio dictionis sermone*m* geminat ad decore*m* † ;

69 Emphasis : i*dest* exaggeratio q*uo*d gradatim crescit §

70 Sinchrisis e*st* . cu*m* causa*m* sua*m* q*ui*s aduersariis nitit*ur* efficere meliore*m* :

71 Ephichirema . exsecutiones u*e*l app*ro*bationes uocare maluerunt ;

72 Anaphora . reuelatio quoties unu*m* u*er*bu*m* per comatum principia repetit*ur* ; quando res secuturę p*ro* preteritis secunt*ur* . 73 Epimone . repetitio .

74 Ironia . i*dest* inrisio quoties aliq*ui*d q*uo*d sub laude d*icit*ur intellectu*m* uituperationis habere monstrat*ur* .

75 Prolemsis . pręoccupatio crebra sermonis quę multa colligit unius uerbi iteratione decursa .

76 Metafora . i*dest* translatio cum

Fol. 28[bb]

mutatur nom*en* aut uerbu*m* ex eo loco in quo propriu*m* est .

77 Sinastrismus . quę uno tractu atq*ue* circuitu cremina¶ multa concludit .

78 Hẏp*er*baton . cu*m* suspensus ordo uerboru*m* inferius explica*tur* .

79 Epexergasia : quoties uni causę duas probationes adponim*us* ;

80 Diaforesis : p*er* qua*m* fit differentia || p*er*sonar*um* ;

81 Per energia*m* : quę actu*m* rei incorpore imaginatione representat ;

82 Efexegresis : id*est* explanatio dicti superioris,

83 Ennoematice ; notio hec una*m*qua*mque* re*m* ‡ p*er* id q*uo*d agit non p*er* id q*uo*d e*st* conat*ur* ostendere ;

84 HẎpotheticus** ; id*est* contionalis sillogism*us*

85 Figura sardismos : quę linguar*um* se*mper* p*er*mixtione formatur ;

86 Epithalamium ; laus thalami †† int*er*p*re*tat*ur* :

87 Yp*er*baton : ide*st* transcensio ;

88 Diatiposis latini exp*re*sio d*icit*ur ubi rebus p*er*sonisue subiectis et formę§§ ipsę et habitus exprimuntur ;

[XXIX] INCIP*IT* UERBOR*UM* IN-T*ERPRE*TAT*IO* ;

1 Allegoria figuralis dictio :

2 Anagogen : superior sensus :

3 Asse . nu*m*mus : 4 autenticu*m*; auctoris ;

5 Augustissimo : famosissimo,

6 Proemium ; prefatio

* The *p* is a correction from some other letter, and is partly written on an erasure.

† MS. has sermonem ad decorem geminat, with three dots over the first *e* of decorem, and over the *i* of geminat, indicating that the words should be transposed.

§ MS. grescit, but the *g* marked by a dot for erasure, and *c* written above it.

¶ MS. nomina, with ÷ above the first *n* of nomina, which refers to a simila mark and the word cremina inserted in the left-hand margin between lines formin a square.

|| Second *f* seems to have been corrected from *i* (*j*).

‡ The *e* has a tag underneath, and above the *e* is a stroke (for *m*) with . above it.

** The *H* has been added in the margin. †† The *h* added above the line.

§§ r corrected from *n*.

7 Nenias : m*en*datiu*m*; 8 Elucubratu*m*; euigilante*m*
9 Quadrans; gen*us* nu*m*mi e*st* habens duo minuta
10 Uiola . herba * : iacinctina;
11 Mauria . de auro facta in tonica ide*st* † . gespan§;
12 Comicus : cantator u*e*l artifex secularium canticor*um* .
Fol. 29[aa]
13 Frixi ciceris : fauę siccate in sole;
14 Lanternis; uasa la*m*padis p*er*lucentia;
15 Batroperite¶ qui portant cibos in utris :
16 Friuolis : frugalis :
17 Emulumentu*m*; mercis labor*um* :
18 Flacidiu*m*; seruum : 19 Fratruel*is*; filius fratris
20 Quisquilia : inmundicia erbar*um* :
21 Curia : ubi ordo *con*siliu*m* iniit;
22 Meatus : uaene modicę :
23 Decipula*m*; tenticula*m* qua aues capiunt*ur* .
24 Inlecti : incitati : 25 Exuuia : spolia :
26 Protoplastru*m* : prima : plamatio :
27 Ideonati : consuetudini :
28 Strofa : fraus : 29 Tecna*m* : artem :
30 Pitatiola : membranula;
31 Decapolim : x· ciuitates in una p*ro*uintia;
32 Nu*m*mismu*m* : solidum :
33 Deuteres : renouationes :
34 Nardum : arbor :
35 Pisticu*m* : herba rubicunda|| . u*e*l nardu*m* pisticu*m* . id*est* spicatu*m* u*e*l fidelis :
36 Siloam : stagnu*m*‡ : 37 Duellionis : belli :
38 Hyinę : nocturnu*m* monstru*m*** similis cani :
39 Prorusu lembo : p*ro*rusu insula p*ro*p*ri*u*m* lembo†† a quo ibi faciunt illa§§ uestim*enta*¶¶;
40 Ferrugineas : pallidus|||; *uel* . rubicundus :
41 Caumate; ardenter;
42 Trapezeta : et nu*m*mularius . et colobista . ide*m* *sunt* qui nummis feneran*tur* et uilis negotiis .
43 Perpera : causa . u*e*l prauitas;
44 Xenodoxior*um*; collectionum;
45 Pragmaticam : negotialis‡‡ : 46 Arue : t*er*ra*m*;
47 Lagona*m*; uas lapideu*m* ollo . id*est* crog;·
48 Cauliculi; ramunculi :
49 Eẏnum : beneuolus;
50 Prathus*** et prapatheian : passio et p*ro*batio
Fol. 29[ab]
51 Epẏuision; perision; Exiareton : p*re*cipuu*m*;
52 Ecacusen; aut in aut in adflix*it* illam;
53 Epiasis : supersanus;
54 Gra*m*mateos; gra*m*matius
55 Emuruse*m* : fluxus sanguinis .
56 Metempschosis; motatio anime alię in alterum hominem :·
57 Agora . foras : 58 Lutugispru*m*; rationabile .

* The *h* added above the line.

† The *d* is a correction from *n*.

§ MS. has horizontal stroke above the *e*.

¶ MS. has a hook (⸢) above the *tr*, which is meant, perhaps, for a *c* which should come after the *a*. The MS. divides Batro perite.

|| The *i* written above the line.

‡ The *g* is a correction from *n*.

** The *str* are written on an erasure.

†† The *e* is blurred, and is now merely a blot.

§§ The first *l* has been added above the line.

¶¶ The top of the *i* has faded away.

||| One or two letters have been erased between *pal* and *lidus*.

‡‡ *otia* written on an erasure.

*** *thu* written on an erasure.

59 Tu thimisiun : plenum irę :
60 Tu epitimitisun ; *con*cupiscibili ;
61 Puruys, uenę ; 62 De citiuis : de insanis ;
63 Ileusun cẏrię ; p*ro*pitius esto d*omi*ne ;
64 Theoritisen . et practicen : *con*templatiuu*m* et actiuu*m* ; 65 Cuimarsus : princeps uille ;
66 Oma corpus 67 sumenumerus quod p*ro* uno om*nes* et pro multis unus :
68 Cataantis : contrarius :
69 Sinthema spica *con*positio
70 Spodasten ; amatorem ; 71 Diatribas : dissensiones : *ue*l disputationes ;
72 Nuymeẏses consiliarius ;
73 Q*ui* dixerit fratri suo racha ; reus erit *con*cilio id*est* reconciliatione ;

[XXX] DE CALOGO HIERONIMI IN PROLOG*O*

1 Peripatthiens : ambulator ;
2 Canitius : qui a canitia p*ro*uintia in gręcia uocat*ur*
3 Ypotheseon . dispositionum* ;
4 Anarchius : ubi nullius potestas ;
5 Monarchia : ubi unius
6 Polarchia : ubi multorum ;
7 Bibliotheca† : nom*en* loci ubi libri ponuntur ;
8 Praxeon : actionum ;
9 Peridion : *con*textu*m* i*dest* unius sensus :
10 Pylominos ; amator ;
11 Diaphonian§ : dissonantia*m* . 12 iereticos sacerdotale ;
13 Peri tes zoes ; theoricas : ide*st*¶ : de hac uit *con*te*m*platiua ;
14 Ho platon : hic plato ;
Fol. 29[ba]
15 Ton philona ; hunc philonem ;
16 Acoloythei : sequit*ur* h ton pla tona aut hunc platone*m*
17 O philon . hec philo ; 18 Archeretoẏs . *con*flictus ;
19 Pantocranto ; omniu*m* :
20 Paturia theo : de potentia d*e*i : continentia eo dic*itur* :
21 Amphitheatru*m*‖ ; circu*m* spectaculum ;
22 Deuterosin : secunda lex ;
23 Apologieticu*m* : excusabile :
24 Philuluguis : uerbi amatoris ;
25 Elegos ; castigatio ;
26 Diatripas . *con*flictus p*ro*p*r*ium nom*en* loci ubi discunt dispuli :
27 De piasma : fractura *ue*l ars :
28 De philoxenia : de amore ospicium ;
29 Capun periens instructio ;
Matuẏtu : de d*e*o corpore induco : *ue*l de peritia d*e*i :
30 Phraẏsi‡ :sensus 31 sub** nomine*m* *con*sintagmata documenta : 32 sẏntagma†† docum*en*tum ;
33 Pseudoephigrapha ; falso sup*er*scribta§§ :

* First *o* corrected from *u*.

† *h* added above the line. Above the : (colon) after Bibliotheca the MS. has ÷, which refers to ÷ nom*en* loci, which is written on the left of the lemma between lines forming a square.

§ The second stroke of the first *a* is written on an erasure.

¶ MS. has id̄ ē, therefore id*est* *est*.

‖ The second *h* is added above the line.

‡ The *h* is added above the line, between the *P* and *r*.

** Of No. 31 the lemma is *sintagmata* ; sub nomine*m* *con* is a misread sub nomine eius, which St Jerome wrote ; see his *Catal.* Ch. XXXII. It is, therefore, neither a lemma, nor an interpretation, and should have had no place in the Glossary.

†† *ntag* written on an erasure ; the *y* is a correction from *i* or *v*.

§§ The *b* corrected from *p*, and the down-stroke of the latter marked by two dots for erasure.

34 Catacesseun : doctrinar*um* 35 uarietas* stromactis desternatione ubi paganor*um* et xp*isti*anor*um*† colleguntu*r* quasi ex lectulo uarietatis; 36 Prosefanesen; ostendit§;
37 Cronographias; te*m*poralis scripturæ¶
38 Archutoman; antiq*ui*tate*m* : u*e*l principatu*m*;
39 Tesseroes : quadris :
40 Extasei excessu : id*est* mentis;
41 Ascesi : intellectui : 42 Chri‖ fiscus; fans :
43 De monogamia; de singularib*us* nuptiis;
44 Catha manthan : secundu*m* matheum;
45 Dialectica : dualis dictio :
46 Arethimetica‡ : numeralis :
47 Musica : modo labiis;
48 Geometrica : terre mensura :
49 Gra*m*matica : literali;
50 Rethorica; eloquentia;
51 Astronomia; sider*um*** lex;
Fol. 29bb
52 Exca (VI) : cai (et)†† : decerida : sedecenalem :
53 Enneafe : decerida decem nouaalem;
54 Et p*ro*comian : narrationum :
55 Erladiocten : operis conpulsorem :
56 Aethimologia : p*ro*prietate : 57 diafonia : dissonantia
58 Genealogia : generatione;
59 Panagericon§§ : laudabilem;
60 Eucharistias : gratiar*um* actiones;
61 Metafrasin : interp*re*tationem;
62 Eortatica; sole*m*nes : 63 Parascheue : p*re*paratione
64 Catheron; mundor*um*
65 Epitomen : memoria : u*e*l breuiarium¶¶;
66 Exenteseon : questionum;
67 Catacesseos : doctrine . 68 Ptocheus : inopie .
69 Sintagmaton : docume*n*torum
70 Monaptolmon : luscus‖‖;
71 Sinphosin : iterariu*m* . *uel* uiarum;
72 Otheporicon; itenerarium :
73 Epimehne‡‡ : memoria u*e*l p*re*uiariv*m****
74 Aceuan : oratio :
75 Eẏaggences; apodoxios . euangelice††† p*re*dicaciones :
76 Euaggences . parasueues : euangelice p*re*parationis
77 Cronicon canuon . te*m*poraliu*m* regular*um* :
78 Tropicon : maralium :
79 Apologus; excusationes
80 Et simcosion : similitudinem;

* Of No. 35 the lemma is [stromactis=] στρωματεῖς, and uarietas the interpretation.

† MS. has ecpianorum, with horizontal stroke over the *p* and *i*; the *e* is marked, by four dots, for erasure, and the *c* corrected into *x*.

§ The *o* is a correction from some other letter.

¶ The *æ* is a combination of the left-hand stroke of an open *a* and an *e*.

‖ MS. should have a stroke over Chri, for *Christi*? but see Cp. C 888.

‡ The first *i* is added below the line, attached to the *h*.

** The *s* has been lengthened by the addition, to its base, of a stroke, the lower part of which has been erased.

†† VI is written in the MS. above *ca*, and et above *cai*, but without ( ).

§§ MS. Pannagericon, but the first *n* marked for erasure.

¶¶ MS. preuiarium, but *p* corrected into *b*.

‖‖ The first *u* seems a correction from *o*.

‡‡ The *h*, which is a correction from some other letter (*n*?), may also be read as *b*.

*** MS. p*re*uiariarium, but above the second *a* is written *v* with a stroke over it (=v*m*), and the remainder of the word has been marked, by five or six dots, for erasure.

††† The *c* has been added above the line.

81 Psichiexodo anime exitu;
82 De entoetromito : deflicto diuersar*um* dispositionu*m*
83 Elegos : castigatio; 84 Monon : unius;
85 Cinticta onitaltaon*; ratio populor*um*
86 Temoẏs . libros;
87 Otheporicon† : iterariu*m* . u*e*l§ uiarum;
88 Catastrofon; *con*uersationem;
89 Ominas; locutiones¶ :
90 Ascetron : intellectum;
91 Peri pthocheas; de paup*er*tate;
Fol. 30[aa]
92 Cataracteras : stilo u*e*l figura;
93 Ypophesion : instructionum :
94 Ortodoxon : gloriosi uel p*er*fecti;
95 Ẏpo (sub) . tyos (hoc)|| . prino‡ prineose secet te :
96 Ẏpo (sub) tos (hoc). scino (scinu)**. scineoose†† scindat te;

[XXXI] DE PONDERIBUS INCIPIT:

1 Gomor maior in ose XU modios :
2 Modicus au*tem* gomor . XXII sextarios;
3 Sextarius au*tem* duo libra et dimedium :
4 Libra . XII uncias§§; 5 Uncia : UI . solid*os*;
6 Solidos tres trẏmisas : sax¶¶ .
7 Libra LXXII solid*os* greci LXXXIIII solid*os* pendica :
8 Emina et cotile|||| medius sextarius;
9 Comor minor septe*m* sextarios . et . U . pars sextarii cotile dimedium :
10 Aquila dix*it* . sextariu*m* III modios :
11 Ephi tres sextarios : Iter*um* ephi in II sextarii et paruu*m*
12 Sata quinquaginta sextarios in liquidis . in aridis uero XXUII sata :·
13 Sarre UII‡‡ sextarios et . u . partem .
14 Hin maior . XUIII sextari*os* Minor UIII :
15 Siclus LXXII siliquas : 16 Regalis XXXUI . siliqua
17 *Grece* i*dest* cercetea; Cercetea IIII grana ordei :
18 Obolus . XUIIII siliquas; 19 Obolus medicinalis III siliq*uas*; 20 Taletu*m* : centu*m* XXU libras :
21 Cathos : sexta pars sextarii;
22 Epiphanius d*icit* dragma XXUIII siliquas;
23 Siliquas argeos i*dest* pendicum;
24 Choros XXX . modios gressus et uestigia ei*us* : i*dest* pes . inter duos . ide*st* duos cubitos;

* The second *a* is not quite clear; it may be read as *ic* or *cc*.

† The *n* is not clear, and appears broken at the top.

§ There is a short perpendicular stroke above the *u*, perhaps the beginning of a wrongly commenced letter.

¶ The *u* may also be read as *a*.

|| sub is written in the MS. above *Ẏpo*, and hoc above *tyos*, but without ( ).

‡ After prino the MS. has some character which may be described as a *c* turned upside down, like the mark of contraction for *con*, except that here there is a dot above it. It is evidently a misread Gr. *υ* belonging to the word prino. A MS. in the Cambridge Univ. Library (Kk. 4. 6), containing Jerome's *Catalogus*, has here ΠΡΙΝΟΙ.

** sub is written in the MS. above *Ẏpo*; hoc above *tos* and scinu above *scino*, but without ( ).

†† The second *o* is added above the line.

§§ MS. has v above the *a*.

¶¶ MS. has v above the *x*.

|||| MS. contile, but *n* marked, by a dot above and underneath, for erasure.

‡‡ Something above the *u* has been erased.

25 Pes uocatur quando una uice . calcat passus id*est* fetim . IIII cubitor*um* :

26 Conurbicus . XXUI uncias :

27 Libra et pondera idem sunt* .

28 Tres argenteos solidu*m* faciunt .

29 Solidus XXIIII† siliq*uas* : 30 Scripulus sex siliq*uas* pensat*ur* ;

Fol. 30[ab]

31 Sextarius : IIII libras pensat ; 32 Sextarius G*rece* duas libras et dimidium pensat§ ;

33 Mina G*rece* mina sex uncias :

34 Statera G*rece* LXXII siliquas ;

35 Cimina romana dimedius sextarius :

36 Sata unu*m* et dimediu*m* modium¶ habens .

37 Hieronim*us* d*icit* statera d*icitur* qui duo didragma habet‖ ;

38 Denarius . p*er* x nummis deputatur ;

39 Chatos‡ . tres . modios . habet :

40 Amphora . III . modios . 41 bathos . III . modios .

[XXXII] DE PONDERIBUS:

1 Dragma pondus e*st* denarii argentei q*uo*d pensat siliq*uas* XUIII a grecis fit sic :

2 C apud latinus fit sic ✳ . ab aliis fit sic ✳

3 Scripulus pensat siliq*uas* sex ab aliq*uibus* fit d*uo*

4 Obolus pensat siliq*uas* III . siliq*uas* . tres fit f** . 5 uncia fit sic : ℩ quę uncia pensat siliq*uas* CXLIIII†† . hoc e*st* solid*os* ui . 6 Ciatos habens pensum sol*i*d*orum* . VI . 7 Acitabulus habens dragm*as* XU . ide*st*§§ scrupulus XLII¶¶ . q*uo*d uncia una semis et scrupulos . UIIII . 8 Cotule habet drag*mas* LXXII id*est* scrupulos‖‖ . ·C·C· XUI‡‡ quod facit UIIII ;

9 Mina habetstateras. XXII***. id*est* dragm*as* . C . scrupulos CCC q*uo*d facit libra*m* unam et semiuncia*m* ; 10 Talentu*m* habet pondera LX††† . q*uo*d facit libras LXXII§§§ : 11 Libra habet scu-

* Over the *s* there is a horizontal stroke with dot above it, to mark the stroke for erasure.

† After XXIIII a long letter or stroke has been erased.

§ The *t* is a correction from *n* or *o*.

¶ The first stroke of the final *m* is a correction from an original *s*.

‖ didragma ha, and the up-stroke of the *b* are written on an erasure. Under the *a* of ha, a comma, which apparently belonged to the erased word, is still visible.

‡ The *h* has been added above the line.

** Through this sign, which has the form of a long thick s, runs the lengthened top stroke of the *t* of fit, with a dot above and underneath, which mark this part of the stroke for erasure.

†† It is possible to read here CXVIII, as the L and first I resemble the capital U elsewhere in the MS.

§§ Above the back of the *d* is the stroke of some wrongly commenced letter still visible.

¶¶ It is possible to read here XVI (see above note ††).

‖‖ The *c* is a correction from *r*.

‡‡ The dots, which are written within the CC, mark them, perhaps, for erasure.

*** May be read as XXV.

††† LX is formed by an L, with a stroke through its bottom-stroke.

§§§ The L and first X are here again combined as above (note ††).

pulos C·C· LXXUIII* . q*uo*d facit dragm*as* . XC·VI† .

[XXXIII] DE PONDERIB*VS SECUNDUM* . EUCHERIUM§;

1 Talentu*m* . hab*et* pond*era* LXII q*uo*d faciunt LXXX libr̨e attice : 2 Mina e*st* libra una et semiuncia 3 talentu*m* hab*et* LX [minas] mina grece latine mine d*icitu*r

4 Drag*ma* hab*et* scrupulos . III 5 dedragma duę¶ Dragmae s*unt* und*e* . miror . q*uo*m*odo* in libro hebraicar*um* question-u*m* semeuncias scribitur .

6 Stat*er* nu*m*mus e*st* habens ut quida*m* adfirmant uncia*m* u-na*m* . ide*st* aureos . VI . ut alii||

Fol. 30[ba]

putant . III ⁝ in euangelio eni*m* p*ro*‡ duob*us* drag*mis* stat*er* datur; 7 Sicel qui latine lingue corruptę siclos d*icitu*r . in questionibus . supra scriptis . uncia** pondus habet ut alibi scriptu*m* repperi†† . scrupula . x . q*uo*d ipse . arbitror : Na*m* siclus ipse u*e*l sicel de p*ro*pinquitate ponderis quasi siclus sonat;

8 Obulus e*st* scrupule dimediu*m* q*uo*d fac*it* siliq*uas* III§§ . In hiezechielo . siclus au*tem* [XX] obolus habet;

9 Chorus e*st* modii . XXX . 10 batus e*st*; Amphora una . id*est* modii . III ; 11 Chatus grece amphora *est* habens urnas . III; 12 Ephi . siue ofa¶¶ . III . modii; Ephi ide*m* me*n*sur̨e habet in aridis et in liquidis; Batus 13 metreta . mensura . una ut q*uida*m d*icu*nt habent sextarios ·C· mensura . a*utem* grece metru*m* d*icitu*r . unde et metreta d*icitu*r : Notandu*m* uero q*uo*d me*n*sura hebraicu*m*|||| nom*en* est; 14 Artab̨e in asaie egyptior*um* me*n*-sur̨e qųe . III . faciunt modios . X .

15 Sata ide*m* s*unt* q*uo*d et ephi . ide*st* modii . III;

16 Gomor me*n*sura est attica . habens ut quida*m* oppinantur . conices III . ide*st* sextarios XII : Alii gomor d*icu*nt sextarios . V . q*uo*d etia[m] ipse sequor eo q*uo*d decima pars sit ephi:

17 Hin‡‡ . sextarios . II . 18 abattidis . V . 19 Nebel . quida*m* putant modios III . in sextariis e*st* liquide speciei : 20 Cola-

* The dots within the cc mark the latter, perhaps, for erasure. The L and first X are again combined as before.

† The dot within the c marks the latter, perhaps, for erasure.

§ See the Vienna *Corpus Scriptt. Ecclesiasticorum Latinorum*, Vol. XXXI, (S. Eucherii Lugdun. *Instructt.* Libri II, p. 158).

¶ Here follows in the MS. s, which seems to have no meaning, and was, perhaps, written by the scribe in place of the usual ;.

|| After alii two or three letters have been erased, and one or two other letters, on the right and left of the erasure, seem to have been wiped away.

‡ The *p* seems a correction from *o*; the mark for *ro* attached to its down-stroke is written on the place of an erased letter of which traces are still visible.

** For unciae.

†† The second *p* added above the line.

§§ The third I has been lengthened by a kind of undulating perpendicular stroke below the line.

¶¶ The *f* is a correction from some other letter (*c*?).

|||| Here the word est followed, but it has been erased.

‡‡ Nos. 17 and 18 do not appear in the printed texts of Eucherius.

mina* *est* : in hiezechielo decim inquid cotilę . gomor† 21 uncia una sol*idi* ui .

22 Semiuncia . III . pensat . 23 libra et pondus ide*m* *sunt* .

24 Urbicus et sextarius ęquali me*n*sura 25 sil*iqua* una . IIII grana ordei pensat 26 sextarius libras IIII 27 siliq*uae* sex scripulu*m* unu*m*; 28 libra LXXII solid*os* pensat

29 Obolus . III . siliq*uas* . solid*os* . XXIIII . 30 siliq*uae* . Tres argenteos solidu*m* faciunt . 31 siliquas sex . scripulum unu*m* pensant§; finit .

Fol. 30[bb]

[XXXIV] DE CASSIANO; 1 Malis : ex maxillis;

2 Letheo; mortali; 3 Spiathio; mattae¶ :

4 Enticam : sublectilem;

5 Xerofagia : herbe quę comedunt*ur* incocte

6 Omofagis : quę non nisi cocte;

7 Asou . integritas‖; 8 Utpute; utest;

9 Causticis; asperis . firmiorib*us*;

10 Auxesin : aucm*entvm*‡ : 11 *Pro*emiis : p*re*facionib*us*;

12 Cenodoxia : inanis gloria .

13 Confutatus; rep*ro*batus; 14 Incentor; suscitator;

15 Scopulosus; petra; 16 Secunda; p*ro*spera :

17 Cautes; lapides; 18 Lentiscere . molliscere ::

19 N*on* officit : n*on* resistit; 20 Catalogu*m*; series nominu*m* :

21 Atauus : IIII : pat*er* : 22 Co*n*fectos : maculatos :

23 Lautiores; pulcriores; 24 Cicona; cecitas;

25 Pinsit; densitudo; 26 Inlecta; suscitata;

27 Oppleta; inpleta; 28 Exaggerare; comulare .

29 Theorice : sup*ernus* intellectus .

30 Inconditos; indisciplinatos; 31 Tabo** : morb*us*;

32 Repagulis; stabulis : 33 Conserto; conposito;

34 Co*m*min*us* : p*ro*pe; 35 Abdicans; contradicans;

36 Gastrimargia; appetitus uentris;

37 Tÿrsamus; p*re*dator; 38 Diruit obruit;

39 Statione; uigilatione;;

40 Prerogatiua††; priuilegium;

41 Nutabundus§§ : mobilis; 42 Indeptu*m* : adq*ui*situ*m*;

43 Rangor : neq*ui*tia; 44 Sillogism*us*; q*ue*stio ineuitabil*is*¶¶

45 Dialecticis . fecundia .; 46 Conicere; intellegere;

47 Sugillatione*m*; iniuriam;

48 Scatentib*us*‖‖ . credenti; 49 Du*m*taxat, maxime

* Cotyla hemina in the printed texts.

† Here the printed texts of Eucherius end.

§ There is an erasure above the *t* in the MS.

¶ MS. has v above the first *t*.

‖ *ta* corrected from *ti*.

‡ MS. aucmenta, but above the final *a* (which is not marked for erasure) there is a v with stroke above it (=v*m*) and a dot on both sides. After the final *a* something has been erased.

** The *a* is a correction from some other letter (*u*?).

†† MS. Preregatiua, with *o* above the second *e*.

§§ The first *u* is a correction from *a*.

¶¶ MS. meuit-, but the first stroke of *m* corrected into *i*.

‖‖ After the *a* some letter has been wiped away; only a yellow spot is now visible.

50 Expers : ignarus : 51 Caracteries :
scripturis*;
52 Degesti *sunt* : congregati sunt;
53 Deflorare; euellare;
54 Condere : abscondere :
55 Eneruatus; inualidus :

Fol. 31[aa]

[XXXV] 1 Tragoedia . bellica cantica . DE EUSEBIO; . *uel*
fabulatio . *uel* hircania† :
trago Hircus§;
2 Coli; dolores uentris : 3 Prorigo :
urido cutis . id*est* gẏccae¶
4 Luridus; pallidus :
5 Hydropicus; aquaticus :
6 Tentigo : tenacitas uentris . id*est*
ebind|| :
7 Toparcha : loci princeps : To-
pus‡; locus;
8 Age; uelociter; 9 C*on*stipatio;
circu*m*stantia;
10 Apparitoriu*m*; auditoriu*m*;
11 Adstipulatio; confirmatio; 12 Cẏati : calices;
13 Consultorib*us* . consiliariis;
14 Diriguere : p*ro* stupore pallescere** :
15 Quadriga; a IIII equis d*icitur* :
16 Stromatum; lector*um* : 17 A
theologia : a dei genilogia :
18 Opperiunt : inueniunt . repperiunt :
19 Miherculi; mifortis††; 20 Magni
sabbati . id*est* paschȩ
21 Subregeris; subieceris :
22 Curione; qui cura*m* gerit; 23
Editionis; puplicationis p*ro*-
positure;
24 Auspiciis; qui aues inspiciunt;
uel . homines obuiantes
25 Thiesteas : commessationes :
26 Oethepia; coitu*m* matris et sororis; sic*ut* manichei in occultis : i*dest* in occulta loca
idolor*um*;
27 Puncto§§; foramine in quo ped*es*
uinctor*um*¶¶ in ligno tenent*ur*
cubitali spatio int*er*iecto inter
uinctos :
28 Muneru*m*; dieb*us* remunerationis
militu*m*;
29 Harene; theatrii : 30 Genefrix :
de frigia : ciuitate
31 Legio; sex milia;
32 Ceteriorem : ulteriorem :
33 Bachantes . turpiter|||| ludentes :
34 Solaria . sedes . *uel* loca alta;
35 Tesseras; tesulas‡‡; 36 Metafrasin : int*er*p*re*tatio;
37 Oraria; mappas . *uel* linteamina;
38 Sinefactas; pudicas . *uel* absti-
nent*es* :
39 Ungula*m*; ferr*um* curuu*m* . ut
digiti;
40 Troclei***; rotis modicis .
Fol. 31[ab]
41 In aculeis; in ferris ligno in t*er*ra
posito infixis et curuis;
42 Stibiis : colorib*us* stibia erba de
quo faci*unt* .

* The *c* is a correction from *s*.

† The first *i* added above the line.

§ The sign or letter before ircus differs not materially from the ordinary capital *h* found in some of the headings of the chapters, and has, therefore, been read here as such. It may also be taken as the ligature for *enim*; but the point cannot be tested, as this ligature does not occur elsewhere in the MS.

¶ MS. has v above the *y*.

|| MS. has v above the *n*.

‡ *p* corrected from *b*.

** MS. palliscere, but the *i* marked by a dot for erasure, and *e* written above it.

†† MS. mifortes, but the *e* marked for erasure, and *i* written above it.

§§ MS. Pungto, but *g* marked by two dots for erasure, and *c* written above it.

¶¶ The *n* added above the line.

|||| MS. has a perpendicular stroke above the *p*.

‡‡ MS. has v above the *e*.

*** The *e* is a correction from *i*.

43 Inextricabiles : inex*terminabiles*;
44 Adortus; inchoans* exortari†;
45 Suppuratis; insania fluentis *uel*
purulentis : 46 Thia§; mat*er*-
tera;
47 Metropolis; mat*er* ciuitatum¶;
48 Compos; particeps; 49 Loculo :
uase ligneo;
50 Asillu*m* : locus refugii *sanctus*;
51 Gesta; scripta; 52 Conibentia :
consensus :
53 Ludus literar*um*; scola paruu-
lor*um* legentiu*m*;
54 Pedissequis : conuiator gegenta||;
55 Lacerta; adexa‡ : 56 Nouella*m*;
noua*m* dimin*itiuum*;
57 Cunabulu*m* : uas in quo iacent
infantes;
58 Uix : statim; 59 Fornice . scelb** :
uel drep††;
60 Bibennem : secure*m* bis acutam :
61 Exedrę; scabelli ad§§ cibos . *uel*
subselli;
62 Pastoforie; modice dom*us*;
63 Fucum; colorem¶¶; 64 Martyriu*m*;
modicu*m* oratoriu*m*
65 Caementaria; ecclesię;
66 Ignis acer; oma|||; 67 Cissura;
sectura;
68 Concidere; incidere;
69 Uixilla et labrum . idem *sunt*
id*est* segin‡‡ :
70 Calonum; nom*en* gentis . cu*m*
francis;
71 Calonu*m*; militum *uel* seruor*um*
72 Lanionib*us* qui*** b*er*bices***
uel porcos incidunt membratim
et uendunt;
73 Codicib*us* : lignis in quib*us* incidunt codex : stofun†††; 74
petigo; tetrafa§§§;
75 Jugeres; gycer¶¶¶ : unius diei
op*us* : aratoris;
76 Fessat : desonat : 77 Subnixis;
subiunctis|||||,
78 Parethis; ministris; 79 Claua;
fuste,
80 Madidu*m*; contusum, *uel* contritum;
81 Uaeri : uirge ferreę;
82 Sub axe pontico; sub illa parte
ubi pontus‡‡‡ e*st*;
Fol. 31^{ba}
83 Ampla*m*; lata*m* . 84 Par*um*;
paruu*m*; 85 Adtracto; breui;
86 Busta****; incisa arbor ramis
trungatis†††† .
87 Afficit; amauit : *uel* onorauit;
88 Panagericis : laudabilibus; 89 Pr*e*-
ditis : ornatis

* The *h* is a correction from some other letter (*i*?).

† Above the second *r* there is a perpendicular stroke hardly larger than a dot.

§ The *T* and left-hand stroke of the *h* written on an erasure.

¶ The second *i* is either blurred or a correction from some other letter.

|| MS. has v above the first *e*.

‡ MS. has v above the *ad*.

** MS. has v above the *e*.

†† MS. has v above the *re*.

§§ The first stroke of the open *a* is a correction from *i*.

¶¶ There is a dot, or the beginning of an unfinished letter, above the *r*.

||| MS. has v above the *m*.

‡‡ MS. has v above the *g*.

*** MS. has quib*us* bices.

††† MS. has v above the *o*.

§§§ MS. has v above the *r*; the final *a* may be read as *ic*.

¶¶¶ MS. has v above the *y*.

||||| The *n* is a correction from some other letter, or from two other letters.

‡‡‡ The *n* has been added above the line.

**** The *a* is a correction from *o* or *u*. Between the *a* and ; one or two letters have been erased.

†††† The *ti* are corrections from *d* (?).

90 Ad ilicem*; gen*us* rubri; 91 Mam-
bre†; nom*en* loci;
92 Processores; excelsi : 93 Molue-
r*unt* : manser*unt* : *uel* senu-
er*unt*,
94 Theomachie; deor*um* pugnę§;
95 Gigantemachie; gigantu*m* pugne;
96 Fas erat; ius erat, *uel* iustu*m* erat;
97 Uatis; p*ro*pheta; 98 Prosapia;
p*ro*genies;
99 Aeditui : ostiarii; 100 Co*mm*ent*a*;
excogitata;
101 Rata; iusta; 102 Fastibus¶ :
libris;
103 Fascib*us* : dignitatib*us* : 104 Gla-
dib*us* . uindictis‖;
105 Arcet‡; depulit; 106 Stephan*us* :
coronatus;
107 Ulcus : lepra** *uel* uulnus :
108 Profusius; habundantius;
109 Perorans; adloquens; 110 Insimularet : accusaret *uel* insultaret;
111 Coniciebant; cogitabant;
112 Constipatio; circumstatio,
113 Concionaretur; loqueretur††;
114 Uecors : malo corde : 115 A*mm*i-
nicula; adiutoria;
116 In p*ro*stibulo; in domo fornicaria;
117 Territoria; loca modica t*er*re,
118 Glebam; cispitem; 119 Coalescant; pascant;
120 Per hironia*m*; p*er* m*en*datiu*m*;
121 Manu*m*; t*ur*ba*m*,
122 Callos; tensam cutem : id*est*
uarras§§;
123 Incusans; accusans; 124 Inconsulto : n*on* int*er*rogato,
125 Probra; obp*ro*bria¶¶; 126 Tropia; signa;
127 Aduentantes; aduenientes;
128 Molitio; meditatio mali‖‖;
129 Adstipulatio : adfirmatio; 130
Amopaga; archisinagogus‡‡ est
131 Multata; p*er*cussa; 132 Fefellit :
fraudulent*er**** m*en*tit*ur*
133 Metru*m* : modiu*m*; 134 Dispicatis; disruptis :
135 Eripisissent; inruissent;
136 Efflabant†††; mortui sunt;
Fol. 31[bb]
137 Sumptu puplico : adiutorium
regali;
138 Tabo; putrido : 139 Infaustiore*m*;
infeliciorem;
140 Portar*um* indum*en*ta; id*est* coria
q*ui*b*us* portę indute s*unt*;
141 Excidium; casum . *uel* discen-
sum§§§;
142 P*ro*ceritas; celsitudo;
143 Per metalla : p*er* diu*er*sas artes
ferri . *uel* alias
144 Enixa e*st*; genuit agnu*m* ab¶¶¶
agno d*icitur* femin*ino*

* The first *i* is attached to the *d* of *Ad* below the line.

† MS. has stroke above the *a*; hence the reading of the MS. is Ma*m*mbre.

§ The *g* is a correction from *n*.

¶ The *i* written on an erasure; the *b* is a correction from *o* or from *ci*.

‖ The *i* and first stroke of the *n* are corrections from the first two strokes of an *m*.

‡ The *r* is a correction from *i*.

** There is an erasure above the *epr*.

†† The *re* have been added above the line.

§§ MS. has v above the first *r*.

¶¶ The *i*, which is combined with the *r*, is written over a *c*.

‖‖ The *a* is written over an erasure.

‡‡ After the *si* a letter has been erased.

*** The bow of *d* is written over the remainder of some other letter the top of which has been erased.

††† After Ef two or three letters have been erased, and a vacant space is left for two more letters.

§§§ After the *n* two or three letters (*dis?*) have been erased. The *s* before the *u* may be read as *f*.

¶¶¶ MS. *ex*, but marked for omission, and *ab* written above it.

145 Numinis : uirtutis ;
146 Luxus ; luxoria : u*e*l lasciuia :
147 Petalu*m* ; in quo scriptu*m* *est* nom*en* dei . u*e*l tetra*gram*m*aton* *
148 Insolentia : inquietudine . *uel* lasciuia ;
149 Consulari delectus ; dignitati adductus ;
150 Facessat ; desinat : 151 Expiscabar ; capieba*m* ;
152 Sceptr*um* ; uirga regalis ;
153 Apologiticum . excusabilem ; 154 Incessere † . incedere §
155 Arcebatur ; inpelebatur ;
156 Ad stadiu*m* ; ad locum certaminis ;
157 Furtuna*m* : fatum ; geuiif ¶ ; 158 Rogus : beel ‖ : *uel* aad ‡ :
159 Confectore*m* : interfectorem ;
160 Idiotae, stulti ; 161 Psaltes ; cythara ;
162 In comminus ; p*ro*pius ; 163 Luculentissime ; splendissime
164 De figm*en*to : de plasmatione hom*inis* ;
165 Fatum ; uyrd** ; 166 Scenas turpes . incesta coinq*ui*nata
167 Eliceret*ur* ; extorq*ue*retur ; 168 Ergastulo ; carcere ;
169 In myrthece ; in domo unguentor*um*
170 Nutatione ; dubitatione .
171 Harene . locus . u*e*l pauim*en*tum theatri ;
172 Nundinas ; negotiationes ;
173 Ouans ; gaudens, 174 Tripudiaret ; uinceret ;
175 Graticulis †† ferreis factis . herst §§
176 Baratr*um* : loh ¶¶ ; u*e*l dal ‖‖,
177 Uesani : insani ;
178 Ea tempestate ; eo tempore ;
179 Horas diurnas . nocturnaq*ue* conputantes . id*est* p*ro* XL ‡‡ diebus . XX statuvnt *** ;
180 Fisco publico ; dominio cesaris ;
181 Regio morb*us* corpus affic*it* colore sic*ut* pedes accipitris,

Fol. 32[aa]

182 Simultantem ; contentionem ;
183 Laciniosa : slitendę :
184 Liberales litera . quas seculares ††† homines legunt ;
185 Expolitum . ornatum ;
186 Infestus, inimicus : u*e*l grauis ;
187 Terebrantes p*er*forantes ;
188 Flagris ; flagellis ; 189 Infestes §§§ : sine barba ;
190 Fibras ; uenas ; 191 Affatibus : dictis,
192 Basis ; omne q*uo*d fundam*en*tu*m* poni sub pote*st*
193 Contribulib*us* : simul contribulatis ;
194 Expolierit . onauerit, u*e*l declarauerit ;

* MS. has tetram, with stroke over the *m* ; the *ra* written over an erasure.

† After Incessere two or three letters have been wiped away.

§ incedere is added above the line, preceded by the usual ſ. The *n* is written over an erased ſ, which shows that the scribe first wrote ſ*cedere* above the line, which was afterwards corrected to ſ*incedere*.

¶ MS. has v over the first *i*.

‖ MS. has v above the first *e*.

‡ MS. has v above the second *a*.

** MS. has v above the *y*.

†† After Graticulis something (; ?) has been erased.

§§ MS. has v above the *e*.

¶¶ MS. has v above the *o*.

‖‖ MS. has v above the *a*.

‡‡ There is a stroke through the upper part of L, but marked by two dots for erasure.

*** The *v* has been added above the line.

††† The final *s* has been added above the line.

§§§ The *I* is a correction from *i*.

195 P*er*ipsima ; purgam*en*tum * : u*e*l q*ui*sq*ui*lea ;

196 Cataceeos : doctrine : 197 Subsaltare : intrepetan :

198 Abiurari ; ab iure aecclesie abicere,

199 Garrientium *per* ludum dicentium ;

200 Reusti : iter*um* usti . 201 Cautere : ferr*um* melius tindre .

202 Exta ; intestina ; 203 Extale, snedil † daerm ;

204 Puplites . hommę ; 205 In metallo : in carcere ;

206 Salariis : pecuniis debitis ;

207 Proscribendo ; damnando ; 208 Fluitans, fluens :

209 Galerius *p*r*op*t*er* nom*en* ;

210 Sexcuplu*m* ; sedecim *pr*o uno sed semiduplu*m* puto ;

211 Cuniculum ; forame*n* u*e*l canalis ;

212 Fautoribus ; adiutorib*us* ; 213 Infenso ; irato ;

214 Obuncans ; obiurgans ; 215 Fragor : uox *ue*l sonitus,

216 Obices ; resistentes : 217 P*er*pera : sine causa ;

218 Anulum ; fidei libertatem ; 219 Co*mm*e*n*ta, petra

220 Globus ; rotunditas ; 221 Munificentia ; largitas.

222 Controuersię ; aduersitates ;

223 Ex pretore ; de pretorio § ; 224 Delubra ; te*m*pla deor*um* :

225 Scuriosa ; sordida : 226 In chaos ; in *p*r*o*fundu*m* : *ue*l in aera ;

227 Aduta, occulta ¶ . 228 Labris ; labris,

229 Dispicatis ; incisis ; 230 Exesum ; subtilis ;

231 Patulis ; ap*er*tis ; 232 Numinis ; diuinitatis

233 Lineolis : dredum ; 234 Suggillato ‖ : inclinato ;

235 Busta ; ubi homines conburuntur.

Fol. 32[ab]

236 Funestare ‡ : cruentare ; 237 Coeme*n*teria ** ; sepulture ;

238 De triuio ; de tribus uiis ;

239 Prefocatus ; strangulatus

240 Angiportus ; angustus locus ;

241 Extorres ; exules de patria ;

242 Ponte moluio †† ; *p*r*op*t*er* pontis iuxta roma ;

243 Eques ; equester ; u*e*l equi ; 244 Fomite ; materia .

245 Conpaginatum ; coniunctum .

246 Spurca : inmunda ; 247 Auditorio, scole legentiu*m* ;

248 Pirgos : §§ turris ; 249 Pompa*m* : risionem ;

250 In exameron ; sex dierum comput*um*

251 Otii ; quieti ; 252 Meandru*m* ; locu*m* u*e*l stagnum ¶¶ ;

253 Solaria ; munera ;

254 De octoade : de nouo testame*n*to ‖‖ ;

255 Conpendiosis ; breuissimis ;

256 Actio : p[*ro*]pt*er* nom*en* ciuit*atis* ; 257 Columellas : diuersis linime*n*tis

* MS. has Purgam*en*tum : P*e*ripsima ; but the two words are each marked for transposition by the marks ÷ above them.

† MS. has v above the *e*.

§ There is an erasure over the *et*.

¶ There is a small perpendicular stroke above the *t*.

‖ The first *g* has been added above the line.

‡ To the top-stroke of F, on the right-hand side, is added ᵓ, without, apparently, any meaning.

** The *a* is a correction from some other letter.

†† The MS. divides Pontem oluio.

§§ The *s* : written on an erasure.

¶¶ The *g* is a correction from *n*.

‖‖ The *st* are written on an erasure.

258 Lenonibus*; *con*ciliatori*bus* mulier*um*†;
259 Gestire; desiderare,
260 Lacessit . p*ro*uocat . u[*e*]l frequent*er* lacerat .
261 Incessit; incurrit; 262 Illo : usq*ue* illuc :
263 Infestus . inruens molestus;
264 Incessere, inpugnare; 265 *Con*cinnant; *con*gregant :
266 Antinoitas; ciu*itas* in egy̆pto;
267 Factioni*bus* sub dolibus; 268 Agellis; te*rr*e partes
269 Plasma, forma : 270 Elogiis; uerbis;
271 Cudat; fabricat;
272 Patricius : senator consiliarius;
273 Delibratu*m* : cogitatum; 274 Axe; polus .
275 Editore; excelsiore§;
276 Reditus; facultates; 277 Iugu*m* montiu*m*; u*er*ticem montiu*m*
278 Litat, sacrificat;
279 Oratoria*m*; sapientia*m* seculariа*m*¶;
280 Infecti : uiciati; 281 Operiremur; expectaremur;
282 Ducennarium; presidem‖
283 Sinisactas; sociatrices : :
284 Consulere : prouidere; 285 Coibat*ur* . exit*ur*;

Fol. 32[ba]

286 Sodalibus; soci*bus*; 287 Adseueratur . adnuntiat*ur*;
288 Nancisci; inueniri; 289 Inuisum; luad‡
290 Effetas; euacuatas; 291 Stipis; esca modica;
292 Ruderibus; mixinnum;
293 Uoti copos xp[*is*]tiana**; 294 Thecis†† custodiis; fabrica*m*§§ de argento
295 Cathanos; mundos; 296 P*er*spicem; ingenium;
297 Exin ؛¶¶. deinde; 298 Spiridon; nom*en* hominis;
299 Cyprius; *pro*uintia; 300 Rata; confirmata;
301 Fruga; modestia;
302 Seminon; honestor*um* conuenticulum;
303 Mulcata : uincta; 304 Pugioni*bus*. mucroni*bus*;
305 Pessum; interitum : 306 Fuco; pigmento;

[XXXVI] DE OROSIO; 1 Iani porte; id*est* porte te*m*pli iane dei paganor*um* quę ante patebant unaqueq*ue* ad gentem suam qu*ando* contraria fuit romanis nomine gentis ipsius scribta sup*er* porta;
2 Armenias pilas : nom*en* montium uel gentis . uel silue : uel clausure;
3 Promontoriu*m*; ubi terra‖‖ intrat‖‖ in mare; 4 Sinu*m*; ubi mare intrat in te*rr*a*m*;
5 Fares : turres custodum;

* MS. Lenonobus, with *i* above the second *o*.

† The *li* are added above the line.

§ The *s* is a correction from *i*.

¶ The second *a* is a correction from some other letter (*u*?).

‖ After the first *e* the MS. has a partly effaced *c* with a little stroke underneath.

‡ MS. has v above the *ua*.

** The sign of contraction for *is* is wanting.

†† After the *s* something has been erased.

§§ Perhaps the stroke over the second *a* is to be expanded by *tis*.

¶¶ After Exin follows a mark (of punctuation?) which resembles a comma, having another comma, turned upside down, on the top of it.

‖‖ MS. intrat terra, but the two words have each been marked by three dots for transposition.

6 Eurus; dexter; 7 Choncis; hebernum* :
8 Scabros; pisces sunt; 9 P*er*uicax : continuu*m*;
10 Uitiginem; bleci†; 11 Musca canina; quę in cane§ habitat¶
12 Foetontis : id*est* sol;
13 Astu; astucia; 14 Uitricu*m*; steuffeder||;
15 Amazones; semiuste,
16 Pellexerat; uocauerat;
17 In lati; in italia; 18 Conmanipulares; id*est* sodales;
19 Stiuam; manubrium;
20 Attica*rum* : athinensium :
21 Laser; pigmentum; 22 Uiteleos; iuuenes;
Fol. 32[bb]

[XXXVII] DE S*A*NC*T*I AGUST*INI*;

1 Obsorio*rum*; negotiationum;
2 ·C· uolles; c· nummos;
3 Fidelia; farris uas tritici :
4 Fidelia; uas . far . gen*us* tritici;
5 Capsaces; lenticula . id*est* uas uitreu*m* simil*e* flasconi;
6 Caligam‡; calciam*en*tu*m*** subtalare,
7 Odonis uita*m*; mihes†† nostlun;
8 Odon; lineum *est* in pede .
9 Tabulas legat . id*est* tabulas matronales; quia omnia scribunt*ur* in curia et substantias disponu*n*t in xii§§ uncias qua*m*uis magnas . u*e*l modicas; et ad maritu*m* p*er*tinent : uiii : ad mulierem iiii; Unde in dialogo gregorii . vi unt*ias* id*est* mediu*m* preciu*m* accip*it* . puella :
10 Mutilabo; dubitabo :
11 Ambieres; munieres;
12 Ore camerato : multu*m* clamante*m* a camera . t*am*en d*icitur*; 13 Passim; p*er* omnia :
14 Sationis; seminis; 15 Uindicat*ur*; defendit*ur*;
16 Taxatio; deputatio;
17 Addicitur; damnatur; 18 Pallebat, timebat
19 Laurus; arbor *est* unde milites coronas sibi faciunt in uictoria;
20 Toga : dignitas;

[XXXVIII] DE CLEMENTE,

1 Examussim; inquisitiue;
2 Dumosis : spinosis; 3 Elocare; collocare;
4 Gattas; muriceps;
5 Chantari; uermes qui cantant nocte sicut locuste;
6 Stragula; curtina pulcra . uarietate depicta¶¶
7 Columnas uitreas . id*est* in simili uitis scalpant*ur*
8 Genesim; natura :
9 Epicurius; uoluptarius corporis
10 Phitagoras : uoluptarius m*en*tis;
Fol. 33[aa]
11 Calistratus; p*ro*p*rium* uiri; 12 Idasteles; p*ro*p*rium* uiri.
13 Diodorus; p*ro*p*er*ter uiri; 14 Adepiades; p*ro*p*rium* uiri;
15 Hygę; quas beluas uocant . id*est* bestie;

* MS. has **v** above the *er*.

† MS. has **v** above the *e*.

§ The *e* seems to be a correction from *a*.

¶ The *h* is a correction from *n*.

|| MS. has **v** above the *u*.

‡ MS. Calicam, but *c* marked by a dot underneath for erasure, and *g* written above it.

** The first stroke of the second *a* is a correction from *i*.

†† MS. has **v** above the line, between the *m* and *i*.

§§ A later hand has inserted : after xii.

¶¶ The *de* are added above the line.

16 Ochimo; herba *est* quę lat*ine* catagoga,
17 Cratera; patena;
18 Creta coma*m* . diptamini mittit;
19 Tholus; tectu*m* de petris sine ligno;
20 Fidiae* opera; opera dei;
21 Anacefaleosin; recapitulatio;
22 Deucalionem : nom*en* regis sub diluuiu*m* factu*m* *est* non generare,
23 Scrupeas : dubitationes;
24 Pyriflegitonta; ignis ebulliens†;
25 Climacteras; partes cęli;
26 Mathesis; doctrina astrologiae :
27 Tetragono; quattuor§ angvlos¶ .
28 Cacodemon*us*; malus demon;
29 Trapezita; qui in m*en*sa nu*m*moru*m* p*er* mutationes uictu*m* querit;
30 Palestris; luctatio;
31 Decanorum‖; qui p*er*‡ x· nu*m*mos auguriantur
32 Thema; doctrina; 33 Scema; figura
34 Paenilopis : uxor; achilis;
35 Ex diametro e regione; medietas anni :
36 Sindetus; ligaturas :
37 Coribantas** : id*est* qui fecer*unt* sonitum
38 Satirum : incubum;
39 Aides : pluto diuitię : 40 Peleu*m*; pat*er* achelis
41 Totegis; procella;
42 Hierufontis†† u*el* p*ro*phetis qui auditis prę*sunt* .
43 Nastologis; mercedes quę dantur nautis; p*ro*pt*er* regim*en* nauis :
44 Epibatis qui p*er*uenient et dant nabulum p*ro* nauigat*ione*;
45 Sitatum : malleu*m* duratum;

Fol. 33[ab]

[XXXIX] DE DIALOGORUM;

1 A primeuo flore§§; a primo flore barbe;
2 Colonus; a colendo;
3 Censura; iuditiu*m*; 4 Balneu*m* ciceronis; a cicerone romano prefecto q*ui* feci*t* illud;
5 Mansionarius; hostiarius qui custodit¶¶ edem‖‖; 6 Fledomum; blodsaex‡‡;
7 Erucę; modici uermes qui mand*unt* folia multos ped*es* hab*ent*
8 In gremio; in medio domus
9 Interorina; p*ro*pt*er* nom*en* loci;
10 Ausaret; *proprium* nom*en* fluminis;
11 Uini fusor; pincerna; 12 Uangas; spaedun***
13 Aurelia; terra e*st*; u*el* p*ro*uincia .
14 Sabanum; linteum ad††† baln*eum*
15 Ferula; baculus arundineus de maiore genere . si feris de ipso ardet et n*on* est libidu*m*

* The second *i* has been added above the line between the *d* and *a*.

† MS. epulliens, but the down-stroke of *p* marked by two dots for erasure, and a stroke (for *b*) added to its top.

§ MS. has quattuos.

¶ MS. angolos, but the first *o* corrected into *v*.

‖ The *D* is a correction from *G*.

‡ Before per a letter (*o* ?) has been erased.

** MS. coribantes, but the *e* subpuncted, and *a* with a dot on its right side written above the line.

†† Here is a hole in the vellum round which this and the next gloss have been written.

§§ MS. frore, but first *r* marked by two dots for erasure, and *l* written above it.

¶¶ MS. custodiunt, but the second *u*, and the *n* marked each by a dot above and underneath for erasure.

‖‖ edem, and the next two words are added in finer writing.

‡‡ MS. has v above the *o*.

*** MS. has v above the *a*.

††† Before ad a letter has been erased.

16 Modernos ; nouos ;
17 Sabura ; in romana urbe ;
18 Paritores : ministros :
19 Freniticus* ; insanus ob dolorem capitis : ad te*mpus* qui multu*m* uigilat †
20 In mare adriatico ; ab adriano . imperatore . qui pensabat hoc§ mare cu*m* catenis in p*ro*fundum
21 rimis . bord¶ remum
22 Presbitera ; uxor|| p*res*b*ite*ri qua*m* habuit ante ordinat*ionem*‡ ;
23 Diaconissa ; qua*m* diac*onus* habuit ;
24 Aduocatus . d*icitu*r qui uocatur in adiutorium alicuius causa . u*e*l p*er* pecunia*m* id*est* dingere ;
25 Uulgari ; huni ;
26 Emorphiu*m* ; *pro*p*rium*
27 Exactio : monung** gaebles†† ;
28 Qui in numero optio fuit numer*us* dic*itu*r quando milites fiunt ;
Optio ; dispensator . qui dispensat stipendia militu*m* : p*re*positus§§ eo*rum* :

Fol. 33[ba]

29 Cassari ; euacuare ; 30 Decrepita*m* ; dobend¶¶ .
31 Carabum ; modica nauis . minor qua*m* scafa ;
32 Dalmatica ; tonica lata habens manicas|||| misalis ;
33 Porta laurenti ; quia p*er* ipsa*m* corp*us* eius portatu*m*‡‡ est ;
34 Angulinis*** ; p*ro*p*er*t term ę calid*ae*
35 Iuuenior : id*est* senior in iuuentute,
36 Sex unt*ias* . mediam parte*m* unius uille, consuetudo est roman*orum* tota*m* substantia*m* XII : unt*ias* dicere siue magna sit siue modica ; 37 Arbor ; maest††† ;
38 Claui . p*er*diti : 39 Rimis : cinum .
40 Paralisin : desolutio§§§ omniu*m* me*m*bro*rum*
41 Crepido ; a crepando d*icitu*r ;
42 Altare : d*icitu*r . q*uo*d alta res : id*est* diuina in eo agit*ur*
43 Duas coronas ·II· panes p*er*tussos similes coronę
44 Glebu*m* : ascensu*m* singularis uia ;
45 Palestra*rum* . luctantium ;
46 Camisa ; lineum ;
47 Sincopin : defectio stomachi ;
48 Calculum d*icitu*r : infirmitas ei*us* qui n*on* pote*st* mingere . q*uasi* lapis obdurat¶¶¶ uirilia ;
49 Coliriu*m* d*icitu*r . multa medicamina in unum collecta ;
50 Sentina d*icitu*r . ubi multe aquę fiunt collecte in naui
51 Byssus . in terra affricana crescit

* The *t* seems a correction from *ct*.

† Above the *t* the MS. has an inkspot, perhaps the top of a wrongly commenced *l* or *b*, or some such letter.

§ The *c* added above the line.

¶ MS. has v above the *o*.

|| The *x* seems to have been corrected from *i*.

‡ The *d* is a correction from *i*.

** MS. has v above the second *n*.

†† MS. has v above the line, between the *a* and *e*.

§§ The down-stroke of the first *p* has the usual curled stroke for *ro*, therefore p*ro*, without any mark of correction ; but above the *p* is the ordinary stroke for *re*. Hence we may read p*ro*- or p*re*-.

¶¶ MS. has v above the *e*.

|||| The first stroke of the first open *a* is a correction from *i*.

‡‡ MS. postatum, but the combined *s* and *t* corrected into *rt*.

*** After the first *i* an *f* or *s* has been erased.

††† MS. has v above the *a*.

§§§ The *t* is a correction from *i*.

¶¶¶ The *d* is a correction from *t*.

in arbustis lana alba sicut nix :
52 Om*nes* dies septimanę sabbata diceba*ntur* ;
53 In pulpito ; in gradu . ubi lectores legunt ;
54 In diocesi : in parrochia ;
55 Scinici : scinnenas* :
56 Ante absida . ante sedem episc*opi* ;
57 Histrionib*us*† ; oroccerum§
58 Pitoicis ; dispensatio pauperum ;
59 Xenodochior*um*¶ : susceptio peregrinor*um* :
Fol. 33[bb]
60 Alae : genus|| . ludi ; 61 Municipii ; tribvtarii‡
62 Filacteria ; scriptura diuersa quę p*ro*p*er*t infirmos habentur ;
63 P*er* pragmatia*m*** formam ; p*er* principalia imperia uel negotia ;
64 Didascalum : doctorale ;
65 Infvlas††; dignitates ; 66 Elicitu*m* ; incitatum
67 Conpotis ; inpletis ;
68 Cataloc*um* : sec*undum* numerum ;
69 Scedule ; carte :
70 Adstipulatione ; congregatione ;
71 Typum : inflationem ;
72 Olografia§§ : totum scriptio ;
73 Autenticum ; auctorale ;

[XL] ITEM INCIP*IUNT* UERB*A*

1 Uiscide . Ineluctabile . i*dest* maius luctu .
2 Fatere . laudare . 3 Deuotatu*m* . male dicturio :. inconparari . 4 Pangebant*ur*¶¶ : iungebt*ur*
5 Alt*er*nandis . inuicem .
6 Palantib*us* . pendentib*us* 7 Crinicuł . funicuł|||| .
8 Ad infirmatione*m* . ad stibulationem . suscitationem . 9 Inperagrata . intransita .
10 Cicima . geometrica . 11 Malua . olus .
12 Fulm*en*tat*ur* . initiat*ur* . 13 Bachal . multi idole foede .
14 Reis . inmundis . 15 Mom*en*taneas . cotidianas .
16 Ollitani . senes . 17 Insigniri‡‡ . inuri‡‡ .
18 Thiarati . diuini . 19 Conpage . porrectione
20 Pallantib*us* ; apparentib*us*
21 Liniam*en*tis*** . signis,

* MS. has **v** above the *e*.

† The second *i* and the *o* are written on an erasure.

§ Before this word a letter (*c*?) has been partly erased and partly effaced. The first *o* resembles the Greek *δ*, and might therefore be read as *d*; but this form for *o* is not uncommon in the MS.; in the present case the top-curl looks fainter than the circle forming the *o*; it has, however, this faintness in common with some other letters in the lines above and below this word.

¶ The *h* has been added above the line between the *c* and *i*.

|| The *g* is a correction from *n*. ‡ MS. tribatarii, but the first *a* corrected into *v*.

** The *p* is a correction from some other letter (o ?).

†† The *v* is a correction from *i*.

§§ The *i* appears to have been added later and crosses the lower part of the first stroke of the second open *a*.

¶¶ MS. plangebantur, but the *l* marked by three dots for erasure.

|||| As the source of this gloss has not been found, the contractions cannot here be expanded.

‡‡ MS. has ÷ above the *I* of Insigniri, and above the *in* of inuri, as marks of transposition.

*** After this word is again the hole mentioned above, p. 40 note ††.

22 Rigentia uigentia .

[XLI] ITEM DE NOMINIB*US* DIUERSIS.

1 Pr*es*b*ite*ri q*ui* s*unt* in agris . epistolas dare n*on* possunt Ad solos tantu*m* uicinos ep*iscop*os litteras distinabunt . 2 Chorep*is*-*co*pi* q*ui* s*unt* inreprehensibiles dare poss*unt* pacificas . i*dest* gene

Fol. 34[aa]

rales epistulas . 3 Sidonicis . hospicia pauperu*m* . 4 Orthodoxa*m* . recte gloriantiu*m* .

5 Diocesis . adiacens domus .

6 Cinico . canino . 7 Iaspis . nigru*m* et uiride*m* colore*m* hab*et*

8 Saphirus . mari simile*m* et quasi aureas stellas habens . 9 Calcidon . ut ignis lucens†

10 Smaragdus . uiride*m* colore*m* hab*et* hoc e*st* prasinu*m* . 11 Sardonix . habet colorem sanguinis q*ui* e*st* onichinus .

12 Sardius . colore*m* puru*m* sanguinis .

13 Crisolitus . auri colore*m* et stellas luculentas habet .

14 Bẏrillus tame*n* ut aqua resplendit .

15 Topation . ut auru*m* micat .

16 Cẏpressus . uiride*m* habet colore*m* ut est porrus et stellas aureas habet .

17 Mastigia . lora cu*m* uncis ferreis .

18 Initiatu*m* . ordinatum .

19 Pagus . possessio magna .

20 Lance . me*n*sura . 21 Obfirmantes . obicientes omne presagio uel signo .

[XLII] INCIP*IT* EX DIUERSIS LIB*RIS*

1 Excipiunt*ur* . separantur .

2 Tapetibus . rihum§

3 Memphitica . regina ¶ egẏpti *uel* ciuit*as*

4 Elleus . ualuẏrt‖ . 5 Neutricis . nouis .

6 Sutrinator ; scoehere ‡ ;

7 Priuigna ; nift ; 8 Paranimphi ; dryctguma ;

9 Ceruerus ; canis qui hostiarius inferni d*icitu*r ;

10 Seuit ; glimith, 11 Pone : post ;

12 Fornaculum ; herth ;

13 Hermofroditus ; androginus homo utriusq*ue* sexus ;

14 Ruscus ; cneholen ; 15 Scithis : speciosas ;

16 Falleras ; falsitates ; 17 Sirte ; harena ;

18 Amphibalu*m* ; coculus . 19 Egre ; difficile** ;

20 In uiridario domus ; in atrio p*ro* uiriditate herbaru*m*

Fol. 34[ab]

21 Basterna . similis curro de coreo tota ; et portat*ur* semp*er* ab asinis . u*el* hominib*us* nullam rota*m* hab*et* ;

22 Typo ; signo ; 23 Quartane . quę quarta die uenit

24 Uectandi : gratia exercendi ;

25 Platonis†† ideas : id*est* species ;

26 Furcifer furci ; id*est* cruci dignus ;

* The *e* is a correction from some other letter.

† The *n* is more like the ordinary *r*.

§ MS. divides ri hum, and has **v** (looking more like **y**) above the *u*.

¶ Before this word a letter has been wiped away, and part of the *r* is written in its place.

‖ MS. divides ualu yrt, and has **v** (or perhaps **y**) with a dot above it, over the second *u*.

‡ MS. has **v** above the *o*.

** The *ci* have been added above the line.

†† After this word something (a sign of punctuation?) has been erased.

27 In pennias; ober* scoeiddo;

[XLIII] IT*EM* DE DIUERSIS NOMINIB*US*

1 Themisto : insula; 2 Calipso; insula;

3 Pan deus; arcadię . u*e*l pastor*um*;

4 Arcades . gens d*icitu*r quę colebat pan*a*;

5 Polideuces; pollux . ulixes . homin*es* fortissimi;†

6 Notha . adultera eo q*uo*d incerti generis;

7 Nepus : filius filii : 8 Nepus : adulter;

9 Nepus : consumptor substantie,

10 Omonima; uaria nomina;

11 Polionima : multiuoca;

12 Cethetica§; possessiua;

13 Agrippa; qui in pedes nascit*ur* ei*us* natura;

14 Comedo; edax; 15 Panpo gen*us* piscis;

16 Micene : nom*en* ciuit*atis* . et plur*ale* sic*ut* Kalend*ae*

17 Nereus; deus maris;

18 Carus; nom*en* hominis¶ qui transportare d*icitu*r . in infernu*m*||; 19 Cruda; ualens;

20 Eunuchus; consul roman*us*

21 Centaurus; nauis unus de naui*bus* ęnie;

22 Forinnadas : interior pars nauis;

·IIII· GENERA POETARUM.

23 Comicus : qui comedia scripsit;

24 Traicus : qui traica scribs*it*

25 Liricus . qui p*er* liram cantat;

26 Saturicus : qui per saturica*m* scribs*it*

27 Frora; mater dear*um*;

28 Bachus lib*er* : pat*er* dionisius no*men* unius hominis e*st*;

Fol. 34[ba]

29 Floralia : bachunalia; saturnalia liberalia : ulcanalia : festiuitate*s* u*e*l sacra paganor*um* e*st*; 30 Emblema; fodor‡;

31 Manes : anime mortuorum;

32 Mactus : magis auctus; 33 Silla; consul;

34 Horno; hoc anno . 35 hac in hac parte;

36 Illac . in illa parte; 37 Cuiatis : huidirrynę**

38 Nostratis; hidirrinę††; 39 Quotus; hu ald§§;

40 Totus;· suæ ald¶¶; 41 Perende; ofer tua nest||||

42 Posttridie; p*ost* III dies : 43 Q*ui*dni; quare . n*on*;

44 Epul . castor; Per pullux; p*er* castor;

45 Pẏtisso; sputu*m* deicio;

46 Piraondes . dom*us* in similitudinem; ignis : na*m* ignis . pirus est;

* MS. has v above the *e*. MS. divides ober sco eiddo, and penni*as* may be read as penni*cis*.

† Above the imi; something has been erased.

§ MS. Cetheetica, but the third *e* is marked by four dots for erasure.

¶ Underneath hominis there is an erasure extending from the *h* till the *q* of qui.

|| The *in* have been added above the line.

‡ MS. has v above the first *o*.

** The *d* is a correction from *r*. The MS. divides huidir rynę, and it has v (which in this case looks more like y) above the line between these two words.

†† MS. divides hidir rinę, and it has v above the second *r*.

§§ MS. has hu ald as one word.

¶¶ MS. has suæ ald as one word, and v above the *æ*.

|||| ofer tua nest is one word in the MS., and there is v, with a dot on its right side, above the *a*.

47 Animalus ; fifaldae* ; 48 Cedo ; dic . u*el* p*er*dono ;

49 Parcę† : q*uae* minime parcant ;

50 Lucus q*uo*d minime luceat ;

51 Piscina ; quę pisces non habet ;

52 Facesso ; facere cesso : u*el* sepe facio ;

53 Eumenides : filię noctis ; i*dest* hegitissę ;

54 Cestus ; arma pictarum ; 55 sis nuis§

56 Aptotu*m* ; inflexibile . *uel* incasale ;

[XLIV] IT*EM* ALIA ; DE CÆLO ; ;

1 Partes . au*tem*¶ . eius ; cous . axis . clima . cardines . conuexa . poli . hiemisperia|| .

2 Cous e*st* quo cęlum contęnetur unde enias uix solum conplere coum terroribus caeli ;

3 Axis : linea recta quę p*er* media*m* pila*m* spere tendit ;

4 Clima cardo u*el* pars celi . ut clima‡ orientalis uel meridiana,

5 Cardines . extreme partes axis sunt ;

6 Conuexa extrema cęli ;

7 Poli ex celestib*us* ciclis cacumina . *Fol.* 34[bb] quo maxime spera nititur alt*er* ad aquilone*m* expectans boreus alt*er* t*er*rę obpositus austronothus dictus e*st*

8 Hiemisperia duo sunt quor*um* alter*um* est sup*er* terra*m* alter*um* sub t*er*ra** ;

9 Cęlum . ab oriente . ad occidentem semel in die et nocte uerti sapientes†† aestimant ;

10 Cardines quoq*ue* axis ipsius sunt extremę§§ . partes sunt quos insertos orbi discribunt sperico ut ipsis cęlum inuoluatur inuisis : et ita polum philosophi ui p*ro*pria semp*er* in suo axe torq*ue*ri arbitrantur . a quibus ignoratur opifex qui mundu*m* in suum orbem absq*ue* ullo axis moderamine eregit ;

11 Clima aliquando . p*ro* cardine accipitur si sepius¶¶ p*ro* qualicumq*ue* celi parte et maxime p*ro* oriente et meridię climas aliqui design*ant* . nos|||| : se*cundum* grec*um* om̄ cęli ad superna conuexas . ita undiq*ue* uocam*us*

12 Arcticos ; septentrionalis‡‡ ab arcto adiectum***

13 Terinos ; id*est* bestialis,

14 Isemerin*us* ; i*dest* meridianus ;

15 Exemerin*us* ; ac si ex meridię remotior

* MS. has v above the second *a*.

† The *r* has been added above the line.

§ sis nuis have been written in finer writing, and are probably a later addition.

¶ au*tem* (aū) has been added above the line between two dots.

|| MS. himesperia, with *e* added above the line between the first *i* and the *m*, and the first *e* altered to *i*.

‡ The *i* is a correction from some other letter.

** Above the *a* the MS. has a stroke, which is marked, by a dot above it, for erasure.

†† MS. has a comma after this word, which has partly been wiped away.

§§ The *x* is a correction from *t*.

¶¶ The *i* written on an erasure.

|||| The *s* has been added above the line.

‡‡ The second *e* had — above it, but it has been erased.

*** MS. has a stroke above the *u*, and the final stroke of the *m* is marked for erasure by a dot above and below; the correction suggests the apparently required word adiectiuum.

16 Antarticus*; artico contrarius hor*um* prim*us* qui est erga arcturum . a polo poreo . IIII muror*um* spatiis distat a quo secundus . u ab eo . III . ui : Item ab eo . IIII . ui . muris distat; Item . u : circulus : u . spatiis ab eo . ad polum australem . IIII . *idest* ad uerticem . IIII sunt moera spatiis . ut figunt astrogi;

17 Cous . d*icitu*r eo q*uo*d sibi inuicem in mundo . IIII . coeunt elementa;

18 Poli summa . cęlor*um* cacumina;
Fol. 35^{aa}

19 Hiemisperium . aput gr*ecos* d*icitu*r q*uo*d nos uertice*m* uocam*us*

20 Anomala : inęqualia;

21 Conuexa; ardua;

22 Pliadę; uii sunt stelle in cauda tauri;

23 Zodiacus; sideralis;

24 Alcian*us*; arbores frangit;

25 Dextera : mutatur quando sibi uertix in circium declinans ad eu*m* subregit austronothum;

26 A tergo . d*icitu*r errare du*m* austronotho in sublimi erecto uertix se in su*m*mu*m* poli demergit;

27 Leua deinde cum se subleuans in boreu*m* uertix austronothum precipitans obiecit† et sursum atq*ue* deorsu*m* dicimus q*uod* cęlum sic*ut* in ortu surgens : eregitur ita et in occasu demergit*ur* :
Hii sunt . UII motus cęli qui solem et luna*m* du*m* polo sunt tardiores in diuersis oriri§ et occidere cogunt orbib*us* .

28 Extremi quoq*ue* duo septentrionales . 29 Axem cęli ipsius dnm̄s : bina hiemisperia *per* medium orbem terrę sed nullus corporalis intellegitur axis q*uod* uirtus diuina cęli globum rotans *per* axem incorporeu*m* in orbem speri contorqueat comminisque . moliri :

[XLV] UERBA DE MULTIS;

1 Gymnasium; locus exercitationis ubi diuerse arte discantur;

2 Eruere; discere; 3 Las . ignis; 4 Fors; uẏrd;

5 Fax . falcis; 6 Glis; egle; 7 Lanx; unde lancis .

8 Pręx unde : pręcis; 9 Far; frume*n*tum;

10 Gyt¶; gen*us* seminis herbis minuta bona in panes mittere;

11 Ops||; aput antiquos terra d*icitu*r unde inops inhumatus; 12 Coa; insula .

13 Massica : mons; 14 Geniu*m*; natura‡
Fol. 35^{ab}

15 Ador : gen*us* frum*enti*; 16 Antes . d*icitu*r . ordo uinear*um* .

17 Toraca; lurica;

18 Pedu*m* . fustis . que*m* pastores habent in modum ʌ.

19 Lanistra; macellarius in macello carnes diuidit : 20 Damma; elha . 21 adsecla minist*er*;

22 Pedissequa; ministra; 23 Uerna; mancipiu*m* .

24 Aleo; teblheri : 25 Alea**; tebl;

* The *i* is a correction from some other letter (a badly formed *i*?).

† The *e* is a correction from some other letter.

§ The *rir* are written on an erasure.

¶ The *y* is a correction from *i*.

|| MS. has a horizontal stroke over the *p*.

‡ Above the *ra* there is a spot, probably caused by effacing something written over the two letters.

** A letter has been erased before the *A*.

26 Histrio; scurres . lees*; 27 Gurgullio; drohbolla;
28 Actio; disputatio; 29 Uligo; te*rr*ę
natural*is*;
30 Mango; comitator equor*um*;
31 Popa; tabernarii qui in domo
tab*er*narii *sunt*

[XLVI] IT*EM* ALIA; 1 Ueru; snaas†;
2 Pugil; milis; 3 Tanaquil; uirga
regalis;
4 Cos . ueostun; 5 Rien§; lumbis;
6 Lien; miltę¶; 7 Tybicen; qui
tibia cantat;
8 Flam*en*; sacer*dos* iouis : 9 Fidicen;
harperi‖;
10 Liricen : qui lira cantat;
11 Lucar : uectical; 12 Lucunar;
camera;
13 Tuber : in dorso cameli :
14 Suber; gen*us* ligni ex hoc cortix
in calcim*en*ta ponitur
15 Laser; gen*us* herbę; 16 Liser;
gen*us* ligni minuti;
17 Semiuir, eunuchus; 18 Fidis :
sner‡;
19 Prepes; auis; 20 Seres, otiosus :
21 Pollis; grot**
22 Scropis : groop††; 23 Astus :
astutus; Uel; cal*lidus*;
24 Situs; lana quę crescit in loco
quę caret sole . u*el* positio;
25 Cliutex : cortix . u*el* lapis;
26 Carex . seic§§; 27 Uarix : om-
prę¶¶ in crurib*us* hominu*m*
28 Matrix . radix . *u*el uterus;
29 Pernix; uelox; 30 Celox . nauis;
31 Epitorta; adbreuiatio;
32 Libertabus : friulactum‖‖
33 Cune; ciltrog . unde cunabula;
34 Inferie; hostie mortuor*um* . 35
Exubię; exuendo .
36 Manubię‡‡; a manu dictę facultates;
37 Magalia . byrae; 38 Glisco; cresco;
39 Si*m*plex; aenli***;
40 Bilex; tili††† : 41 Triplex .
drili§§§; 42 Paturu*m* . fc-
tor¶¶¶ :
43 Abctape; tysse‖‖‖ .

Fol. 35[ba]
[XLVII] IT*EM* ALIA;
1 Abellana : hel‡‡‡ : 2 Usq*ue*qua-
q*ue* . multum :
3 Rigor . frigor inflexibilis;
4 Ancones; untinos; 5 Corimbis :
nauibus;
6 Cirris; crinib*us*; 7 Calomaucus :
het**** :
8 Muscus; bestia; et sanguis ei*us*
boni odoris e*st*;

* MS. has v above the first *e*.
† MS. has v above the first *a*.
§ The *i* is written over an erasure.
¶ MS. has v above the *t*.
‖ MS. has over the *ar* a waving stroke, corrected into v.
‡ MS. has v, with a dot above it, over the *ne*.
** MS. has v above the *ro*.
†† MS. has v above the first *o*.
§§ MS. has v above the *i*.
¶¶ MS. has v above the *p*.
‖‖ MS. has v above the *a*.
‡‡ The first stroke of the open *a* is a correction from *i*.
*** MS. has v above the *en*.
††† MS. has v above the first *i*.
§§§ MS. has v above the *ri*.
¶¶¶ MS. has v, with a dot above it, over the *o*.
‖‖‖ This gloss has been added at the foot of the column.
‡‡‡ MS. has v above the *e*.
**** MS. has v above the *e*.

9 Platissu : folc; 10 Balera : hron* :
11 Uiuarium; piscina; 12 Caefalus † : haerdhera;
13 Perna; flicci§; 14 Umbrellas :
stalo to fuglam :
15 Tappula; uermis qui currit super
aquas;
16 Uertigo; eduallę¶; 17 Buculus;
nordbaeg‖,
18 Truffulus; felospric; 19 Famfelvcas ‡ : laesungae**;
20 Inuolucrus; uuluc††;
21 Mordatius : clox : 22 Erpica;
egida§§;
23 Alga : uuac; 24 Osma : odor :
25 pessul . leer ¶¶;
26 Opilauit; gigisdae; 27 Colostrum :
beust;
28 Saburica‖‖ . *dicitur* quando
mittuntur in nauem quando
alia non habent;
29 Isica; tyndri; 30 Sicunia; gi-
breci‡‡;
31 Reuma; streum*** : 32 Mustacra :
gronae††† .
33 Uicias : fuglues§§§ . benae¶¶¶;
34 Manticum : hondful baeues;
35 Maulistis; scyhend : 36 Berruca;
uaertę‖‖‖
37 Argella laam‡‡‡; 38 Accearium;
stel****;
39 Scarpmat; scribid : 40 Byrseus;
ledir uyrcta††††;
41 Tubolo fala; 42 andeda brond-
ra;
43 Uaricat; stritęd : 44 Battat . gi-
nat§§§§;
45 Lurdus, lemphald : 46 Terebellus;
nębugaar
47 Dolabella; bradacus;
48 Scalpellum; biriis; 49 Ciscillus;
haerdhaeu;
50 Auriculum; dros : 51 Garallus,
hroc¶¶¶¶ :
52 Parula : masae; 53 Sturnus; stęr :
54 Noctua; necthtrefn‖‖‖‖;
55 Turdella‡‡‡‡; drostlae*****; 56
Ciconia; storhc :
57 Arpa; arngeus††††† . 58 Scorelus;
emaer§§§§§;
59 Acega; holthona; 60 Cucuzata;
laepiuincę;

* MS. has v above the *ro*.

† A letter has been erased between the second *a* and the *l*.

§ MS. has v above the first *c*.

¶ MS. has v above the *u*.

‖ MS. has v above the *a*.

‡ The *v* is a correction from *u*, or two *ii*.

** MS. has (more *y* than) v above the first *e*.

†† MS. has v above the third *u*.

§§ MS. egldae, with v above the *a*. But the *l* and final *e* are marked, each by three dots, for erasure, and an *i* has been added above the *g*.

¶¶ MS. has v above the first *e*.

‖‖ The *ri* added above the line.

‡‡ MS. has v above the *re*.

*** MS. has stroke over the *m*.

††† MS. has v above the *n*.

§§§ MS. has v above the second *u*.

¶¶¶ MS. has v above the *n*.

‖‖‖ To the upper stroke of the *r*, whereby it is joined to the *t*, is apparently added a v written sideways, with its top towards the left.

‡‡‡ The second *a* has been added above the line, and a v above the first *a*.

**** There is a stroke through the *l*.

†††† MS. has v above the *y*.

§§§§ MS. has v above the *n*.

¶¶¶¶ MS. has v above the *o*.

‖‖‖‖ MS. has v above the second *t*.

‡‡‡‡ The *r* is a correction from *l*, and the *d* seems a correction from *n* or *c*.

***** MS. has v above the *a*.

††††† Arpa and arngeus are underlined in the MS. with faint ink.

§§§§§ MS. has v above the *ma*.

61 Tilaris; laurice; 62 Ruscinia;
nectigalae;
Fol. 35[bb]
63 Turdus : scruc; 64 Perdvlu*m**;
hragra †;
65 Sticulus; gaeuo§; 66 Picus :
higrę¶ :
67 Marsopicus : uinu||; 68 Ficetula :
suca,
69 Fringella : uinc ‡; 70 Cardella .
distyltige**
71 Tinct slii : 72 lupus breuis; 73
Porco piscis; stẏra †† :
74 Sardin*us*; heringas§§; 75 Ginis-
culas¶¶ . idem :
76 Furunculas; maerth;
77 Netila : herma||||; 78 Musi-
ran*us*; scraeua‡‡;
79 Talpa : uoond : 80 Striga haeg-
tis;
81 Incuba; maerae*** . *uel* saturus;
82 Taban*us*†††; brimisa§§§; 83 Ca-
comican*us*; logdor;
84 Lendina; hnitu; 85 Aquilius :
onga :
86 Auricula : ęruigga¶¶¶;
87 Castorius : bebor||||||; 88 Scira;
acurna‡‡‡;
89 Bulin*us*; uermis . lacertę similis
in chomacho hominis habit*at*;
90 Maruca; snægl**** : 91 Maialis :
bęrg;
92 Porcastru*m*; foor; 93 Scrufa††††;
sugu§§§§;
94 Bęrrus : baar¶¶¶¶; 95 Philocain :
gr*ece*||||||| . scopon‡‡‡‡ .
96 Acrifoliu*m*; holera ::
97 Acerafulus; mapaldurt***** :
98 Inuoluco; uudubindlae; 99 Al-
n*us*†††††; alaer;
100 Tilio : lind§§§§§ : 101 almenta .
alerholt¶¶¶¶¶
102 Putat; snędit; 103 Ruscus; cre-
holegn; finit|||||||| .

[XLVIII] IT*EM* DE CASSIANO : 1 E-
regan*tur*‡‡‡‡‡ : loquan*tur*
2 Adscitus; inuitatus;
3 Inextricabiles . anatreten****** :
4 Uacillante*m*; fugante*m* . 5 Questus; substantia
6 Flagitior*um*; adulterior*um*;
7 Biothanti : laquei; 8 Inpegit :
trudit;
9 Dirimit : diuidit;

* The *v* is a correction from some other letter (*o*?).

† MS. has v above the first *r*.

§ MS. has v (which resembles *x*) above the *e*.

¶ MS. has v above the *r*.

|| MS. has v above the *i*.

‡ MS. has v above the *i*.

** MS. has v above the second *i*.

†† The *ẏ* is a correction from *i*.

§§ The *h* has been added above the line.

¶¶ The *G* is an ordinary small *g* written largely to make a capital. On its top there is a perpendicular stroke, suggesting an attempt to write first an *h*.

|||| MS. has v above the *r*.

‡‡ MS. has v above the first *a*.

*** MS. has v above the first *e*.

††† The second *a* is a correction from *u*.

§§§ MS. priusa; but *p* corrected into *b*. The *u* is marked for erasure by a small, fine dot underneath, and above it is written *mi*, in small fine writing, and hence brimisa. The lemma and its interpretation are underlined in faint ink.

¶¶¶ MS. has v above the *i*.

|||||| MS. has v above the *e*.

‡‡‡ The *r* is a correction from some other letter (*i*?).

**** MS. has v above the *æ*.

†††† The *c* is an alteration from *i*.

§§§§ MS. has v above the *ug*.

¶¶¶¶ MS. has v above the *aa*.

||||||| The lower part of *g* written on an erasure.

‡‡‡‡ MS. has v above the *op*.

***** MS. has v above the *u*.

††††† The right-hand stroke of the *n* is an alteration from *c*.

§§§§§ MS. has v above the *n*.

¶¶¶¶¶ MS. has v above the *e*.

|||||||| This word is written in faint ink, or perhaps an attempt was made to efface it.

‡‡‡‡‡ Between the *E* and *r* a *g* has been erased or wiped away.

****** MS. has a stroke over *treten*.

10 Corpulentioribus : crassioribus .
11 Gestiunt : uolunt ; 12 Frugalitas ;
penuria
13 Cassuae* ; ruinae ;
14 Fastus . inflatio . u*e*l timor ;
Fol. 36[aa]
15 Iubar : lum*en* : u*e*l splendor ; 16
Man*us* ; turba,
17 Conpellare ; fraudare† ; 18 Inhibere ; p*ro*hibere ;
19 Prerogatiua ; excellentia ;
20 Abdicare ; abicere : 21 Lepore*m* ;
decorem ;
22 Inmunitatis ; castitatis ;
23 Expolita ; famata ; 24 Indolem ;
ingenium iuuentutis ; 25 Acron ;
ciuitas ;
26 Effebor*um* ; studior*um* ; 27 Tesbites ; castella ;
28 Insolescit ; unstillit§ ; 29 Delecto
ei*us* . legationes ; ei*us*
30 Adfecit ; distauit ; 31 P*er*nities :
uelocitas ;
32 Conciderat ; acciderat ; 33 P*er*-
peti ; ueloces ;
34 Adfectanda, adficienda ;
35 Expertim¶ : ignorari || ; 36 Faus-
tus ; sup*er*bia ;
37 Postere : portę : 38 Contiguis :
iugis . *uel* conpetentes
39 Libet ; inuidet :
40 Excellentiores : gipparre ; ;
41 Synaxeos ; cura ; 42 Scita : documenta ;
43 Scandere, ascendere ; 44 Distabui ;
tabefactus ;
45 Reditus ; substantia ; 46 Fautore*m* ;
laudatore*m* ;
47 Distrauntur ; uendentur‡ ;
48 Co*m*mectar*um* . tractatores ; 49
Uersu*m* contra ;
50 Suffusione, circu*m*fusione ; 51 Sanguessuges ; lexas ;
52 Inmunes : mundi ; 53 Aborsu*m* ;
abiectio infantis ;
54 Citra ; bihina** ; 55 Suricus : brooc ;
56 Extores ; extraneos
57 Classica ; tuba : 58 Opere *pre*-
ciu*m* ; necessariu*m*
59 Telopagere : bibere ; 60 Reddibitiones ; retributiones†† ;
61 Multhra ; celdre§§ ; 62 Nanctus ;
nuens¶¶ ;
63 Aspeleo ; bethlem|||| 64 sarculum ;
65 Infestante ; iniuria*m* faciente‡‡ :
66 Scalpeum boor***
67 Ocilis ; uelotius ; 68 Sinaxeos :
celebrationes ;
69 Ceno ; luto ; 70 Entheta*m* : subpellectilem ;
71 Apologis ; excusationib*us* ; 72
Coalescere : adolescere ;
73 Adulti ; maturi : 74 Emolum*en*ta ;
lucra ;

Sicut Inueni scripsi : ne reputes
scriptori

* The second *a* is unlike the other open *a* of the MS., and might be read as *cc* or *ic* ; the text has here "casus ac ruinas."

† The first *r* has been added above the line.

§ MS. has stroke over nstil. The final *t* has been added above the line.

¶ A stroke (for *er*) through the foot of the *p* is still visible though an attempt has been made to efface it.

|| MS. ignorare, but the *e* is marked by a point on its top for erasure, and underneath it is a stroke to make *i*.

‡ The second *n* has a dot above and underneath for erasure (?).

** MS. has a waving stroke over ina. †† After the *u* a letter (*m* ?) has been erased.

§§ MS. has a waving stroke over this word which goes right through the upper strokes of the *l* and *d*.

¶¶ The upper parts of the *ns* are written on an erasure.

|||| The *hle* are written on an erasure.

‡‡ After the final *e* the MS. has a stroke which may be read as *i*.

*** MS. has a waving stroke over the *oo*.

INDEX (*Latin*).

A List of the *abbreviations* of proper names, titles of quoted books &c. will be found at the end of the Preface.

a for *ae* (tabul*a* for tabul*ae*).—for *au* (*a*rugo for *au*rugo) —for *e* (caementar*i*a for coemet*e*ria; pan*a*gerius and pan*a*gericon for pan*e*gyricis &c.).—for *h* (aabita for *h*abita).—for *i* (inn*a*taris for inn*i*taris).—for *o* (call*a*s for call*o*s; c*a*nto for c*o*nto; infrunit*a* for infrunit*o*; m*a*ralium for m*o*ralium).—for *u* (b*a*cula for b*u*cula; coalesc*a*nt for -*cu*nt; S*a*lamitis for S*ul*-).—*a* omitted (labrum for lab*a*rum).

a, prep. I. 2, 15, 68; II. 35, 53; III. 62; IV. 94, 114 (bis); X. 5; XI. 5, 14, 16; XIII. 3, 6, 37, 58; XVI. 13, 18; XIX. 53, 64; XXI. 19; XXII. 16; XXIV. 6, 12, 16; XXVII. 16; XXVIII. 18, 41, 57; XXIX. 39; XXX. 2; XXXII. 1; XXXV. 15, 17 (bis); XXXVII. 12; XXXIX. 1 (bis), 2, 4, 41; XLIV. 10, 16 (bis), 26; XLVI. 36.—See also *abene* (for *a bene*); *aspeleo* (for *a speleo*).

aabita, dicta constituta, II. 87 (*Bened. reg.* 58, 24 *habita* [41 habita, abita] secum deliberatione).

ab, II. 149 (bis); VIII. 9; XI. 16; XVI. 15 (bis); XXVIII. 33; XXXII. 2, 3; XXXV. 144, 198; XXXIX. 20; XLII. 21; XLIV. 9, 12, 16 (ter).—*ab ustum*, IV. 100 for *ambustum*?

abattidis v. [add *sextarios*?], XXXIII. 18 (*Euch. De Pond.*?). This word does not appear in the printed texts of Eucherius; nor is it in the Brit. Mus. MS.

abba, syrum pater genitor, II. 4 (*Bened. reg.* 2, 7 [8]). See Cp. Int. 33; Ef.[2] 259, 4.

abbatem, II. 161, see *sarabaite*.

abctape, tysse, XLVI. 43 (*Alia*=*Ars Phocae*?). Kluge (*A. S. Leseb.* p. 11) suggests *tapetia** for *abctape*; but Schlutter (*Journ. Germ. Phil.* I. 63 and *Anglia*, XXVI. 301) *amphitape*, and it seems=Aldh. p. 290 *amphitapete* genus vestimenti utrinque villosum et hirsutum; see also Non. 540; (cf. Cp. A544 amphitare [Ep. 2A12 and Ef.[1] 339, 56 amphitape], genus uestimenti utrimque uillosum). Cf. Isid. *Etym.* XIX. 26, 5. Schlutter (*Anglia*, l.c.) thinks that *tysse* answers to the O.H.G. *zussa*, which explains *lodix* in Steinm. II. 375, 32.

abdicans, contradicans, XXXIV. 35 (*De Cass.*?). According to the order in which this gloss occurs in the Glossary, *abdicans* is to be looked for between Ch. X. 3 and XII. 3 of *Cass. Inst.*, and Glogger refers to X. 12 non gladio carnali eos *addicens*, sed...uitae eis *interdicens* substantiam; a St. Gallen MS. reads *addicans*, *contradicens*.—See further *abdicare*.

abdicare, abicere, XLVIII. 20 (*De Cass.*, *Inst.* V. 11, 2 non ualuit *abdicare*; VII. 30 quae...*abdicare* deuouimus; IV. 36, 1 *abdicasti*; V. 32, 2 *abdicauit*; VII. 12 *abdicarat*).

abellana, hel, XLVII. 1 (*Alia*=?)=auellanus, [hael, and s added above the line=] haesl, Cp. A895; a-, aesil, Ep. 2A31; a-, haesl, Ef.[1] 340, 18. Cf. *abelena*, haeselhnutu, Cp. A2; *abilina*, hrutu, Ep. 1A26; *a*-, hnutu, Ef.[1] 338, 48.

abene, corrigia frenorum, XI. 9 (*Sap.* V. 22 tamquam *a bene* curvato arcu nubium exterminabuntur). The glossator read (*h*)*abene*; and the Cambridge MS. KK. 4. 6 has actually: *habene* corrigię frenorum. Cf. Steinm. *AHG.* I. p. 554. 13, 556. 34, 559. 20, 560. 26; IV. p. 277. 10.

abenis, halsledir, III. 37 (*De S. Mart. Stor.*=*Sulp. Sev. Dial.* I. 18, 4 totis *habenis*). Cf. *habenis* geþaldleðrum, Cp. H37.

ab exitu sermonis, ab exordio sermonis, XVI. 15 (*Dan.* IX. 25 *ab exitu sermonis*).

abhominatio, I. 3, see *anathema*. Cf. *abom*-.

abhominatus, VI. 26, see *perossus*.

abicere, XXXV. 198, see *abiurari*; XLVIII. 20, see *abdicare*.

abiectio, XLVIII. 53, see *aborsum*.

abire, II. 61, see *excedere*.

abita, see *aabita*.

abiurari, ab iure aecclesie [ecclesiae] abicere, XXXV. 198 (*Ruf.* VII. 26 fol. 129 b necessarium est...hunc...abijci et *abiurari*).

ablata, II. 144, see *remota*.

aboleri, a memoria tolli, I. 15 (*De

Canon.; *Decret. Innoc.* LII p. 208[b] *aboleri*; Cf. ibid. XIII p. 197 *aboletur*). See Cp. A85, 90, 91; Ef.[2] 259, 10, 11, 34.

abominatio, XII. 26, see *aporia*; *abhominatio.*

aborsum, abiectio infantis, XLVIII. 53 (*De Cass.*?). The word does not seem to occur in Cassianus' works. Cf. Rufin. (Origen.) in *Num.* VII. 3; in *Cant.* III p. 53 (Lomm., Vol. 15); in *Exod.* hom. x. 2; Aug. *Serm.* 97 § 3; *Thesaur. L. Lat.* (*abortus*) &c.

abra, ancilla, XXI. 6 (*Judith* VIII. 32 ego exeam cum *abra* mea; x. 10 *abra* ejus; x. 2 and XVI. 28 *abram* suam &c.) = *abra* ancella, Cp. A10; Ep. 2C21; *abra*, ancilla, Ef.[1] 340, 47.

abscondere, XXXIV. 54, see *condere.*

abscondunt, XV. 11, see *preteriola.*

absida, XXXIX. 56, see *absidam.*

absidam, grece sedem episcopalem, I. 6 (*De Canon.*); **ante absida**, ante sedem episcopi, XXXIX. 56 (not *Greg. Dial.* but = *Can. Conc. Afric.* XLIII p. 150 *ante absidem* manus ei imponatur).

absidem, see *absidam.*

absinthi [for *absinthii*], XXV. 15, see *hysopo.*

absinthii, see *hysopo.*

absolue, XXIV. 4, see *dimitte eam.*

absque, XLIV. 10, see *cardines.*

abstinentes, XXXV. 38, see *sinefactas.*

abstinentie, II. 190, see *parcitate.*

abstrahit, II. 71, see *extollit.*

absurdum, inconueniens turpem indignum, II. 11 (*Bened. reg.* 65, 9 [16] Quod quam sit *absurdum*). Cf. *absorduum*, indignum, Cp. A95; *absurdus*, rusticus indignus, ibid. A76 and Ef.[2] 259, 17.

abtet, see *aptet.*

abundantia, XII. 39, see *plestia.*

ac, IV. 11; XLIV. 15.

acaetum [acet-], VIII. 2, see *coacuerint.*

acbochnrotan, see *cinticta.*

Accaron, see *Acron.*

accearium, stel, XLVII. 38 (*Alia* = ?) = *a-*, steli, Cp. A127 and Ef.[1] 340, 17; *a-*, steeli, Ep. 2A30. For (*accearium* =) *aciarium*, see Körting, *Wörterb.* 125. For *stel* [or stele, or steli, as the MS. has stroke through *l*] see Bosw. T. (*stēle, stīle*, steel; O.H.G. *stahal, stāl*, &c.).

accega, accëia, see *acega.*

accensores, IV. 116, see *acoluthos.*

accersire, I. 52, see *exhibere.*

acciderat, XLVIII. 32, see *conciderat.*

accidiosus, see *acidiosus.*

accipiens, IV. 48, see *munerarius.*

accipimus, X. 3, see *odor ungentorum.*

accipit, XXXVII. 9, see *tabulas legat.*

accipitres, haefuc, XIX. 36 (*Job* XXXIX. 13 Penna struthionis similis est pennis... *accipitris*). *haefuc*, a hawk, Bosw. T. (*hafoc*); Skeat; Oxf. D. (*hawk*).

accipitris, XIV. 19, see *arugo*; XXXV. 181, see *regio morbus*; see also *accipitres.*

accipitur, XLIV. 11, see *clima.*

accipiunt, XVI. 27, see *malefici.*

accito, uocato, XX. 4 (*Tobias*; *Praef. Hieron.* p. XIII.[b] and Migne, *Patr. L.* XXIX col. 26[A], *accito* notario).

acclamatione, see *epiphonima.*

accola, see *adcola.*

accommodantes, see *accommorante.*

accommodentur, prestantur [praest-], II. 22 (*Bened. reg.* LIII. 36 ut...solacia *accomodentur* eis [62] *adcommodentur, accomm-*).

accommorante, conhabitantes, XII. 46 (*Eccles.* XXXVIII. 39 *accommodantes* animam suam). The gloss (conhab-) agrees with *accommorante* of the Glossary, not with *accommodantes* of the text.

accomodentur, see *accommodentur.*

accrescit, XXVIII. 32, see *climax.*

accusans, XXXV. 123, see *incusans.*

accusare, IV. 39, see *incessere.*

accusaret, XXXV. 110, see *insimularet.*

acdocroaton, see *cinticta.*

acediosus, see *acidiosus.*

acega, holthona, XLVII. 59 (*Alia* = ?) = *a-*, h-, Cp. A125; *a-*, holthana, Ep. 2A22; *accega*, holtana, Ef.[1] 340, 9. For *acega* (a snipe; also written *acegia*, see Cp. A138 *Acegia*, snite, and Bosw. T. in voce *snite*) see Körting, No. 84 (*accëia*); for *holt-hana, holt-hona* &c. (*holt*, a holt, wood + *hana*, a cock), a wood-cock, see Bosw. T. (holt-hana). Cf. cardiolus, uudusnite, Cp. C258.

acegia, see *acega.*

acephalo, see *epimehne.*

acer, XXXV. 66, see *ignis acer*; see also *acerafulus.*

acerabulus, see *acerafulus.*

acerafulus, mapaldurt, XLVII. 97 (*Alia* = ?) = *aerabulus*, mapuldur, Cp. A120; *acerabulus*, mapuldur, Ep. 2A14; *acterabulus*, maefuldur, Ef.[1] 340, 1. The readings of the Cp., Ep. and Ef.[1] Glossaries suggest *acerabulus* (prob. a dim. of *acer*, the maple-tree, Germ. *Ahorn-baum*), see Körting, 113. For *mapaldurt, mapuldur* &c. see Bosw. T. (*mapulder*), and Kluge, *Wrtb.* (*ahorn*; *maszholder*).

aceruo, aceruum, VIII. 8, see *in aceruo Mercurii.*

acetum, see *acętum*; *coacuerint.*

acętum [acet-], VIII. 17, see *nitrum.*

aceuan, oratio, XXX. 74 (*Cat. Hier.*?) = Cp. A156 aceuon, oratio. According to the order in which this gloss occurs in the Glossary, the lemma should occur in Ch.

LXXX or LXXXI, but there is nothing in Migne's or Richardson's texts corresponding to it; unless it be ἀκεφάλῳ (ἀκέφαλον, Migne) in Ch. LXXX, for which the Glossator perhaps read ἀκοήν or εὐχήν.

aceuon, see *aceuan*.

achalantis, see *ruscinia*.

achediosus, see *acidiosus*.

Achelis [for *Achillis*], XXXVIII. 40, see *Peleum*.

Achilis [for *Ulixis*], XXXVIII. 34, see *Paenilopis*.

Achillis, see *Peleum*.

aciarium, see *accearium*.

acide, triste, XII. 6 (*Eccles.* IV. 9 non *acide* feras in anima tua).

acidiosus [altered from aced-], ociosus [ot-] instabilis tristis uagus, II. 9 (*Bened. reg.* 48, 33 frater *acediosus*; [58] f. *achediosus*, *accidiosus*, *acediosus*).

aciem, IV. 120, see *bibennem*.

acisculus, see *ciscillus*.

acitabulus habens dragmas XU idest scrupulus XLII quod uncia una semis et scrupulos UIIII, XXXII. 7 (*De ponder.*?). Cf. Blume, I. 375, 3; 374, 28.

ackesoy, see *ascesi*.

acola, XIII. 55, see *adcola*.

acoloythei, XXX. 16, see *ho platon*.

acoluthos, accensores, IV. 116 (*Ruf.* VI. 33 fol. 115[a] videbat...*acolythos*). For *accensor* see *Thes. L. Lat.*; Georges, *Wrt.*

acolythos, see *acoluthos*.

acrifolium, holera, XLVII. 96 (*Alia*=?) =*acrifolus*, holegn, Cp. A123; Ep. 2A15; Ef.[1] 340, 2. In Lewis and Short's Dict. *acrifolium* (*acer*+*folium*) is said to be *an unknown tree of ill omen*. The reading *holegn* of the Cp., Ep. and Ef.[1] Glossaries is the same word as *holen* (*holly*), which is seen in (*cne*)*holegn* of the present Glossary (for which see *ruscus*) and (*cnio*) *holen* of the Cp. Gloss.; see Bosw. T. (*holen*); the Oxf. D. (*hollin*, *hollen*). The above *holera* suggests the plur. of *holus* (see Steinm. in *Zeitschr. f. d. Alt.* XXXIII p. 249 note), cabbage, colewort.

acrifolus, see *acrifolium*.

acriter, see *alacriter*.

Acron, ciuitas, XLVIII. 25 (*De Cass.*, *Inst.* I. 1, 2 Beelzebub deum *Accaron* consulere destinasset).

actenus, VI. 3, see *eatenus*.

acterabulus, see *acerafulus*.

Actiaco, see *Actio*.

actio, disputatio, XLV. 28 (*Uerba de multis*=*Ars Phocae*, p. 413, 12 *actio*).

Actio, propter [proprium] nomen ciuitatis, XXXV. 256 (*Ruf.* VI. 13 fol. 103[b] in *Actiaco* littore).

actione, VIII. 9, see *Lamuhel*.

actiones, XXX. 60, see *eucharistias*.

actionum, XXX. 8, see *praxeon*.

actiuum, XXIX. 64 (*theoritisen*).

actum, I. 77, see *negotia*; XXVIII. 81, see *per energiam*.

actus, XXVIII. 43, see *caracterismos*.

actuum, see *praxeon*.

acuent [for *acuunt*], XIV. 20, see *scalpellum*.

aculeis, XXXV. 41 [either a different reading for, or a corruption from, *eculeis*], see *in aculeis*.

aculeus, see *aquilius*.

acuta, XXVIII. 16, see *argula*.

acutam, XXXV. 60, see *bibennem*.

acuunt, see *scalpellum*.

ad, II. 10(bis); III. 21; IV. 117(bis); VIII. 17, 19; IX. 5; XI. 11, 14; XII. 35, 45; XIII. 1(bis); XIV. 32; XV. 48; XVI. 9; XXI. 19; XXV. 8; XXVII. 4; XXVIII. 56, 58, 68; XXXV. 61, 156(bis); XXXVI. 1; XXXVII. 9 (bis); XXXIX. 14, 19; XL. 8(bis); XLI. 1; XLIV. 7, 9, 11, 16 (bis), 25.

ad aestum, see *uitulam consternantem*.

adamans; **adamantino**, XIV. 9, see *in unge adamantino*.

adbreuiatio, XLVI. 31, see *epitorta*.

adclamatio, XXVIII. 65, see *epiphonima*.

ad coemetoria, ad ecclesia [!], IV. 117, see *coementeria*.

adcola et acola idem sunt, XIII. 55 (*Isai.* LIV. 15 *accola* veniet).

adcommodentur, see *accommodentur*.

addenda [-do], XXVIII. 31, see *ausesis*.

addicans, addicens, see *abdicans*.

addicitur, damnatur, XXXVII. 17 (*S. Aug.*?). See *Thes. Ling. Lat.* I. 575, 46–9.

adduc, VIII. 20, see *offer*.

adductus, XXXV. 149, see *consulari delectus*.

Adepiades [for *Asclepiades*?], proprium [nomen] uiri, XXXVIII. 14 (*Clem.*), see *Calistratus*.

adeptus, consecutus indeptus, I. 9 (*De Canon.*; *Can. Conc. Carth.* LIII dominatu *adepto*). Cf. *adeptus*, adsecutus, Cp. A197; *adeptus*, consecutus, Ef.[2] 261, 8.

adesse, I. 52, see *exhibere*.

adfecit, distauit, XLVIII. 30 (*De Cass.*, *contra Nest.* V. 1 sacrilegii iniuria deum *afficit*). *distauit* for *ditauit*? see also *afficit*.

adfectanda, adficienda, XLVIII. 34 (*De Cass.*, *Inst.* I. 10 illa...a nobis quoque *adfectanda* censemus). See ibid. *adfectatis*, I. 2, 1; *adfectatur*, IV. 14; *adfectare*, VII. 12; *adfectanda*, id. *Conl.* I. 8. 1.

adficienda, XLVIII. 34, see *adfectanda*.

adfirmant, XXXIII. 6, see *stater*.

adfirmatio, XXXV. 129, see *adstipulatio*; see also (XL. 8) *ad infirmationem*.

adflictio, xx. 11, see *angor.*
adflixit, xxix. 52, see *ecacusen.*
adhibenda, prestanda [praest-], ii. 19 (*Bened. reg.* 36, 2 cura...*adhibenda* est).
adiacens, xli. 5, see *diocesis.*
adiacentia, see *diocesis.*
adiaciens, i. 36, see *diocesis.*
adiectum [for *adiectiuum*?], xliv. 12, see *clima.*
adigent, surgentes, iv. 112 (*Ruf.* iii. 6 fol. 36[b] praeacutas sudes per...verenda *adigentes*). Therefore leg. *adigentes*, urgentes; cf. id. v. 16, fol. 86[a] daemone... *adigente.*
adigentes, see *adigent.*
ad ilicem, genus rubri [rubi], xxxv. 90, see *ilix* (for *ilex*).
ad infirmationem, ad stibulationem suscitationem, xl. 8 (*Uerba*?). Perhaps leg.: *adfirmationem, adstipulationem, sustentationem.* See *adstipulatio*; *adstipulatione* sub voce *stipulatio.*
adipe, xiv. 5, see *placentas.*
aditum, introitum, ii. 18 (*Bened. reg.* 29, 8 [12] reuersionis *aditum* denegari).
adiutoria, xxxv. 115, see *amminicula.*
adiutoribus, xxxv. 212, see *fautoribus.*
adiutoriis, iv. 115, see *auspiciis.*
adiutorio, iv. 26, see *adstipulatione.*
adiutorium, xxxv. 137, see *sumptu puplico*; xxxix. 24, see *aduocatus.*
ad leuicandum, leuem facere, xv. 48 (*Ezech.* xxi. 11 dedi eum *ad leuigandum*).
adloquens, xxxv. 109, see *perorans.*
adluuio, lauatio, xix. 34 (*Job* xiv. 19 *alluvione*...terra consumitur).
adminicula, see *amminicula.*
administrare, ii. 78, see *fungi.*
ad missas, ad[fi]nitas, ii. 10, see *missas.*
admittere, exequere [=exequi, see Georges, *Wörterb.*], i. 10 (*De Canon.*; *Decret. Innoc.* li Nos....nouerit vestra dilectio, haec penitus non *admittere*).
adnisus, conatus, i. 11 (*De Canon.*; *Can. Conc. Calch.* xii qui hoc *adnisus* fuerit); see nisus, conatus, Cp. N104.
adnuntiatur, xxxv. 287, see *adseueratur.*
adolantur, adolator, see *adolatur.*
adolatur, plandus [for *blandus*?] adsentatur, ii. 23 (*Bened. reg.* 65, 17 hi...dum *adolantur* [32 *adulantur*] partibus). If the Glossator meant adulatur, *plandus* may be read as *blanditur*, or, perhaps, *plaudit*; if adulator, adsentatur should be adsentator. Cf. adsentator, adolator, blanditor, Cp. A258; ads-, ad-, blanditur, Ep. 4A29; adserator, adolator blanditur, Ef.[1] 344, 13; adsentatur, adolatur, blanditur, Ef.[2] 261, 38.
adolescentulae, see *aduliscentulę.*
adolescere, xlviii. 72, see *coalescere.*
Adonai, dominus exercituum uel omnipotens, xxi. 17 (*Judith* xvi. 16 *Adonai* Domine). Cf. *Adonai*, adoneus dominus, Cp. Int. 1.
ador, genus frumenti, xlv. 15 (*Uerba de multis*=*Ars Phocae*, p. 416, 9 hoc *ador*) =a-, genus farao frumenti, Cp. A243; *a*-, g. uarris uel frumenti, Ep. 5C20; *a*-, g. farris uel f-, Ef.[1] 346, 45. Cf. Non. 53 *ador* frumenti genus.
adortus, inchoans exortari, xxxv. 44 (*Ruf.* viii. 17 fol. 145[a] virgines...*adortus*; cf. *id.* vii. 25 fol. 126[b]: *adortus*que eum).
adpetitus, see *gastrimargia.*
adponimus, xxviii. 79, see *epexergasia.*
adquisitum, xxxiv. 42, see *indeptum.*
Adriano; **Adriatico**, xxxix. 20, see *in mare adriatico.*
adrogantia, iv. 46, see *procacia.*
adscitus, inuitatus, xlviii. 2 (*De Cass., Inst.* xii. 21, 1 Ioas...*adscitus* in regnum).
adsecla, minister, xlv. 21 (*Uerba de multis*=*Ars Phocae*, p. 412, 21 hic *assecla*). Cf. *adsaeclum*, þegn, minister turpitudinis, Cp. A209; *adsaeculam*, thegn, Ep. 2E29; adsexulam, degn, Ef.[1] 341, 33.
adsecutus, see *adeptus.*
ad seduforum, pro similitudinem fori, iii. 21 (*S. Mart. Stor.*=*Sulp. Sev. Dial.* iii. 14, 1 *ad pseudoforum*; pseudothyrum *in note*).
adsentator, see *adolatur.*
adsentatur [for *adsentator*?], ii. 23, see *adolatur.*
adserator, see *adolatur.*
adseueratur, adnuntiatur, xxxv. 287 (*Ruf.* ix. 3 fol. 148[a] *asseueratur*...deus... dedisse responsa).
adsignato, tradito uel deputato, ii. 21 (*Bened. reg.* 42, 15 [24] in *adsignato* sibi commisso).
ad stadium, ad locum certaminis, xxxv. 156 (*de Eus.*), see *stadium.*
ad stibulationem, xl. 8 [for **adstipulationem**?], see *ad infirmationem* (for adfirmationem?). See *stipulatio.*
adstipulatio, confirmatio, xxxv. 11 (*De Eus.*); **adstipulatio**, adfirmatio, xxxv. 129 (*De Eus.*); **adstipulatione**, adiutorio, iv. 26 (*Eccl. Hist.*); **adstipulatione**, congregatione, xxxix. 70 (*not* Greg. Dial., but *Can. Conc. Carth.*), see *stipulatio.*
adtentos, xix. 45, see *adtonitos.*
adtonitis, intentis, ii. 1 (*Bened. reg.*, Prol. 20 [28] *adtonitis* auribus).—**adtonitos**, adtentos, xix. 45 (*Job* xv. 12 *attonitos* habes oculos). Cf. *adtonitus*, hlysnende,

Cp. A228; *attoniti*, hlysnende, afyrhte, id. 876; *attonitus*, intentus, Ef.[2] 269. 13.

adtonitos, adtentos, XIX. 45; see *adtonitis.*

adtracto, breui, XXXV. 85 (*Ruf.* XI. 26 fol. 190[a] *attracto* collo).

adtributa, II. 56, see *exhibita.*

aduenientes, XXXV. 127, see *aduentantes.*

aduentantes, aduenientes, XXXV. 127 (*Ruf.* II. 25 fol. 33[b]: ambo...simul *aduentantes*).

aduersariis, XXVIII. 70, see *sinchrisis.*

aduersitates, XXXV. 222, see *controuersię.*

adulantur, see *adolatur.*

adulator, see *adolatur.*

aduliscentulę, ecclesię uel animę de numero gentium, X. 7 (*Cant.* I. 2 *adolescentulae* dilexerunt te).

adulter, XLIII. 8, see *nepus.*

adultera, XLIII. 6, see *notha.*

adulterio, XI. 5, see *uitulamina*; XVI. 14, see *ex latere regni.*

adulteriorum, XLVIII. 6, see *flagitiorum.*

adulti, maturi, XLVIII. 73 (*De Cass.*, *Inst.* VI. 13 *adulti*...ualidiores insurgent). Cf. *adulti*, inmaturi, Cp. A191; Ep. 2A4; Ef.[1] 339, 48; *adultus*, maturus, Cp. A192; Ep. —, Ef. —.

adunata, XXVIII. 19, see *sympsalma.*

aduocatus, dicitur qui uocatur in adiutorium alicuius causa uel per pecuniam idest dingere, XXXIX. 24 (*Greg. Dial.* IV. 26 col. 360[A] quidam *advocatus* qui...defunctus est). = *aduocatus*, þingere, Cp. A283; cf. Napier 2587. For *dingere*, þingere (an advocate, intercessor), see Bosw. T. in voce *þingere*; cf. Steinm. II. 244, 13.

adusque, VI. 30, see *quoad.*

aduta, occulta, XXXV. 227 (*Ruf.* XI. 24 fol. 188[b] in illis, quę dicebant ἄδυτα).

adytis, see *editus*; *hierufontis.*

ae for diphth., used XXX. 37, otherwise usually *e* or *ę*;—for *e*: ac*ae*tum (for ac*e*tum); *ae*cclesie (for eccl-); *ae*thimologia (etym-); c*ae*leuma (cel-); u*ae*na (uena); u*ae*ne (uenae);—for *e* (for *i*): l*ae*tania (letania = l*i*t-);—for *oe*: c*ae*mentaria (c*oe*meteria).

aecclesie [ecclesiae], XXXV. 198, see *abiurari.*

aedem, see *mansionarius.*

aedificant, see *perpendiculum.*

aeditionis, for *editionis* (q.v.).

aediti regis, see *editus.*

aeditui, ostiarii, XXXV. 99 (*Ruf.* I. 4 fol. 9[a] filius, templi Apollinis *aeditui*; I. 6 fol. 11[a] cuiusdam *aeditui* filium). = *aeditui*, hostiarii, Cp. A325; Ep. 3C18; Ef.[1] 342, 41; *editui*, hostiarii, Cp. E42; Ep. —; Ef.[1] 359, 3. See also *editus.*

aegre, see *egre.*

Aegypti, Aegyptiaca, -ptiorum, -pto, see *Egypti &c.*

aemulationes, see *emulatione.*

aemulum, eiusdem rei studiosum quasi imitatorem, I. 12 (*De Canon.*; *Vetus Defin. fidei Conc. Chalc.*, ap. Mans. VII. 750[E] hunc...adversus *æmulum* nobis concessit principem). Cf. Isid. *Etym.* X. 7 (*aemulus*, eiusdem rei studiosus quasi imitator); *aemulus*, imitator, Cp. A293 and Ef.[2] 262, 30.

Aeneae, see *centaurus.*

aeneum, XI. 10, see *signum.*

aeoytyerosen, see *deuterosin.*

aephi, see *ephi.*

aequali, see *ęquali.*

aera, XXXV. 226, see *in chaos.*

aerabulus, see *acerafulus.*

aeramento, see *cacabus*; *olla*; *speties ęris.*

aere, XIII. 7, see *discriminalia*; see also *electrum.*

aerea, see *urceos.*

aeri, haue, XXII. 3 (*Esther* I. 6 pendebant ex omni parte tentoria *aerij* coloris) = Cp. A356 (*aeri*, iacintini; with which cf. below *iacyntini*). For *haue* (blue, azure) see Bosw. T. (*hæwen*); Oxf. Dict. (*haw*, a.); Steinm. I. 488, 7; and the present Glossary XXII. 6 (iacyntini, syitor heuuin).

aerii, see *aeri.*

aerii uirgae, see *pusti.*

aeris, see *speties ęris.*

aeste [for *aestuantem*?], XIV. 34, see *uitulam....*

aestimant [text *existimant*], XLIV. 9, see *cęlum.*

aestiuo, see *opago tempore.*

aestuantem (?); aestum, see *uitulam consternantem.*

aethimologia, proprietate, XXX. 56 (*Cat. Hier.* LXIII col. 675[A] Hebraica *etymologia*; B: hebraica *ethimologia*; C: hebraica [blank]) = *ethimologia*, proprietas, Cp. E318; Ep. —; *ethomologia*, proprietas, Ef.[1] 358, 29.

aetilogia, idest cause redditio quoties promisse rei ratio decora subiungitur, XXVIII. 46 (*Cass. Psalm.* XV. 10 figura... *ætiologia*, id est causæ r.q. præmissæ rei r.d.s.).

aetiologia, see *aetilogia.*

affatibus, dictis, XXXV. 191 (*Ruf.* VII. 11 fol. 120[a]...dignis remuneratur *affatibus*).

affer, see *offer.*

afficit, ditauit, IV. 118 (*Eccl. Istor.*); **afficit**, amauit uel onorauit [hon-], XXXV. 87 (*De Euseb.*) = (*Ruf.* IX. 4 fol. 148[a] multisque eos...muneribus *praeficit*). Cacciari,

p. 512 muneribus *afficit*, adding, in not., "Vulgati *praeficit*." Cf. *Ruf.* ix. 10 fol. 156ª paribus suppliciis *afficit*; *afficit*, amauit honorat, Cp. A370. See also above *adfecit*, distauit (for ditauit?). For *afficit* (xxxv. 181), see also *regio morbus*.

Affricana [Afr-], xxxix. 51, see *byssus*.

Affrice, see *sinphosin*.

age, uelociter, xxxv. 8 (*Ruf.* ii. *prooem.*, fol. 18ª *Age* iam nunc). = Cp. A404. See also *auo*.

agellis, terre [-rae] partes, xxxv. 268 (*Ruf.* vi. 7 fol. 100ª in...*agellis* secretioribus); **agellum**, agrum, iii. 25 (*S. Mart. Stor.* = *Sulp. Sev. Dial.* ii. 12, 2 praeter *agellum*...praeteriret); **in agillo**, in agro, xxviii. 2 (*Lib. Anton.* iii col. 128ᴬ erat... *in agello* vicino senex).

agello, xxviii. 2, see *agellis*.

agellum, agrum, iii. 25 (*S. Mart. Stor.*), see *agellis*.

aggerem, congregationem de lignis uel lapidibus, xvi. 21 (*Dan.* xi. 15 comportabit *aggerem*).—**per aggerem** [sine interpret. ?], iii. 14 (*De S. Mart. Stor.* = *Sulp. Sev. Dial.* 2, 3, 2 interim *per aggerem* publicum plena militantibus uiris fiscalis raeda ueniebat).—**riui aggerum**, congregatio aquarum, xiii. 32 (*Isai.* xix. 6 siccabuntur *rivi aggerum*).

aggerum, xiii. 32, see *riui aggerum*, sub v. *aggerem*.

agillo [for *agello*], xxviii. 2, see *in agillo* sub v. *agellis*.

agiografa, sancta scriptura, xvi. 23 (*Dan.*, *Praef. Hieron.* p. xvi.ᵇ qui *hagiographa* conscripserunt..., et in *hagiographa*; Migne xxviii col. 1294ᴬ 'Ἁγιόγραφα). = *agiographae*, sancta scriptura, Cp. A381; Ep. 2C19; *agograffa*, s.s., Ef.[1] 340, 45. The Cambr. MS.: *agiographa*, idest sancta scriptura.

agit, xix. 5, see *eschematismenos*; xxviii. 83, see *ennoematice*.

agitatus, iii. 28, see *nutabundus*.

agitur, iv. 47, see *stadium*; xxxix. 42, see *altare*.

agno, xxxv. 144, see *enixa est*.

agnomen, viii. 9, see *Lamuhel*.

agnum, xxxv. 144, see *enixa est*.

agon, see *diatripas*.

agoniare, certare, xii. 43 (*Eccles.* iv. 33 Vulg.: pro iustitia *agonizare* pro anima tua). Sab., in note, *agoniare* from MS. S. Germ. 15.

agonizare, see *agoniare*.

agora, foras, xxix. 57 (*Uerb. Interpr.* = *Hier. in Matth.* xi. 16 col. 73ᴮ sederunt in foro, sive ἐν ἀγορᾷ).

agrestes, xiii. 35, see *uiciam*.

agri, xxvii. 28, see *in georgicis*.

Agrippa, qui in pedes nascitur eius natura, xliii. 13 (*De div. nominibus* = Donati *Ars gramm.*, p. 376, 11 *Agrippa*) = *Agrippa* (Agrippago, Ef.[2] 263, 29) q.i.p.n. Cp. A392; Ep. 4C19; Ef.[1] 344, 44.—*eius natura* for *contra naturam*? see Non. 556 Agrippae, qui cum labore matris eduntur, hoc est per pedes *contra naturam* &c.; cf. Loewe, *Prodr.* 396.

agris, xli. 1, see *presbiteri*.

agro, xxviii. 2, see *in agillo* sub v. *agellis*.

agrum, iii. 25, see *agellum* sub v. *agellis*.

Agustini [Aug-], xxxvii *tit.*

aiatkibas, see *diatripas*.

aides, **pluto** diuitię, xxxviii. 39 (*Clem. Rom. Recognitt.* x. 32 quia invisibilis facta est, *Aides* appellata est, qui et Orcus vel *Pluto* nominatur; x. 18 filius quem *Aiden* appellarunt). See Goetz, vi. 510 (*Hades*).

alabastrum, proprium nomen lapidis et uas sic nominatur de illo lapide factum, xxiv. 13 (*Math.* xxvi. 7 mulier habens *alabastrum* unguenti) = *alabastrum*, uas de gemma propri nomen lapidis et uas nominat de illo lapide factum, Cp. A442; *a*-, uas de gemma, Ep. 2C27; Ef.[1] 340, 53.

alacriter [for *acriter*], sine gratia, amariter, xii. 13 (*Eccles.* xviii. 18 stultus *acriter* improperabit). The Cambridge MS.: *echariter* sine gratia idest amariter.

alae, genus ludi, xxxix. 60 (*not* Greg. Dial., but *Can. Apostt.* xlii); see *alea*.

alauda, see *tilaris*.

alba, xxxix. 51, see *byssus*.

albo, xxiv. 5, see *mocum*.

albri, uas apium, vi. 12 (*Breu. exsol.* ?).

album, xii. 19, see *calbanus*.

alcianus, arbores frangit, xliv. 24 (*Alia; de cœlo* = Isid. *de nat. rerum* xxxvii. 5 col. 1008 duo...spiritus magis quam venti, aura et *altanus*). See *alcanus* (for *alt*-), boden, Cp. A482. For þoden, see Bosw. T. in v.

alea, ludum tabulę a quodam mago, i. 2 (*De Canon.*); **alae**, genus ludi, xxxix. 60 (*not* Greg. Dial., but) = (*Can. Apostt.* xlii Episcopus...*aleae*...deseruiens; ib. xliii tit. si permanserint in *alea*).—**alea**, tebl, xlv. 25 (*Uerba de multis*). This latter gloss (which = *alea*, tebl, Cp. A414; *a.*, teblae, Ep. 1A36; *a.*, tefil, Ef.[1] 338, 19; Ef.[3] 273, 18) seems to be merely a further explanation of *aleo* (q.v.) in *Ars Phocae*, p. 413, 5.—For *tebl* (from Lat. *tabula*, *a board* for the playing of a game, and *a game* played on such a board), see Bosw. T. (*tæfl*).—See *alea*, prodigus, Cp. A465; Ep. 4C29; Ef.[1] 344, 54; Ef.[2] 264, 3 (adding *origine*); Ef.[3] 269, 12.—Cf. Landgraf, in *Arch. f. L. L.* ix. 362, 363.

aleae, see *alea.*

aleator, ludor cupiditatis, i. 1 (*Can. Apostt.* xlii tit. Quod Episcopus...*aleator*...esse non debeat) = a-, lusor c., Cp. A466; Ep. 4C30; Ef.[2] 264, 5; *a-*, lussor c., Ef.[1] 344, 55. See also *aleo.*

alectat, for *allectat*, q.v.

aleo, teblheri, xlv. 24 (*Uerba de multis = Ars Phocae*, p. 413, 5 hic ganeo *aleo* labeo). *teblheri = tæflere*, a gamester, dicer, see Bosw. T. Glogger suspects the *h* to have arisen from a long ſ (for *Saxonice*?) above the line. See *aleator*, teblere, Cp. A416; Ep. 1A37; Ef.[1] 338, 20. See also *aleator.*

alga, uuac, xlvii. 23 (*Alia* = ?) = *alga*, paar, Cp. A434; *a-*, [paar, corr. to] uaar, Ep. 2A28; *a-*, uar, Ef.[1] 340, 15. For (*uuac*, wrongly for) *uuar* = wār (sea-weed, waur, *wore*), see Bosw. T. (*wār*); Oxf. Dict. (ore[5]); Napier, 23, 13.

alia, xiii. 11; xv. 36; xliv *tit.*; xlvi *tit.*; xlvii *tit.*, 28.

(aliae), xxix. 56.

aliarum, x. 21.

alias, alibi uel interdum uel nonnumquam, i. 4 (*De Canon.*; *Can. Conc. Nicaen.* i inueniuntur...*alias* dignissimi; ib. ii per necessitatem aut *alias* cogentibus hominibus). See also (ii. 157) *sin alias*; (xxxv. 143) *per metalla.*

alibi, i. 4; xxxiii. 7.

alicuius, i. 77, see *negotia*; xxxix. 24, see *aduocatus.*

alię [-ae], xxix. 56.

alienam, i. 84, see *peruadere.*

alienatis, ii. 136, see *priuatis.*

alii, xxxiii. 6, 16.

aliis, ii. 149; iii. 56; xxxii. 2.

alimentis, cibis, ii. 20 (*Bened. reg.* 37, 6 [8] in *alimentis*).

alio, xxiii. 13, see *nemias.*

alioquin, ii. 158, see *si quo minus.*

aliqua, xxviii. 38.

aliquam, xxviii. 51, 55.

aliquando, xii. 9, see *cacabus*; xliv. 11, see *clima.*

aliquem, xxviii. 26.

aliqui, xiii. 43; xliv. 11.

aliquibus, xxxii. 3.

aliquid, xxii. 12; xxviii. 74.

aliquis, xxviii. 43.

aliter, i. 117; ii. 157. For *alter*? see (xiv. 11) *perdix.*

aliud, iv. 17; xix. 5 (bis); xxviii. 39 (bis), 53 (bis).

alium, xxviii. 44.

allectat, expectat, i. 8 (*De Canon.*; cf. *Can. Conc. Calched.* iii quidam, qui in clero uidentur *allecti*). = *alectat*, spectat, Cp. A470; Ep. 4C34; Ef.[1] 344, 59; *all-*, Ef.[2] 264, 17; see Steinm. *AHG.* ii. 101. 1 (allecti, electi).

allecti, see *allectat.*

allegare, allegaremus, allegarentur, allegat, allegatum, allegauerunt, see *alligare.*

allegoria, idest inuersio aliud dicens aliud significans, xxviii. 39 (*Cass. Psalm.*, praef. vii schema...*allegoria*, i. i. a. d. a. s.; see also xxxi. 13). **allegoria**, figuralis dictio, xxix. 1 (*Uerb. Int.* = *Hier. Comm. in Matth.* xi. 16 col. 73[A] *allegoriæ* interpretatio). = *allegoria*, figuralis dictio aliud dicere et aliud intelligere, Cp. A413.

allegoriae, see *allegoria.*

alleluia, laudate dominum siue pater filius spiritus sanctus, ii. 7 (*Bened. reg.* 9, 20 cum *Alleluia* [32 all-]; id. 11, 15 [23]). Cf. *A.*, laudate dominum, Cp. Int. 19; Eucher. *Instructt.* 145, 12.

allidentem, xiv. 28, see *sternentem* sub v. *stratores.*

alligare [*allegare*], insinuare mittere, i. 7 (*De Canon.*; cf. *Can. Concil. Afric.*, Praef. p. 142[a] proferatur commonitorium quod fratres...in actis...*allegauerunt*; xlvii *allegaremus* scripta; xcvi cum...legationes diuersarum prouinciarum *allegarentur*; cvi *alleget*; cxxxiv p. 171[b] *allegatum*). Cf. *allegat*, insinuat, mittit, Cp. A473; Ep. 4C37; Ef.[1] 345, 3; Ef.[2] 264, 22; *allegare*, uerba imperatoris ad iudicem ciuitatis mittere, Cp. A457; Ep. 3C34, 35 (*alligare*); Ef.[1] 342, 57 (*alligare*).

alluvione, see *adluuio.*

almenta, alerholt, xlvii. 101 (*Alia* = ?) = *alneta*, alerholt, Cp. A433; *almeta*, alter holt, Ep. 2A27; *almeta*, alerholt, Ef.[1] 340, 14. (*Almenta*, for) *alneta* (*alnus*, an alder), a place full of alders, an alder-wood = *aler-holt*, for which see Bosw. T. (*aler-*, *alor-holt*); Kluge, *Wrtb.* (*erle*).

almeta, alneta, see *almenta.*

alnus, alaer, xlvii. 99 (*Alia* = ?) = *a-*, aler, Cp. A428; Ef.[1] 340, 3; *a-*, alaer, Ep. 2A16. For *alaer*, *aler*, the alder, see Bosw. T. (*aler*, *alor*); Kluge, *Wrtb.* (*erle*).

aloe, x. 18, see *murra.*

alta, xxxv. 34; xxxix. 42.

altanus, see *alcianus.*

altare, dicitur quod alta res idest diuina in eo agitur, xxxix. 42 (*Greg. Dial.* iii. 17 col. 264[B] ab *altaris* crepidine; ib. iii. 3 col. 224[B] ab *altari* exiens).

altari, altaris, see *altare.*

alter, xiv. 11, see *perdix*; xliv. 7 (bis), see *poli.*

altera, xiv. 20, see *scalpellum.*

alternandis, inuicem, xl. 5 (*Uerba*?).

alterum, xv. 3; xxix. 56; xliv. 8 (bis).

altilia, saginata de auibus tantum dicitur, xxiv. 10 (*Math.* xxii. 4 *altilia* occisa sunt). Cf. *altilia*, foedils, Cp. A467; *a.*, uolatilia, Ef.[2] 264, 61, and Goetz vi. 55 (*altilis*).

altior, xv. 29; xxiii. 17.

altioribus, xvi. 17, see *castrum*.

alueum, see *uertigo*.

alueus, see *suricus*.

aluginatio, xi. 3, see *lanugo*.

Amana et **libanus sanir** et **hermon** montes sunt, x. 14 (*Cant.* iv. 8 Vulg.: veni de *Libano*...veni coronaberis de capite *Amana* de vertice *Sanir* et *Hermon*).

amarescit, viii. 17, see *nitrum*.

amariter, xii. 13, see *alacriter*.

amarum, xxv. 2, see *murratum*.

amator, xxx. 10, see *pylominos*.

amatorem, xxix. 70, see *spodasten*.

amatores, see *philuluguis*.

amatorie, ars philophie [philophiliae?], iv. 44 (*Ruf.* iv. 8 fol. 56[b] perorabat de *amatoriis*).

amatoriis, see *amatorie*.

amatoris [for *amatores*], xxx. 24, see *philuluguis*.

amauit, xxxv. 87, see *afficit*.

amazones, semiuste[-tae], xxxvi. 15 (*Oros.* i. 15, 3 feminas...nutriunt inustis... dexterioribus mammillis...unde *Amazones* dictae; i. 2, 50 regio...*Amazonum*; i. 21, 2 *Amazonum* gentis incursus).

Ambianensium, see *Ambiensium*.

Ambiensium, provintie [-ciae], iii. 2 (*De S. Mart. Stor.*=*Sulp. Sev. Vit. S. Mart.* 3, 1 in porta *Ambianensium* ciuitatis).

ambieres, munieres, xxxvii. 11 (*S. Aug.*?).

ambigua, xxviii. 61, see *amphibolia*.

ambitum, perh. for (per)*ambulabat*, xvii. 7, see *Niniue*.

ambone, analogio, i. 5 (*De Canon.*; *Can. Conc. Laod.* cxviii tit. in *ambone*, id est in pulpito).

ambonem, v. 11, see *labrum*.

ambrones, deuoratores, vi. 7 (*Breu. ex-sol.*?)=*ambrones*, deuoratores, Ep. 2A6 & 4E17; Ef.[1] 339, 50 & 345, 21; Ef.[2] 265, 9; cf. *ambrones*, gredge, Cp. A519. Much has been said on the meaning and derivation of the lemma; see DuC., in voce *ambro*; Forcellini, in his Lex. and Onomast. Sonny (*Arch. f. Lat. Lex.* x. 366) sees in *ambrones* the Gr. Ἄβρων (from ἁβρός) of the Gr. proverb Ἄβρωνος βίος (Suid. s. v.; *Paroemiogr. Gotting.* i. pp. 2, 180). Cf. Heinr. Zimmer, *Nennius Vindicatus*, p. 104, and for interpretations of the word in A. S. see A. S. Napier, *O. E. Glosses* (index).—It may be observed that the Cambridge (1705) and Oxford (1834) editions of Suidas print Ἄβρωνος with the smooth breathing. Liddell & Scott print it in the same way; so also God. Bernhardy in his reprint of the Oxf. edition, but he says in a note leg. Ἅβρωνος (with rough breathing). See also Henr. Stephanus' *Thesaurus Gr. Linguae*, and *Etymol. Magnum*, ed. Gaisford 765, 2. The editors (Leutsch & Schneidewin) of the *Paroemiogr. Graeci* (Gött. 1839) print (pp. 2, 180) the word with the rough breathing in their texts, relegating the reading with the smooth breathing to their notes.

ambulantes, viii. 8, see *in aceruo m-*.

ambulator, xxx. 1, see *peripatthiens*.

ambustum, see *bustus*.

amfibalo, see *anfibula*.

amictalum, arbor nucum, ix. 4 (*Eclesiast.* xii. 5 florebit *amygdalus*; Heyse *migdalum*, *amigdalum* in note). Cf. *amigdalinas*, quidam arbor, Cp. A531.

amicto [-tu], iii. 5, see *amiculo*.

amictu, see *amiculo*.

amiculo, amicto [-tu], iii. 5 (*De S. Mart. Stor.*=*Sulp. Sev. Dial.* i. 15, 7 *amiculo* circumtectus). Cf. *amiculo*, hręgli, Cp. A546; *a.*, hraecli, Ep. 2E8; *a.*, hraegl, Ef.[1] 341, 13, but this more likely from Oros. v. 9, 2 (detracto *amiculo*): see Schlutter in *Arch. f. Lat. Lexic.* x. 366. For *hręgli* &c., a garment, robe, rail, see Bosw. T. (hrægel); Skeat (*rail*[4]).

amigdalum, see *amictalum*.

Aminab, proprium nomen uiri, x. 23 (*Cant.* vi. 11 *Aminadab*).

Aminadab, see *Aminab*.

amissam, i. 110, see *resipiscant*.

amissas, ii. 110, see *missas*.

amminicula, adiutoria, xxxv. 115 (*Ruf.* ii. 13 fol. 24[a] *adminicula*...maiora suppeditans). Cf. *amminiculum*, adiutorium, Cp. A511; Ef.[2] 265, 22.

amopaga, archisinagogus [archisyn-] est, xxxv. 130; see *ariopagitis*.

amore, xxx. 28, see *de philoxenia*; see also *peri pthocheas*.

amphibalo, amphibalum, see *amphibalum*.

amphibalum, coculus, xlii. 18 (*Ex div. libris*); **anfibula**, oberlagu, iii. 11 (*De S. Mart. Storia*=*Sulp. Sev. Dial.* ii. 1, 5 p. 181, 8 intra *amphibalum* sibi tunicam latenter eduxit; indutum *amphibalo*, ib. ii. 1, 7; *amfibalum*, *amphimalum*, *amfibalo*, in note). coculus=cocula (q. v.)=cuculla (q. v.), a mantle. Cf. *amphibalus*, hircus bellosus, Cp. A551; Ep. 3E10; Ef.[1] 343, 13.

amphibolia, idest dictio ambigua dubium faciens pendere sententiam, xxviii. 6

(*Cass. Psalm.* xx. 12 schema...*amphibologia*, id est d. a. dubiam f. p. s.).

amphibologia, see *amphibolia*.

amphimalum, see *amphibalum*.

amphitape, see *abctape*.

amphitheatro, see *amphitheatrum*.

amphitheatrum, circumspectaculum, xxx. 21 (*Cat. Hier.* xvii in *amphitheatro*).

amphora, iii modios, xxxi. 40 (*De ponder.*?). Cf. Blume, i. 376, 9. For *amphora* see also (xxxiii. 10) *batus*; (xxxiii. 11) *chatus*.

amplam, latam, xxxv. 83 (*Ruf.* x. 12 fol. 167b *amplam* temporis...occasionem).

amurca, see *auriculum*.

amussim, see *examussim*.

amygdalus, see *amictalum*.

anacefaleos, recapitulatio, ix. 6 (*Eclesiast.*? Cf. *Cassiod. in Psalm.* cxiii. 22 quae figura dicitur *anacephaleosis idest recapitulatio*; *S. Hier. in Ez.* vii. 36, in Migne's *Patr. Lat.* xxv col. 222D: facta *anacephalæosi*).—**anacefaleosin**, recapitulatio, xxxviii. 21 (*Clem. Recognitt.* viii. 39 *anacephalaeosin* facere eorum quae dicta sunt). Cf. *anacephaleosin*, repetitionem uel recapitulatio, Cp. A628; *an-*, rep-, Ep. 4E28 & Ef.[1] 345, 31 & Ef.[2] 265, 47.

anacephalaeosin, -sis, see *anacefaleos*.

anachoreta, see *anachorita*.

anachorita [-reta], graece heremita [er-], ii. 2 (*Bened. reg.* 1, 4 [5] genus...*anachoritarum*).

anachoritarum, see *anachorita*.

anadiplosis, congeminatio dictionis sermonem geminat ad decorem, xxviii. 68 (*Cass. Psalm.* xxiii. 11 *anadiplosis*...cong. d.; xxiv. 2 per figuram *anadiplosin*, quae Latine dicitur congeminatio d. s. g. a. d.).

anagogen, superior sensus, xxix. 2 (*Uerb. interpr.*=*Hier. Comm. in Matth.* x. 9, 10 col. 63B secundum *anagogen*)= *anagogen*, superior sensus, Cp. A634.

analogio, i. 5, see *ambone*.—**analogium**, lectorium ligneum in quo leguntur libri, ii. 6 (*Bened. reg.* 9, 11 [15] super *analogium*).

anaphora, reuelatio quoties unum uerbum per comatum principia repetitur, quando res secuturę pro preteritis secuntur, xxviii. 72 (*Cass. Psalm.* xxvi. 5 figura...*anaphora*, quoties u. v. per *commatum* p. r.; xliii. 15 per figuram *anaphoram*, quae Latine *relatio* dicitur, verbum ipsum iteratum; lii. 2 *anaphora*, id est *relatio*, quoties u. v. frequenti iteratione repetitur).—quando res sec. &c. belongs to (xxviii. 75) *prolemsis* q. v.

anapxias, anarchias, see *anarchius*.

anarchius, ubi nullius potestas, xxx. 4 (*Cat. Hier.* ii col. 611A occasione ἀναρχίας concilium congregauit; B: occ. *anarchias*, idest principatus conc. cong.; C: occ. *anapxias* conc. cong.; E: αναρκιας, idest sine principatu;—**monarchia**, ubi unius, xxx. 5. This latter gloss is, it seems, a further explanation of the preceding *anarchias*; so also **polarchia**, ubi multorum, xxx. 6. This latter is not in the *Catalogus* at all, but *monarchia* occurs in Chapt. xxiii col. 641 (*monarchia* Dei) and in Ch. xxxv col. 640 (de *monarchia*). The whole=*Anarchias* sine principatu uel ubi nullius potestas; monarchia ubi unius; polarchia ubi multorum, Cp. A591; anarchias sine principatu, Ep. 3C4 and Ef.[1] 342, 26; cf. monarchia, anwald, Cp. M253; Ep. 14C25; E[1]. 371, 4.

anastrophe, idest peruersio quando promimus ordine conuerso sententiam, xxviii. 67 (*Cass. Psalm.* xxiii. 6 *a., id est p.* &c.).

anathema, abhominatio, i. 3 (*De Canon.*; *Can. Conc. Gangr.* lix, lx &c. *anathema* sit; *Conc. Laod.* cxxxii *anathema* sint a Christo) = *anathem*, abhominatio, Cp. A658; cf. *anathema*, abhominabilis deiectus, Cp. A583.—**In anathema**, in obliuione in separatione idest a se uel in dona ad templum, xxi. 19 (*Judith* xvi. 23 Judith universa vasa bellica Holofernis...et conopaeum quod ipsa sustulerat de cubili ipsius obtulit *in anathema oblivionis*).

ancilla, xxi. 6, see *abra*.

ancillis, animalibus figl, xix. 63 (*Job* xl. 24 Numquid illudes ei quasi avi, aut ligabis eum *ancillis* tuis). On this quotation Jerome says (*Exposit. Interlin. libri Job*, Migne *Patr. L.* xxiii col. 1465C): "In tantum Deo humiliabitur draconis istius fortitudo, ut omnino pro nihilo erit, et ab *animabus sanctis* deludetur, quae sunt *ancillae* Christi," and (*Comm. in lib. Job*, Migne, *P.L.* xxvi col. 788D): "Sic itaque alligatur atque illuditur a *sanctis animabus* Dei, quae sunt *ancillae* Christi." These quotations would suggest *animabus* for *animalibus* and *figuraliter* for *figl* (over which the MS. has a stroke) in the Leiden Glossary.—Steinm. (*Zeitschr. f. d. Alterth.* xxxiii. 249) referring to the same gloss, quotes (*Germania* viii. 389) from a Paris MS. (2685, olim Colbert 4951) *ancellis*, annalibus figuli, and regards *figuli* as Latin. But then the gloss would remain unintelligible.—Jerome's translation of the book of Job (Migne, *Patr. Lat.* xxviii col. 1120C) has: "Numquid illudes ei quasi avi [h. passeri] aut ligabis cum [*Al.* eum] *aucillis* [h. puellis] tuis." Migne's *aucillis* (which would=*aucellis*) is printed *ancillis* in

Vallarsius' ed. of 1738 col. 1150. If *aucillis* (little birds) is not a misprint, but actually found in Migne's MS. or MSS., it would agree with the Glossary if we altered *ancillis* into *aucillis*, and regard *figl* (adding some letter or letters to represent the stroke over the *g*) as a form (nom. or oblique?) of the ordinary A.S. *fugel*, *fugol*, *fugul* (a bird).—It is to be noted that the Hebrew has וְתִקְשְׁרֶנּוּ לְנַעֲרוֹתֶיךָ, but the Septuagint *ἢ δήσεις αὐτὸν ὥσπερ στρουθίον* (sparrow) *παιδίῳ* for *aut ligabis eum ancillis tuis* of the Vulg., and Jerome knew this reading of the Sept. as, in his *Comm.*, he says (Migne XXVI col. 789[A]): "Alii dixerunt Alligabis eum sicut *passerem* infantulo, quod est, ab infantulo teneatur praecepto imperii mei, et velut ligatus in potestatem tradetur. Hic est ille infans, de quo Isaias ait: Infans ab ubere in foramine aspidum manum mittet &c." See also Migne, *Patr. Lat.* LXXIII col. 177, note 41. It seems, therefore, clear that there was a Latin text in Jerome's time agreeing with the Sept., and, perhaps, the Glossary refers to this text in the present instance. All the MSS. of the Vulg. at Cambridge, and in the Brit. Mus., which I have examined have *ancillis*.

ancones, untinos [uncinos], XLVII. 4 (*Alia* = ?) = *anconos*, urcenos, Cp. A575; *a*-, uncenos, Ep. 2A32 & Ef.[1] 340, 19.

andeda, brondra, XLVII. 42 (*Alia*=?) =*a*-, brandrod, Cp. A562; *a*-, brandrad, Ep. 1A21; *a*-, brondrad, Ef.[1] 338, 3. For (*andeda*, for) *andena*, a gridiron, see Du C., and Goetz, VI. 68; for *brondrad*, *brandrad*, *brandrod* (=O.N. *brand-reið*, a grate, from *brand-r*, brand, burning + *reið*, carriage, vehicle), see Oxf. D. *brandreth*.

andena, see *andeda*.

androginus [-gynus], XLII. 13, see *hermofroditus*.

anfibula, oberlagu, III. 11, see *amphibalum*.

angariati, portati, II. 17; **angarizanti**, cogenti uel conpellenti, II. 3 (*Bened. reg.* 7, 97 *angarizati* [in note, and 157 *angariati*] milliario vadunt et duo). For *angarizanti* see Edm. Schmidt, *Regula*, p. 20, note *κ*.

angarizanti, cogenti uel conpellenti, II. 3, see *angariati*.

angarizati, see *angariati*.

Ange, see *arge*.

angiportos, nomen porti, IV. 93; **angiportus**, angustus locus, XXXV. 240 (*Ruf.* IX. 8 fol. 151[a] per plateas omnes et *angiportus*) = *angiportus*, angustus locus, Cp. A615; Ep. 2C22. On the *Gen. Sing.* porti, see Lewis & Sh.

angiportus, see *angiportos*.

angor, adflictio, XX. 11 (*Tobias?* not in the Vulg.?). For angor see also (I. 133) *scrupulum*.

anguile [for *anguillae*], XIX. 8, see *murenula*.

anguillae, see *murenula*.

Angulanis, see *Angulinis*.

Angulinis, propert [for *proprium nomen?*] termę calidae, XXXIX. 34 (*Greg. Dial.* IV. 40 col. 397[B] in *Angulanis* thermis lavari debuisset) = *Angulinis*, proprium nomen, Cp. A629.

angulos, XXXVIII. 27, see *tetragono*.

angusti, XIV. 14, see *calati*.

angustiosus, II. 12, see *anxius*.

angustum, XIII. 38, see *artum*.

angustus, XXXV. 240, see *angiportus*.

animae, see *manes*; *psichiexodo*.

animalibus, XIX. 63, see *ancillis*.

anime [-mae], XXIX. 56, see *metempschosis*; XXX. 81, see *psichiexodo*; XLIII. 31, see *manes*.

animę, X. 7, see *aduliscentulę*.

animalus, fifaldae, XLIII. 47 (*De div. nominibus?*). This gloss appears in the Glossary among a number of words occurring in Donati *Ars gramm.*, but the lemma is not found in the printed texts of this work. Glogger suggests that *animalus* may be a corruption for *animulus* (= *ψυχάριον*, dim. of *ψυχή*, a butterfly, Goetz, VI. 71) meant as an interpretation of an omitted lemma *papilio* (Don. *Ars* p. 376, 18). Cf. Cp. P168; Ep. 21A28; Ef.[1] 384, 44; Steinm. IV. 181, 17. For *fifaldae* (butterfly) see Bosw. T. (*fiffealde*, *fiffalde*); Kluge, *Etym. Wrtb. D. Spr.* (*Falter*).

animi, II. 153, see *scrupolositas*; XXVIII. 42, see *idea*.

animo, II. 125, see *magnopere*.

animulus, see *animalus*.

anni, XXXVIII. 35, see *ex diametro*.

anno, IV. 99, see *quadraplas*; XLIII. 34, see *horno*.

anomala, dissimilia, XXVII. 14 (*Lib. Rot.*); **anomala**, inęqualia, XLIV. 20 (*Alia, de cælo*) = (*Isid.*, *Lib. de nat. rer.* XXII. 3 Sidera, aut *anomala* fiunt, aut retrograda; XXIII. 3 *anomala* efficiuntur) = *a*-, dissimilia, Cp. A623 & Ef.[1] 342, 37; *anomalo*, d-, Ep. 3C15.

antarticus [-arcticus], XLIV. 16, see *arcticos*.

ante, IV. 35; X. 6; XXII. 12; XXIII. 10; XXXVI. 1; XXXIX. 22, 56 (bis).

antea, I. 104.

ante absida, ante sedem episcopi, XXXIX. 56; see *absidam*.

antefana, antefanas, antefanis, see *antiphona*.

antefrasin, see *cataantis*.

antelucanos, see *antelucanum*.

antelucanum, ante calli [galli] cantus, iv. 35 (*Ruf.* iii. 32 fol. 50^b *antelucanos* hymnos & vi. 2 fol. 95^a cum...eum...*antelucanum* prorumpere...praesensisset).

antequam, x. 12; xxii. 16 (bis).

antes, dicitur ordo uinearum, xlv. 16 (*Uerba de multis*=*Ars Phocae*, p. 428, 6 hi *antes*).=*a*-, extremi ordines uiniarum, Cp. A626 & Ef.[1] 346, 46; *a*-, extrime ordines uinearum, Ep. 5C21.

antesignano, see *antesignato*.

antesignato, signatore suspectum, iv. 119 (*Ruf.* xi. 22 fol. 187^a deligunt Olympum quendam...quo *antesignano* arcem defenderent). On the gloss cf. Goetz, vi. 75 *antesignanus*, propugnator signorum &c.

antichristus, see *anticristus*.

anticristus [antichr-], viii. 13, see *in sublime*.

antifrasin, see *cataantis*.

Antinoitas, ciuitas in egypto [aeg-], xxxv. 266 (*Ruf.* vi. 9 fol. 100^b epistolis...ad *Antinoitas* scriptis).

antiphona, uox reciproca, ii. 5 (*Bened. reg.* 9, 7 cum *antefana* [8 *antiphona*]); cf. 9, 9 [11] cum *antefanis* [cum *antiphonas*]; xi. 11 [16] cum *antefanas* [cum *antiphonas*]; xii. 4 & xiii. 5 sine *antefana* [*antiphona*] &c.

antiphonas, see *antiphona*.

antiquitatem, xxx. 38, see *archutomam*.

antiquos, xlv. 11, see *ops*.

Antoni [sine interpret.], iii. 52 (*De S. Mart. Stor.*=*Sulp. Sev. Dial.* i. 17, 1 duo beati *Antoni* [*Antonii*, in 3 MSS.] monasteria adii). The Glossary has this word and 14 other glosses under the heading *Uerba de Sancti Martyni Storia*. But, though *Antoni* actually occurs in Sulp. Sev. as above, the word seems to be nothing but the remains of some such heading as "Antoni Vita" or "Antoni Storia" as 11 or 12 of the other glosses following the word *Antoni* are excerpted from this *Vita* (see *Antonii*).

Antonii (In Libro), xxviii tit. (=*Vita B. Antonii Abb.*, auctore S. Athanasio, interpr. Evagrio; Migne, *P. L.* lxxiii.).

anulum fidei, libertatem, xxxv. 218 (*Ruf.* x. 28 fol. 174^a *anulum fidei* recipit) =*anulum* fidei, libertatem fidei, Cp. A616; Ep. 2C23; Ef.[1] 340, 49.

anxietas, ii. 153, see *scrupolositas*; see also *axietas*, in v. *scrupulum*.

anxius, angustiosus, ii. 12 (*Bened. reg.* 64, 30 [54] non sit...*anxius*). Cf. *anxius*, sorgendi, Cp. A617; Ep. 2E3; Ef.[1] 341, 8, and Bosw. T. (*sorgian*).

aoteȝoȝoy, see *psichiexodo*.

Apadno, Apedno, see *Apethno*.

aperiantur, x. 12, see *ficus protulit*.

apertis, xxxv. 231, see *patulis*.

apertus, xxiv. 17, see *clibanus*.

Apethno, proprium nomen loci, xvi. 19 (*Dan.* xi. 45 figet tabernaculum...*Apadno*). Heyse; Sabat., in notes; Migne, xxviii col. 1318^c, and the Cambr. MS. *Apedno*.

apium, vi. 12, see *albri*.

aplestia, see *plestia*.

apo tu ptsaum, a tangendo est inde quidam psalmum uolunt dici cognosce uero quod isti tantum pro excellentia sui dicantur psalmi, xxviii. 18 (*Cass. Psalm.*, Praef. iv col. 15^D ἀπὸ τοῦ ψαύειν, hoc est *a tangendo*; for *cognosce—psalmi*, see id. Praef. iv col. 15^c).

apodoxios, xxx. 75, see *eyaggences a*-.

apoliȝeon, see *eyaggences apod*-.

Apollo, xxvii. 15, see *Mappanus*.

apollogeticus, excusans, iv. 23 (*Ruf.* ii. 18 fol. 29^a *apologeticus* liber).—**apologieticum**, excusabile, xxx. 23 (*Cat. Hier.* xx col. 639^A volumen...*apologeticum* pro Christianis; B: *Apologeticon* idest *excusabilem* p. cristianis; C: *apologeticum* pro cristianis). Cf. ib. lxxv col. 685^A: Scripsit...*Apologeticum* pro Origene; B: *apologeticon*, id est *excusabilem* pro origine; C: *apologeticum* pro origene.—**apologiticum**, excusabilem, xxxv. 153 (*Ruf.* iv. 3 fol. 54^b *Apologeticum* librum obtulit)=apologiticum, excussabilem, Cp. A691; Ep. 3C7; Ef.[1] 342, 29.

apologeticon, see *apologieticum*.

apologeticum, see *apologieticum*, *-giticum*.

apologeticus, see *apollogeticus*.

apologieticum, excusabile, xxx. 23 (*De Cat. Hier.*), see *apollogeticus*.

apologiis, see *apologis*.

apologim, see *apologus*.

apologis [-giis], excusationibus, xlviii. 71 (*De Cass.* ?).—**apologus**, excusationes, xxx. 79 (*Cat. Hier.* lxxxi col. 689^B ἀπολογίας pro Origene libri sex; B: *apologim* pro origine libros sex; C: [blank] pro origene li. vi.)=*apologias*, excusationes, Cp. A693; *a*-, excussationes, Ep. 3C14 & Ef.[1] 342, 36; *apototyas*, excusationes, Cp. A697; *apothias*, excussationes, Ef.[1] 346, 48.

apologiticum, excusabilem, xxxv. 153 (*De Eus.*), see *apollogeticus*.

apologus, excusationes, xxx. 79 (*Cat. Hier.*), see *apologis*.

aporia, abominatio subitania [-nea], xii. 26 (*Eccles.* xxvii. 5 *aporia* hominis in cogitatu illius).

aposiopesis, idest dictio cuius finis reticetur, xxviii. 54 (*Cass. Psalm.* xvii. 46).

apostata, discessus a fide, xix. 64 (*Job* xxxiv. 18 qui dicit regi, *apostata*) = Cp. A692; Ep. 3C13; Ef.[1] 342, 35.

apostatare, retrorsum ire, ii. 8 (*Bened. reg.* 40, 14 [24] uinum *apostatare* facit... sapientes).

apostoli, x. 2, see *ubera*.

apostolos, x. 11, see *tigna*.

apostropei, idest conuersio quoties ad diuersas personas crebro uerba conuertimus, xxviii. 58 (*Cass. Psalm.* xix. 6 figura... *apostrophe* i. c. q. &c.).

apostrophe, see *apostropei*.

apotecas, cellaria, xiii. 45 (*Isai.* xxxix. 2 ostendit...*apothecas* supellectilis suae).

apothecas, see *apotecas*.

apotu [= ἀπὸ τοῦ], see *ypo* (sub) *tyos* (hoc) &c.

apparabilis, ministratio, iii. 46 (*S. Mart. Stor.* = *Sulp. Sev. Dial.* ii. 6, 5 conponitur castus reginae manibus *apparatus*).

apparatus, see *apparabilis*.

apparentibus, xl. 20, see *pallantibus*.

apparitores, see *paritores*.

apparitorium, auditorium [for *auditorum* or *adiutorum*?], xxxv. 10 (*Ruf.* ii. 13 fol. 25[a] ex *apparitorum* suorum numero) = *apparitorium*, adiutorium, Cp. A664; Ep. 1A18; *apparatorium*, adiutorium, Ef.[1] 337, 18.

apparitorum, see *apparitorium*.

appellans, vi. 21, see *conueniens*.

appellant, xiv. 3, see *uorith*.

appetentes, i. 21, see *conpetentes*.

appetitus, xxxiv. 36, see *gastrimargia*.

applicari, xxviii. 34, see *figura m-*.

apponuntur, xxviii. 24, see *ypozeuxis*.

approbationes, xxviii. 71, see *ephichirema*.

appuli, see *appulli*.

appulisse, see *apulisse*.

appulli, huuitabar [for *hinuitabar*, for *inuitabar*?], iii. 15; **appulli**, inuitabant [for *inuitabar*?], iii. 30 (*De S. Mart. Stor.* = *Sulp. Sev. Vita S. Mart., Prol.* 1, 5 cum primum animum ad scribendum *appuli*). Cf. Steinmeyer, in *Zeitschr. f. D. Alt.* xxxiii. 249; see also below *apulisse*.

a primeuo flore, a primo flore barbe, xxxix. 1 (*Greg. Dial.* i *Prol.* col. 149[B] mihi *a primævo* juventutis *flore*...obstrictus).

apta, i. 62, see *idonea*; xxviii. 24, see *ypozeuxis*.

aptet, congruet implet, ii. 16 (*Bened. reg.* 2, 71 [107] Ita se omnibus conformet et *aptet* ut...). Cf. abtet uos, impleat uos Cp. A64; Ep. 3E30; Ef.[1] 343, 33; Ef.[2] 259, 2; aptet uos, impleat uos, Cp. A698.

aptis, ii. 91, see *inconpententibus*.

aptoton, see *aptotum*.

aptotum, inflexibile uel incasale, xliii. 56 (*De div. nominibus* = Donati *Ars grammat.* p. 376, 16 aut trium generum est *aptoton*, ut frugi nihili; in note *aptotum*). *Incasale* for *incasuale*; cf. Hagen *Ars Anon. Bern.* p. 109 unum nomen *aptoton*, hoc est *incasuale*; see *casualis* (Lewis & Sh.).

aptus, ii. 31, see *congruus*.

apud, ii. 189; xvi. 11, 27; xxxii. 2; see also *aput*.

apulisse, pulsasse, iv. 113 (*Ruf.* iii. 24 fol. 46[a] *appulisse* animum traduntur); see above *appulli*.

aput, xliv. 19; xlv. 11; see also *apud*.

aqua, viii. 12, see *uaena*, 14, see *blena*; x. 22, see *areola*; xi. 11, see *in aqua ualebat*; xli. 14, see *byrillus*.

aquae, see *gurgitum*; *sentina*; *taermę*.

aquam, xiv. 36, see *urceos*.

aquarum, xiii. 32, see *riui aggerum*.

aquas, xlvii. 15, see *tappula*.

aquaticus, xxxv. 5, see *hydropicus*.

aque [aquae], xix. 53, see *gurgitum*; xx. 8, see *taermę*.

aquę [aquae], xxxix. 50, see *sentina*.

aquila, see *arpa*.

Aquila dixit **sextarium** iii modios, xxxi. 10, see *sextarius*.

aquilium, see *aquilius*.

aquilius, onga, xlvii. 85 (*Alia* = ?) = *aquilium*, onga, Cp. A715; *a-*, anga, Ep. 2A24 and Ef.[1] 340, 11. Goetz (vi. 20) identifies the lemma with *aculeus*, a sting. For *anga*, *onga* (O.H.G. *ango*), a sting, see Bosw. T. (*onga*).

aquilonem, xliv. 7, see *poli*.

aquiloni, vi. 5, see *boriali*.

aquilonis, xxvii. 33, see *artofilax*.

aquis, xix. 51, see *fabula*; xxvii. 31, see *tethis*.

ara, xvi. 25, see *arioli*.

arachaisitetos, see *archeretoys*.

araneus (mus), see *musiranus*.

aras, xvi. 7, see *aruspices*.

aratoris, xxxv. 75, see *iugeres*.

arbitrantur, xliv. 10, see *cardines*.

arbitror, xxxiii. 7, see *sicel*.

arbor, ix. 3, see *amictalum*; x. 10, see *cyprus*, 17, see *fistola*; xii. 17, see *platanus*; xiii. 48, see *myrtus*; xiv. 10, see *miricę*; xv. 10, see *ebor*; xvi. 4, see *ilicus*, 5, see *lentiscus*; xix. 58, see *iuniper*; xxix. 34, see *nardum*; xxxv. 86, see *busta*; xxxvii. 19, *laurus*. See also *tigna*.

arbor, maest, xxxix. 37 (*Greg. Dial.* iii. 36 col. 304[C] ex navi clavi perditi, *arbor* abscissa est). For *maest* (a pole, mast) see Bosw. T. (*mæst*).

arbore, x. 19, see *gutta*; xiii. 37, see *malus nauis*, 51, see *calamum*; xiv. 6, see *resina*; xv. 14, see *hebenenos*; xxv. 8, see *byssus*.

arbores, xvii. 20, see *myrteta*; xliv. 24, see *alcianus*.

arboribus, xii. 21, see *ungula*.

arboris, xxv. 6, see *de siliquis*.

arborum, x. 11, see *tigna*, 21, see *elatę palmarum*.

arbustis, xxxix. 51, see *byssus*.

arcades, gens dicitur quę colebat pana, xliii. 4, see *Themisto*.

arcadię [-diae], xliii. 3, see *Pan*.

arcae, arce [arcae], xiii. 47, see *plaustrum*.

arcebatur, inpelebatur [inpell-], xxxv. 155 (*Ruf.* iv. 6 fol. 55[b] ab omni regione... *arcebatur*). Cf. *arcebat*, repellebat, Cp. A733.—**arcet**, depulit, xxxv. 105 (*Ruf.* i. 12 fol. 14[a] hunc *arcet* officio). = *arcet*, depulit, Ep. 2C24; Ef.[1] 340, 50; cf. *arcet*, uetat *depulit* prohibet, Cp. A767.

archeretoys, conflictus, xxx. 18 (*Cat. Hier.* xiii col. 629[C] scripsit...libros...duos Ἀρχαιότητος adversum Appionem; B: scr....l....d. *arachaisitetos* idest conflictus adv. app.; C: scr....li....duos [blank] adv. app.; E: αρχηωρηθος). As the Gr. word signifies *antiquity*, the notion of the gloss "conflictus" refers, perhaps, to the word "adversum."—By this passage we have the key to Cp. A725 *archioritas* conflictus (= Cp. A812 and Ep. 3C20 *arcoretos* conflictus), and Ef.[1] 342, 43 *arcoretos* conflictos, and Cp. A779 and Ef.[1] 346, 47 *archioretis* libros duo = Ep. 5C22 archioretys libros duo.

archikronan, see *archutomam*.

archimandritis, see *arcimandritis*.

archis [for *arx Sion*?], xxiii. 17, see *ciuitas dauid*.

archisinagogus [archisyn-], xxxv. 130, see *amopaga* sub v. *ariopagitis*.

archisynagogus, see *amopaga* sub v. *ariopagitis*.

archutomam, antiquitatem uel principatum, xxx. 38 (*Cat. Hier.* xxxviii col. 653[B] qui in similitudinem Josephi ἀρχαιογονίαν Moysi et Judaicae gentis asseverant; B: qui i. s. iosephi *archikronan* idest principio temporum moysi et iudaice gentis asseruerint; C: qui i. s. iosephi [blank] m. et i. g. asseuerant) = *arxhotanian*, a. uel p., Cp. A811; *arxhotoniam*, a. u. p., Ep. 3C8, and *arcsotonian*, antiquitatum, 3C21; *arcxotonian*, a. u. p., Ef.[1] 342, 30 and *arcsotoniam*, antiquitatum, Ef.[1] 342, 44. For *principatum* we have to read, it seems, *principia temporum*, which is found in text B (*principio t.*), and in F (*principia t.*).

arcimandritis [sine interpretat.], i. 14 (*De Canon.* = *Decret. Horm.* iv tit., fol. 271[b] Hormisda presbyteris...*archimandritis*); cf. *archimandrita*, princeps ouilium, Ef.[2] 267, 25.

arcticos, septentrionalis ab arcto adiectum [adiectiuum?], xliv. 12; **Terinos**, idest bestialis, xliv. 13; **isemerinus**, idest meridianus, xliv. 14; **Exemerinus**, ac si ex meridię [-die] remotior, xliv. 15; **antarticus**, artico [arct-] contrarius horum primus qui est erga arcturum a polo poreo [boreo] iiii murorum [moerorum] spatiis distat a quo secundus u ab eo iii ui Item ab eo iiii ui muris [moeris] distat Item u circulus u spatiis ab eo ad polum australem iiii idest ad uerticem iiii sunt moera spatiis ut figunt astrogi [astrologi], xliv. 16 (*Alia*; *de cælo* = Isid. *de nat. rerum* x. 1, col. 978 circulus *Arcticus*... circulus *Therinus*...circulus *Isemerinus*... circulus *Chimerinus*...circulus *Antarcticus*...; 2 *Horum primus* septentrionalis est). Cf. also Isid. *Etym.* xiii 6, 2—6.

arcticus, see *arcticos*.

arcto, xliv. 12, see *clima*.

arctophylax, see *artofilax*.

arctum, see *artum*.

arcturum, septentrio, xix. 33 (*Job* ix. 9 Qui facit *Arcturum*; cf. ibid. xxxvii. 9 *Arcturo*; xxxviii. 31 *Arcturi*) = *archturus*, septem, Cp. A742. See also (xliv. 16) *antarticus*.

ardea, see *perdulum*.

ardenter [for *ardore*?], xxix. 41, see *caumate*.

ardentes, iv. 106, see *candentes*.

ardentissimo, ii. 79, see *feruentissimo*.

ardet, xxxix. 15, see *ferula*.

ardia, see *perdulum*.

ardore, see *caumate*.

ardua, xliv. 21, see *conuexa*.

area sitiens, siccans in tritura, xvii. 1 (*Joel* i. 20 *area sitiens*).

arenae, see *calculus*; *harene*; *sabuli*.

arene [-nae], xv. 20, see *sabuli*.

arenę, xii. 12, see *calculus*.

arenosa, iii. 33, see *in sirtim*.

areola, dicitur ubi aqua diriuatur [der-] in ortum [hort-] et stat in modico stagnello ipse [ipsa?] dicitur ereola [ar-] propter inrigationem ubi crescunt aromata, x. 22 (*Cant.* v. 13 genae illius sicut *areolae* aromatum; vi. 1 descendit...ad *areolam*). Cf. *areoli*, aromatum orti, Cp. A723; Ep. 1C6; Ef.[1] 338, 29.

areolae, areolam, see *areola*.

areopagitam, see *ariopagitis*.

arepticium, arepticius, see *arreptitium*.

arethimetica, numeralis, xxx. 46, see

dialectica. Cf. *arthimetica*, diuinitio uel numeralis, Cp. A719; *arethimetica*, definitio, Ep. 1A15 and Ef.[1] 337, 15; *arithimetica*, numeralis, Ep. 3C10 and Ef.[1] 342, 32.

Arge, nomen montium, xxi. 4 (*Judith* ii. 12 venit ad magnos montes *Ange*).

argella [=*argilla*, white clay], laam, xlvii. 37 (*Alia*=?)=*a*-, laam, Cp. A730; Ep. 2A29; *a*-, sram, Ef.[1] 340, 16. See hoc *argillum*, lam (Napier, 28, 32), and Wright W. (index). For *laam* (O.H.G. *leim*, Germ. *lehm*), loam, see Bosw. T. (lām); Kluge, *Etym. Wrtb.* (*lehm*).

argentei, xxxii. 1, see *dragma.*

argenteis, viii. 16, see *mala aurea...*

argenteos, xxxi. 28, see *tres argenteos*; xxxiii. 30, see *siliquae tres.*

argento, xiii. 6, see *lunulas*, 7, see *discriminalia*, 9, see *olfactoriola*; xv. 37, see *electrum*; xxxv. 294, see *thecis*; see also *periscelidas.*

argentum, viii. 10, see *conflatorium.*

argeos, xxxi. 23, see *siliquas.*

argilla, argillum, see *argella.*

argula, acuta, xxviii. 16 (*Lib. Anton.* xlvi col. 158[D] *arguta* sophismatum interrogatione). Cf. argute, acute, Cp. A737; Ep. 2C25; Ef.[1] 340, 51. See also *arguta.*

argumenta, see *arguta.*

argumentum, i. 129, see *suspicio.*

arguta, ordancas, iii. 65 (not *De S. Mart. Stor.*, but *Vita S. Anton.* xlvi col. 158[D] niterentur *arguta* sophismatum interrogatione de divina cruce eum illudere). The lemma, if it refers to this quotation, would require *orþance* (abl. of the adj. *orþanc*, cunning, skilful) as interpretation, whereas *ordancas* (for orþ-) is the plur. of the subst. *orþanc* (wit, understanding, artifice, device). Steinmeyer (*Alth. Gl.* ii. 746, 33) would read *argumenta*, which occurs *Vit. S. Ant.* xlviii col. 160[C], and actually glosses *orþancas* in other texts (see Bosw. T. *orþanc*). Glogger suggests *argutia*[*e*]. See *argumento*, mit orþance (Napier, *Aldh. Gl.* 1389, 3214; cf. ib. 3016, 3399), and also above *argula* (for *arguta*).

ariculum, see *auriculum.*

aridis, xxxi. 12, see *sata*; xxxiii. 12, see *ephi.*

ariel, arihel, see *arihellio.*

arihellio [written as one word], xv. 27 (*Ezech.* xliii. 15, 16 *Ariel* quatuor cubitorum: et ab *Ariel* usque ad sursum... et *Ariel* duodecim cubitorum). *arihel*= אֲרִיאֵל, hearth, altar of God. If *lio* is meant as an interpretation, it may be for *leo*, lion (which is the meaning of the Hebr. אֲרִי; see Gesenius), or, as Glogger suggests, for A. S. hlēo(w), protection, shelter.

arioli, qui in ara coniecturam faciunt, xvi. 25 (*Dan.* ii. 2 ut convocarentur *arioli*; *Dan.* ii. 27 and iv. 4 *arioli*; *ariolos* i. 20; *ariolo* ii. 10; *ariolorum* iv. 6)= *arioli*, q.i.a.c.f., Cp. A823.

ariopagitis, princeps sinagogae [syn-], iv. 27 (*Eccl. Istor.*); **amopaga**, archisinagogus [archisyn-] est, xxxv. 130 (*De Euseb.*)=(*Ruf.* iii. 4 fol. 35[a] Dionysium *Areopagitam*)=*aripagita*, archisynagogus, Cp. A750; *ariopagita*, archisinagogus, Ep. 1A20 and Ef.[1] 338, 2.

arismeticam, arismetrica, arismetricam; see *dialectica.*

Aristoteles, see *Calistratus.*

arithimetica, see *arethimetica.*

arithmeticam, see *arethimetica.*

arma, xii. 42, see *uasa*; xliii. 54, see *cestus.*

Armenias pilas, nomen montium uel gentis uel silue [-uae] uel clausure [-rae], xxxvi. 2 (*Oros.* i. 2, 40 ad *Armenias pylas*; in three MSS. *pilas*). Cf. *Armenias pilas*, nomen loci, Cp. A738.

armilla, ermboeg, xix. 43 (*Job* xl. 21 *armillâ* perforabis maxillam eius). For *ermboeg* (an arm-ring, bracelet) see Bosw. T. (*earm-beah*).

armillas, xiii. 8, see *periscelidas.*

aromata, x. 22, see *areola.*

aromatizans, redolens, xii. 20 (*Eccles.* xxiv. 20 sicut...balsamum *aromatizans*).

arpa, arngeus, xlvii. 57 (*Alia*=?)=*a*-, earngeot, Cp. A759; *a*-, earngeat, Ep. 2A21; *a*-, aerngeup, Ef.[1] 340, 8. For *arpa* (=Gr. ἅρπη, a bird of prey, milvus ater, the Egyptian kite, Liddell & Sc.) see Du C. (*arpa* 1 & 2; *harpa*[2]. falcon). As to *arngeus*, *earngeot*, *earngeat*, *aerngeup*, *ærengeat* (Wright W. 117, 24), *eargeat* (ibid. 258, 4; 351, 14), all explaining *arpa* and *earngeap* glossing *vultur* (ib. 132, 19) and *asapa* (for *arpa*? Cp. A862), seem to be not compounds, but two different, alternative words, the first of which (*arn*, *earn*, *aern*, *æren*, *ear*) means an eagle (Oxf. D. *erne*), and as such is a gloss to *aquila* (Wright W. 131, 10; 258, 3; 284, 3; 317, 44; 351, 12). The second (*geus*, *geup*, *geap*, *geot*, *geat*) seems to be the Gr. γύψ Latinised as *geus* (instead of gūps) or γῦπα Latinised as *geup* (instead of gūp-). The form *geop* arose from *eu* being Anglicised as *eo*, and this gave rise to the corrupted *geot*, and finally *geat*.—Bosw. T. explains *earngeāp* as *a vulture, species of falcon* (*earn*, an eagle + the adj.

geāp, now usually written gēap, *shrewd, cunning*), and *earn-geāt*, as a goat-eagle, vulture. But A.S. ēa does not become E. *oa*, and in any case the compound would mean eagle-goat, not goat-eagle. Kluge (*Ags. Leseb.* p. 172) explains the simple *earn* as *adler* (eagle), but the compound *earn-geat* (-geup) as *geier* (vulture). —Egilsson (*Lex poët.*) gives o. N. *gaupi, gauti*, a sea-king, pirate, which may, for its sense, rest on γυπ-α, associated, by popular etymology, with o. N. *gaupa*, a lynx (cf. A. S. gēap) and o. N. *gautr*, A. S. Gēat, a Goth.

arreptitium, demoniosum [daem-], xiv. 17 (*Hier.* xxix. 26 super omnem virum *arreptitium*) = *arepticium*, dem-, Cp. A795; *arepticius*, furiosius, Ep. 1E29 and Ef.[1] 339, 35; cf. *repticius*, demoniosus, Ef.[1] 386, 57.

arrura, xvii. 4, see *torris*.

ars, iv. 44, see *amatorie*; xxx. 27, see *de piasma*.

arserunt, xi. 7, see *pentapolim*.

artabę, in asaie egyptiorum mensurę quę iii faciunt modios x, xxxiii. 14 (*Euch. De Pond.* p. 159, 8 *Artabae* in Esaia Aegyptiorum mensurae quae tres f. m. x.). Cf. *artaba*, modi iii, Cp. A813; Ep. 3C36; Ef.[1] 343, 2. Euch. refers to Isai. v. 10; cf. Hier. in id. (ed. Vall. iv. 75). For *artabę* see also (xvi. 22) *trinte*.

arte [for *artes*], xlv. 1, see *gymnasium*.

artem, xvi. 26, see *magi*; xxix. 29, see *tecnam*.

artes, xxxv. 143, see *per metalla*; see also *gymnasium*.

arthimetica, see *arethimetica*.

arthro, see *cuimarsus*.

artico [arctico], xliv. 16, see *antarticus*.

artifex, xxix. 12, see *comicus*.

artifices, xv. 12, see *bibli*.

artofilax, custos aquilonis, xxvii. 33 (*Lib. Rot.* = Isid. *Lib. de nat. rer.* xxvi. 5 *arctophylax*).

artum, angustum, xiii. 38 (*Isai.* xxx. 20 dabit...Dominus panem *arctum*).

arua, terra, xiv. 18 (*Hierem.* xxiii. 10 arefacta sunt *arva* deserti; xxv. 37: conticuerunt *arva* pacis).—**arue**, terram, xxix. 46 (*Uerb. Interpr.* = *Hier. in Matth.* v. 43 cum subjecta sibi *arva* riget).

arugo, color sicut pedes accipitris, xiv. 19 (*Hierem.* xxx. 6 conversae sunt universae facies in *auruginem*; Cambr. MS. *aurugo* sicut p. a.).

aruina, pinguitudo, xix. 47 (*Job* xv. 27 de lateribus eius *aruina* dependet). Cf. *aruina*, risel (= rysel, D. reuzel), Cp. A796.

arundineus, xxxix. 15, see *ferula*.

aruspices, qui aras inspiciunt, xvi. 7; **aruspices**, qui exta inspiciunt et ex his futura predicant [praed-], xvi. 30 (*Dan.* ii. 27 magi, arioli et *aruspices* nequeunt indicare; cf. *aruspices* iv. 4; v. 7; principem *aruspicum* v. 11). Cf. Cp. A818, 821. The Cambr. MS. adds: *Auruspices* qui aues inspiciunt; see *auspices*.

arx, see *ciuitas dauid*.

asaie [Esaia], xxxiii. 14, see *artabę*.

asapa [for arpa?], see *arpa*.

ascecon, see *ascetron*.

ascendere, xlviii. 43, see *scandere*.

ascensum, xxxix. 44, see *glebum*.

ascesi, intellectui, xxx. 41 (*Cat. Hier.* xli col. 657A epistolae auctoris sui ἀσκήσει et vitae congruentes; B: ep. a. s. *ackesoy* idest intelligentie et vite cong.; C: ep. auct. sui [blank] et vite cong.) = *arcesi*, intellectui, Cp. A775; *archesi*, intellectui, Ep. 3C9; *ascesui*, intellectui, Cp. A836; *ascesu*, intellectui, Ep. 1A32; *ascessu*, intellectui, Ef.[1] 338, 15; arcessi, intellectui, Ef.[1] 342, 31.—**ascetron**, intellectum, xxx. 90 (*Cat. Hier.* cxvi col. 707C elaborauit...et ἀσκητικὸν; B: el...et *ascecon*, idest *intellectum*; C: el. et *a* [blank]) = *ascetron*, intellectum, Cp. A848; Ep. 3C11; Ef.[1] 343, 33.

ascetron, intellectum, xxx. 90, see *ascesi*.

asciculus, see *ciscillus*.

Asclepiades, see *Calistratus*.

ascopa, similis utri, xxi. 13 (*Judith* x. 5 imposuit...abrae suae *ascoperam* vini; Heyse, in note; Migne, *Patr. Lat.* xxix col. 52 note [b], and Sabat. *ascopam*). Cf. *ascopa*, kylle (= cyll = Lat. culleus, culeus, a leather bottle, flagon), Cp. A852; *ascopa*, in similitudinem utri, Ep. 3E3 & Ef.[1] 343, 6.

ascoperam, see *ascopa*.

asilium diuinum, iv. 16 (*Ruf.* ii. 10 fol. 22b nisi *diuinum* affuisset *auxilium*). If this reference to ii. 10, where the lemma should occur, according to the order in which the gloss appears in the MS., is correct, *asilium diuinum* seems to be a lemma without interpretation. But it is possible that the glossator having explained *asylum* by *sanctum* (see *asitum*, iv. 14 in v. *asillum*), interpreted *auxilium* by *diuinum*.

asillum, locus refugii sanctus, xxxv. 50 (*De Euseb.*); **asitum**, sanctum, iv. 14 (*Eccl. Ist.*) = (*Ruf.* ii. 6 fol. 21b templum...quod... perdurauerat *asylum*). Cf. asilum, templum refugii, Cp. A846; Ep. 2E37; Ef.[1] 341, 41.

asilo, asilus, see *tabanus*.

asinis, xlii. 21, see *basterna*.

asino, xiii. 42, see *epocentaurus*.

asinus, XIX. 24, see *onager*.

asitum, sanctum, IV. 14, see *asillum*.

askeseon, see *ptocheus*.

asolatis, plane factis, XVII. 9 (*Nahum* I. 5 colles *desolati sunt*). From the gloss (plane fact*is*) it seems clear that the final *s* of the lemma was regarded as belonging to it. There is, apparently, a stroke in the MS. over the *s* (therefore *sunt*), but a point above it marks it for erasure. *Asolati* (for *assolati*?) points to a reading different from the Vulgate.

ason, integritas, XXXIV. 7 (*De Cass.*, *Inst.* VI. 4 in affectum integritatis uel incorruptionis transire, quod dicitur ἀγνὸν; in note *asNON*; *autNON*).

aspaltum, spaldur, XII. 18 (*Eccles.* XXIV. 20 sicut cinnamomum et *balsamum aromatizans* odorem dedi). Sab. points out in note that the Gr. has ἀσπάλαθος ἀρωμάτων, and the MS. Sangerm. 15 *aspaltum aromatizans*. *Aspaltum* is also in Heyse's text (note). The Corp. Gl. A839 has *aspaltum, spaldur*; Ep. 2A36 *asfaltum, spldr* with *a* added above the line; Ef.[1] 340, 23 *asfaltum, spaldur*. It is, therefore, possible that *spaldur* is an A. S. spelling for *asphaltum*, but the Cambridge MS. Kk. 4. 6 has *aspaltum, squalor*; a Leiden MS. (Voss. Lat. fol. 24) *asfaltum, spalor* (Steinm., IV. 278, 1), and other MSS. *sypaldor* and *spalor* (Steinm. I. 561, 1 and notes 1 & 2). The Gr. ἀσπάλαθος means a prickly shrub yielding a fragrant oil, but a confusion between this word and *asphaltum* is apparent.

aspeleo, bethlem, XLVIII. 63 (*De Cass.*, *Inst.* IV. 31 non longe fuit *a spelaeo*, in quo dominus noster ex uirgine nasci dignatus est; in note *speleo, spelunca*). See *speleum*, saxum cauum, Cp. S485 and Ef.[1] 393, 46; *sepelleum*, saxum cauum, Ep. 25C36.

asperis, XXXIV. 9, see *causticis*.

asperum, II. 48, see *dirum*.

asse, nummus, XXIX. 3 (*Uerb. Interpr.* = *Hier. Comm. in Matth.* X. 29 col. 66C Nonne duo passeres *asse* ueneunt). Cf. *as* assis, genus nummi, Cp. A854; Ep. 3E12; Ef.[1] 343, 15.

assecla, see *adsecla*.

assolati, see *asolatis*.

ast, statim, VI. 8 (*Breu. exsol.*?). Cf. *Ast* hominem non terra parit..., *Dracont.* I. 333; *ast* uerum uel statim, Cp. A842; *ast* statim aut uerum, Ef.[2] 268, 34.

aste [for *hastae*]. XVII. 12, see *fulgorantes*.

-aster [termination], see *porcastrum*.

asteriscis, stellis, XIX. 2 (*Job*; *Praef. Hieron.* p. XIVa, and Migne, *P.L.* XXVIII col. 1079A volumina Origines obelis *asterisc*isque distinxerit) = *asteriscus*, stellis, Cp. A849; *asteriscis*, stellis, Ep. 3C12; *asteristis*, stellis, Ef.[1] 342, 34; *asteriscus*, stella, Ef.[2] 268, 32. The Cambr. MS. *asteriscus*.

astrogi [astrologi], XLIV. 16, see *antarticus*.

astrologi, see *antarticus*.

astrologiae, XXXVIII. 26, see *mathesis*.

astronomia, siderum lex, XXX. 51 (*Cat. Hier.* LIV; not in Migne's nor in Richardson's text, but in the Utrecht ed. [B]; see the quotation sub v. *dialectica*). Cf. *astronomia*, lex astrorum, Cp. A827; Ep. 1A16; Ef.[1] 337, 16.

astu, astucia [-tia], XXXVI. 13 (*Oros.* I. 8, 7 and II. 7, 2 *astu*). Cf. *astu*, facni (Bosw. T: *fácne*, *fácen*) uel fraefeli (Bosw. T. *fræfele*), Cp. A844; *astu*, facni, Ep. 2E7; Ef.[1] 341, 12.—**astus**, astutus uel callidus, XLVI. 23 (*Alia* = *Ars Phocae*, p. 420, 6 hic cultus luxus senatus *astus* rictus...). Cf. *astus*, calliditas, Cp. A855; Ep. 5C19; Ef.[1] 346, 44.

astucia [-tia], XXXVI. 13, see *astu*.

astus, astutus uel callidus, XLVI. 23, see *astu*.

astutia, see *astu*.

astutus, XLVI. 23, see *astus*.

asylum, see *asilium*; *asillum*; *asitum*.

asyndetus, see *sindetus*.

atauus, IIII pater, XXXIV. 21 (*De Cass.*, *Inst.* XI. 11 regis *atauus*).

a tergo, XLIV. 26, see *dextera*.

atersatha, XXIII. 13, see *nemias*.

Atheniensium, see *Atticarum*.

a theologia, a diuina generatione, IV. 114 (*Eccl. Istor.*); **a theologia**, a dei genilogia [geneal-], XXXV. 17 (*De Euseb.*) = (*Ruf.* III. 24 fol. 46b *a theologia*...sumit exordium) = *theologia*, dei genelogia, Cp. T137; Ep. 26A35; Ef.[1] 395, 8.

Athersatha, see *Nemias*.

Athinensium [Atheniens-], XXXVI. 20, see *Atticarum*.

atque, II. 134; XXVIII. 77; XLIV. 27.

atramentarium, uas atramenti, XV. 1 (*Ezech.* IX. 2 *atramentarium* scriptoris; also IX. 3 & 11).

atramenti, VIII. 17, see *nitrum*; XV. 1, see *atramentarium*.

atriis, XIV. 12, see *domatibus*.

atrio, XLII. 20, see *in uiridario domus*.

atris, nigris tetris, XXVII. 26 (*Lib. Rot.* = Isid. *Lib. de nat. rer.* I. 4 *atri* dies sunt). Glogger suggests a connexion with Isid. *Lib. de nat. rer.* XXXIX. 2 vlceribus *tetris*, in which case signs of transposition must have been omitted in the MS. But as the Glossator, while quoting (xxvii. 28 q.v.) *in Georgicis* from Isidore's *Lib. de nat. rer.* x. 1, excerpts (without Isidore quoting it) *uia secta* from Virg. *Geo.* i. 238, it seems possible that the above *atris* is likewise quoted from *Geo.* i. 236 (imbribus atris). Cf. also Goetz, vi. 109 (*ater*).

atroces, i. 16, see *barbari.*

atrumque [for *utr-*?], viii. 17, see *nitrum.*

Attica, xxxiii. 16, see *gomor.*

Atticarum, athinensium [atheniens-], xxxvi. 20 (*Oros.* ii. 13, 2 legum *Atticarum* gratia).

Attice [-cae], xxxiii. 1, see *talentum.*

attracto, see *adtracto.*

au for a: *au*ditis, for *a*dytis; see above *a* for *au.*

aucellas, xiii. 25, see *de radice.*

aucellatores, viii. 4, see *aucupes.*

aucmenta [augm-], xxviii. 31, see *ausesis.*

aucmentum [augm-], xxxiv. 10, see *auxesin.*

auctorale, i. 13 and xxxix. 73, see *autenticum.*

auctoris, xxix. 4, see *autenticum.*

auctoritas, see *autenticum.*

auctus, xliii. 32, see *mactus.*

aucupes, aucellatores, viii. 4 (*Salam.* vi. 5 de manu *aucupis*).

aucupis, see *aucupes.*

auditis [for *adytis*], xxxviii. 42, see *hierufontis.*

auditores, i. 22, see *caticumini.*

auditorio, scole [-lae] legentium, xxxv. 247 (*Ruf.* vi. 3 fol. 96^{a} cum praeesset *auditorio*; xi. 9 fol. 182^{a} ambo de *auditorio* digressi). Cf. *auditorium*, locus legendi, Cp. A960.

auditorium [for *auditorum*?], xxxv. 10, see *apparitorium.*

auditorum, see *apparitorium.*

aues, xvi. 32, see *auspices*; xxix. 23, see *decipulam*; xxxv. 24, see *auspiciis.*

augmenta, see *ausesis.*

augmentum, xxviii. 56, see *auxesis*; see also *auxesin.*

auguria, auspicia, xxvi. 11 (*Isid. Offic.* i. 41, 2 *auguriis* profanantur). For *auguria*, see also (xv. 38) *conectura.*

auguriantur (!), xxxviii. 31, see *decanorum.*

auguriis, see *auguria.*

Augustini, see *De sancti Agustini.*

augustissimo, famosissimo, xxix. 5 (*Uerb. Interpr.* = *Hier. in Matth.* xxi. 12, 13 col. 150^{B} *augustissimo* in toto orbe templo Domini) = Cp. A956.

auibus, xxiv. 10, see *altilia.*

auis, xiv. 11, see *perdix*; xlvi. 19, see *prepes.*

auo, ·i· utj eza, septemplici, v. 8 (*Ruf.*?). The MS. has Auo, but the place where it occurs in the alphabetically arranged Ch. v. would suggest *Duo* or *Euo*, and ·i· usually stands for *idest.* Glogger thinks that *auo* may be a corrupt *age* (*Ruf.* ii., prooem. fol. 18^{a} or iii. 24 fol. 45^{b}) interpreted by *uti.—eza* perhaps = ἐξαπλᾶ (*Ruf.* vi. 13 fol. 103^{b} exemplaria ipsa nominauit ἐξαπλᾶ, idest *sexiplici* ordine conscripta; Cacciari, p. 348: εξαπλα, idest *sex simplici* ordine conscripta), which the Glossator might have wished to explain by *septemplici*, and correctly so, as there are actually *seven* not *six* texts; see Cacciari's note e, p. 348, and Migne's *P. Gr.* xx col. 558 note 3.

auocare, occupare, xii. 31 (*Eccles.* xxxii. 15 illic *avocare* et illic lude).

aurea, iv. 34, see *petulum*; viii. 16, see *mala aurea*; xxii. 10, see *diadema.*

aureas, xli. 8, see *saphirus*; xli. 16, see *cypressus.*

aurei, xxii. 8, see *lecti aurei.*

aureis, xxi. 5, see *cum coronis.*

Aurelia. terra est uel prouincia, xxxix. 13 (*Greg. Dial.* iii. 17 col. 261^{C} & ^{D} in... *Aureliae* partibus ..; in *Aurelia*).

aurem, xix. 23, see *susurrat.*

aureos, xxxiii. 6, see *stater.*

aureum, xxii. 12, see *urna.*

auri, xli. 13, see *crisolitus.*

aurichalcum, see *auriculum.*

auricula, ęruigga, xlvii. 86 (*Alia* = ?) = *auriculum*, earpicga, Cp. A891; *auriculum*, earuuigga, Ep. 2A25; *auriculum*, aeruuica, Ef.[1] 340, 12. The Oxf. D. (v. *earwig*) mentions an insect, forficula *auricularia* (auricularis, Bosw. T.), so called from the notion that it penetrates into the head through the ear, and it is possible that this adj. gave rise to the above lemma, though Cp., Ep. and Ef.[1] all have *auriculum.* A Harl. MS. 1002, quoted in the *Prompt. Parv.*, 143 note, has *auriolus.*—See also *auriculum.*

auricularia, auricularis, see *auricula.*

auriculum, dros, xlvii. 50 (*Alia* = ?) = *a-*, dorsos, Cp. A889; *a-*, dros, Ep. 2A20; *ariculum*, dros, Ef.[1] 340, 7. The Cp. Gloss. interprets *auriculum* not only by *dorsos* (A889), but also by *earpicga* (A891), and a Glossary of the 11th cent. (Wright W. 350, 36) has *auriculum*, earwicga, oððe dros, and again (353, 20) *auriculum*, dros. On the other hand, *dros*, *drosna*, *drosne*, (dross) interprets *faex* (grounds, dregs; see Wright W. 129, 7; 238, 25; 330, 34; 549, 4), also *auricula* and *amurca* (Bosw. T. *dros*, *dross*, *drosna*). The *Promptor. Parv.* (of c. 1440) explains *ruscum*, *rus-*

culum by *drosse* or fylthe. The Oxf. D. (*Dross*, sb.) understands *dros*, which interprets *auriculum*, to be *the scum* thrown off from metals in the process of melting, which would make *auriculum = aurichalcum* (for orichalcum; see the form *ariculum* in Ef.[1]).

auriculum (earwig), see *auricula*.

auriolus, see *auricula*.

auro, VIII. 16, see *mala aurea* XIII. 6, see *lunulas*, 7, see *discriminalia*, 9, see *olfactoriola*; XIV. 16, see *inclusor*; XV. 37, see *electrum*; XXIX. 11, see *mauria*.

auruginem, see *arugo*.

aurum, XLI. 15, see *topation*.

auruspices, see *aruspices*.

Ausaret, proprium nomen fluminis, XXXIX. 10 (*Greg. Dial.* III. 9 col. 233[c] *Auseris* fluvius; some MSS. have *Ausaris*; cf. Migne's note *h*).

Ausaris, Auseris, see *Ausaret*.

ausesis, quę addenda quedam nomina per membra singula rerum aucmenta congeminat, XXVIII. 31 (*Cass. Psalm.* III. 2 col. 44[c] schema quod Graece dicitur *auxesis*, quae addendo quaedam n. p. m. s. r. augmenta c.).—**auxesin**, aucmentvm [augm-], XXXIV. 10 (*De Cass.*, *Inst.* x. 8, 1 increpationis *auxesin* facit).—**auxesis**, augmentum paulatim enim ad superiora concrescit, XXVIII. 56 (*Cass. Psalm.* XVIII. 13 schema...*auxesis*, Latine augmentum p. e. a. s. c.).

auspices, qui aues inspiciunt, XVI. 32 (*Dan.?*). It is not in the Vulg., and seems to be merely a further explanation of *aruspices* (q.v.) in XVI. 7 and 30. For *auruspices* qui aues inspiciunt of the Cambr. MS., see above *aruspices*.

auspicia, XXVI. 11, see *auguria*.

auspiciis, auxiliis, IV. 55 (*Eccl. Istor.*); **auspiciis**, adiutoriis, IV. 115 (*Eccl. Istor.*); **auspiciis**, qui aues inspiciunt uel homines obuiantes, XXXV. 24 (*De Euseb.*) = (*Ruf.* IV. 26 fol. 70[b] obseruantiae huius *auspiciis* eleuatum). Cf. *aruspices*, qui intendunt signa corporis uel obuiantes hominum &c., Cp. A821; Ep. 5A28; Ef.[1] 346, 14.

australem, XLIV. 16, see *antarticus*.

austronotho, XLIV. 26, see *a tergo*.

austronothum, XLIV. 25, see *dextera*, 27, see *leua*.

austronothus, XLIV. 7, see *poli*.

aut, XIV. 34; XV. 3 (bis); XXVIII. 26, 43 (bis), 45 (bis), 76; XXX. 16.

aut in aut in [the first *aut in* for the Gr. αὐτῆν; the second is dittography], XXIX. 52, see *ecacusen*.

autem, XVI. 27; XXXI. 2, 3; XXXIII. 8, 13; XLIV. 1.

autenticum, auctorale, I. 13 (*De Canon.*); **autenticum**, auctorale, XXXIX. 73 (*not* Greg. Dial. but) = (*Can. Conc. Carth.*, praef. p. 142[b] *authenticum* concilium) = *autenticum*, auctorale, Cp. A910; Ep. 3A25; Ef.[1] 342, 9.—**autenticum**, auctoris, XXIX. 4 (*Uerb. Interpr.* = *Hier. in Matth.* XII. 13 col. 78[A] in Evangelio...quod vocatur a plerisque Matthæi *authenticum*). See Ef.[2] 270, 6 *auctenticum*, auctoritas.

autexusio, see *psichiexodo*.

authenticum, see *autenticum*.

auxesin, aucmentum, XXXIV. 10; **auxesis**, augmentum paulatim &c., XXVIII. 56, see *ausesis*.

auxiliis, IV. 55, see *auspiciis*.

auxilium, see *asilium*.

axe, polus, XXXV. 274 (*Ruf.* VII. 25 fol. 125[b] sub...Septentrionis *axe*). For *axe* see also (XXXV. 82) *sub axe pontico*; (XLIV. 10) *cardines*.—**axem** cęli &c., XLIV. 29, see *extremi*.—**axis**, linea recta quę per mediam pilam spere tendit, XLIV. 3 (*Alia*; *de cælo* = Isid. *de nat. rerum*, XII. 3 col. 983 *Axis*, *l. r. quæ p. m. p. sphæræ tendit*). Cf. *aether* polum axis caelum, Cp. A340. For *axis* see also (XLIV. 1) *partes*; (XLIV. 5, 10) *cardines*; (XLIV. 29) *axem*.

axietas [anx-], I. 133, see *scrupulum*.

axis, linea recta &c., XLIV. 3, see *axe*.

azimorum [azym-], VII. 2, see *pro octaua*.

azymorum, see *azimorum*.

b for *f*: *b*ornacula (for *f*orn-);—for *p*: bi*b*ennem (bi*p*-); pu*b*lite for po*p*lite; scri*b*sit, scri*b*ta, scri*b*tos, scri*b*turae (scri*p*-); superscri*b*ta (-*p*ta).—for *u* (v): *b*erruca (uer-); coni*b*entes (coni*u*-); coni*b*entia (coniu-); gle*b*um (for cli*u*um); li*b*idum (li*u*idum).

bacchanalia, see *bachus*.

bacchantes, see *bachantes*.

bacchus, see *bachus*.

bachal, multi idole foede, XL. 13 (*Uerba?*).

bachantes, turpiter ludentes, XXXV. 33 (*Ruf.* V. 16 fol. 85[b] contra fidem Christi *bacchantes*). Cf. *bachans*, ludens, Cp. B10; *bachans*, turpiter ludens uel discurrens, Ep. 6A11; Ef.[1] 347, 22; *bachantes*, uuoedende (Bosw. T. *wēdan*), Cp. B48.

bachunalia [for *bacchanalia*], XLIII. 29; see *bachus*.

Bachus [Bacchus], liber pater dionisius [Dionysus] nomen unius hominis est, XLIII. 28; **floralia, bachunalia** [*bacchan-*], **saturnalia, liberalia, ulcanalia** [uulc-], festiuitates uel sacra paganorum est, XLIII. 29 (*De div. nominibus* = Donati *Ars grammat.*, p. 376, 32 *Floralia Saturnalia*; ib. p. 379, 11 *Saturnalia Vulcanalia*, Conpitalia). Gloss No. 28 (with which cf. bachum liberum patrem, Cp. B5) is, apparently, a further explanation to *bacchanalia* and *liberalia* of No. 29, which two terms do not seem to occur in the current texts of *Donatus*.

Bactroperitae, see *batroperite*.

bacula, uacca, III. 26 (*De S. Mart. Stor.* = *Sulp. Sev. Dial.* II. 9, 4 sensus in *bucula*) = *bucula*, uacca, Cp. B218.

baculus, XXXIX. 15, see *ferula*.

badare, see *battat*.

baerrus, see *bęrrus*.

balaena, balena, see *balera*.

balera, hron, XLVII. 10 (*Alia* = ?) = *ballena*, horn, Cp. B21; *b*-, hran, Ep. 6C3; *b*-, hron, Ef.[1] 347, 48. Cf. Napier (Index, *balena*). *Balera* (for *balena*, *balaena*), a whale; for *hran*, *hron*, a whale, see Bosw. T. (*hran*).

ballena, see *balera*.

balnea, XX. 8, see *taermę*.

balneum, XXXIX. 14, see *Sabanum*.

balneum ciceronis, a cicerone romano prefecto qui fecit illud, XXXIX. 4 (*Greg. Dial.* I. 4 col. 165B monasterii quod appellatur *Balneum Ciceronis*).

balsamum, X. 19, see *gutta*.

baptismate, X. 3, see *odor ungentorum*.

baptismi, X. 1, see *osculetur me*.

barathrum, see *baratrum*.

baratrum, loh uel dal, XXXV. 176 (*Ruf.* V. 15 fol. 85a in...*barathrum* deducebant) = *baratrum*, dael, Cp. B49; cf. *baratrum*, sepulcrum, Cp. B39. For (O. H. G.) *loh*, = A. S. *loc*, *an enclosure*, *fold*, *hole*, *abyss*, *pit*, *lock*, see Bosw. T. (*loc*); Kluge, *Et. Wrtb.* (*Loch*); Skeat (*lock*); Oxf. D. (*lock*, sb[2]). For *dal* (A. S. *dæl*, G. *thal*, D. *dal*) *a dale*, *vale*, *valley*, *pit*, *gulf*, see Bosw. T. (*dæl*); Skeat (*dale*); Oxf. D. (*dale*[1]).

barba, XXXV. 189, see *infestes*.

barbari, feroces inmites atroces, I. 16 (*De Canon.*; *Can. Conc. Nic.* I si quis ...a *barbaris* abscisus; cf. *Can. Conc. Carth.* LXXII multos...a *barbaris* redimunt).

barbarus [sine interpretat.], I. 18 (*De Canon.*?), see *barbari*.

barbe [barbae], XXXIX. 1, see *a primeuo flore*.

basiliscus, XIII. 25, see *de radice*.

basis, omne quod fundamentum poni sub [for subponi?] potest, XXXV. 192 (*Ruf.* VII. 14 fol. 121a *basis* quaedam). Cf. *basis*, syl, Cp. B50.

basterna, similis curro de coreo tota et portatur semper ab asinis uel hominibus nullam rotam habet, XLII. 21 (*Ex div. libris* = *Vita S. Eug.* 3; Migne LXXIII col. 608A juxta *basternam*...et vacua pertranseunte *basterna*) = *basterna*, s. c. de corio t. e. p. s. a hominibus uel asinis nullam ratam (rotam) habens, Ep. 5E31; Ef.[1] 348, 5. Cf. *basterna*, beer, Cp. B9; Ep. 6A10; Ef.[1] 347, 21; *basterna*, scrid, Cp. B25.

batat, see *battat*.

bathos, III modios, XXXI. 41 (*De ponder.*?).—**batus** est amphora una idest modii III, XXXIII. 10 (*Euch. de Pond.* p. 159, 2 *batus* amphora una id est modi tres). Cf. Ezech. 45, 11, 14. For *batus* (E. *bath*) see also (XXXIII. 12) *ephi*. Cf. Blume, I. 376, 6 sq.

batroperite, qui portant cibos in utris, XXIX. 15 (*Uerb. Interpr.* = *Hier. in Matth.* X. 9, 10 col. 63A arguit philosophos, qui vulgo appellantur *Bactroperitæ*).

battat, ginat, XLVII. 44 (*Alia* = ?) = *b*-, geonath, Cp. B24; *batat*, ginath, Ep. 6C6; *battat*, ginath, Ef.[1] 347, 50. For *battat*, *batat* (from °badare, to open the mouth, to yawn) see Körting, *Wörterb.* 1150; for *geonath*, *ginat*, *ginath*, yawneth, see Bosw. T. (*geonian*, *ginian*); Kluge, *Et. Wörterb.* (*gähnen*), Goetz, VI. 132.

batus est amphora &c., XXXIII. 10, see *bathos*.

Behemoth, see *Veemoth*.

Bel, see *del*.

bella, XII. 42, see *uasa*.

belli, XXIX. 37, see *duellionis*.

bellica, XXXV. 1, see *tragoedia*.

bellum, IV. 40, see *duellis*.

beluas, XXXVIII. 15, see *hygę*.

bene, see *abene* (for *a bene*).

beneuolus, XXIX. 49, see *eynum*.

benigne, I. 82, see *operam*.

berbaticas, see *uorith*.

berbices, XXXV. 72, see *lanionibus*.

berillus, see *byrillus*.

berruca [for *uerruca*, a wart], uaertę, XLVII. 36 (*Alia* = ?) = *b*-, uearte, Cp. B71; *b*-, uueartae, Ep. 6C11; *b*-, uaertae, Ef.[1] 348, 2. For *uaertę* &c. see Bosw. T. (*wearte*).

berrus = *uerrus*, see *bęrrus*.

bęrrus, baar, XLVII. 94 (*Alia* = ?) = *berrus*, baar, Cp. B70; Ep. 6C8; Ef.[1] 347, 53. *Bęrrus* (for *bærrus*), *berrus* = *uerrus* = class. *verres*, *verris*, a male swine, boar-pig; for *baar* (*a boar*) see Bosw. T. (*bār*) and below, *porcastrum*.

beryllus, see *byrillus*.

bestia, XIX. 37, see *ueemoth*; XLVII. 8, see *muscus*.

bestiae, see *hygę*.

bestialis, XLIV. 13, see *Terinos*.

bestie [bestiae], XXXVIII. 15, see *hygę*.

beth, see *chatus*.

bethlem, XLVIII. 63, see *aspeleo*.

bibennem, securis binam aciem habens, iv. 120 (*Eccl. Ist.*); **bibennem** securem bis acutam, xxxv. 60 (*De Eus.*)=(*Ruf.* xi. 23 fol. 188[a] correptam *bipennem*...inlidit)= *bipennem*, securem bis acuatem, Cp. B132.

bibere, xlviii. 59, see *telopagere*.

biberes, potiones, ii. 15 (*Bened. reg.* 35, 18 singulas *biberes*; [30] singulos *biberes*). Cf. Wölfflin in *Archiv f. Lat. Lex.*, x. 550; Du C., sub v. *biberis*.

bibli, artifices qui faciunt trapezitas uel proprium nomen gentis, xv. 12 (*Ezech.* xxvii. 9 Vulg.: Senes *Giblij*; Heyse, in note: *bibli*; Sabat., vers. ant.: senes *Biblii*. The Cambr. MS.: *Bibli*, art. q.f. *tapetas* &c.). Conf. 3 *Reg.* 5. 18 Giblij praeparauerunt ligna et lapides. For trapezitas probably leg. *trapetias*, or any of the other forms [=tapeta] found in Du C. and Dief.

Biblii, see *bibli*.

biblioteca, reconditorium librorum, ii. 13 (*Bened. reg.* xlviii. 28 de *bibliotheca*, [50] *biblyotheca*).—**bibliotheca**, nomen loci ubi libri ponuntur, xxx. 7 (*Cat. Hier.* iii col. 613[B] in Caesariensi *bibliotheca*). Cf. *bibliotheca*, librorum reposi[ti]o, Cp. B101.

bibliotheca, biblyotheca, see *biblioteca*.

bifarius, see *uiuarium*.

bigae, see *bige equitum*.

bige equitum, duorum exercitum, [Cambr. MS. exercituum], xiii. 33 (*Isai.* xxi. 9 ecce iste venit ascensor vir *bigae equitum* et respondit. On this passage cf. the various translations and commentaries).

bigerimam, bigerricam, bigerrigam, bigerrimam, see *bigiricum*.

bigiricum, breuem, iii. 12 (*De S. Mart. Stor.*=*Sulp. Sev. Dial.* 2, 1, 8 *bigerricam* [*bigerimam*, *bigerrimam*, *bigerrigam*, in note] uestem...rapit).

bilex, tili, xlvi. 40; **triplex**, drili, xlvi. 41 (*Alia*=*Ars Phocae*?). As *bilex* and *triplex* do not occur in the current texts of Phoca (*bilex* for *duplex*, p. 421, 3?), they are, perhaps, further explanations of (xlvi. 39) *simplex* (q.v.). *Tili* for *twīli* (double, twill; Bosw. T.); drili=þrili (triple, Bosw. T.). See Cp. Int. 322 trilex, ðrili; cf. Goetz, vi. (*biplex*, *bilex*, *bilix*); vii. (*trilex*).

bina, xliv. 29, see *axem*.

binam, iv. 120, see *bibennem*.

biothanati, see *biothanti*.

biothanti, laquei, xlviii. 7 (*De Cass.*, *Inst.* vii. 14, 2 Judas...uitam...*biothanati* morte conclusit). Cf. *biothanatas*, seolfbonan (a suicide), Cp. B118.

bipennem, see *bibennem*.

birrum, see *byrrum*.

birrus, see *byrrus*.

bis, xxxv. 60, see *bibennem*.

bissextus, iv. 99, see *quadraplas*.

bithalassa loca; bithalassum, see *situtum*.

bl for u: *bl*ena (q.v.) for *u*ena.

blanditur, see *adolatur*.

blandus, see *plandus*.

blena, dicitur per quam aqua currit, viii. 14, see *uaena* (for *uena*).

bona, ix. 5, see *capparis*; xiii. 1, see *cucumerarium*; xiv. 32, see *croceis*; xlv. 10, see *gyt*.

bonam escam, manna quae soluebatur a sole non ab igne, xi. 16 (*Sap.* xix. 20 flammae...non...dissolvebant illam, quae facile dissolvebatur sicut glacies, *bonam escam*).

boni, x. 17, see *fistola*; xii. 1, see *euergetis*, 17, see *platanus*; xiii. 48. see *myrtus*; xlvii. 8, see *muscus*.

bono, xix. 62, see *uiri cordati*.

boreo, see *antarticus* (sub v. *arcticos*).

boreum, xliv. 27, see *leua*.

boreus, xliv. 7, see *poli*.

boriali, aquiloni, vi. 5 (*Breu. exsol.*?).

borit [=borith, Hebr. בֹּרִית], xvii. 19, see *herba fullonum*.

borith, see *herba fullonum*; *uorith*.

bornacula, genus ignis, iii. 22, see *fornacula*.

boues, xiii. 36, see *in serris*.

bracas, see *lumbare*.

brachii, xix. 49, see *lacertos*.

bracile, zona, ii. 14 (*Bened. reg.* lv. 30 [54] *bracile*).

bragas [bracas], xiv. 8, see *lumbare*.

branchiam, see *brantie*.

brantie, chyun, xx. 3 (*Tobias* vi. 4 Apprehende *branchiam* ejus) = *braciae*, cian, Cp. B189; *branciae*, cian, Ep. 6C22; *brancie*, cian, Ef.[1] 348, 13. See Steinm. i. 475. 3, 4 (cyan, chyun), 10 (kio); 476. 1 (cheuon), 4 (cheuun); 478. 43 sqq.; 480. 3; Kluge, *Ang. Les.* 166; id. *Wörterb. d.d. Sprache* (*Kieme*); Franck, *Woord. Ned. T.* (*kieuw*).

breuem, iii. 12, see *bigiricum*.

breui, xxviii. 55, see *metaforan*; xxxv. 85, see *adtracto*.

breuiarium, xxx. 65, see *epitomen*; see also *epimehne*.

breuis, i. 17, see *byrrus*, sub v. *byrrum*; iii. 7, see *byrrum*; vi *tit.*; xix. 6, see *comma*.

breuis (error for A.S. *brers*=*baers*, a perch), xlvii. 72, see *lupus*.

breuissimis, xxxv. 255, see *conpendiosis*.

breuitas, xxvii. 8, see *bruma*.

breuiter, xxviii. 65, see *epiphonima*.

bruma, breuitas, xxvii. 8 (*Lib. Rot.* = Isid. *Lib. de nat. rer.* vi. 2 Principium... anni alii a *bruma* putant) = bruma, breuitas, Cp. B180; Ep. 5E33; Ef.[1] 347, 6.

buccula, see *buculus*.

bucellis, vi. 10, see *crusticis*.

bucula, see *bacula*.

buculus, nordbaeg, xlvii. 17 (*Alia* = ?) = *buculus*, rondbaeg, Cp. B208; *b*-, randbeag, Ep. 6C11; *baculus*, rondbaeg, Ef.[1] 348, 1. Buculus = buccula, the boss of a shield; (*nord* for rond =) *rand* (a brink, edge, margin; shield); *baeg* = *beag*, *beah* (a ring, bracelet, collar); hence *rand-beag*, the boss of a shield, or a shield; see Bosw. T. (*rand-beáh*).

Bulgar, see *uulgari*.

bulimus, see *bulinus*.

bulinus [for *bulimus*, as in Cp., Ep., Ef.[1]], uermis lacertę [-tae] similis in chomacho [for *stom*-] hominis habitat, xlvii. 89 (*Alia* = ?) = *bulimus*, u. sim. lacertae in stomacho h. habitans, Cp. B209; Ep. 6C14; Ef.[1] 348, 4.

busta, incisa arbor ramis trungatis [truncatis], xxxv. 86; **busta**, ubi homines conburuntur, xxxv. 235 (*De Eus.*); **bustus**, tumulum uel ab ustum, iv. 100 (*Eccl. Stor.*) = (*Ruf.* xi. 27 fol. 190[a] ueternosa *busta* deiecta sunt; xi. 28 fol. 190[b] si... *busta* reperiri potuerunt). Q[y] *bustus* for bustum? and *ab ustum* for *ambustum*? The gloss xxxv. 86 = *busta*, incisa arbor ramis, Cp. B203.

bustus, tumulum uel ab ustum, iv. 100; see *busta*.

butros, x. 10, see *cyprus*.

byrillus tamen ut aqua resplendit [-det], xli. 14 (*De nomin. div.* = *Apoc.* xxi. 20 *berillus*; see also *Exod.* xxviii. 20, xxxix. 13; *Ezek.* xxviii. 13 *beryllus*) = *birillus* ut aqua splendet, Cp. B97; *bir*-, tantum u. a. spl., Ep. 5E32; Ef.[1] 347, 5.

byrrum, cocula [*cuculla*] breuis, iii. 7 (*De S. Mart. Stor.* = *Sulp. Sev. Dial.* i. 21, 4 ut *byrrum* rigentem...texat; *birrum* in note). **byrrus**, cuculla breuis, i. 17 (*De Canon.*; *Can. Conc. Gangr.* lxx qui... *birris*...utuntur).

byrseus [= βυρσεύς, a tanner], ledir uyrcta, xlvii. 40 (*Alia* = ?) = *b*-, leðeruyrhta, Cp. B232; *b*-, lediruuyrcta, Ep. 6C13; *byrreus*, lediruyrhta, Ef.[1] 348, 3. For leðer-wyrhta (leðer, *leather* + wyrhta, *a wright, workman*) see Bosw. T.

bysso, see *byssus*.

byssus, in arbore nascitur ad uestimentum, xxv. 8 (*Luc.* xvi. 19 induebatur purpura et *bysso*).—Cf. *byssum*, siricum retortum, Cp. B113; *byssum*, tuin, Cp. B230; *byssum*, tuum, Ep. 6A14; *byssum*, tuigin, Ef.[1] 347, 25; *byssum*, tortum siricum, Cp. B233.—**byssus**, in terra affricana [afric-] crescit in arbustis lana alba sicut nix, xxxix. 51 (*Greg.* [not Dial., but] *Reg. Past.* ii. 3 col. 29[A] superhumerale ex auro, hyacintho...et torta fieri *bysso* praecipitur; col. 30[A] torta *byssus*). Id. *Dial.* iv. 33 col. 373[B] (quoting *Luc.* xvi. 19) dives, qui induebatur purpura et *bysso*.

bythalasma, see *sitatum*.

c for *cc*: sacelli (for saccelli).—for *ch*: anticristus (anti*ch*r-); Caldeos (*Ch*-); caracteries (*ch*ar-); caracterismos (*ch*ar-); carcamis (*ch*-); caticumini (catec*h*umini); choncis (conc*h*is); colera (c*h*ol-); conca (conc*h*a); cronographias (*ch*ron-); moloncolia (melanc*h*olia); scema (sc*h*ema); scismatici (sc*h*ism-); scola, scolasticus (sc*h*ol-); tecnam (tec*h*nam); troclei (troc*h*leis).—for *ct*: mulcata (mulc*t*ata).—for *g*: amictalum (for amy*g*dalum); aucmentum (au*g*m-); calbanus (*g*alb-); catalocum (-lo*g*um); circumuacantium (-ua*g*antium); congrecacio (-*g*atio); congrecauimus (congre*g*-); creacras (crea*g*r-); leuicandum (leui*g*-); licant (li*g*-); octoade (o*g*d-); prodicus (prodi*g*-).—for *t*: astucia; cicius; congregacio; dificiones; induco (indu*t*o); iniciatus; inicium; inficiabor; inmundicia; lucubraciuncula; milicie; ociosus; ocii; ospicium; precium; prefacione; praefacionibus; predicaciones; uiciati.—for Gr. κ: paraprosdocia (-δοκια).—for Gr. π: simcosion (sym*p*osium).—c *omitted*: artum (arctum, in text); bachantes (bac*c*hantes); exolantes (excol-); dialeticam, dyal- (for dialecticam); pitatiola (pict- = pitt-).—c *inserted*: iacinctino, iacincto (hyacinthino, -cintho).

c apud latinus [-nos] fit sic ✳ ab aliis fit sic ✱, xxxii. 2 (*De ponder.*?).

caballi, xiii. 43, see *lamia*.

cacabus, de testa est duas manubrias [!] habens aliquando de ęręmento [aeram-] sicut et olla, xii. 9 (*Eccles.* xiii. 3 Quid communicabit *cacabus* ad ollam). The Cambridge MS. omits *de* before *testa*. Cf. *caccabum*, cetil, Cp. C6; Ep. 6E29; Ef.[1] 349, 31, and Bosw. T. (*cetel*).

cacastrofon, see *catastrofon*.

cacodaemon, -monem, see *cacodemonus*.

cacodemonus, malus demon [daemon], xxxviii. 28 (*Clem. Recognitt.* ix. 17 *cacodaemon* Venus; ix. 22 *cacodaemonem* Venerem...habuere).

cacomicanus [= Gr. κακομήχανος, mischief plotting, malicious], logdor, xlvii. 83 (*Alia* = ?) = *c*-, logðor, Cp. C123; Ep. —; *c*-, logdor, Ef.[1] 353, 53. For *logdor* &c. (which also glosses *marsius*, Wright W.

443, 9) plotting mischief, crafty, see Bosw. T. (*logđor*).

cacosprobon, see *catastrofon.*

cacumina, XLIV. 7, 18, see *poli.*

cadere, XVII. 3, see *occumbere.*

cadus, see *chatus*, sub v. *cathos.*

caeca, caecitas, see *cicona.*

caefalus, haerdhera, XLVII. 12 (*Alia*=?) =cefalus, heardhara, Cp. C314; Ep. —; Ef.[1] 353, 55. Caefalus=Gr. κέφαλος, a large-headed sea-fish, perhaps a kind of *mullet* (Liddell & Sc.). Haerdhera, heardhara (=heardra, Bosw. T.), the name of a fish (mulus vel mugilis, Aelfr. Gl. in Wright W. 180. 31; mullus ibid. 319, 14; cf. *mugil*, heardhara, Cp. M339). Cf. Grimm, *Wörtb.* (*Harder*); Kluge (*Etym. Wörtb.* v. *Harder*) is of opinion that the A. S. forms indicate a compound *hart-hase* (=E. *hard hare*); cf. id. in v. *hart* and *Asche*[2]; Goetz, VI. 178 (*capito*).

caeleuma, exortatio [exhort-] in naue, XIV. 15 (*Hier.* XXV. 30 *celeuma* [Heyse *caeleuma* in note] quasi calcantium concinętur; XLVIII. 33, LI. 14 *celeuma*).

caeli, XLIV. 2, see *cous*; see also *celi, cęli*; *clima*; *climacteras*; *conuexa*; *uasa castrorum.*

caelo, XLIV tit.

caelorum, see *cęlorum.*

caelum, see *celum, cęlum*; *laquearia.*

caementa, see *cementa.*

caementaria, ecclesię, XXXV. 65, see *coementeria.*

caementariis, see *cymentarii.*

caemento, see *commenta.*

caeno, see *ceno.*

caeporicon, see *otheporicon*, sub v. *sinphosin.*

Caesaris, see *fisco.*

caestus, see *cestus.*

cai, XXX. 52, see *ex ca.*

calamaucus, see *calomaucus.*

calamum, pigmentum ex arbore, XIII. 51 (*Isai.* XLII. 3 *calamum*...non conteret; XLIII. 24 non emisti...*calamum*; XIX. 6 *calamus*; XXXV. 7 viror *calami*).

Calanan, XIII. 22, see *carcamis.*

calanne, calano, see *carcamis.*

calathi, calathus, see *calati.*

calati, canistri de uirgis fiunt angusti in prodis [Cambr. MS. *profundis*] lati in ore, XIV. 14 (*Hier.* XXIV. 1 duo *calathi* pleni ficis; XXIV. 2 *calathus* unus).

calbanus, pigmentum album, XII. 19 (*Eccles.* XXIV. 21 quasi storax, et *galbanus.* The Cambridge MS. *galbanum*).

calcat, XXXI. 25, see *pes.*

calcauerit, see *excesserit.*

calce, calces, see *calles.*

calciamenta, XXI. 10, see *sandalia*; see also *suber.*

calciamentum, XXXVII. 6, see *caligam.*

calcidon, ut ignis lucens, XLI. 9 (*De nomin. div.*=*Apoc.* XXI. 19 *calcidonius*; cf. *calcido*, ut ignis lucet. haec est prasinum, Cp. C77; Ep. 8C11; Ef.[1] 352, 21. For *hoc est prasinum* in the present Glossary see *smaragdus*).

calcimenta [calciam-], XLVI. 14, see *suber.*

calculum (?), see *scriptionem.*

calculum, dicitur infirmitas eius qui non potest mingere quasi lapis obdurat uirilia, XXXIX. 48 (*Greg. Dial.*?). *Calculum* does not seem to occur in Gregory's *Dial.* Glogger suggests that it may be a further explanation to (XXXIX. 47) *sincopin* (q. v.). The Corpus Gl. (C127) and Ef.[1] (353, 58) have *calculum* (-lus) infirmitas dicitur (quae) non potest migare (mitigari) quasi lapis *obturat* (obdurat) uirilia.—**calculus**, minutissima petra arenę, XII. 12 (*Eccles.* XVIII. 8 *calculus arenae*). The Cambridge MS.: *calculus* arenę ipsę minutę petrę.

calcum [=calculum?], IV. 107, see *scriptionem.*

caldarius, XV. 41, see *lebes.*

caldeos [Chaldaeos], XVI. 11, see *saraballa.*

calefaciendo, XIII. 44, see *fouit.*

calices, XXXV. 12, see *cyati.*

calicis, XXIV. 1, see *fiole.*

calidae, XXXIX. 34, see *angulinis*; see also *taermę.*

calide [-dae], XX. 8, see *taermę.*

caligam, calciamentum subtalare, XXXVII. 6 (*S. Aug. Serm.* 29, 5 Migne *P.L.* XXXVIII col. 187 quaeris...*caligam*; 72, 5 ibid. col. 469 velis habere...*caligam*; 339, 5 ibid. col. 1482 *caligam* non vis habere malam); see also Serm. 82, 14 *caligas*; 107, 6 *caligam*; cf. *caligo*, scoh (*shoe*), Cp. C141.

caligine, see *cicona.*

Calipso [-ypso], insula, XLIII. 2, see *Themisto.*

Calistratus, proprium [add: *nomen*] uiri, XXXVIII. 11; **Idasteles**, proprium uiri, XXXVIII. 12; **Diodorus**, properter uiri, XXXVIII. 13; **Adepiades**, proprium uiri (*Clem. Recognitt.* VIII. 15 *Callistratus*... Alcmaeon..., Anaximandrus..., Anaxagoras..., *Diodorus*..., *Asclepias* [*Asclepiades* in Migne's note]...*Aristoteles*).

calix, XXIII. 7, see *cratera.*

callas, uarras, IV. 24, see **callos.**

calles, lapides, IV. 90 (*Ruf.* X. 37 fol. 176[b] *calce* cementoque, in editt. 1548 & 1535; Cacciari, p. 64: *calces*, cæmentaque); cf. (IV. 91) *cementa.*

calli (for *galli*), IV. 35, see *antelucanum.*

callidus, XLVI. 23, see *astus*.
Callistratus, see *Calistratus*.
callos, tensam cutem idest uarras, XXXV. 122 (*De Euseb.*); **callas**, uarras, IV. 24 (*Eccl. Istor.*) = (*Ruf.* II. 23 fol. 31[a] orando *callos* faceret in genibus). = *callos*, peorras uel ill, Cp. C161; *callus*, paar, Cp. C255. For *uarras*, *peorras* see Bosw. T. (*wearr*, a piece of hard skin); = *ill*, in Cp., see Bosw. T. (*ile* = o. Fris. *ili*, D. *eelt*; see Franck, *Woord. Ned. T.*).
calomachus, calomacus, see *calomaucus*.
calomaucus, het [a hat], XLVII. 7 (*Alia* = ?) = *calomachus*, haet, Cp. C124; Ep. —; *calomacus*, haeth, Ef.[1] 353, 54.—Schlutter (*Journ. Germ. Phil.* I. 326), referring to the glosses *galerum*, pylleum (= pileum) pastorale deiuuco factum (Goetz, v. 458, 24) and *galeros*, *calamaucos* (ib. v. 458, 25), thinks that *calamaucus* is connected with the late Gr. καλυμαύκιον, and (by metath.) καμηλαύκιον, shortened to καμηλαύκι in modern Greek (a monk's cap), and that the word may have developed from καλυμμάτιον. Cf. Du C. in v. *camelaucum*; *Archiv*, VI. 113; Goetz, VI. 165.
calones, saltantium turba, IV. 81 (*Eccl. Istor.*); **calonum**, nomen gentis cum francis, XXXV. 70; **calonum**, militum uel seruorum, XXXV. 71 (*De Euseb.*) = (*Ruf.* IX. 9 fol. 154[a] turbis...*calonum*). As *calonum* occurs only once in Ruf., 70 is, perhaps, a further explanation of 71 by the Glossator, referring to *Catalaunum* (Châlons-sur-Marne) or *Cabillonum* (Chalon-sur-Saône). Cf. *calones*, gabar militum, Cp. C190; Hildebrand, p. 42; *Archiv f. Lat. Lex.* IX. 368; X. 205.
Calypso, see *Themisto*.
cameli, XIII. 60, see *dromedarię*; XLVI. 13, see *tuber*.
camera, XXXVII. 12, see *ore camerato*; XLVI. 12, see *lucunar*.
camerae, see *camerum*.
camerato, XXXVII. 12, see *ore camerato*.
camerum, tectum, IV. 50 (*Ruf.* IV. 15 fol. 63[b] in modum *camerae*).
caminus, a caumando dicitur, XXIV. 16 (*Math.* XIII. 42 in *caminum* ignis); *caumando* for *caumate?*
camisa [for *camisia?*], lineum, XXXIX. 46 (*Greg. Dial.?*). Glogger suggests *Dial.* I. 9 col. 197[A] sine *linea*...sine tunica revertebatur; so that *lineum* may have been meant as lemma. Cf. *camisa*, haam, Cp. C109; Ep. 8E31; *camissa*, haam, Ef.[1] 353, 24.
camisia, see *camisa*.
canalis, XXXV. 211, see *cuniculum*.
Cananea [-naea], XXV. 3, see *sirofenissa*.
cancri, XXV. 5, see *scorpiones*.
candela, a candendo dicitur, II. 35 (*Bened. reg.* 22, 6 [9] *candela*...ardeat).
candendo, II. 35, see *candela*.
candentes, ardentes, IV. 106 (*Ruf.* V. 1 fol. 75[a] *candentes* laminas aeris et ferri... adhibebant). See also *veri candentes* (*Ruf.* VIII. 13), sub voce *pusti*.
candidum, X. 25, see *uinum candidum*.
cane, XXXVI. 11, see *musca canina*.
canes, VI. 20, see *molosi*.
cani, XXIX. 38, see *hyinę*.
canina, XXXVI. 11, see *musca canina*.
caninas, see *musca canina*.
canino, XLI. 6, see *cinico*.
canis, XLII. 9, see *ceruerus*.
canistri, XIV. 14, see *calati*.
Canitia, XXX. 2, see *Canitius*.
Canitius, qui a canitia prouintia [-cia] in gręcia uocatur, XXX. 2 (*Cat. Hier.*, Prol. 603[A] Antigonus *Carystius*; texts B & C *Caristius*).
CANONIBUS, I *tit.*, see GLOSAE.
canonicas, regulares horas, II. 37 (*Bened. reg.* 37, 7 [9] praeveniant horas *canonicas*; 67, 6 [9] per omnes *canonicas* horas).
canonum, see *cronicon*.
cantant, XXXVIII. 5, see *chantari*.
cantantes, XXI. 5, see *cum coronis*.
cantat, XLIII. 25, see *liricus*; XLVI. 7, see *tybicen*, 10, see *liricen*.
cantatis, II. 109, see *modulatis*.
cantator, XXIX. 12, see *comicus*.
Canthari, see *Chantari*.
cantica, XXXV. 1, see *tragoedia*.
CANTICO, X *tit.*
canticorum, XXIX. 12, see *comicus*; CANTICORUM, X *tit.*
canto, uectis, V. 4 (*Ruf.* XI. 33 fol. 192[a] proximos quosque *conto*, telis...sternit).
cantor, see *psaltes*.
cantum, XIX. 55, see *concentum*.
cantus, II. 135, see *psalmus*; IV. 35, see *antelucanum*; see also *psaltes*.
canuon, XXX. 77, see *cronicon canuon*.
caotastrifon, caotostrifon, see *catastrofon*.
capiantur, I. 70, see *mancipantur*.
capiebam, XXXV. 151, see *expiscabar*.
capite, XXII. 16, see *ueredarii*; XXIII. 1, see *exedra*.
capitella, I. 49, see *epistilia*.
capitibus, XXI. 5, see *cum coronis*.
capitio, haubit loh, XIX. 26 (*Job* XXX. 18 *capitio* tunicae succinxerunt me). Haubit loh is the O.H.G. *houbitloh* [see Schade], neut., opening for the head. The Cambr. MS. has: *capitio* summitas tunicę.
capitis, XXXIX. 19, see *freniticus*.
capiuntur, XXIX. 23, see *decipulam*.
capparis, erba [herba] bona ad com-

messationem nascitur in montibus, IX. 5 (*Eclesiast.* XII. 5 dissipabitur *capparis*).

capsaces [=Gr. καψάκης], lenticula idest uas uitreum simile flasconi, XXXVII. 5 (*S. Aug.*); see *fidelia farris.*

captiuitate, XXIII. 2, see *filii f-.*

capud [caput], IV. 97, see *thoraces.*

capun periens instructio **Matuytu** de deo corpore induco [-to] uel de peritia dei, XXX. 29 (*Cat. Hier.* XXIV col. 643B περὶ 'Ενσωμάτου Θεοῦ librum; a Vat. MS. ΚΑΙΤΟΙΤΕΡΙΕΝCΩΜΑΤΟΥ; B *kaitonperien goo atoythyo* librum; C [blank]). Hence *leg.* (as in Rich.): καὶ τὸν περὶ ἐνσωμάτου θεοῦ [which reading is clearly traced in B], instructio de deo corpore induto uel de peritia dei; see Migne's note.

caput, XIII. 37, see *malus nauis*, 43, see *lamia*; see also *thoraces.*

carabum, modica nauis minor quam scafa [scapha], XXXIX. 31 (*Greg. Dial.* IV. 57 col. 424B post nauem *carabum* regebat, ...cum eodem *carabo*).

caracteres, see *caracteries.*

caracteries, scripturis [-turas?], XXXIV. 51 (*De Cass. Inst.* XII. 29 *characteres* eius ...exprimamus; in note *caracteres*).—**cataracteras**, stilo uel figura, XXX. 92 (*Cat. Hier.* CXVII col. 709A Secutus est...Polemonem dicendi *charactere*; Richardson: Secutus est...Polemonium dicendi χαρακ: τῆρα; B: Secutus est...polemonium dicendi *character*; C: Sec. est...polemonium dicendi [blank])=*caracter*, stilus uel figura, Cp. C68; Ep. 8A37; Ef.[1] 352, 10.

caracterismos, quando aliquis aut per formam discribitur aut per actus propriores indicatur, XXVIII. 43 (*Cass. Psalm.* IX. 25 *characterismos*, q. a. a. p. f. describitur, a. p. a. proprios i.). See also id. XX. 3; XXXVI. 32.

carbasini, color gemme [-mae] idest uiridis, XXII. 7 (*Esther* I. 6 tentoria aërij coloris et *carbasini*).

carbunculi, poccas, V. 5 (*Ruf.* IX. 8 fol. 150b humana corpora vlceribus...qui dicuntur *carbunculi* replerentur). For *poccas* (plur. of *pocc*, a pock, pustule, ulcer) see Bosw. T. (*pocc*).

Carcamis, nomen loci uel ciuitatis; **Calanan**, similiter, XIII. 21 & 22 (*Isai.* x. 9 Vulg. numquid non ut *Charcamis*, sic *Calano*). Heyse, note: *carchamis* sic *chalam*; Sab., vers. ant. *Chalane*; Cambr. MS. *Calanne.*

carcere, XXXV. 168, see *ergastulo*; 205, see *in metallo*; **carcere**, XI. 13, see *in carcere.*

Carchamis, see *carcamis.*

cardella, distyltige, XLVII. 70 (*Alia*=?) =*c-*, þisteltuige, Cp. C122; Ep. —; *c-*, thistil, Ef.[1] 353, 51. The lemma, perh. a dim. of *cardus* the thistle, seems another form of *carduelis*, the thistle-finch, goldfinch. For distyltige, þisteltuige (from *þistel*, a thistle, and *twige*, perh. from *twiccian*, to pluck, twitch, for which see Skeat, in vv. *twitch, tweak*) see Bosw. T. (*þistel, þistel-twige*); Steinm. III. 462, 11 (O.H.G. *distilziu*), 463, 46 (O.H.G. *distilzuui*).

cardine, XLIV. 11, see *clima.*

cardines, extreme partes axis sunt, XLIV. 5 (*Alia*; *de cælo*=Isid. *de nat. rerum* XII. 3 col. 983 *cardines extremae axis partes sunt*). A further explanation of the above is, perhaps, XLIV. 10: **cardines** quoque axis ipsius sunt extremę partes sunt quos insertos orbi discribunt sperico [descr- sphaerico] ut ipsis cęlum inuoluatur inuisis et ita polum philosophi ui propria semper in suo axe torqueri arbitrantur a quibus ignoratur opifex qui mundum in suum orbem absque ullo axis moderamine eregit [erigit]. See also (XLIV. 1) *partes.*

cardo, XLIV. 4, see *clima.*

carduelis, cardus, see *cardella.*

carectum, hreod, XIX. 16 (*Job* VIII. 11 *carectum*)=*carectum*, hreod, Cp. C129; Ep. —; Ef.[1] 354, 33. For *hreod*, a reed, see Bosw. T.

caret, XLVI. 24, see *situs.*

carex, seic, XLVI. 26 (*Alia*=*Ars Phocae*, p. 420, 31 haec *carex*)=*carix*, secg, Cp. C110; Ep. —; *carix*, sech, Ef.[1] 353, 34. *Seic*=A.S. *secg* (Bosw. T.), E. *sedge.*

caricis, see *carricibus.*

Caristius, see *Canisius.*

carmina, I. 90, see *philacteria.*—**carmina in nocte**, laudes in tribulatione, XIX. 50 (*Job* XXXV. 10 qui dedit *carmina in nocte*). On the gloss see Hieron. *Comm. in Job* XXXV. 10 (Migne, *Patr. Lat.* XXVI col. 732C), and id. *Expos. interl. in Job* XXXV. 10 (Migne, *P.L.* XXIII col. 1456B) consolationem in tribulatione.

carne, XI. 3, see *lanugo*; XIV. 7, see *lignum.*

carnes, XLV. 19, see *lanistra.*

carnium, IV. 58, see *oedipia*, in voce *thesteas.*

carpenta, carra, VII. 7 (1 *Paral.* XX. 3 fecit super eos...ferrata *carpenta* transire). Cf. *carpentum*, carrum, Cp. C182; Ep.—; Ef.[1] 355, 21; Ef.[2] 274, 23.

carperetur, consumeretur, I. 34 (*De Canon.*; *Can. Conc. Carth.* LVI ut ex massa dioecesium nulla *carperetur*).

carra, VII. 7, see *carpenta.*

carricibus, genus ligni, III. 39 (*De S. Mart. Stor.*=*Sulp. Sev. Dial.* I. 20, 4 hic ...sex...*caricis* sustentari).

carrum, XV. 3, see *uas transmigrationis.*

cartas, XIII. 31, see *papiri*; XIV. 20, see *scalpellum.*

carte [-tae], XXXIX. 69, see *scedule.*

cartilago, see *cartillago.*

cartillago, uuldpaexhsue uel grost, XIX. 59 (*Job* XL. 13 *cartilago* illius quasi laminæ ferreæ; Heyse, in note, *cartillago*). *uuldpaexhsue*, in another MS. *yulpa exhsaey* (for wuldwaexhsae = A. S. wealdweax? = O.H.G. *waltowahso*), nervus, a sinew, tendon, nerve; cf. Oxf. D. (*paxwax*); Steinm. I. 497; Graff I. 689; Schade 1085; Schmeller II. 838; Grimm (*Gesch. der d. Spr.* 666); Kluge (*Ang. Leseb.* 216ᵇ wealdweax); Schlutter (*Journ. Germ. Phil.* I. 63); Holthausen (*Anglia* XXI. 239).—*grost* (= O.H.G. *grostila*, *chrustula*; see Steinm. I. 507, 19—25), in another MS. *grist* = A.S. *grystle*, *gristle*; cf. cartilago, *naesgristle*, Cp. C14; cartilaga (cartalago), *naesgristlae*, Ep. 7A5 & Ef.[1] 349, 45 (i.e. *nose-gristle*).

Carus, nomen hominis qui transportare dicitur in infernum, XLIII. 18; **cruda**, ualens, XLIII. 19 (*De div. nominibus* = Donati *Ars grammat.* [Hagen, *Comm. Einsidl. in Don.*, p. 233, 27] ut Virgilius [*Aen.* VI. 304] de *Charone*: Iam senior [Keil's Vol. IV., p. 374, 32 ut iam senior &c.] sed *cruda* deo uiridisque senectus).

Carystius, see *Canisius.*

case, see *magalia.*

casia, see *cassia.*

cassa, uacua, IX. 2 (*Eclesiast.* II. 26 *cassa* solicitudo mentis).

cassae, see *cassuae.*

cassari, euacuare, XXXIX. 29 (*Greg. Dial.* IV. 44 col. 404ᴰ ante illum judicis justi conspectum orationis suae meritum *cassari* refugiunt).

cassia, erba [herba] est similis coste, X. 20 (*Cant.*?). Together with the glosses X. 18 & 19, we may perhaps refer to Psalm XLIV. 9: myrrha [*murra*, vers. ant.] et gutta et *casia* [cassia, vers. ant.]; coste for cost*o*, or, perhaps, for a dat. cost*ae*, fem. of cost*os*.—**cassia**, pigmenta, XIX. 46 (*Job* XLII. 14 nomen secundae *Cassiam*; Heyse, in note, *Cassia*; Migne, *Patr. L.* XXVI col. 800ᴰ *Casia*).

cassiam, see *cassia.*

CASSIANO, XXXIV *tit.*; XLVIII *tit.*

cassidie [for *cassidile*], cassidile, cassidili, see *de cassidie.*

cassu, see *cassuae.*

cassuae, ruinae, XLVIII. 13 (*De Cass.*, *Inst.* VII. 13 qui innumeros diuersorum *casus ac ruinas* experti sunt). If the Glossary refers to this passage, the above words are two lemmata without any interpretation. A St Gallen MS. has *cassae*, ruinae, with which cf. Cassian. *Inst.* VII. 22 fructus...*cassae* uoluntatis uitio perdi disse; ib. IV. 16 *casu* [al. *cassu*] aliquo.

castella, XLVIII. 27, see *tesbites.*

castigatio, XXX. 25, 83, see *elegos.*

castigationis, see *elegos*; *eortatica.*

castitatis, XLVIII. 22, see *inmunitatis.*

castor, see *castorius.* **castor**, XLIII. 44 (bis), see *epul.*

castorius, bebor, XLVII. 87 (*Alia* = ?) = *c*-, beber, Cp. C126; Ep. —; *c*-, bebir, Ef.[1] 353, 57. *Castorius*, a deriv. of *castor*, *the castor*, *beaver* (see Goetz, VI. 187). For *bebor* &c., the beaver, see Bosw. T. (*beber*, *befer*, *beofer* &c.), and Oxf. D. (*beaver*[1]).

castrati, XIII. 60, see *dromedarię.*

castro, see *castrum.*

castrorum, XII. 42, see *uasa castrorum.*

castrum, modica ciuitas altioribus muris, XVI. 17 (*Dan.* VIII. 2 cum essem in Susis *castro*).

castus [for *cantus* or *cantor*?], IV. 53, see *psaltes.*

casu, see *cassuae*; *fortuitu.*

casulas, domunculas, XXVI. 2 (Isid. *Offic.* II. 16, 1 faciebant sibi *casulas*).

casum, XXXV. 141, see *excidium.*

casus, XXVIII. 40, see *silemsis*; see also *cassuae.*

cataantis, contrarius, XXIX. 68 (*Uerb. Interpr.* = *Hier. in Matth.* XXVI. 50 Verbum, Amice, vel κατὰ ἀντίφρασιν intelligendum). Cf. antifrasin (antefrasin), contraria locutio, Cp. A561; Ep. 1A14; Ef.[1] 337, 14. Glogger refers also to XVI. 22 *Satanas* interpretatur adversarius, sive *contrarius*; but *satanas*, a well-known word, would hardly be corrupted into *cataantis.*

cataceeos, doctrine [-nae], XXXV. 196 (*De Eus.*); **catacesseos**, doctrinarum, IV. 102 (*Eccl. Istor.*) = (*Ruf.* VI. 19 fol. 108ᵇ Heraclae...κατηχήσεως auditorium derelinquens; VI. 22 fol. 109ᵃ auditorium κατηχήσεως...tradidit). **catacesseos**, doctrine, XXX. 67 (*Cat. Hier.* CXII col. 707ᴬ Exstant ejus κατηχήσεις; B: Extant eius *catheseon* idest doctrinarum opuscula; C: Extant eius [blank]. Cf. *Cat. Hier.* LXIX col. 677ᶜ scholam κατηχήσεων... tenuit; B: scolam doctrinarum...tenuit; C: scolam [blank] tenuit).—**catacesseun**, doctrinarum, XXX. 34 (*Cat. Hier.* XXXVIII col. 653ᴬ κατηχήσεων magister; B: catecheseon idest docte marum magister; C: [blank] magister) = *cataceseis*, doctrinae, Cp. C76; Ep. 8C8; *catacesseis*, doctrinae, Ef.[1] 352, 18; *catacesion*, doctrinarum, Cp. C62; *cataceseon*, doctrinarum, Ep. 8A31; *catacesseon*, doctrinarum, Ef.[1] 352, 4.

catacesseos, doctrinarum, IV. 102; **cata-**

cesseos, doctrine, xxx. 67; **catacesseun**, doctrinarum, xxx. 34; see *cataceeos*.

catafrigarum [sine interpretat.], I. 23 (*De Canon.*; *Can. Conc. Laod.* CXI conuertuntur ab haeresi quae dicitur *Cataphrygarum*; ib. *tit.* ab haeresi *Cataphrygarum*). Cf. *catafrigia*, genus hereticorum in frigia, Cp. C25; Ep. 7A33; Ef.[1] 350, 15; *catafrigas*, secundum frigas, Cp. C63; Ep. 8A32; Ef.[1] 352, 5.

catagoga, XXXVIII. 16, see *ochimo*.

catalocum, secundum numerum, XXXIX. 68, see *catalogo*.

CATALOGO, XXX *tit.*, see *De Catalogo*.—**catalogum**, series nominum, XXXIV. 20 (*De Cass.*, *Inst.* XI. 10, 1 ut praeteream uirtutum...*catalogum*).—**catalocum**, secundum numerum, XXXIX. 68 (*not* in Greg. Dial., but *Can. Apostt.* IX. p. 112 ex sacerdotali *catalogo*).

cata mane, iuxta mane, XV. 30 (*Ezech.* XLVI. 14, 15).

cataplasmarent, contritos [add: *ficos?*] inponerent, XIII. 46 (*Isai.* XXXVIII. 21 jussit Isaias ut tollerent massam de ficis et *cataplasmarent* super vulnus).

cataracteras [for *charactere*], stilo uel figura, XXX. 92, see *caracteries*.

catas. prophon, see *catastrofon*.

catastam, lupam, VI. 11 (*Breu. exsol.?*). Cf. *catasta*, genus supplicii, Cp. C51; Ep. 8A4; Ef.[1] 351, 36; *catasta*, geloed, Cp. C98; *c*-, gloed, Ep. 8E3; *c*-, geleod, Ef.[1] 352, 49. For *catasta* see Napier, 4485; 2, 340; Goetz, VI. 189.

catastrofon, conuersationem, XXX. 88 (*Cat. Hier.* CXI col. 705[B] quod vocavit καταστροφὴν, sive Πεῖραν; B: quod vocauit *katascrophen* idest *conuersationem* siue peran idest peram; C: quod uocauit [blank] siue peram)=*catastrofon*, conuersationem, Cp. C69; Ep. 8C1; *cacastrofon*, c-, Ef.[1] 352, 11. Cf. *catas. prophon*, conprehensio uel pena, Cp. C146; *cacos probon*, conprehensio uel opera, Ef.[1] 354, 60, 61;—*caotostrifon*, uterem, Cp. C84; *caotastrifon*, uterem, Ep. 8C20; Ef.[1] 352, 30; *-trofon*, conuersationem, Cp. T256; Ep. 26C37; Ef.[1] 395, 48; see Schlutter, *Journ. Germ. Phil.* I. 313.

catecheseon, see *catacesseun*.

catechizatur, see *catezizatur*.

catechumeni, see *caticumini*.

catenis, XXXIX. 20, see *in mare adriatico*.

catenulas, XIII. 10, see *murenulas*.

catepenon, latini per laudem, XXVIII. 50 (*Cass. Psalm.* XVII. 1 Hic duodecima species definitionis est, quae Graece dicitur κατ' ἔπαινον, Latine per l.).

catezizatur, inbuitur, I. 20 (*De Canon.*; *Can. Conc. Nic.* II ei, qui *catechizatur*).

catha manthan, secundum matheum, XXX. 44 (*Cat. Hier.* LIV col. 665[B] κατὰ Ματθαῖον; B: iuxta *matheum*; C: *cathamatheon*)=*catamasion*, secundum matheum, Cp. C81; *catamaqoon*, secundum matheum, Ep. 8C16; Ef.[1] 352, 26.

cathamatheon, see *catha manthan*.

cathanos, mundos, XXXV. 295 (*Ruf.* X. 6 fol. 162[a] Et *Catharos*; VI. 33 fol. 114[b] καθαροὺς, id est mundos).—**catheron**, mundorum, XXX. 64 (*Cat. Hier.* LXX col. 681[A] Novatianorum, quod Graece dicitur Καθαρῶν dogma; B: nouat. quod greco d. *kathareo* id est *mundorum* dogma; C: nouac. q. grece d. [blank] dogma)= *Cataron*, mundorum, Cp. C70; Ep. 8C4; Ef.[1] 352, 14.

Cataphrygarum, see *catafrigarum*.

catharos, see *cathanos*.

catheseon, see *catacesseos*, sub v. *cataceeos*.

catholica, catholicæ, catholicam, see *catholicus*.

catholicus, grece, latine uniuersalis, I. 31 (*De Canon.*; cf. *Can. Conc. Nic.* VIII ad Ecclesiam *Catholicam*; *Catholicæ*... Ecclesiae dogmata; IX *Catholica*...Ecclesia).—**catholicus**, uniuersalis, II. 34 (*Bened. reg.* 9, 19 [28] a nominatis doctorum orthodoxis *catholicis* patribus; 73, 11 [16] liber sanctorum *catholicorum* patrum). Cf. catholica, uniuersalis, Cp. C78; Ep. 8C14; Ef.[1] 352, 24.

cathos, sexta pars sextarii, XXXI. 21; **chatos** tres modios habet, XXXI. 39 (*De ponder.?*).—**chatus** grece amphora est habens urnas III, XXXIII. 11 (*Euch. De Pond.* p. 159, 3 *cadus* Graeca a. e. habet u. tres). The Brit. Mus. MS. adds: Beth in paralypemenonis tria sata capit. Satum uero mensura est XLVIII sextariorum quod facit modii III. Cf. also Wotke, in note to Euch. Cf. *cados*, ambras, Cp. C9; Ep. 6E35; Ef.[1] 349, 37. See E. *cade* in Oxf. D. (sb[1]).

caticumini, grece, latine instructi uel auditores, I. 22 (*De Canon.*; *Can. Conc. Ancyr.* XXXI tit. cum essent *catechumeni*; cf. *Can. Conc. Nic.* XIV De *catechumenis*; *Neocaes.* XLIX De *catechumenis*, *catechumenus*; *Laod.* CXXII super *catechumenos* &c.). Cf. *catecominus*, deforis audiens, Cp. C73; Ep. 8C7; Ef.[1] 352, 17; *catecuminus*, instructus, Cp. C74.

catino, see *catinum*.

catinum, discum modicum ligneum uel lapideum, XXV. 1 (*Marc.* XIV. 20 intingit... manum in *catino*; cf. *Luc.* XI. 39 *catini*) =*catinus*, discus modicus, Cp. C61; Ep. 8A29; *castinus*, d.m., Ef.[1] 352, 2.

catinus, see *catinum*.

cattas, see *gattas*.

cauatum, IV. 108, see *excessum*.

cauda, XXV. 5, see *scorpiones* ; XLIV. 22, see *pliadę*.

caudex, see *cliutex*.

cauliculi, ramunculi, XXIX. 48 (*Uerb. Interpr.* = *Hier. in Matth.* XXIV. 32, 33 quando teneri fuerint in arbore ficus *cauliculi*. Cf. Migne's note, col. 179).

caumando [for *caumate*? heat], XXIV. 16, see *caminus*.

caumate, ardenter, XXIX. 41 (*Uerb. Interpr.* = *Hier. in Matth.* XXV. 8 exorto *caumate*, arefiunt). Q^y *ardenter* for *ardore*? see Napier 3244, 3779, *chaumate*, idest ardore. Cf. *caumati*, suole, Cp. C237 ; see Bosw. T. (*swōl*) ; Franck, *Woord. Ned. T.* (*zwoel*). For *caumate* see also *caminus*.

caupo, qui uinum permiscet ad perdendum, XII. 45 (*Eccles.* XXVI. 28). Cf. *caupo*, qui uinum cum aqua miscet, Cp. C20 ; Ep. 7A29 ; *causo*, q.u.c.a.m., Ef.[1] 350, 11.

causa, I. 95, see *portentuose* ; II. 182, see *uerbi gratia* ; XXIX. 43 and XXXV. 217, see *perpera* ; XXXIX. 24, see *aduocatus*.

causae, see *aetilogia*.

causam, XXVIII. 70, see *sinchrisis*.

cause [-sae], XXVIII. 46, see *aetilogia* ; causę [-sae], XXVIII. 79, see *epexergasia*.

causetur, murmuretur, II. 24 (*Bened. reg.* 2. 78 [119] ne *causetur* de minore forte substantia).

causticis, asperis firmioribus, XXXIV. 9 (*De Cassiano, Inst.* X. 7, 6 *causticis* medicamentis sanare).

caute, II. 141, see *prouide*.

cäutere, tunderi, IV. 77 (*Eccles. Istor.*); **cautere**, ferrum melius tindre, XXXV. 201 (*De Euseb.*) = (*Ruf.* VIII. 13 fol. 142[a] poplite...*cauterio* debilitato). Cf. *cautere*, aam, Cp. C16 ; *cautere*, ferrum id est haam, Ep. 7A8; *cautere*, ferrum fam, Ef.[1] 349, 48. For *tunderi*, *tindre* (perh. *instr.* of *tunder*, or = *tundre*, G. *Zunder*, D. *tondel*, tinder, fuel), see Bosw. T. (*tynder*) ; Franck, *Woord. Ned. T.* (*tondel*).

cauterio, see *cautere*.

cautes, lapides, XXXIV. 17 (*De Cass.*, *Inst.* XI. 4 nos perniciosis...*cautibus* inlidendos).

cautibus, see *cautes*.

cecinit, XXVII. 28, see *in georgicis*.

cecitas [caec-], XXXIV. 24, see *cicona*.

cedo, dic uel perdono, XLIII. 48 (*De div. nominibus* = Donati *Ars grammat.* p. 385, 4 Sunt verba defectiva alia per modos, ut *cedo* ; ibid. 383, 16 and 385, 7 *cedo*). Cf. Hagen, *Comm. Einsidl. in Don.* 255. 13 and 257, 31 *cedo*. id est dic.

cedri, X. 11 (bis), see *tigna*.

cedrina, cedrus, see *tigna*.

cefalus, see *caefalus*.

celebrationes, XLVIII. 68, see *sinaxeos* ; see also *synaxeos cura*.

celestibus [coel-], XLIV. 7, see *poli*.

celeuma, see *caeleuma*.

celi [caeli], XLIV. 4, 11, see *clima*.

cęli [caeli], XII. 42, see *uasa* ; XXXVIII. 25, see *climacteras* ; XLIV. 6, see *conuexa*, 11, see *clima*, 27, see *dextera*, 29 (bis), see *axem*.

cęlis [caelis], XXVIII. 28, see *metonymia*.

cellaria, XIII. 45, see *apotecas*.

cęlorum [cael-], XLIV. 18, see *poli*.

celox, nauis, XLVI. 30 (*Alia* = *Ars Phocae*, p. 421, 22 haec *celox* quod scapham significat [*nauis*]). Cf. *celox*, ceol (E. *keel*), Cp. C293 ; Ep. 8E4; *caelox*, ceol, Ef.[1] 352, 50.

celsitudo, XXXV. 142, see *proceritas*.

celum [caelum, coelum], III. 41, see *laquearia*.

cęlum, ab oriente ad occidentem semel in die et nocte uerti sapientes aestimant, XLIV. 9 (*Alia* ; *de cælo* = Isid. *de nat. rerum*, XII. 4 col. 984 *Coelum* autem ab O. ad O. s. i. d. e. n. u. s. existimant). For *cęlum*, see also (XLIV. 2) cous ; (XLIV. 10) *cardines* ; (XLIV. 27) *leua*.

cementa, gluttina, IV. 91 (*Eccl. Istor.*); **commenta**, petra, XXXV. 219 (*De Euseb.*) = (*Ruf.* X. 37 fol. 176[b] calce *cemento*que adhibitis, in editt. 1548 & 1535; Cacciari, p. 64 : calces *cæmenta*que adhibita) ; cf. (IV. 91) *calles*.—**cementa**, petre molliores, XII. 15 (*Eccles.* XXII. 21 *caementa* sine impensa posita...non permanebunt). Cf. *cementum*, liim lapidum, Cp. C320; cementum, limlidum, Ef.[1] 354, 32.

cemento, see *cementa*.

cenas, see *scenas turpes*.

ceno, luto, XLVIII. 69 (*De Cass.*, *Inst.* VI. 6 de terrae *caeno* ; in note *ceno*) = *caenum*, lutum, Cp. C29 ; cf. *caenum*, pase, Cp. C128.

cenobita, graece in commune uiuens, II. 33 (*Bened. reg.* 1, 3 & 28 [38] genus... *coenobitarum* [*coenouitarum*]).

cenodoxia, inanis gloria, XXXIV. 12 (*De Cass. Inst.* V. 1 septimum [uitium] *cenodoxiae*, quod sonat uana seu inanis gloria; XI. 1 contra spiritum κενοδοξίας quam nos uanam siue inanem gloriam possumus appellare).

censeri, II. 164, see *suadere*.

censo, II. 138, see *penso*.

censum, quod repente indicitur, XXIV. 9 (*Math.* XVII. 24 accipiunt...*censum* ; XXII. 17 *censum* dare).

censura, iuditium [-cium], XXXIX. 3

(*Greg. Dial.* i. 1 col. 156[c] magistri intimi *censura* non desit).

centaurus, nauis unus de nauibus enie [Aeneae], xliii. 21, see *eunuchus*.

centum, xxxi. 20, see *taletum*; see also *c. uolles*.

cephalus, see *caefalus*.

cerberus, see *ceruerus*.

cercetea, xxxi. 17, see *Grece idest cercetea*.

certaminis, xxxv. 156, see *ad stadium*.

certare, xii. 43, see *agoniare*.

certe, ii. 132, see *plane*, 165, see *sane*.

certissime [-mis], xxviii. 34, see *figura metopoea*.

ceruerus [cerb-], canis qui hostiarius inferni dicitur, xlii. 9 (*Ex div. libris?*).

ceruicatus, superbus, xii. 10 (*Eccles.* xvi. 11 si unus fuisset *ceruicatus*).

ceruicis, x. 8, see *redimicula*.

cesae, see *magalia*.

Cesaris, xxxv. 180, see *fisco*.

cespitem, see *glebam*.

cesso, xliii. 52, see *facesso*.

cessura, see *cissura*.

cestus, arma pictarum [pyct-], xliii. 54 (*De div. nominibus*; not in Donati *Ars gramm.*, but Keil iv, Probi *Cathol.* 30, 12—14 [and note] hic *cestus*, tunica Veneris, huius *cesti*, hic *caestus pugilum* huius caestus: Vergilius [*A.* v. 410] "quid siquis caestus ipsius" et orthographia distant et declinatione). With this gloss Glogger would connect *sis nuis* of xliii. 55, perhaps corrupted from A. S. *sīma*, a cord, rope (Bosw. T. sima; Kluge, *Etym. D.* Saite). He suggests that the gloss originally may have been *siima s*(axonice); see note § on p. 45 of the present Glossary.

ceteriorem, ulteriorem, xxxv. 32 (*Ruf.* v. 10 fol. 83[a] ad Indiam *citeriorem*).

cethetica [for *ctetica*], possessiua, xliii. 12; see *omonima*.

ch for *c*: *ch*atos, *ch*atus (for cadus); *ch*oncis (for conchis); enc*h*enia (encaenia); oc*h*imo (ocimo).—for *h*: parc*h*redis (par*h*edris).—for *st*: *ch*omacho (*st*om-).

chalam, chalane, see *carcamis*.

Chaldaei, see *Chaldei*.

Chaldaeos, see *malefici*; *saraballa*.

Chaldei sunt quos uulgus mathematicos uocat, xvi. 29 (*Dan.* ii. 2 ut convocarentur ...*Chaldaei*). Also *Chaldaei* ii. 4, 10; iii. 8; iv. 4.—*Chaldaeorum*, i. 4.—*Chaldaeis*, ii. 5 &c.

Chaldeos [-daeos], xvi. 27, see *malefici*.

chantari, uermes qui cantant nocte sicut locuste [-tae], xxxviii. 5 (*Clem. Recognitt.* vi. 10 quod etsi lex de his non admonuisset, nos ut *canthari* libenter volveremur in stercore?). For *canthăris*, ĭdis = κανθαρίς?

chaos, xxxv. 226, see *in chaos*.

character, charactere, see *cataracteras*.

characteres, see *caracteries*.

characterismos, see *caracterismos*.

charcamis, see *carcamis*.

Charone, see *Carus*.

chatos tres modios habet, xxxi. 39; **chatus**, grece amphora est habens urnas iii, xxxiii. 11, see *cathos*.

chaumate, see *caumate*.

chimerinus, see *exemerinus*.

chinou, chisau, see *ypo* (sub) *tyos* (hoc) &c.

cholera, see *colera*.

chomacho [for *stom-*], xlvii. 89, see *bulinus*.

choncis, hebernum, xxxvi. 7 (*Oros.* i. 3, 4 lapidum, quos...*conchis* et ostreis scabros ...uisere solemus: in note *conchis*, *concis*); *hebernum*, abl. plur., *with crabs* (literally with sea-houses, from *heb* = hæf, sea, and *ern* = ærn, an habitation, house), see Kluge, *A. S. Les.* p. 181 (*hæf* & *hæférn*); cf. *concis*, scellum, Cp. C758.

chorepiscopi, xli. 2 (*De nomin. div.*); see *presbiteri*.

choris, xxi. 5, see *cum coronis*.

choros xxx modios gressus et uestigia eius idest pes inter duos idest duos cubitos, xxxi. 24 (*De ponder.*); **chorus** est modii xxx, xxxiii. 9 (*De pond. Euch.*, p. 159, 2 *corus* [al. *chorus*] est modi [al. *modii*] xxx) = *chorus*, xxx modios habet, Cp. C364; Ep. 8A19; Ef.[1] 351, 51. Cf. Blume, i. 376, 12, 13.

chorus, see *choros*.

choum, see *cous*.

chous, see *cous*; *partes*.

Chri fiscus, fans [for fraus; see Cp. C888, F158], xxx. 42 (*Cat. Hier.* liv col. 663[B] Rem familiarem ob confessionem *Christi fiscus* occupaverat; B: Rem f. ob *cristi* conf. *fiscus* occupauerat; C: R. f. ob conf. *Cristi fiscus* occ.). This reading of the text suggests *Christi* for *Chri*, by the omission of a stroke. But a comparison with Cp. C888 (cristonografon siriem fiscus fraus regalis) would also suggest that *chri* may be the remainder of some such gloss as χρονογραφεῖον [XPO = Christo], *seriem temporum*; see below *cronographias*.

chrisma, x. 6, see *unguentum exinanitum*.

chrismam, x. 5, see *nomen tuum*.

chrisme, x. 6, see *unguentum exinanitum*.

Christi, see *chri fiscus*.

Christiana, see *uoti compos*, and *xpistiana*.

Christiani, Christianiam, Christo, see *nomen tuum*.

chronicorum, see *cronicon.*

chrono, chronographias, see *chronographias.*

chrysolithus (-tus), see *crisolitus.*

ciatos habens pensum solidorum VI, XXXII. 6, see *cyati*; for *ciatos* see also (XXII. 12) *urna.*

cibis, II. 20, see *alimentis.*

cibo, XXIII. 12, see *memores salis.*

cibos, XV. 11, see *preteriola*; XXIX. 15, see *batroperite*; XXXV. 61, see *exedrę.*

ciceris, XXIX. 13, see *frixi ciceris.*

Cicerone, XXXIX. 4; **Ciceronis**, XXXIX. 4, see *balneum ciceronis.*

cicima, geometria, XL. 10 (*Uerba?*).

cicius [citius], XXIII. 1, see *exedra*; see also *citius.*

ciclis [for *cyclis*, or *circulis*], XLIV. 7, see *poli.*

cicona, cecitas [caec-], XXXIV. 24 (*De Cassiano?*). According to the order in which *cicona* occurs in the Glossary, it should be looked for in *Inst.* XI. 13 to 15. But it is not found there. Could it refer to V. 34 oculi...a suffusione uel *caligine* caecitatis inmunes?; or to nocte caeca, *Inst.* XI. 9?

ciconia, storhc, XLVII. 56 (*Alia*=?)=*c*-, storc, Cp. C405 and Ef.[1] 353, 43; Ep.—. For *storhc*, *storc*, a stork, see Bosw. T. (*storc*); Schade (*storhc*).

cicuanus, see *picus.*

cimbalis [cymb-], VII. 1, see *in nablis.*

cimina romana, dimedius sextarius, XXXI. 35 (*De ponder.?*).

cinamum, cortix [-tex] dulcis, VIII. 11 (*Salam.* VII. 17 aspersi cubile meum... *cinnamomo*). Cf. *cinnamomum*, cymiu resina, Cp. C437.

cincinnos, crines, XXI. 14 (*Judith* XVI. 10 colligavit *cincinnos* suos mitra).

cineris, see *cyneris.*

cingulo, XI. 14, see *poderis.*

cinico, canino, XLI. 6 (*De nomin. div.* = *Can. Conc. Constant.* CLXV p. 133, De Maximo *Cynico*).

cinnamomo, see *cinamum.*

cinticta onitaltaon [or *-talticon*, or *-taltccon*], ratio populorum, XXX. 85 (*Cat. Hier.* XCVIII col. 699 elaboravit in Ecclesiasten decem et septem volumina, et *συμμίκτων ζητημάτων* sex; B: elab. in eccl. xviij volumina et *sinokte ȝetnyaton* idest *dogmata populorum* sex; C: elab. in ecc. x et vij volumina et [blank] sex). ¶ In § 62 (p. xl) of my preface to the Cp. Glossary I connected the above gloss with ΛΑΩΒΗΤΟΝ, ratio populorum, found in the Cp. Gloss. among the A words (A 593). But at that time I had not studied, and thought it unnecessary to study, St Jerome's *Catalogus.* The above reading of Text B clearly points to *συμμίκτων ζητημάτων*, and the Leiden *cinticta oni* may be identified with *συμμίκτων.* But there is difficulty in connecting the Leiden *taltaon* (or *talticon*, or *taltccon*) with *ζητημάτων*; it rather seems to be the remains of *μονόφθαλμον*, of which the Glossator explained *monon* (q.v.) in the preceding gloss (XXX. 84). If this be so, there was, perhaps, another text of the *Catalogus* which had ΛΑΩΒΗΤΟΝ, ratio populorum of the Cp. Gloss. (= *acbochnrotan*, Ep. 3C26, and acdoēroaton, Ef.[1] 342, 49).

cinyris, see *cyneris.*

circa, XIII. 13.

circino, ferrum duplex unde pictores faciunt circulos idest gaborind, XIII. 53 (*Isai.* XLIV. 13 in *circino* tornavit illud). = *circinno*, gabulrond, Cp. C416; *c*-, gabelrend, Ef.[1] 354, 36. Gaborind, gabulrond &c. for the Irish *gabolrind*, see Cormac's Glossary in W. Stokes' *Three Irish Glossaries*: Cercenn...idest a circino, idest ogabulrind; cf. Windisch, *Irische Texte*, I. 585 (*gabul*, G. Gabel), and Bosw. T. (*geafel*, *gaflas*; *gabul-roid* for *gabul-rond*, *gafol-rand*), a pair of compasses.

circium, XLIV. 25, see *dextera.*

circuitu, VIII. 16, see *mala aurea*; XXVIII. 77, see *sinastrismus.*

circulis, XXI. 5, see *cum coronis*; see also *poli.*

circulos, XIII. 53, see *circino.*

circulus, XLIV. 16, see *antarticus.*

circumdarent, IV. 41, see *pessimos darent.*

circumfusione, XLVIII. 50, see *suffusione.*

circumiens, IX. 1, see *lustrans.*

circumspectaculum, XXX. 21, see *amphitheatrum.*

circumstantia, XXXV. 9; circumstatio, XXXV. 112 [a surrounding crowd or troop, a circle], see *constipatio.*

circumuacantium [circumuag-], II. 80, see *girouagum.*

cirris, crinibus, XLVII. 6 (*Alia*=?)=Cp. C409; Ep.—; Ef.[1] 353, 62.

ciscillus, haerdhaeu, XLVII. 49 (*Alia*=?) =*cisculus*, heard heau, Cp. C408; Ep.—; *ciscillus*, heardheui, Ef.[1] 353, 47. For *ciscillus*, *cisculus* (?=*acisculus*, perh. for *asciculus*, a little adze, chisel, see Lewis & Sh.), see Körting, *Wrtb.* 2216 (*cisellus). Haerd-haeu, heard-heau, heard-heui (prop. a hardy, strong hewer), from *heard*, hardy, strong+*heaw*, *heawa*, a hewer, hoe; see Bosw. T. (*heard-heāwa* & *heāwan*); Oxf. D. (*hard* and *hoe sb.*[2]).

cisculus, cisellus, see *ciscillus.*

cispitem [cesp-], xxxv. 118, see *glebam*.

cissura, sectura [for *secutura*?], xxxv. 67 (*Ruf.* ix. 8 fol. 150[b] prospere cuncta *cessura*...promiserat). If *sectura* were correct, the Glossator must be supposed to have thought of *scissura*.

citeriorem, see *ceteriorem*.

cithara, see *psaltes*.

citharis, xii. 40, see *cyneris*.

citiuis, xxix. 62, see *de citiuis*.

citius, ii. 77, see *facile*; xxi. 20, see *labastes*; see also *cicius*; *exedra*.

citra, bihina, xlviii. 54 (*De Cass. Inst.* v. 36, 2 *citra* Nili fluminis alueum). Cf. *citra*, ultra, Cp. C380; Ep. 7E15; Ef.[1] 351, 10. Bihina = A.S. *bi-heonan*, *be-heonan* (O.H.G. *hinana*), on this side; see Bosw. T. (*bi-heonan*).

citro, iii. 64, see *ultro*.

ciuitas, iv. 4, see *mambre*; xiii. 26, see *Gabaa*; xvi. 17, see *castrum*; xxiii. 17 (bis), see *ciuitas dauid*; xxiv. 15, see *Sidon*; xxv. 10, see *Salim*; xxxv. 266, see *Antinoitas*; xlii. 3, see *memphitica*; xlviii. 25, see *Acron*.

ciuitas dauid, archis in hierusalem modica ciuitas altior, xxiii. 17 (2 *Esdr.* iii. 15 usque ad gradus qui descendunt de *Civitate David*; *ibid.* xii. 36 in gradibus *civitatis David*.—Archis in hierusalem, for "arx Sion in Jerusalem"? See 2 *Reg.* v. 7; 3 *Reg.* viii. 1; 1 *Paral.* xi. 5 &c.).

ciuitate, xxxv. 30, see *genefrix*; see also *ciuitas dauid*.

ciuitates, xi. 7, see *pentapolim*; xxix. 31, see *decapolim*.

ciuitatis, vi. 14, see *Dum*; xiii. 21, see *Carcamis*; xvii. 15, see *Pile*; xxxv. 256, see *actio*; xliii. 16, see *Micene*. See also *ciuitas*.

ciuitatum, xxxv. 47, see *metropolis*.

cladem inferens, iii. 29 (*De S. Mart. Stor.*?). *Cladem* does not seem to occur in *Sulp. Sev.*, and, perhaps, the gloss is, like *nutabundus*, agitatus [iii. 28], a further explanation of *furibundus* [iii. 27]. For "Bellum inferens" cf. *Sulp. Sev. Vit.* 20. 8; "recens fraternae *cladis* feruebat inuidia" *id. Dial.* i. 7, 6.

cladibus, see *gladibus*.

cladis, iv. 11, see *tragoedia*; and on nom. sing. *cladis*, see Georges, *Lat. Wörterb.*

clamantem, xxxvii. 12, see *ore camerato*.

clare, i. 64, see *insigne*.

classica, tuba, xlviii. 57 (*De Cass.*?) = *clasica*, tuba, Cp. C493; *classica* tubae sonus, Cp. C468; Ef.[1] 354, 45; cf. Goetz, vi. 1 p. 220 (*classica*; *classicum*).

claua, fuste, xxxv. 79 (*Ruf.* iv. 16 fol. 64[b] spero baculo aut *claua* feriendum). Cf. *claua*, steng, Cp. C450; *claua*, stegn, Ep. 7E7; *claua*, stęng, Ef.[1] 351, 2; prov. E. *stang*.

claui perditi [sine interpret.], xxxix. 38 (*Greg. Dial.* iii. 36 col. 304[c] ex navi *clavi perditi*, arbor abscissa est).

claustro, vi. 28, see *clustello*.

clausulis, xxviii. 24, see *ypozeuxis*.

clausurae, see *Armenias*.

clausure [-rae, gen., of a castle, fort], xxxvi. 2, see *Armenias pilas*.

Clemente, xxxviii *tit.*

clibanus, desuper apertus, xxiv. 17 (*Math.* vi. 30 foenum agri...in *clibanum* mittitur). Perhaps the gloss should read *clibanus*, furnus des. ap.—Cp. C459 has *clibanus*, fornax.

clima, cardo uel pars celi [caeli] ut clima orientalis uel meridiana, xliv. 4 (*Alia*; *de cælo* = [?] Isid. *de natura rerum* xii; but not found in the texts known at present). It would seem that a further explanation the Glossator gives xliv. 11: **clima**, aliquando pro cardine accipitur si sepius [saep-] pro qualicumque celi [caeli] parte et maxime pro oriente et meridię [-die] climas aliqui designant nos secundum grecum [graec-] om̄ [*omnes*? and suppl. *partes*?] cęli [caeli] ad superna conuexas ita undique uocamus. For *clima* see also (xliv. 1) *partes*.

climacteras, partes cęli [caeli], xxxviii. 25 (*Clem. Recognitt.* ix. 12 *climacteras* quosdam introducunt...; *Climacteras*.. dicunt quasi periculi tempus; x. 12 ut *climacteras* dicerent).

climas, xliv. 11, see *clima*.

climax, gradatio quando quibusdam gradibus semper accrescit, xxviii. 32 (*Cass. Psalm.* iii. 2 figura quae dicitur *climax*, Latine gradatio, q. positis quibusdam g., ...semper a.) = *climax*, gradatio, Cp. C470.

cliutex, cortix [-tex] uel lapis, xlvi. 25 (*Alia* = *Ars Phocae*, p. 420, 29 [?] hic *codex* [= caudex] codicis). Cf. caudix, cortix, Cp. C113; see further *codicibus*.

clivum, see *glebum*.

cluditur, iii. 19, see *pessuli*.

clustello, claustro, vi. 28 (*Breu. exsol.*?). Cf. *clustella*, clustorloc, Cp. C466; *caustella*, clustorlocae, Ep. 8C22; *clustella*, cluster locae, Ef.[1] 352, 32.

clusum, xxii. 12, see *urna*.

Coa, insula, xlv. 12 (*Uerba de multis* = *Ars Phocae*, p. 427, 23 vina *Coa* dicimus).

coacuerint, uersę sunt in acaetum [acet-], viii. 2 (*Salam.*; *Praef. S. Hieron.* scripta ...quae non in tertium vas transfusa *coacuerint*).

coadunatio, II. 151, see *sinaxis*.

coagmentare, congregare, IV. 2 (*Ruf. Prooem.*, fol. 1b Quaecunque...*coagmentare* tentauimus).

coalescant, pascant, XXXV. 119 (*Ruf.* II. 17 fol. 27a ad perfectam...vitam studiis iugibus *coalescunt*) = *coalescunt*, pascunt, Cp. C737; Ep.—; Ef.[1] 354, 13.—**coalescere**, adolescere, XLVIII. 72 (*De Cass.*, *Inst.* VI. 9 ne intrinsecus quidem *coalescere*...patiamur).

coalescunt, see *coalescant*.

coccum, see *coccus*.

coccus, uuyrmbaso, XXII. 18 (*Esther?* not in Vulg., and perhaps, only a further explanation of XXII. 17 *purpura*, q.v.). *Coccus* = coccum, *scarlet*; for *uuyrm* (worm)-*baso* (blue-red, purple, carmoisin), see Bosw. T. (*wurma*, *wyrma*, *wyrm*, *wyrm-basu*); cf. *coccum*, bis tinctum piolocread, Cp. C520; coccum, bis tinctum uuilocread, Ep. 6E34; c.b.t. uuslucreud, Ef.[1] 349, 36; cf. E. *cochineal* (Oxf. D.).

cochleas, for the corrupt *conolas* (q.v.).

coclea, see *maruca*.

cocte [-tae], XXXIV. 6, see *omofagis*.

cocto [for *cocta* ?], XII. 41, see *lino crudo*.

cocula [for *cuculla*], III. 7, see *byrrum*; III. 8, see *lacernam*; III. 56, see *ependiten*.

coculam [sine interpr.], II. 38 (*Bened. reg.* 55, 6 & 7 [10 & 11] sufficere credimus monachis *cucullam*; 16 [28] *cucullas*; 21 [37] *cucullae*, 30 [53] *cuculla*).

coculus, XLII. 18, see *amphibalum*.

Cocyti, see *Coquiton*.

codex, XXXV. 73, see *codicibus*; see also *cliutex*.

codices, see *codicibus*.

codicibus, liminibus, IV. 82 (*Eccl. Istor.*); **codicibus**, lignis in quibus incidunt [*add*: codices? see Cod. Ambros. in Goetz' *Corp. Gl. Lat.* V. 427, 52; or litteras?] codex stofun, XXXV. 73 (*De Eus.*) = (*Ruf.* IX. 10 fol. 158a omnes...*codicibus* superpositos). See also *cliutex*. For *stofun* (a stem, stump of a tree), see Bosw. T. (*stofn*); it = prov. E. *stoven*, *stovin*, *stoving*, *stowan*. See Engl. Dial. Dict.

coel-, see also *cael-*, *cel-*, *cęl-*.

coelestibus, see *poli*.

coelis, see *metonymia*.

coelo (cælo), XLIV *tit.*

coelum, see *cęlum*; *cous*; *laquearia*.

coementeria, sepulture [-rae], XXXV. 237 (*De Eus.*); **caementaria**, ecclesię, XXXV. 65 (*De Eus.*); **ad coemetoria**, ad ecclesia [!], IV. 117 (*Eccl. Ist.*) = (*Ruf.* IX. 2 fol. 147b *ad coemiteria* conuenirent; Cacciari, p. 510 *ad coemeteria*).—**cymiteria**, sepulture, I. 24 (*De Canon.*; *Can. Conc. Laod.* CXII ad haereticorum *coemeteria*; cf. *Decr. Innoc.* V per *coemeteria*).

coemeteria, see *coementeria*.

coemetoria [coemeteria], IV. 117, see *ad coemetoria* in v. *coementeria*.

coemiteria, see *coementeria*.

coenas, see *scenas turpes*.

coenobiis, see *coenobium*.

coenobita, coenobitarum, see *cenobita*.

coenobium, ex greco et latino conpositum esse dicitur: est enim habitaculum plurimorum, II. 188 (*Bened. reg.* 5, 21 [31] in *coenobiis* degentes).

coenouitarum, see *cenobita*.

coetu, see *coetus*.

coetus, conuentus uel congrecacio [-gatio] uel socius, I. 28 (*De Canon.*; *Can. Conc. Carth.* Praef., p. 142a de tantae congregationis *coetu*; id. II in hoc *coetu* glorioso; id. LIII statutum a *coetu* sacerdotali est); *uel socius* seems to belong to I. 30 (*collega* &c. q.v.). For *coetus* see also (I. 19) *concilium*; (I. 114) *synodus*.

coeunt, XLIV. 17, see *cous*.

cogenti, II. 3, see *angarizanti*.

cogitabant, XXXV. 111, see *coniciebant*.

cogitamus, I. 132, see *satagimus*.

cogitatum, XXXV. 273, see *delibratum*.

cognitio, I. 118, see *simbulum*.

cognoscant, I. 47, see *experiuntur*.

cognosce, XXVIII. 18, see *apo tu-*.

cognoscit [-citur], XXVIII. 34, see *figura metopoea*.

cogunt, XLIV. 27, see *dextera*.

cohum, see *partes*.

coibatur, exitur, XXXV. 285 (*Ruf.* VII. 25 fol. 125b *Coibatur* a fratribus...non ad capiendos pisces).

coinquinata, XXXV. 166, see *scenas turpes*.

coitum, XXXV. 26, see *oethepia*.

colamina est in hiezechielo decim inquid cotilę gomor, XXXIII. 20 (*Euch. De Pond.* p. 159, 15 *Cotyla hemina* est in Ezechiele: Decem, inquit, cotylae sunt gomor). Eucherius refers to Ezek. XLV. 11 (see the Hebr. and Gr. texts).

colando, see *exolantes*.

colebat, XLIII. 4, see *arcades*.

colendo, XXXIX. 2, see *colonus*. For *colando* (?), XXIV. 12, see *exolantes*.

colera, nausia, XII. 30 (*Eccles.* XXXI. 23 *cholera*; XXXVII. 33 ad *choleram*. Cambr. MS.: *Colera*, n. idest gutta pessima).

coli, dolores uentris, XXXV. 2 (*Ruf.* I. 8 fol. 12b doloribus...*coli*...cruciabatur; ibid. *coli*...dolor) = *coli* deleres uentris, Cp. C634; *coli*, dolores uentris, Ep. 8C10 and Ef.[1] 352, 20.

colirium, dicitur multa medicamina in unum collecta, XXXIX. 49 (*Greg.* [not Dial., but] *Reg. Past.* I. 11 col. 25A [quoting from *Apoc.* III. 18] *collyrio* inunge oculos tuos, [and adding] *collyrio*...oculos ut videamus inungimus).

collationes, collationum, see *conlationes.*

collecta, XXXIX. 49, see *colirium.*

collectae, IV. 98, see *comellas.*

collectam, congregationem, XXIII. 15 (2 *Esdr.* VIII. 18 fecerunt...in die octavo *collectam* juxta ritum).

collecte [-tae], XXXIX. 50, see *sentina.*

collectio, II. 151, see *sinaxis.*

collectionum, XXIX. 44, see *xenodoxiorum.*

collega, conmanipularius uel conscius, I. 30 (*De Canon.*; *Can. Conc. Carth.* LIV frater et *collega* noster; LXVIII id.). The explanation *uel socius*, which is out of place in I. 28 (see *coetus*), is probably to be connected with this gloss; cf. *commanipularius*...uel conscius socius collega, Cp. C695; Ep.—; commanipularius, conscium conlega, Ef.[2] 279, 16.

collegit, XIV. 29, see *ficarius.*

colleguntur [collig-], XXX. 35, see *uarietas stromactis.*

colligit, XXVIII. 75, see *prolemsis.*

colligitur, XXV. 6, see *de siliquis.*

colliguntur, XXVIII. 63, see *sinatrismos.*

collo, XIII. 6, see *lunulas.*

collocare, XXXVIII. 3, see *elocare.*

collocet, see *reculicet.*

collybistas, see *trapezeta.*

collyrio, see *colirium.*

colobista (for *collybista*), XXIX. 42, see *trapezeta.*

colobostrum, see *colostrum.*

colomellas, lomum, V. 2 (*De Eccl. Stor.*); **columellas**, diuersis linimentis [lineam-], XXXV. 257 (*De Euseb.*); **comellas** h[oc est] uniuscuiusque interpretis translatio in unum collectae et e regione posite, IV. 98 (*Eccl. Istor.*) = (*Ruf.* VI. 13 fol. 103b per singulas *columnulas* [*columellas*, in edit. 1535, & edit. Cacciari, p. 348], è regione separatim opus interpretis uniuscuiusque descripsit). *Lomum* (V. 2) is clearly not the instr. pl. of *loma*, a tool (for which see Bosw. T. *loma*, *and-gelóman*, *and-lóman*, *gelóman*; Kluge, *A. S. Leseb.* gelóma, rarely *lóm*, m. *gerät*, *geschirr*); nor of *leoma*, a ray of light, radiance, for which see Napier, index (*leoma*). Schlutter (*Anglia* XXVI. 304) would read *lonum*, from *lone* = *lane*, *lanu*, a lane, narrow path; he also suggests *limum* (limbs) for *lomum.* But the gloss *diuersis linimentis* (for *lineamentis*, lines or strokes) of XXXV. 257 rather points to *lomum* for *leomum* from *leoma* (also written *lema*), from A. S. *lim*, a limb, joint, especially *a branch.*

colonus, a colendo, XXXIX. 2 (*Greg. Dial.* I. 1 col. 153c *colonus*).

color, VIII. 15, see *flauescit*; XIV. 19, see *arugo*; XXII. 7, see *carbasini.*

colore, XV. 10, see *ebor*; XIX. 15, see *tigris*; XXIV. 5, see *mocum*; XXXV. 181, see *regio morbus.*

colorem, XXXV. 63, see *fucum*; XLI. 7, see *iaspis*, 10, see *smaragdus*, 11, see *sardonix*, 12, see *sardius*, 13, see *crisolitus*, 16, see *cypressus.*

coloribus, XXXV. 42, see *stibiis.*

colostrum, beust, XLVII. 27 (*Alia* = ?) = *colostrum*, beost, Cp. C658; Ep.—; *colobostrum*, beost, Ef.[1] 353, 46. For *beust*, *beost* (biest, biestings, beestings) see Bosw. T.; Oxf. D.; Skeat, Dict.; Kluge, *A. S. Leseb.* (beost).

colubri, XIII. 25 (bis), see *de radice.*

columellas, diuersis linimentis [lineam-], XXXV. 257, see *colomellas.*

columnarum, I. 49, see *epistilia.*

columnas uitreas, idest in simili uitis scalpantur, XXXVIII. 7 (*Clem. Recognitt.* VII. 12 & 26 videndi...gratia...*columnas viteas*) = *columnas uiteas*, idest uitearum similitudines scluptae [sculptae] erant, Cp. C642; Ep. 8E2; Ef.[1] 352, 48. For "in simili uitis scalpantur" another MS. has "in similitudinem uitis sculpentur."

columnulas, see *colomellas.*

comam, XXXVIII. 18, see *creta comam-.*

comatum [commatum], XXVIII. 72, see *anaphora.*

comedendum, see *croceis.*

comedentem, see *edacem.*

comedia [comoedias], XLIII. 23, see *comicus.*

comedo, edax, XLIII. 14 (*De div. nominibus* = Donati *Ars grammat.*, p. 374, 18 *comedo*). Cf. *comedo*, forax **edax**, Cp. C547; Ef.[2] 279, 24.

comeduntur, XXXIV. 5, see *xerofagia.*

comellas h[oc est] uniuscuiusque interpretis translatio &c., IV. 98, see *colomellas.*

comessationibus, see *commessationes.*

comicus, cantator uel artifex secularium canticorum, XXIX. 12 (*Uerb. Interpr.* = *Hier. Comm. in Matth.* VII. 18 col. 48c *Comicus* dixerit).—**comicus**, qui comedia [comoedias] scripsit; **traicus** [tragicus], qui traica [tragica] scribsit; **liricus** [lyr-], qui per liram [lyr-] cantat; **saturicus** [satyr-], qui per saturicam scribsit, XLIII. 23—26 (*De diuersis nominibus*). The last four glosses, preceded, in the MS., by the heading "IIII *genera poetarum*" seem to be further explanations of the passage from Donati *Ars grammat.* quoted sub v. *eunuchus*, q.v. The first of the four = *comicus* qui comedia scribit, Cp. C803.

cominus, see *in comminus*.
comissationes, see *commessationes*.
comitantur, I. 89, see *prosequantur*.
comitator (?), XLV. 30, see *mango*.
comitatus, I. 114, see *synodus*.
comma, breuis pars, XIX. 6 (*Job*; *Praef. Hieron.* p. XIV^b, and Migne, *P.L.* XXVIII col. 1082 parvum *comma* quod remanet). Cf. *comma*, breuis dictio, Cp. C817.
commandit, manducat, VIII. 21 (*Salam.* XXX. 14 *commandit* molaribus suis).
commatum, see *anaphora*.
commectarum, tractatores, XLVIII. 48 (*De Cass.*, *Inst.* V. 34 labores suos erga *commentatorum* libros inpendere...nec eos *commentatorum* [*commentorum*, in note] institutionibus indigere).
commedentem [comed-], II. 64, see *edacem*.
commendatitiis, II. 102, see *literis commendatitiis*.
commendatum, II. 39, see *commissum*.
commenta, excogitata, XXXV. 100 (*Ruf.* I. 6 fol. 10^a *commenta* quaedam). Cf. *commenta*, atinuenta, Cp. C638.—**commenta** [for *caementa*], petra, XXXV. 219, see *cementa*.
commentarium, see *sub nominem*.
commentata, see *commentatus*.
commentatorum, see *commectarum*.
commentatus, tractatus, IV. 8 (*Ruf.* I. 6 fol. 11^a haec ... non ... *commentata* sunt).
commentorum, see *commectarum*.
commessationem, IX. 5, see *capparis*.
commessationes [comissationes], luxosa [luxuriosa] conuiuia cum meretribus [meretricibus], I. 25 (*De Canon.*; *Can. Conc. Laod.* CLVIII *tit.* Non congruere... Christianis *comessationibus* interesse. Quod non oporteat sacerdotes...ex collatis, vel *comessationibus* conuiuia celebrare). Cf. *commesatio*, conuiuio meretricum, Cp. C687; *conmesatio*, comuiuia cum meretricibus mixta, Ef.[2] 280, 55.—For *commessationes* see also (XXXV. 25) *thiesteas*, and *scenas turpes*.
comminisque, XLIV. 29, see *axem*.
comminus, prope, XXXIV. 34 (*De Cass.*, *Inst.* X. 3 *comminus*) = *comminus*, prope, Cp. C864.—**in comminus**, propius, XXXV. 162 (*Ruf.* V. 18 fol. 88^a *in cominus* ueniant; IV. 24 fol. 69^b *cominus* perurgendo).
commissum, commendatum, II. 39 (*Bened. reg.* 31, 28 [58] officium sibi *commissum*; 63, 4 [6] gregem sibi *commissum*; see also 42, 15 [24] adsignato sibi *commisso*).
commissuras, ligaturas uel conposituras, VII. 3 (1 *Paral.* XXII. 3 ad *commissuras*). Cf. *commisura*, flycticlað, Cp. C507.
commodare, II. 67, see *expedire*.
commodum, II. 59, see *expedit*.
commolita, molata, XXVI. 1 (*Isid. Offic.* I. 18, 6 grana...*commolita*) = *commilita*, molata, Cp. C739; Ep.—; Ef.[1] 354, 16. For *molata* v. Du C. (*molare* = molere; *molatio*, &c.). See also *commolitus*.
commolitis, see *commolitus*.
commolitus, exterminatus, XIII. 5 (*Isai.* III. 15 Quare atteritis populum meum et facies pauperum *commolitis*). See also *commolita*.
commonitorium, see *communitorium*.
commune, II. 33, see *cenobita*.
communione [for *-ore*], XXVIII. 57, see *figura*.
communis, XVI. 27, see *malefici*.
communitorium, munitionem, XXVI. 3 (*Isid. Offic.* II. 22, 2 Istis...salutare symbolum traditur, quasi *commonitorium* fidei; cf. Goetz VI. 240 *commonitorium* and 241 *communitorium*). Cf. *commonicarium*, pastiarium, Cp. C833.
comoedia, see *eunuchus*.
comoedias, see *comicus*.
comor minor, septem sextarios et u [quinta] pars sextarii cotile dimedium, XXXI. 9, see *gomor*.
compaginatam, see *conpaginatum*.
compitis, see *in pago*.
componitis, see *conpotis*.
compos, particeps, XXXV. 48 (*De Eus.*) = *compos*, particeps, Cp. C755; **uoti compos**, xpistiana, IV. 84 (*Eccl. Ist.*); **uoti copos**, xpistiana, XXXV. 293 (*De Eus.*) = (*Ruf.* X. 8 fol. 163^b regina voti *compos* effecta).
computum, XXXV. 250, see *in exameron*.
comulare [cum-], XXXIV. 28, see *exaggerare*.
con [the beginning of an unfinished interpretation], II. 25 (*Bened. reg.*).
conando, IV. 94, see *coniculum*.
conatur, XXVIII. 83, see *ennoematice*.
conatus, I. 11, see *adnisus*.
conburuntur, XXXV. 235, see *busta*.
conca [concha], XXIV. 5, see *mocum*.
concentum, cantum, XIX. 55 (*Job* XXXVIII. 37 *concentum* cæli quis dormire faciet); concentus, I. 19, see *concilium*.
conceptio, XXVIII. 60, see *enthimema*.
concha, see *mocum*.
conchilia [for the corrupt *contia*], see *conolas*.
conchis, see *choncis*.
conciderat, acciderat, XLVIII. 32 (*De Cass.*, *Inst.* I. 1, 2 de lecto...in quo *conciderat*).—**concidere**, incidere, XXXV. 68 (*Ruf.* IX. 8 fol. 151^a in medio conatus inualidi...*concideret*).

concidisti, occidisti, xvii. 13 (*Habac.* ii. 10 *concidisti* populos multos).
conciliare, i. 82, see *operam.*
conciliatoribus, xxxv. 258, see *lenonibus.*
concilio, xxix. 73, see *qui dixerit...*
concilium, grece, latine consilium conuentus uel concentus coetus, i. 19 (*De Canon.*; cf. *Dionys.* Praef. p. 101 regulas ...*conciliorum*...digessimus; *ibid.* Calchedonensis *Concilij* decreta &c.; *Can. Apostt.* xxxviii Episcoporum *Concilia* celebrentur; *Can. Conc. Nic.* ii contra magnum *Concilium* se efferens).
concinnant, consonant, i. 29 (*De Canon.*; cf. *Can. Conc. Carth.* liii presbyteri... conviviis sibi *concinnantes* plebem......; *ibid.* propter...praue *concinnata* consilia). If this gloss *consonant* refers to these quotations it seems clear that the Glossator was thinking of *concinere* (not *concinnare*) to sing together, or, in an active sense, to cause to sing together, to cause anyone to agree.—**concinnant**, congregant, xxxv. 265 (*Ruf.* vi. 7 fol. 100ᵃ *concinnant*... aduersum eum infame... crimen).
concionaretur, loqueretur, xxxv. 113 (*Ruf.* ii. 10 fol. 22ᵇ de sublimi *concionaretur*).
concionem, see *contionem.*
concitamus, xxviii. 42, see *idea.*
conclauia, porticos [!], iii. 40 (*S. Mart. Stor.* = *Sulp. Sev. Dial.* i. 21, 4 construit multa *conclauia*).
concludit, xxviii. 77, see *sinastrismus.*
concluduntur, xxviii. 45, see *zeuma.*
conclusione, xii. 38, see *sophistice.*
concrescit, xxviii. 56, see *auxesis.*
concrescunt, iv. 99, see *quadraplas.*
concubina, x. 24, see *Salamitis.*
concubitas, iv. 57, see *thesteas.*
concupiscibili (-le), xxix. 60, see *tu epitimitisun.*
condatur, reponatur, ii. 30 (*Bened. reg.* 52, 3 nec ibi quicquam...*condatur*).—**condere**, abscondere, xxxiv. 54 (*De Cass., Inst.* v. 4, 2 monachum spiritalia mella *condere* cupientem).
conditionalis, see *hypotheticus.*
condito, see *uinum candidum.*
condixerunt, xxii. 12, see *urna.*
conductores [sine interpretat.], i. 26 (*De Canon.*; *Can. Conc. Calched.* iii *conductores* alienarum possessionum; *Conc. Carth.* xvi Episcopi...non sint *conductores*).
conectura, auguria, xv. 38 (*Ezech.* xxi. 19 manu capiet *conjecturam*).
confectorem, interfectorem, xxxv. 159 (*Ruf.* iv. 15 fol. 63ᵇ iusserunt propius accedere *confectorem*).
confectos, maculatos, xxxiv. 22 (*De Cass., Inst.* xi. 11 conspicis duos uiros tam iustos...triumphis suis...fuisse *confectos*).
conferentes [for *conferentiae*, or *conferentias*?] ii. 29, see *conlationes.*
conferentiae, conferentias, see *conlationes.*
confice, xvii. 14, see *subigens.*
conficitur, i. 111, see *sicera.*
confidens, iii. 45, see *fretus.*
confidentes, xiii. 20, see *inniti.*
configent, crucifigent, xvii. 21 (*Zachar.* xiii. 3 *configent* eum).
confirmata, xxxv. 300, see *rata.*
confirmatio, xxxv. 11, see *adstipulatio.*
confisi, xiii. 20, see *inniti.*
conflatorio, see *conflatorium.*
conflatorium, ubi ferrum uel argentum conflatur, viii. 10 (*Salam.* xxvii. 21 probatur in *conflatorio* argentum).
conflatur, viii. 10, see *conflatorium.*
conflictus, xxx. 18, see *archeretoys*, 26, see *diatripas.*
conformatio, xxviii. 57, see *figura.*
confutatus, reprobatus, xxxiv. 13 (*De Cass., Inst.* xi. 2 *confutatus* incentor).
congeminat, xxviii. 31, see *ausesis.*
congeminatio, xxviii. 68, see *anadiplosis.*
congrecacio [congregatio], i. 28, see *coetus.*
congrecauimus [congreg-], ii. 47, see *digessimus.*
congregamus, xxviii. 40, see *silemsis.*
congregant, xxxv. 265, see *concinnant.*
congregare, iv. 2, see *coagmentare.*
congregatae, see *in exaplois.*
congregate [-tae], xix. 11, see *in exaplois.*
congregati, xxxiv. 52, see *degesti sunt.*
congregatio, xiii. 32, see *riui aggerum*; xix. 53, see *gurgitum*; xxviii. 63, see *sinatrismos*; see also *coetus.*
congregatione, xxxix. 70, see *adstipulatione.*
congregationem, xvi. 21, see *aggerem*; xxiii. 15, see *collectam.*
congregationes, xv. 6, see *struices.*
congregauimus, see *digessimus.*
congruet, ii. 16, see *aptet.*
congruus, aptus, ii. 31 (*Bened. reg.* 53, 4 [5] omnibus *congruus* honor exhibeatur; cf. 24, 12 [20] satisfactione *congrua*; 43, 39 [65] ad emendationem *congruam*).
conhabitantes, xii. 46, see *accommorante.*
conibentes, consentientes uel conspirantes, i. 27 (*De Canon.*; *Can. Conc. Chalc.* xxvii cooperantes aut *conniuentes* raptoribus); see also *conibentia.*
conibentia, consensus, xxxv. 52 (*Ruf.* x. 22 fol. 172ᵃ ordinationis *conuenientia*

maculatur; Cacciari p. 47 *conniventia*); see also *conibentes.*

conicere, intellegere, xxxiv. 46 (*De Cass., Inst.* xii. 27, 4 tacita intra se cordis uolutatione *coniectat*).—**coniciebant**, cogitabant, xxxv. 111 (*Ruf.* ii. 6 fol. 21ᵇ *coniiciebant*...ex hoc) = coniciebant, cogitabant, Cp. C738; Ep. —; Ef.[1] 354, 14.

conices, xxxiii. 16, see *gomor.*

coniciebant, cogitabant, xxxv. 111; see *conicere.*

coniectat (!), see *conicere.*

coniectura, i. 129, see *suspicio.*

coniecturam, xvi. 25, see *arioli*; see also *conectura.*

coniiciebant, see *coniciebant*, in voc. *conicere.*

coniculum, a conando [cun-?], iv. 94, see *cuniculum.*

coniuentia, see *conibentia.*

coniunctio, xxviii. 45, see *zeuma*, 52, see *epizeusis.*

coniunctos, xv. 43, see *puluillos.*

coniunctum, xxxv. 245, see *conpaginatum.*

coniuratio, consensio conuentio, i. 32 (*De Canon.*; *Can. Conc. Calch.* xviii *tit.* de *coniuratione*; *ib. coniurationis* crimen).

conix, xxi. 16, see *conopeum.*

conlationes, conlocutiones conferentes [*conferentiae* or *conferentias*?] ii. 29 (*Bened. reg.* 42, 7 [9] legat unus *collationes*; 73, 12 [19] *Conlationes Patrum*... quid aliud sunt nisi...; 42, 12 [19] ad lectionem *collationum*).

conlocet, see *reculicet.*

conlocutiones, ii. 29, see *conlationes.*

conmanipulares, idest sodales, xxxvi. 18 (*Oros.* ii. 9, 4 cognati et *commanipulares* ...occubuerant; in note *comm-*, *cumm-*, *conm-*). Cf. *commanipulares*, conmilitones, Cp. C856; cf. ibid. C695.

conmanipularius, i. 30, see *collega.*

conniuentes, see *conibentes.*

conniuentia, see *conibentia.*

conolas, quę contia uocant, v. 3 (*Ruf.* iv. 15, p. 82, ed. 1535, and Cacciari, p. 206: marinas *cochleas*, *quæ conchilia uocant*; the ed. of 1548, fol. 61ᵃ: marinas *cochleas* quos murices vocant. The Glossator, therefore, has added no interpretation of his own). Cf. *cocleas*, uuiolocas [E. *whelks*], Cp. C660; Ep. —; *cocleas*, uuylocas, Ef.[1] 353, 52.

conopeum, in similitudine retis contextum propter muscas et culices nam culix [culex] conix hebraice dicitur, xxi. 16 (*Judith* xiii. 10 abstulit *conopoeum* eius a columnis; see also xiii. 19 *conopoeum* illius; xvi. 23 *conopoeum*; x. 19 in *conopoeo*). *Conix* perh. for Gr. κώνωψ, a gnat. Cf. *conopeum*, rete muscarum, Cp. C531; Ep. 7C5; Ef.[1] 350, 24; *conopeum*, retiaculum sub quo solent [ho]mines dormire, Ef.[2] 281, 25. Cf. Skeat (*canopy*).

conpactis, v. 28, see *simbulis.*

conpage, porrectione, xl. 19 (*Uerba*?).

conpaginatum, coniunctum, xxxv. 245 (*Ruf.* ix. 10 fol. 155ᵇ *compaginatam* machinam).

conparatio, xxviii. 48, see *parabole*; 59, see *syncrisis.*

conparatur, xxviii. 62, see *tapynosin.*

conpellare, fraudare, xlviii. 17 (*De Cass., Inst.* vii. 23 nisi...solitus fuisset creditos sibi loculos *conpilare*; vii. 24 loculos clancule *conpilare*). The interpretation (*fraudare*) agrees only with *conpilare*, not with *conpellere*, which occurs ii. 17 (quamuis eum consuetudo diurna hora solita euigilare *conpellat*); v. 23, 1 (quae canonicam refectionis horam praeueniri *conpellit*); vii. 9, 2 (*conpellit* utilitas); vii. 10 (laborare *conpellit*); vii. 14, 1 (desiderare *conpellit*); viiii. 6 (peccare *conpellitur*). Conpellare is not found in Cass. Cf. *conpilat*, spoliat, Cp. C632; *conpilat*, stilith (steals), Cp. C859.

conpellenti, ii. 3, see *angarizanti*; conpellere, see *conpellare.*

conpendiosis, breuissimis, xxxv. 255 (*Ruf.* vi. 11 fol. 102ᵇ Scripturam...*compendiosis* dissertionibus explanauit).

conpetentes, appetentes, i. 21 (*De Canon.*; *Conc. Can. Antioch.* xiii ap. Migne, *Patr. L.* lxxxiv col. 126ᴬ quoslibet actus illi Ecclesiae *competentes*). Cf. Isid. *Etym.* vii. 14. 8; id. *de Offic. Eccles.* xxii. For *conpetentes* see also (xlviii. 38) *contiguis.*

conpetis [= compitis], iii. 31, see *in pago.*

conpilare, see *conpellare.*

conpingebantur, pinguiscebant, xix. 27 (*Job* xxxviii. 38 quando...glebae *compingebantur*).

conplentur, xxviii. 12, see *stipantur.*

conplere, xliv. 2, see *cous.*

conplosi, plausum feci, xv. 8 (*Ezech.* xxii. 13 *complosi* manus meas). Cf. *conplosi*, iubilati, Cp. C742; *conplori*, iub-, Ef.[1] 354, 26.

conpluta, xv. 7, see *non conpluta.*

conposita, xxviii. 25, see *scema.*

conpositio, xxv. 14, see *lithostrotus*; xxix. 69, see *sinthema.*

conpositione, xxii. 1, see *themate.*

conposito, xxxiv. 33, see *conserto.*

conpositores, xiv. 27, see *stratores.*

conpositum, ii. 188, see *coenobium.*

conposituras, vii. 3, see *commissuras.*

conpotis, inpletis, xxxix. 67 (not Greg. Dial., but, perhaps, *Decr. Bonif.* p. 213ª qui cuncta aequa moderatione *componitis*).

conprehensio, see *catastrofon.*

conprobetur, ii. 147, see *ratiociniis.*

conpulsorem, xxx. 55, see *erladiocten.*

conputantes, xxxv. 179, see *horas diurnas.*

conscius, i. 30, see *collega.*

consecutus, i. 9, see *adeptus.*

consensio, i. 32, see *coniuratio*; i. 33, see *conspiratio.*

consensus, xxxv. 52, see *conibentia.*

consentientes, i. 27, see *conibentes.*

consentientibus, iv. 95, see *fautoribus*,

conserto, conposito, xxxiv. 33 (*De Cass., Inst.* x. 3 *conserto* proelio).

considas, viii. 3, see *ne innataris.*

consiliariis, xxxv. 13, see *consultoribus.*

consiliarius, xxix. 72, see *nuymeyses*; xxxv. 272, see *patricius.*

consiliis, v. 28, see *simbulis.*

consilio, ii. 172, see *temere.*

consilium, i. 19, see *concilium*; xxix. 21, see *curia.*

consintagmata [for *sintagmata*], xxx. 31, see *sub nominem.*

consistunt, x. 11, see *tigna.*

consonant, i. 29, see *concinnant.*

conspicientes, ii. 25, see *contuentes.*

conspiciunt, v. 13, see *operiunt.*

conspirantes, i. 27, see *conibentes.*

conspiratio, consensio, i. 33 (*De Canon.*; *Can. Conc. Calch.* xviii *tit.* De...*conspiratione*; ib. *conspirationis* crimen).

consternantem, xiv. 34, see *uitulam consternantem.*

constipatio, circumstantia, xxxv. 9 (*De Euseb.*); **constipatio**, circumstatio, xxxv. 112 (*De Euseb.*)=(*Ruf.* ii. 6 fol. 22ª plurimi...propria *constipatione* perculsi).

constipatione, see *constipatio.*

constituta, ii. 87, see *aabita.*

construpauerunt, contaminauerunt, xiv. 1 (*Hier.* ii. 16 filii...*constupraverunt* te).

constuprauerunt, see *construpauerunt.*

consuetudinem, viii. 8, see *in aceruo m-.*

consuetudini, xxix. 27, see *ideonati.*

consuetudo, xvi. 27, see *malefici*; xxxix. 36, see *sex untias.*

consul, xliii. 20, see *eunuchus*, 33, see *silla.*

consulari delectus, dignitati adductus, xxxv. 149 (*Ruf.* iii. 32 fol. 50ª Christianus *consulari delatus*, in editt. 1535 & 1548; Cacciari p. 163: Christianus Attico *Consulari delatus*). The MS. has distinctly *delectus*, though there seems to be some erasure above the second *e*; perhaps an attempt was made to erase the top of *e* and so make *a* out of *e* and *c*.

consulere, prouidere, xxxv. 284 (*Ruf.* vii. 25 fol. 126ᵇ *consulere* simulacrum Apollinis mos erat).

consulibus, consulis, i. 100, see *proconsolaris.*

consultoribus, consiliariis, xxxv. 13 (*Ruf.* iii. 6 fol. 38ª pessimis...*consultoribus*).

consumeretur, i. 34, see *carperetur.*

consumptor, xliii. 9, see *nepus.*

contaminauerunt, xiv. 1, see *construpauerunt.*

contegnatio, tectio domus, ix. 3 (*Eclesiast.* x. 18 *contignatio*).

contemplatiua, xxx. 13, see *iereticos.*

contemplatiuum, xxix. 64, see *theoritisen.*

contempto, pertinax durus superbus, ii. 26 (*Bened. reg.* 23, 4 [6] si quis...*contemptor* repertus fuerit; 65, 34 [66] *contemptor*, contemtor sanctae Regulae).

contemptor, contemtor, see *contempto.*

contendimus, xxviii. 51, see *hyperthesis.*

contęnetur [contin-], xliv. 2, see *cous.*

contentionem, xxiii. 18, see *contionem*; xxxv. 182, see *simultantem.*

contentus, patiens sufficiens, ii. 32 (*Bened. reg.* 7, 112 [179] omni vilitate... *contentus* sit Monachus; 61, 5, 7 [5, 9] *contentus* est).

conternante, see *uitulam consternantem.*

contextum, xxi. 16, see *conopeum*; xxx. 9, see *peridion.*

contia [for *conchilia*], v. 3, see *conolas.*

conticiscit, i. 44, see *dissimulat.*

contigit, vii. 8, see *obtigit.*

contignatio, see *contegnatio.*

contiguis, iugis uel conpetentes, xlviii. 38 (*De Cass., Inst.* ii. 5, 5 *contiguis* uersibus).

continentes, iv. 56, see *encratiani.*

continentia, xxx. 20, see *pantocranto.*

continetur, see *cous.*

contingunt, xvi. 27, see *malefici.*

continuanda, iugiter semper perpetuo, ii. 28 (*Bened. reg.* 41, 8 [13] prandii sexta ...*continuanda* erit).

continuatio, xxviii. 20, see *diapsalma.*

continuum, xxxvi. 9, see *peruicax.*

contionalis [for *condit-*], xxxviii. 84, see *hypotheticus.*

contionem, contentionem tumultuosam, xxiii. 18 (2 *Esdr.* v. 7 congregavi adversum eos *concionem* magnam). This is the only instance in Esdras of *contio*, but meaning *assembly*, which disagrees with *contentio. Contio*, however, also meaning a *discourse*, *oration*, would agree with *contentionem* which occurs 2 *Esdr.* ix. 17 (quasi per *contentionem*); so that possibly *contentionem* was intended to be the lemma, and *contionem tum-* the interpretation.

contis, xxi. 9, see *in contis*.
conto, see *canto*.
contorqueat, xliv. 29, see *axem*.
contra, i. 117, see *secus*; vi. 4, see *uersus*; xvii. 12, see *fulgorantes*; xlviii. 49, see *uersum*.
contracta, xiii. 27, see *flaccentia*.
contradicans, xxxiv. 35, see *abdicans*.
contradicat, iii. 55, see *inuitiat*.
contradicens, see *abdicans*.
contradico, iii. 4, see *inficiabor*.
contradictor, ii. 36, see *contumax*.
contraria, xxxvi. 1, see *Iani*.
contrarius, xxix. 68, see *cataantis*; xliv. 16, see *antarticus*.
contribulatis, xxxv. 193, see *contribulibus*.
contribulibus, simul contribulatis, xxxv. 193 (*Ruf.* ii. 5 fol. 20b pro *contribulibus* suis Iudaeis).
contritae, see *malagma*.
contrite [-tae], xi. 12, see *malagma*.
contritos, xiii. 46, see *cataplasmarent*.
contritum, xxxv. 80, see *madidum*.
contriuit, xxvii. 22, see *fatescit*.
controuersiae, see *controuersię*.
controuersię, aduersitates, xxxv. 222 (*Ruf.* xi. 21 fol. 186b multae *controuersiae* ...commotae).
contuentes, conspicientes con [sic], ii. 25 (*Bened. reg.* 40, 5 [6] infirmorum *contuentes* inbecillitatem).
contumacia, see *contumax*.
contuma[x], contradictor, ii. 36 (*Bened. reg.* 23, 2 [1] frater *contumax*; 71, 16 [29] si *contumax* fuerit; cf. 62, 18 [31] contumacia).
contusum, xxxv. 80, see *madidum*.
conueniens, appellans, vi. 21 (*Breu. exsol.*?).
conuenientia, see *conibentia*.
conuenit, ii. 123, see *non expedit*.
conuenticulum, xxxv. 302, see *seminon*.
conuentio, i. 32, see *coniuratio*.
conuentus, i. 19, see *concilium*; 28, see *coetus*; iv. 7, see *curia*.
conuersationem, xxx. 88, see *catastrofon*.
conuersio, xxviii. 58, see *apostropei*.
conuerso, xxviii. 67, see *anastrophe*.
conuertimus, xxviii. 58, see *apostropei*.
conuexa, extrema cęli, xliv. 6 (*Alia*; *de cælo* = Isid. *de nat. rerum* xii. 3 col. 983 *Convexa, extrema cœli*). A further explanation of this gloss is, perhaps, **conuexa**, ardua, xliv. 21. For *conuexa* see also (xliv. 1) *partes*.
conuexas, xliv. 11, see *clima*.
conuiator, xxxv. 54, see *pedissequis*.
conuincendos, see *ypo* (sub) *tyos* (hoc) &c.
conuiuia, i. 25, see *commessationes*.
conuoluulus, see *inuoluco*.
conurbicus, xxui uncias, xxxi. 26 (*De ponder.*?).
coopertis, xiii. 59, see *feretri*.
copos [compos], xxxv. 293, see *uoti compos*, sub voc. *compos*.
copulatio, xxviii. 19, see *sympsalma*.
coquiton, fluuius infernorum, xix. 22 (*Job* xxi. 33 dulcis fuit glareis *Cocyti*).
coquuntur, xvi. 1, see *pistrinum*.
cordati, xix. 62, see *uiri cordati*.
corde, xix. 62, see *uiri cordati*; xxxv. 114, see *uecors*.
cordis, ii. 179, see *typo*.
coreo, xlii. 21, see *basterna*.
coria, xxxv. 140, see *portarum indumenta*.
coribantas, idest qui fecerunt sonitum, xxxviii. 37 (*Clem. Recognitt.* x. 18 *Corybantas* quosdam cymbala fecit ac tympana percutere).
corimbis [corymb-; carved clusters for the ornamenting of ships], nauibus, xlvii. 5 (*Alia* = ?) = *Corimbus*, nauibus uel cacumen, Cp. C661; Ep. —; *corimbis*, n-, Ef.[1] 353, 60. Cf. *corimbos*, leac trogas, Cp. C656; *corimbus*, leac trocas, Ep. 8E34 & Ef.[1] 353, 27. The A. S. *lēac-trog* properly means *vegetable-basket*, see Bosw. T. (*leac*, a garden herb, and *trog*, a trough, tub, vessel); Engl. Dial. Dict. (tray, sb[1], sense 1).
corio, xv. 18, see *inuoluere*.
corium, xxi. 10, see *sandalia*.
cornu 1. *an oil cruet*, iii. 19, see *pessuli*. —2. *a horn*, xix. 31, see *rinocerus*.—3. *a horn, trumpet*, xxv. 7, see *symphonia*.
corona, xxii. 10, see *diadema*; see also *teristra*.
coronae, see *duas coronas*.
coronas, xxxvii. 19, see *laurus*; xxxix. 43, see *duas coronas*.
coronatus, xxxv. 106, see *stephanus*.
coronę [-nae], xxxix. 43, see *duas coronas*.
coronis, xxi. 5, see *cum coronis*.
corpora, xvi. 27, see *malefici*.
corporalis, xliv. 29, see *axem*.
corpore [for *corporeo*], xxx. 29, see *capun periens*.
corporis, xxxviii. 9, see *epicurius*.
corpulentioribus, crassioribus, xlviii. 10 (*De Cass.*, *Inst.* v. 7 qui ab escis *corpulentioribus*...temperarent). Cf. below *excellentiores*.
corpus, xiii. 43, see *lamia*; xxix. 66, see *oma*; xxxv. 181, see *regio morbus*; xxxix. 33, see *porta laurenti*.
corrigia, xi. 9, see *abene* (for *a bene*).
corrigię, see *abene* (for *a bene*).
corrupte, corruptę[-te], xxxiii. 7, see *sicel*.
cortex, see *cinamum*; *cliutex*; *suber*.

cortina, XIII. 59, see *feretri*.

cortix [-tex], VIII. 11, see *cinamum*; XLVI. 14, see *suber*, 25, see *cliutex*.

corus, see *chorus*.

corybantes, see *coribantas*.

corymbus, see *corimbis*.

cos, ueostun, XLVI. 4 (*Alia* = *Ars Phocae*, p. 419, 4 haec *cos*, haec dos). For *ueostun* = hwet-stān (= O. H. G. *wezi-stein*, *wezzi-stein*; Germ. *wetz-stein*; D. *wet-steen*), a whetstone, see Bosw. T. (*hwet-stān*); for the missing *h*, see Siev. *Gr.* § 217; for the missing *t*, cf. E. *best* = A. S. *betst*.

costae [dat. of costos?], see *cassia*.

coste [for costo, or costae], X. 20, see *cassia*.

costo, see *cassia*.

cothurno, see *turnodo*.

cotidianas, XL. 15, see *momentaneas*.

cotile [for *cotula*, or *cotyla*], XXXI. 8, see *emina*, 9, see *comor*.

cotilę [cotylae], XXXIII. 20, see *colamina*.

cotula, see *comor*, *emina*.

cotule habet dragmas LXXII idest scrupulos CCXVI &c., XXXII. 8, see *emina*.

coturno, see *turnodo*.

cotyla, see *colamina*; *comor*; *emina*.

cotylae, see *colamina*.

coum [choum, cohum], XLIV. 2, see *cous*.

cous est quo cęlum contęnetur unde enias uix solum conplere coum terroribus caeli, XLIV. 2 (*Alia*, *de cælo* = Isid. *de nat. rerum*, XII. 3 col. 983 *Chous* quod coelum continet [*quo coelum continetur*, in note]. Unde Ennius [Ann. 545 (ed.[2] Vahlen); 550 (ed.[1] Vahlen); 570 (Postgate, *Corp.* I)]: "Vix solum complere choum terroribus coeli"). A further explanation seems to be: **cous**, dicitur eo quod sibi inuicem in mundo IIII coeunt elementa, XLIV. 17. For *cous* (= χοῦς, mound, heap?) see also (XLIV. 1) *partes*. Cf. Forcell. (*cohum*).

cragacus, see *porco piscis*.

crapula, ingluuies uel uomitum [sic], II. 27 (*Bened. reg.* 39, 12 [21] remota... *crapula*; cf. ib. 14, 16 [24, 26]).

crassioribus, XLVIII. 10, see *corpulentioribus*.

cratera, patena siue calix, XXIII. 7 (1 *Esdr.* VIII. 27 *crateres* aureos; Heyse, in note, *crateras*).—**cratera**, patena, XXXVIII. 17 (*Clem. Recognitt.* VIII. 27 in *cratere* aliquo, ...omnibus ex *cratere* sumtis).

crateras, cratere, crateres, see *cratera*.

craticula for *latriuncula*, q.v.

craticulis, see *graticulis*.

cratorias, see *pantocranto*.

creacras, fuscinulas, VII. 5 (2 *Paral.* IV. 11, 16 fecit...*creagras*).

creagras, see *creacras*.

crebra, XXVIII. 75, see *prolemsis*.

crebro, XXVIII. 58, see *apostropei*.

credenti (?), XXXIV. 48, see *scatentibus*.

cremina, XXVIII. 77, see *sinastrismus*.

crepando, XXXIX. 41, see *crepido*.

crepido, a crepando dicitur, XXXIX. 41 (*Greg. Dial.* III. 17 col. 264[B] ab altaris *crepidine* pulverem collegit).

crescit, XIII. 1, see *cucumerarium*, 41, see *paliurus*, 57, see *saliuncula*; XXVIII. 69, see *emphasis*; XXXIX. 51, see *byssus*; XLVI. 24, see *situs*.

cresco, XLVI. 38, see *glisco*.

crescunt, X. 22, see *areola*; XII. 48, see *pululent*.

crestrum, see *tabanus*.

Creta comam diptamini mittit, XXXVIII. 18 (*Clem. Recognitt.*, Rufini Praef. *Creta comam dictamni mittit*). There is no interpretation. On *dipt-*, see Goetz, VI. 340 (voce *dictamnus*); Oxf. D.; Skeat, D. (*dittany*).

crimen, II. 117, see *noxa*.

crimina, see *sinastrismus*.

crines, XIII. 7, see *discriminalia*; XXI. 14, see *cincinnos*.

crinibus, XLVII. 6, see *cirris*.

crinicu┼, funicu┼, XL. 7 (*Uerba*?). As the source of this gloss has not yet been traced, the contractions cannot be expanded. Cf. inculta *criniculorum* cæsarie (Aldh. de laud. Virg. p. 17); rasis cincinorum *criniculis* (*id.* p. 58) glossed by *locca* and *loccum* (Napier, 1211, 4173).

crisma, see *nomen tuum*.

crisolitus, auri colorem et stellas luculentas habet, XLI. 13 (*De nomin. div.* = *Apoc.* XXI. 20 *chrysolitus*; see also *Exod.* XXVIII. 20, XXXIX. 13; *Ezek.* XXVIII. 13 *chrysolithus*) = crisolitus (crys-) auricolorem et stellas habet, Cp. C886; Ep. 8C12 & Ef.[1] 352, 22. For *luculentas* in Cp., Ep. and Ef.[1] see below *sardonix*.

crispantes, VI. 23, see *raucos*.

cristi, see *chri fiscus*.

cristonografon, see *chri fiscus*.

croceis, erba [herba] bona ad medicinam, XIV. 32 (*Hier.* = *Thren.* IV. 5 nutriebantur in *croceis*). The Cambr. MS.: *crocus* herba bona ad comedendum.

crocus herbe [-bae] flos est modice [-cae] mire [for *miri*?] odoris, X. 16 (*Cant.* IV. 14 nardus et *crocus*). See also *croceis*.

cronicon canuon, temporalium regularum, XXX. 77 (*Cat. Hier.* LXXXI col. 689A *Chronicorum Canonum*... historia; B: In *cronicorum canonum*...hystoriam; C: *chronicorum canonum*...historiam). The lemma is evidently taken from the Gr. text: χρονικων κανόνων ... ἱστορίας. Cf. *cronicon*, temporale, Cp. C885; Ep. 8C9; Ef.[1] 352, 19.

cronicorum, see *cronicon.*

cronographias, temporalis scribturae [script-], xxx. 37 (*Cat. Hier.* xxxviii col. 653B Meminit...et Casiani cujusdam χρονογραφίας; B: M...et Cassiani c. *cronographie*; C: M...et cassiani c. *chrono*) = *cronografias*, breuis scriptura, Cp. C896; cf. *cronograffum*, temporalis scriptura, Cp. C883; *cronografum*, temporalis scripturis, Ep. 8C2; *cinocrafum*, tempora uel scripturis, Ef.[1] 352, 12.

cronographie, see *cronographias.*

crucem, xiv. 7, see *lignum.*

cruci, xlii. 26, see *furcifer.*

crucifigent, xvii. 21, see *configent.*

cruda, ualens, xliii. 19, see *Carus.*

crudelem, ii. 173, see *tirannidem.*

crudo, xii. 41, see *lino crudo.*

cruentare, xxxv. 236, see *funestare.*

crura, xvi. 11, see *saraballa.*

cruribus, xlvi. 27, see *uarix.*

crusticis, bucellis, vi. 10 (*Breu. exsol.*?).

crypta, spelunca peruia, xvi. 3 (*Dan., Praef. Hier.* p. xvi[b], and Migne xxviii col. 1292B per *cryptam* ambulans).

ctetica, see *cethetica.*

cubat, xiii. 44, see *fouit.*

cubitales, xv. 13, see *pigmei.*

cubitali, xxxv. 27, see *puncto.*

cubiti, xv. 11, see *preteriola*; xv. 13, see *pigmei.*

cubitorum [for *cubitos*?], xxxi. 25, see *pes.*

cubitos, xxxi. 24, see *choros.*

cubitum, elin, xvi. 28 (*Dan.* iii. 1 fecit statuam...altitudine *cubitorum* sexaginta; *cubitis* ib. iii. 47). For *elin*, an ell, see Bosw. T. (*eln*).

cucu, see *cucuzata.*

cuculla, i. 17, see *byrrus*; see also *byrrum*; *coculam*; *ependiten*; *lacernam.*

cucullae, cucullam, cucullas, see *coculam.*

cuculus, see *sticulus.*

cucumerarium, hortus in quo cucumerus [Cambr. MS. *cucumeris*] crescit bona erba [herba] ad manducandum siue ad medicinam xiii. 1 (*Isai.* i. 8 tugurium in *cucumerario*) = *cucumerarium*, h. i. q. cucumeris c. b. herba a. m. s. a. m., Cp. C964.

cucumeris, see *cucumerarium.*

cucumerus, xiii. 1, see *cucumerarium.*

cucurata, see *cucuzata.*

cucuzata, laepiuincę, xlvii. 60 (*Alia* = ?) = *c*-, lepeuuince, Cp. C951; Ep. —; *c*-, laepaeuincae, Ef.[1] 353, 49. *cucuzata* is also written *cucurata* (Wright W. 285, 11). For laepi-uincę &c. (a lapwing, which also glosses *cucu*, Wright W. 260, 2; 367, 29, and *upipa*, Prompt. Parv.), see Bosw. T. (*hleāpe-wince*); Oxf. D.; Skeat, D. (*lapwing*); see also Kluge, *Etym. Wrtb.* (kibitz).

cudat, fabricat, xxxv. 271 (*Ruf.* vii. 1 fol. 116[b] Septimum nobis ecclesiasticae historiae librum...*cudat*...Dionysius) = *cudit*, fabricat, Cp. C924; *cudat*, fabricat, Ep. 6E33; Ef.[1] 349, 35.

cuiatis, huidirrynę, xliii. 37; **nostratis**, hidirrinę, xliii. 38 (*De div. nominibus* = Donati *Ars grammat.* p. 379, 30 in note, in one MS. *cuiatis nostratis*; ibid. 380, 32 *cuiatis nostratis*). For *huidirrynę* (= *hwider* = whither, and *rynę*, a course, run, running) whither-running, whither-derived or originating, and *hidir-rynę* (= *hider* = hither, and *rynę*) hither-running, from our country, see Bosw. T.

cuimarsus, princeps uille [-lae], xxix. 65 (*Uerb. Interpr.* = *Hier. in Matth.* xxi. 10 Propheta, quem et Moyses similem sui dixerat esse venturum, et qui proprie apud Graecos *cum arthro* scribitur). According to the order in which this gloss follows in the Glossary, *cuimarsus* can only refer to the above quotation, *cum arthro* being, perhaps, misunderstood by the Glossator, who was, evidently, thinking of κωμάρχης; or it may be that his text had this latter word.

cuius, i. 111; xi. 14; xxviii. 54.

culices, xxi. 16, see *conopeum.*

culicet, see *reculicet.*

culinae, see *culine.*

culine, fornacula, xv. 42 (*Ezech.* xlvi. 23 *culinae* fabricatae erant...).

culix [-lex], xxi. 16, see *conopeum.*

culmen, iv. 52, see *monarchia.*

culpa, ii. 117, see *noxa.*

culpauerit, ii. 57, see *excesserit.*

culpetur, ii. 127, see *obiurgetur.*

cultura, xii. 8, see *rusticatio*; xxvii. 28, see *in georgicis.*

cum, i. 25, 95; xiii. 23, 43; xxviii. 25, 42, 51, 53, 55, 64, 65, 70, 76, 78; xxxv. 70; xxxix. 20; xli. 17; xliv. 27.

cum arthro, see *cuimarsus.*

cum coronis, circulis aureis in capitibus eorum significantes uictoriam eius uel in choris cantantes, xxi. 5 (*Judith* iii. 10 excipientes eum *cum coronis*...ducentes choros).

cumulare, see *exaggerare.*

cunabula, xlvi. 33, see *cune.*

cunabulis, see *cunabulum.*

cunabulum, uas in quo iacent infantes, xxxv. 57 (*Ruf.* vi. 2 fol. 94[b] ex ipsis *cunabulis*; also in ed. of 1535; Cacciari, p. 319: ex ipsis *incunabulis*). According to the place where the word occurs in the Glossary, it might refer to xi. 16 fol. 185[a] ab *incunabulis*, where also a reading *cunabulis* may have existed.

cune, ciltrog unde cunabula, XLVI. 33 (*Alia*=*Ars Phocae*, p. 428, 8 *cunae*). Cf. *cunae*, cildclaðas, Cp. C966; curae (for cunae) statum infantum, Cp. C954. For *ciltrog* (=cild-trog, a child's cradle) see Bosw. T. (*cilda trog* and *trog*).

cuniculum, foramen uel canalis, XXXV. 211 (*De Eus.*); **coniculum**, a conando [cun-?], IV. 94 (*Eccl. Istor.*)=(*Ruf.* X. 13 fol. 168ª in secessus *cuniculum*)=*cuniculum*, f. u. c., Cp. C922; Ep. 6E32; Ef.[1] 349, 34.

cuniculus, see *maruca*; *suricus*.

c. uolles, c. nummos, XXXVII. 2 (*S. Aug. Serm.* 45, 2 [Migne, *P. L.* XXXVIII col. 263] qui contemnit *centum folles*...invenisti eum contemnentem *folles centum*; *Serm.* 389, 3 [Migne, *P. L.* XXXIX col. 1704] *centum folles*...jussit erogari). For other instances from Aug. see Lew. and Sh. (*follis*, C²).

cupiditatis, I. 1, see *aleator*.

cupiens, II. 46, see *desidens*.

cura, XLVIII. 41, see *synaxeos cura*.

curae, see *synaxeos cura*.

curam, XXXV. 22, see *curione*.

curatoris, I. 101, see *procuratores*.

curculio, see *gurgullio*.

curia, conuentus, IV. 7 (*Ruf.* I. 3 fol. 8ᵇ ex consessu *curiae*; cf. *curia* ibid. VIII. 16 fol. 143ᵇ).—**curia**, ubi ordo consilium iniit, XXIX. 21 (*Uerb. Interpr.*=*Hier. in Matth.* XIV. 11 a censoribus pulsum *curia*). For *curia* see also (XXXVII. 9) *tabulas legat*.

curione, qui curam gerit, XXXV. 22 (*Ruf.* IV. 15 fol. 63ª misso...*Curione*). Cacciari, p. 210, note x: *praecone*, *decurione*.

curiosa, see *scuriosa*.

currit, VIII. 12, see *naena*, 14, see *blena*; X. 19, see *gutta*; XLVII. 15, see *tappula*.

curro, XLII. 21, see *basterna*.

currunt, XXII. 16, see *ueredarii*.

currus, XIII. 59, see *feretri*.

curtina, XIII. 12, see *teristra*; XXXVIII. 6, see *stragula*.

curuis, XXXV. 41, see *in aculeis*.

curuum, XXXV. 39, see *ungulam*.

custodes, I. 40, see *defensores*.

custodia, IV. 31, see *prestatio*.

custodiis, IV. 85 and XXXV. 294, see *thecis*.

custodire, II. 180, see *tueri*.

custodit, XXXIX. 5, see *mansionarius*.

custodum, XXXVI. 5, see *fares*.

custos, XXVII. 33, see *artofilax*.

cutem, XXXV. 122, see *callos*.

cutis, XXXV. 3, see *prorigo*.

cuturno, see *turnodo*.

cyathi, see *cyati*.

cyati, mensum minutum, V. 1 (*Eccl. Stor.*); **cyati**, calices, XXXV. 12 (*De Euseb.*) =(*Ruf.* III. 6 fol. 36ᵇ unius panis, aut *cyathi* farinae).—**ciatos** habens pensum solidorum VI, XXXII. 6 (*De ponder.*?). Cf. Blume, I. 375, 25 (*cyatos*); **374**, **27** (*ciatum*); 375, 1 (*ciati*).—Cf. further *cyatos* (II. 86, sub v. *himina*); *urna*; and *cyatus*, calix, Cp. C972; Ep. 6E28; *cietas*, calix, Ef.[1] 349, 30.

cyclis (?), see *ciclis*.

cymbalis, see *in nablis*.

cymentarii, qui minores [lapides] dolant, XXIII. 4 (1 *Esdr.* III. 7 Dederunt... pecunias latomis et *cæmentariis*; III. 10 fundato...a *cæmentariis* templo). See also *latomi*.

cymiteria, sepulture, I. 24, see *coementeria*.

cyneris, nablis, idest citharis longiores quam psalterium nam psalterium triangulum fit theodorus dixit, XII. 40 (*Eccles.* XXXIX. 20 Vulg. confitemini illi in voce labiorum vestrorum, et in canticis labiorum et *citharis*). Sab. records in a note that a Sangerm. MS. has *cinyris* for *citharis*. The Cambr. MS. has: *Cineris*, nablis. It is difficult to say who "Theodorus" was. Glogger suggests either Th. of Heraclea, who died about A.D. 355; or Th. of Mopsuestia, d. about A.D. 428, or Th. of Tharsus, Archbp. of Canterbury, who died A.D. 695.

CYNXPONON, unius temporis, XVIII. 1 (*Ose*; *Praef. Hier. in XII Proph.*, p. XVIIª Osee *synchronon* Isaiae; Migne, *P. L.* XXVIII col. 1016ᴬ σύγχρονον).

cypressus, uiridem habet colorem ut est porrus et stellas aureas habet, XLI. 16 (*De nomin. div.*=*Apoc.* XXI. 20 *chrysoprasus*)=*cyprassus*, uiridem h. c. aureum hoc est et stellas, Cp. C977; Ep. 8C13; Ef.[1] 352, 23. For *ut est porrus* in Cp., Ep. and Ef.[1] see the present Glossary in voce *topation*.

cypri, see *cyprus*.

cyprius, prouintia [-cia], XXXV. 299 (*Ruf.* X. 5 fol. 160ᵇ Spiridion *Cyprius* episcopus).

cyprus, arbor est similis salice [salici] habens flores miri odoris et butros sicut erba [herba] pratearum [pratorum? as in the Cambridge MS.], X. 10 (*Cant.* I. 13 Vers. ant. Sab.: Nardus *cypri*; ib. Vulg.: Botrus *cypri*).

cyrię, XXIX. 63, see *ileusun cyrię*.

cyrieleison, see *kyrieleison*.

cythara [cith-], XXXV. 161, see *psaltes*.

d for *g*: urido (for urigo).—for *t*: capud (caput); ridhmus (rhythmus).

daefecatior, see *defecatior*.

daemones, see *manius*.
daemoniosum, see *arreptitium*.
dalatura, see *dolabella*.
dalmatica, tonica lata habens manicas misalis [=missalis, -les, of or belonging to the *missa*], XXXIX. 32 (*Greg. Dial.* IV. 40 col. 397A *dalmaticam*...tetigit)=*Dalmatica*, tunica latas manicas habens, Cp. D10; Ep. —; Ef.[1] 356, 72.
damma, elha, XLV. 20 (*Uerba de multis* =*Ars Phocae*, p. 412, 20 masculini generis, hic...*damma*)=*damma*, bestia idest eola, Cp. D12; Ep. —; Ef.[1] 357, 4. For *elha*, *eola*, an elk, see Bosw. T. (*eolh*).
damnando, XXXV. 207, see *proscribendo*.
damnatur, XXXVII. 17, see *addicitur*.
Dan, proprium nomen gentis, XV. 15 (*Ezech.* XXVII. 19 *Dan* et Graecia; cf. ibid. XLVIII. 1, 2, 32).
DANIELEM, XVI *tit.*
Danihelis, see *ypo* (sub) *tyos* (hoc) &c.
dant, XXXVIII. 44, see *epibatis*.
dantur, I. 112, see *stipendiis*; XXXVIII. 43, see *nastologis*.
dapes, IV. 58, see *oedipia*, sub v. *thesteas*.
dapulas [for *stipulas*?], III. 54, see *enrusa*.
dare, XLI. 1, see *presbiteri*, 2, see *chorepiscopi*; **dare**, I. 82, see *operam dare*.
darent, IV. 41, see *pessimos darent*.
datione, XII. 33, see *de traiectione*.
datur, XXVIII. 57, see *figura*; XXXIII. 6, see *stater*.
daturque, XXII. 16, see *ueredarii*.
dauid, X. 24, see *Salamitis*; XXIII. 17, see *ciuitas dauid*.
de, I *tit.*; II *tit.*; III *tit.*; IV. 79 (bis); V *tit.*; 6 (bis), 14; VI. 16, 29; VIII. 16, 18, 19; X. 7, 19, 26; XI. 5; XII. 9 (bis), 21, 33 (bis); XIII. 6–9, 25 (bis), 40, 56; XIV. 3, 5, 6, 14; XV. 14, 22, 37, 45; XVI. 14, 21; XVII *tit.* (bis), 4; XIX. 40 (bis), 44 (bis), 48; XXI. 18, 20; XXII. 4, 16; XXIII. 1; XXIV. 10, 13; XXV. 3, 4, 7; XXVI. 13; XXVII. 28; XXIX. 11, 62 (bis); XXX. 13, 20, 27, 28 (bis), 29 (bis), 35, 43 (bis), 82 (bis), 91; XXXIII. 7; XXXV. 30, 42, 164 (bis), 223, 238 (bis), 241, 254 (bis), 294; XXXVIII. 19; XXXIX. 15 (bis); XLI *tit.*; XLII. 21; XLIII *tit.*, 21; XLIV *tit.*; XLV *tit.*; XLVIII *tit.*
de, see *delecto eius* (for *de lecto*).
dea, XIII. 43, see *lamia*.
dearum, XLIII. 27, see *frora*.
deauratum, XXII. 8, see *lecti aurei*.
debitis, XXXV. 206, see *salariis*.
debuerunt, XXII. 11, see *mundum m-*.
decani, a decim [decem] nominantur, II. 53 (*Bened. reg.* 21, 4 constituantur *decani*; 6 [8] *decani* tales elegantur; 8 [13] *decani*; cf. 21 *tit.*, De *decanis*; 62, 12 [21] a *decanis*; 65, 21 [42] per *decanos*).—**decanorum**, qui per x nummos auguriantur (!), XXXVIII. 31 (*Clem. Recognitt.* IX. 26 secundum numerum *decanorum*). Goetz (VI. 306) suggests to read *numeros* for *nummos*.
decanis, decanos, see *decani*.
decanorum, qui per x nummos auguriantur, XXXVIII. 31, see *decani*.
decapolim, x ciuitates in una prouintia [-cia], XXIX. 31 (*Uerb. Interpr.*=*Hier. in Matth.* IV. 24, 5 de Galilæa et *Decapoli*; Vulg. *Decapolim*).
DE CASSIANO, XXXIV *tit.*
de cassidie, pera pastoralis, XX. 9 (*Tobias* VIII. 2 protulit *de cassidili* suo partem jecoris; Heyse, in note, *de cassidile*). Cf. *cassidele*, pung (a bag, purse), Cp. C136; Ep. —; Ef.[1] 354, 40.
DE CA[TA]LOGO HIERONIMI IN PROLOGO, XXX tit. [*in prologo* seems to refer to the first two lemmata (*peripatthiens* and *Canitius*) of the Chapter, which are extracted from St Jerome's Preface to his *Catalogus*, or *Liber de illustribus viris*; see the "Admonitio" in Migne's ed., col. 597, and note [a] on col. 601 ibid.].
decem, see *colamina*; *decani*.
december, XXII. 14, see *Tebetht*.
decem iugera uinearum, x iugeres uel diurnales, XIII. 15 (*Isai.* V. 10 *decem... jugera vinearum* facient lagunculam unam). For *iugeres* see also below sub v. *iugeres*; Forcellini; Maii *Spicil.* IX ad fin., Gloss. nov. Lat. p. 34 (*iuger*, ris, gen. masc. Opusc. vet. MS. in Isaiam Decem iugeres vel diurnales).
decemnoualem, XXX. 53, see *enneafe decerida*, sub v. *ex ca*.
decerida, XXX. 52, 53, see *ex ca*.
decim [decem], II. 53, see *decani*; XXXIII. 20, see *colamina*.
decima, XXXIII. 16, see *gomor*.
decimas, XXI. 18, see *sancta domini*.
decipulam, tenticulam [tend-] qua aues capiuntur, XXIX. 23 (*Uerb. Interpr.*=*Hier. in Matth.* XIX. 1 col. 134A ut *decipulam* eorum transeat). Cf. *decipula*, bisuicfalle, Cp. D33.
decisio [sine interpretat.], I. 42 (*De Canon.*; *Can. Conc. Carth.* LIX *decisio* clericorum).
de citiuis, de insanis, XXIX. 62 (*Uerb. Interpr.*=*Hier. in Matth.* XV. 31 De κυλλοῖς tacuit; XV. 29, 30 κυλλούς and κυλλός).
declarauerit, XXXV. 194, see *expolierit*.
DE CLEMENTE, XXXVIII *tit.*
declinans, XLIV. 25, see *dextera*.
decora, XXVIII. 46, see *aetilogia*.
decore, XXVIII. 25, see *scema*.

decorem, xxviii. 68, see *anadiplosis*; xlviii. 21, see *leporem*.

decorticantur, viii. 18, see *ptisanas*.

decrepita, fracta uel uetorosa [ueternosa], xxvi. 9 (*Isid. Offic.* ii. 7, 4 propter *decrepitam* senectutem).—**decrepitam**, dobend, xxxix. 30 (*Greg. Dial.* iv. 52 col. 413B usque ad aetatem *decrepitam*) = *decrepita*, dobgendi, Cp. D46; Ep. —; *decrepita*, dobendi, Ef.[1] 356, 6. For *dobend* &c., doting, see Bosw. T. *dofung* (dotage), *dufian* (to sink); Kluge, *A. S. Leseb.* 170 (*dofian*, toben); Franck, *Woord. Ned. T.* (*doof*).

decurio, princeps super x homines, xxv. 9 (*Marc.* xv. 43 nobilis *decurio*; *Luc.* xxiii. 50 qui erat *decurio*).

decurione, see *curione*.

decursa, xxviii. 75, see *prolemsis*.

decus, i. 57, see *genuinum decus*.

De Dialogorum, xxxix *tit.*

dedicationes, xxv. 11, see *enchenia*.

dedictum [for *dedicatum*?], x. 6, see *unguentum exinanitum*.

dedragma duę Dragmae sunt unde miror quomodo in libro hebraicarum questionum semeuncias scribitur, xxxiii. 5 (*Euch. De pond.*, p. 158, 11 *didragma* dragmae duae, unde m. q. in l. H. quaestionum *semuncia* s.). The Brit. Mus. MS. adds: *didragma* habet scripula vi. Cf. Wotke's note (ibid.); cf. *dedragmae*, duae mensurae, Cp. D149, and see below *didragma*.

deduco, see *deducor*.

deducor [for *deduco*], i. 102, see *prosequor*.

de ecclesiastico, xii *tit.*

de eclesiasten, ix *tit.*

de entoetromito, deflicto [for *de ficto*? for *fictus* cf. Cp. F44, 312; S313] diuersarum dispositionum, xxx. 82 (*Cat. Hier.* lxxxv col. 691C de *Engastrimytho*; Migne's Gr. text: περὶ Ἐγγαστριμύθου; Richardson: De ἐγγαστριμύθῳ; B: de *entasrimeiteon*; C [blank]). *Diuersarum dispositionum* is here out of place; it clearly refers to *Cat. Hier.* lxxxvi col. 693A: multaque *diuersarum* ὑποθέσεων scripsit volumina, where B has: m. *diuersarum expositionum* s. vol.; and C: multaque *diuersarum* [blank] s. vol. Cf. *ypoteseon*, dispositionum, Cp. Y1; Ef.[1] 401, 5.

De [e]odem libro [heading to a second collection from the *Lib. Rotarum* = *Isid. Lib. de natura rerum*], xxvii. 18.

De Ester, xxii *tit.*

De Eusebio, xxxv *tit.*

defatiget, see *deficiet*.

defecatior, purior, iv. 109 (*Ruf.* xi. 26 fol. 189b aqua...*defecatior* ac *purior* redditur; Cacciari, ii. p. 108: *dæfecatior*). Further explanations of this gloss seem to be iv. 110: **defecatum**, liquidam, and iv. 111: **purum**, extersum. See also *defecatum*, uinum purificatum, Cp. D79; Ep. —; Ef.[1] 356, 56.

defecatum, liquidam, iv. 110, see *defecatior*.

defectio, xxvii. 1, see *deliquium*, 21, see *eclipsis*; xxxix. 47, see *sincopin*.

defectionis, see *obductionis*.

defenditur, xxxvii. 15, see *uindicatur*.

defensor, i. 87, see *presul*.

defensores, custodes presides [praes-], i. 40 (*De Canon.*; *Can. Conc. Carth.* lxxv ut *defensores* eis...delegentur; de *defensoribus* Ecclesiarum, ib. *tit.*; dent facultatem *defensores* constituendi, ib. xcvii.). Cf. *Can. Conc. Calched.* ii & xxiii (*defensorem*).

defetimur, renitimur, vi. 25 (*Breu. exsol.*?).

deficientes, i. 37, see *delirantes*.

deficiet, fatiget, xxviii. 1 (*Lib. Anton.* xv.; Migne, *P.L.* lxxiii col. 135B non vos aut tædium *defatiget*) = *defitiget*, fatiget, Cp. D51; Ep. —; *defiget*, fatiget, Ef.[1] 356, 15. Cf. *defatiget*, suenceth, Cp. D52.

de figmento, de plasmatione hominis, xxxv. 164 (*Ruf.* iv. 26 fol. 70a *De figmento*). Cf. *figmenta*, plasmatio hominum, Cp. F174.

definita, see *secus*.

definitio, see *dogma*.

definitiones, see *sanctiones*.

definiuit, see *sanxit*.

defixiezodo, see *psichiexodo*.

deflicto (for *de ficto*?), xxx. 82, see *de entoetromito*.

deflorare, euellare (!), xxxiv. 53 (*De Cass. Inst.* v. 4, 2 unamquamque uirtutem ...*deflorare*; two MSS. have *deplorare*).

deforma [deformis?], iii. 10, see *hispida*; for deforma = *deformia*, xv. 44, see *prophana*.

deformis, see *hispida*.

degessimus, see *digessimus*.

degesti sunt, congregati sunt, xxxiv. 52; see *digessimus*.

degradauerit, deposuerit, ii. 42 (*Bened. reg.* 63, 14 [24] hos quos...abbas...*degradaverit*).

dei, xxx. 20, see *pantocranto*, 29, see *capun periens*; xxxv. 17, see *a theologia*, 147, see *petalum*; xxxvi. 1, see *Iani*; xxxviii. 20, see *fidiae opera*; see also *epimelne*, sub v. *epitomen*.

deicio, xliii. 45, see *pytisso*.

deificum lumen, diuinum lumen, ii. 40 (*Bened. reg.* Prol. 20 [28] ad *deificum* lumen); cf. Ef.[2] 286, 12 (*deficum*, diuinum).

deinde, xxxv. 297, see *exin*; xliv. 27, see *leua*.

De Iohel uel de prophetis minoribus, xvii *tit.*

delatus, see *consulari delectus*.

delectabilia, x. 15, see *emissiones tuę*.

delectionis, see *obductionis*.

delecto eius, legationes eius, xlviii. 29 (*De Cass.*, *Inst.* i. 1, 2 prior...missus ad increpandos nuntios Ochoziae...eo quod ...propheta descensum *de lecto* ei [*eius*, in three MSS.] in quo conciderat denegasset, decumbenti regi exposita uestitus qualitate conpertus est). It is clear that the Glossator regarded *de lecto* as one word referring to the *messengers* of King Ochozias to Elijah; see iiii *Reg.* i. 1 sq.

delectus [for *delatus*?], xxxv. 149; see *consulari delectus*.

Del et hnabot [sine interpret.], xiii. 54 (*Isai.* xlvi. 1 confractus est *Bel*, contritus est *Nabo*; Heyse in note *Naboth*).

delibamus [deliberamus], i. 132, see *satagimus*.

deliberamus, see *satagimus*.

deliberatio [sine interpret.], ii. 55 (*Bened. reg.* 58, 24 [41] habita secum *deliberatione*). Cf. *deliberatio*, ymbðriodung, Cp. D62; *d*-, ymbdritung, Ef.[1] 356, 36, and Bosw. T. (*ymb-þreodian*, *ymb-þreodung*).

deliberatione, see *deliberatio*.

deliberatum, see *delibratum*.

delibratum, cogitatum, xxxv. 273 (*Ruf.* vii. 12 fol. 120[b] continuo sibi et *deliberatum* asserit, et...confirmatum).

delibutus, unctus, xxvi. 4 (*Isid. Offic.* ii. 26, 2 mystico vnguento est *delibutus*). Cf. *delibutus*, perunctus infusus, Cp. D38; *d*-, perunctus uel perfusus, Ef.[2] 283, 58 and Goetz, vi. 318[b] (*delibutus*).

deliquium, defectio, xxvii. 1 (*Lib. Rot.* = *Isid. de nat. rer.*, xxiv. 1 solis *deliquium*) = Cp. D95; Ep. —; Ef.[1] 356, 58.

delirantes, mente deficientes, i. 37 (*De Canon.*; *Vet. Defin. fid. Chalc.*, Mans. vii. 754[b] Ipsis...figuram *delirantes* vel insanientes dicimus; 755[a] *delirantes* exterminat).

delubra, templa deorum, xxxv. 224 (*Ruf.* xi. 28 fol. 190[b] quae...stare *delubra* potuerunt; xi. 22 fol. 187[a] impuritates *delubri*; xi. 23 fol. 187[b] Interioris *delubri* parietes). Cf. *delubra*, templa idolorum, Cp. D201.

De Marco et Luca et Iohanne, xxv *tit.*

demergit, xliv. 26, see *a tergo*.

demergitur, xliv. 27, see *leua*.

deminut-, see diminit-.

demon [daemon], xxxviii. 28, see *cacodemonus*.

demones [daem-], iv. 104, see *manius*.

demoniosum [daem-], xiv. 17, see *arreptitium*.

de monogamia, de singularibus nuptiis, xxx. 43 (*Cat. Hier.* liii col. 663[A] texuit volumina de pudicitia...*de monogamia*). Cf. *monogamia*, singularis nuptiae, Cp. M250; Ep. 14C13; Ef.[1] 370, 46.

demum, postea, ii. 54 (*Bened. reg.* 2, 22 [31]; 73, 19 [33] tunc *demum*).

denarii, xxxii. 1, see *dragma*.

denarius per x nummis deputatur, xxxi. 38 (*De ponder.*). Cf. Blume, i. 374, 1 sqq.

densitudo, xxxiv. 25, see *pinsit*.

denso, xxvii. 32, see *opago tempore*.

dentes, xiii. 18, see *sarculum*, 36, see *in serris*, 47, see *plaustrum*; xix. 56, see *molas*.

deo, i. 109, see *religio*; xxx. 29, see *capun periens*.

de octoade, de octaua die, v. 6 (*Eccl. Stor.*); **de octoade**, de nouo testamento, xxxv. 254 (*De Eus.*); see *ogdoade*.

deodem [for *de eodem*], xxvii. 18.

De Orosio, xxxvi *tit.*

deorsum, x. 21, see *elatę palmarum*; **deorsum**, xliv. 27, see *dextera*.

deorum, xxxv. 94, see *theomachie*, 224, see *delubra*.

De Ose spetialiter [spec-], xviii *tit.*

de paralipomenon, vii *tit.* [otherwise entit. *Chron.* i. & ii.].

dependisset, sustinuisset, iv. 32 (*Ruf.* iii. 6 fol. 37[b] supplicium ciuitas *dependisset*).

de philoxenia, de amore ospicium [hospitium], xxx. 28 (*Cat. Hier.* xxiv col. 643[B] *de philoxenia* [de φιλοξενίᾳ, Rich.] librum; B: *de philogenia* idest hospitalitate librum; C: de hospitalitate librum).

de piasma, fractura [factura?] uel ars, xxx. 27; see *plasma*.

depicta, xxxviii. 6, see *stragula*.

depingit, depinguit, see *pinsit*.

De ponderibus, xxxii *tit.*; De ponderibus incipit, xxxi *tit.*; De ponderibus secundum Eucherium, xxxiii *tit.*

deposuerit, ii. 42, see *degradauerit*.

depromsimus, protulimus, i. 38 (*De Canon.*; *Can. Conc. Carthag.*, Praef. p. 143[a] Praeter ista, quae *depromsimus* actis).

depteronomium, see *deuteronomii*.

depulit, xxxv. 105, see *arcet*.

deputatio, xxxvii. 16, see *taxatio*.

deputato, ii. 21, see *adsignato*.

deputatur, xxxi. 38, see *denarius*.

de radice colubri nascitur regulus qui manducat aucellas idest basiliscus secundum historiam dicitur de colubri nasci, xiii. 25 (*Isai.* xiv. 29 *de radice*...

colubri egredietur regulus; Cambr. MS.: *De colubro nascitur regulus* q. m. a. Nascitur represents, perhaps, another reading; or it may be a gloss to *egredietur*). Cf. E. *basilisk*, Oxf. D.

derelictum, II. 65, see *excussum*.

deriguere, see *diriguere*.

deriuatur, see *areola*.

DE SALAMONE, VIII *tit*.

DE SANCTI AGUSTINI [Aug-], XXXVII *tit*.

DE SAPIENTIA, XI *tit*.

descendentes, XXII. 16, see *ueredarii*.

describitur, see *caracterismos*.

describunt, see *cardines*.

desertator, II. 156, see *stirpator*.

deserto, XIV. 11, see *perdix*.

deses, see *seres*.

desidens, negligens uel otium cupiens, II. 46 (*Bened. reg.*?). The lemma does not seem to occur in the *Reg. Bened.*; it is, perhaps, a further explanation of *desidia* (q. v.); see also *desidiosus*.

desiderare, XXXV. 259, see *gestire*.

desidia, ignauia, II. 45 (*Bened. reg.* Prol. 5 [6] per inoboedientiae *desidiam*).

desidiam, see *desidia*.

desidiosis, see *desidiosus*.

desidiosus, ignauus pigrus [sic], II. 41 (*Bened. reg.* 48, 41 [72] Si quis...*desidiosus* fuerit; cf. 73, 16 [26] Nobis...*desidiosis* ...rubor confusionis est).

designant, XLIV. 11, see *clima*.

designauimus, II. 177, see *taxauimus*.

de siliquis, fructus arboris colligitur porcis, XXV. 6; see *siliqua*.

desinat, XXXV. 150, see *facessat*.

desolati sunt, see *asolatis*.

desolutio, XXXIX. 40, see *paralisin*.

desonat, XXXV. 76, see *fessat*.

desperabilis, see *obstinatus*.

despicatis, see *dispicatis*.

despiciendo, II. 163, see *spernendo*.

destinabunt, see *presbiteri*.

destruitur, see *menstruum*.

desuper, III. 56, see *ependiten*; XIII. 59, see *feretri*; XXI. 10, see *sandalia*; XXIV. 17, see *clibanus*.

detegere, II. 118, see *non detegere*.

deterrens, XXVIII. 26, see *paradigma*.

detineri, I. 63, see *inhibere*.

de traiectione, de datione, ideŝt malum, XII. 33 (*Eccles.* XXXVII. 12 tracta...cum negotiatore *de trajectione*).

de triuio, de tribus uiis, IV. 79 and XXXV. 238, see *triuium*.

deucalionem, nomen regis sub [quo] diluuium factum est non generare, XXXVIII. 22 (*Clem. Recognitt.* VIII. 50 Deus diluvium mundo induxit, quod vos sub *Deucalione* factum dicitis). Cf. Goetz, VI. 335. Glogger suggests that *Non generare* may be for *non generale*, that is *not the general deluge*.

deuocari [sine interpretat.], I. 43 (*De Canon.*; *Can. Conc. Carth.* LIX non liceat clericum in iudicium...*deuocari* eum, qui...).

deuoratores, VI. 7, see *ambrones*.

deuotatum, male dicturio inconparari, XL. 3 (*Uerba*?). Cf. *deuotaturi*, maledicturi, Cp. D180.

deus, I. 39, see *diuus*; XXVIII. 52 (bis), see *epizeusis*, 53 (bis), see *paraprosdocia*; XLIII. 3, see *Pan*, 17, see *Nereus*.

deuteres, renouationes, XXIX. 33 (*Uerb. Interpr.* = *Hier. in Matth.* XXII. 23 Pharisæi traditionum et observationum, quas illi δευτερώσεις vocant, justitiam præferebant).

deuteronomii, secunda lex, II. 52 (*Bened. reg.* 13, 14 canticum *Deuteronomii*; [22 canticum *deutheronomium*; in note deuter-, and depteronomium]) = Deuteronomium, s. l., Cp. Int. 83 (Euch. 105).

deuteronomium, see *deuteronomii*.

deuterosin, secunda lex, XXX. 22 (*Cat. Hier.* XVIII col. 637B Hic dicitur mille annorum Judaicam edidisse δευτέρωσιν; B: *aeoytyerosen*, idest nouitatem; C [blank]).

deutheronomium, see *deuteronomii*.

dexter, XXXVI. 6, see *eurus*.

dextera, mutatur quando sibi uertix [-tex] in circium declinans ad eum subregit austronothum, XLIV. 25;—**a tergo**, dicitur errare dum austronotho in sublimi erecto uertix se in summum poli demergit, XLIV. 26;—**leua**, deinde cum se subleuans in boreum uertix austronothum precipitans obiecit et **sursum** atque **deorsum** dicimus quod cęlum sicut in ortu surgens eregitur ita et in occasu demergitur. Hii sunt uii motus cęli qui solem et lunam dum polo sunt tardiores in diuersis oriri et occidere cogunt orbibus, XLIV. 27 (*Alia*; *de cælo* = Isid. *de nat. rerum* XII. 5 quod motum inerrabilem habeat, siquidem sex alii motus errabiles sunt, *ante*, *a tergo*, *dextra*, *laevaque*, *sursum*, *deorsum*).

diaconico, ministerio, I. 41 (*De Canon.*; *Can. Conc. Laod.* CXXIV *tit.* a *diaconico* id est a secretario; *ibid.* non oporteat subdiaçonos habere locum in *diaconico*).

diaconissa, quam diaconus habuit, XXXIX. 23 (*Greg. Dial.*?). The word *diaconissa* does not seem to occur in Gregory's *Dial.*, and the present gloss is, perhaps, merely a further explanation of the preceding *presbitera* (q. v.). Cf. *Can. Conc. Calched.* 15 De *diaconissis* mulieribus. *Diaconissam* non ordinandam.

diaconus, XXXIX. 23, see *diaconissa*.

diadema, corona aurea, XXII. 10 (*Esther* II. 17 posuit *diadema* regni in capite ejus;

vi. 8 regium *diadema*; i. 11 posito...*diademate*).

diafonia, dissonantia, xxx. 57; see *diaphonian.*

diaforesis, per quam fit differentia personarum, xxviii. 80 (*Cass. Psalm.* xxxvi. 22 *diaphoresis* p.q.f.d.p.).

dialectica, dualis dictio, xxx. 45 [=Cp. D259; Ef.[1] 356, 11]; **arethimetica**, numeralis, xxx. 46; **musica**, modo labiis [for *modulabilis*?], xxx. 47; **geometrica**, terre mensura, xxx. 48; **grammatica**, literali, xxx. 49 [=gr-, litteralis, Cp. G144]; **rethorica**, eloquentia, xxx. 50 [=rethorica, praeclara eloquentia, Cp. R62]; **astronomia**, siderum lex, xxx. 51 [cf. *a-*, lex astrorum, Cp. A827] (*Cat. Hier.* liv col. 665c *dialecticam*...et *geometriam*, et *arithmeticam*, *musicam*, *grammaticam* et *rhetoricam*, omniumque philosophorum sectas...didicit [*διαλεκτικὴν, καὶ γεωμετρικὴν, ἀριθμητικὴν, μουσικὴν, γραμματικὴν, καὶ ῥητορικὴν, καὶ πάντων*...]; B: *dyaleticam*...et *geometriam* et *astronomiam* et *arismetricam*, *musicam*, *grammaticam* et *rethoricam*, omniumque phil. s. d.; C: *dialeticam*...et *geometricam*, *arismeticam*, *musicam*, *grammaticam* et *rhetoricam* omniumque ph. s. d.). Cf. *Cat. Hier.* lxxiii col. 683B: *arithmetica*, *geometria*, *astronomia*, *grammatica*, *rhetorica*, *dialectica*; B: in *arismetrica*, *geometria*, *astronomia*, *gramatica*, *rethorica*, *dyaletica*; C: in *arismetricam*, *geometricam*, *astronomiam*, *grammaticam*, *rhetoricam*, *dialeticam.*

dialecticam, see *dialectica.*

dialecticis, fecundia, xxxiv. 45 (*De Cass., Inst.* xii. 19 syllogismis *dialecticis* et Tulliana *facundia*). According to Glogger a St Gallen MS. has *facundis* instead of *fecundia.*

dialetica, see *dialectica.*

dialogo, xxxvii. 9, see *tabulas legat.*

DIALOGORUM, xxxix *tit.*

diametro, xxxviii. 35, see *ex diametro.*

Diana, filia iouis, xxviii. 11 (*Lib. Anton.* xlvii col. 160A *Dianam*).

Dianam, see *Diana.*

diaphonian, dissonantiam, xxx. 11 (*Cat. Hier.* ix col. 623B res...*διαφωνίαν* (dissonantiam)...tollit; B: res *diaphonian* id est *dissonantiam*...tulit; C: res et [blank] idem *dissonanciam*...tollit).—**diafonia**, dissonantia, xxx. 57 (*Cat. Hier.* lxiii col. 675A super *διαφωνίᾳ*...disputat; B: super *dyaphonia*...disputat; C: super [blank]... disputat). Cf. also *Cat. Hier.* lxxxi col. 689A de Evangeliorum *Diaphonia*; B: de E. *dyaphonia*, idest *dissonantia*; C: de euangeliis [blank])=Cp. D248; Ep. —; Ef.[1] 355, 49.

diaphoresis, see *diaforesis.*

diapsalma, uero sermonum rupta continuatio, xxviii. 20 (*Cass. Psalm.*, Praef. xi. d., u. s. r. c.; see also id. *in Ps.* iv. 4 *diapsalmatis* silentium; ix. 16 canticum *diapsalmatis*) = *diapsalma*, sermonum rupta continuatio, Cp. Int. 87; cf. sympslma, diapsalma, Ep. 23C31, and sympsalma, diapsalma, Ef.[1] 389, 32. In the latter two Glossaries, therefore, we have merely two lemmata without the interpretations; see *sympsalma*; *uero* in the above gloss refers to the preceding clause in the text.

diatiposis, latini expresio dicitur ubi rebus personisue subiectis et formę ipsę et habitus exprimuntur, xxviii. 88 (*Cass. Psalm.* xxx. 11 figura *diatyposis*, quae *Latine expressio* d. u. r. p. s. e. formae ipsae e. h. e. See also ibid. 14).

diatribas, dissensiones uel disputationes, xxix. 71 (*Uerb. Interpr.*).—**diatripas**, conflictus proprium nomen loci ubi discunt dispuli [discipuli], xxx. 26 = (*Cat. Hier.* xxiii col. 641c: cum in ùrbe Roma haberet *διατριβάς*; B: cum in u. R. h. *aiatkibas* idest *dissentiones* et *conflictus*; C: cum in v. rōna h. [blank]). There is nothing in the above readings militating against the various meanings of *διατριβή*, and in Cp. D262 and Ef.[1] 356, 14 we find *Diatrifas*, conflictus. But Glogger suggests that a lemma has fallen out, namely: gymnicus agon (*γυμνικὸς ἀγών*) which occurs xxii col. 641A; cf. Cp. G192 (=Ep. 10C26; Ef.[1] 363, 3): Gymnicus agon locus ubi leguntur diuersae artes.

diatrifas, see *diatripas*, sub v. *diatribas.*

diatripas, conflictus &c., xxx. 26, see *diatribas.*

diatyposis, see *diatiposis.*

dic, xliii. 48, see *cedo.*

dicantur, xxviii. 18, see *apo tu-.*

dicebantur, xxxix. 52, see *omnes dies....*

dicenda, xxviii. 64, see *epitrocasmos.*

dicens, xxviii. 39, see *allegoria.*

dicentium, xxxv. 199, see *garrientium.*

dicere, xxxix. 36, see *sex untias.*

dici, xxviii. 18, see *apo tu-.*

dicimus, xliv. 27, see *leua.*

dicit, xxxi. 22, 37.

dicitur, ii. 35, 161, 188; iii. 62; viii. 12, 14; x. 6, 22 (bis); xi. 4; xii. 42; xiii. 25, 36, 43; xiv. 10; xv. 22; xvi. 13; xxi. 16; xxii. 4, 11; xxiii. 20; xxiv. 10, 12, 16; xxviii. 49, 52, 62, 74, 88; xxx. 20; xxxi. 37; xxxiii. 3, 7, 13 (bis); xxxv. 15, 144; xxxvii. 12; xxxix. 24, 28, 41, 42, 48–50; xlii. 9; xliii. 4, 18; xliv. 17, 19, 26; xlv. 11, 16; xlvii. 28.

dicitur, xiii. 47, for *dicuntur*, see *plaustrum.*

dico, II. 170, see *uerbotenus*.

dicta, II. 87, see *aabita*, 146, see *regula*; XXVIII. 44, see *hypallage*.

dictamni, see *creta comam-*.

dictare, I. 97, see *preces dictare*.

dictę, XLVI. 36, see *manubię*.

dicti, XXVIII. 64, see *epitrocasmos*, 82, see *efexegresis*.

dictio, XXVIII. 33, see *tropus*, 54, see *aposiopesis*, 61, see *amphibolia*; XXIX. 1, see *allegoria*; XXX. 45, see *dialectica*.

dictionis, XXVIII. 25, see *scema*, 57, see *figura*, 68, see *anadiplosis*.

dictis, XXXV. 191, see *affatibus*.

dictum, XXVI. 13, see *uaruassi*.

dicturio, XL. 3, see *deuotatum*.

dictus, XLIV. 7, see *poli*.

dicunt, XXVIII. 55; XXXIII. 13, 16.

dicuntur, X. 12; XI. 5; XIII. 6, 58; XXII. 16; see also *plaustrum*.

didascalicum, see *didascalum*, sub v. *didascalium*.

didascalium, magisteriale, XX. 12 (*Tobias*? not? in the Vulg.). Perhaps = **didascalum**, doctorale, XXXIX. 64 (*not* in Greg. Dial., but *Decr. Innoc.* VIII p. 196[b] regularum hunc librum, quasi *didascalicum* atque monitorem...insinuare).

didragma, XXXI. 37, see *statera*; didragmis, see *stater*; see also *dedragma*.

die, V. 6, see *de octoade*; VII. 2, see *pro octaua*; XLII. 23, see *quartane*; XLIV. 9, see *cęlum*.—**die**, IV. 99, see *quadraplas die*.

diebus, XXXV. 179, see *horas diurnas*; **diebus**, XXXV. 28, see *munerum diebus*.

diei, XXVIII. 52, see *epizeusis*; XXXV. 75, see *jugeres*.

diem, XVII. 7, see *Niniue*.

dieperdulum, see *perdulum*.

dierum, XVII. 7, see *Niniue*; XXXV. 250, see *in exameron*.

dies, XXVIII. 52, see *epizeusis*; XXXIX. 52, see *omnes dies...*; XLIII. 42, see *posttridie*.

differentia, XXVIII. 80, see *diaforesis*.

difficile, XLII. 19, see *egre*.

difiniciones [definit-], I. 122, see *sanctiones*.

difinita [def-], I. 117, see *secus*.

difinitio [def-], I. 35, see *dogma*.

difiniuit [def-], I. 125, see *sanxit*.

digessimus, congrecauimus [congreg-] ordinauimus, II. 47 (*Bened. reg.* 17, 3 [2] *degessimus* ordinem psalmodiae; *digessimus*, in note).—**digesti**, dispositi excocti, II. 51 (*Bened. reg.* 8, 5 [7] iam *degesti* surgant; cf. 18, 39 [70] *digesto* ordine).—**degesti sunt**, congregati sunt, XXXIV. 52 (*De Cass., Inst.* v. 1 post... libellos, qui...*digesti sunt*).

digesti, dispositi excocti, II. 51, see *digessimus*; digesti sunt, see *degesti sunt* sub v. *digessimus*.

digiti, XXXV. 39, see *ungulam*.

digitis, I. 95, see *portentuose*.

dignitas, XXXVII. 20, see *toga*.

dignitate, VII. 9, see *in fastu*.

dignitates, XXXIX. 65, see *infulas*.

dignitati, XXXV. 149, see *consulari delectus*.

dignitatibus, XXXV. 103, see *fascibus*.

dignus, XLII. 26, see *furcifer*.

dilectiones [for *dilectionis*, or *delectionis*?], XII. 3, see *obductionis*.

dilectionis, see *obductionis*.

diluuium, XXXVIII. 22, see *deucalionem*.

dimedium, XXXI. 3, see *sextarius*, 9, see *comor*, 36, see *sata*; XXXIII. 8, see *obulus*.

dimedius, XXXI. 35, see *cimina*.

dimidians? see *dnm̄s*, sub v. *extremi*.

dimidium, XXXI. 32, see *sextarius*.

diminitiue [deminut-], XIII. 6, see *lunulas*.

diminitiui [deminut-], XVII. 6, see *sacelli*.

diminitiuum [deminut-], XVII. 10, see *geniculorum*; XIX. 60, see *lagunculas*; XXXV. 56, see *nouellam*.

dimitte eam, absolue eam, XXIV. 4 (*Math.* XV. 23 *dimitte eam*).

Dinae, see *femur uirginis*.

dinę [for *Dinae*], XXI. 7, see *femur uirginis*.

diocesem, see *diocesim*.

dioceseos [dioeceseos], I. 93, see *primatem*.

diocesi, XXXIX. 54, see *in diocesi* sub voce *diocesim*.

diocesim, gubernationem, II. 43 (*Bened. reg.* 64, 10 ad cuius *dioecesim* pertinet locus ipse [17 *diocesim*, *diocesem*]).—**diocesis**, parrochiis [paroecia] idest adiaciens domus uel gubernationibus, I. 36 (*De Canon.*); **diocesis**, **adiacens domus**. XLI. 5 (*De nomin. diu.*) = (*Decr. Hil.* p. 251[a] semper huius ciuitatis Ecclesiae fuisse *dioecesis* constet; cf. *Can. Conc. Antioch.* XXCVII p. 126[a] ad suam *dioecesim*; *Can. Conc. Constant.* CLXIV p. 133 De ordine singularum *dioeceseon*...; super *dioecesim* Episcopi...*dioeceseos* Episcopi...in Asiana *dioecesi* &c.; *Can. Conc. Carth.* LVI in *dioecesibus*..., *dioecesim*, *dioeceses*, in *dioecesi* &c.). Cf. *diocisa*, gubernatio, Cp. D261 & Ef.[1] 356, 17; *parochia*, loca adiacentia ecclesiae, Cp. P24; Ep. 18E6; Ef.[1] 379, 33.—**massa diocesium** [sine interpret.], I. 74 (*De Canon.*; *Can. Conc. Carth.* LVI ut ex *massa dioecesium* nulla carperetur.—**in diocesi**, in parrochia [parœcia], XXXIX. 54 (*Greg. Dial.* IV. 55 col. 417[A] *in dioecesi* Centumcellensis urbis). It is possible that reference is here made *not* to Greg. Dial., but to *Can. Conc. Constant.* CLXIV p. 133 (see above), or *Can. Conc. Carth.* LXXI ad...Ecclesiam *in dioecesi* constitutam; or *ib.* CXVII Ecclesiae *in dioecesi* constitutae; or *Decr. Siricii* XV qui *in* tua sunt *dioecesi*; or *Decr. Hil.* p. 251^{a} *in dioecesi* sua. On gubernationem, gubernationibus, see *Can. Concil. Const.* CLXIV.

diocesis, parrochiis idest adiaciens domus uel gubernationibus, I. 36; **diocesis**, adiacens domus, XLI. 5; see *diocesim.*

diocesium [diœcesium], I. 74, see *massa diocesium*, sub v. *diocesim.*

diocisa, see *diocesim.*

Diodorus, properter [for *proprium*] uiri, XXXVIII. 13 (*Clem. Recognitt.* VIII. 15); see *Calistratus.*

dioeceseos, see *dioceseos.*

dioeceses, see *diocesim.*

dioecesi, see *in diocesi*, sub v. *diocesim.*

dioecesibus, dioecesim, dioecesis, see *diocesim.*

dioecesium, see *massa diocesium*, sub voce *diocesim.*

dionisius [for *Dionysus*], XLIII. 28, see *bachus.*

Dionysus, see *bachus.*

diptamini [=dictamni], XXXVIII. 18, see *creta comam-.*

diriguere [der-], pro stupore pallescere, XXXV. 14 (*Ruf.* III. 6 fol. 38^{b} immanes quanuis animi *diriguere*) = *diriguere*, pallescere, Cp. D260; Ep. —; Ef.^{1} 356, 20.

dirimit, diuidit, XLVIII. 9 (*De Cass*, *Conl.* XXIV. 26, 3 [?] fratrum *dirimit* facultatem contentiosa diuisio).

diriuatur [der-], X. 22, see *areola.*

diruit, obruit, XXXIV. 38 (*De Cass.*, *Inst.* XII. 3 ciuitatem *diruit*).

dirum, asperum, durum, II. 48 (*Bened. reg.* 2, 52 [75] *dirum* magistri, pium patris ostendat affectum).

discantur, XLV. 1, see *gymnasium.*

discensum [for *discessum?*], XXXV. 141, see *excidium.*

discere, XLV. 2, see *eruere.*

discernuntur, XIII. 7, see *discriminalia.*

discessum, see *excidium.*

discessus, XIX. 64, see *apostata.*

dis[ci]puli, XXX. 26, see *diatripas.*

discoferum, see *discoforum.*

discofor[u]m, discum portantem, XVI. 6 (*Dan.*, *Praef. Hieron.* p. XVI.^{b} and Migne XXVIII col. 1293^{B} *discophorum* lectitaret). Migne records a reading *discumferentem*; the Cambr. MS. has *discoferum.*

discophorum, see *discoforum.*

discordans, see *lingua tertia.*

discordians [discordans], XII. 29, see *lingua tertia.*

discrepantes, XXVIII. 40, see *silemsis.*

discretio, seperatio [separ-] diuisa [diuisio?; but see G. Körting, no. 3051] II. 44 (*Bened. reg.* 64, 34 [63] cogitans *discretionem* sancti Jacob; 37 [68] testimonia *discretionis*; 70, 11 [17] sine *discretione*).

discretione, discretionem, discretionis, see *discretio.*

discribitur [descr-], XXVIII. 43, see *caracterismos.*

discribunt [descr-], XLIV. 10, see *cardines.*

discriminalia, unde discernuntur crines de auro uel argento uel aere, XIII. 7 (*Isai.* III. 20 auferet Dominus...*discriminalia*).

discriminauit, diuisit, XXI. 8 (*Judith* X. 3 *discriminavit* crinem).

discum, XVI. 6, see *discoforum*; XXV. 1, see *catinum.*

discumferentem, see *discoforum.*

discunt, XXX. 26, see *diatripas.*

discussio, examinatio, II. 50 (*Bened. reg.* 2, 13 [18] facienda erit *discussio*; 87 [133] timens...futuram *discussionem*).

discussione, II. 62, see *examine.*

discussionem, see *discussio.*

dispensat, XXXIX. 28, see *qui in numero....*

dispensatio, XXXIX. 58, see *pitoicis.*

dispensationibus, I. 91, see *ptochiis.*

dispensator, XXXIX. 28, see *qui in numero....*

disperabilis [desp-], II. 128, see *obstinatus.*

dispicatis, diuisis, IV. 30 (*Eccl. Istor.*); **dispicatis**, disruptis, XXXV. 134 (*De Eus.*) =(*Ruf.* III. 6 fol. 36^{b} *despicatis* foribus). Cf. *despicatus*, disruptus, Cp. D21; Ep. —; Ef.^{1} 355, 52.—**dispicatis**, incisis, XXXV. 229 (*Ruf.* XI. 24 fol. 189^{a} vinecatis paruulis, *despicatis*que...virginibus).

disponunt, XXXVII. 9, see *tabulas legat.*

dispositi, II. 51, see *digesti.*

dispositionum, XXX. 3, see *ypotheseon*, 82, see *de entoetromito.*

dispuli [for discipuli], XXX. 26, see *diatripas.*

disputatio, XLV. 28, see *actio.*

disputationes, XXIX. 71, see *diatribas.*

disputationum, see *ypotheseon.*

disruptis, XXXV. 134, see *dispicatis.*

dissensatores, I. 119, see *scismatici.*

dissensiones, XXIX. 71, see *diatribas.*

dissentiones, see *diatripas*, sub v. *diatribas.*

dissimilia, XXVII. 14, see *anomala.*

dissimulans, dissimulet, see *dissimulat.*

dissimulat, conticissit preterita [praet-] neglegiter [neglegenter], I. 44 (*De Canon.*;

cf. *Can. Conc. Sard.* v si conuentus literis tacuerit, et *dissimulauerit*; *Can. Conc. Carth.* LXV ut de haereticorum...insidiis ...nullo modo *dissimulemus*; XCIII [p. 162b] qui...*dissimulant*; *Can. Conc. Nic.* X per ordinantium *dissimulationem*).—**dissimulat**, preterita [praet-] neglegit, II. 49 (*Bened. reg.* 2, 56 [82] Neque *dissimulet* peccata; 74 [112] ne *dissimulans* [112 *dissimulet*, in note] salutem animarum). Cf. dissimulat, miđiŏ, Cp. D272.

dissipator, II. 137, see *prodicus*.

dissonantia, XXX. 57, see *diafonia*.

dissonantiam, XXX. 11, see *diaphonian*.

distabui, tabefactus, XLVIII. 44 (*De Cass., Inst.* V. 30, 1 languore *distabui*).

distat, XLIV. 16 (bis), see *Antarticus*.

distauit, XLVIII. 30, see *adfecit*.

distinabunt [dest-], XLI. 1, see *presbiteri*.

distollit, see *extollit*.

distrahuntur, see *distrauntur*.

distrauntur, uendentur, XLVIII. 47 (*De Cass., Inst.* IV. 14 quae tribus uix denariis ...*distrahuntur*).

distruitur [destr-], XXVII. 20, see *menstruum*.

ditauit, IV. 118, see *afficit*.

ditione, potestate, XVI. 16 (*Dan.* XI. 5 dominabitur *ditione*; II. 38 sub *ditione*).

diuersa, I. 90, see *philacteria*; XXVIII. 24, see *ypozeuxis*; XXXIX. 62, see *filacteria*.

diuersae, see *gymnasium*.

diuersarum, XXX. 82, see *de entoetromito*.

diuersas, XXVIII. 58, see *apostropei*; XXXV. 143, see *per metalla*.

diuerse [-sae], XLV. 1, see *gymnasium*.

diuersis, XXXV. 257, see *columellas*; XLI, XLII, XLIII *titt.*; XLIV. 27, see *dextera*.

diuidere, XXVIII. 47, see *parenthesin*.

diuidit, XLV. 19, see *lanistra*; XLVIII. 9, see *dirimit*.

diuina, IV. 114, see *a theologia*; XXXIX. 42, see *altare*; XLIV. 29, see *axem*.

diuinatio, XIX. 48, see *necromantia*.

diuini, XL. 18, see *thiarati*.

diuinitatis, XXXV. 232, see *numinis*.

diuinum, II. 40, see *deificum*; IV. 16, see *asilium*, 21, see *fas*.

diuisa [for *diuisio*?], II. 44, see *discretio*.

diuisio, see *discretio*.

diuisis, IV. 30, see *dispicatis*.

diuisit, XXI. 8, see *discriminauit*.

diuisura, XIII. 4, see *fissura*.

diuite, I. 68, see *liberalitas*.

diuitiarum, XV. 19, see *gazarum*.

diuitię, XXXVIII. 39, see *aides*.

diurnales, XIII. 15, see *decem iugera*.

diurnas, XXXV. 179, see *horas diurnas*.

diuturna, II. 113, see *morosa*.

diuus imperator qui post mortem ut deus habetur, I. 39 (*De Canon.*?)=*diuus* imperator qui post mortem quasi deus factus est, Cp. D305; cf. *diuus* deus uel imperator qui post mortem quasi deus est, Ef.[2] 286, 20. Cf. Isid. *de diff. Verbb.* I. 168 Inter *Deum* et *Diuum* quod *Deus* semper est, *Diuus* fit.

dixerit, XXIX. 73, see *qui dixerit*.

dixit, XII. 40; XXXI. 10.

dnm̄s [? for dimidians ?], XLIV. 29, see *axem*, sub v. *extremi*.

-do, see *turnodo*.

doctorale, XXXIX. 64, see *didascalum*.

doctrina, I. 35, see *dogma*; XXXVIII. 26, see *mathesis*, 32, see *thema*.

doctrinae, see *cataceeos*.

doctrinam, XXIII. 12, see *memores salis*.

doctrinarum, IV. 102, see *catacesseos*; XXX. 34, see *catacesseun*, sub v. *cataceeos*.

doctrine [-nae], XXX. 67, see *catacesseos*, sub v. *cataceeos*; XXXV. 196, see *cataceeos*.

doctrix, see *eletrix*.

documenta, XXX. 31, see *sub nominem*; XLVIII. 42, see *scita*.

documentorum, XXX. 69, see *sintagmaton*.

documentum, *leg.* for *dorium* (q.v.)?

documentum, XXX. 32, see *sub nominem*.

dogma, doctrina uel difinitio [def-], I. 35 (*De Canon.*; *Can. Apostt.* XXXVIII ut... *dogmata* pietatis explorent; *Can. Conc. Nic.* VIII Ecclesiae *dogmata*).

dogmata, see *cinticta*; *dogma*.

dolabella, bradacus, XLVII. 47 (*Alia*=?) = *dolatura*, braadlast-ęcus, Cp. D346; Ep. —; *dalaturae*, braedlaestu aesc, Ef.[1] 356, 5. For *dolabella* (*a small pick-axe, hatchet*, dim. of *dolabra*) see Lewis & Sh.; for *dolatura* of Cp. & Ef.[1] see Du C.—*Bradacus* (from A.S. *brād*, broad + *acus* = *æx*, an ax, for which *ęcus*, for *æcus* in Cp., and *aesc* in Ef.[1] = O.H.G. *acus*) = *broad-ax* (an ax with a broad head), Oxf. D. (earliest quot. A.D. 1352), and Bosw. T. (*brād-æx*). *Braadlast* in Cp. and *braedlaestu* in Ef.[1] may, perhaps, have the same meaning as the simple *brad* (from *braad*, *braed*, broad), and *last*, *laestu*, a foot, track, *a last*; see Oxf. D. (*broad*; *last*, sb.[1]); Kluge, *Et. D.* (*Leisten*).

dolant, XXIII. 4, see *cymentarii*.

dolatura, see *dolabella*.

dolorem, XXXIX. 19, see *freniticus*.

dolores, XXXV. 2, see *coli*.

[**domate**] **in domate suo**, in solario suo, XXIII. 14 (2 *Esdr.* VIII. 16 fecerunt...tabernacula unusquisque *in domate suo*).—**domatibus**, porticibus uel atriis quę non tegent, XIV. 12 (*Hier.* XIX. 13 & XXXII. 29

in ... *domatibus*).—**domatis**, domus sine tecto uel spinarum, VIII. 7 (*Salam.* XXI. 9 & XXV. 24 in angulo *domatis*). Cf. *domatibus*, solaris, Cp. D350; Ep. —; Ef.[1] 356, 22; *domatis*, huses, Cp. D352.

domine, II. 98, see *Kyrieleison*; XXVIII. 33, see *tropus*; XXIX. 63, see *ileusun cyrię*.

domini, III. 24, see *sacro tegmini*; XXI. 18, see *sancta domini*.

dominio, XXXV. 180, see *fisco p-*.

dominum, II. 7, see *alleluia*.

dominus, XXI. 17, see *Adonai*.

domo, XXXV. 116, see *in prostibulo*, 169, see *in myrthece*; XLV. 31, see *popa*.

domorum, XIII. 41, see *paliurus*.

domuncula, XIII. 2, see *tugurium*; XV. 11, see *preteriola*.

domunculas, XXVI. 2, see *casulas*.

domus, I. 36, see *diocesis*; V. 10, see *exedre*; VIII. 7, see *domatis*; IX. 3, see *contegnatio*; XXIV. 18, see *pretorium*; XXXV. 62, see *pastoforie*; XXXIX. 8, see *in gremio*; XLI. 5, see *diocesis*; XLII. 20, see *in uiridario domus*; XLIII. 46, see *piraondes*.

dona, II. 115, see *munuscula*; XXI. 19, see *in anathema*.

donatio, I. 68, see *liberalitas*.

donum, *leg.* for *dorium* (q. v.)?

donum, X. 3, see *odor ungentorum*.

dorium, indiculum, V. 7 (?*Ruf.* ? for *donum*? Cf. eucharistiæ suscipiens *donum*, VII. 8 fol. 118^{b}—or for *documentum*?: tentationum *documentis* probatus, XI. 21 fol. 186^{b}). Cf. Gallée 338, 61.

dorix, idest proprium nomen fluminis, XII. 24 (*Eccles.* XXIV. 41 ego quasi fluvij *Dioryx* [= διῶρυξ, a trench, conduit, canal]).

dorso, XLVI. 13, see *tuber*.

dragma pondus est denarii argentei quod pensat siliquas XVIII a grecis fit sic:, XXXII. 1 (*De ponder.*).—**dragma** habet scrupulos III, XXXIII. 4 (*De pond. Euch.* p. 158, 10 *d.* h. *scriptula* tria). The Brit. Mus. MS. has *d.* h. *scripula* tria, and adds: sil[iquas] XVIII, LXXII dragmae efficiunt libram, draugma denarium significat, octo denarii, id est dragmae, efficiunt unciam, VI oboli faciunt dragma·/·—See also Wotke, in note.—**Epiphanius** dicit **dragma** XXVIII siliquas, XXXI. 22 (*De ponder.*?). Cf. Blume, I. 373 sqq.

dragmae, XXXIII. 5, see *dedragma*.

dragmas, XXXII. 7, see *acitabulus*, 8, see *cotule*, 9, see *mina*, 11, see *libra*.

dragmis [al. *didragmis*], XXXIII. 6, see *stater*.

dromedarię [-riae], castrati cameli; dromedarius unus, XIII. 60 (*Isai.* LX. 6 *dromedarii*; Heyse *dromedariae* in note).

dromedarii, see *dromedarię*.

dromedarius, XIII. 60, see *dromedarię*.

dualis, XXX. 45, see *dialectica*.

duas, XII. 9, see *cacabus*; XXI. 20, see *labastes*; XXVIII. 79, see *epexergasia*; XXXI. 32, see *sextarius*.

duas coronas, II panes pertussos similes coronę, XXXIX. 43 (*Greg. Dial.* IV. 55 col. 417^{B} *duas*...oblationum *coronas* detulit).

dubiam, see *amphibolia*.

dubietas, II. 153, see *scrupolositas*.

dubio, I. 86, see *prorsus*.

dubitabo, XXXVII. 10, see *mutilabo*.

dubitaret, XX. 7, see *nutaret*.

dubitatione, XXXV. 170, see *nutatione*.

dubitationes, XXXVIII. 23, see *scrupeas*.

dubium [for *dubiam*], XXVIII. 61, see *amphibolia*.

ducenarium, see *ducennarium*.

ducennarium, presidem, XXXV. 282 (*Ruf.* VII. 26 fol. 128^{a} se magis *Ducenarium* quam episcopum videri vellet). Cf. *ducenarius*, praeses, Cp. D371; Ep. —; Ef.[1] 355, 53.

ducens, I. 88, see *paruipendens*.

ducit, II. 146, see *regula*.

duę, XXXIII. 5, see *dedragma*.

duellionis, belli, XXIX. 37 (*Uerb. Interpr.* = *Hier. in Matth.* XXVII. 24 *perduellionis* mihi contra Cæsarem crimen impingitur).

duellis, bellum, IV. 40 (*Ruf.* IV. 6 fol. 55^{b} fame ac siti *perduellibus* intrinsecus ad extremum internitionis adductis).

dulce, XXIII. 19, see *mulsum*.

dulces, XIV. 5, see *placentas*.

dulcis, VIII. 11, see *cinamum*; XIX. 10, see *ridhmus*.

dum, XIX. 5; XLIV. 26, 27.

Dum, nomine ciuitatis, VI. 14 (*Breu. exsol.*?).

dumosis, spinosis, XXXVIII. 2 (*Clem. Recognitt.* III. 14 in *dumosis* ac repletis sentibus locis).

dumtaxat, maxime, XXXIV. 49 (*De Cass., Inst.* XII. 28 in hac *dumtaxat* regione). See also ib. I. 11, 3; II. 4; III. 7, 2; IV. 15, 1; VIII. 19, 3.

duo, XXIII. 2; XXIX. 9; XXXI. 3, 37; XXXII. 3; XLIV. 8, 28; see also *auo*.

duobus, XXII. 12, see *urna*; XXXIII. 6, see *stater*.

duorum, XIII. 33, see *bige*.

duos, XIII. 18; XV. 43; XXXI. 24 (bis).

dupla, I. 115, see *sescopla*.

duplex, XIII. 53, see *circino*; see also *bilex*.

duratum [?], XXXVIII. 45, see *sitatum*.

durissima, XIV. 9, see *in unge*.

duriter, II. 173, see *tirannidem*.

durum, II. 48, see *dirum*.

durus, II. 26, see *contempto*.

dyaletica, dyaleticam, see *dialectica*.

dyaphonia, see *diafonia*.

e for *a*: colendo (for colando); eloquentie (-tia); ereola (ar-); myrthece (myrotheca); oratorie (-ria); pastoforie (-phoria); seperatio, seperatis, seperatores (separ-).—for *ae* (*gen.*, *dat. sing.* or *nom. pl.*): aecclesie (for ecclesiae); ęnie (for Aeneae); anguile (-llae); anime (-mae); aque (aquae); arce (arcae); arene (-nae); aste (hastae); barbe; batroperite (-tae); bestie (-tiae); brantie (branchiae); calide (-dae); carte (-tae); clausure (-rae); cocte (-tae); collecte; congregate; contrite; culine; diuerse; doctrine; exedre; facule; gemme; gigantemachie; hostie; harene; herbe; indute; inferie; infrenate; infrunite; inopie; ipse; kalende; liquide; locuste; lune; Mambre; marine; materie; Micene; milicie; modice; multe; opere; parue; petre; Pile; porte; postere; prophete; propositure; prouintie; pugne; quartane; regine; scedule; scole; semiuste; sepulture; silue; sirene; spere (sphaerae); subiecte; subnixe; subposite; substantie; tede; terre; theomachie; uaene (uenae); uirge; uille.—So also in various other positions: cementa, cemento (for caem-); ceno (caeno); cesaris (caes-); Caldeos, Chaldei, Chaldeos (Chaldae-); demon, demones, demoniosum (daem-); edem (aed-); egypti, egyptiaca, egypto (aeg-); emulatione (aem-); enchenia (encænia); eramento (aer-); grecorum, grecos (graec-); hebreum (hebraeum); hereticum (haer-); manichei (-chaei); meandrum (Mae-); palestrarum, palestris (palaes-); pigmei (-maei); pre always for the prefix prae-; but see ę for *ae*; primeuo (-maeuo); que (quae); quedam (quaed-); querit (quaer-); questio, questionum, questus (quaest-); sepe (saepe); seuit (saeuit); unaqueque (-quaeque).—for *i*: accipitres (for -tris); ceteriorem (cit-); colleguntur (collig-); contegnatio (contign-); degesti (dig-); eregitur (erig-); fatescit (fatiscit); glebum (for cliuum); ideonati (idiomati); indegeries (indig-); inhibere (-ri); itenerarium (itin-); mire (miri); Oethepia (Oedipia); quisquilea (-lia); salice (-ci); sterelis (-rilis); subregeris (subrig-); trapezeta (-zita).—(through *ae*) laetania (for letania, for litania).—for *o*: gigantemachie (giganto-); preteriola (praetor-).—for *oe*: cenobita (for coen-); comedia (comoed-); effetas (effoet-); proemio (prooem-).—for *u*: acuent (-unt); pingent (-unt).—for *y*: cyneris (cinyris); panagericis, panagericon, pannigericis (panegyr-).—e *prefixed*: exenia (for xenia). —*omitted*: kyrieleison (for kyrieel-).

ę for *a*: ęręmento (for aera-).—for *ae*: aduliscentulę (-lae); animę; aquę; arenę; artabę; bęrrus; cęli; controuersię; coronę; Dinę; ecclesię; elatę; ęnie; ęquali; ęre; ęręmento; ęris; erucę; ęstiuo; exedrę; fabę, fauę; ferreę; inęqualia; lacertę; lętitia; mirtę; modicę; multę; parcę; paschę; peritię; portę; pręoccupatio; pręrogatiua; pręsunt; prouintię; pugnę; pulcrę; quę; secuturę; siluę; substantię; taermę (for thermae); termę; tuę.—for *e*: eccləsiastes (eccles-); prefacionę (-ne); pręx, pręcis (prex, precis); tęde (tedae).—for *i*: contęnetur (contin-). —for *oe*: cęlis, cęlum (coel-).

e (prep., *e* regione), IV. 98; XXXVIII. 35.

ea, XIII. 43; XXVIII. 64; XXXV. 178.

eam, I. 109; XXIV. 4 (bis).

ea tempestate, eo tempore, XXXV. 178 (*Ruf.* V. 21 fol. 89ᵇ *ea tempestate*; V. 23 fol. 90ᵃ &c.).

eatenus, actenus, VI. 3 (*Breu. exsol.* ?).

ebenum, see *ebor*.

eberenos, XV. 14, see *hebenenos*.

ebor, arbor inputribilis nigro colore, XV. 10 (*Ezech.* XXVII. 6 ex *ebore* Indico). Cf. *ebor*, elpendbaan, Cp. E3. The gloss does not agree with the lemma *ebor* (*ebur*), but with *hebenus*; the Cambr. MS. has eben*um* and *uel or* above the line; see also (XV. 14) *hebenenus*.

ebore, see *ebor*; *hebenenos*.

ebulliens, XXXVIII. 24, see *pyriflegitonta*.

ebulo, see *elleus*.

ebur, XXII. 4, see *eburneis*; see also *ebor*.

eburneis, de ossibus elefantis ebur os eius dicitur, XXII. 4 (*Esther* I. 6 qui *eburneis* circulis inserti erant).

eburneos, see *hebenenos*.

ecacusen, aut in aut in [second *aut in*, repetition] adflixit illam, XXIX. 52 (*Uerb. Interpr.* = *Hier. in Matth.* VI. 34 Sara afflixit Agar ancillam suam, quod...Graece dicitur ἐκάκωσεν αὐτήν).

ecastor, see *epul*.

ecclesia, IV. 117, see *ad coemetoria*.

ecclesiae, see *abiurari*; *diocesis*; *osculetur me*. See further *ecclesię*.

eccləsiastes, VIII. 9, see *Lamuhel*.

ecclesiastica, I. 77, see *negotia*; ECCLESIASTICA, V *tit.*; ECCLESIASTICĘ, IV *tit.*

ecclesiasticis, see *negotia*.

ECCLESIASTICO, XII *tit.*

ecclesiasticorum, see *negotia*.

ecclesię [-siae], IV. 37, see *trallis*; X. 7, see *aduliscentulę*; XXXV. 65, see *caementaria*. See also *ecclesiae*.

ECLESIASTEN, ix *tit.*

eclipsis, defectio, xxvii. 21 (*Lib. Rot.* = *Isid. Lib. de nat. rer.* vi. 3 quod dicitur *eclipsis*; *ib.* xviii. 4 *eclipsis* fieret; xx *tit.* De *eclipsi* solis; *ib.* xx. 3 *eclipsis* mysterium; *ib.* xxi *tit.* De lunae *eclipsi*). =*eclipsis*, defectio, Ef.[1] 357, 21. Cf. *eclipsis*, defectio solis aut luminis, Cp. E14; Ep. —.

ecstasi, see *extasei.*

ecthetas, see *hecthetas.*

eculeis, see *in aculeis.*

edacem, commedentem [comed-], ii. 64 (*Bened. reg.* 4, 22 [31] Non esse superbum...non multum *edacem*). Cf. *edax*, commedens, Cp. E34.

edax, xliii. 14, see *comedo.*

edem [aedem], xxxix. 5, see *mansionarius.*

edepol, see *epul.*

edificant [aed-], xiii. 40, see *perpendiculum.*

editiones, xix. 11, see *in exaplois.*

editiones, thestisuir, v. 21 (*De Eccl. Stor.*); **editionis**, puplicationis [publ-] propositure [for *praepositurae*?], xxxv. 23 (*De Eus.*)=(*Ruf.* iv. 15 fol. 63^a quia iam *aeditionis* [*editionis*, Cacciari, p. 211] suae munus [the performance, or management, of his gladiatorial show or exhibition; the Gr. has ἐπεπλήρώκει τὰ κυνηγέσια] explesset). As *editio* means an exhibition, show, spectacle, *publicationis praepositurae* may signify "the office of the superintendent of a public show."—As to *thestisuir* (for which a Berne MS. has *hestiuis*) it may be for *thyestaeas*, and if so it would be an unexplained lemma like *editiones*. Schlutter (in *Journ. for Germ. Phil.* i. 321) suggests *ambihtes sciir.*—Cf. *editiones* duplicationes [for *public-*], Cp. E25; Ep. —; Ef.[1] 357, 24.

editionis, puplicationis [publ-] propositure [for praepos- ?], xxxv. 23; see *editiones.*

editiore, see *editore.*

edito, iv. 25, see *in edito.*

editore, excelsiore, xxxv. 275 (*Ruf.* vii. 14 fol. 121^a in loco *editiore*).

editum, templum, iv. 6 (*Eccl. Ist.*); see **editus.**

ęditus, see *editus.*

editus, ostiarius, iv. 6 (*Eccl. Ist.*). This gloss appears in Ch. iv before gloss 7: **curia** (conuentus), which *Ruf.* has in i. 3 (fol. 8^b of Rhenanus' ed. of 1548). If, therefore, it is not out of place, the Glossator seems to have mistaken *editus* (born, created), which occurs in *Ruf.* i. 1, and is printed *ęditus* by Rhenanus on fol. 6^b, corresponding to *aediti* regis on fol. 12^a (*Ruf.* i. 7). And hence, "*editum*, templum," which follows in the MS. after *ostiarius*, was, perhaps, added by the Glossator as a further explanation of "editus, ostiarius." On the other hand, *aeditui* (q.v.) occurs *Ruf.* i. 4 fol. 9^a, and again i. 6 fol. 11^a, while "editum, templum" we may, perhaps, refer to ab ipsis quidem *adytis*, *Ruf.* i. 5 fol. 9^b. Cf. *editui*, hostiarii, Cp. E42; Ep. —; Ef.[1] 342, 41, 359, 3.

efexegresis, idest explanatio dicti superioris, xxviii. 82 (*Cass. Psalm.* xxxviii. 2 figura est *epexegesis*, id est e. d. s. The same vii. 3; see also xx. 5 schema... *epexegesis*, Latine explanatio; xxix. 11 schema...*e.* L. e., ubi priora dicta verbis subsequentibus exponuntur).

effeborum, studiorum, xlviii. 26 (*De Cass., Inst.* v. 12, 2 de *epheborum* luctamine; in note *effeborum*, *efoeborum*). Goetz, vi. 392, suggests *studiosorum* for *studiorum.*

efferatus est, a ferocitate dicitur, xvi. 13 (*Dan.* viii. 7 *efferatus est* in eum).

efferente [for *offerentes*], xxviii. 42, see *idea.*

effetas, euacuatas, xxxv. 290 (*Ruf.* ix. 8 fol. 150^a *ęffoetas*...segetes derelinquit).

efficaciter, uelotiter [ueloc-], ii. 63 (*Bened. reg.*, Prol. 4 admonitionem pii patris...*efficaciter* comple; cf. Woelfflin in *Arch. f. Lat. Lexic.* x. 550)=efficaciter, uelociter fromlice, Cp. E88.

efficere, xxviii. 70, see *sinchrisis.*

efflabant, mortui sunt, xxxv. 136 (*Ruf.* iii. 6 fol. 37^a multi...*efflabant*)=Cp. E62; Ep. —; Ef.[1] 357, 23.

effoetas, see *effetas.*

effrenatę, see *infrunite.*

effugere, see *excedere.*

effugire [effugere], ii. 61, see *excedere.*

effusio, xii. 47, see *offusio.*

effusius, xxviii. 64, see *epitrocasmos.*

effusum, see *unguentum.*

egre, difficile, xlii. 19 (*Ex div. libris*= *Sulp. Sev. Dial.* i. 14, 4 p. 166, 24 *aegre* patiebatur; *ib.* ii. 3, 3 p. 183, 9 *aegre* expediuntur; *ib.* iii. 1, 7 p. 199, 13 *aegre*...obtinui). Cf. *egre*, earfedlice, Cp. E94; *egre*, erabedlicae, Ef.[1] 357, 47, and Bosw. T. (*earfoþlice*).

Egypti [Aeg-], xlii. 3, see *memphitica.*

Egyptiaca [Aeg-], ii. 161, see *sarabaite.*

Egyptiorum [Aeg-], xxxiii. 14, see *artabę.*

Egypto [Aeg-], xxxv. 266, see *Antinoitas.*

ei, x. 24.

eis, xxii. 12, 16.

eius, viii. 8; xxi. 5; xxii. 4; xxiii. 1;

xxviii. 53; xxxi. 24; xxxix. 33, 48; xliii. 13; xliv. 1; xlvii. 8.

eius, xlviii. 29 (bis), see *delecto eius*.

eiusdem, i. 12, see *aemulum*.

elatae, see *elatę*.

elatę palmarum, folia palmarum quę eleuentur sursum quia non pendent deorsum sicut aliarum arborum, x. 21 (*Cant.* v. 11 Vulg. comae eius sicut *elatae palmarum*).

Elcesæi, see *Naum*.

electri, see *electrum*.

electrix, xi. 8, see *eletrix*.

electrum, de auro et argento et ęrę [for *aere*], xv. 37 (*Ezech.* i. 4 species *electri*, 27 vidi speciem *electri*; viii. 2 visio *electri*). Cf. *electrum*, elotr, Cp. E116; *electirum*, elothr, Ef.[1] 359, 20; *electrum*, aurum et argentum mixtum, Cp. E118 and Ef.[1] 359, 9.

elefantis [eleph-], xxii. 4, see *eburneis*.

elegos, castigatio, xxx. 25 (*Cat. Hier.* xxiii col. 641B: quartum [volumen] adversus Gentes, cui titulum praenotauit ἔλεγχος; B: cui t. p. *eletchos*; C: cui t. p. [blank]).—**elegos**, castigatio, xxx. 83 (*Cat. Hier.* ?) = *elegoos*, castigatio, Cp. E145; *elegcos*, castigatio, Ef.[1] 358, 37. According to the order in which this gloss occurs in the present Glossary it should be looked for in, or after, Ch. lxxxvi. But neither Migne's nor Richardson's text record it there. The Utrecht ed. (B), however, has in Ch. lxxxvii: *eortastikai* id est *castigationis* epistola, which seems to show that either "id est castigationes" of B strayed away from Ch. xxiii (see above), or that ἔλεγχος was again in Ch. lxxxvii in some text, together with ἑορταστικαὶ (see below *eortatica*), which is in Migne's and Rich. text, but which, meaning festive, could not be glossed by *castigatio*.

elementa, xliv. 17, see *cous*.

elenchos, see *elegos*.

elephantis, see *eburneis*.

eletchos, see *elegos*.

eletrix, electrix, xi. 8 (*Sap.* viii. 4 [sapientia] doctrix enim est disciplinae Dei, et *electrix* operum illius). There is here dittography in the MS., or *electrix* was added as a correction of *eletrix*; or *doctrix*, intended to be glossed, was perhaps omitted, and a wrong word written in its place, causing the omission of the glosses.

eleuaris, v. 24, see *subrigeris*.

eleuentur, x. 21, see *elatę palmarum*.

eliceretur, extorqueretur, xxxv. 167 (*Ruf.* v. 1 fol. 74b quo...tale aliquid *eliceretur* a nobis esse commissum) = Cp. E117; Ep.—; Ef.[1] 359, 1.—**elicitum**, incitatum, xxxix. 66 (not in Greg Dial., but *Decr. Innoc.* lvi p. 210b id...*elicitum* per insidias demonstratis).

elisa, iii. 59, see *explosa*.

elleus, ualuyrt, xlii. 4 (*Ex diu. libris* = ? *Sulp. Sev. Vit. S. Mart.* 6, 5 p. 117, 2 *helleborum* [other MSS. *eleborum*, *elebori*] uenenatum, ut ferunt, gramen). For *ualuyrt* (lit. foreign root; wallwort, dwarfelder) see Bosw. T. (*wealh-wyrt*). Most of the lemmata of Ch. xlii have been excerpted from Sulp. Sev. *Dial.*, and it is possible that the above was taken from his *Vit. S. Mart.*, though it seems identical with *ebulo*, wælwyrt of Aldhelm's *Aenigm.* (p. 266, 14), for which see Napier, p. 195. Cf. *ebulum*, paluyrt, Cp. E11; Ef.[1] 359, 45.

elocare, collocare, xxxviii. 3 (*Clem. Recognitt.* iii. 73 ne...mortem meam per insidias *elocaret*).

elogiis, uerbis, xxxv. 270 (*De Eus.*); **elogis**, uerbis, iv. 68 (*Eccl. Istor.*) = (*Ruf.* vii. 1 fol. 116b cudat *elogiis*) = *elogiis*, uerbis, Cp. E138; *elogis*, uerbis, Ef.[1] 359, 52.

elogis, uerbis, iv. 68; see *elogiis*.

eloquentia, xxx. 50, see *rethorica*.

eloquentie, iv. 51, see *oratorie*.

eloquia, xxvii. 2, see *faria*.

elucubratam, see *elucubratum*.

elucubratum, euigilantem, xxix. 8 (*Uerb. Interpr.* = *Hier. in Matth.*, Prol. col. 21A *elucubratam* scribendi diligentiam). Cf. *elucubratum*, euigilatum, Cp. E112; Ep.—; Ef.[1] 357, 72.

emancipent, manum mittent, i. 50 (*Can. Conc. Carth.* xxxv *tit.* Ut Episcopi...non facile filios suos *emancipent*). Cf. *emancipat*, manum mittit, Cp. E177.

emblema, fodor, xliii. 30 (*De div. nominibus* = Donati *Ars grammat.* p. 379, 12 quae a Graecis sumpsimus, ut *emblema* epigramma...) = *emblema*, fothr, Cp. E160; *emlemma*, fothr, Ef.[1] 358, 27.—emblema, inlaid work; fōdor, foddor, fothr (see Bosw. T.) = O. H. G. *fuotar* (Graff, *Sprachsch.* iii. 378 sqq.; Schade, *Altd. Wrt.*); Germ. *futter*.

emenides, see *eumenides*.

emergentes, see *emergit*.

emergit, surgit uel exuperat, i. 45 (*De Canon.*; cf. *Can. Apostt.* xxxviii *emergentes* ...contentiones amoueant; *Can. Conc. Calched.* xix corrigere singula, si qua... *emerserint*; *Can. Conc. Carth.* vi si quis... *emerserit*; *Decret. Symm.* ii, p. 258b de quibus certamen *emerserit*). Cf. *emersit*, exsurgit, Cp. E152; *emergit*, exsurgit, Ef.[1] 357, 42.

emerserint, emerserit, see *emergit*.

emina et cotile [*cotula*, or *cotyla*], medius sextarius, xxxi. 8 (*De ponder.* ?).—**himina**, medius sextarius **cyatos** [cyathos] iii, ii. 86 (*Bened. reg.* 40, 5 [8] credimus *eminam* vini...sufficere; Edm. Schmidt, *Regula*, p 44 *heminam*).—**cotule** habet dragmas lxxii idest scrupulos ccxvi quod facit viiii, xxxii. 8 (*De ponder.* ?). For *emina* cf. Blume i. 375. 2, 4, 7; for *cotile*, Fann. [Prisc.] 12 [67].

eminam, see *himina*, sub v. *emina*.

emissarius, xii. 35, see *equus emissarius*.

emissiones tuę, munera delectabilia, x. 15 (*Cant.* iv. 13 *emissiones tuae* paradisus malorum punicorum).

emolumenta, lucra, xlviii. 74 (*De Cass., Inst.* vi. 13, 2 *emolumenta* laborum).—**emulumentum**, mercis [merces] laborum, xxix. 17 (*Uerb. Interpr.*=*Hier. in Matth.* xiii. 3 absque *emolumento* populi; xiii. 44 mundi *emolumenta* contemnere). Cf. *emolomentum*, lucrum mercis laboris, Cp. E155; Ep.—; *emolomentum*, mercis laboris, Ef.[1] 357, 74; *emolumentum*, mercis laborum uel lucris, Ef.[2] 289, 18.

emorphium, proprium [add *nomen*], xxxix. 26 (*Greg. Dial.* iv. 35 col. 377[c] vidua ... *Eumorphium* ... juvenem filium habebat; *Eumorphii*, ibid. *tit.* col. 376[c]; *Eumorphius*, ibid. col. 380[A]).

emphasis, idest exaggeratio quod gradatim crescit, xxviii. 69 (*Cass. Psalm.* xxiv. 6; xliii. 10 and lix. 1 *emphasis*, id est exaggeratio; xxxvii. 20 hoc schema dicitur *emphasis*, *quod gradatim crescit* ad motum animi concitandum).

emulatione, zeli, ii. 73 (*Bened. reg.* 65, 13 Hinc suscitantur invidiae ... *aemulationes*; [25 *emulationes*]).

emulationes, see *emulatione*.

emulumentum, mercis laborum, xxix. 17, see *emolumenta*.

emurusem, fluxus sanguinis, xxix. 55 (*Uerb. Interpr.*=*Hier. in Matth.* ix. 27 de *hæmorrhousa*...muliere; xx. 20, 21 quomodo et in *hemorrhousa*). The original may have had *emuruse* (=αἱμοῤῥοοῦσα) ē (=est), and hence the stroke (for *m*) on the *e* after the *s*, in the MS. Goetz (v. 417, 6) actually prints *emurus est*.

encænia, see *enchenia*.

enchariseon, see *panagericon*.

enchenia, dedicationes, xxv. 11 (*Joh.* x. 22 facta sunt...*Encænia*; Wordsw. and White *encenia* in text, *enchenia*, &c. in note). Cf. *encenia*, initia ut dedicationes, Cp. E213.

encratiani, continentes, iv. 56 (*Ruf.* iv. 28 fol. 71[b] ad haeresim, quae dicitur *Encratitarum*...hi, qui vocantur *Encratitae*) =*encratitae*, continentes, Cp. E199; *encratitu*, continentes, Ef.[1] 358, 38.

encratitae, encratitarum, see *encratiani*.

energiam, xxviii. 81, see *per energiam*.

eneruatus, inualidus, xxxiv. 55 (*De Cass., Inst.* v. 5, 2 esus...*eneruatus*).

engastrimytho, see *de entoetromito*.

Enias [for *Ennius*], xliv. 2, see *cous*.

Enie [Aeneae], xliii. 21, see *centaurus*.

enim, ii. 188, 189; xii. 42; xxviii. 56; xxxiii. 6.

enixa est, genuit agnum ab agno dicitur feminino, xxxv. 144 (*Ruf.* iii. 8 fol. 40[a] vitula...*enixa est agnam*; from this it appears that the word *agnam* has been omitted after *est* or after *genuit*: cf. *enixa est* genuit agnam, Cp. E216).

enneafe decerida, decemnoualem, xxx. 53 (*Cat. Hier.* lxi); see *ex ca*.

ennelaecaterim, see *ex ca*.

Ennius, see *cous*.

ennoematice, notio hec unamquamque rem per id quod agit non per id quod est conatur ostendere, xxviii. 83 (*Cass. Psalm.* xxxix. 4 per...speciem definitionis exprimitur, quae Graece *ennoematice*, Latine *notio* nuncupatur. Haec unamquamque r. p. i. q. a. n. p. i. q. e. c. o.). See further v. 6; xiii. 6; xl. 1 and Praef. in Ps. i species definitionis quae Graece ἐννοηματικὴ dicitur, Latine notio.

enrusa, dapulas, iii. 54 (*Vit. S. Antonii* [auctore S. Athanasio, Evagrio interpr.] 16, Migne, *P. L.* lxxiii col. 138[C] Dominus ad Iob dicens: Arbitratur enim ferrum ut paleas, æramentum ut lignum putridum, *maria ut terram*, tartarum profundi tanquam captivum aestimavit). "*Maria ut terram*" in this quotation is an addition to Job xli. 18 [27] wanting in the Vulg., which reads: Reputabit enim quasi paleas ferrum, et quasi lignum putridum aes; [31] Fervescere faciet quasi ollam profundum mare, et ponet quasi cum unguenta bulliunt.—This addition is also found in the texts of the *Vita* published at Basle in 1552 (p. 77[A] Append. to *Liber de Passione D. N. Jesu Christi*, &c. ed. Wolfg. Lazius), at Antwerp in 1615 (p. 42[b] Herib. Rosweydi *Vitae Patrum*) and 1643 (*Acta SS. Jan.* tom. ii. p. 126[b]). But in Athanasii *Opp.* ed. Monach. Ord. S. Ben. e Congreg. S. Mauri (Par. 1698), Vol. i. p. 2, where by the side of the Gr. ἥγηται δὲ θάλασσαν ὥσπερ ἐξάλειπτρον, a Latin translation gives *mare* reputat quasi *vas unguentarium*, the *versio Evagrii*, at the foot of the page, has *maria ut erasa*, with a note appended: "Sic quidam MSS. Bollandus *ut terra*, alia MSS. *ut aëra*, quae postrema non quadrant cum Graecis." This text was reprinted in 1857 in Migne's *Patr. Gr.*

Vol. XXVI col. 880A. The same reading *maria ut erasa* is found in a Cambridge Un. Libr. MS. (Mm. IV. 28 fol. 7bb) of the 12th cent. And a third reading: *maria ut sata erasa* occurs in D. Athanasii *Opp*. Colon. 1548 (fol. 163B) and Paris. 1572 (col. 1002).—To account for these differences in the Latin translations of Athanasius' Vita S. Ant., we must, perhaps, ascribe one version to Evagrius, to whom the translation is commonly attributed, and another to S. Jerome, who is likewise said to have translated it (see Acta SS., Jan. II. 114). Our Glossator seems to have had Evagrius' text maria ut *erasa* (hence *enrusa*) before him, and to account for *dapulas*, for which we must, perhaps, read *stipulas*, we may further assume that he was aware of some text which had *sata erasa*.—The Gr. ἐξάλειπτρον (an unguent-box) agrees with the Hebr. text מִרְקָחָה (a pot of ointment), but the former is liable to misconstruction, as a derivative from ἐξαλείφω (1) to plaster or wash over; (2) to wipe out or obliterate; and it would seem that Evagrius has taken it in this sense.

entasrimeiton, see *de entoetromito.*

enthecam, see *enthetam.*

enthetam, subpellectilem [supell-], XLVIII. 70; **enticam**, sublectilem, XXXIV. 4 (*De Cassiano, Inst.* IV. 14 totam *enthecam* coenobii).

enthimema, interpretatur mentis conceptio, XXVIII. 60 (*Cass. Psalm.* XX. 7 *enthymema*, quod Latine interpretatur m. c.).

enthymema, see *enthimema.*

enticam, sublectilem, XXXIV. 4, see *enthetam.*

entoetromito, XXX. 82, see *de entoetromito.*

enumerationis, XXVIII. 30, see *epembasis.*

eo, I. 76, 111; II. 146; XXVIII. 33, 76; XXX. 20; XXXIII. 16; XXXV. 178; XXXIX. 42; XLIII. 6; XLIV. 16 (ter), 17.

EODEM, XXVII. 18, see *deodem.*

eologias, see *eulogias.*

eortastikai, see *elegos*; *eortatica.*

eortatica, solemnes, XXX. 62 (*Cat. Hier.* LXIX col. 679B Est ejus ad Dionysium et ad Didymum altera epistola, et ἑορταστικαὶ de Pascha plurimae...conscriptae; B: Est e. a. d. e. ad d. altera epistola *eortatikai* idest solempnis de pascha plurima... conscripta; C: Est e. et ad d. et a. d. altera epistola [blank] de pasca plurime... conscripte) = *eortatice*, solemnes, Cp. E223; *eortaticę*, s., Ef.[1] 357, 13; *eortasticai*, solemnes, *id.* E227; eortasicai, s-, Ef.[1] 358, 46; cf. *eortasitasi*, epistularum, Cp. E226; Ef.[1] 358, 45. Conf. *Cat. Hier.* LXXXVII col. 693B et ἑορταστικαὶ epistola; B: eortastikai idest castigationis epistole; C: [blank] epistule. For "id est castigationis," which text B has here in the wrong (?) place, cf. *elegos.*

eortatikai, see *eortatica.*

eorum, XXI. 5; XXXIX. 28.

epembabis, iteratio enumerationis studio uerba repetens, XXVIII. 30 (*Cass. Psalm.* III. 1 Haec figura locutionis dicitur *epembasis*, en. st. u. r.; XXI. 5 *epembasis*, Latine *iteratio*).

ependiten, tonica [tunica] uel cocula [cuculla], uel omnis uestis desuper aliis uestibus pendens, III. 56 (*not* S. Mart. Stor., but *Vit. S. Anton.* XXIII col. 147C lavit *ependyten* suum). Cf. ependiten, cop, Cp. E262, 289; Ef.[1] 359, 33 and Bosw. T. (*cōp*).

ependyten, see *ependiten.*

epexegesis, see *efexegresis.*

epexergasia, quoties uni causę duas probationes adponimus, XXVIII. 79 (*Cass. Psalm.* XXXVI. 21 *epexergasia*, q. u. causae d. p. a.).

epheborum, see *effeborum.*

ephi tres sextarios iterum ephi in II sextarii et paruum, XXXI. 11 (*De ponder.* ?); **ephi** siue ofa III modii Ephi idem mensurę habet in aridis et in liquidis Batus, XXXIII. 12 (*Euch. De Pond.* p. 159, 3: *Oephi* siue Oepha modii tres. Oephi i. mensurae h. i. a., quod i. l. Batus). Cf. Blume, I. 376, 10 (*oephi*, Hebr. *ephah*). Cf. *oephi* et batus aequalia, Cp. O132. For *ephi* see also (XXXIII. 15) *sata*, (XXXIII. 16) *gomor.*

ephichirema, exsecutiones uel approbationes uocare maluerunt, XXVIII. 71 (*Cass. Psalm.* XXVI. 3 *epichirema* Latini e. u. a. u. m. See also XXXVI. 2).

ephigrapha, XXX. 33, see **pseudo ephigrapha.**

ephod, superumerale [superhum-], V. 9 (*Ruf.* X. 14 fol. 169a ad portandum post se *ephod* sacerdotale).

epiasis, supersanus, XXIX. 53 (*Uerb. Interpr.* = *Hier. in Matth.* VIII. 14 ut ἐπίτασις fortitudinis indicetur).

epibatis, qui peruenient et dant nabulum pro nauigatione, XXXVIII. 44 (*Clem. Rom. Epist. ad Jacobum* in Migne's *Patr. L.* CXXX col. 24D *epibatis*...totius fraternitatis multitudo similis sit; col. 25A ibid. *epibatae* id est laici).

epichirema, see *ephichirema.*

Epicurius, uoluptarius corporis, XXXVIII. 9 (*Clem. Recognitt.* VIII. 7 *Epicuri* scholas frequentavi; VIII. 15 *Epicurus*; VIII. 16 qui erit *Epicuro* locus).

Epicurus, see *Epicurius*.

epimehne, memoria uel preuiarium [br-], xxx. 73, see *epitomen*.

epimone, repetitio, xxviii. 73 (*Cass. Psalm.* xxviii. 2 figura...*epimone*, Latine *repetitio*; cf. id. cxliii. 1). The additional explanation of this figura, in Migne's text col. 199A "crebra sermonis quae multa colligit unius uerbi iteratione decursa," is in the Leiden MS. wrongly under *prolemsis* (q. v.), xxviii. 75. See also Cass. xii. 1 *epimone*, quando similia dicta crebra repetitione geminantur.

Epiphanius dicit **dragma** xxviii siliquas, xxxi. 22; see *dragma*.

epiphonema, see *epiphonima*.

epiphonima, idest adclamatio quę post narratas rebus breuiter cum exclamatione prorumpit, xxviii. 65 (*Cass. Psalm.* xxii. 9 *epiphonema*, id est a....quae p. n. *res* b. c. *acclamatione* p.). Cf. *ib.* xxx. 32 *epiphonema*, id est a. quae p. n. *res* b. c. *exclamatione* prorumpit.

episcopalem, i. 6, see *absidam*.

episcopi, xxxix. 56, see *ante absida*.

episcopos, xli. 1, see *presbiteri*.

epistelia, see *epistilia*.

epistilia, grece quae super capitella columnarum ponuntur, i. 49 (*De Canon.*?). The interpretation points to *epistylium*, a cross-beam that rests on columns, the architrave; but this word does not seem to occur in the Canones. Could the original Glossator have extracted *epistolia* (*Can. Conc. Calch.* xi *tit.*), and another, mistaking the word, added the interpretation? See also *epistolio* in *Can. Concil. Carth.* cxxxiv p. 171a. Cf. Eucherii *Instructt.* ii p. 148, 9; Isid. *Etym.* xv. 8, 15, xix. 10, 24; and *epistelia*, capitella, Cp. E235 and Ef.[1] 358, 23; Ep. —.

epistolas, xli. 1, see *presbiteri*.

epistolia, see *epistilia*.

epistulas, xli. 2, see *chorepiscopi*, in voc. *presbiteri*.

epistylium, see *epistilia*.

epithalamium, laus thalami interpretatur, xxviii. 86 (*Cass. Psalm.* xliv Praef. *Epithalamium* interpretatur l. t.).

epithoma [epitoma], see *epitorta*.

epitimitisun, xxix. 60, see *tu epitimitisun*.

epitomen, memoria uel breuiarium, xxx. 65 (*Cat. Hier.* lxx col. 681B ἐπιτομὴν operis Tertulliani faciens; B: *epitomen* idest *breuiarium* vel *memoriam* operis terculliani faciens; C: [blank] op. Terculliani f.).—**epimehne**, memoria uel preuiarium [for breu-], xxx. 73 (*Cat. Hier.* lxxx col. 687B Habemus...et ἐπιτομὴν ejusdem operis in libro uno acephalo [ἀκεφάλῳ, Rich.]; B: Hab.... *epitomen* idest *breuiarium* eiusdem operis in libro *iaketalo* idest *visionis vel memorie dei*; C: Hab....[blank] eiusdem operis libro [blank]) = *Epitomem*, memoria uel breuiarum, Cp. E237, Ef.[1] 358, 31; *epome*, memoria, Cp. E232; *epitomen*, breuiarum, Ef.[1] 358, 44; *epinome*, memoria, Ef.[1] 357, 11. As to the reading of text B, see Siatta sapodimeos de praedicatione uisionis dei, Cp. S347.—**epitorta**, adbreuiatio, xlvi. 31 (*Alia = Ars Phocae*, p. 425, 24 note chalybis *epithoma*) = *epithoma*, adbreuiatio, Cp. E241.

epitorta, adbreuiatio, xlvi. 31, see *epitomen*.

epitrocasmos, idest dicti rotatio cum succincte ea quę sunt effusius dicenda perstringit, xxviii. 64 (*Cass. Psalm.* xxii. 9 figura...*epitrochasmos* id est d. r. c. s. ea quae s. e. d. p.).

epitrochasmos, see *epitrocasmos*.

epizeusis, quę latine coniunctio dicitur ut est dies diei et deus deus meus, xxviii. 52 (*Cass. Psalm.* xvii. 12 *epizeuxis*, quae Latine c. d. [*ut est*, the Glossator's addition] d. diei....et d. d. m. See also xxxiv. 24).

epizeuxis, see *epizeusis*.

epocentaurus, equo; **onocentaurus** asino mixtum, moster [for *monstrum*? as in Cambr. MS.], xiii. 42 (*Isai.* xxxiv. 14 occurrent dæmonia *onocentauris*; Heyse *onocentaurus*, in note; *epocentaurus* [= hippoc-], *equo* is perhaps added as a further explanation). Cf. *onocentaurus*, asino permixtum, Cp. O177.

eptaticum, septem librorum uel septenarium, ii. 69 (*Bened. reg.* 42, 8 legat...non *Eptaticum*, [11] *eptaticum*, in note *heptaticum*) = heptateuchos.

epul, **castor**, per pullux, per castor, xliii. 44 (*De div. nominibus* = Donati *Ars gramm.* p. 386, 15 adverbia...iurandi, ut *edepol*, *ecastor*).

epyuision perision Exiareton precipuum [praec-], xxix. 51 (*Uerb. Interpr.* = *Hier. in Matth.* vi. 11–13 Quod nos superstantialem expressimus, in Graeco habetur ἐπιούσιον, quod verbum lxx interpretes περιούσιον...transferunt. Consideravimus ergo in Hebræo, et ubicumque illi περιούσιον expresserunt, nos invenimus sgolla (סגולה), quod Symmachus ἐξαίρετον, id est *praecipuum*, vel egregium transtulit).

ęquali [aeq-], xxxiii. 24, see *urbicus*.

eques, equester uel equi, xxxv. 243 (*Ruf.* ix. 9 fol. 152b *eques* ac praecursor).

equester, equi, xxxv. 243, see *eques*.

equis, xiii. 59, see *feretri*; xxii. 16 (bis), see *ueredarii*; xxxv. 15, see *quadriga*.

equitum, xiii. 33, see *bige*.

equo, XIII. 42, see *epocentaurus*.
equorum, XLV. 30, see *mango*.
equos, XXII. 16, see *ueredarii*.
equuleis, see *in aculeis*.
equus, XXII. 16, see *ueredarii*.
equus emissarius, qui mittitur ad iumenta, XII. 35 (*Eccles*. XXXIII. 6).
-er- for rae: perpeti for *praepeti*.
eramento [aer-], XV. 22, see *speties ęris*; XIX. 40, see *olla*.
erant, see *erunt*.
erat, XXXV. 96 (ter).
erba [herba], IX. 5, see *capparis*; X. 10, see *cyprus*, 20, see *cassia*; XIII. 1, see *cucumerarium*, 41, see *paliurus*, 57, see *saliuncula*; XIV. 3, see *uorith*, 32, see *croceis*; XXXV. 42, see *stibiis*.
erbarum [herb-], XXIX. 20, see *quisquilia*.
erbaticas, XIV. 3, see *uorith*.
ęrę [for *aere*], XV. 37, see *electrum*.
erea [aer-], XIV. 36, see *urceos*.
erecto, XLIV. 26, see *a tergo*.
eregantur, loquantur, XLVIII. 1 (*De Cass*., *Inst*. IV. 41, 2 si tibi uel cuiquam conuicia, si *inrogantur* iniuriae, esto inmobilis...; *id*., *ibid*. VIII. 8, 3 lapides et maledicta...*inrogaret*; *not*, it seems *id*. *ibid*. II. 7, 3 cum is, qui orationem collecturus est, e terra surrexerit, omnes pariter *eriguntur*). Cf. Löfstedt, in *Archiv f. L. L.* XIV. 134, who would read *eleganter*, eloquenter.
eregit [erigit], XLIV. 10, see *cardines*.
eregitur [erig-], XLIV. 27, see *leua*.
ęręmento, XII. 9, see *cacabus*.
eremita, see *anachorita*; *heremita*.
ereola [ar-], X. 22, see *areola*.
erepsissent, see *eripisissent*.
erga, XLIV. 16, see *antarticus*.
ergastulo, carcere, XXXV. 168 (*Ruf*. V. 2 fol. 75[b] in *ergastulis* consumuntur; *ibid*. fol. 76[b] non in *ergastulo*...conclusi).
erigitur, see *eregitur*.
eriguntur, see *eregantur*.
eripisissent, inruissent, XXXV. 135 (*Ruf*. III. 6 fol. 36[b] si qui...*erepsissent*) = *erepsissent*, inruissent, Cp. E270; Ep. —; Ef.[1] 357, 22.
ęris, XV. 22, see *speties ęris*.
erit, XXIX. 73, see *qui dixerit-*.
erladiocten, operis conpulsorem, XXX. 55 (*Cat. Hier*. LXI col. 673[A] ἐργοδιώκτην eum Origenes vocat; B: *ertoauogten* idest operis expulsorem eum O. vocat; C: [blank] eum Origenes vocat).
erodis [Her-], IV. 17, see *fadus*.
erotema, interrogatio, XXVIII. 27 (*Cass. Psalm*. I. 1 haec figura Graece dicitur *erotema*, Latine *interrogatio*; cf. also XIV. 1) = *erotema*, interrogatio, Cp. E280; Ep. —; *eroteria* grece interrogatio, Ef.[1] 359, 27.
erpica, egida, XLVII. 22 (*Alia* = ?) = *erpica*, egðe, Cp. E293; Ep. —; *erpica*, egdae, Ef.[1] 359, 47. For *erpica* (a harrow) see Körting, *Wört*., No. 4576 (*hirpex*), and *hirpex*, *irpex* (Lewis & Sh.). The O. H. G. *egida* (Schade, p. 125) is, in the present Glossary, an alteration from an original *egldae* (for *egidae*? see note §§ on p. 48). Cf. the A. S. *egeðe*, *egþe* (Bosw. T.); M. E. *eythe*; Germ. and D. *Egge*.
errare, XLIV. 26, see *a tergo*.
ertoauogten, see *erladiocten*.
erucę, modici uermes qui mandunt folia multos pedes habent, XXXIX. 7 (*Greg. Dial*. I. 9 col. 197[A] hortum, magna... *erucae* multitudine invenit esse coopertum; ...ad easdem *erucas*).
eruere, discere, XLV. 2 (*Uerba de multis* = *Ars Phocae*, p. 411, 10 veterum *eruere* commentarios).
erunt [for *erant*], I. 100, see *proconsolaris*.
erynnis, see *striga*.
Esaia, see *artabę*.
esca, XXXV. 291, see *stipis*. See also *isica*.
escam, XI. 16, see *bonam escam*.
eschematismenos, idest dum aliud loquitur aliud agit, XIX. 5 (*Job*; *Praef. Hieron*. p. XIV[b], and Migne, *P. L.* XXVIII col. 1081[A] ἐσχηματισμένος dumque aliud loquitur, aliud agit).
esculentiores, see *excellentiores*.
ESDRA, XXIII *tit*.
esocem, esohascem, see *merocem*.
esse, I. 52; II. 188.
essentia, substantia, I. 46 (*De Canon*.; *Can. Conc. Carth*. CXXXVII [*Def. fidei Conc. Nic*.] ex alia substantia, vel *essentia*; *Ep. S. Cyr. Alex*., p. 177[b] de illius *essentia*; *Def. fid. Chalc*. ap. Mans. VII. 752[a] de *essentia*).
est, I. 111; II. 59, 188, 189 (bis); IV. 99; VIII. 8; X. 6, 10, 11, 13, 16, 17, 20; XI. 3, 14; XII. 9, 17; XIII. 39; XIV. 3, 6, 10, 20; XVI. 4, 13; XVII. 7; XIX. 51; XXIII. 1; XXVIII. 18, 25, 28, 33 (quater), 52, 53, 57, 70, 76, 83; XXIX. 9; XXXII. 1, 5; XXXIII. 2, 6, 8–11, 13, 16, 19, 20; XXXV. 82, 130, 144, 147; XXXVII. 8, 19; XXXVIII. 16, 22; XXXIX. 13, 15, 33, 36; XLI. 10, 11, 16; XLIII. 28, 29, 46; XLIV. 2, 7, 8, 16; XLVII. 8.
ESTER, XXII *tit*.
ęstiuo [aest-], XXVII. 32, see *opago tempore*.
esto, XXIX. 63.
et, I. 80, 111; II. 149, 169, 188; IV. 97, 98; IX. 1; X. 1, 5, 10, 14 (bis), 18, 22; XI. 3, 4, 14 (bis); XII. 9, 21, 42; XIII. 11, 39, 43 (bis), 47, 54, 55; XIV. 3, 5 (bis), 6, 20; XV. 37 (bis); XVI. 5, 27 (ter), 30; XIX. 15,

39, 40; xx. 8; xxi. 16, 18; xxii. 11; xxiv. 13; xxv *tit.* (bis), 7; xxviii. 36 (bis), 52, 57, 88 (bis); xxix. 42 (ter), 50 (bis), 64 (bis), 67; xxx. 35, 52; xxxi. 3, 8, 9, 11, 13, 24, 27, 32, 36; xxxii. 7, 9; xxxiii. 2, 12, 13, 15, 23, 24; xxxv. 26, 41, 69, 72; xxxvii. 9 (bis); xxxviii. 44; xxxix. 15; xli. 7, 8, 13, 16; xlii. 21; xliii. 16; xliv. 9, 10, 11 (bis), 27 (quater); xlvii. 8.

et, see *expolita.*

ethecas, see *hecthetas.*

ethimologia, see *aethimologia.*

etiam, xxxiii. 16.

etodeporicon, etodiforicon, see *otheporicon,* sub v. *sinphosin.*

et procomian, narrationum, xxx. 54 (*Cat. Hier.* lxi col. 671B Hippolytus... scripsit...*et* Προσομιλίαν de laude Domini Salvatoris [Richardson, *id.*]; B: *epicoïa,* id est *narrationē* iā de laude saluatoris; C: [blank] et de laude domini saluatoris). The Gr. text of Migne and Gebh. (= Sophron.) has: προσομιλιῶν περὶ τῶν ἐπαίνων τοῦ κυρίου ἡμῶν Ἰησοῦ Χριστοῦ. And in a note Migne remarks "that a Verona MS. has *prosaomelian,* from which we may read with Fabricius προσομιλίαν, and that former edd. had wrongly πρὸς ὁμιλιῶν, or περὶ ὁμιλιῶν". = *prosomean,* narrationem, Cp. P566; *prosomian,* narrationem, Ep. 17E17; *prosonam,* narrationem, Ef.[1] 377, 38. Cf. *promaean,* narrationem, Cp. P569; *prosepion,* narrationem, Cp. P624. The gloss "narrationum" of the present Glossary would agree with προσομιλιῶν, but the ending -ean, -ian, -nam of the lemmata, and the accus. form "narrationem" of all the kindred Glossaries, distinctly point to προσομιλίαν as the true reading.

et simcosion, similitudinem, xxx. 80; see *sinphosin.*

etymologia, see *aethimologia.*

euacuare, xxxix. 29, see *cassari.*

euacuatas, xxxv. 290, see *effetas.*

euaggences parasueues, euangelice preparationis, xxx. 76, see *eyaggences.*

euangelicae; euangelicarum; euangelice [-cae], xxx. 75, 76, see *eyaggences apod.*

euangelio, xxxiii. 6, see *stater.*

eucharistias, gratiarum actiones, xxx. 60, see *panagericon,* sub v. *panagericis.*

Eucherium, xxxiii *tit.*

euellare [for *euellere* ?], xxxiv. 53, see *deflorare.*

euentus, vi. 13, see *for.*

Euergetis, boni operis uel factoris, xii. 1 (*Eccles.*, Prol., p. 586 of Antwerp ed.: in...temporibus Ptolemaei *Evergetis* regis). For *operis* the Cambr. MS. Kk. 4. 6 has *operantis.*

euigilantem [!], xxix. 8, see *elucubratum.*

euigilatum, see *elucubratum.*

eulogias, salutationes, ii. 58 (*Bened. reg.* 54, 4 Nullatenus liceat...*eulogias*... accipere, [4] eologias, eul- and eul- in *tit.* for *litteras,* in some MSS.; cf. Edm. Schmidt, *Regula,* p. 54). Cf. Woelfflin in *Arch. f. Lat. Lexic.* x. 550.

eum, xxviii. 33; xliv. 25; see also *stratores.*

eumenides, filię noctis idest hegitissę, xliii. 53 (*De div. nominibus* = [*not* ? Donati *Ars grammat.*, but] Hagen *Ars Anon. Bern.*, p. 132, 23 note *eymenides* eymenidos, 24 *eminides* eminidis) = *Eumenides,* furie iii, Cp. E353; Ep. —; Ef. —; *Eumenides,* haehtisse, ib. E354; Ep. —; Ef. —. For *hegitissę, haehtisse,* see Bosw. T. (*hægtesse,* a witch, hag, fury); Oxf. D. (*hag,* sb.[1]). See also *striga.*

Eumorphium, see *emorphium.*

eunuchus, xlvi. 17, see *semiuir.*

eunuchus, consul romanus, xliii. 20; **centaurus,** nauis unus de nauibus ęnie [Aeneae], xliii. 21 (*De div. nominibus* = Donati *Ars grammat.*, p. 375, 24, 25 sunt ...alia sono masculina, intellectu feminina, ut *Eunuchus* comoedia [Terent. Af.], Orestes tragoedia [Eurip.], *Centaurus* navis [Virg. A. v. 122]).

euo, see *auo.*

eurus, dexter, xxxvi. 6 (*Oros.* i. 2, 13 ad *Eurum*; ib. 61 in *eurum*; ib. 55, 57, 58, 63, 68 ab *euro*).

Eusebio, xxxv *tit.*

ex, i. 111; ii. 188; iii. 41; xiii. 51; xiv. 20; xvi. 14, 30; xix. 39, 60; xxi. 11; xxviii. 76; xxx. 35; xxxiv. 1; xxxv. 223; xxxviii. 35; xlii *tit.*; xliv. 7, 15; xlvi. 14.

exactio, monung gaebles, xxxix. 27 (*Greg. Dial.* iv. 30 col. 369A *exactionem* canonis egerat) = *exactio,* geabules monung, Cp. E518; *exactio,* geblesmonung, Ef.[1] 359, 46. For *monung,* (a claiming or exaction of debt, tribute), see Bosw. T. (*manung*); O. H. G. *manunga* (Schade); for *gaebles, geabules, gebles* (tribute, tax), Bosw. T. (*gæfel, gafol, gafel,* &c.).

exaetasmos, idest exquesitio, xxviii. 66 (*Cass. Psalm.* xxiii. 3 figura...*exetasmos,* idest exquisitio).

exaggerare, comulare [cum-], xxxiv. 28 (*De Cass., Inst.* viii. 18 uitia non solum seruare, uerum etiam *exaggerare* consueuit; x. 7, 9; x. 8, 3; x. 11 &c. *exaggerat*).

exaggeratio, xxviii. 69, see *emphasis.*

exaggerationis, xxviii. 38, see *per figuram y-.*

exallage, see *exallege*.

exallege, permotatio, xxviii. 29 (*Cass. Psalm.* ii. 6 *exallage*, Latine *permutatio*; see also xviii. 4)=*exallage*, permotatio, Cp. E466; Ep. —; *exallage*, grece permotatio, Ef.[1] 359, 28.

examinatio, ii. 50, see *discussio*.

exameron [hex-], xxxv. 250, see *in exameron*.

examine, iudicio discussione, ii. 62 (*Bened. reg.* 1, 8 [11] fraterna *ex acie*; but fraterno *examine*, Hattemer, *Denkmahle*, i. 34 and Paul Piper, *Nachträge*, p. 34, 18, 19).

examussim, inquisitiue, xxxviii. 1 (*Clem. Recognitt.* x. 47 si quis cupit *examussim* veritatem...agnoscere). See also iii. 58: accipio quod de veritate ad *amussim* requiris.

exaplois, xix. 11, see *in exaplois*.

ex ca (vi) **cai** (et) **decerida**, sedecenalem [-cennalem], xxx. 52; **enneafe decerida**, decemnoualem, xxx. 53 (*Cat. Hier.* lxi col. 671AB sedecim annorum circulum quem Græci ἐκκαιδεκαετηρίδα vocant...; decem et novem annorum circulum, id est ἐννεακαιδεκαετηρίδα; B: sed. ann. cir. q. greci *eʒacaterim* idest sex et decem annorum vocant...nouemdecim ann. cir. *ennelaecaterim* idest decem nouenalem; C: xvi annorum cir. q. greci [blank] vocant...x et viiij annorum circulum id est [blank])=*exacaide*, *ceterida*, sedecennalem, Cp. E413; *exacaidae ceterida*, sedecennalem, Ef.[1] 358, 40, 41; *enneacaide ceterida*, decennouenalem, Cp. E201; *ennecaide ceterida* decennouenalem, Ef.[1] 358, 41.

excarptio, see *scarpmat*.

excedere, abire effugire [effugere], ii. 61 (*Bened. reg.* 68, 5 [8] si...uirium suarum mensuram uiderit pondus oneris *excedere*).

excellentia, xxviii. 18, see *apo tu-*; xlviii. 19, see *prerogatiua*.

excellentiores, gipparre, xlviii. 40 (*De Cass.*, *Inst.* Praef. 2 *excellentior* progenies; v. 36 ordinem, qui *excellentior* habetur). The form *excellentiores* occurs neither in the *Inst.*, nor in the *Conl.*, which latter only gives *excellentior* (i. 11, 2), *-oris* (xv. 8), *-orem* (xi. 12, 7; xxi. 1, 2. 23, 3), *-ore* (xi. 13, 1). But *Inst.* v. 7 we find *esculentiores* cibi, for which three MSS. have *excolentiores*, and v. 23, 1 accuratioribus epulis et *esculentioribus*. Can this be the word that was meant to be glossed? it was more likely to require explanation than the well-known *excellentior*. *Gipparre* seems to be another form of the A. S. geappre (comp. of gēap) which=the Lat. *callidior* in Gen. 3. 1 (Bosw. T. *geap*) and with an Umlaut would appear as gīeppre, gīppre; gēap answers to the M. E. ʒēp (see ʒeap in Stratmann); see Wright W. *Voc.* (*geap*, geaplice, in index). Cf. above *corpulentioribus*.

excelsi, xxxv. 92, see *processores*.

excelsiore, xxxv. 275, see *editore*.

excelso, iv. 25, see *in edito*.

exceptis, xxii. 12, see *urna*.

excesserit, oblitus fuerit culpauerit, ii. 57 (*Bened. reg.* 46, 6 [7] Si quis...aliquid *excesserit*; cf. 67, 7 [12] excessus, excessos; 45, 5 excessisse). Cf. *excesserit*, culpauerit, Cp. E410; excesserit, calcauerit, Ef.[1] 358, 24, and below, *excussum*. See Woelfflin in *Arch. f. Lat. Lexic.* x. 550.

excessos, see *excesserit*; *excessus*.

excessu, xxx. 40, see *extasei*.

excessum, cauatum, iv. 108, see *exesum*.

excessus, extulit se, ii. 60 (*Bened. reg.* 67, 7 [12] propter *excessus* [*excessos*]; cf. 45, 4 excessu). With this lemma "extulit se" does not agree. If the latter were correct, the lemma might be "excessit," which, however, does not occur in the Regula [but see above *excesserit*]. Cf. ectasi, excessum, expello, Cp. E17; *excesus*, egylt, Cp. E500. For *egylt*, a fault, trespass, see Bosw. T. (*egylt*, *ægylt*).

excetra, see *exedra*.

excidium, casum uel discensum [for *discessum*?], xxxv. 141 (*Ruf.* iii. 7 fol. 39[a] post vrbis *excidium*...de bello...atque *excidio* ciuitatis; iii. 11 fol. 41[b] ciuitatis *excidium*). Cf. *excidium*, discidium, Cp. E378; *excidium*, expugnatio, Cp. E379.

excipiuntur, separantur, xlii. 1 (*Ex div. libris*=*Sulp. Sev. Dial.* ii. 3, p. 183, 8 misera ipsa animalia conglobantur... dumque aegre *expediuntur*).

exciso, xxiii. 5, see *lapide inpolito*.

excisum, see *exesum*.

excitandum, xvi. 9, see *malleolis*.

exclamatione, xxviii. 65, see *epiphonima*.

excocti, ii. 51, see *digesti*.

excogitata, xxxv. 100, see *commenta*.

excolantes, see *exolantes*.

excoriandi, xx. 6, see *extentera*.

excubiae, see *exubię*.

excusabile, xxx. 23, see *apologieticum*.

excusabilem, xxxv. 153, see *apologiticum*.

excusans, iv. 23, see *apollogeticus*.

excusationes, xxx. 79, see *apologus*.

excusationibus, xlviii. 71, see *apologis*.

excussum, obliuionem uel derelictum, ii. 65 (*Bened. reg.* 4, 34 [51] risum multum aut *excussum* non amare; q[y] for *excessum*? see *excesserit* oblitus fuerit, in ii. 57, and cf. Woelfflin in *Arch. f. Lat. Lexic.*, x. 550).

ex diametro, e regione medietas anni, xxxviii. 35 (*Clem. Recognitt.* x. 11 aliquis annum tuum aspexit *ex diametro* aut conjunctus aut in centro). Cf. *diametro*, duplici mensura, Cp. D255; Ef.[1] 355, 62; Goetz, vi. 411 (*ex diametro*).

execlesie [for *ecclesiae*], x. 1, see *osculetur me.*

exedra, serpens est si occiditur surgent de capite eius plures serpentes nisi cicius [cit-] incenditur, xxiii. 1 (*Esdras*; *Hieron. Praef.*, p. xiii^b licet *hydra* sibilet; Heyse, p. xlviii^a licet et *excetra* sibilet; Migne, *Patr. Lat.* xxviii col. 1406^A licet et *excetra* sibilet, and in note *hydra*; *serpens*; *extra cittara*).

exedrae, see *exedre*.

exedre, parue domus, v. 10 (*Eccl. Stor.*); **exedrę**, scabelli [!] ad cibos uel subselli [!], xxxv. 61 (*De Eus.*) = (*Ruf.* xi. 23 fol. 187^b spatia occupant *exhedrae*, in ed. 1548; *exhedrę*, in ed. 1535, p. 255; *exedrae*, Cacciari ii. p. 102). Cf. *exedrę*, scabelli ad cibos, Cp. E420; cf. also Cp. E366, 415, 562, and Goetz vii. 411 (*exedram*).

exemerinus [for *Chimerinus* = χειμερινός], ac si ex meridię [-die] remotior, xliv. 5; see *arcticos*.

exempla, xxviii. 26, see *paradigma*.

exempli, i. 95, see *portentuose*.

exempta, uiolenter sublata, i. 51 (*De Canon.*; *Can. Conc. Carth.* lvi *exempta* de fasce multarum). Cf. *exemta*, suciata (for sublata ?), Cp. E536; Goetz, vi. 411 (*exemptus*).

exenia, madmas, iii. 66 (*Vit. S. Anton.* xxvii col. 150^{CD} *xenia*; but in note 65, col. 181 *exenia*). For *madmas* (precious things, ornaments) see Bosw. T. (*ma-đum*).

exentera, see *extentera*.

exenteseon, questionum, xxx. 66 (*Cat. Hier.* lxxv col. 685^A viginti quinque ἐξηγήσεων Origenis volumina; B: viginti q. *eȝeseon* idest *questionum* o. v.; C: xxv [blank] orig. v.) = *exentesion*, expositio quaessionum, Cp. E412; *exentession*, quaestion, Ef.[1] 358, 32.

exequere [= *exequi*], i. 10, see *admittere*.

exequi, see *exequere*.

exercendi, xlii. 24, see *uectandi*.

exercitationis, xlv. 1, see *gymnasium*.

exercitu, iii. 14, see *per aggerem*, and note † on p. 7.

exercitum [-tuum], xii. 42, see *uasa*; xiii. 33, see *bige*.

exercitus, xxi. 1, see *in expeditione*.

exercituum, xxi. 17, see *Adonai*. See also *bige equitum*; *uasa castrorum*.

exertum, sollicitum, xv. 39 (*Ezech.* iv. 7 brachium tuum erit *extentum*; Heyse, in note *exertum*) = *exertum*, sollicitum, Cp. E382. The Hebrew has חֲשׂוּפָה (made naked). Cf. Wright W. i. 230, 37, and Steinm. i. 642, 50.

exesum, subtilis, xxxv. 230 (*De Eus.*); **excessum**, cauatum, iv. 108 (*Eccl. Istor.*) = (*Ruf.* xi. 25 fol. 189^a simulachrum...a tergo *exesum*; Rhenanus' ed. of 1535 has *excisum*; Cacciari, ps. ii. p. 106 *exesum*, alias *excisum*) = *exesum*, suptile, comsumtum, Cp. E520.

exetasmos, see *exaetasmos*.

exhedrae, exhedrę, see *exedre*.

exhibere, accersire [-siri] adesse uel presto [praesto] esse, i. 52 (*De Canon.*; *Can. Conc. Carth.* lxxxvii ut...suam praesentiam non differat *exhibere*).

exhibita, adtributa prestita [praest-], ii. 56 (*Bened. reg.* 2, 18 [25] cura *exhibita*).

exhortatio, see *caeleuma*.

exiareton [for ἐξαίρετον], xxix. 51, see *epyuision*.

exigerit, poposcerit uel petierit, ii. 70 (*Bened. reg.* 48, 13 [23] Si...necessitas loci...*exegerit* [and correctly ?] *exigerit*).

exiit, xxii. 12, see *urna*.

exin, deinde, xxxv. 297 (*Ruf.* i. 9 fol. 13^a; ix. 9 fol. 152^a; x. 11 fol. 167^b *exinde*).

exinanitum, x. 6, see *unguentum exinanitum*.

exinde, see *exin*.

existimant, see *cęlum*.

exitiali, mortali, iv. 29 (*Ruf.* iii. 5 fol. 35^b *exitiali* quadam manu; iii. 8 fol. 39^b *exitialibus* flammis).

exitu, xvi. 15, see *ab exitu sermonis*; xxx. 81, see *psichiexodo*.

exitur, xxxv. 285, see *coibatur*.

exitus, xxviii. 53, see *paraprosdocia*.

ex latere regni, de adulterio regine, xvi. 14 (*Dan.* vi. 4 principes...quaerebant occasionem ut invenirent Danieli *ex lateri regis*; Heyse, and Migne xxviii col. 1308, in notes, *ex latere regni*) = *ex latere regni*, de adulterio reginę, Cp. E409 & Ef.[1] 358, 22; Ep. —.

exolantes, mundantes a colendo [colando ?] dicitur, xxiv. 12 (*Math.* xxiii. 24 duces cæci, *excolantes* culicem) = *exolantes*, mandantes, Cp. E362; Ep. —; *exolantes*, mundantes, Ef.[1] 357, 16.

exordio, xvi. 15, see *ab exitu sermonis*.

exortari, xxxv. 44, see *adortus*.

exortatio, xiv. 15, see *caeleuma*.

expectans [for *spectans*], xliv. 7, see *poli*.

expectaremur, xxxv. 281, see *operiremur*.

expectat [for *exspectat*], i. 8, see *allectat*.

expediat, see *expedit*.

expedire, prodesse uel commodare, ii. 67 (*Bened. reg.* 64, 28 [51] ut viderit cuique *expedire*; cf. 65, 19 [38], 26 [50]; 68, 9 [17]).

expedit, prodest commodum est, ii. 59 (*Bened. reg.* 6, 17 [23 marg. & not.] ne videatur plus loqui quam *expedit*; 36, 13 [20] quotiens *expedit*; cf. xxxix. 12 [19] *expediat*).—**non expedit**, non conuenit, ii. 123 (*Bened. reg.* 66, 14 [26] quia...*non expedit* animabus eorum).

expeditione, expeditionem, xxi. 1, see *in expeditione*.

expediuntur, see *excipiuntur*.

expenso, expleto, ii. 68 (*Bened. reg.* 18, 17 [28] *expenso* ergo psalmo).

experimento, probamento, ii. 72 (*Bened. reg.* 59, 17 [27] quod *experimento* didicimus).

experiri, see *expertim*.

experiuntur, explicantur uel cognoscant, i. 47 (*De Canon.*; *Can. Conc. Antioch.* xcviii omnes Synodi *experiantur* examen).

expers, ignarus, xxxiv. 50 (*De Cass.*, *Inst.* xii. 29, 3 *expers* patientiae est; ii. 3, 5 *expertes*).

experta, iii. 59, see *explosa*.

expertem, expertes, see *expertim*.

expertim, ignorari, xlviii. 35 (*De Cass.*, *Inst.* ii. 3, 5 seniorum institutionis *expertes*). If *expertes* is the Glossator's lemma, *ignorari* is perhaps corrupted from *ignari*. There is *expertem* caelestis panis, ibid. v. 21, 3; qui innumeros diuersorum casus ac ruinas *experti sunt*, ibid. vii. 13; nec spiritales pugnas merebimur *experiri*, ibid. v. 19, 2. The latter two quotations would suggest *experiri, non ignorare*.

expiscabar, capiebam, xxxv. 151 (*Ruf.* iii. 39 fol. 52^{b} ab ipso sedulo *expiscabar*).

explanatio, xxviii. 82, see *efexegresis*.

expleto, ii. 68, see *expenso*.

explicantur [sine interpret.], ii. 66 (*Bened. reg.* 5, 16 [23] ambae res...citius *explicantur*). For *explicantur* see also (i. 47) *experiuntur*.

explicatur, xxviii. 53, see *paraprosdocia*, 78, see *hyperbaton*.

explosa, elisa uel experta, iii. 59; **explosa**, mortua, iii. 61 (*not* De S. Mart. Stor., but *Vit. S. Anton.* xliii col. 158^{A} cum...puella jaceret *explosa*) = explosa, elisa, Cp. E447. See also *explosi*.

explosi, extincti, xxvii. 6 (*not* in Isid. Lib. Rot.); **explosi**, extincti, xxviii. 14 = (*Lib. Anton.* xxvi col. 150^{A} Ista...*explosi* mors atque enecati prodigii) = *explosi*, extincti, Cp. E363; Ep. —; Ef.^{1} 357, 18.

expolierit, onauerit [ornauerit] uel declarauerit, xxxv. 194 (*Ruf.* vi. 18 fol. 108^{a} Graeco eam (epistolam)...sermone, non tamen sensibus *expoliuerit*).

expolita, famata, xlviii. 23 (*De Cass.*, *Inst.* Praef. 5 quae...discussa non fuerint *et polita*; one MS. has *et expolita*). For famata Goetz, vi. 420, suggests *formata*; cf. *politum*, limatum, Cp. P521.

expolitum, ornatum, xxxv. 185 (*Ruf.* vi. 15 fol. 105^{a} ingenium...*expolitum* uiciauit).

expoliuerit, see *expolierit*.

exponi, xix. 28, see *iubilo*.

expositionis, see *eyaggences apod-*.

expositionum, see *de entoetromito*; *ypophesion*.

expresio [expressio], xxviii. 88, see *diatiposis*.

ex pretore, de pretorio, xxxv. 223 (*Ruf.* xi. 21 fol. 186^{b} *ex praetore* Vrbano catechumenus).

exprimebant, i. 127, see *striones*.

exprimuntur, xxviii. 88, see *diatiposis*.

expulsorem, see *erladiocten*.

expulsus, i. 48, see *extorris*.

exquesitio [exquisitio], xxviii. 66, see *exaetasmos*.

exquisitio, see *exaetasmos*.

exsecutiones, xxviii. 71, see *ephichirema*.

exsolutio, vi *tit.*

exspectat, see *expectat*.

exsuperare, xxviii. 51, see *hyperthesis*.

exsurge, xxviii. 33, see *tropus*.

exta, intestina, xxxv. 202 (*Ruf.* viii. 16 fol. 143^{b} *exta*...perscrutabantur). Cf. *exta*, iesen, Cp. E439. For *exta*, see also (xvi. 30) *aruspices*, and *extale*.

extale, snedil-daerm, xxxv. 203 (*Ruf.* ?). Q^{y} for *extalis*? (see Lewis & Sh.; Forcell.), and, perhaps, together with the Germanic words, a further explanation of *exta* (q.v.), intestina. For *snedildaerm* (the great gut) see Bosw. T. (*snædel, snædelþearm*) = *extale*, snaedilþearm, Cp. E419; *extale*, snaedil uel thearm, Ef.^{1} 359, 5.

extalis, see *extale*.

extasei, excessu idest mentis, xxx. 40 (*Cat. Hier.* xl col. 655^{B} quae scripsit περὶ ἐκστάσεως [De ἐκστάσει, Rich.]; and liii col. 663^{A} de *ecstasi*; B (xl): quae scripsit de *excessu mentis*; (liii: de *extasi*); C (xl): quae scripsit [blank]; (liii: de *extasi*). Cf. *extaseos*, celsa, Cp. E402).

extasi, see *extasei*.

extemplo, see *extimplo*.

extendi, xxviii. 38, see *per figuram yperbolen*.

extensa, xix. 20, see *tympanum*.

extensos, vi. 24, see *intentos*.

extentera, inicium [init-] excoriandi, xx. 6 (*Tobias* vi. 5 *exentera* hunc piscem; Heyse, in note, *extentera*). See Lewis & Short, in voce *exintero*; cf. *exintera*, ansceat (the bowels, Bosw. T.); *extentera*, anseot, Ef.[1] 358, 26.

extentum, see *exertum*.

exterminat, xx. 5, see *extricat*.

exterminatus, xiii. 5, see *commolitus*.

extersum, iv. 111, see *purum*.

extimplo, statim, xxviii. 4 (*Lib. Anton.* ix col. 132D corporis dolor *extemplo* deletus est) = Cp. E429.

extincti, xxvii. 6 and xxviii. 14, see *explosi*.

extollatur, see *extollit*.

extollit, abstrahit, ii. 71 (*Bened. reg.* 48, 35 alios *extollit* [61 *distollit*; cf. ibid. *note*]; cf. 34, 7 [9] *extollatur*; 57, 4 [5] *extollitur*).

extollitur, see *extollit*.

extores, extraneos, xlviii. 56, see *extorris*.

extorqueretur, xxxv. 167, see *eliceretur*.

extorrem, see *extorris*.

extorres, exules de patria, xxxv. 241, see *extorris*.

extorris, ui expulsus quasi exterris, i. 48 (*De Canon.*; *Conc. Gangr.*, Praef., ap. Migne, *Patr. Lat.* lxxxiv col. 112D ab ecclesia habeatur *extorris*).—**extores**, extraneos, xlviii. 56 (*De Cass.*, *Inst.* v. 38, 1 qui uniuersis facultatibus paternis esset *extorris*; id. *Conl.* xxi. 9, 1 *extorrem* facere).—**extorres**, exules de patria, xxxv. 241 (*Ruf.* ix. 8 fol. 151b *extorres* patria). Cf. Isid. *Etym.* x. 86, 87; and *extorres*, praeccan, Cp. E515.

extra, i. 111, see *sicera*.

extraneos, xlviii. 56, see *extores*.

extrema, xliv. 6, see *conuexa*.

extremas, xiv. 33, see *lacinias*.

extreme [-mae], xliv. 5; extremę, xliv. 10, see *cardines*.

extremi quoque duo septentrionales, xliv. 28; **axem cęli ipsius dnm̄s** [dimidians?] bina hiemisperia per medium orbem terrę sed nullus corporalis intellegitur axis quod uirtus diuina cęli globum rotans per axem incorporeum in orbem speri contorqueat comminisque moliri, xliv. 29 (*Alia*; *de cælo*?). These two articles are, perhaps, in further explanation of the twenty-seven preceding glosses of Ch. xliv.

extremum, xi. 6, see *supremum*.

extricat, exterminat foras mittit, xx. 5 (*Tobias* vi. 8 *extricat* omne genus daemoniorum).

extulit, ii. 60, see *excessus*.

exuberat, iii. 49, see *lugoria*.

exubie, exuendo, xlvi. 35, see *exuuia*.

exuendo, xlvi. 35, see *exubię*.

exules, xxxv. 241, see *extorres*.

exuperat, i. 45, see *emergit*.

exurit, xxvii. 12, see *uaporat*.

exuuia, spolia, xxix. 25 (*Uerb. Interpr.* = *Hier. in Matth.* xxii. 11, 12 vestem pollutam, id est veteris hominis *exuvias*) = *exugiae*, spolia, Cp. E525; *excubiae*, spolia, Ef.[1] 359, 57; *exuuiae*, spoliae, Ef.[2] 292, 7. Cf. *exubiae*, uestes mortuorum, Cp. E524. — **exubię**, exuendo, xlvi. 35 (*Alia* = *Ars Phocae*, p. 428, 8 *exuviae*; in note *excubiae*, *exubiae*).

exuuiae, see *exuuia*.

exuuias, see *exuuia*.

eyaggences apodoxios, euangelice [-cae] predicaciones [-nis], xxx. 75; **euaggences parasueues**, euangelice [-cae] preparationis [praep-], xxx. 76 (*Cat. Hier.* lxxxi col. 689A Εὐαγγελικῆς Ἀποδείξεως libri viginti, Εὐαγγελικῆς Προπαρασκευῆς [Εὐαγ- προδείξεως παρασκευῆς, in Migne's Gr. text] libri quindecim; B: euangelice *apoliʒeon*, idest *euangelice expositionis* libri viginti *euangelica eproparaskenes* idest *euangelicarum preparationum* libri quindecim; C: [blank] libri viginti [blank] libri viginti quinque) = *Euaggelices apodixeos*, euangelicae ostensiones, Cp. E358; *Euanggelices parasceues*, euangelicae praeparationes, Cp. E342; *Euangellices apodixeos*; *Euangelicae praeparationes*, Ef.[1] 358, 34, 35.

eymenides, see *eumenides*.

eynum, beneuolus, xxix. 49 (*Uerb. Interpr.* = *Hier. in Matth.* v. 25 Pro... consentiens, in Graecis scriptum est Εὐνοῶν, quod interpretatur *benevolus*).

eza, v. 8 [for ἐξαπλᾶ?], see *auo*.

eʒacaterim, see *ex ca*.

Ezechiele, see *colamina*; *obulus*.

f for *p*: e*f*exegresis (for e*p*-).—for *ph*: agiogra*f*a (hagiogra*ph*a); anace*f*aleos, -*f*aleosin (anace*ph*); arto*f*ilax; cae*f*alus; Cata*f*rigarum; dia*f*oresis; ele*f*antis; *f*alleras; *f*ares; *f*aros; *f*idiae; *f*ilacteria; *f*ledomum; *f*oetontis; *f*reniticus; *f*rix; *f*rigia; gazo*f*ilatia; hermo*f*roditus; hieru*f*ontis; meta*f*ora; meta*f*rasin; pasto*f*oria; pyri*f*legitonta; sca*f*a; siro*f*enissa; so*f*ismatum; stro*f*a; ti*f*on.—for *u* (= v): *f*ates: in*f*estes.—*ff* for *ph*: ę*ff*eborum (e*ph*eb-).

fabae, see *frixi ciceris*; *mocum*.

fabarum, see *leguminum*.

fabę, xxiv. 5, see *mocum*.

fabricam [for *fabricatis*?], xxxv. 294, see *thecis*.

fabricat, xxxv. 271, see *cudat*.

fabricatis, see *thecis*.

fabula poetarum est gigantes terram

sustentare sub aquis, xix. 51 (*Job* xxvi. 5 Ecce *gigantes* gemunt sub aquis).

fabulatio, xxxv. 1, see *tragoedia*.

fac, xvii. 18, see *tene laterem*.

facere, i. 82, see *operam*; xv. 48, see *ad leuicandum*; xliii. 52, see *facesso*.

facessat, lacessat [for *lassescat* ?], iv. 38 (*Eccl. Istor.*); **facessat**, desino, xxxv. 150, and **fessat**, desonat [for *desinat* ?], xxxv. 76 (*De Eus.*) = (*Ruf.* iii. 36 fol. 51[b] *facessat* inuidia); cf. *facessit*, desinat, Cp. F112; *fessat*, desonat, Cp. F116; see also *fessat*.

facesso, facere cesso uel sepe [saepe] facio, xliii. 52 (*De div. nominibus* = Donati *Ars gramm.* p. 385, 5, 7 *facesso*). Cf. *facessit*, duo sunt, idest facere cessat et frequenter facit, Cp. F98.

faciat, viii. 19, see *si usque ad*.

faciens, xxviii. 61, see *amphibolia*.

faciente, xlviii. 65, see *infestante*.

facile, citius uelociter, ii. 77 (*Bened. reg.* 65, 9 [17] *facile* advertitur).

facio, xliii. 52, see *facesso*.

facit, xxxii. 8–11; xxxiii. 8.

facitur, x. 26, see *mustum*.

faciunt, x. 9; xiii. 31, 53; xiv. 3, 5; xv. 12; xvi. 22, 25, 26; xvii. 19; xix. 44; xxi. 20; xxiv. 6; xxix. 39; xxxi. 28; xxxiii. 1, 14, 30; xxxv. 42; xxxvii. 19.

facta, xxix. 11, see *mauria*.

factionibus, subdolibus, xxxv. 267 (*Ruf.* vi. 7 fol. 100[a] *factionibus* circumuenire parant eum). Q[y] subdolibus for *sodalibus* or *sodaliciis* ?

factis, xvii. 9, see *asolatis*; see also *fastibus*.

factis [for *flectis* ?], xxxv. 175, see *graticulis*.

factoris, xii. 1, see *euergetis*.

factum, xxiv. 13, see *alabastrum*; xxxviii. 22, see *deucalionem*.

factura, see *de piasma*.

faculae, see *tęde*.

facule [-lae], xix. 44, see *tęde*.

facultates, xxxv. 276, see *reditus*; xlvi. 36, see *manubię*.

facundia, facundis, see *dialecticis*.

fadus, aliud nomen erodis [Her-], iv. 17 (*Ruf.* ii. 11 fol. 24[a] Fado, *abl.*, and Fadus).

faeu-, see *fen-*; *foen-*.

faex, see *auriculum*.

fala, xlvii. 41, see *tubolo*.

falcis, xlv. 5, see *fax*.

fallacia, fallatia, iv. 63, see *pompa*.

falleras, falsitates, xlii. 16 (*Ex div. libris* = *Sulp. Sev. Dial.* i. 27, 3, p. 179, 21 inanes sermonum *faleras*...contemnere; in note *phaleras*). Cf. *farelas* (for *faleras*) hryste, Cp. F111. For *hryste* see Bosw. T. (*hyrst*, an ornament, trapping).

false, see *pseudo ephigrapha*.

falsitates, xlii. 16, see *falleras*.

falso, xxx. 33, see *pseudo ephigrapha*.

falx, see *fax*.

famata [for *formata* ?], xlviii. 23, see *expolita*.

famfaluca, see *famfelucas*.

famfelvcas, laesungae, xlvii. 19 (*Alia* = ?) = *famfaluca*, faam, leasung, Cp. F25; *f-*, leasung uel faam, Ep. 9C12; *f-*, laesung uel faam, Ef.[1] 360, 46. For *leasung* (leasing, lying, vain or frivolous speech, deception, artifice), see Bosw. T. For famfelucas (trifles, fineries), see Körting, *Wört.* 3620. The derivation of this word from Gr. πομφόλυξ is strengthened by the additional gloss *faam*, foam, a water-bubble, in Cp., Ep. and Ef.[1]

famosissimo, xxix. 5, see *augustissimo*.

fanonem, see *labrum*.

fans [for *fraus*], xxx. 42, see *chri fiscus*.

far, xxxvii. 4, see *fidelia farris*.—**far**, frumentum, xlv. 9 (*Uerba de multis* = *Ars Phocae*, p. 412, 5 neutri generis...fas *far* git). Cf. *far*, genus frumenti, Cp. F87; Ep. 10A18; Ef.[1] 362, 14.

faram, see *fares*.

fares, turres custodum, xxxvi. 5 (*Oros.* i. 2, 71 altissimam *pharum*; in note *farum*, *faram*).

faria, eloquia, xxvii. 2 (*Lib. Rot.* = *Isid. de nat. rer.*, iii. 1 *Feria* quoque a fando dicta est, quasi fari) = Cp. F24; Ep. 9C21; Ef.[1] 360, 54; cf. Goetz vi. 435, 6; Isid. *Lib. Gloss. faria*, verba multa.

farina, xxi. 15, see *polenta*.

faros, xxiii. 2, see *filii faros*.

farris, xxxvii. 3, see *fidelia farris*.

farum, see *fares*.

fas, diuinum, iv. 21 (*Ruf.* ii. 20 fol. 29[b] ius *fas*que).—**fas erat**, ius erat uel iustum erat, xxxv. 96 (*Ruf.* i. 1 fol. 2[b] quantum *fas erat*; ibid. fol. 5[a] quantum...*fas erat*).

fascia pectoralis, uestis [Cambr. MS. adds quę] circa pectus uoluitur, xiii. 13 (*Isai.* iii. 24 erit...pro *fascia pectorali* cilicium).

fascibus, onoribus [hon-], iv. 13 (*Eccl. Istor.*); **fascibus**, dignitatibus, xxxv. 103 (*De Eus.*) = (*Ruf.* ii. 5 fol. 21[a] omnibus qui Romanis *fascibus* subiacent). See also *fastibus*.

fascinatio, laudatio stulta, xi. 1 (*Sap.* iv. 12 *fascinatio*...nugacitatis obscurat bona).

fastibus, libris, iv. 9 (*Eccl. Istor.*); and id. xxxv. 102 (*De Eus.*) = (*Ruf.* i. 6 fol. 11[b] nullis conscriptionum *fastibus*). Cacciari, p. 34, prints *fascibus*, and says that 3 Vatican MSS. have *factis*.

fastis, fastos, see *in fastu*.

fastu, vii. 9, see *in fastu*.

fastus, inflatio uel timor [*tumor* ?], XLVIII. 14; **faustus**, superbia, XLVIII. 36 (*De Cass.*, *Inst.* V. 10 superbiae calcandus est *fastus*; II. 3, 3 *fastus* uitae; IV. 5 omni *fastu* deposito mundiali) = *fastus*, superbia, Cp. F16; *fastus*, superbia uel liber, Ep. 10A20; Ef.[1] 362, 16. See also *in fastu*.

fastus, acc. plur. 4th decl. of *fasti*, see *in fastu*.

fatere, laudare, XL. 2 (*Uerba?*).

fates, propheta, IV. 5; see *uatis*.

fatescente, fatiscente, see *fatescit*.

fatescit, briudid, III. 34 (*S. Mart. Stor.* = *Sulp. Sev. Dial.* I. 11, 2 corpus media *fatiscebat*; *ibid.* I. 16, 3 stomacho iam *fatiscente* [*fatescente*, in note]). Steinmeyer (*Alth. Glossen*, II. 746) refers the gloss to *facessat* a quoquam qui sub Deo uiuit, ista suspicio (*Dial.* III. 5, 5); remarking that *briudid* is connected with O.H.G. *brôdi*, crippled, weak (see Schade, in voce). For *briudid*, gone to ruin, come to grief, from A.S. brēoþan (Bosw. T.) prop. intransitive, but sometimes also trans. to ruin, destroy, cf. Oxf. D. (sub v. *brothel*).—**fatescit**, soluit contriuit, XXVII. 22 (*Lib. Rot.* = *Isid. Lib. de nat. rer.* VII. 3 terra *fatiscit* in puluerem). Cf. *fatescit*, resoluitur, Cp. F46 and Ef.[2] 293, 14.

fatiget, XXVIII. 1, see *deficiet*.

fatiscebat, fatiscit, see *fatescit*.

fato, see *fatum*.

fatores, XIV. 22, see *in fatores*.

fatum, uyrd, XXXV. 165 (*Ruf.* IV. 30 fol. 72ᵃ de *fato*...dialogus). For *fatum* see also (XXXV. 157) *furtunam*. For *uyrd* see Bosw. T. (*wyrd*, fate, fortune), and below, *fors*.

fauę [fabae], XXIX. 13, see *frixi ciceris*.

fauor, plausus, I. 55 (*De Canon.*; *Can. Conc. Carth.* LIII illicito *fauore*; *Decret. Innoc.* VIII p. 196ᵇ fin. populi *fauorem* sequentes). Cf. *plausus*, fauor, Cp. P444.

fauorum [fabarum ?], II. 106; see *leguminum*.

faustus, superbia, XLVIII. 36, see *fastus*.

fautorem, laudatorem, XLVIII. 46 (*De Cass.*, *Inst.* V. 31 fabularum diabolum esse *fautorem*...declarauit).—**fautoribus**, consentientibus, IV. 95 (*Eccl. Istor.*); **fautoribus**, adiutoribus, XXXV. 212 (*De Eus.*) = (*Ruf.* X. 15 fol. 169ᵃ *fautoribus*... indulget).

fax, falcis, XLV. 5 (*Uerba de multis* = *Ars Phocae*, p. 412, 1 feminini generis...gens *falx fax* faex).

fecerunt, XXXVIII. 37, see *coribantas*.

feci, XV. 8, see *conplosi*.

fecit, XXXIX. 4, see *balneum ciceronis*.

fecundia [for *facundia* ? or *facundis* ?], XXXIV. 45, see *dialecticis*.

fefellerant, see *fefellit*.

fefellit, fraudulenter mentitur, XXXV. 132 (*Ruf.* III. 10 fol. 41ᵇ Nec me de eorum testimonio *fefellit* opinio; III. 6 fol. 36ᵃ de his qui *fefellerant*).

feliciter, VIII. 13, see *in sublime*.

fellis, XXVII. 30, see *moloncolia*.

feminarum, I. 127, see *striones*.

feminino, XXXV. 144, see *enixa est*.

femur uirginis, idest dinę [Dinae; see *Genes.* XXXIV., and Steinm. I. 481 note 1], XXI. 7 (*Judith* IX. 2 denudaverunt *femur virginis*).

fenerantur, XXIX. 42, see *trapezeta*.

fenus, see *foenus*.

ferculum lectum est quod portari potest, X. 13 (*Cant.* III. 9 Vulg. *ferculum* fecit sibi rex Salomon).

feretri, in quibus portantur filię nobilium super IIII equis coopertis desuper cortina sicut currus, XIII. 59 (*Isai.* ? not in the Vulg.; perhaps a further explanation of XIII. 58 *in lecticis*. Conf. *feretrum* 2 *Reg.* 3. 31).

feretrum, see *feretri*.

feria [sine interpret.], II. 74 (*Bened. reg.* 13, 8 [11] secunda *feria*; cf. 18, 9 [13] primam ... secundae *feriae* [ferię] &c.; 41, 5 [7] sexta *feria*). See also *faria*.

feriatus, sanctus uel requies, XXVII. 19 (*Lib. Rot.* = *Isid. Lib. de nat. rerum*, III. 1 dies sabbati ab initio *feriatus* habetur; cf. ib. I. 4 *feriati* dies) = *feriatus* sanctus requies, Cp. F126; Ep. 9C20; Ef.[1] 360, 53.

ferię, see *feria*.

feris, XXXIX. 15, see *ferula*.

feroces, I. 16, see *barbari*.

ferocitate, XVI. 13, see *efferatus est*.

ferreę, XXXV. 81, see *uaeri*.

ferreis, XXXV. 175, see *graticulis*; XLI. 17, see *mastigia*.

ferri, XXXV. 143, see *per metalla*.

ferris, XXXV. 41, see *in aculeis*.

ferro, XI. 13, see *in carcere*...

ferrugineas, pallidus uel rubicundus, XXIX. 40 (*Uerb. Interpr.* = *Hier. in Matth.* XXVII. 45 *ferrugineas* fecisse tenebras). Cf. *feruginius*, greig (gray), Cp. F115.

ferrum, VIII. 10, see *conflatorium*; XIII. 18, see *sarculum*, 52, see *lima*, 53, see *circino*; XIV. 20, see *scalpellum*; XVII. 2, see *ligones*, 5, see *trulla*; XXXV. 39, see *ungulam*, 201, see *cautere*.

feruens, III. 27, see *furibundus*.

feruentes, I. 69, see *lasciuientes*.

feruentissimo, ardentissimo, II. 79 (*Bened. reg.* 72, 6 [6] hunc...zelum *feruentissimo* amore exerceant).

ferula, baculus arundineus de maiore

genere si feris de ipso ardet et non est libidum [liuidum], XXXIX. 15 (*Greg. Dial.* III. 26 col. 281A quos...*ferula*...caedebat; ictus *ferulae* pertimescebant).

ferunculus, see *furunculas.*

fessat, desonat [*desinat*?], XXXV. 76; see *facessat.*

festinanter, festinatio, XXII. 16, see *ueredarii.*

festiuitates, XLIII. 29, see *bachus.*

fetida, IV. 88, see *purulenta.*

fibrarum, darmana, V. 22 (*Ruf.* XI. 24 fol. 189a ob *fibrarum* inspectionem; XI. 33 fol. 191b ex *fibrarum* praescientia).—**fibras,** intestinas, IV. 70 (*Eccl. Istor.*); **fibras,** uenas, XXXV. 190 (*De Eus.*) = (*Ruf.* VII. 9 fol. 119a humanas rimari...*fibras*) = *fibras*, uenas, Cp. F175. For *darmana* (Gen. pl.) see Bosw. T. (*þearm*, a gut, an intestine).

ficariis, see *ficarius.*

ficarius, qui ficos collegit, XIV. 29 (*Hier.* L. 39 dracones cum faunis *ficariis*).

ficetula, suca, XLVII. 68 (*Alia* = ?) = *f*-, sugga, Cp. F176 and Ep. 9C8; *f*-, sucga, Ef.[1] 360, 42. The lemma (= *ficedula* or *ficecula*), a small bird, the fig-pecker (Lewis & Sh.); for suca, sugga, sucga (the name of *a bird*) see Bosw. T. (*sucga*).

ficos, XIV. 29, see *ficarius*; XXI. 20, see *labastes.* See also *cataplasmarent.*

ficto, fictus, see *de entoetromito.*

ficus protulit grossos suos, flore [flores] ipsius antequam aperiantur sic dicuntur, X. 12 (*Cant.* II. 13 *ficus protulit grossos suos*).

fide, III. 50, see *neotricis*; XIX. 64, see *apostata.*

fidei, XXXV. 218, see *anulum fidei.*

fidelia farris, uas tritici, XXXVII. 3; **fidelia,** uas; far, genus tritici, XXXVII. 4; **capsaces,** lenticula, idest uas uitreum simile flasconi, XXXVII. 5 (*S. Aug.*). These glosses evidently refer to the reading "*fidelia farris* non deficiet et *capsaces* olei non minuet" in I (III) *Reg.* 17. 14 recorded by Cyprianus (*de op. et eleem.* c. 17, in *Corp. Scriptt. Eccl. Latin.* III pt. 1, p. 387; see also Sabat.), for which the Vulg. has: "*hydria farinae* non deficiet, nec *lecythus* olei minuetur." August. treating of this passage (Serm. 239, 3; Migne XXXVIII col. 1128) says Benedixit sanctus Elias hydriam farinæ, et capsacem olei. For *capsaces* see also Migne LXVII. 618A (Facundi *Def.*).

fidelis, XXIX. 35, see *pisticum.*

fides (*a string* of a musical instrument), see *fidis.*

fidiae opera, opera dei, XXXVIII. 20 (*Clem. Recognitt.* VII. 12 Erant...in aede quadam positae, in qua *Phidiae opera*... habebantur).

fidicen, harperi, XLVI. 9 (*Alia* = *Ars Phocae*, p. 415, 4 hic *fidicen*). Cf. Cp. F180; Ep. 9E22; Ef.[1] 361, 34. For harperi = hearpere, a harper, see Bosw. T.

fidis, sner, XLVI. 18 (*Alia* = *Ars Phocae*, p. 417, 9 [?] *fides* fidei, spes spei). It is possible that this reference is wrong, and that the present gloss is a further explanation to *fidicen* (q.v.). For *snēr*, the string of a musical instrument (D. *snaar*), see Bosw. T.; also ib. *snearu*; Kluge, *A. S. Leseb.* (p. 204) *snearh* obl. *snēare*, f. strick, saite.

figl [for *figuraliter*? or A.S. *figul*?], XIX. 63, see *ancillis.*

figmento, XXXV. 164, see *de figmento.*

figulus, XIII. 49, see *plastes.*

figunt, XLIV. 16, see *antarticus.*

figura, XXVIII. 25, see *scema*; XXX. 92, see *cataracteras*; XXXVIII. 33, see *scema.*

figura est sicut nomine ipso datur intellegi quedam conformatio dictionis a communione remota quam ostentationem et habitum possumus nuncupare, XXVIII. 57 (*Cass. Psalm.* II. 1 *Figura* est s.n.i.d. intelligi, quaedam c. d. a communione [for *communiore*?] r. quae interioribus oculis velut aliquid vultuosum semper offertur, quam traditione majorum ost. e.h. p.n.). See *figura* a confirmatione, Cp. F182; Ep. 9E34; Ef.[1] 361, 45.—**figura metopoea,** que personis semper cognoscit certissime applicari, XXVIII. 34 (*Cass. Psalm.* IV Praef., col. 47D sub *figura mythopœia*, Ecclesiam dicamus loqui, quae p.s. cognoscitur certissimis applicari). —**figura sardismos,** quę linguarum semper permixtione formatur, XXVIII. 85 (*Cass. Psalm.* XLI. 11 *figuram* fecerunt *sardismos*, quae l. s. p. f.—Cf. LIX. 6 *figuram* faciunt *sardismos* quae fit diversarum commixtione linguarum).

figuralis, XXIX. 1, see *allegoria.*

figuram, XXVIII. 38, see *per figuram y*-.

filacteria, scriptura diuersa quę propert [for *propter*] infirmos habentur, XXXIX. 62; see *philacteria.*

filia, XXVIII. 11, see *Diana*, 13, see *Ionan.*

filiae, see *feretri.*

filię [filiae], XIII. 59, see *feretri*; XLIII. 53, see *eumenides.*

filii, I. 80, see *omousion*; XI. 5, see *uitulamina*; XXI. 12 (bis), see *filii titan*; XLIII. 7, see *nepus.*—**filii faros,** duo milia generationis numerat qui in captiuitate nati sunt, XXIII. 2 (1 *Esdr.* II. 3 *Filii Pharos*, duo millia centum septuaginta duo).—**filii titan,** filii solis qui sunt fortiores hominibus, XXI. 12 (*Judith* XVI. 8 *filii Titan* percusserunt eum).

filius, II. 7, see *alleluia*; XXVIII. 7, see *tifon*, 23, see *Iouis*; XXIX. 19, see *fratruelis*; XLIII. 7, see *nepus*.

filo, XIII. 40, see *perpendiculum*.

finibus, XXII. 12, see *urna*.

finis, XXVIII. 54, see *aposiopesis*.

finit, XXXIII. 31; XLVII. 103.

finitae, see *missas*.

[fi]nitas, II. 10, see *ad missas* sub voce *missas*.

finite [for *finitae*, or *finitas*?], II. 110, see *missas*.

fiola, fiolae, see *fiole*.

fiole, in similitudinem calicis, XXIV. 1 (*Math.* ? not in the Vulg., but as the words, collected from the Gospel of Matthew, follow in the Glossary immediately after those extracted from Esdras, this gloss is perhaps misplaced, and *fiole* =*phialae*, in 1 Esdr. I. 9 *phialæ* aureæ). Cf. *fioli*, similitudo calicis, Cp. F177; *fiola*, similitudo calicis, Ep. 9C18; *fiolae* similitudo calicis, Ef.[1] 360, 51.

fioli, see *fiole*.

firmioribus, XXXIV. 9, see *causticis*.

fisco, publico dominio cesaris, XXXV. 180 (*De Eus.*); **fiscum**, tributum, IV. 64 (*Eccl. Istor.*) = (*Ruf.* VI. 2 fol. 95[b] census paternus...*fisco*...sociatus est) = *fisco*, puplico, Cp. F161; *fusco*, puplico, Ep. 9A14; fisso, publico, Ef.[1] 360, 9.—*fisco* puplico, domini caesaris, Cp. F183; *fisco* puplico, dominio cesaris, Ep. 9E26; *fisco* publico, domino caesaris, Ef.[1] 361, 37.

fiscum, tributum, IV. 64, see *fisco*.—**fiscus**, XXX. 42, see **chri fiscus**.

fissura, scissura diuisura, XIII. 4 (*Isai.* II. 21 ingredietur *scissuras* petrarum; Heyse records, in note, *fissuras*).

fissuras, see *fissura*.

fistola, arbor est boni odoris non boni saporis, X. 17 (*Cant.* IV. 14 *fistula*).

fistula, see *fistola*.

fit, I. 68; IV. 99; XI. 2; XII. 40; XIX. 40; XXIV. 8; XXVIII. 36, 80; XXXII. 1, 2 (bis), 3–5.

fiunt, VIII. 18, see *ptisana*; XIV. 14, see *calati*; XXXIX. 28, see *qui in numero*..., 50, see *sentina*.

flabris, see *labris*.

flaccentia, contracta, XIII. 27 (*Isai.* XIX. 10 erunt irrigua eius *flaccentia*) = *flacentia*, contracta, Cp. F217; *flaccentia*, contracta, Ep. 9C25; Ef.[1] 360, 59.

flaccidum, see *flacidium*.

flacidium, seruum, XXIX. 18 (*Uerb. Interpr.* = *Hier. in Matth.* XIII. 32 col. 90[B] nihil vitale demonstrat, sed totum *flaccidum* marcidumque). *Seruum* seems a corruption; cf. *flaccidum, contractum*, Cp. F215; Ep. 9A22; Ef.[1] 360, 18.

flagella, II. 185, see *uerbera*.

flagellis, III. 42, see *flagris*, 43, see *mautigia*; XXXV. 188, see *flagris*.

flagitiorum, adulteriorum, XLVIII. 6 (*De Cass.*, *Inst.* V. 6 ad...*flagitiorum* praecipitium).

flagris, flagellis, III. 42 (*De S. Mart. Stor.* = *Sulp. Sev. Dial.* II. 3, 4, 6 Martinum *flagris* urguere coeperunt).—**flagris**, flagellis, XXXV. 188 (*De Eus.* = *Ruf.* VI. 31 fol. 113[a]: *flagris* hinc inde uerberantibus; VIII. 7 fol. 137[a] *flagris*...Dei martyres carpebantur; VIII. 10 fol. 139[b] verberabantur ...*flagris*). Cf. *flagris*, suiopum, Cp. F222, and Bosw. T. (sub v. *swipu*).

flamen, sacerdos iouis, XLVI. 8 (*Alia* = *Ars Phocae*, p. 415, 3 hic *flamen* [sacerdos Iovis]).

flasconi [= Gr. φλάσκων], XXXVII. 5, see *capsaces*.

flauescit, color olei, glitinot, VIII. 15 (*Salam.* XXIII. 31 vinum quando *flavescit*). Cf. *flauescit*, glitinat albescit, Cp. F252; *flauescit*, albescit, Ef.[2] 295, 14. For *glitinot*, *glitinat* (from glitinian, to glitter, glisten) see Bosw. T. (*glitinian*); Sievers, *Gr.* § 357 n. 1 and 2, and § 412 n. 5.

flebiles [weak, Fr. *faible*], II. 92, see *inbicilles*.

fledomum, blodsaex, XXXIX. 6 (*Greg. Dial.* I. 4 col. 169[B] in lingua mea medicinale ferramentum, id est *phlebotomum* posuit) = *flebotoma*, blodsaex, Cp. F255. For *blod-saex* (= blod-seax, *a blood-knife, lancet*), see Bosw. T. (sub v.v. *blōd-seax*; *blōd*; *seax*).

flegma, see *sicunia*.

Flora, see *frora*.

floralia, XLIII. 29; see *bachus*.

flore, XXXIX. 1 (bis), see *a primeuo flore*.

flore [for *flores*], X. 12, see *ficus protulit*.

flores, X. 10, see *cyprus*; see also *ficus protulit*.

flos, X. 16, see *crocus*.

fluens, XXXV. 208, see *fluitans*.

fluentis, XXXV. 45, see *suppuratis*.

fluitans, fluens, XXXV. 208 (*Ruf.* VIII. 17 fol. 144[a] omni dissolutionum genere *fluitans*).

fluminis, XII. 24, see *Dorix*; XXIII. 6, see *Stabur*; XXXIX. 10, see *ausaret*.

fluuius, XIX. 22, see *coquiton*.

fluxus, XXIX. 55, see *emurusem*.

fodi, see *foedi*.

fodientur, XIII. 19, see *sarientur*.

foede, XL. 13, see *bachal*.

foederamni [for *foederaui*?], XV. 34, see *foedi*.

foederaui, XVIII. 4, see *foedi*.

foedi, foederamni [for *foederaui*], xv. 34 (*not* in Hiezech.); **foedi**, foederaui, xviii. 4 (*De Ose*) = (*Osee* iii. 2 *fodi* eam mihi quindecim argenteis).

foenus [= fenus = faenus], usura uel lucrum, i. 54 (*De Canon.*; *Can. Conc. Carth.* v nec...liceat...*foenus* accipere; *Decret. Leon.* iv *foenus*, ter). Cf. *foenus*, borg, Cp. F129; fenus, usura debitum, Cp. F133.

foetontis, idest sol, xxxvi. 12 (*Oros.* i. 10, 19 *Phaethontis* fabulam texuerunt; MSS. *foetontis*). Cf. *Foeton*, Solis et Climenæ filius, Cp. F130; Ef.[1] 360, 10; *feton*, solis et climinae filius, Ep. 9C36.

folia, x. 21, see *elatę palmarum*; xiii. 41, see *paliurus*; xvi. 4, see *ilicus*, 5, see *lentiscus*; xxiii. 20, see *frondes*; xxxix. 7, see *erucę*.

folles, see *C. uolles*.

follicantes, see *folligantes*.

folligantes, uestis grossior, xxvi. 5; **follicantes**, uestis grossior, xxvi. 12 (*Isid. Offic.* ii. 16, 10 affectata sunt...omnia, fluxae manicae, caligae *follicantes*, *vestis grossior*, crebra suspiria; see Hier. Ep. 22, 34) = *folligantes*, uestis grossior, Cp. F287.

fomenta, nutrimenta, ii. 75 (*Bened. reg.* 28, 8 [13] si exhibuit *fomenta*, si unguenta adhortationum).

fomite, materia, xxxv. 244 (*Ruf.* ix. 9 fol. 154b ex eo *fomite*).

fomitis, xvi. 10, see *nappa*.

for [for *fors*?], euentus, vi. 13 (*Breu. exsol.* ?). See below *fors*.

foramen, xxii. 12, see *urna*; xxxv. 211, see *cuniculum*.—**foramina**, ubi mittunt gemmas, xv. 21 (*Ezech.* xxviii. 13 *foramina* tua...praeparata sunt. The Cambr. MS.: f. u. mittuntur gemmę).

foramine, xxxv. 27, see *puncto*.

foraminibus, xxii. 12, see *urna*.

foras, xx. 5, see *extricat*; xxix. 57, see *agora*.

forficula, see *auricula*.

fori, iii. 21, see *ad seduforum*; see also *forinnadas*.

foribus, xi. 15, see *in foribus iusti*.

forinnadas, interior pars nauis, xliii. 22 (*De div. nominibus* = Donati *Ars grammat.*, p. 375, 29–31 sunt...nomina in singulari numero alterius generis et alterius in plurali, ut balneum Tartarus...locus iocus *forum*; in note, in MS. L: ioca *fori nauium* [*forum*, or *fori*, the gangways of a ship, see Lewis & Sh.]; the MS., followed by the Glossator, had, perhaps, *forum nauis*).

forma, i. 92, see *pragmatica*; xxxv. 269, see *plasma*.

formam, xxviii. 43, see *caracterismos*; xxxix. 63, see *per pragmaticam formam*; see also *pragmatica*.

formata, see *expolita*.

formatur, xxviii. 85, see *figura sardismos*.

formę [-mae], xxviii. 88, see *diatiposis*.

fornacula [sine interpret.], xv. 28 (*Ezech.* ?). As *fornacula* (small oven, hearth) does not occur in Ezech. it is perhaps a gloss to xv. 27 *arihel* (Ezech. xliii. 15, 16; see *arihellio*); cf. *fornacula*, cyline, heorðe, Cp. F289. The Cambr. MS. has: *fornacula* in quibus faciunt focum ad coquendum.—**fornaculum**, herth, xlii. 12 (*Ex div. libris*); **bornacula**, genus ignis, iii. 22 (*De S. Mart. Stor.* = *Sulp. Sev. Dial.* iii. 14, p. 213, 3 ad *fornaculam*; id. *Epist.* i. 11 super *fornaculam*). Cf. *fornaculum*, here, Cp. F306. For herth (= heorþ), a hearth, fire-place, see Bosw. T. (*heorþ*). For *fornacula*, see also (xv. 42) *culine*. For the above quoted *cyline* (an oven, kiln), a loan-word from the Lat. *culina*, see Bosw. T. (*cylen*); Skeat (*kiln*).

fornaculam, see *fornacula*.

fornicaria, xxxv. 116, see *in prostibulo*.

fornicationis, iv. 72, see *prostipulum*.

fornice, scelb uel drep, xxxv. 59 (*Ruf.* xi. 23 fol. 187b cuncta...quo ad summum pauimentorum euadatur, opere *forniceo* constructa). Is *fornice* perhaps another reading? The meaning of the word, recorded only from this source by Forcellini, is evidently *arched*, *vaulted*.—Scelb occurs as *scelf*, *scelp*, *scelb* in Steinm. *Ahd. Gl.* i. 449. 1 (ad camaram pastorum i.e. *scelf*), ii. 597. 8 (fornice *scelb* uel drep; *scelp*, f. uel derbs); ib. 598. 18 (fornice *scelb* uel dreb). It seems the same as A.S. *scylf* (Bosw. T.) a peak, crag, turret, pinnacle, or *scilfe*, a shelf, ledge, floor; see Grimm, in *Germ.* iii. 4; Kluge, *E. Et.* (shelf); Skeat (*shelf*); *drep* may = Lat. *trabs*, O. Fr. *tref* (a beam, a timber, roof); E. *thrave* (Skeat), a number of sheaves of wheat; see Grimm, l. c. p. 5.

fornicem, signum uictorię, viii. 6 (*Salam.* xx. 26 incurvat super eos *fornicem*).

forniceo, see *fornice*.

foro, otio, i. 56 (*De Canon.*; *Can. Conc. Sardic.* xiii si...aut diues, aut scholasticus de *foro*, aut ex administratione Episcopus fuerit postulatus). The interpretation of *foro* by *otio* becomes clear by *Can. Conc. Carth.* xcvii ut dent facultatem defensores constituendi scholasticos qui *in actu* sunt, vel in munere defensionis causarum.

fors, uyrd, xlv. 4 (*Uerba de multis* = *Ars*

Phocae, p. 412, 3 feminini generis...res spes *sors*) =*fors*, pyrd, Cp. F285; cf. sortem, pyrd, condicionem, Cp. S433, and Goetz vii. 281 (*sors*). Cf. *for*, and for *uyrd* see also above *fatum*.

forte, ii. 182, see *uerbi gratia*.

forti, ii. 125, see *magnopere*.

fortia [Fr. *force*; see Körting, *Lat.-rom. Wört.* in voce], ii. 181, see *uiolentia*.

fortiores, xxi. 12, see *filii titan*.

fortissimi, xliii. 5, see *polideuces*.

fortiter, xii. 28, see *solide*.

fortuito, see *fortuitu*.

fortuitu, subito, ii. 76 (*Bened. reg.* 38, 3 [2] *fortuito* casu; *fortuitu* casu, in notes).

fortunam, see *furtunam*; *furtunatam*.

forum, see *forinnadas*.

fossa, xxiv. 2, see *perna*.

fossorium, xiii. 18, see *sarculum*; see also *ligones*.

fouit, cubat calefaciendo, xiii. 44 (*Isai.* xxxiv. 15 *fovit* in umbra). For *fouit* see also (xiv. 11) *perdix*.

fracta, xxvi. 9, see *decrepita*.

fractura [for *factura* ?], xxx. 27, see *de piasma*.

fragile, fragilis, see *friuolis*.

fragor, uox uel sonitus, xxxv. 215 (*Ruf.* x. 17 fol. 170[b] *fragor* omnium... attollitur).

francis, xxxv. 70, see *calonum*.

frangent [for frangunt], xiii. 47, see *plaustrum*.

frangit, xliv. 24, see *alcianus*.

frangunt, see *plaustrum*.

frasi, see *effrasi*, sub v. *phraysi*.

fraterna, fraterno, see *examine*.

fratri, xxix. 73, see *qui dixerit fratri*, &c.

fratris, xxix. 19, see *fratruelis*.

fratruelis, filius fratris, xxix. 19 (*Uerb. Interpr.* = *Hier. in Matth.* xiii. 52, quoting from *Cant.* vii. 13 nova et vetera, *fratruelis* meus, servavi tibi; cf. *note*[d], Migne, *P. L.* xxvi. 95, and Sabatier). Cf. *fratuelis*, geaduling, suhterga, broðorsunu, Cp. F318–320, for which see Bosw. T. (*gædeling*; *suhteriga*; *broðor + sunu*).

fraudare, xlviii. 17, see *conpellare*.

fraudulenter, xxxv. 132, see *fefellit*.

fraus, xxix. 28, see *strofa*; see also *Chri fiscus*.

freniticus, insanus ob dolorem capitis ad tempus [temple of the head] qui multum uigilat, xxxix. 19 (*Greg. Dial.* iii. 35 col. 301[c] mente captus...quem medici... *phreneticum* appellant) = *freniticus*, insanus ex dolore capitis, Cp. F330; Ep. 9C7; Ef.[1] 360, 41.

freno, xii. 34, see *infrunita*.

frenorum, xi. 9, see *abene*.

frequenter, xxxv. 260, see *lacessit*.

fretus, confidens, iii. 45 (*De S. Mart. Stor.* = *Sulp. Sev. Dial.* ii. 5, 8 *fretus* auxilio).

-frigia [Phrygia], xxxv. 30, see *genefrix*.

frigilla, see *fringella*.

frigor, xlvii. 3, see *rigor*.

fringella, uinc, xlvii. 69 (*Alia* = ?) = *fringella*, finc, Cp. F331; Ep. 9C9; Ef.[1] 360, 43. For *fringella* (*fringilla*, *frigilla*, *fringuilla*, perh. *the robin-redbreast*, or *the chaffinch*) see Lewis & Sh. For *uinc*, *finc* see Bosw. T. (*finc*).

fringilla, fringuilla, see *fringella*.

friuolis, frugalis, xxix. 16 (*Uerb. Interpr.* = *Hier. in Matth.* xii. 36, 37 de rebus *frivolis* loquamur). Cf. fribolum, fragile, Cp. F321 and Ep. 9A21; fribolum, *fragillae*, Ef.[1] 360, 17; Goetz iv. 519, 22 (Glossae affatim) friuulus, uilis *fragilis*; id. v. 296, 32 (Ef.[2]) fribula *frigulis* &c.

friuolus, see *truffulus*.

frixi ciceris, faue [fabae] siccate [-tae] in sole, xxix. 13 (*Uerb. Interpr.* = *Hier. in Matth.* xxi. 12, 13 munuscula...*frixi ciceris*) = frixi ciceris, fauae siccatę in sole, Cp. F343.

frondes dicitur quando folia habet, xxiii. 20 (2 *Esdr.* viii. 15 afferte *frondes* olivae, et *frondes* ligni pulcherrimi &c.).

frora, mater dearum, xliii. 27 (*De div. nominibus*; perhaps for *Flora*, and, as such, a further explanation of xliii. 29); see *floralia*.

fruatur, ii. 186, see *utatur*.

fructuosae, xvii. 20, see *myrteta*.

fructus, xvi. 5, see *lentiscus*; xxv. 6, see *de siliquis*.

fructusque, xvi. 4, see *ilicus*.

fruga, modestia, xxxv. 301 (*Ruf.* ii. 16 fol. 26[a] *frugi* eorum sobriaque conuiuia) = *frugi*, modestia, Cp. F354; *frui*, modestia, Ef.[2] 296, 27.—**frugis**, parcus, xii. 32 (*Eccles.* xxxi. 19 homo *frugi*).

frugali, larga uel lata, xxvii. 3 (*Lib. Rot.* = *Isid. de nat. rer.*, but not found there); **frugali**, larga uel lata, xxviii. 6 (*Lib. Anton.* ?). Cf. *frugalis*, largus, Cp. F333; Ep. 9C19; Ef.[1] 360, 52.

frugalis, xxix. 16, see *friuolis*.

frugalitas, penuria, xlviii. 12 (*De Cass.*, *Inst.* v. 9 tantum...*frugalitatis* indicere).

frugalitatis, see *frugalitas*.

frugi, see *fruga*; *frugis*.

frugis, parcus, xii. 32, see *fruga*.

frumenti, xlv. 15, see *ador*.

frumentorum, i. 111, see *sicera*.

frumentum, xlv. 9, see *far*.

fuco, pigmento, xxxv. 306 (*Ruf.* iv. 8 fol. 57[a] adulterino maledicorum *fuco*).—

fucum, colorem, xxxv. 63 (*Ruf.* xi. 25 fol. 189ᵃ adulterii *fucum*).
fuerit, ii. 57; viii. 19; x. 6.
fugantem, xlviii. 4, see *uacillantem.*
fugerit, see *si usque ad lacum f-.*
fuit, xxxvi. 1; xxxix. 28.
fulgorantes aste, quando fulgurant contra solem, xvii. 12 (*Nahum* iii. 2, 3 vox...*fulgurantis hastae*; *Habac.* iii. 11 in splendore *fulgurantis hastae*; cf. Migne, *P.L.* xxix col. 1028ᴮ&ᶜ *fulgurantes hastae*).
fulgura, xi. 11, see *in aqua.*
fulgurant, xvii. 12, see *fulgorantes.*
fulgurantis, see *fulgorantes.*
fuligo, see *uligo.*
fullonum, xvii. 19, see *herba fullonum.*
fulmentatur, initiatur, xl. 12 (*Uerba* =?).
fundamentum, xxxv. 192, see *basis.*
funestare, cruentare, xxxv. 236 (*Ruf.* xi. 28 fol. 190ᵃ mori gratius habentes quam...piaculo *funestari*).
funestari, see *funestare.*
funestis, mortiferis uel scelestis, i. 53 (*De Canon.*; *Can. Conc. Ancyr.* xxiii *funestis* sacrificiis admoverent).
fungantur, i. 101, see *procuratores.*
fungi, administrare, ii. 78 (*Bened. reg.* 62, 3 [4] qui dignus sit sacerdotio *fungi*).
funicu†, xl. 7, see *crinicu†.*
funis, xii. 37, see *lor*; xxi. 11, see *restis.*
furci (!), xlii. 26, see *furcifer.*
furcifer, furci (!) idest cruci dignus, xlii. 26 (*Ex div. libris* = *Vita S. Eug.* 14, Migne lxxiii col. 613ᴰ Dic nunc, *furcifer*, quae te temeritas coegit) = *furcifer*, cruci dignus, Cp. F373; Ep. 9C13; Ef.¹ 360, 47.
furia, see *striga.*
furibunda, see *furibundus.*
furibundus, feruens, iii. 27 (*De S. Mart. Stor.* = *Sulp. Sev. Dial.* iii. 15, 2 Brictio *furibundus* inrupit; *Dial.* ii. 9, 2 uacca... *furibunda*).
furnus, see *clibanus.*
furtunam, fatum geuiif, xxxv. 157 (*De Eus.*); **furtunatam**, prosperitatem, iv. 49 (*Eccl. Istor.*) = (*Ruf.* iv. 15 fol. 62ᵇ iura *fortunam* Caesaris...; ibid. vt *fortunam* Caesaris iuraret &c.). For *geuiif* (for *geuuif*) a web; fate, fortune, see Bosw. T. (*ge-wef, gewife*).
furtunatam, prosperitatem, iv. 49, see *furtunam.*
furunculas, maerth, xlvii. 76 (*Alia* = ?) = *furuncus*, mearð, Cp. F383; *f-*, mearth, Ep. 9C11; *f-*, meard, Ef.¹ 360, 45; (*furunculas*, for) *furunculus* is known already in Class. Lat. as meaning *a petty thief*; see Lewis & Sh. In this case it is apparently a dim. of *furuncus* in the Cp., Ep. and Ef.¹ Glossaries, and means a little ferret (Germ. *Frettchen*, see Kluge, *D.*). For *maerth*, *mearð* &c. (a marten, kind of weasel, Germ. *Marder*, see Kluge, *D.*), see Bosw. T., where some forms *fer-* are recorded.
furuncus, see *furunculas.*
fuscinulas, vii. 5, see *creacras.*
fusor, xxxix. 11, see *uini fusor.*
fusoris, see *uini fusor.*
fusorium [for *fossorium*?], xvii. 2, see *ligones.*
fuste, xxxv. 79, see *claua.*
fusticellus, xv. 5, see *paxillus.*
fustis, xlv. 18, see *pedum.*
fusum, x. 6, see *unguentum exinanitum.*
futura, xii. 42, see *uasa*; xvi. 30, see *aruspices.*
future [-rae], xxviii. 42, see *idea.*

g for *c*: bra*g*as (for bracas); folli*g*antes (follic-); *g*attas; *g*ladibus; *g*lebum (for cliuum); *g*raticulis; opa*g*o; ran*g*or; trun*g*atis.—for *ch*: tro*g*leis (troc*h*leis).—for *z*: scandali*g*eris (-lizeris).—g *omitted*: tra*i*ca, tra*i*cus (tra*g*ica &c.); zeuma (zeu*g*ma); see also su*g*illat- or su*gg*-.
Gabaa, ciuitas Saulis, xiii. 26 (*Isai.* x. 29 *Gaba* sedes nostra...*Gabaath* Saulis fugit).
Gabaath, see *Gabaa.*
galbanum, galbanus, see *calbanus.*
Galerius, propter [proprium] nomen, xxxv. 209 (*Ruf.* viii. 19 fol. 146ᵃ *Galerius* Maximianus).
galeros, galerum, see *calomaucus.*
galli, see *antelucanum.*
gallina, see *scarpmat.*
ganniret, quasi cum ira inrideret, xiii. 23 (*Isai.* x. 14 aperiret os et *ganniret*) = *ganniret*, cum ira quasi ridet, Cp. G2.
garallus, hroc, xlvii. 51 (*Alia* = ?) = *grallus*, hrooc, Cp. G154; Ep. 10E4; Ef.¹ 363, 18. For (*garallus*, *grallus* =) *graculus*, a jackdaw, see Körting, 4310; Goetz, vi. 499 (*graculus*). For *hroc*, *hrooc* see Bosw. T. (*hrōc*, a rook, raven), Kluge & Lutz, *Engl. Et.* (*rook*); Skeat.
garrientium, per ludum dicentium, xxxv. 199 (*Ruf.* viii. 10 fol. 139ᵃ *garrientium* dicta).
gastrimargia, appetitus uentris, xxxiv. 36 (*De Cass., Inst.* xii. 3, 2 *gastrimargia*, id est *adpetitus uentris*; see ibid. v. 1 sqq.).
gattas, muriceps, xxxviii. 4 (*Clem. Recognitt.* v. 20 alii bovem...colendum tradidere, alii hircum, alii *cattas*).
gaudens, xxxv. 173, see *ouans.*
gazarum, diuitiarum, xv. 19 (*Ezech.* xxvii. 24 *gazarum*que pretiosarum). Cf. *gaza*, diuitiae, Cp. G16; *gaza*, census uel diuitiae, Ep. 10E3; Ef.¹ 363, 17; *gesiae* (for *gazae*), diuitiae, Cp. G70; *gesieae*

[second *e* marked for erasure], diuitiae, Ep. 11A2; *gessiae*, diuitiae, Ef.[1] 363, 55.

gazofilatia [gazophylacia], IV. 92, see *pastoforia*.

gazophylacia, see *pastoforia*.

geminat, XXVIII. 68, see *anadiplosis*.

gemmae, see *carbasini*.

gemmas, XIV. 16, see *inclusor*; XV. 21, see *foramina*.

gemme [-mae], XXII. 7, see *carbasini*.

genealogia, generatione, XXX. 58 (*Cat. Hier.* LXIII col. 675A in *genealogia* Salvatoris; B: in *geneologia* s.; C: inni [blank]) = *genealogia*, generatio, Cp. G35; *gen-*, generatione, Ep. 10C10; *gaenelogia*, generatio, Ef.[1] 362, 44. For *genealogia* see also *a theologia*.

genefrix, de frigia [Phrygia] ciuitate, XXXV. 30 (*Ruf.* V. 3 fol. 77b Alexander quidam *genere Phryx*).

genera, XLIII. 23, see IIII.

generale, see *deucalionem*.

generales, XLI. 2, see *chorepiscopi*, in voc. *presbiteri*.

generare [for *generale*?], XXXVIII. 22, see *deucalionem*.

generatione, IV. 114, see *a theologia*; XXX. 58, see *genealogia*.

generationis, XXIII. 2, see *filii*.

generatus, XIX. 39, see *leopardus*.

genere, XXXIX. 15, see *ferula*; see also *genefrix*.

generis, XLIII. 6, see *notha*.

genesim, natura, XXXVIII. 8 (*Clem. Recognitt.* VIII. 4 *genesim* dico esse; VIII. 7 introduxi *genesim*; VIII. 57 extra *genesim*; *genesim*, IX. 26).

genethliaci, see *genthliatici*.

geniculorum, genuum dimiuitiuum, XVII. 10 (*Nahum* II. 10 dissolutio *geniculorum*).

geniculum, see *giniscula*s.

genilogia [geneal-], XXXV. 17, see *a theologia*.

genis, XIII. 56, see *uellentibus*.

geniscula, genisculae, genisculas, see *giniscula*s.

genitor, II. 4, see *abba*.

genium, natura, XLV. 14 (*Uerba de multis* = *Ars Phocae*, p. 427, 26 pulvis sanguis *genius*....).

genius, see *genium*.

gens, XIV. 26, see *Lidii*; XXI. 3, see *subal*; XLIII. 4, see *arcades*.

gentem, XXXVI. 1, see *Iani*.

genthliatici, gentiles, XXVII. 17; **genthliatici**, gentiles uel naturalium scriptores, XXVII. 27 (*Lib. Rot.* = *Isid. Lib. de nat. rer.* XXVI. 13 *Genethliaci*...dicunt) = *genthliatici*, gentiles, Cp. G56; Ep. 10E7; *genthiliatici*, g-, Ef.[1] 363, 21.

gentiles, XXVII. 17, 27, see *genthliatici*.

gentis, XV. 12, see *bibli*, 15, see *Dan*; XXXV. 70, see *calonum*; XXXVI. 1, see *Iani*, 2, see *Armenias pilas*.

gentium, X. 7, see *aduliscentulę*.

genuinum decus, naturale uel intimum, I. 57 (*De Canon.*; *Can. Conc. Gangr.*, praef., ap. Maassen *Canon. Recht*, I. 936 *genuini decoris*; Migne, *Patrol. Lat.* LXXXIV col. 111D *id.*). Cf. *genuinum*, intimum, Cp G76; *genuino*, tusc naturale, Cp. G62; Ep. —; *genuinum*, intimum uel dens id est tusc, Ef.[1] 363, 56; *genuinum*, initium uel dens qui interius in ore hominis, Ef.[2] 297, 54. For *tusc* (tusk) see Bosw. T. & Skeat, in voce.

genuit, XXXV. 144, see *enixa est*.

genus, II. 106; III. 6, 22, 39, 43; XII. 36; XVI. 10; XIX. 15; XXIX. 9; XXXV. 90; XXXVII. 4; XXXIX. 60; XLIII. 15; XLV. 10, 15; XLVI. 14, 15, 16.

genuum, XVII. 10, see *geniculorum*.

geometriam, see *geometrica* sub v. *dialectica*.

geometrica, terre mensura, XXX. 48; = *gaeometrica*, terrae mensuratio, Cp. G1; *geometria*, terrae mensuratio, Ep. 10C8; *geometrica*, terrae mensuratio, Ef.[1] 362, 42; see sub v. *dialectica*. For *geometrica*, see also (XL. 10) *cicima*.

georgicis, XXVII. 28, see *in georgicis*.

gerit, XXXV. 22, see *curione*.

gesta, scripta, XXXV. 51 (*Ruf.* X. 17 fol. 170b *gesta* in hunc modum ficta).—**gesta municipalia**, uel publica, I. 58 (*De Canon.*; *Can. Conc. Carth.* LXIX per *gesta*...*municipalia*).

gestantes, portantes, II. 82 (*Bened. reg.*?).

gestire, desiderare, XXXV. 259 (*Ruf.* VI. 16 fol. 106b *gestire* coepit; X. 9 fol. 164b *gestire* ut...).—**gestiunt**, uolunt, XLVIII. 11 (*De Cass.*, *Inst.* VII. 16 ad suum desiderium *gestiunt* deprauare).

gestus, I. 127, see *striones*.

Giblij, see *bibli*.

gigantemachie, gigantum pugne, XXXV. 95 (*Ruf.* I. 1 fol. 3b *Gigantomachiae* exortae sunt) = *gigantomacie*, gigantum pugna, Cp. G98; *gigantomacię*, gigantum pugnae, Ep. 10C8; *gigantomaciae*, gigantium pugnae, Ef.[1] 363, 22.

gigantes, XIX. 51, see *fabula*.

gigantomachiae, see *gigantemachie*.

gigantum, XXXV. 95, see *gigantemachie*.

ginisculas, idem, XLVII. 75 (*Alia* = ?) = *genisculus* [for -las], muscellas, Cp. G55; *genisculas*, muscellas, Ep. 10E5; *genisculae*, muscellae, Ef.[1] 363, 19. As this gloss follows after *sardinus* [for -nas], heringas, the word *idem* (if it be not a corruption, or does not refer to some omitted lemma) may indicate that *genisculae* (gin-) were also regarded as herrings. Goetz (vi. 488) inserts the present gloss under *geniculum*, and regards *muscellae* (*-las*) as A.S., which would agree with Wright W. 261, 34 geniscula, muxle; 293, 21 & 413, 37 geniscula, mucxle. See also Bosw. T. (*muscelle*).

girouagum, circumuacantium [circumuag-], ii. 80 (*Bened. reg.*, 1, 21 Quartum... genus ... monachorum ... nominatur *gyrouagum*; [29] *id.*, in note *girouagum*).

git, see *gyt*.

gladiatores, iv. 19, see *sicarii*.

gladibus, uindictis, xxxv. 104 (*Ruf.* ii. 5 fol. 20[b] ubi de Iudaeorum *cladibus* refert; ii. 7 fol. 22[a] *cladibus* cruciatus est). There is: ne *gladiis*...vterentur, ii. 6 fol. 22[a], and: ceruices suas persecuutorum *gladiis* obiicere, i. 1 fol. 6[b], but *cladibus* is no doubt the right word; cf. *cladibus*, uindictio, Cp. C453.

gladiis, see *gladibus*.

gladius, iv. 20, see *pungios*.

glandes, see *ilicus*.

glandi (!), xvi. 4, see *ilicus*.

glarea, lapides modici, xix. 21 (*Job* xxi. 33 dulcis fuit *glareis* Cocyti; xxx. 6 super *glaream*). Cf. *glarea*, cisilstan, Cp. G111; *glarea*, cisil, Ep. 10C21; *glare*, cisal, Ef.[1] 362, 54. For the A.S. words in Cp., Ep., Ef. see Bosw. T. (*ceōsel*, *cisil-stān*, gravel, sand); Verdam, *Woordenb.* (*Kesel*; *Keselsteen* = D. *Kiezelsteen*); Franck, *Etym. Woordenb.* (*Kiezel*).

glaream, glareis, see *glarea*.

glebam, cispitem [cesp-], xxxv. 118 (*Ruf.* ii. 17 fol. 27[a] ad...patriae *glebam*). Cf. *gleba*, cespes dura, Cp. G103.

glebum, ascensum singularis uia, xxxix. 44 (*Greg. Dial.* iii. 6 col. 229[B] ad Fundanum *clivum* perveniens) = *clibum*, ascensus uiae singularis, Cp. C465; *clibum*, ascensus singularis uiae, Ep. 8A18; *cliuium*, ascensus singularis uiae, Ef.[1] 351, 50.

glis, egle, xlv. 6 (*Uerba de multis* = *Ars Phocae*, p. 412, note 1 fax fraus fex lens *glis* [text *glos*] lux lex; note 2 [glos] glix, *glis*) = Cp. G104 (*glis*, egle); Ep. 10E6 (*glis*, eglae); Ef.[1] 363, 20 (*glis*, egilae). As the well-known Lat. *glis* (gliris) means a dormouse, *egle* &c. have been taken in the same sense; see ex. gr. Kluge (*A.S. Leseb.* p. 172) ëgle, spitzmaus. But Schlutter (*Anglia*, xix. 474) is of opinion that *egle* &c. = E. *ail*(s), the awn of barley or other corn (Germ. *Achel*), for which see *Oxf. D.*; *Cent. Dict.* This is confirmed by other glosses as *glumula*, scale uel hule, uel egle (*Zeitschr. f. d. Alt.* ix. 439); *arista*, egla (Alfr. Vocab., in Wright W. 148, 28); *fistucam*, strewu, eglan (ib. 405, 33 & 479, 25); *aresta*, egle (ib. 273, 22); *glis*, fonfyr [for furfur?] oððe egle (ib. 413, 12); *aristis*, eglum oððe earum (ib. 347, 29); *gliribus*, eglum (ib. 414, 28; 533, 33). It is to be observed that the texts of Phocas vary between *glos*, *glis* and *glix*, and that of *glis* at least three meanings are recorded: (1) *glis*, gliris, a dormouse; (2) *glis*, glitis, humus tenax; (3) *glis*, glissis, incrementum. As regards *glix* (for which some would read *glis*), a Gloss. Lat. Gr. has ἵππουρος ἰχθύς a sea-fish, for which Du C. proposes to read ἵππουρις, a water-plant, mare's-tail = *equisetum*. It is, therefore, not impossible that egle &c. may have had more meanings than one; see *egel*, in Verdam, *Mid. Ned. Woordenb.* (1) hedgehog; (2) = hirudo, a leech. See further Forcellini; De Vit, Gloss. p. 615; Diefenbach; Du Cange.

glisco, cresco, xlvi. 38 (*Alia* = *Ars Phocae*, p. 436, 24 *glisco*).

glix, see *glis*.

globum, xliv. 29, see *axem*.

globus, rotunditas, xxxv. 220 (*Ruf.* x. 39 fol. 177 *globus* quidam ignis; xi. 15 fol. 184[b] armatorum *globum*...mittit) = globus, pila rotunditas, Cp. G110.

gloria, xxxiv. 12, see *cenodoxia*.

gloriantium, xli. 4, see *orthodoxam*.

gloriosi, xxx. 94, see *ortodoxon*.

gloriosis, ii. 129, see *ortodoxis*.

glos, see *glis*.

GLOSAE UERBORUM DE CANONIBUS, I *tit.*

gnauiter, see *nauiter*.

gnostici, scientes, iv. 43 (*Ruf.* iv. 8 fol. 56[b] qui *Gnostici* appellantur).

gomor, mensura est attica habens ut quidam oppinantur conices iii idest sextarios xii Alii gomor dicunt sextarios v quod etiam ipse sequor eo quod decima pars sit ephi, xxxiii. 16 (*Euch. De Pond.*, p. 159, 10 *gomor* m.e.A.h.u.q. opinantur c. tres i.s. xii a.g.d. paulo minus a sextariis quinque, q. &c.).—**gomor maior** in ose [iii. 2, Hebr. & Gr. texts] xu modios, xxxi. 1; **modicus** autem **gomor**, xxii sextarios, xxxi. 2 (*De ponder.*?). Cf. Blume, i. 376, 12.—**comor** [gomor] **minor** septem sextarios et u [quinta] pars sextarii cotile dimedium, xxxi. 9 (*De ponder.*).—For *gomor*, see also (xxxiii. 20) *colamina*.

gorgonicum, gorthonicum, gortonicum, see *toronicum*.

graciarum, see *panagericon*.

graculus, see *garallus*.

gradatim, xxviii. 69, see *emphasis*.

gradatio, gradibus, xxviii. 32, see *climax*.
gradu, i. 65 and xxxix. 53, see *in pulpito*.
gradu suo, honore priuato, ii. 81 (*Bened. reg.?* Cf. in ultimo *gradu* recipiatur, 29, 5 [6]; *gradum* bonum sibi adquirit, 31, 12 [21]). De *gradu suo* deiecerint eum occurs *Can. Conc. Carth.*, *Prol.* p. 142b, and it is possible that this gloss may have strayed from its proper place in Ch. i. of the Glossary into Ch. ii.
graece, see *grece*.
graecorum, see *Saturnus*.
graecos, see *hiemisperium*.
graecum, see *clima*.
grallus, see *garallus*.
grammateos, grammatius [-ticus?], xxix. 54 (*Uerb. Interpr.*=*Hier in Matth.* viii. 19, 20 litterator erat, quod significantius Graece dicitur γραμματεύς).
grammatica, literali [for *literalis*?], xxx. 49 (=*grammatica* litteralis, Cp. G144; Ep. 10C9; Ef.[1] 362, 43), see *dialectica*.
grammaticam, see *grammatica*.
grammaticus, see *grammateos*.
grammatius [-ticus?], xxix. 54, see *grammateos*.
grana, viii. 18, see *ptisanas*; xvi. 5, see *lentiscus*; xxxi. 17, see *Grece*; xxxiii. 25, see *siliqua una*.
granatis, x. 26, see *mustum*.
granis, see *lentiscus*.
graphium, xiv. 20, see *scalpellum*.
gratia, x. 1, see *osculetur me*; xii. 13, see *alacriter*; xlii. 24, see *uectandi*.—**gratia**, ii. 182, see *uerbi gratia*.
gratiarum, xxx. 60, see *eucharistias*.
graticulis, ferreis factis [flectis, abl. plur. of *flecta*, a hurdle?] herst, xxxv. 175 (*Ruf.* v. 3 fol. 78b ut...*craticulis* exusta gauderet). For *herst* (=hearst, hierst, a small hurdle?), gridiron, see Bosw. T. (*hearste*); Wright W. 214, 40.
grauem, i. 106, see *querimoniam*.
grauis, xxxv. 186, see *infestus*.
grauitas, modestia, ii. 83 (*Bened. reg.* 7, 136 [219]; 22, 12 [21]; 42, 21 [37]; 43, 5 [5]; 47, 8 [14] cum *grauitate*).
grauitate, see *grauitas*.
grece [graece], i. 6, see *absidam*, 19, see *concilium*, 22, see *caticumini*, 31, see *catholicus*, 49, see *epistilia*, 80, see *omousion*, 114, see *synodus*, 118, see *simbulum*; ii. 2, see *anachorita*, 33, see *cenobita*, 107, see *monachus*; xxxi. 17, 32, see *sextarius*, 33, see *mina*, 34, see *statera*; xxxiii. 3, see *talentum*, 11, see *chatus*, 13, see *metreta*; xlvii. 95, see *philocain*.
Grece [Graece] **idest cercetea**, cercetea iiii grana ordei, xxxi. 17 (*De ponder.?*).
greci [graeci], xxxi. 7, see *libra*.
gręcia [graecia], xxx. 2, see *Canisius*.
grecis [graecis], xxxii. 1, see *dragma*.
greco [graeco], ii. 188, see *coenobium*.
grecorum [graec-], xxviii. 9, see *Saturnus*.
grecos [graecos], ii. 189, see *monasterium*; xliv. 19, see *hiemisperium*.
grecum [graec-], xliv. 11, see *clima*.
gregorii, xxxvii. 9, see *tabulas legat*.
gremio, xxxix. 8, see *in gremio*.
gressus, xxxi. 24, see *choros*.
grossa, xiii. 41, see *paliurus*.
grossior, xix. 8, see *murenula*; xxvi. 5, see *folligantes*, 12, see *follicantes*.
grossos, x. 12, see *ficus protulit grossos*...
gubernatio, see *diocesis*.
gubernationem, ii. 43, see *diocesim*.
gubernationibus, i. 36, see *diocesis*.
gurdonicum, see *toronicum*.
gurgitum, modica congregatio aque a pluuie, xix. 53 (*Job* xxxvi. 27 effundit imbres ad instar *gurgitum*).
gurgulio, see *gurgullio*.
gurgullio, drohbolla, xlv. 27 (*Uerba de multis*=*Ars Phocae*, p. 413 *curculio*; in note *gurgulio*)=*gurgulio*, ðrotbolla, Cp. G180; Ef.[1] 362, 45; *gurgulio*, throtbolla, Ep. 10C11. *Drohbolla* &c.=þrot-bolla (Bosw. T.), the gullet, windpipe (*ðrotu*, the throat, +*bolla*, a round vessel, cup, bowl), cf. E. *thropple*.
gurgustium, chelor, xix. 38 (*Job* xl. 26 Numquid implebis sagenas pelle eius, et *gurgustium* piscium capite illius?). *Gurgustium*, a small dwelling, hovel, hut; *chelor*, O.H.G. (see Schade, in vv. *cĕlur*, *kĕla*)=A.S. *ceolor* (=Germ. *Kehle*, throat, *Keller*, cellar, see Schlutter, in *Anglia* xix. 493) from the Lat. *cellarium* (see Kluge, *Angels. Lesebuch* 166). Cf. Steinm. iii. 7, 41 gurgustium, celur; *id.* i. 497, 6 gurgustium, chelor (celor, caelor, cilor). The Cambr. MS. has: gurgustium, ubi pisces mittunt capti. Cf. Cp. G176, 177, 181, 183, 187.
gurtonicum, see *toronicum*.
gutta, de arbore currit idest balsamum, x. 19 (*Cant.* v. 2 caput meum plenum est rore, et cincinni mei *guttis* noctium). For *gutta* see also (xii. 21) *ungula et gutta*; *cassia*.
guttis, see *gutta*.
gymnasium, locus exercitationis ubi diuerse [-sae] arte [artes] discantur, xlv. 1 (*Uerba de multis*=*Ars Phocae*, p. 411, 6 *gymnasium* sapientiae).
gymnicus agon, see *diatripas*.
gyrouagum, see *girouagum*.
gyt, genus seminis herbis minuta bona in panes mittere, xlv. 10 (*Uerba de multis*

=*Ars Phocae*, p. 412, 5 neutri generis... fas far *git*). Cf. *git*, olus, Cp. G89; Ep. 10C12; Ef.[1] 362, 46. Cf. E. *gith* (Oxf. D.).

h *inserted*: ab*h*ominatio (for abom-); et*h*imologia (etymol-); scit*h*is (scitis).—*dropped* or *omitted*: abenis (*h*ab-); agiografa (*h*ag-); arcimandritis (arc*h*-); autenticum (aut*h*-); aste (*h*astae); biblioteca (-t*h*eca); ciatos, cyati, cyatos (-t*h*os, -t*h*i, -t*h*os); distrauntur (-*h*untur); eptaticum (*h*ept-); erba, frequently (*h*e-); erodis (*H*er-); exortatio (ex*h*ort-); iacincto, iacinctino, iacyntini (*h*yacint*h*ini &c.); omonima (*h*om-); onorauit (*h*on-); onoribus (*h*on-); ortans (*h*o-); ortodoxis (ort*h*-); ortum (*h*o-); ospicium (*h*os-); ridhmus (r*h*ythm-); rinocerus (r*h*in-); scismatici (sc*h*ism-); superumerale (super*h*-); teristra (t*h*er-); torax (t*h*or-); ueendo (ue*h*endo); yperbolen (*h*yp-); ypozeuxis (*h*yp-).—*prefixed*: *h*arene (ar-); *h*eremita (er-); *h*ibicum (ib-); *h*ironiam (ir-).—*transposed*: c*h*antari (cant*h*ari).

h[*oc est*, or *autem*], IV. 98, see *comellas*.

h [=ἤ], XXX. 16, see *ho platon*.

habebant, VIII. 8, see *in aceruo m-*.

habebantur, XI. 14, see *poderis*.

habene, see *abene* (for *a bene*).

habenis, see *abenis*.

habens, I. 88; IV. 120; X. 10; XI. 4; XII. 9; XIII. 18, 36, 41, 43, 47, 57; XVI. 4, 5; XXII. 12; XXIX. 9; XXXI. 36; XXXII. 6, 7; XXXIII. 6, 11, 16; XXXIX. 32; XLI. 8.

habent, XIII. 6, 9, 47; XIV. 20; XV. 43; XXI. 10; XXII. 16; XXXIII. 13; XXXIX. 7; XLV. 18; XLVII. 28.

habentes, XI. 10, see *signum habentes*; XXII. 12, see *urna*.

habentque, XIV. 3, see *uorith*.

habentur, I. 90; XVI. 27; XXXIX. 62.

habere, II. 161; XXVIII. 74.

habet, XIX. 31; XXIII. 20; XXXI. 37, 39; XXXII. 8–11; XXXIII. 1, 3, 4, 7, 8, 12; XLI. 7, 10, 11, 13, 16 (bis); XLII. 21; XLIII. 51.

habetur, I. 39; VIII. 17.

habilis, I. 62, see *idonea*.

habita, see *uabita*.

habitaculum, II. 188, see *coenobium*.

habitat, XXVIII. 28, see *metonymia*; XXXVI. 11, see *musca canina*; XLVII. 89, see *bulinus*.

habitatio, II. 189, see *monasterium*.

habitum, XXVIII. 57, see *figura*.

habitus, XXVIII. 88, see *diatiposis*.

habuerunt, see *presbiteras*.

habuit, XXXIX. 22, 23.

habundantius, XXXV. 108, see *profusius*.

hac, XXX. 13, see *ieretícos*; XLIII 35, see *hac*.—**hac**, in hac parte, XLIII. 35; **illac**, in illa parte, XLIII. 36 (*De div. nominibus* =Donati *Ars gramm*. p. 386, 22 adiciunt quidam etiam per locum, ut *hac illac*).

Hades, see *aides*.

haecthetas, see *hecthetas*.

haemorrhousa, see *emurusem*.

haeresis, see *secta*.

haereticam, see *hereticum*.

hagiographa, see *agiografa*.

harena, XLII. 17, see *sirte*.

harene, theatri, XXXV. 29 (*De Eus.*); **harene**, locus uel pauimentum theatri, XXXV. 171 (*De Eus.*)=(*Ruf.* v. 2 fol. 76[b] in medio *arenae*; id. ibid. v. 3 fol. 78[a])= *harenae*, pauimentum theatri, Cp. H22; *harenae*, locus uel pauimentum theatri, Ep. 11C10; *harenae*, lacus uel pauimentum theatri, Ef.[1] 364, 44, 45.

harpa, see *arpa*.

hastae, see *fulgorantes aste*.

hebenenos uel **eberenos**, de arbore hebore, XV. 14 (*Ezech*. XXVII. 15 dentes *eburneos* et *hebeninos* commutauerunt). For *hebore*, ebore, see also *ebor*.

hebeninos, see *hebenenos*.

hebenus, see *ebor*.

hebore, XV. 14, see *hebenenos*.

hebraeum, see *sicera*.

hebraicarum, XXXIII. 5, see *dedragma*.

hebraice, XXI. 16, see *conopeum*.

hebraicum, XXXIII. 13, see *metreta*.

hebreum [hebraeum], I. 111, see *sicera*.

hec [=haec], XXVIII. 83, see *ennoematice*; XXX. 17, see *ho platon*.

hecthetas [sine interpret.], XV. 25 (*Ezech*. XLI. 15, 16 mensus est...*ethecas* ex vtraque parte centum cubitorum...fenestras obliquas et *ethecas* in circuitu; Heyse, in note, *ecthetas* in 15 & 16; Migne, *Patr. Lat.* XXVIII col. 1001, note b *hecthetas*, *haecthetas* &c.).

hederam, ibaei, XVII. 11 (*Jonas* IV. 6 praeparauit...Deus *hederam*; *hederam* also IV. 7, 10; IV. 6, 9 super *hedera*). Cf. *eder*, ifegn, Cp. E33; Ep. —; *edera*, ifeg, Ef.[1] 359, 40; Steinm. I. 676. 1, 677. 41; for *ibaei* (=O.H.G. ëba-hewi, M.H.G. ëphöu, G. epheu; A.S. ifiȝ, short for if-hiȝ) see Kluge, *E. Etym.* (*ivy*); Bosw. T. (*ifig*); Kluge, *Et. Wrt.* (*epheu*).

helcesei, XVII. 8, see *naum*.

hemina, see *colamina*.

heminam, see *himina*, sub v. *emina*.

hemisphaeria, see *hiemisperia*; *partes*.

hemisphaerium, see *hiemisperium*.

hemorrhousa, see *emurusem*.

heortasticae, see *eortatica*.

heptateuchos, see *eptaticum*.

heptaticum, see *eptaticum*.

herba, XXIX. 10, see *uiola*, 35, see *pisticum*; XXXVIII. 16, see *ochimo*. See also *capparis*; *cassia*; *cucumerarium*; *cyprus*; *erba*; *paliurus*; *saliuncula*; *uorith*.

herba fullonum, borit [=borith, Hebr. בְּרִית] quia inde faciunt saporem [for *saponem*], XVII. 19 (*Malach.* III. 2 quasi *herba fullonum*).

herbae, see *crocus*; *malagma*; *murra*.

herbarum, XLII. 20, see *in uiridario domus*. See also *quisquilia*.

herbe [-bae], X. 16, see *crocus*, 18, see *murra*; XI. 12, see *malagma*; XXXIV. 5, see *xerofagia*.

herbę [-bae], XLVI. 15, see *laser*.

herbis, XXI. 11, see *restis*; XLV. 10, see *gyt*.

hercule, see *miherculi*.

heremita, remota, II. 84 (*Bened. reg.* 1, 5 [6] genus...anachoritarum, id est *heremitarum*). For *heremita* [=*eremita*] see also (II. 2) *anachorita*.

heresis [haer-], I. 121, see *secta*.

hereticum [sine interpret.], III. 19 (*De S. Mart. Stor.*=*Sulp. Sev. Dial.* II. 12, 9 uirginem...*haereticam* iudicasset).

hermaphroditus, see *hermofroditus*.

hermofroditus [hermaphr-], androginus [-gynus] homo utriusque sexus, XLII. 13 (*Ex div. libris?*)=*herma.froditus*, androgi, Cp. H88.

Hermon, X. 14, see *amana*.

herodii, see *herodion*.

herodion, ualchefuc, XIX. 35 (*Job* XXXIX. 13 Penna struthionis similis est pennis *herodij*)=*herodius*, palch habuc, Cp. H83; *horodius* uualh'hebuc, Ep. 11C35; *horodius* uualh haebuc, Ef.[1] 365, 11. Cf. Wright W. (index). The Cambr. MS. has *herodion*, genus accipitris.—For *ualc-hefuc*, foreign hawk, see Bosw. T. (*wealh-hafoc*, *hafoc*); Kluge, *Etym. Wrtb. d. Spr.* (*Habicht*).

Herodis, see *fadus*.

hexameron, see *in exameron*.

hibernis, see *hiebernis*.

hibicum, firgingata, XIX. 29 (*Job* XXXIX. 1 tempus partus *ibicum*; Heyse, in note, *hibicum*. The Cambr. MS. has: *Ibix*, capra montuosa)=*ibices*, firgengaet, Cp. I12; Ep. 12E33; Ef.[1] 367, 50. For *firgingata* (=of mountain-goats), see Bosw. T. (*firgen-gāt*, *firgin-gāt*).

hic, XXX. 14, see *ho platon*.

hiebernis, hiemalibus, XXVII. 24 (*Lib. Rot.*=*Isid. Lib. de nat. rer.* VII. 2 *hibernis* flatibus; cf. Virg. *Geo.* II. 339).

hiemalibus, XXVII. 24, see *hiebernis*.

hiemisperia duo sunt quorum alterum est super terram alterum sub terra, XLIV. 8 (*Alia*; *de cælo*=*Isid. de nat. rerum*, XII. 3 note *hemisphaeria* duo s. q. a. e. s. t. a. *subter terram*). For *subter terram* see (text) note ** on p. 45. See also XLIV. 1 (*partes*), and (XLIV. 29) *axem*. Perhaps a further explanation of the above is: **hiemisperium** [hemisphaerium] aput grecos dicitur quod nos uerticem uocamus, XLIV. 19.

HIEREMIA, XIV *tit.*

Hieronimi, XXX *tit.*, see *De Catalogo*.

Hieronimus dicit **statera** dicitur &c., XXXI. 37; see *statera*.

hierophantis, see *hierufontis*.

hierufontis, uel prophetis qui auditis pręsunt, XXXVIII. 42 (*Clem. Rom. Recognitt.* I. 5 *hierophantis vel prophetis qui adytis praesunt*, amicus efficiar).

hierusalem, XXIII. 17, see *ciuitas dauid*.

HIEZECHIEL, XV *tit.*

hiezechielo [Ezech-], XXXIII. 8, see *obulus*, 20, see *colamina*.

hii, XLIV. 27, see *leua*.

himina, medius sextarius cyatos iii, II. 86; see *emina*.

hin, sextarios II, XXXIII. 17 (*Euch. De Pond.?*). *Hin* does not appear in the printed texts of Eucherius, but the Brit. Mus. MS. has: Nebel quidam putant modii III. *Hin* sextarius est liquidae speciei. See below *nebel*, where *in sextariis* is, perhaps, to be read as *hin*, *sextarius*.—**hin maior** XUIII sextarios Minor UIII, XXXI. 14 (*De ponder.?*).

hinuitabar [for *inuitabar*], see *appulli*.

hippocentaurus, see *epocentaurus*.

hircania, XXXV. 1, see *tragoedia*.

hircus, XXXV. 1, see *tragoedia*.

hironiam, XXXV. 120, see *per hir-*.

hirpex, see *erpica*.

his, XVI. 30.

hispida, deforma [?*deformis*?] nodis, III. 10 (*De S. Mart. Stor.*=*Sulp. Sev. Dial.* 2, 3, 2 ueste *hispida*; cf. *Dial.* 1, 3, 5 herbam *hispidam*, and 2, 1, 8 uestem *hispidam*).

hispidam, see *hispida*.

historiam, XIII. 25, see *de radice*.

histrio, scurres. lees, XLV. 26 (*Uerba de multis*=*Ars Phocae*, p. 413, 8 *histrio* centurio). *Scurres lees* perhaps=*scurrilis* (es). But *lees* being marked as A.S. in the MS., *scurres* may be for *scurra*, or *scurrus*, or *scurrax* (see Goetz, vol. VII. p. 246), and *lees*=A.S. *leas*, loose, false, deceitful, as subst. a deceiver (Bosw. T.).—**histrionibus**, oroccerum, XXXIX. 57 (not in Greg. Dial., but *Can. Concil. Afric.* XLV p. 150 Vt scenicis atque *histrionibus*...gratia vel reconciliatio non negetur). *Oroccerum* (misread *droccerum*), a derivation, perhaps, from *orc* (Lat. *orcus*), the infernal regions; cf. Bosw. T. in vocc. *orc*, *orcen* (a sea-monster); Kluge, *Altg. Dial.* p. 341; id. (in Paul & Braune's *D. Sprache*, IX. 188).—**striones**, qui muebri [muliebri] indumento gestus inpudicarum feminarum exprimebant, I. 127 (*De Canon.*; *Can. Conc. Carth.* CXXIX Omnes...*histriones*; cf. *ibid.* XLV, and LXIII *histrionibus*).

hnabot, XIII. 54, see *del.*

hoc, IV. 99; XXX. 95; XXXII. 5; XXXIX. 20; XLI. 10; XLIII. 34; XLVI. 14.

hodiporitum, see *sinphosin.*

hodoeporicon, see *sinphosin.*

holera (q^y? plur. of Lat. *holus*, cabbage, colewort; or corruption of A.S. *holen, holegn*, holly?), XLVII. 96, see *acrifolium.*

holografia, see *olografia.*

homelias, homilias, see *ominas.*

hominem, X. 6, see *unguentum exinanitum*; XXIX. 56, see *metempschosis.*

homines, XV. 13, see *pigmei*, 24, see *pollinctores*; XXV. 9, see *decurio*; XXXV. 24, see *auspiciis*, 184, see *liberales l.*, 235, see *busta*; XLIII. 5, see *polideuces.*

hominibus, XXI. 12, see *filii titan*; XLII. 21, see *basterna.*

hominis, XXXV. 164, see *de figmento*, 298, see *spiridon*; XLIII. 18, see *carus*, 28, see *bachus*; XLVII. 89, see *bulinus.*

hominum, XVI. 11, see *saraballa*; XLVI. 27, see *uarix.*

homo, IV. 4, see *mambre*; XLII. 13, see *hermofroditus.*

homofagiis, homofagis, see *omofagis.*

homonyma, see *omonima.*

honestorum, XXXV. 302, see *seminon.*

honorauit, see *afficit.*

honore, II. 81, see *gradu*; VIII. 8, see *in aceruo m-.*

honores, see *solaria.*

honoribus, see *fascibus.*

ho platon, hic plato, xxx. 14; **ton philona**, hunc philonem, xxx. 15; **acoloythei**, sequitur **h ton platona** aut hunc platonem, xxx. 16; **o philon**, hec philo, xxx. 17 (*Cat. Hier.* XI col. 629A De hoc [Philo Judæus] vulgo apud Graecos dicitur *ἢ Πλάτων φιλωνίζει ἢ Φίλων πλατωνίζει*, idest Aut Plato Philonem sequitur aut Platonem Philon.—B: De hoc vulgo apud Grecos dicitur platon philonizein philon platonizein id est aut plato philonem sequitur aut philo platonem sequitur.—C: De h. v. a. g. d. [blank line] idest aut p. p. seq. a. platonem philo). It is clear that the Glossator had a text before him which read, or which he interpreted to read, *ἢ ὁ Πλάτων τὸν Φίλωνα ἀκολουθεῖ, ἢ τὸν Πλάτωνα ὁ Φίλων.*—E has: ΗΟ· ΠΛΑΤΟΝ· ΤΩΗΤΩ· ΦΙΛΩΝΑ; ЄΚΩΩΙϹ· ΤΗΙΩΙϹ· ΤΗϹΗΤΩΝ· ΠΙΛΘΟΝΑ· ΦΙΛΟΝ· id est aut plato phylonem sequitur . aut filo platonem.

horas, II. 37, see *canonicas.*

horas diurnas nocturnaque conputantes, idest pro XL diebus XX statuunt, XXXV. 179 (*Ruf.* v. 24 fol. 91^b quidam... putant uno tantum die obseruari debere ieiunium...nonnulli etiam quadraginta, ita ut *horas diurnas nocturnasque computantes*, diem statuant).

horę, IV. 99, see *quadraplas.*

horno, hoc anno, XLIII. 34 (*De div. nominibus* = not Donati Ars grammat., but Serv. *Comm. in Donat.*, p. 438, 14, 15 *horno*...nihil est aliud nisi *hoc anno*). Cf. *horno*, þys gere, Cp. H137, 142; *horno*, thys geri, Ep. 11C18; Ef.[1] 364, 51.

hortans, see *paradigma.*

hortari, II. 164, see *suadere.*

hortum, see *areola.*

hortus, XIII. 1, see *cucumerarium.*

horum, XLIV. 16, see *antarticus.*

hospicia, XLI. 3, see *sidonicis.*

hospitalitate, hospitium, see *de philoxenia.*

hostiarius [ost-], XXXIX. 5, see *mansionarius*; XLII. 9, see *ceruerus.*

hostie [-tiae], XLVI. 34, see *inferie.*

huc, II. 134, see *passim.*

humanum, IV. 22, see *ius.*

humiliatio, XXVIII. 62, see *tapynosin.*

humilissimus [for *humillimis*], XXVIII. 62, see *tapynosin.*

humillimis, see *tapynosin.*

humor, XXVII. 30, see *moloncolia.*

hunc, XXX. 15, 16, see *ho platon.*

huni (may be for Lat. *Hunni*, or for A.S. *Hūne*, or O.H.G. *Huni*), XXXIX. 25, see *uulgari.*

Hunni (Lat.), see *uulgari.*

huuitabar [for *hinuitabar, inuitabar*], III. 15; see *appulli.*

hyacinthina, see *uiola.*

hyacinthini, see *iacyntini.*

hyacinthino, hyacintho, see *iacincto.*

hyadas, a tauri similitudine, XXVII. 16 (*Lib. Rot.* = *Isid. Lib. de nat. rer.* XXVI. 1 [quoting *Job* IX. 9] Qui facit arcturum, et Orionem, et *hyadas*) = *hiadas*, a tauri similitudine, Cp. H104; hiadas, a tauris similitudine, Ep. 11C30 & Ef.[1] 365, 6. Cf. *hyadas*, raedgasram, Cp. H162; Ep. 11C1; Ef.[1] 364, 34; also the note to Isid. XXVI. 5 (p. 39 in Areval's ed.): Alii addunt... *Hyades* sunt quinque...in fronte *Tauri* positae.

hyaenae, see *hygę*; *hyinę.*

hydra, see *exedra.*

hydria, see *fidelia farris.*

hydropicus, aquaticus, XXXV. 5 (*Ruf.* I. 8 fol. 12^b *hydropis*...tumor).

hydropis, see *hydropicus.*

hygę, **quas beluas uocant** idest bestie, XXXVIII. 15; see *hyinę.*

hyinę, nocturnum monstrum similis

cani, xxix. 38 (*Uerb. Interpr.* = *Hier. in Matth.* xxiii. 38 col. 175A [quoting Jer. xii. 8] facta est mihi hæreditas mea quasi spelunca *hyænæ*) = *hynę*, n. m. s. c., Cp. H166, and cf. *hyna*, naectgenge (night-goer, Bosw. T. *niht-genge*), Cp. H130. The Vulg. has quasi leo in sylva. See Migne's note, ibid., and Sabatier.—**hygę, quas beluas uocant** idest bestie [bestiae], xxxviii. 15 (*Clem. Recognitt.* viii. 25 *hyaenae, quas beluas* [*belluas*, Migne] vocant).

hymnum, laudem, ii. 85 (*Bened. reg.* 11, 18 incipiat abbas *ymnum* [29 *hymnum*; and *ymnum*, in note], 21 [35] subsequatur ...abbas *hymnum*).

hypallage, idest permutatio quoties in alium intellectum uerba quę dicta sunt transferuntur, xxviii. 44 (*Cass. Psalm.* xiii. 5 schema dicitur *hypalage* id est p.q. i.a.i.u. quae d.s.t. See xxix. 1 *hypallage*). Cf. *ypallage*, uerbum pro uerbo, Cp. Y5; Ef.[1] 401, 11.

hyperbaton, cum suspensus ordo uerborum inferius explicatur, xxviii. 78 (*Cass. Psalm.* xxxvi. 10 *hyperbaton*, c.s.o.u.i.e.).
—**yperbaton**, idest transcensio, xxviii. 87 (*Cass. Psalm.* xliv. 14 *hyperbaton*, i.t.).

Hyperberetæi, Hyperberetaeon, see *mensis yperberetheus*.

hyperbolen, see *per figuram y-*.

hyperthesis, idest superlatio cum aliquam rem opinione omnium nota sententia nostra exsuperare contendimus, xxviii. 51 (*Cass. Psalm.* xvii. 12 *hyperthesis* idest s.c. a.r.o.o. notam s.n.e.c. And again l. 8).

hypotheseon, see *ypophesion*.

hypotheticus, idest contionalis sillogismus, xxviii. 84 (*Cass. Psalm.* xl. 1 *hypotheticus*...id est *conditionalis syllogismus*; idem vii. 5).

hypozeuxis, see *ypozeuxis*.

hysopo, in similitudinem absinthi [-thii], xxv. 15 (*Joh.* xix. 29 spongiam plenam aceto, *hyssopo*; Wordsw. & White *hysopo*).

hyssopo, see *hysopo*.

i for *a*: l*i*ciniosa (for lac-)—for *ae*: trop*i*a (for troph*ae*a)—for *e*: adul*i*scentulę (for adul*e*scentulae); ag*i*llo (ag*e*llo); all*i*gare (all*e*g-); amator*i*s (-r*e*s); anachor*i*ta (-r*e*ta); apolog*i*ticum (apolog*e*t-); ariopag*i*tis (areopag*i*tam); cat*i*cum*i*ni (cat*e*chum*e*ni); c*i*spitem (c*e*sp-); c*i*ssura (c*e*ss-); cort*i*x (cort*e*x); cym*i*teria (coem*e*teria); dec*i*m (dec*e*m); d*i*finiciones, d*i*finita, &c. (d*e*f-); d*i*riguere, d*i*riuatur (d*e*r-); d*i*scribitur, -bunt (d*e*scr-); d*i*sperabilis, d*i*spicalis (d*e*sp-); d*i*stinabunt, d*i*struitur (d*e*st-); ent*i*cam (enth*e*cam); er*i*p- (er*e*p-); ext*i*mplo (ext*e*m-); h*i*mina (h*e*m-); inb*i*cilles (inb*e*c-); interf*i*ci (-f*e*ci); lag*i*na (lag*e*na); lent*i*scere (-t*e*scere); mausil*i*o (-l*e*o); moll*i*scere (-l*e*scere); m*i* hercul*i* (m*e* hercul*e*); pan*i*gericis (pan*e*gyricis); peripsima (-s*e*ma); pyrifleg*i*tonta (-g*e*thonta); red*i*gerit (red*e*g-); sc*i*nici (sc*e*n-); subitan*i*a (-n*e*a); supr*i*ma (-r*e*ma); uat*i*s (uat*e*s); uert*i*x (-t*e*x); u*i*xilla (u*e*x-).—for *o*: maus*i*lio (maus*o*leo).—for *y*: aeth*i*mologia (et*y*m-); androg*i*nus (-g*y*nus); archis*i*nagogus (archis*y*n-); artof*i*lax (arctoph*y*lax); as*i*llum (as*y*l-), as*i*tum (as*y*lum); aud*i*tis (ad*y*tis); az*i*morum (az*y*m-); Cal*i*pso (Cal*y*-); c*i*atos (c*y*athos); c*i*mbalis (c*y*mb-); col*i*rium (coll*y*r-); Cor*i*bantas (Cor*y*b-); cor*i*mbis (cor*y*mb-); diat*i*posis (diat*y*p-); epend*i*ten (-d*y*ten); epist*i*lia (-t*y*lia); f*i*lacteria (ph*y*l-); fr*i*x, fr*i*gia (Phr*y*-); gazof*i*latia (gazoph*y*l-); g*i*rouagum (g*y*r-); *i*acincto, *i*acinctino (h*y*ac-); l*i*ra, l*i*ricus (l*y*r-); L*i*dii (L*y*d-); M*i*cene, m*i*rtę (m*y*-); omon*i*ma (-n*y*ma); on*i*chinos (on*y*ch-); pap*i*ri (-p*y*ri); paral*i*sin (-l*y*sin); ph*i*lacteria (ph*y*l-); ph*i*tagoras (P*y*thag-); p*i*ctarum (p*y*ct-); Pol*i*deuces (Pol*y*d-); pol*i*on*i*ma (pol*y*on*y*ma); presb*i*tera, presb*i*teri &c. (presb*y*t-); sat*i*rum (sat*y*-); S*i*lla (S*y*-); s*i*llogismus (s*y*ll-); s*i*mbulis, s*i*mbulum (s*y*mbo-); s*i*mcosion (s*y*mp-); s*i*nagogae, s*i*ncopin, s*i*naxis, s*i*nchronon, s*i*necdochen (s*y*n-); s*i*nphosin (s*y*mposium); s*i*ntagmata (s*y*nt-); S*i*riis (S*y*riis); S*i*rofenissa (S*y*r-); S*i*rte (S*y*rten); Teth*i*s (-h*y*s); th*i*esteos (Th*y*-); th*i*miamateria (th*y*m-); t*i*fon (T*y*phon); t*i*rannidem, -des (t*y*r-).—i *omitted*: conectura (con*i*-); editore (edi*t*iore); elogis (-giis); Spiridon (-d*i*on); uestmenta (uest*i*m-).—i *inserted*: apparitor*i*um (-torum); auditor*i*um (-torum); erip*i*sissent (erepsissent); strangu*i*llato (-gulato).

·i·, v. 8 [=*idest*?]; see *auo*.

iacent, xv. 9, see *transtra*; xxxv. 57, see *cunabulum*.

iacinctina [*hyacinthina*], xxix. 10, see *uiola*.

iacinctino [*hyacinthino*], xv. 45, see *iacincto*.

iacincto, idest de pelle iacinctino [hyacinthino], xv. 45 (*Ezech.* xxiii. 6 vestitos *hyacintho*).

iactare, viii. 8, see *in aceruo m-*.

iacynthini, see *iacyntini*.

iacyntini, syitor heuuin, xxii. 6 (*Esther* i. 6 tentoria aerij coloris, et carbasini ac *hyacinthini*; Heyse, in note, *iacynthini*; viii. 15 vestibus regiis, *hyacinthinis*). *Syitor* for swiðor (?) comp. of swiðe, very much (see Bosw. T.); *heuuin* = hæwen (Bosw. T.), blue, azure. See Steinm. i. 488, 12; iv. 273, 4; and the present Glossary xxii. 3 (*aeri*, haue); see also *Aeri* iacintini, Cp. A356.

iaketalo, see *epimehne*.

iane (!), xxxvi. 1, see *Iani porte*.

Iani porte, idest porte templi iane [!] dei paganorum quę ante patebant unaqueque ad gentem suam quando contraria fuit romanis nomine gentis ipsius scribta [scripta] super porta, xxxvi. 1 (*Oros.* i. 1, 6 *Iani portae* clausae sunt).

iaspis, nigrum et uiridem colorem habet, xli. 7 (*De nomin. div.* = *Apoc.* xxi. 19 fundamentum primum *jaspis*; see also *Exod.* xxviii. 18, xxxix. 11; *Ezek.* xxviii. 13) = *iaspis*, n. e. u. c. h., Ep. 11E9; Ef.[1] 365, 21; Cp. —.

ibi, xi. 14; xxix. 39; see also *ubi et ubi*.

ibicum, see *hibicum*.

icon, xxviii. 49, see *periscema icon*.

id, xxviii. 83 (bis).

Idasteles [for *Aristoteles*?], proprium [add: *nomen*] uiri, xxxviii. 12 (*Clem. Recognitt.* viii. 15); see *Calistratus*.

idea, cum speciem rei future uelut oculis efferente motum animi concitamus, xxviii. 42 (*Cass. Psalm.* xvii. 9 Hoc schema dicitur *idea*, cum s. r. futurae u. o. offerentes m. a. c. Cf. *ib.* xxxii. 13 *idea*, Latine species dicitur, quando velut effigiem rei futurae oculis *offerentes*, animi *votum* ad audiendi studium concitamus; *ib.* xlvii. 15 *idea*, Latine species, quando aliquid futurum velut oculis offerentes, notum animi concitamus).

ideas, xlii. 25, see *Platonis ideas*.

ideonati, consuetudini, xxix. 27; see *idioma*.

idioma, proprietas, xix. 7 (*Job*; *Praef. Hieron.* p. xiv^{b}, and Migne, *P.L.* xxviii col. 1081^{B} propter linguæ *idioma*) = *idioma*, proprietas linguae, Cp. I19; *iodioma*, pr-, Ep. 11E10; *iodiama*, proprietas, Ef.[1] 365, 22. The Cambr. MS.: *idioma* proprietas uniuscuiusque linguae.—**ideonati**, consuetudini, xxix. 27 (*Uerb. Interpr.* = *Hier. in Matth.* xxii. 30 Latina consuetudo Graeco *idiomati* non respondet).

idiomati, see *idioma*.

idiotae, stulti, xxxv. 160 (*Ruf.* iv. 16 fol. 65^{a} imperiti uel *idiotae* obseruant).

idole, xl. 13, see *bachal*.

idolorum, xxxv. 26, see *oethepia*.

idolum, xv. 35, see *teraphin*.

idem, xi. 3; xiii. 39, 55; xxix. 42; xxxi. 27; xxxiii. 12, 15, 23; xxxv. 69.

idem, xlvii. 75, see *genisculas*.

idest, i. 36; v. 11; viii. 13, 16, 19; x. 19, 26; xi. 5, 15; xii. 3, 24, 33, 40–42; xiii. 24, 25, 35, 53; xv. 13, 45; xvi. 5, 18; xvii. 2, 20; xix. 5, 12; xxi. 7, 19; xxii. 7, 9, 12–15; xxviii. 21, 37, 39, 44–47, 51, 54, 58, 61, 64–67, 69, 74, 76, 82, 84, 87; xxix. 11, 35, 47, 73; xxx. 9, 13, 40; xxxi. 17, 23, 24 (bis), 25; xxxii. 7–9; xxxiii. 6, 10, 15, 16; xxxv. 3, 6, 20, 26, 69, 122, 140, 179; xxxvi. 1, 12, 18; xxxvii. 5, 9 (bis); xxxviii. 7, 15, 37; xxxix. 24, 35, 42; xl. 1; xli. 2; xlii. 25, 26; xliii. 53; xliv. 13, 14, 16.

i[dest?], v. 8; see *auo*.

idonea, apta utilis habilis, i. 62 (*De Canon.*; *Can. Conc. Sard.* xv *idonea* praedia habere cognoscuntur).

ie for *e*: apologi*e*ticum (apologet-).

iereticos, sacerdotale, xxx. 12 (*De Catal.*); **peri tes zoes theoricas**, id est de hac uit[a] contemplatiua, xxx. 13 (*De Catal.*). In these cases the original Glossator had, perhaps, two, somewhat different, versions of the *Cat. Hieron.* before him. As regards "iereticos, sacerdotale" it may refer to *Cat. Hier.* ii col. 612^{A} de genere sacerdotali (*Gr. transl.* γένους ἱερατικοῦ) or to xi col. 625 de genere sacerdotum (Gr. γένους ἱερέων). But as the Glossator apparently made his extracts from a Latin text (or texts), in which the Greek words were written in Latin characters, and the order in which the present glosses appear in the Glossary suggests an extract from ch. xi, or thereabout, of the *Catal.*, the two glosses 12 & 13 seem to refer to *Cat. Hier.* xi col. 629^{A} liber...de apostolicis viris quem et inscripsit περὶ βίου θεωρητικοῦ ἱκετῶν. If this be the case *iereticos* (of 12) refers, perhaps, to ἱκετῶν, and the *ti* may be misplaced, and belong to *theoricas* (of 13), to make *theoriticas*. For βιου of the present texts some MS. must have had ζοης or ζωης, which appears in the Glossary. The Utrecht ed. (B) has traces of these two words in "librum...de apostolicis viris quem et inscripsit *periso oythe yroti koy* id est *de vita contemplatiua*," where *so* (of periso) points to ζο- or ζω-, and *oy* (of oythe) to ου (of βιου). The Augsburg ed. (C) sheds further light on the gloss (13), it having: "librum...de apostolicis viris quem et inscripsit [blank] de *hac* vita contemplatiua." E has: πηρι της ζωης θεοσηκας.

ignari, see *expertim*.

ignarus, xxxiv. 50, see *expers*.

ignauia, ii. 45, see ***desidia***.

ignauus, ii. 41, see ***desidiosus***.

igne, xi. 16, see ***bonam escam***; xvii. 4, see ***torris***.

ignem, xvi. 9, see ***malleolis***.

ignis, iii. 22, see ***bornacula***; xxxviii. 24, see ***pyriflegitonta***; xli. 9, see ***calcidon***; xliii. 46 (bis), see ***piraondes***; xlv. 3, see *las*; **ignis**, xi. 11, see *in aqua ualebat ignis.*

ignis acer, oma, xxxv. 66 (*Ruf.* ix. 8 fol. 150^b vlceribus...quae *ignis sacer* appellantur) = *igni sacrum*, oman, Cp. I27. For *oma*, *oman*, erysipelas, see Bosw. T. (*oman*).

ignorari [!], xlviii. 35, see *expertim.*

ignoratur, xliv. 10, see *cardines.*

ignota, xix. 37, see *ueemoth.*

ileusun cyrię, propitius esto domine, xxix. 63 (*Uerb. Interpr.* = *Hier. in Matth.* xvi. 22, 23 ἵλεώς σοι, Κύριε...hoc est propitius sis tibi, Domine [*propitius esto Domine*, Migne in note [a]]).

ilex, see *ilix.*

ilice, see *ilicus.*

ilicem, see *ilix*; **ilicem**, xxxv. 90, see *ad ilicem*, sub v. *ilix.*

ilico, see *ilicus.*

ilicus, arbor est folia modica habens fructusque sicut glandi modici, xvi. 4 (*Dan.*, *Praef. Hieron.* p. xvi^b and Migne xxviii col. 1293^A ut, verbi gratia, dicamus ab arbore *ilice* dixisse eum, *ilico* [Migne *Illico*] pereas). The Glossator mistook the adverb *ilico*, used by St Jerome to illustrate the false etymology in his preceding sentence, for the name of the tree *ilice* (ilex). The Cambr. MS. has: *Ylex*, a. e. f. m. h. f. s. *glandes modicę.*

ilix, nomen ligni, iv. 3 (*Eccles. Ist.*); **ad ilicem**, genus rubri [rubi], xxxv. 90 (*De Eus.*) = (*Ruf.* i. 1 fol. 2^b sedenti ad *ilicem* Mambrae). In xxxv. 90 the MS. has *adilicem*, which = *adilicem* genus rubi, Cp. A184; Ep. 1A31 and Ef.[1] 338, 14. See also *ilicus.*

ill-, see *inl-*.

illa, xxi. 3; xxix. 39; xxxv. 82; xliii. 36.

illac, in illa parte, xliii. 36; see *hac.*

illam, xxix. 52, see *ecacusen.*

illico, see *ilicus.*

illo, xxiv. 13.—**illo usque**, illuc, xxxv. 262 (*Ruf.* vi. 15 fol. 105^b Origenem *illo usque* orante emitti).

illos, xiv. 3.

illuc, ii. 134, see *passim*; xxxv. 262, see *illo usque.*

illud, xxii. 11; xxxix. 4.

imaginatio, xxviii. 49, see *periscema.*

imaginatione, xxviii. 81, see *per energiam.*

imagines, v. 32, see *thoraces.*

imb-, see *inb-*.

imitatio, xxvii. 5, see *scina.*

imitatorem, i. 12, see *aemulum.*

immolat, iv. 73, see *litat.*

immolatio, mactatio, i. 60 (*De Canon.*; *Decret. Leon.* xii p. 227^a multorum agnorum occisio illius *immolatione* finita est; cf. *Can. Conc. Ancyr.* xxi, xxii immolauerunt; immolantes &c.; Isid. *Etym.* vi. 19. 31).

imp-, see *inp-*.

impendiis, see *inpendiis.*

imperator, i. 39, see *diuus.*

imperatore, xxxix. 20, see *in mare adriatico.*

imperia, i. 92, see *pragmatica*; xxxix. 63, see *per pragmaticam formam.*

impingaris, see *inpingaris.*

impios, xi. 11, see *in aqua....*

implanauit, see *inpl-*.

impleat, see *aptet.*

implet, ii. 16, see *aptet.*

improbos, improbus, see *inprobus.*

impunitas, see *in pennias.*

in, i. 65 (bis), 91, 100; ii. 6, 33, 95 (bis), 161; iii. 31 (bis), 33; iv *tit.*, 1, 25 (bis), 98, 99; vii. 1 (bis), 2, 6 (bis), 9 (bis); viii. 2, 8 (ter), 13, 16 (bis), 17 (bis), 18; ix. 5; x *tit.*, 3, 22 (bis), 24; xi. 3, 11 (bis), 12, 13 (bis), 14, 15; xii. 25 (bis), 42, 48; xiii *tit.*, 1, 6, 30 (bis), 36, 37, 40, 41, 47 (bis), 57–59; xiv *tit.*, 2, 7 (bis), 9, 11, 14 (bis), 15, 22, 30, 36; xv *tit.*, 5, 9 (bis), 11 (bis), 18 (bis), 33, 43; xvi *tit.*, 25; xvii. 1, 7; xviii. 3; xix *tit.*, 11, 20, 23, 31, 50 (bis); xx *tit.*, xxi *tit.*, 1 (bis), 5 (bis), 9 (bis), 16, 19 (quater), 20; xxii. 12 (ter), 16 (bis); xxiii *tit.*, 2, 14 (bis), 17; xxiv *tit.*, 1, 5; xxv. 3, 5, 8, 13, 15; xxvi *tit.*; xxvii *tit.*, 28; xxviii *tit.*, 2 (bis), 25, 28, 33 (ter), 38, 40, 44, 47, 63, 76; xxix. 11, 13, 15, 31, 56; xxx *tit.*, 2; xxxi. 1, 11, 12 (bis); xxxiii. 5–8, 12 (bis), 14, 20; xxxv. 26 (bis), 27 (bis), 41 (ter), 57, 73, 116 (bis), 147, 162, 169 (bis), 205 (bis), 226 (ter), 250, 266; xxxvi. 3, 4, 11, 17 (bis); xxxvii. 8, 9 (ter), 19; xxxviii. 7, 29; xxxix. 8 (bis), 17, 20 (bis), 24, 28, 35, 42, 49, 50, 51 (bis), 53 (bis), 54 (bis); xli. 1; xlii. 20 (bis), 27; xliii. 13, 18, 35, 36, 46; xliv. 9, 10 (bis), 17, 22, 25, 26 (bis), 27 (ter), 29; xlv. 10, 18, 19, 31; xlvi. 13, 14, 24, 27; xlvii. 28, 89.

in [for *hin*?], xxxiii. 19, see *nebel.*

in, xxix. 52 (bis; the first to be joined to *aut* = αὐτήν, the second, dittography).

in aceruo mercurii, consuetudinem habebant ambulantes in uia ubi sepultus est mercurius lapidem iactare in aceruum ipsius unusquisque pro honore eius, viii. 8 (*Salam.* xxvi. 8 Sicut qui mittit lapidem *in acervum Mercurij*).

in aculeis, in ferris ligno in terra posito infixis et curuis, xxxv. 41 (*Ruf.* viii. 10 fol. 140^a *in eculeis* exigebant; *in equuleis*, Cacciari p. 483) = *in eculeis*, in ferreis ligno infixis et curbis in terra positis, Cp. I85, 86; Ep. 11E22; Ef.[1] 365, 34.

Equuleus, or eculeus, *a wooden rack* (Lewis & Sh.).

inaequalia, see *anomala.*

in agillo, in agro, xxviii. 2 (*Lib. Anton.*), see *agellis.*

in anathema, in obliuione, &c., xxi. 19 (*Judith* xvi. 23), see *anathema.*

inanis, xxxiv. 12, see *cenodoxia.*

inaptius, iii. 47, see *indecentius.*

in aqua ualebat ignis, fulgura in pluuia ad impios missa, xi. 11 (*Sap.* xvi. 17 *in aqua,* quae omnia extinguit, plus *ignis valebat.* See *Sap.* xix. 19 ignis in aqua valebat, and for the gloss cf. *Exod.* ix. 23, 24, and Wace's *Apocr.* p. 516).

inbecilles, inbecillibus, see *inbicilles.*

inbicilles [inbec-], ii. 192, see *pusillanimes.*—**inbicilles,** infirmi, flebiles, ii. 92 (*Bened. reg.* 35, 5 [6] *Inbecillibus*... procurentur solacia).

inbuitur, i. 20, see *catezizatur.*

incantatores sunt qui rem uerbis peragunt, xvi. 31 (*Dan.* v. 11 principem magorum, *incantatorum*...constituit eum).

incantatorum, see *incantatores.*

IN CANTICO CANTICORUM, x *tit.*

in carcere sine ferro, in mare rubro, xi. 13 (*Sap.* xvii. 15 custodiebatur *in carcere sine ferro*).

incasale [for *incasuale*], xliii. 56, see *aptotum.*

incasuale, see *aptotum.*

incedere, xxxv. 154, see *incessere.*

incedit, viii. 13, see *in sublime.*

incenditur, xxiii. 1, see *exedra.*

incensum, xii. 22, see *storax.*

incentor, suscitator, xxxiv. 14 (*De Cass., Inst.* xi. 2 confutatus *incentor*).

incerti, xliii. 6, see *notha.*

incesserat, see *incessit.*

incessere, accusare, iv. 39 (*Eccles. Istor.*); **incessere**, incedere, xxxv. 154 (*De Eus.*); **incessere**, inpugnare, xxxv. 264 (*De Eus.*) =(*Ruf.* iv. 3 fol. 54^b quidam homines... nostros nitebantur *incessere*).—**incessit,** incurrit, xxxv. 261 (*Ruf.* vi. 6 fol. 99^a animos *incesserat*)=*incessit,* incurrit, Cp. I448.

incesta, xxxv. 166, see *scenas turpes.*

in chaos, in profundum uel in aera, xxxv. 226 (*Ruf.* xi. 23 fol. 188^a terra... solueretur *in chaos*).

inchoans, xxxv. 44, see *adortus.*

incidere, xiv. 30, see *pedalis*; xxxv. 68, see *concidere.*

incidunt, xiv. 20, see *scalpellum*; xxiii. 3, see *latomi*; xxxv. 72, see *lanionibus,* 73, see *codicibus.*

INCIPIT, xxxi *tit.*; INCIPIT BREUIS EXSOLUTIO, vi *tit.*—EX DIUERSIS LIBRIS, xlii *tit.*—IN DANIELEM, xvi *tit.*—IN HIEREMIA, xiv *tit.*—IN ESDRA, xxiii *tit.*—IN HIEZECHIEL, xv *tit.*—IN JOB, xix *tit.*—IN JUDITH, xxi *tit.*—IN LIBRUM ECCLESIASTICE ISTORIAE, iv *tit.* —IN MATHEUM [Matthaeum], xxiv *tit.*—IN TOBIA, xx *tit.*—UERBORUM INTERPRETATIO [=Hieron. *Comm. in Matthaeum*], xxix *tit.*

incipitur, ii. 149, see *responsoria.*

INCIPIUNT, xl *tit.*

incisa, xxxv. 86, see *busta.*

incisis, xxxv. 229, see *dispicatis.*

incisus, xiv. 21, see *torta panis.*

incitati, xxix. 24, see *inlecti.*

incitatum, xxxix. 66, see *elicitum.*

inclinato, xxxv. 234, see *suggillato.*

includit, see *inclusor.*

inclusit, xiv. 16, see *inclusor.*

inclusor, qui gemmas inclusit [Cambr. MS. *includit*] auro, xiv. 16 (*Hier.* xxix. 2 faber et *inclusor*; xxiv. 1 fabrum et *inclusorem*).

incocte [-tae], xxxiv. 5, see *xerofagia.*

in comminus, propius, xxxv. 162, see *comminus.*

incompetentibus, see *inconpentententibus.*

inconditos, indisciplinatos, xxxiv. 30 (*De Cass., Inst.* viii. 16 *inconditos* mores nostros...emendare).

incongruis, ii. 91, see *inconpententibus.*

inconparari, xl. 3, see *deuotatum.*

inconpententibus, non aptis incongruis, ii. 91 (*Bened. reg.* 48, 38 [68] horis *inconpetentibus*).

inconpetentibus, see *inconpententibus.*

inconsulto, non interrogato, xxxv. 124 (*Ruf.* ii. 23 fol. 32^b se *inconsulto*).

in contis, in lancis, xxi. 9 (*Judith* ix. 9 confidunt...in curribus suis et *in contis,* et in scutis...et *in lanceis* gloriantur). It may be that *in lancis* (for *in lanceis*) is meant as a gloss to *in contis,* as *contus* (a pole, pike) also means *a weapon* (see Lewis & Sh. in voce); otherwise the above quotation suggests two lemmata without interpretations.

inconueniens, ii. 11, see *absurdum.*

incorpore [for *incorporeae*], xxviii. 81, see *per energiam.*

incorporeae, see *per energiam.*

incorporeum, xliv. 29, see *axem.*

increpetur, ii. 127, see *obiurgetur.*

increuit, i. 59, see *inoleuit.*

incuba, maerae uel saturus, xlvii. 81 (*Alia* = ?)=*incuba,* maere, Cp. I225; *i-,* mera uel satyrus, Ep. 12E14; *incuba,* merae uel saturnus, Ef.^{1} 367, 30. *Incuba* = *incubus,* a nightmare, incubus. For maerae, maere, mera, merae, an incubus, (night)mare, see Bosw. T. (*mæra, mære*). For *saturus, saturnus* leg. *satyrus,* as in Ep.

incubi, XIII. 24, see *pilosi.*
incubum, XXXVIII. 38, see *satirum.*
incubus, see *incuba.*
incumberis, VIII. 3, see *ne innataris.*
incunabulis, see *cunabulum.*
incurrit, XXXV. 261, see *incessit.*
incus, osifelti, XIX. 41 (*Job* XLI. 15 malleatoris *incus*) = *incuda*, onfilti, Cp. I137; see Steinm. I. 497. 18, besides the above also *ysifolto*, *ueliti*, *anaboz* = O.H.G. *anafalz*, Mod. G. *Amboss*; *id.* I. 507, 62; 509, 33; Wright W. 141, 23 incus, *anfilte*; *id.* 426, 31 incus, *onfilte*; *id.* 627, 35 incus, *anfeld*, D. *aanbeeld.* Cf. Bosw. T. in voce *anfilt* (an *anvil*).
incusans, accusans, XXXV. 123 (*Ruf.* II. 23 fol. 32^b quos...contra legem gerere *incusans*).
inde, XVII. 7, 19; XXII. 16; XXVIII. 18.
indecentius, inaptius, III. 47 (*De S. Mart. Stor.* = *Sulp. Sev. Dial.* II. 8, 3 uirginem adulescenti cuidam...*indecentius* adhaerentem).
indegeries [indig-], XII. 39, see *plestia.*
indeptum, adquisitum, XXXIV. 42 (*De Cass.*, *Inst.* XII. 11, 1 intellegemus eum... tantam beatitudinem...dono dei miserentis *indeptum*).
indeptus, I. 9, see *adeptus.*
indicationem, II. 167, see *suggessionem.*
indicatur, XXVIII. 43, see *caracterismos.*
indicitur, XXIV. 9, see *censum.*
indiculum, V. 7, see *dorium.*
indigeries, ingluuies, II. 90 (*Bened. reg.* 39, 13 [22] ut numquam subripiat monacho *indigeries*). For *indigeries* see also *plestia.*
indignum, II. 11, see *absurdum.*
in diocesi, in parrochia [parochia], XXXIX. 54; see *diocesim.*
indisciplinatos, XXXIV. 30, see *inconditos.*
indiscretas, IV. 57, see *thesteas.*
indolem, ingenium iuuentutis, XLVIII. 24 (*De Cass.*, *Inst.* V. 12, 1 *indolem* suae iuuentatis ostentet; in note *iuuentutis*). Cf. *indolem*, iuuentutem, Cp. I208; Ep. 12C19; Ef.[1] 366, 52.
induco [for *induto*], XXX. 29, see *capun periens.*
indui, XXII. 11, see *mundum m-.*
indumenta, XXXV. 140, see *portarum indumenta.*
indumento, I. 127, see *striones.*
indutae, see *portarum.*
indute [-tae], XXXV. 140, see *portarum.*
induto, see *induco.*
inebriare, I. 111, see *sicera.*
in edito, in excelso, IV. 25 (*Ruf.* II. 23 fol. 31^b vt *in edito* positus appareas omnibus).
ineluctabile, XL. 1, see *uiscide.*
inęqualia [inaeq-], XLIV. 20, see *anomala.*
inequiperabilis [sine interpret.], VI. 31 (*Breu. exsol.*?).
ineuitabilis, XXXIV. 44, see *sillogismus.*
in exameron, sex dierum computum, XXXV. 250 (*Ruf.* V. 13 fol. 84^b *in Hexameron* commentarius). Cf. *exameron*, VII dierum conputatio, Cp. E522; *exameron*, VI dierum conputatio, Ef.[1] 359, 51; Goetz VI. 568 (*in exaimeron*).
in exaplois, ui editiones congregate [-tae], XIX. 11 (*Job*; *Praef. Hieron.* p. XIV^b, and Migne, *P.L.* XXVIII col. 1082^B in Ἑξαπλοῖς).
in expeditione, in preparatione [praep-] exercitus, XXI. 1 (*Judith* II. 7 dinumeravit viros *in expeditionem*; Heyse, in note, *in expeditione*). Cf. *expeditio*, praeparatio, Cp. E558.
inexterminabiles, XXXV. 43, see *inextricabiles.*
inextricabiles, inexterminabiles, XXXV. 43 (*Ruf.* VIII. 15 fol. 142^b *inextricabiles* languores).—**inextricabiles**, anatreten, XLVIII. 3 (*De Cass.*, *Inst.* III. 3, 6 penetrans *inextricabiles* Tartari tenebras; *ib.* VII. 6 *inextricabilis* nequitiae fomes). *Anatreten* for *un-a-treden* unpassed, untrodden, inaccessible, see Bosw. T. (*tredan*; *a-tredan*; *be-tredan*, &c.); cf. Schlutter, in *Journ. Germ. Phil.* I. 62.
infantes, XXXV. 57, see *cunabulum.*
infantibus, XIX. 48, see *necromantia.*
infantis, XLVIII. 53, see *aborsum.*
infantium, IV. 58, see *oedipia*, sub v. *thesteas.*
in fastu, in dignitate, VII. 9 (1 *Paral.* XXVII. 24 non est relatus in *fastos* regis David; *id.* Heyse, but *in fastus* in note). Hieron. quotes this passage (Migne, XXIII col. 1388) as: *in fastis* regis David. The Glossator seems to have used a text which had the accus. pl. *fastus* (= *fastos*), and mistook this for *fastus*, pride, haughtiness. The Cod. Colb. 4951 (Migne, *Patr. Lat.* XXIII col. 1554) and a Bern MS. have "*in fastos*, dignitates."
in fatores, nomen loci, XIV. 22 (*Hier.* XLIV. 15 omnis populus habitantium in terra Aegypti *in Phatures*; XLIV. 1 in terra *Phatures*).
infausti, see *inuastum.*
infaustiorem, infeliciorem, XXXV. 139, see *inuastum.*
infecti, uiciati [uit-], XXXV. 280 (*Ruf.* VII. 26 fol. 128^a qui...tali doctrina *infecti* sunt).
infeliciorem, XXXV. 139, see *infaustiorem.*
infenso, irato, XXXV. 213 (*De Eus.*); **infensus**, inoffensus [for *offensus*?], IV. 87 (*Eccl. Istor.*) = (*Ruf.* X. 17 fol. 169^b omnes ...*infenso* animo...conueniunt).

infensus, inoffensus [for *offensus?*], IV. 87, see *infenso.*

inferens, III. 29, see *cladem.*

inferie, hostie [-tiae] mortuorum, XLVI. 34 (*Alia*=*Ars Phocae*, p. 428, 8 *inferiae*). Cf. *inferiae*, sacra mortuorum, Cp. I265; *inferiale*, sacra mortuorum, Ep. 12E30; *inferiale*, sacramentu, Ef.[1] 367, 47.

inferius, XXVIII. 78, see *hyperbaton.*

inferni, XLII. 9, see *ceruerus.*

infernorum, XIX. 22, see *coquiton.*

infernum, XLIII. 18, see *carus.*

infestante, iniuriam faciente, XLVIII. 65 (*De Cass.*, *Inst.* VI. 2 puritatem nostri corporis *infestante*).

infestationibus, see *infestionibus.*

infestes, sine barba, XXXV. 189 (*Ruf.* VII. 9 fol. 119ª pueros *inuestes* iugulari iubebat)=*inuestis*, sine barba, Cp. I343. Cf. Cacciari, VII. 9, p. 410, note *e*, who says that some Vatic. MSS. have *imberbas*, and three other MSS. pueros *infantes*, which latter he prefers, as agreeing better with "atque in teneris visceribus" &c.

infestionibus, iniuriis, XXVIII. 3 (*Lib. Anton.* XXIV col. 148ᴬ filia immundi spiritus *infestationibus* quatiebatur). Cf. *infestationes*, tionan (see Bosw. T. *teōna* harm, annoyance), Cp. I369.

infestus, inimicus uel grauis, XXXV. 186 (*De Eus.*); **infestus**, inruens molestus, XXXV. 263 (*De Eus.*)=(*Ruf.* VI. 29 fol. 111ᵇ *infestus* esset Philippo). Cf. *infestus*, molestus, Cp. I400.

inficiabor, contradico, III. 4 (*De S. Mart. Stor.*=*Sulp. Sev. Dial.* I. 12, 3 nec...*infitiabor* iustas illi causas irarum fuisse).—**infitiandi**, negandi, XXVIII. 5 (*Lib. Anton.*), and **inuitiat**, contradicat, III. 55 (not S. Mart. Stor., but)=(*Vit. S. Anton.* XXVIII col. 151ᶜ vetus delictum novo *inficiandi* augere delicto)=*infitiandi*, negandi, Cp. I189; *inuitiandi*, negandi, Ep. 12A38; Ef.[1] 366, 34.

inficiandi, see *infitiandi* sub v. *inficiabor.*

infirmationem, XL. 8, see *ad infirmationem* (for *adfirmationem?*).

infirmi, II. 92, see *inbicilles.*

infirmitas, XXXIX. 48, see *calculum.*

infirmos, I. 90, see *philacteria*; XXXIX. 62, see *filacteria.*

infitiabor, see *inficiabor.*

infitiandi, negandi, XXVIII. 5; see *inficiabor.*

infixis, XXXV. 41, see *in aculeis.*

inflatio, II. 179, see *typo*; XLVIII. 14, see *fastus.*

inflationem, XXXIX. 71, see *typum.*

inflexibile, XLIII. 56, see *aptotum.*

inflexibilis, XLVII. 3, see *rigor.*

in foribus iusti, idest loth, XI. 15 (*Sap.* XIX. 16 percussi sunt...cæcitate sicut illi *in foribus iusti*; cf. *Sap.* X. 6 and *Gen.* XIX. 11).

informacionum (-tionum), see *ypotheseon.*

informatur, I. 59, see *inoleuit.*

infrenatae, see *infrunite.*

infrenate [-tae], XII. 16, see *infrunite.*

infrunita sine freno uel moderatione, XII. 34 (*Eccles.* XXXI. 23 tortura viro *infrunito*).—**infrunite**, infrenate [-tae], XII. 16 (*Eccles.* XXIII. 6 animae irreverenti et *infrunitae* ne tradas me). The Cambridge MS. has *infrunitę effrenatę.*

infrunitae, see *infrunite.*

infrunito, see *infrunita.*

infula, ornamenta, XX. 10 (*Tobias* ? not ? in the Vulg., and perhaps the same as **infulas**, dignitates, XXXIX. 65; not in Greg. Dial., but *Decr. Innoc.* LI p. 208ª ad *infulas* summi sacerdotii). Cf. Cp. I98, 117 (=Ep. 11E32; Ef.[1] 365, 45), 420, 425.

infundunt, XVII. 16, see *infusuria.*

infusoria, see *infusuria.*

infusuria, olearia uasa unde infundunt lucernas, XVII. 16 (*Zachar.* IV. 2 septem *infusoria* lucernis).

ingenium, XXXV. 296, see *perspicem*; XLVIII. 24, see *indolem.*

in georgicis, ubi de cultura agri cecinit, **uia secta**, iringesuuec, XXVII. 28 (*Lib. Rot.* =*Isid. Lib. de nat. rer.* X. 1 Has [zonas] Virgilius *in Georgicis* [I. 233] ostendit, dicens: Quinque tenent caelum zonae...). *Uia secta*, which is a separate line in the Glossary, occurs five lines further down in Virg. *Geo.* (I. 238), but is not quoted by Isidore. uia secta, iringesuuec=Cp. U174; Ep. 28A6; Ef.[1] 398, 40. Iringesuuec, milky way; cf. Bosw. T. in voce; Grimm, *D. Myth.* (297) 332; id. *D. Heldens.* 394.

ingluuies, II. 27, see *crapula*, 90, see *indigeries.*

ingratus, II. 89, see *inprobus.*

in gremio, in medio domus, XXXIX. 8 (*Greg. Dial.* III. 7 col. 229ᶜ *in gremio* loci).

inhibere, detineri morare [=morari, see Dictt.], I. 63 (*De Canon.*; *Can. Conc. Carth.* LVI hoc...*inhiberi*...debet).—**inhibere**, prohibere, XLVIII. 18 (*De Cass.*, *Inst.* V. 20 adpetitus *inhibere* non potuit).

inhiberi, see *inhibere.*

inhumatus, XLV. 11, see *ops.*

iniciatus, sanctificatus, IV. 86 (*Ruf.* X. 10 fol. 166ª nondum *initiatus* in sacris).—**initiatum**, ordinatum, XLI. 18 (*De nomin. div.?*).

inicium [init-], XX. 6, see *extentera.*

iniit, XXIX. 21, see *curia.*

inimicus, xxxv. 186, see *infestus*.

iniquas, ii. 178, see *tirannides*.

initiatum, ordinatum, xli. 18, see *iniciatus*.

initiatur, xl. 12, see *fulmentatur*.

initiatus, see *iniciatus*.

initio [initium], ii. 116, see *materia*.

initium, see *extentera*; *materia*.

iniuriam, xxxiv. 47, see *sugillationem*; xlviii. 65, see *infestante*.

iniuriis, xxviii. 3, see *infestionibus*.

in lati, in italia, xxxvi. 17 (*Oros.* ii. 4, 12 oppida...*in Latio*).

inlecebris, inlicitis sollitationibus [sollicitat-], ii. 93 (*Bened. reg.* 1, 24 [34] gulae *inlecebris* servientes). Cf. *inlecebris*, tychtingum, Cp. I135; *i-*, tyctinnum (instr. pl. of *tyhten*[*n*], allurement, bait), Ep. 12A15; Ef.[1] 366, 12. See Bosw. T.

inlecta, suscitata, xxxiv. 26 (*De Cass., Inst.* xi. 15 anima...cogitationum *inlecta* dulcedine).—**inlecti**, incitati, xxix. 24 (*Uerb. Interpr.*=*Hier. in Matth.* xvi. 18 per quas *illecti* homines ducuntur).

in lecticis, a similitudine lecti dicuntur, xiii. 58 (*Isai.* lxvi. 20 adducent...fratres vestros...*in lecticis*).

IN LIBRO ANTONII, XXVIII *tit.*—LIBRO ISAIE PROPHETE, XIII *tit.*—LIBRO OFFICIORUM [=Isidor. *de eccles. officiis*], XXVI *tit.*—LIBRO ROTARUM [=Isidor. *Lib. de natura rerum*], XXVII *tit.* [On the title *Liber Rotarum*, cf. Areval's ed. of Isidore's Opera, tom. i. p. 659.]

inlicitis, ii. 93, see *inlecebris*.

inluminans, ix. 1, see *lustrans*.

inluminatio, xxvii. 13, see *lustrum*.

in mare adriatico, ab adriano imperatore qui pensabat hoc mare cum catenis in profundum, xxxix. 20 (*Greg. Dial.* iii. 36 col. 304B *in mari Adriatico*).

in mausilio, in monumento, vii. 6 (2 *Paral.* xxxv. 24 sepultus *in mausoleo*).

in metallo, in carcere, xxxv. 205, see *metalla*.

inmisit, xii. 4, see *inplanauit*.

inmites, i. 16, see *barbari*.

inmunda, iv. 80, and xxxv. 246, see *spurca*.

inmundicia, xxix. 20, see *quisquilia*.

inmundis, xl. 14, see *reis*.

inmunditia, see *quisquilia*.

inmunes, mundi, xlviii. 52 (*De Cass., Inst.* v. 34 si...fuerint a caligine caecitatis *inmunes*).

inmunitatis, castitatis, xlviii. 22 (*De Cass., Inst.* v. 12, 1 *inmunitatis* priuilegio decoratam).

in myrthece, in domo unguentorum, xxxv. 169 (*Ruf.* v. 2 fol. 76b *in myrotheca* conclusi)=*in merothece*, in domo unguentorum, Cp. I142; *in merothecę*, in d. u., Ep. 12A21; Ef.[1] 366, 18. Cf. also Cp. M132, 138; Ep. 14C36 & 14E33; Ef.[1] 371, 14, 51.

in nablis, in cimbalis [cymb-] quę per pedes ponuntur, vii. 1 (1 *Paral.* xv. 16, 20 constituerent cantores *in* organis musicorum, *nablis* videlicet, et lyris et cymbalis). See *nablium*, *nablum* in Lew. & Sh.; Gesenius נֵבֶל & נֶבֶל.

innataris, viii. 3, see *ne innataris*.

inniti, confisi confidentes, xiii. 20 (*Isai.* x. 20 *inniti* super eo).

inoffensus [for *offensus*?], iv. 87, see *infensus*.

inoleuerant, see *moluerunt* sub v. *inoleuit*.

inoleuit, increuit informatur, i. 59 (*De Canon.*; not found). Cf. *inolescere*, crescere, Cp. I321; *inolescit*, iungit, Cp. I315.—**moluerunt**, manserunt uel senuerunt, xxxv. 93 (*Ruf.* i. 1 fol. 3b si qua...in ipsis boni semina ... *inoleuerant*) = *ioluerunt*, manserunt, Cp. I470 & Ef.[1] 365, 25; *ioluerunt* [corr. from *ioloerunt*], manserunt, Ep. 11E13.

inopiae, see *inopie*.

inopie [-ae], xxx. 68, see *ptocheus*; see also *peri pthocheas*.

inopinatus, xxviii. 53, see *paraprosdocia*.

inops, xlv. 11, see *ops*.

in ormentum, in ornamentum, xii. 25 (*Eccles.* xxvi. 21 *in ornamentum* domus). If there is no dittography here, the gloss is, perhaps, *a correction*, not an interpretation, of the lemma. See *Eccles.* xxxii. 7 *in ornamento* auri. The Cambridge MS. agrees with the present Glossary.

in pago, in uico conpetis [=compitis], iii. 31; see *pagi*.

inpegit, trudit, xlviii. 8 (*De Cass., Inst.* v. 6 illos...nimietas panis...*inpegit*).

inpelebatur [inpell-], xxxv. 155, see *arcebatur*.

inpellebatur, see *inpelebatur*.

inpelleris, xii. 44, see *inpingaris*.

in peluem, uas rotundum ligneum, xxv. 13 (*Joh.* xiii. 5 mittit aquam *in pelvim*; Wordsw. & White *in peluem*, &c.).

inpendiis, rebus, xii. 11 (*Eccles.* xxi. 9 qui aedificavit domum suam *impendiis* alienis).

in pennias, ober scoeiddo, xlii. 27 (*Ex div. libris*=? *Vita S. Eugen.* 14, Migne, lxxiii col. 614B ipsa *impunitas* ad hoc eum perduxit, ut etiam dominae meae... cubiculum impudenter ingressus). Glogger, who suggests *impunitas* (safety from punishment, or hurt, dissoluteness) for *in pennias* or *in pennicis*, further proposes ofersc(a)eþþu (over, exceeding scathe, insolence, mischief), f. for *oberscoeiddo*; cf. sceþþ[u], hurt, injury (Bosw. T.), from sceaþa (scathe, harm, injury), sceaþan (to scathe, hurt, injure). For the ending *o* see Siev. *Gr.* § 253, note 2.

inpensa, xv. 4, see *litura.*

inperagrata, intransita, xl. 9 (*Uerba?*).

inpingaris, inpelleris, xii. 44 (*Eccles.* xiii. 13 ne improbus sis, ne *impingaris*). For *inpingere* see also *inpolastis.*

inpinguastis, xxviii. 17, see *inpolastis.*

inplanauit, seduxit inmisit, xii. 4 (*Eccles.* xv. 12 ille me *implanavit*).

inpleta, xxxiv. 27, see *oppleta.*

inpletis, xxxix. 67, see *conpotis.*

inpolastis, inpugnastis uel inpinguastis [*inpingere?*], xxviii. 17 (*Lib. Anton.* xlvi col. 159D Haec omnia Scripturis divinis, quas *interpolatis*, inserta sunt). Acta SS., xvii Jan., p. 136 has *interpellatis*, and in note g, p. 137, *interpellastis.*

inpolito, xxiii. 5, see *lapide inpolito.*

inpolluta, xxviii. 53, see *paraprosdocia.*

inponerent, xiii. 46, see *cataplasmarent.*

inportunitas, ii. 96, see *inprobitas.*

inportunus, i. 67, see *insolens*; ii. 89, see *inprobus.*

inpotens, i. 67, see *insolens.*

inprobitas, procacitas, i. 61 (*De Canon.*; *Can. Conc. Sard.* ix Episcoporum *improbitas*; *Can. Conc. Carth.* xciii p. 163a *improbitas* eius).—**inprobitas**, procacitas, inportunitas, ii. 96 (*Bened. reg.* 52, 6 [9] non inpediatur alterius *inprobitate*).

inprobitate, see *inprobitas.*

inprobus, ingratus procax inportunus, ii. 89 (*Bened. reg.* 23, 9 sin *inprobus* est [15 impr-]; 2, 60 [90 *inprobos*] *improbos* coerceat).

in prostibulo, in domo fornicaria, xxxv. 116; see *prostipulum.*

inpudicarum, i. 127, see *striones.*

inpugnare, xxxv. 264, see *incessere.*

inpugnastis, xxviii. 17, see *inpolastis.*

in pulpito, in gradu ubi lectores legunt, i. 65 (*De Canon.*); **in pulpito**, in gradu ubi lectores legunt, xxxix. 53 (*not* in Greg. Dial., but) = (*Can. Conc. Laod.* cxviii tit. p. 130 in ambone, id est *in pulpito* psallere).

inputribili, x. 11, see *tigna.*

inputribilis, xv. 10, see *ebor.*

inquid [-quit], xxxiii. 20, see *colamina.*

inquietudine, xxxv. 148, see *insolentia.*

inquilini, ministri, xix. 18 (*Job* xix. 15 *inquilini* domus meae...habuerunt me).

inquisitiue, xxxviii. 1, see *examussim.*

inreprehensibiles, xli. 2, see *chorepiscopi* sub v. *presbiteri.*

inreuocabilis, ii. 128, see *obstinatus.*

inridebit, xxviii. 28, see *metonymia.*

inrideret, xiii. 23, see *ganniret.*

inrigationem, x. 22, see *areola.*

inrisio, xxviii. 74, see *ironia.*

inrogantur, see *eregantur.*

inrogatis [sine interpret.], ii. 94 (*Bened. reg.* 7, 80 [127] in...*inrogatis* iniuriis).

inruens, xxxv. 263, see *infestus.*

inruissent, xxxv. 135, see *eripisissent.*

insani, xxxv. 177, see *uesani.*

insania, xxxv. 45, see *suppuratis.*

insanis, xxix. 62, see *de citiuis.*

insanus, xxxix. 19, see *freniticus.*

insaturabilia, see *offer.*

in scamnis, in subselliis, ii. 95 (*Bened. reg.* 9, 10 [13] *in scamnis*; 11, 6 [7] *in subselliis*; cf. above, p. 5, note §). Cf. *subsellia*, scamma, Cp. S643; *s*-, scamnia, Ep. 24A25; *s*-, scamna, Ef.[1] 390, 48.

insecutio, i. 121, see *secta.*

in serris, serra dicitur lignum habens multas dentes quod boues trahent [-hunt], xiii. 36 (*Isai.* xxviii. 27 non...*in serris* triturabitur gith).

insertos, xliv. 10, see *cardines.*

insigne, nobile clare, i. 64 (*De Canon.*; *Can. Conc. Carth.* liii *insigne* mentis tuae tenemus votum).

insigniri, xl. 17, see *inuri.*

insimularet, accusaret uel insultaret, xxxv. 110 (*Ruf.* ii. 5 fol. 21a cum in caeteris...*insimularet* Iudaeos). Cf. *insimulat*, accussat, Cp. I82; Ep. 11E18; *i*-, accusat, Ef.[1] 365, 30.

insinuare, insinuat, i. 7, see *alligare.*

in sirtim, mare arenosa [!], iii. 33; see *sirte.*

insolens, inportunus inpotens intollerandus, i. 67 (*De Canon.*; *Can. Conc. Carth.* lxxix propter...*insolentem* insultationem haereticorum).—**insolentia**, inquietudine uel lasciuia, xxxv. 148 (*Ruf.* iii. 32 fol. 49b ex *insolentia* populi). Cf. *insolentia*, inquietudo, Cp. I84; Ef.[1] 365, 33; *insilentia*, i-, Ep. 11E21.

insolescit, unstillit, xlviii. 28 (*De Cass., Inst.* v. 14 lasciuiam carnis, quae fotu escarum uehementius *insolescit*). *unstillit*, from *unstillan*, to be restless, not still, see Bosw. T. (*un-stillan*, *unstillian*); cf. *agitatio*, unstilnis, Cp. A399.

insolubile, xiv. 9, see *in unge.*

inspectio, i. 126, see *spectacula.*

inspiciunt, xvi. 7, 30, see *aruspices*, 32, see *auspices*; xxxv. 24, see *auspiciis.*

instabilis, ii. 9, see *acidiosus.*

instar, viii. 17, see *nitrum.*

institis, suithelon, xxv. 12 (*Joh.* xi. 44 prodiit qui fuerat mortuus, ligatus pedes et manus *institis*). Cf. *instites*, sueðelas,

Cp. I119; *instites*, suedilas, Ep. 12A4; Ef.[1] 366, 2. *suithelon* (Instr. plur.), from *suithel* = A.S. *sweþel*, *sweoþol* (Bosw. T.), a swaddling-band; O.H.G. *swidel*, *swithel*; D. *swachtel*.

instructi, I. 22, see *caticumini*.

instructio, XXX. 29, see *capun periens*.

instructionum, XXX. 93, see *ypophesion*.

instruitur, XXVII. 20, see *menstruum*.

instrumenta, peritię utensilia uel materie [materiae], II. 88 (*Bened. reg.*, 4 *tit. instrumenta* bonorum operum, 50 [76] *instrumenta* artis spiritalis; 73, 15 [25] *instrumenta* virtutum).

in sublime, idest anticristus [antichr-] qui quasi feliciter incedit, VIII. 13 (*Salam.* XXX. 32 Est qui stultus apparuit postquam elevatus est *in sublime*; cf. *ib.* XXX. 29 Tria sunt quae bene gradiuntur et quartum quod *incedit feliciter*).

insula, XXIV. 14, see *Tyrus*; XXIX. 39, see *prorusu*; XLIII. 1, see *Themisto*, 2, see *Calipso*; XLV. 12, see *Coa*.

insultaret, XXXV. 110, see *insimularet*.

integra, II. 166, see *sincera*.

integritas, I. 131, see *sinceritas*; XXXIV. 7, see *ason*.

intellectui, XXX. 41, see *ascesi*.

intellectum, XXVIII. 44, see *hypallage*, 74, see *ironia*; XXX. 90, see *ascetron*.

intellectus, XXXIV. 29, see *theorice*.

intellegatur, XXII. 16, see *ueredarii*.

intellegere, XXXIV. 46, see *conicere*.

intellegi [intelligi], XXVIII. 57, see *figura*.

intellegitur, XLIV. 29, see *axem*.

intelligentie, see *ascesi*.

intentis, II. 1, see *adtonitis*.

intentos, extensos, VI. 24 (*Breu. exsol.*?).

inter, XXXI. 24; XXXV. 27.

interdicens, see *abdicans*.

interdum, I. 4, see *alias*.

interfeci, see *succidi*.

interfectorem, XXXV. 159, see *confectorem*.

interfici [for *interfeci*], XVII. 17, see *succidi*.

interiecto, XXXV. 27, see *puncto*.

interior, XLIII. 22, see *forinnadas*.

interitum, XXXV. 305, see *pessum*.

Interocrina, see *interorina*.

interorina, propter [for *proprium*] nomen loci, XXXIX. 9 (*Greg. Dial.* I. 12 col. 212[B] In eo etiam loco *Interorina* vallis dicitur, quae a multis verbo rustico *Interocrina* nominatur).

interpellastis, interpellatis, interpolatis, see *inpolastis*.

interponentes, XXI. 20, see *labastes*.

interpositionem, XXVIII. 47, see *parenthesin*.

interpretatio, XXXV. 36, see *metafrasin*; INTERPRETATIO, XXIX *tit.*; INTERPRETATIO SERMONUM DE REGULIS, II *tit.*

interpretationem, XXX. 61, see *metafrasin*.

interpretatur, XXVIII. 60, see *enthimema*, 86, see *epithalamium*.

interpretis, IV. 98, see *comellas*.

interrogatio, XXVIII. 27, see *erotema*, 36, see *peusis*.

interrogato, XXXV. 124, see *inconsulto*.

intestina, XXXV. 202, see *exta*.

intestinas, IV. 70, see *fibras*.

intimare, suggerere, I. 66 (*De Canon.*; *Can. Conc. Carth.*, praef. p. 142[a] ad sedem venerandam...*intimare* possitis; id. LVI, p. 154[a] ut...valeat *intimare*).

intimi, XIX. 56, see *molas*.

intimum, I. 57, see *genuinum*.

intollerandus, I. 67, see *insolens*.

intransita, XL. 9, see *inperagrata*.

intrat, XXXVI. 3, see *promontorium*, 4, see *sinum*.

in triuiis, in tribus uiis, XIII. 30, see *triuium*.

introitum, II. 18, see *aditum*.

intus, XIII. 47 and XXII. 12, see *urna*.

inualidus, XXXIV. 55, see *eneruatus*.

inuastum, inuisum, IV. 33 (*Eccl. Istor.*) = (*Ruf.* III. 8 fol. 40[a] viri...*infausti* pręsagii indignatione commoti).—**infaustiorem**, infeliciorem, XXXV. 139 (*De Eus.*) = (*Ruf.* III. 6 fol. 37[b] *infaustiorem*...protulisset aetatem). Cf. *infastior*, infelicior, Cp. I83; *infaustior*, infelicior, Ep. 11E20; Ef.[1] 365, 32.

inueni, XLVIII. 74.

inueniens, see *nanctus*.

inueniri, XXXV. 288, see *nancisci*.

inuenitur, VIII. 17; XIV. 2, see *nitrum*; XV. 31, see *salinas*.

inueniunt, XXXV. 18, see *opperiunt*.

inueniuntur, XXIV. 5, see *mocum*.

inuentus, see *nanctus*.

inuersio, XXVIII. 39, see *allegoria*.

inuestes, see *infestes*.

inuestigatio, II. 160, see *sagatitas*.

inuicem, XL. 5, see *alternandis*; XLIV. 17, see *cous*.

inuidet, XLVIII. 39, see *libet*.

in uiridario domus, in atrio pro uiriditate herbarum, XLII. 20; see *uiridarium*.

inuisis, XLIV. 10, see *cardines*.

inuisum, luad, XXXV. 289 (*Ruf.* IX. 7 fol. 150[a] *inuisum*...hominum genus; IX. 10 fol. 155[b] Maximinus...Deo atque hominibus *inuisus*) = *inuisus*, lath, Cp. I229; Ef.[1] 367, 20; *inuisus*, laath, Ep. 12E5. For *inuisum* see also (IV. 33) *inuastum*. For (*luad* for *laad* =) lād, hateful, hated, loathed, see Bosw. T. (*lād*, adj.).

inuitabant [for *inuitabar*?], III. 30, see *appulli*.

inuitabar, see *appulli*.
inuitat, x. 1, see *osculetur me*.
inuitatus, XLVIII. 2, see *adscitus*.
inuitiat, contradicat, III. 55; see *inficiabor*.
in unge adamantino quamuis modicum sit sicut ungula tamen insolubile sicut adamans petra durissima, XIV. 9 (*Hier.* XVII. 1 Peccatum Juda scriptum est...*in ungue adamantino*).
inuoluatur, XLIV. 10, see *cardines*.
inuoluco, uudubindlae, XLVII. 98 (*Alia* =?)=*i*-, uudubinde, Cp. I236; *i*-, uuidubindlae, Ep. 12E15; *inuolucu*, uuydublindae, Ef.[1] 367, 31. The lemma and its meaning suggest a formation like that of *convolvulus* (a plant, bind-weed), perh. *involvola*. For *uudubinde*, &c. *woodbine*, see Bosw. T. (*wudubind*, *wuduwinde*).
inuolucris, see *inuolucrus*; *inuoluere*.
inuolucrus, uuluc, XLVII. 20 (*Alia*=?) =*inuolucus*, uulluc, Cp. I. 235; *inuolucus* [*c* altered from *r* or *s*], uuluc, Ep. 12E13; *i*-, uulluc, Ef.[1] 367, 29; *i*-, weoluc, Wright W. 422, 19.—Schlutter (*Journ. Germ. Phil.* I. 329 and *Anglia* XXVI. 303) refers this lemma to Ezek. XXVII. 24 Ipsi negotiatores tui multifariam *involucris* hyacinthi..., which is glossed, in a St Gallen MS., *inuoluclis* dicitur quando inuoluitur vestimentum idest *vulluch* (Steinm. I. 640, 15 & 16; cf. id. III. 301, 62 *inuoluculum*, conuolutio uestium, id est *uuolloch*), and hence *uuluc &c. a wrapper* (Germ. *Wickeltuch*); cf. Kluge, *A. S. Les.* p. 220; Schade, p. 1209 (*wulluh*, *wulluch*). It seems that the above A.S. *uuluc*, *uulluc* (O.H.G. *vulluch*, *uuolloch*) are the same word as *weoluc*=weoloc, a whelk (in Prov. E. more correctly *wilk*), though it may also mean "inuolucrum" from a root *wil*-, Indogerm. *wel*, with a gradation *wol*, as in Lat. uol-u-ere; hence *weoloc* and *inuolucrum* are from the same root. The original form was perhaps **wiluc*, which becomes *weoluc*, as *i* becomes *eo* by u-umlaut (cf. A.S. *meoloc*, *meoluc*, milk= Goth. *miluks*, from **miluc*), and might also become *wuluc*, by the action of *w*, just as the old A.S. *widu* (wood) usually appears as *wudu*. So that **wiluc*, *weoluc*, *wuluc* are equivalents, meaning (1) a thing twisted; (2) Lat. *inuolucrum*, a wrapper, covering, cloth, G. *Wickel*(-tuch); (3) a twisted shell, hence a whelk-shell, and finally the whelk itself.
inuolucus, see *inuolucrus*.
inuoluere, quando inuoluitur uestimentum in corio uel in sago, XV. 18 (*Ezech.* XXVII. 24 negotiatores tui multifariam *inuolucris* hyacinthi...gazarumque pretiosarum). See also *inuolucrus*.
inuoluitur, XV. 18, see *inuoluere*.
inuri, insigniri, XL. 17 (*Uerba?*).
IOB, XIX *tit.*
iocus, IV. 47, see *stadium*.
IOHANNE, XXV *tit.*
IOHEL, XVII *tit.*
ioluerunt, see *moluerunt*.
ionan, filia uulcani, XXVIII. 13 (*Lib. Anton.* XLVII col. 160A semiclaudem Vulcanum...ignem, *Junonem* aerem...interpretantes).
Iouis, filius saturni nouissimus, XXVIII. 23 (*Lib. Anton.* XLVI col. 159C parricidium *Iouis*; XLVII libidinum principem *Iouem*). For *Iouis* see also (XXVIII. 11) *Diana*; (XLVI. 8) *flamen*.
ipsa, XIV. 3; XXVII. 9; see also *areola*.
ipsae, see *calculus*; *plaustrum*.
ipsam, XXXIX. 33.
ipse, XXXIII. 7 (bis), 16.—[for *ipsa?*], X. 22; [for *ipsae*], XIII. 47.
ipsę [ipsae], XXVIII. 88.
ipsis, XLIV. 10.
ipsius, VIII. 8; X. 12; XVII. 8; XXXVI. 1; XLIV. 10, 29.
ipso, XXVIII. 57; XXXIX. 15.
ira, XIII. 23, see *ganniret*.
irae, see *tu thimisiun*.
irato, XXXV. 213, see *infenso*.
ire, II. 8, see *apostatare*.
irę [irae], XXIX. 59, see *tu thimisiun*.
ironia, idest inrisio quoties aliquid quod sub laude dicitur intellectum uituperationis habere monstratur, XXVIII. 74 (*Cass. Psalm.* XXVII. 4 *ironia*, id est irrisio q. a. q. s. l. d. i. u. h. m. See also XXI. 8; XXXIX. 20).
ironiam, see *per hironiam*.
irpex, see *erpica*.
irr-, see *inr*-.
irrisio, see *ironia*.
ISAIE, XIII *tit.*
isca, see *isica*.
Isemerinus [=ἰσημερινός], idest meridianus, XLIV. 14; see *arcticos*.
isica, tyndri, XLVII. 29 (*Alia*=?)=*isca*, tyndrin, Cp. I491; *i*-, tyndirm, Ep. 13A7; *i*-, tyndrin, Ef.[1] 367, 27. Isica (isca)= Lat. *esca*. For *tyndri* &c. (=Germ. *Zunder*, D. *tonder*, &c.) see Bosw. T. (*tynder*, tinder, fuel).
isocem, see *merocem*.
ista, X. 1.
isti, XXVIII. 18.
ISTORIAE, IV *tit.*
ita, XLIV. 10, 11, 27.
italia, XXXVI. 17, see *in lati*.
item, XLIV. 16 (bis).
ITEM ALIA, XLVI *tit.*; XLVII *tit.*; ITEM

ALIA, XV. 36, is perhaps title to ch. XV. 32–36.

ITEM ALIA; DE CÆLO, XLIV *tit.* [=S. Isidori Hisp. *de natura rerum*, cap. XII tit. (col. 981) *De cælo*].

ITEM DE CASSIANO, XLVIII *tit.*—DE DIUERSIS NOMINIBUS, XLIII *tit.*—DE ECCLESIASTICA STORIA, V *tit.*—DE NOMINIBUS DIUERSIS, XLI *tit.*—INCIPIUNT UERBA, XL *tit.*

itenerarium [for *itin-*], XXX. 72, see *otheporicon*.

iter, XVII. 7, see *Niniue*.

iterarium [for *itiner-*], XXX. 71, see *sinphosin*, 87, see *otheporicon*.

iteratio, XXVIII. 30, see *epembabis*, 37 see *metabole*.

iteratione, XXVIII. 75, see *prolemsis*.

iterum, XXXI. 11, see *ephi*; XXXV. 200, see *reusti*.

itilaris, for *tilaris* (q.v.).

itinerarium, see *otheporicon*; *sinphosin*.

itineris, XXII. 16, see *ueredarii*.

iubar, lumen uel splendor, XLVIII. 15 (*De Cass.*, *Inst.* VIII. 12 spiritus sancti splendidissimum *iubar*).

iubilo, lętitia quę non potest uerbis exponi, XIX. 28 (*Job* XXXIII. 26 videbit faciem eius in *jubilo*; cf. VIII. 21 *jubilo*).

iudex, I. 87, see *presul*.

iudicationes, I. 122, see *sanctiones*.

iudicaturia, XXIV. 18, see *pretorium*.

iudicauit, I. 125, see *sanxit*.

iudices, XXIII. 16, see *senatores*.

iudicio, II. 62, see *examine*.

iudicium, see *censura*.

IUDITH, XXI *tit.*

iuditium [-cium], XXXIX. 3, see *censura*.

iugera, XIII. 15, see *decem iugera*....

iugeres, gycer unius diei opus aratoris, XXXV. 75 (*Ruf.* III. 20 fol. 43ᵃ in quadraginta *iugeribus*). For *iugeres* see also (XIII. 15) *decem iugera*; and cf. Papias (ap. Du C.) who has this gloss except *gycer*, which latter, from its *y*, seems to be an A.S. form; it may be of Germanic origin and cognate with *iuger*, or else borrowed so early that *g* became *c* (cf. Lat. *ager*, A.S. *æcer*). Cf. G. *Juchert*, *Jauchert* (Kluge, *Wrtb.*); D. *juk* (Franck, *Woordenb.*); E. *yoke* (Skeat, *Dict.*).

iuge sacrificium, legale officium, XVI. 24 (*Dan.* VIII. 11 ab eo tulit *juge sacrificium*; cf. also VIII. 12, 13; XI. 31; XII. 11).

iugis, XLVIII. 38, see *contiguis*.

iugiter, II. 28, see *continuanda*.

iugum montium, uerticem montium, XXXV. 277 (*Ruf.* VII. 25 fol. 126ᵃ ad summum alpium *iugum*).

iumenta, XII. 35, see *equus emissarius*.

iungebtur, XL. 4, see *pangebantur*.

iunioris, see *iuuenior*.

iuniper, arbor, XIX. 58 (*Job* XXX. 4 radix *juniperorum* erat cibus eorum).

iuniperorum, see *iuniper*.

Iunonem, see *ionan*.

iure, XXXV. 198, see *abiurari*.

ius, XXXV. 96, see *fas erat*.—**ius**, humanum, IV. 22 (*Eccl. Istor.*=*Ruf.* II. 20 fol. 29ᵇ *ius* fasque), see *fas*.

iussit, I. 125, see *sanxit*.

iusta, XXXV. 101, see *rata*.

iuste, II. 108, see *merito*, 141, see *prouide*.

iusti, XI. 15, see *in foribus iusti*.

iustum, XXXV. 96, see *fas erat*.

iuuenes, XXXVI. 22, see *uiteleos*.

iuuenior, idest senior in iuuentute, XXXIX. 35 (*Greg. Dial.*? Glogger suggests III. 38 col. 316ᴬ Joannis *junioris* praedecessoris mei tempore).

iuuentatis, see *indolem*.

iuuentute, XXXIX. 35, see *iuuenior*.

iuuentutis, XLVIII. 24, see *indolem*.

iuxta, XV. 30, see *cata mane*; XXXV. 242, see *ponte moluio*.

kaitonperien goo atoythyo, see *capun periens*.

kalendae, XLIII. 16, see *Micene*; see also *kalende*.

kalendas, see *kalende*.

kalende [-dae], uocationes, II. 97 (*Bened. reg.* 8, 2 a *kalendis* novembris, [2 a *kalendas* nobembres; a *kalendis* nouembribus]; 8 [12] ad *kalendas* novembris; 10, 3 [1] ad *kalendas* novembris).

kalendis, see *kalende*.

katascrophen, see *catastrofen*.

kathareo, see *catheron*.

kyrie eleison, see *kyrieleison*.

kyrieleison, domine miserere nobis, II. 98 (*Bened. reg.* 9, 22 supplicatio letaniae, id est *Kyrie eleison* [36 *kyrieleison*, in marg., & *quirie eleison*, in text]; 17, 9, 12, 20 *Kyrie eleison* [13, 18, 35 *quirie eleison*, in text, and *cyrieleison*, in marg.]) =Cp. *Int.* 186.

l for *ll*: anguile (for anguil*l*ae); cocu*l*a (cucu*ll*a); co*l*irium (co*ll*yrium); co*l*obista (co*ll*yb-); inpe*l*ebatur (inpe*ll*-); pu*l*ulent (pu*ll*-).—l for *t*: argu*l*a (argu*t*a).—l *doubled*: apo*ll*ogeticus (apo*l*og-); asi*ll*um (asy*l*um); carti*ll*ago (carti*l*ago); fa*ll*eras (pha*l*eras); strangui*ll*ato (-gu*l*ato).—l *omitted*: cassidie (-di*l*e).

labarum, see *labrum*; *uixilla*.

labastes, in similitudine sculdre de ligno duas tales faciunt interponentes ficos ne citius putrescant, XXI. 20 (*Judith* X. 5 imposuit...abrae suae ascoperam vini et vas olei, et polentam et *palathas* et panes; Heyse, in note, and Migne, *Patr. Lat.* XXIX col. 52 note[b] *lapates*; Sabat., in note, *lapsaces*; the Sept. παλάθης). Some MSS. have *lapates*, idest in similitudine *palae* (shoulder-blade) idest sculdrę; cf. Steinm. I. 481, 5, 18 (*lapastes*, caricę); 484, 3; 487, 47. *Palatha* of the Vulg. means a cake of preserved fruit, usually figs; but "de ligno" in the above gloss would suggest that the Glossator understood the word to be *lebetas*, basins, pots or jars; see *lapates*, ollę minores, brocco, Steinm. I. 486, 27. For sculdre, sculdrę, see Bosw. T. (*sculdor*, shoulder).

labefacare, agleddęgo, III. 63 (*Vit. S. Anton.* XVI col. 140[B] non potes *labefactare* constantiam). The MS. has this gloss in a Chapter entitled Uerba de S. Martyni Storia, and hence Steinmeyer refers (II. 746, 30) to *Sulp. Sev. Dial.* III. 11, 3 totis animis *labefactati* mussitare et trepidare coeperunt. But as the gloss occurs among a number of glosses all derived from *Vit. S. Anton.*, it is here referred to the above quotation. A verb *agleddian* is not recorded, but *gleddian*, to spatter, is quoted by Bosw. T. from Lchdm. III. 292, 14. Glogger (p. 14) suggests that *agleddaego* may be a causat. of *glīdan*, to cause to glide or slip, or totter; cf. a-glīdan (to glide or slip), labascere, Bosw. T.

labefactare, see *labefacare*.

labiis, XXX. 47, see *musica*; see also *labris*.

laborum, XXIX. 17, see *emulumentum*.

labris [for *labiis*?], XXXV. 228, see *labris*.

labris, labris [for *labiis*?], XXXV. 228 (*Ruf.* XI. 24 fol. 188[b] ibi infantum capita desecta inauratis *labris* inuenta).

labris, uentis nomen, V. 12 (*Ruf.* ?). According to the gloss, the lemma could not be *labris* [lips] which occurs in Ruf. IX. 10 fol. 155[a], and XI. 24 fol. 188[b]. Perhaps for *flabris* [not found in Ruf., but] cf. *flabra*, flatus uentorum, Cp. F231, and *flabris*, uentus [for uentis] tempestas, *id.* F253; *flabris*, uentis tempestatibus, Ef.[2] 295, 17.

labrum [labarum], XXXV. 69; see *uixilla et labrum*.

labrum, ambonem, id est haet, V. 11 (*Ruf.* IX. 9 fol. 152[a] signum quod in coelo sibi fuerat demonstratum, in militaria vexilla transformat, ac *labarum* quem dicunt in speciem dominicæ crucis exaptat). *Ambonem* (a pulpit or reading desk) cannot explain *labarum*, a military standard, and may be a lemma without an interpretation, or, perhaps, a corruption for *fanonem* [for which see Du C.], or for *umbonem*, the full part or swelling of a garment, and a toga; *haet*, a hood, hat, would, in case it is meant to gloss labarum, probably signify a head-band, coif. Cf. *labrum*, segn [a sign, token, see Bosw. T.], Cp. L4; *labarum*, seng, Ep. 13A30; *labarum*, segn, Ef.[1] 368, 25; see Schlutter, in *Journ. Germ. Phil.* I. 323.

labruscas, see *lambruscas*.

lacerat, XXXV. 260, see *lacessit*.

lacernam, prolixor [-xior] cocula [*cuculla*], III. 8 (*De S. Mart. Stor.*=*Sulp. Sev. Dial.* I. 21, 4 haec ut fluentem texat *lacernam*).

lacerta, adexa, XXXV. 55 (*Ruf.* XI. 7 fol. 181[b] oculi...quos...*lacertae* habent)=*lacerta*, aðexe, Cp. L45. For *adexa* (for *aðexa*), a lizard, newt, see Bosw. T. (*aðexe*), and for its final *-a*, see Sievers, *O. E. Gr.* § 276 note 5.

lacertae, see *bulinus*; *lacerta*.

lacertę, XLVII. 89, see *bulinus*.

lacertos, pars brachii, XIX. 49 (*Job* XXII. 9 *lacertos* pupillorum comminuisti).

lacessat [for *lassescat* ?], IV. 38, see *facessat*.

lacessit, prouocat uel frequenter lacerat, XXXV. 260 (*Ruf.* V. 3 fol. 78[b] Beata... Blandina...innumeris ictibus *lacessita*).

lacessita, see *lacessit*.

lacetur, VI. 17, see *lanio*.

lacinias, extremas partes uestium, XIV. 33 (*Hier.*=*Thren.* IV. 14 tenuerunt *lacinias* suas).

laciniosa, slitendę, XXXV. 183 (*De Eus.*); **liciniosa**, questiosa [for *quaestuosa*, lucrative, abundant ?], IV. 65 (*Eccl. Istor.*) =(*Ruf.* VI. 11 fol. 102[a] libros suos στρωματέας appellauit, idest *laciniosa* quadam et uaria diuersitate contextos). For *slitendę* (patched; ptc. of *slītan*, to slit, tear, rend), see Bosw. T. (*slītan*).

lacum, VIII. 19, see *si usque ad lacum...*

lacuna, floda, III. 53 (*Vita S. Anton.* 27, col. 150[B] quaerunt saltem collectam pluviis *lacunam*)=*lanucar*, flode, Cp. L37; *lacunar*, flodae, Ep. 13E13; Ef.[1] 369, 31. For *floda* (which is, perhaps, the original form) &c., a channel, sink, gutter, see Bosw. T. (*flode*); for the final *e*, instead of *a*, see Sievers § 276, note 5; cf. *cloacarum*, flodena (Wright W. 372, 1, and also their index, *flode* &c.).

lacunar, see *lucunar*.

laena, see *lena*.

laetania, rogatio, postulatio, II. 99 (*Bened. reg.* 9, 22 [35] supplicatio *letaniae*, [35 *litanię*]; 12, 9 [12] *letania*, *litania*; 13, 19 *letania*, [32 *litania*, *letania*, *laetania*]; 17, 17 [28] *letania*, *litania*).

laetitia, see *iubilo*

laeua, see *leua*.

lagena, see *lagunculas*.

lagenam, see *lagonam*.

lagina [lagena], xix. 60, see *lagunculas*.

lagonam, uas lapideum ollo [olla] idest crog, xxix. 47 (*Uerb. Interpr.*=*Hier. in Matth.* xxvi. 18 [quoting] Et invenietis ibi quemdam, portantem *lagenam* aquæ. Cf. *Marc.* xiv. 13)=*laogoena*, crog, Cp. L21; *lagoena*, croog, Ep. 13C25; Ef.[1] 369, 4. For *crog*, a small vessel, or bottle, a crock, see Bosw. T. (*crog, croc*).

lagunculas, ex lagina [lagena] diminitiuum croog, xix. 60 (*Job* xxxii. 19 *lagunculas* novas disrumpit). For *croog*, a small vessel, flask or bottle, a crock (Germ. *Krug*; D. *kruik*) see Bosw. T. (*crog, croc*); see above *lagonam*.

lambent, see *lumbire*.

lambruscas, malas uuas, xiii. 14 (*Isai.* v. 2, 4 fecit *labruscas*). Cf. *labrusca*, arida uba, Cp. L51; Goetz, vi. (sub v. *labrusca*).

lamia, dea siluę dicitur habens pedes similes caballi caput et manus totum corpus pulcrę mulieris et uiderunt multi aliqui manserunt cum ea, xiii. 43 (*Isai.* xxxiv. 14 ibi cubavit *lamia*)=*lamia*, d. s. d. h. p. s. c. c. manus et t. c. pulchrum simili mulieris, Cp. L29. The Cambr. MS.: Lamia d. s. d. h. p. s. c. caput uero et m. et totum c. pulchrum simile mulieris; it omits the rest. The Author. Vers. has *screech-owl*.

lamina, see *petulum* [for *petalum*].

lampadis, xxix. 14, see *lanternis*.

Lamuhel, agnomen salamonis sicut ecclęsiastes ab actione, viii. 9 (*Salam.* xxxi. 1 uerba *Lamuelis* regis; ibid. 4 ô *Lamuel*; Heyse in both places *Lamuhel*). The Author. Vers. has *Lemuel*.

lana, xxxix. 51, see *byssus*; xlvi. 24, see *situs*.

lance, mensura, xli. 20 (*De nomin. div.* ?). Cf. *lancis*, mensuratio, Cp. L42; Ep. 13E24; Ef.[1] 369, 42. See also *lanx*.

lanceis, see *in contis*.

lancis [for *lanceis*], xxi. 9, see *in contis*.

lancis, xlv. 7, see *lanx*.

languida, ii. 111, see *morbida*.

lanio, lacetur, vi. 17 (*Breu. exsol.* ?). Cf. *lanio*, qui lacerat, Cp. L17; Ep. 13C31; Ef.[1] 369, 10.

lanionibus, qui berbices uel porcos incidunt membratim et uendunt, xxxv. 72 (*Ruf.* ix. 10 fol. 157[b] iubebat...*lanionibus* dari). Cf. *lanioses*, qui berbices incidunt, Cp. L2; *laniones*, qui berbices incidunt uel porcos, Ep. 13A15; Ef.[1] 368, 10.

lanista, see *lanistra*.

lanistra, macellarius in macello carnes diuidit, xlv. 19 (*Uerba de multis*=*Ars Phocae*, p. 412, 20 hic *lanista*).

lanternis, uasa lampadis perlucentia, xxix. 14 (*Uerb. Interpret.*=*Hier. in Matth.*, but not found). Glogger suggests that the Glossator may have found *lanternis* in xxvi. 55 (col. 201[A]) after "cum gladiis et fustibus," just as in *Joann.* xviii. 3 (venit illuc cum *lanternis* et facibus et armis), and that Jerome's "in nocte quasi latitantem" may refer to this.

lanuginatio, see *lanugo*.

lanugo et aluginatio pene idem est, squalor lanugo in carne, xi. 3 (*Sap.* v. 15 spes impii tamquam *lanugo* est). The Cambr. MS. Kk. 4. 6 has: "*lanugo* uel *lanuginatio* pene idem sunt idest *squalor lanugo* in carne, *lanuginatio* in vellere." Perhaps leg. *lanugo squalor*...

lanx, unde lancis, xlv. 7 (*Uerba de multis*=*Ars Phocae*, p. 412, 2 feminini generis...*lanx* mors merx...). See also *lance*.

Laodes, nomen regine [-nae], xxviii. 15 (*Lib. Anton.* xlvi col. 159[c] ille modulatus ales *Ledæos* petivit amplexus).

lapates, see *labastes*.

lapide, xxiv. 13, see *alabastrum*.

lapidea, xx. 8, see *taermę*.

lapide inpolito, ungebatne stane non exciso, xxiii. 5 (1 *Esdr.* v. 8 ad domum Dei...quæ ædificatur *lapide impolito*; vi. 4 de lapidibus impolitis). *Ungebatne stane* =*ungebēatne stāne*, unbeaten stone, instrum., see Bosw. T. (*ge-beātan*; *stān*).

lapidem, viii. 8, see *in aceruo m-*.

lapideo, viii. 18, see *ptisanas*.

lapides, iv. 90, see *calles*; xix. 21, see *glarea*; xxiii. 3, see *latomi* and *cymentarii*; xxxiv. 17, see *cautes*.

lapides onichinos, dunnę, vii. 4 (1 *Paral.* xxix. 2 *lapides onychinos*); dunnae [sc. *stānas*], from *dun*, black-brown, swarthy, dusky; Engl. *dun*.

lapideum, xxv. 1, see *catinum*; xxix. 47, see *lagonam*.

lapidibus, xvi. 21, see *aggerem*.

lapidis, xxiv. 13, see *alabastrum*.

lapidum, xxv. 14, see *lithostrotus*.

lapis, xxxix. 48, see *calculum*; xlvi. 25, see *cliutex*.

lappa, clitę, xv. 36; **lappa**, clate, xviii. 2 (*Osee*, ix. 6 *lappa* in tabernaculis eorum; x. 8 *lappa* et tribulus ascendet)=*lappa*, clibe, Cp. L54; *lappa*, cliþae, Ep. 14A12; *lappa*, clifae, Ef.[1] 370, 7. For *clitę*, *clate* (clibe, cliþae, clifae), the herb clot- (or more correctly clote-) bur, see Bosw. T. (*clāte, clite*); Oxf. Dict. (*clote*).

lapsaces, see *labastes*.

laquearia, celum [caelum, coelum] ex

lignis, III. 41 (*De S. Mart. Stor.* = *Sulp. Sev. Dial.* I. 21, 4 erigit celsa *laquearia*).
laquei, XLVIII. 7, see *biothanti*.
larga, XXVII. 3 & XXVIII. 6, see *frugali*.
largitas, XXXV. 221, see *munificentia*.
Lars, see *las*.
las, ignis, XLV. 3 (*Uerba de multis* = *Ars Phocae*, p. 411, 33 masculini generis as dens...fons *Lars* mons...; in note *las*).
lasciuia, XXXV. 146, see *luxus*, 148, see *insolentia*.
lasciuiantem, XIV. 34, see *uitulam*...
lasciuientes, feruentes, I. 69 (*De Canon.*; *Can. Conc. Carth.* LX feminarum pudor... iniuriis *lasciuientibus* appetatur).
lasciuientibus, see *lasciuientes*.
laser, pigmentum, XXXVI. 21 (*Oros.* I. 2, 43 ubi...*laser* nascitur).—**laser**, genus herbę, XLVI. 15 (*Alia* = *Ars Phocae*, p. 415, 16 hoc *laser*).
lassescat, see *facessat*.
lata, XXVII. 3; XXVIII. 6, see *frugali*; XXXIX. 32, see *dalmatica*.
latam, XXXV. 83, see *amplam*.
latere, XVI. 14, see *ex latere regni*.
laterem, XVII. 18 (bis), see *tene laterem*.
lateria, VI. 19, see *modoli*.
lateribus, XXII. 12, see *urna*.
lati, XIV. 14, see *calati*.
lati [for *Latio*], XXXVI. 17, see *in lati*.
latina, see *sicel*.
latine, I. 19, see *concilium*, 22, see *caticumini*, 31, see *catholicus*, 80, see *omousion*, 114, see *synodus*, 118, see *simbulum*; II. 107, see *monachus*; XIV. 10, see *miricę*; XXVIII. 52, see *epizeusis*, 53, see *paraprosdocia*, 62, see *tapynosin*; XXXIII. 3, see *talentum*; XXXVIII. 16, see *ochimo*; see also *catepenon*; *diatiposis*.
latine [for *latina*], XXXIII. 7, see *sicel*.
latini, XXVIII. 55, see *metaforan*; latini for *Latine*, XXVIII. 49, see *periscema*, 50, see *catepenon*, 88, see *diatiposis*.
latino, II. 161, see *sarabaite*, 188, see *coenobium*.
latinos, see *C* apud lat-.
latinum, I. 111, see *sicera*.
latinus [-nos], XXXII. 2, see *C* apud lat-.
Latio, see *in lati*.
latomi, qui maiores lapides incidunt, XXIII. 3 (1 *Esdr.* III. 7 Dederunt...pecunias *latomis* et cæmentariis). See also *cymentarii*.
latomis, see *latomi*.
latriuncula, herst, IV. 75 (*Ruf.* VIII. 12 fol. 140[b] *craticulas* prunis impositas; cf. *craticulis* exusta, *id.* V. 3 fol. 78[b]). For *herst* = hearst (a small hurdle?), a small gridiron, see Bosw. T. (*hearste-*, *hierste-panne*, a frying-pan).
latum, XIV. 20, see *scalpellum*; XVII. 5, see *trulla*.
lauatio, XIX. 34, see *adluuio*.
laudabilem, XXX. 59, see *panagericon*.
laudabilibus, XXXV. 88, see *panagericis*.
laudare, XL. 2, see *fatere*.
laudate, II. 7, see *alleluia*.
laudatio, XI. 1, see *fascinatio*.
laudatorem, XLVIII. 46, see *fautorem*.
laude, XXVIII. 74, see *ironia*.
laudem, II. 85, see *hymnum*; XXVIII. 50, see *catepenon*.
laudes, XIX. 50, see *carmina in nocte*.
laudibus, IV. 1, see *pannigericis*.
laurenti [-tii], XXXIX. 33, see *porta laurenti*.
Laurentii, see *porta laurenti*.
laurus, arbor est unde milites coronas sibi faciunt in uictoria, XXXVII. 19 (*S. Aug.* ?).
laus, XXVIII. 86, see *epithalamium*.
lautiores, pulcriores, XXXIV. 23 (*De Cass.*, *Inst.* XI. 13 corpore *lautiores*).
lebes, caldarius, XV. 41 (*Ezech.* XI. 3, 7 haec est *lebes*). For *lebes* (lebetas) see also *labastes*.
lecti, II. 100, see *lectisternia*; XIII. 58, see *in lecticis*.
lecti aurei, berian beed deauratum, XXII. 8 (*Esther* I. 6 *lectuli* quoque *aurei* et argentei...dispositi erant; Sabat. *lecti*). Q[y] *berian* from *beran*, to bear, carry, like the O.H.G. *traga bethi*, *tragabetti*; cf. *Lectuli aurei*, berian bed gildi bilegid, i.e. traga bethti &c. (Steinm. I. 488, 16). See Schlutter in *Anglia* XXVI. 303.
lecticis, XIII. 58, see *in lecticis*.
lectis, VIII. 16, see *mala aurea*...
lectisternia, uestmenta [uestim-] lecti uel ordo lectorum, II. 100 (*Bened. reg.* 22, 2 [2] *lectisternia*...accipiant; and 53 ubi sint *lecti strati* [67 note *lectisternia*]).
lecto, see *delecto eius*.
lectores, I. 65; XXXIX. 53, see *in pulpito*.
lectorium, II. 6, see *analogium*.
lectorum, II. 100, see *lectisternia*; VIII. 16, see *mala aurea*...; XXXV. 16, see *stromatum*.
lectuli, see *lecti aurei*.
lectulo, XXX. 35, see *uarietas stromactis*.
lectum, X. 13, see *ferculum*.
lecythus, see *fidelia farris*.
Ledæos, see *Laodes*.
legale, XVI. 24, see *iuge sacrificium*.
legat, XXXVII. 9, see *tabulas legat*.
legationes, XLVIII. 29, see *delecto eius*.
legentium, XXXV. 53, see *ludus literarum*, 247, see *auditorio*.
legerunt, XXIII. 8, see *recenserunt*.
legio, sex milia, XXXV. 31 (*Ruf.* V. 5 fol. 80[b] in *legione* quadam) = *legio*, ui milia, Cp. L131; Ep. 13E23; Ef.[1] 369, 41.

legione, see *legio*.

leguminum, omne genus fauorum [*fabarum*], II. 106 (*Bened. reg.* 39, 7 [10] unde poma aut nascentia *leguminum*).

legunt, I. 65; XXXIX. 53, see *in pulpito*; XXXV. 184, see *liberales litera*.

leguntur, II. 6, see *analogium*.

lembo, XXIX. 39, see *prorusu lembo*.

lena [laena], toscia [=toga], II. 101 (*Bened. reg.* 55, 25 sagum et *lena* et capitale; *lina* in note [43 *lena, laena*]). As regards *toscia* = *toxa*, cf. Du C.; Kluge, *Angels. Lesebuch*, 3e Aufl., p. 10, who regards *toscia* as A.S. = *tysce*, mantel. It is doubtful, however, whether *toscia* could be A.S., as there are no A.S. glosses in Ch. II. See Schlutter, in *Anglia*, XXVI. p. 301, who gives further references to Steinmeyer &c.

lendina, hnitu, XLVII. 84 (*Alia* = ?) = *lendina*, hnitu, Cp. L127; Ep. 13E5; Ef.[1] 369, 22. *Lendina* (deriv. from *lens*, lendis) a louse's egg, *a nit*; for *hnitu* see Bosw. T. in voce.

lenonibus, conciliatoribus mulierum, XXXV. 258 (*Ruf.* VI. 5 fol. 98a eam...*lenonibus* traderet). Cf. *lenones*, conciliatores meretricum, Cp. L103; Ep. 13A17; Ef.[1] 368, 12.

lens, see *lendina*.

lentescere, see *lentiscere*.

lenticula, XXXVII. 5, see *capsaces*.

lentiscere, molliscere [mollesc-], XXXIV. 18 (*De Cass., Inst.* XI. 8 *lentescere* solent).

lentisco, see *lentiscus*.

lentiscus, arbor folia modica habens et fructus sine grana idest muras rubras ursi, XVI. 5 (*Dan., Praef. Hieron.* p. XVIb, and Migne XXVIII col. 1293A a *lentisco*). For *muras* perhaps leg. *moras*, another form for *morum*, a mulberry, a blackberry. The Cambr. MS. has: lentiscus, a. est f. m. h. e. f. sine *granis* i. *moras* rubras.—*Ursi* is not clear; it may be a misreading (see Steinm. I. 656, 3 rubsr), or a corrupt A.S. word. Glogger, on account of the reading *uisi* in Bern MS. fo. 15 b/1, suggests *uiri* = *wir*, myrtle.

leo, see *arihellio*.

leone, VI. 16, see *leonine*; XIX. 39, see *leopardus*.

leonine, de leone, VI. 16 (*Breu. exsol.* ?).

leonis, XIX. 15, see *tigris*.

leopardus, ex leone et pardo generatus, XIX. 39 (*Job*? Not in the *Vulg.*). In Job IV. 11, we read *tigris* periit, for which, according to Hieron. (*Comm. in libr. Job*, IV, Migne, *Patr. Lat.* XXVI col. 628A) another text (which see in Sabatier) has "*myrmicoleon*, id est, formica et leo." Cf. *myrmicaleon*, formicaleo uel formicarum leo, Cp. M379.

leporem, decorem, XLVIII. 21 (*De Cass., Inst.* Praef. 3 non *leporem* sermonis inquirens).

lepra, IV. 12, see *uncus*; XXXV. 107, see *ulcus*.

leprositas, IV. 89, see *morbo regio*.

lesera, see *pessul*.

letania, letaniae, see *laetania*.

lethaeo, see *letheo*.

letheo, mortali, XXXIV. 2 (*De Cassiano Inst.* V. 31, note 8 *Letheo* quodam sopore).

lętitia, XIX. 28, see *iubilo*.

leua [laeua], XLIV. 27, see *dextera*.

leuem, XV. 48, see *ad leuicandum*.

leuicandum [for *leuigandum*], XV. 48; see *ad leuicandum*.

leuigandum, see *ad leuicandum*.

leuiter, II. 134, see *passim*.

lex, II. 52, see *deuteronomii*; XXX. 22, see *deuterosin*, 51, see *astronomia*.

lexas, XLVIII. 51, see *sanguessuges*.

li for *u*: oci*lis* for ocius.

Libanus, X. 14; see *Amana* et *libanus*.

Liber, XLIII. 28, see *Bachus*.

liberales litera, quas seculares homines legunt, XXXV. 184 (*Ruf.* VI. 15 fol. 104b si ...in *liberalibus literis*...exercerentur). Cf. in *liberalibus literis*, II. 5 fol. 20b; eruditione...*liberalium litterarum*, VIII. 10 fol. 139a &c.

liberalia, XLIII. 29, see *Bachus*.

liberalibus, see *liberales litera*.

liberalitas, donatio quę a diuite fit, I. 68 (*De Canon.*; *Can. Conc. Carth.* XXXII Si...ipsis...aliquid *liberalitate* alicuius... obuenerit; *Decret. Symm.* IV p 263a cum *liberalitati* illi alia itinera reseruentur).

liberant, XXII. 16, see *ueredarii*.

libertabus, friulactum, XLVI. 32 (*Alia* = *Ars Phocae*, p. 427, 8 *libertabus*) = *libertabus*, frioletan, Cp. L177. For *friulactum* (for *friulætum* f., from *friulæte*? a freedwoman) see Bosw. T. (*freolæta*, *frioleta*, m., a freedman); Kluge, *A.S. Leseb.* p. 177 (freolæt, m.).

libertatem, XXXV. 218, see *anulum*.

libet, inuidet, XLVIII. 39 (*De Cass., Inst.* V. 22 hic, dum *liuet* [*libet*, in note], paruulum...se probat).

libet, quibuscumque, II. 104 (*Bened. reg.* 7, 80 [127]; 32, 4 [3] *quibus libet* inrogatis iniuriis).

libidum [for *liuidum*], XXXIX. 15, see *ferula*.

libra, XXXI. 3, see *sextarius*; XXXIII. 2, see *mina*.—**libra**, LXXII solidos pensat, XXXIII. 28 (*Euch. De Pond.* ?).—**libra** et **pondera** idem sunt, XXXI. 27 (*De ponder.*?). —**libra** et **pondus** idem sunt, XXXIII. 23

(*Euch. De Pond.* ?).—**libra** habet scupulos [scrup-] CCLXXUIII quod facit dragmas XCVI, XXXII. 11 (*De ponder.* ?).—**libra** LXXII solidos greci LXXXIIII solidos pendica, XXXI. 7 (*De ponder.* ?).—**libra** XII uncias, XXXI. 4 (*De ponder.* ?). Cf. Blume, I. 374 sqq. As the MS. has a **v** above uncias, Glogger thinks that it may refer to an original A.S. *ynce* (an inch), or the O.H.G. *unza.*

libram, XXXII. 9, see *mina.*

libras, XXXI. 20, see *taletum,* 31, see *sextarius,* 32, see *sextarius* ; XXXII. 10, see *talentum* ; XXXIII. 26, see *sextarius.*

librę, XXXIII. 1, see *talentum.*

libri, II. 6, see *analogium* ; XXX. 7, see *bibliotheca.*

libris, IV. 9, see *fastibus* ; XXXV. 102, see *fastibus* ; LIBRIS, XLII *tit.*

libro, XXVII. 18, see *De eodem libro* ; XXXIII. 5, see *dedragma* ; LIBRO, XIII *tit.* ; XXVI *tit.* ; XXVII *tit.* ; XXVIII *tit.*

librorum, II. 13, see *biblioteca,* 69, see *eptaticum.*

libros, XXX. 86, see *temoys.*

LIBRUM, IV *tit.*

licant [for *ligant*], XIII. 40, see *perpendiculum.*

licet, quamuis, II. 103 (*Bened. reg.* 37, 2 [1] *Licet* ipsa natura humana trahatur ad misericordiam; cf. 40, 11 [17]; 49, 2 [1]). For *licet* see also (I. 111) *sicera.*

liciniosa, questiosa [for *quaestuosa*, lucrative, abundant ?], IV. 65 ; see *laciniosa.*

Lidii, gens, XIV. 26 (*Hier.* XLVI. 9 *Lydij* arripientes...sagittas).

lien, miltę, XLVI. 6 (*Alia*=*Ars Phocae*, p. 415, 1 hic *lien* lienis)=*lien*, milte, Cp. L172 ; *lien*, multi, Ep. 13E10 ; *lien*, milti, Ef.[1] 369, 27. For *miltę*, the milt, spleen (=A.S. *milte*, O.H.G. *milzi*, Germ. *Milz*) see Bosw. T. in voce.

ligamen, XIX. 19, see *pedica.*

ligamentum, XII. 14, see *loramentum.*

ligant, see *perpendiculum.*

ligaturas, VII. 3, see *commissuras* ; (for *ligatus* ?) XXXVIII. 36, see *sindetus.*

ligneo, XXXV. 49, see *loculo.*

ligneum, II. 6, see *analogium* ; XXV. 1, see *catinum,* 13, see *in peluem.*

ligni, III. 6, see *toronicum,* 39, see *carricibus* ; IV. 3, see *ilix* ; XLVI. 14, see *suber,* 16, see *liser.*

lignis, III. 41, see *laquearia* ; XVI. 21, see *aggerem* ; XIX. 20, see *tympanum* ; XXXV. 73, see *codicibus.*

ligno, XIX. 44, see *tęde* ; XXI. 20, see *labastes* ; XXXV. 27, see *puncto,* 41, see *in aculeis* ; XXXVIII. 19, see *tholus.*

lignum, XIII. 36, see *in serris.*

lignum in pane, crucem in carne, XIV. 7 (*Hierem.* XI. 19 mittamus *lignum in panem* eius). Cf. Hieron. in *Jer.*, Migne, *P.L.* XXIV col. 756[B].

ligones, ferrum fusorium [for *fossorium*] idest tyrfahga, XVII. 2 (*Joel,* III. 10 Concidite...*ligones* vestros in lanceas ; *Mich.* IV. 3 concident...hastas suas in *ligones*). Cf. *ligones*, meottucas, Cp. L161 ; *ligones*, mettocas, Ep. 13E1 ; *lagones*, metocas, Ef.[1] 369, 18. See Steinm. I. 678 note 3.—Bosw. T. record *turf-haga* an enclosed place covered with turf, a grassy enclosure ; but the above *tyrf-ahga* evidently means a mattock, hoe, from *tyrf*, a turf, sod, piece of earth with grass on it, and *ahga*, a mattock, hoe=D. & G. *egge* ; see Verdam (*egge*, *egede*, which latter, =A.S. egeþe, has an additional suffix).

lima, qua limatur ferrum fiil, XIII. 52 (*Isai.* XLIV. 12 lima operatus est)=*lima*, fiil, Cp. L251. For *fiil*, fil (=*feol*, f. Germ. *Feile*, D. *vijl*), a file, see Bosw. T. (*feol*).

limati, mundati, XV. 47 (*Ezech.* XXI. 15 gladii...*limati* ad fulgendum).

limatur, XIII. 52, see *lima.*

limax, see *maruca.*

limbo, see *prorusu.*

liment, XVII. 5, see *trulla.*

liminibus, IV. 82, see *codicibus.*

linea, XLIV. 3, see *axis* ; see also *camisa.*

lineamentis, see *columellas.*

lineolis, dredum, XXXV. 233 (*Ruf.* XI. 25 fol. 189[a] *linteolis* obductis ; Cacciari, II. p. 106 *lineolis* obductis). The reading *lineol-* (dimin. of linea, a line, thread) is also in other edd. of Ruf. For *dredum* (instr. plur. of ðrēd, ðrǣd, a thread) see Bosw. T. (*þrǣd*).

lineum, XXXVII. 8, see *odon* ; XXXIX. 46, see *camisa.*

lingua, II. 161, see *sarabaite.*—**lingua tertia**, discordians [*discordans*, as in the Cambr. MS.] lingua uel rixosa, XII. 29 (*Eccles.* XXVIII. 16, 19 *lingua tertia*) ; for *lingua* see also *sicel.*

linguarum, XXVIII. 85, see *figura sardismos.*

lingue [-gua], XXXIII. 7, see *sicel.*

liniamentis, signis, XL. 21 (*Uerba* ?).

linimentis [lineam-], XXXV. 257, see *columellas.*

lino crudo, idest uiride non cocto [!] ueste, XII. 41 (*Eccles.* XL. 4 usque ad eum qui operitur *lino crudo*. Cambr. MS.: Lino crudo. Viride necdum cocta ueste).

linteamen, I. 81, see *orarium.*

linteamina, XXXV. 37, see *oraria.*

linteolis, see *lineolis.*

linteum, XXXIX. 14, see *sabanum.*

lio, XV. 27 [for *leo*, lion, or the A.S. *hlēo*(*w*), protection, shelter ?] ; see *arihellio.*

liquidam, IV. 110, see *defecatum*.

liquide [-dae], XXXIII. 19, see *nebel*.

liquidis, XXXI. 12, see *sata*; XXXIII. 12, see *ephi*.

lira, XLVI. 10, see *liricen*, for *liticen*?

liram [lyr-], XLIII. 25, see *liricus*.

liricen [?], qui lira cantat, XLVI. 10 (*Alia*=*Ars Phocae*, p. 415, 4 hic *liticen*). Cf. *liticen*, qui cum lituo canit, Cp. L179; *liciter* qui cum lituo canit, Ep. 14A5.

liricus [lyr-], qui per liram [lyr-] cantat, XLIII. 25; see *comicus*.

liser, genus ligni minuti, XLVI. 16 (*Alia* =*Ars Phocae*, p. 415, 16 hoc *siler*, hoc iter, hoc cicer, hoc *siser*). Cf. *siler* (a kind of brook-willow), genus ligni, Cp. S360; Ep. 25A35; Ef.[1] 393, 6.

litania, litanię, see *laetania*.

litat, immolat, IV. 73 (*Eccl. Istor.*); **litat**, sacrificat, XXXV. 278 (*De Eus.*)=(*Ruf.* VII. 25 fol. 126[b] iterum *litat*).

litera [literis], XXXV. 184, see *liberales l.*

literali [for *literalis*?], XXX. 49, see *grammatica*.

literalis, see *grammatica*.

literarum, XXXV. 53, see *ludus literarum*.

literas (litteras) commendaticias (-titias), see *literis commendatitiis*.

literis, see *liberales litera*.

literis commendatitiis [sine interpret.], II. 102 (*Bened. reg.* 61, 28 Caveat...abbas, ne...monachum...suscipiat sine consensu abbatis eius aut *littera commendaticias* [49 *literas conmendaticias*, in note *litteris commendaticiis*]); cf. Edm. Schmidt *Regula*: *literas commendatitias*, *literis commendatitiis*.

lithostrotos, see *lithostrotus*.

lithostrotus, conpositio lapidum, XXV. 14 (*Joh.* XIX. 13 in loco qui dicitur *Lithostrotos*; Wordsw. & White *lithostrotus*).

liticen, see *liricen*.

litteras, XLI. 1, see *presbiteri*; see also *codicibus*.

litura, inpensa lim uel clam, XV. 4 (*Ezech.* XIII. 12 ubi est *litura*). For *lim* (lime; Germ. *Leim*, D. *lijm*), see Bosw. T. (*līm*); Kluge, *Etym. W. d. Sprache* (leim); for clām (cloam, clay; Germ. & D. *Klei*) see Bosw. T. (*clam*); Oxf. Dict. (*cloam*); Kluge (*Klei*).

liuet, see *libet*.

liuidum, see *ferula*.

loca, XV. 31, see *salinas*; XXXV. 26, see *oethepia*, 34, see *solaria*, 117, see *territoria*; see also *diocesis*.

loci, XIII. 21, see *carcamis*, 29, see *mede*; XIV. 22, see *in fatores*; XV. 23, see *Syeres*; XVI. 19, see *apethno*; XXX. 7, see *bibliotheca*, 26, see *diatripas*; XXXV. 7, see *toparcha*, 91, see *Mambre*; XXXIX. 9, see *interorina*.

loco, XXVIII. 33, see *tropus*, 76, see *metafora*; XLVI. 24, see *situs*.

loculo, uase ligneo, XXXV. 49 (*Ruf.* X. 15 fol. 169[b] brachium *loculo* delatum).—**loculum**, portatorium de tabulis, XXV. 4 (*Luc.* VII. 14 tetigit *loculum*).

locum, XXVIII. 33, see *tropus*; XXXV. 156, see *ad stadium*, 252, see *meandrum*.

locus, IV. 72, see *prostipulum*; XV. 29, see *thalamus*; XXXV. 7, see *toparcha*, 50, see *asillum*, 171, see *harene*, 240, see *angiportus*; XLV. 1, see *gymnasium*.

locustae, see *chantari*.

locuste [-tae], XXXVIII. 5, see *chantari*.

locutionem, XV. 40, see *oraculum*.

locutiones, XXX. 89, see *ominas*.

logismoi, see *pantocranto*.

longa, II. 113, see *morosa*; XXV. 5, see *scorpiones*.

longiores, XII. 40, see *cyneris*.

longis, XIX. 9, see *untialibus*.

longum, XXII. 12, see *urna*.

loquacitate, uerbositate, II. 105 (*Bened. reg.* 49, 14 [24] de *loquacitate*).

loquantur, XLVIII. 1, see *eregantur*.

loquendi, see *pantocranto*.

loqueretur, XXXV. 113, see *concionaretur*.

loquitur, XIX. 5, see *eschematismenos*, 23, see *susurrat*.

lor, funis, XII. 37 (*Eccles.* XXXII. 27 jugum et *lorum* curvant collum).

lora, XLI. 17, see *mastigia*.

loramentum, ligamentum, XII. 14 (*Eccles.* XXII. 19 *loramentum* ligneum).

lordicare, see *lurdus*.

lorica, see *toraca*; *torax*.

lorum, see *lor*.

Loth, XI. 15, see *in foribus iusti*.

LUCA, XXV *tit.*

lucar, uectical [-gal], XLVI. 11 (*Alia* =*Ars Phocae*, p. 415, 8 hoc *lucar*). Cf. *lucar*, uectigal puplicum, Cp. L306.

luceat, XLIII. 50, see *lucus*.

lucens, XLI. 9, see *calcidon*.

lucernas, XVII. 16, see *infusuria*.

lucra, XLVIII. 74, see *emolumenta*.

lucrum, I. 54, see *foenus*.

luctantium, XXXIX. 45, see *palestrarum*.

luctatio, XXXVIII. 30, see *palestris*.

luctu, XL. 1, see *uiscide*.

luctus, IV. 11, see *tragoedia*.

lucubraciuncula, unius noctis uigilantia, XXI. 2 (*Judith*; *Praef. Hieron.*, p. XIV[a], and Migne, *Patr. L.* XXIX col. 39[A] huic unam *lucubratiunculam* dedi).

lucubratiunculam, see *lucubraciuncula*.

luculentas, XLI. 13, see *crisolitus*.

luculentissime, splendissime [splendidiss-], xxxv. 163 (*Ruf.* iv. 25 fol. 69b libros ...*luculentissime* conscriptos).

lucunar, camera, xlvi. 12 (*Alia*=*Ars Phocae*, p. 415, 9 hoc *lacunar*).

lucus, quod minime luceat, xliii. 50 (*De div. nominibus*=Donati *Ars gramm.* p. 402, 4 *lucus* eo quod non luceat).

ludentes, xxxv. 33, see *bachantes*.

ludi, xxxix. 60, see *alae*.

ludor, i. 1, see *aleator*.

ludum, i. 2, see *alea*; xxxv. 199, see *garrientium*.

ludus literarum, scola [schola] paruulorum legentium, xxxv. 53 (*Ruf.* x. 32 fol. 175a *ludos literarum*...patere decernit) =*ludus litterarum*, scola legentium, Cp. L271; Ep. 13A11; *l-*, *l-*, scola litterarum legentium, Ef.[1] 368, 6.

lugoria, exuberat, iii. 49 (*De S. Mart. Stor.*=*Sulp. Sev. Dial.* ii. 10, 4 herbis fecunda *luxuriat*, foeni in ea fructus *exuberat*). Qy. are there here two lemmata without explanations, or is *exuberat*, which also appears in the text, meant to be a gloss to (luxoriat=) luxuriat? cf. *exuberat*, habundat, Cp. E454; *exuberat*, exundat, superfluit, Cp. E498. One MS. has *luxuriatur*.

lumbare, bragas [bracas] modicas, xiv. 8 (*Hier.* xiii. 1 posside tibi *lumbare* lineum; also xiii. 2, 4, 6, 7 &c. *lumbare*, the accus.).

lumbi, see *lumbire*.

lumbire [sine interpret.], xix. 13 (*Job*?). Perhaps: *Job* xxxix. 30 pulli *lambent* sanguinem. Or perhaps corrupted for *lumbi*, see *lumbos* Job xvi. 14, xxxviii. 3, xl. 2.

lumbis [for *lumbus*?], xlvi. 5, see *rien*.

lumbus, see *rien*.

lumen, ii. 40, see *deificum lumen*; xlviii. 15, see *iubar*.

lumina [for *lamina*], iv. 34, see *petulum*.

luna, xii. 42, see *uasa*; xxvii. 20, see *menstruum*.

lunae, see *quartane*.

lunam, xliv. 27, see *dextera*.

lune, iii. 3, see *quartane*.

lunę, xiii. 6, see *lunulas*.

lunulas, quas mulieres in collo habent de auro uel argento a similitudine lunę diminitiue dicuntur, xiii. 6 (*Isai.* iii. 18 auferet Dominus...*lunulas*). The Cambr. MS.: lun. q. m. i. c. h. d. a. u. a. ad similitudinem lunę.

lupam, vi. 11, see *catastam*.

lupercal, templum panos, xxvii. 11; see *Luperci*.

lupercales, xxvii. 7, see *Luperci*.

lupercalia, ipsa sacra, xxvii. 9; see *Luperci*.

Luperci, sacerdotes lupercales, xxvii. 7 (*Lib. Rot.*=*Isid. Lib. de nat. rer.* iv. 4 Februarium...a februis sacris *lupercorum* appellauerunt)=*luperci*, sacerdotes lupercales, Cp. L317. See also xxvii. 9 **Lupercalia**, ipsa sacra (=*lupercalia*, ipsa sacra, Cp. L336) and xxvii. 11 **Lupercal**, templum panos (cf. *lupercal*, haerg, Cp. L325), which are further explanations of *Luperci*. For haerg=A.S. *hearh*, a temple, an idol, see Bosw. T.

lupus, breuis, xlvii. 72 (*Alia*=?)=*lupus*, brers, Cp. L297; *l-*, baers, Ep. 13E7 and Ef.[1] 369, 24. For *lupus* (the wolf-fish or pike) see Lewis & Sh.; for (*breuis*, error for *brems*?) *baers* see Bosw. T. (*bærs*, *bears*, a perch); Oxf. Dict. (*bass*, sb.[1]); Skeat (*bass*[2]); Kluge, *Et. Wrtb.* (*Barsch*).

lurdus, lemphald, xlvii. 45 (*Alia*=?) =*l-*, lemphalt, Cp. L296; *l-*, laempihalt, Ep. 13E4; *lurdur*, lemphihalt, Ef.[1] 369, 21. For *lurdus* (from *luridus*? pale yellow, ghastly; putrefied; slow; limping) see Körting, *Wörterb.* 5750; Du C. *lurdus*, and *lordicare* (which he derives from the Gr. λορδός, bent supinely). For *lemp-hald*, *lemp-halt*, *laempi-halt* (limping-lame) see the Oxf. D. *limphalt* and *halt*; Bosw. T. (*lemp-healt*).

lurica [lor-], xi. 4, see *torax*; xlv. 17, see *toraca*.

lurida, pox, iii. 57 (not *De S. Mart. Stor.* but, like **luridam**, luto sordidam, xxviii. 10=*Lib. Anton.* xx col. 144D Illico *luridam* faciem serpentis agnovi). Cf. *luridam*, luto pollutam, Cp. L301; Ep. 13E21; Ef.[1] 369, 39. *pox* for **þox*?=A.S. *dox* (translating Lat. *flauus*, Wright W. 239, 26), E. *dusk* (Skeat, *Conc. Etym. D.*, ed. 1901, and Oxf. D., sub v. *dusk*). Cf. Napier, p. 15, note to 532; Schlutter, in *Anglia* xxvi p. 301, who refers to *geþuxsað*, *Be Dóm.* D105, for which see Bosw. T. (*þuhsian*). For þ and d, cf. E. *dim*, O. Sax. *thimm.*—**luridus**, pallidus, xxxv. 4 (*Ruf.* i. 8 fol. 12b humor liquidus et *luridus*)=*luridus*, pallidus, Cp. L273; Ep. 13A22; Ef.[1] 368, 17. For *luridus* see also *lurdus*.

luscinia, see *ruscinia*.

luscus, xxx. 70, see *monaptolmon*.

lusor, lussor for *lusor*, see *aleator*.

lustrans, circumiens et inluminans, ix. 1 (*Eclesiast.* i. 6 *lustrans* universa).

lustrum, inluminatio, xxvii. 13 (*Lib. Rot.* =*Isid. Lib. de nat. rer.* vi. 6 *lustrum* quinquennii tempus est) = Cp. L302; Ep. 13E22; Ef.[1] 369, 40.

luto, xxviii. 10, see *luridam*; xlviii. 69, see *ceno*.

lutugisprum, rationabile, xxix. 58 (*Uerb. Interpr.*=*Hier. in Matth.* xiii. 33 τὸ λογικὸν [other MSS. τὸ λογιστικὸν] quod nos possumus interpretari *rationabile*).
luxoria [luxuria], xxxv. 146; see *luxus*.
luxoriat, see *lugoria*.
luxosa [luxuriosa], i. 25, see *commessationes*.
luxuria, see *luxus*.
luxuriat, luxuriatur, see *lugoria*.
luxuriosa, see *commessationes*.
luxus, luxoria [luxuria] uel lasciuia, xxxv. 146 (*Ruf.* iii. 23 fol. 44[b] quibus *luxus*...cordi est).
Lydii, see *Lidii*.
lyra [?], see *liricen*.
lyram, see *liricus*.
lyricen [?], see *liricen*.
lyricus, see *liricus*.

m for *in*: *m*oluerunt (for *in*oleuerant).—for *n*: buli*n*us (buli*m*us).—for *re*: amopaga (a*re*opagita).—m *inserted*: la*m*bruscas (labruscas).—*omitted*: copos (co*m*pos).—*doubled*: com*m*edentem (comed-).
macellarius, xlv. 19, see *lanistra*.
macello, xlv. 19, see *lanistra*.
macera, xvii. 14, see *subigens*.
machomenus [sine interpretat.], i. 72 (*De Canon.*). This word, which has not been found in the Canons, seems to answer to the Gr. part. μαχόμενος. The Glossary has it between two lemmata taken from the *Can. Apostt.*, but it is probably not a corruption for *eunuchus*, Can. Apostt. xxi.
mactatio, i. 60, see *immolatio*.
mactus, magis auctus, xliii. 32 (*De div. nominibus*=Donati *Ars grammat.* p. 378, 2 ut dignus munere, *mactus* virtute).
maculatos, xxxiv. 22, see *confectos*.
madefacti, see *madidum*.
madidum, contusum uel contritum, xxxv. 80 (*Ruf.* vii. 14 fol. 121[a] haustu... *madefacti* salutaris graminis).
Maeandrum, see *Meandrum*.
magalia, byrae, xlvi. 37 (*Alia*=*Ars Phocae*, p. 428, 12 *magalia*)=*mapalia*, byre, Cp. M46; *mapalia*, cesae postorum, Ep. 15C3; *m*-, case pastorum, Ef.[1] 372, 27; *magalia*, byre, Cp. M81. For *bȳrae* (cottages, dwellings) see Kluge, *A. S. Leseb.* p. 165 (bȳre n. stall, O. H. G. bûri); Oxf. D. (*byre*).
magi, qui magicam artem faciunt siue philosophiam, xvi. 26 (*Dan.* ii. 2 ut convocarentur...*magi*. See also ii. 27, iv. 4, v. 14 *magi* &c.). For *magi* see also (xvi. 27) *malefici*.
magicam, xvi. 26, see *magi*.
magis, xliii. 32, see *mactus*.
magisteriale, xx. 12, see *didascalium*.
magna, xxxix. 36, see *sex untias*; xli. 19, see *pagus*.
magnas, xxxvii. 9, see *tabulas legat*.
magnato, magno, xii. 5 (*Eccles.* iv. 7 *magnato* humilia caput tuum).
magni sabbati, idest paschę, xxxv. 20 (*Ruf.* iv. 15 fol. 62[a] cum esset dies *magni sabbati*).
magnitudinem, xxviii. 38, see *per figuram yperbolen*.
magnitudo, xxviii. 62, see *tapynosin*.
magno, xii. 5, see *magnato*.
magnopere, forti animo uel maiore opere, ii. 125 (*Bened. reg.* 27, 11 [17] *Magnopere*...debet sollicitudinem gerere abbas).
mago, i. 2, see *alea*.
magos, xvi. 27, see *malefici*.
maialis, bęrg, xlvii. 91 (*Alia* = ?) = *maiales*, bearug, Cp. M38; *maialis*, bearug, Ep. 15A29; Ef.[1] —. *M*-, a gelded boar, a barrow-hog; for bęrg, *bearug*, a castrated boar, a barrow-pig, see Bosw. T. (*bearg*); Kluge, *Wrtb.* (*Barch*); Oxf. D. (*barrow*, *sb*[2]).
maior, xxxi. 1, see *gomor maior*, 14, see *hin maior*.
maiore, ii. 125, see *magnopere*; xxxix. 15, see *ferula*.
maiores, xxiii. 3, see *latomi*.
maius, xl. 1, see *uiscide*.
mala, xi. 14, see *poderis*.
mala aurea in lectis argenteis, mila idest poma de auro in circuitu lectorum pro ornamento, viii. 16 (*Salam.* xxv. 11 *mala aurea in lectis argenteis*). The Bern MS. has (fo. 13 b/11) *mala*; but mila (if it be not a repetition of part of the lemma which alone is to be glossed) may=the Gr. μῆλα or mela; cf. Körting, *Wörterb.* No. 5851.
malagma, multe [-tae] herbe [-bae] contrite [tae] in una massam uulnerum, xi. 12 (*Sap.* xvi. 12 neque *malagma* sanavit eos).
malas, xiii. 14, see *lambruscas*.
male, xl. 3, see *deuotatum*; see also *sitatum*.
malefici, qui sanguine et uictimis et sepe contingunt corpora mortuorum consuetudo autem et sermo communis magos pro meficiis [maleficis?] accipiunt Magi uero apud chaldeos [chaldaeos] philosophi habentur, xvi. 27 (*Dan.* ii. 2 ut convocarentur...*malefici*).
maleficis, see *malefici*.
mali, xxxv. 128, see *molitio*.
malis, x. 26 (bis), see *mustum*.
malis, ex maxillis, xxxiv. 1 (*De Cass., Inst.* ii. 10, 1 dissutis *malis*).

malleolis, quodcumque tunguitur ad excitandum ignem, XVI. 9 (*Dan.* III. 46 succendere fornacem naphtha, et stuppa et...*malleolis*). The Gr. has καίοντες τὴν κάμινον νάφθαν καὶ...κληματίδα bundles of wood, faggot-wood. The Glossator seems to have regarded *malleolis* as anything that could be tinged, besmeared (t*u*nguitur for t*i*nguitur?) for stimulating the fire. Cf. *malleolus*, genus fomenti aput persas, Cp. M2; Ep. 14C19; Ef.[1] 370, 52. Coverdale translated *faggottes*.

malleum [?], XXXVIII. 45, see *sitatum*.

malo, XXXV. 114, see *uecors*.

malua, olus, XL. 11 (*Uerba?*). Cf. *malua* [E. *mallow*], hocc, cottuc uel gearpan leaf, Cp. M42; *malua*, cotuc uel georcmant lab, Ep. 15A32. For *hocc*, *cottuc*, *cotuc* (mallow), see Bosw. T. in vv.; for *gearpan leaf* &c. (yarrow), see Bosw. T. (*gæruwe, gearwe*); Skeat, *D.* (yarrow).

maluerunt, XXVIII. 71, see *ephichirema*.

malum, XII. 33, see *de traiectione*.

malus, XXVIII. 28, see *cacodemonus*.

malus nauis, caput in arbore nauis a similitudine milui, XIII. 37 (*Isai.* XXX. 17 relinquamini quasi *malus navis*).

Mambrae, see *Mambre*.

Mambre, homo uel ciuitas, IV. 4 (*Eccl. Istor.*); **Mambre**, nomen loci, XXXV. 91 (*De Eus.*)=(*Ruf.* I. 1 fol. 2[b] ad ilicem *Mambrae*). For Mambre, *homo*, see Gen. XIV. 13, 24.

mancipantur, manu capiantur, I. 70 (*De Canon.*; *Can. Apostt.* XVIII quae publicis spectaculis *mancipantur*; cf. *Can. Conc. Nic.* XV manciparit, XVI mancipatur &c.).

manciparunt, tradiderunt, XX. 1 (*Tobias: Praef. Hieron.* p. XIII[b] [Migne, *Patr. L.* XXIX col. 24A] librum...quem Hebraei...his quae hagiographa memorant, *manciparunt*).

mancipatur, see *mancipantur*.

mancipium, XLV. 23, see *uerna*.

manducandum, XIII. 1, see *cucumerarium*.

manducant, XXII. 16, see *ueredarii*.

manducat, VIII. 21, see *commandit*; XIII. 25, see *de radice*.

mandunt, XXXIX. 7, see *eruce*.

mane, XV. 30 (bis), see *cata mane*.

manes, anime mortuorum, XLIII. 31 (*De div. nominibus* = Donati *Ars grammat.* p. 376, 26 semper pluralia, ut *manes* Quirites...). Cf. Hildebrand, *Glossar. Lat.* p. 205 (*manes*, dii mortuorum inferi).—**manius**, demones [daem-], IV. 104 (*Ruf.* VII. 27 fol. 130[a] *Manes* quidem). Cf. *manes*, deae, Cp. M10.

mango, comitator equorum, XLV. 30 (*Uerba de multis*=*Ars Phocae*, p. 413, 23 hic *mango*). Cf. *mango*, negotiator, Cp. M48; Ef.[1] 372, 30; *mango*, negotiatur, Ep. 15C7. Q[y] comitator for *commutator*, a barterer? from *commutare*, to barter.

manicas, XI. 4, see *torax*; XXXIX. 32, see *dalmatica*.

manichaei, see *Oethepia*.

manichei [manichaei], XXXV. 26, see *Oethepia*.

manicis, XI. 4, see *torax*.

manifestare, II. 118, see *non detegere*.

manifestauerit, II. 191, see *prodiderit*.

manifeste, I. 84, see *peruadere*.

manipulus, see *manticum*.

manius, demones [daem-], IV. 104; see *manes*.

manna, XI. 16, see *bonam escam*.

manserunt, XIII. 43, see *lamia*; XXXV. 93, see *moluerunt*.

mansionarius, hostiarius qui custodit edem [aedem], XXXIX. 5 (*Greg. Dial.* I. 5 col. 177B De...*mansionario*...; *mansionarii* functus officio; III. 25 col. 280 *mansionario*; *mansionarium*).

manthan, XXX. 44, see *cata manthan*.

mantica, see *manticum*.

manticum, hondful baeues, XLVII. 34 (*Alia* = ?)=*m* , hondful beopes, Cp. M32; *m-*, handful beouuas, Ep. 15A21; *m-*, handful beouaes, Ef.[1] 372, 19. As the A. S. interpretation means *a handful of corn* or *barley* (A.S. *handfull*, and *baeues*, *beopes*, &c. grain, gen. of *baew*, *beow*, cf. Sievers, *A.S. Gramm.* § 250 (1)), the lemma *manticum* seems to point to *mantica* (a bag for the hand, wallet) or *manipulus* (the Roman pole with a handful of hay or straw twisted about it), or *manua* (a handful; see Lewis & Sh.).

manu, I. 70, see *mancipantur*, 76, see *manumissio*; XLVI. 36, see *manubię*.

manua, see *manticum*.

manubię, a manu dictę facultates, XLVI. 36 (*Alia*=*Ars Phocae*, p. 428, 8 *manubiae*).

manubrias [! for *manubria*?], XII. 9, see *cacabus*.

manubrium, XXXVI. 19, see *stiuam*; see also *manubrias*.

manum, I. 50, see *emancipent*.—**manum**, turbam, XXXV. 121 (*Ruf.* II. 20 fol. 29[b] conquirentes...perditorum iuuenum...*manum*).—**manus**, turba, XLVIII. 16 (*De Cass.*, *Inst.* XI. 18 nec episcopi euadere *manus* potui; cf. I. 1, 5 tradent in *manus* gentium [from *Act.* XXI. 11]).

manumissio, eo quod manu mitterentur, I. 76 (*De Canon.*; *Can. Conc. Carth.* LXIV De *manumissionibus*; XXCII *ib.*, *id.*).

manumissionibus, see *manumissio*.

manus, xiii. 43, see *lamia.*—**manus**, turba, xlviii. 16; see *manum.*

mapalia, see *magalia.*

mappam, i. 81, see *orarium.*

mappanus, apollo, xxvii. 15 (*Isid. Lib. Rot.*?). See Goetz, vi. 680, who refers, at the suggestion of Schlutter, to J. Rhys, *Celtic Britain*, p. 228; Holder 414.

mappas, xxxv. 37, see *oraria.*

mappula, ii. 112, see *matta.*

mapula, see *matta.*

maralium [mor-], xxx. 78, see *tropicon.*

Marco, xxv *tit.*

mare, iii. 33, see *in sirtim*; xi. 13, see *in carcere*; xxxvi. 3, see *promontorium*, 4, see *sinum*; xxxix. 20 (bis), see *in mare adriatico.*

mare [for *mari*], xxxix. 20, see *in mare adriatico.*

mari, xli. 8, see *saphirus*; see also *in mare adriatico.*

marinam, vi. 9, see *thiticum.*

marine, xiii. 28, see *sirene.*

marinus, xix. 8, see *murenula.*

maris, xliii. 17, see *nereus.*

maritum, xxxvii. 9, see *tabulas legat.*

marpicus, see *marsopicus.*

marruca, see *maruca.*

marsius, see *cacomicanus.*

marsopicus, uinu, xlvii. 67 (*Alia*=?)=*m-*, fina, Cp. M35; Ep. 15A25; *marpicus*, pina, Ef.[1] 372, 22. Goetz (vi. 181, *marpicus*) thinks the lemma to be *Martius picus* (=Germ. *Marsspecht*), a woodpecker. For *uinu* (leg. *uina*=) *fina*, which latter glosses also *picus* [q. v.] in Cp., Ep. & Ef.[1], and *sturfus* (Wright W. 49, 2), see Bosw. T. (*fina*).

martini, iii. 24, see *sacro tegmini.*

Martius, xxii. 13, see *Nisan*; see also *marsopicus.*

Martyni, iii *tit.*

martyrium, modicum oratorium, xxxv. 64 (*Ruf.* xi. 27 fol. 190 ex uno latere *martyrium*, ex altero consurgit ecclesia).

maruca, snægl, xlvii. 90 (*Alia*=?)=*marruca*, snegl, Cp. M37; *maruca*, snegl, Ep. 15A28; Ef.[1]—. The lemma is, perhaps, a deriv. of *murex*, the purple fish, or for *murena*, the murena. For *snægl*, *snegl*, which also glosses *coclea*, *cuniculus*, and *limax*, see Bosw. T. (*snægel*, *snegel*, a snail).

massa diocesium [sine interpretat.], i. 74, see *diocesim.*

massam, xi. 12, see *malagma.*

Massica, mons, xlv. 13 (*Uerba de multis*=*Ars Phocae*, p. 427, 24 vina Coa dicimus et *Massica*).

mastigia, lora cum uncis ferreis, xli. 17 (*De nomin. div.*); **mautigia**, genus flagellis [!], iii. 43 (*De S. Mart. Stor.*)=(*Sulp. Sev. Dial.* ii. 3 p. 183, 24 consumit Gallicas mularum poena *mastigias*).

mastigias, see *mastigia.*

mater, xxxv. 47, see *metropolis*; xliii. 27, see *frora.*

materia, xxxv. 244, see *fomite.*—**materia**, origo uel initio [initium?], ii. 116 (*Bened. reg.* 65, 10 [18] ab ipso initio ordinationis *materia* ei datur superbiendi).

materiae, see *instrumenta.*

materie [materiae], ii. 88, see *instrumenta.*

matertera, xxxv. 46, see *thia.*

mathematicos, xvi. 29, see *chaldei.*

mathesis, doctrina astrologiae, xxxviii. 26 (*Clem. Recognitt.* ix. 12 qui...calculis *mathesis* decipiunt; ix. 18 unumquodque schema *mathesis*; ix. 26 disciplina *mathesis*).

matheum, xxx. 44, see *cata manthan*; Matheum [Matthæum], xxiv *tit.*

matricis [sine interpretat.], i. 75 (*De Canon.*; *Can. Conc. Carth.* xxxiii *tit.* Vt...nulli Episcopo liceat rem tituli *matricis* Ecclesiae vsurpare...; nec Episcopo liceat *matricis* Ecclesiae...rem tituli sui vsurpare).

matrimoniales, see *tabulas legat.*

matris, xxxv. 26, see *Oethepia.*

matrix, radix uel uterus, xlvi. 28 (*Alia*=*Ars Phocae*, p. 421, 8 haec *matrix*).

matronales [for *matrimoniales*?], xxxvii. 9, see *tabulas legat.*

matta, mappula [two lemmata, without interpret.? see note ‡ on p. 5], ii. 112 (*Bened. reg.* 55, 24 [43] stramenta...lectorum sufficiat *matta*...; 31 [55; also *mapula*] *mappula*).

mattae, xxxiv. 3, see *spiathio.*

Matthæum, see *Matheum.*

maturi, xlviii. 73, see *adulti.*

maturitas [sine interpret.], ii. 114 (*Bened. reg.* 66, 3 [4] senex...cuius *maturitas* eum non sinat vagare).

matuytu, xxx. 29, see *capun periens.*

maulistis [=μαυλιστής, a pandar], scyhend, xlvii. 35 (*Alia*=?)=*m-*, scyend, Cp. M40; *m-*, scyhend, Ep. 15A30; Ef.[1]—. For *scyhend*, *scyend*, a seducer, corrupter, part. sb. of *scyhan*, *scyan*, to persuade, see Bosw. T. (*scȳan*).

mauria, de auro facta in tonica [tunica] idest gespan, xxix. 11 (*Uerb. Interpr.*=*Hier. in Matth.* vii. 28—30 col. 46A violae uero purpuram, nullo superari *murice*)=*murica*, gespon, Cp. M296; *murica*, gespan aureum in tunica, Ep. 14C30; *murica*, gespon aureum in tonica, Ef.[1] 371, 8. From these readings it would seem that the above *mauria* stands for *maurica* or *murica*, a development of *murex*, the secondary meanings of which are (1) a pointed rock or stone; (2) a sharp murex-shell used for a bridle-bit; (3) a caltrop with sharp points; (4) a spike of iron (see Lewis & Short, *Lat. Dict.*), and hence, possibly, murica = the A. S. *gespan* (see Bosw. T.), a clasp.

mauritani, xv. 16, see *mozel*.

mausilio [-soleo], vii. 6, see *in mausilio*.

mausoleo, see *in mausilio*.

mautigia, genus flagellis [!], iii. 43; see *mastigia*.

maxillis, xxxiv. 1, see *malis*.

maxime, xxxiv. 49, see *dumtaxat*; xliv. 7, see *poli*, 11, see *clima*.

maximis, ii. 193, see *precipuis*.

me, x. 1, see *osculetur me*.

Meandrum, nomen montis, iv. 36 (*Eccl. Istor.*) = (*Ruf.* iii. 36 fol. 51[a] ciuitati, quae supra *Maeandrum* iacet). — **Meandrum**, locum uel stagnum, xxxv. 252 (*De Eus.*) = (*Ruf.* v. 16 fol. 86[b] apud Apamiam, quę est supra *Meandrum* posita).

meatus, uaene [uenae] modicę [-cae], xxix. 22 (*Uerb. Interpr.* = *Hier. in Matth.* xv. 17, 18 per occultos *meatus* corporis) = *m.*, uenae modicae, Cp. M143.

Mede, nomen loci, xiii. 29 (*Isai.* xxi. 2 obside *Mede*).

mediam, xxxix. 36, see *sex untias*; xliv. 3, see *axis*.

medicamina, xxxix. 49, see *colirium*.

medicinalis, xiii. 57, see *saliuncula*; **medicinalis**, xxxi. 19, see *obolus medicinalis*.

medicinam, xiii. 1, see *cucumerarium*; xiv. 32, see *croceis*.

medietas, xxxviii. 35, see *ex diametro*.

medio, xxviii. 47, see *parenthesin*; xxxix. 8, see *in gremio*.

meditatio, xxxv. 128, see *molitio*.

medium, xxxvii. 9, see *tabulas legat*; xliv. 29, see *axem*.

medius, ii. 86, see *himina*; xxxi. 8, see *emina*.

meficiis [for *maleficis*?], xvi. 27, see *malefici*.

megale [= mygale], see *netila*.

me hercule, see *miherculi*.

melancholia, see *moloncolia*.

meliora, xiii. 11, see *mutatoria*.

meliorata, ornata, vi. 6 (*Breu. exsol.*?).

meliorem, xxviii. 70, see *sinchrisis*.

melius, xxxv. 201, see *cautere*.

mellatum, x. 25, see *uinum candidum*.

melle, xiv. 5, see *placentas*.

melodia, modulatio, xxvi. 10 (*Isid. Offic.* ii. 12, 2 Vox...habens...*melodiam* sanctae religioni congruentem).

melodiam, see *melodia*.

membra, xxviii. 31, see *ausesis*.

membrano, vi. 15, see *perigamini*.

membranula, xxix. 30, see *pitatiola*.

membratim, xxxv. 72, see *lanionibus*.

membrorum, xxxix. 40, see *paralisin*.

memores salis, pro cibo posuit sal uel doctrinam, xxiii. 12 (1 *Esdr.* iv. 14 nos... *memores salis* quod in palatio comedimus).

memoria, sepulcrum, iii. 58 (*Vit. S. Anton.* vii col. 131[B/C] cum in una *memoria* supra dictus frater eum clausisset). For *memoria* see also (i. 15) *aboleri*; (xxx. 65) *epitomen*; (xxx. 73) *epimehne*.

memorie, see *epimehne*.

memphitica regina egypti [Aeg-] uel ciuitas, xlii. 3 (*Ex div. libris* = *Sulp. Sev. Dial.* i. 23 p. 176, 11 hic Aegyptum... ac tota *Memphitica* regna transiuit).

mendacium, see *nenias*; *per hironiam*.

mendatium [-cium], xxviii. 35 & xxix. 7, see *nenias*; xxxv. 120, see *per hironiam*.

mensa, xxxviii. 29, see *trapezita*.

menses, xxii. 12, see *urna*.

mensis, xxii. 13, see *nisan*.

mensis yperberetheus [sine interpretat.], i. 73 (*De Canon.*; *Can. Apostt.* xxxviii secundò verò xii. die *mensis Hyperberetæi*; cf. *Can. Conc. Antioch.* xcviii mensis Octobris, quem Hyperberetaeon Graeci cognominant).

menstruum, quando luna distruitur [destr-] uel instruitur, xxvii. 20 (*Lib. Rot.* = *Isid. Lib. de nat. rer.* xviii. 5 luna...*menstruis* completionibus deficit).

mensum, v. 1, see *cyati*.

mensura, ii. 142, see *quantitas*; xiv. 30, see *pedalis*; xxx. 48, see *geometrica*; xxxiii. 13 (ter), see *metreta*, 16, see *gomor*, 24, see *urbicus*; xli. 20, see *lance*.

mensurae, see *artabę*.

mensurę [-rae], xxxiii. 12, see *ephi*, 14, see *artabę*.

mente, i. 37, see *delirantes*.

mentis, xxviii. 60, see *enthimema*; xxx. 40, see *extasei*; xxxviii. 10, see *phitagoras*.

mentitur, xxxv. 132, see *fefellit*.

mercatis, xv. 17, see *nundinis*.

mercedes, xxxviii. 43, see *nastologis*.

merces, see *emulumentum*.

mercis [merces], xxix. 17, see *emulumentum*.

mercurii, viii. 8, see *in aceruo mercurii*.

mercurius, viii. 8, see *in aceruo m-*.

meretribus [for *meretricibus*], i. 25, see *commessationes*.

meretricibus, see *commessationes*.

meridiana, xliv. 4, see *clima*.

meridianus, xliv. 14, see *Isemerinus*.

meridię [-die], xliv. 11, see *clima*, 15, see *exemerinus*.

merito, iuste, II. 108 (*Bened. reg.* 7, 47 [76] Docemur...*merito* nostram non facere uoluntatem).

merocem, nomen piscis, III. 20 (*De S. Mart. Stor.*=*Sulp. Sev. Dial.* III. 10, 4 immanem *esocem*; esohascem, isocem, *in note*. The initial *m* of the lemma arose, perhaps, from the final *m* of immanem).

metabole, idest iteratio unius rei sub uarietate uerborum, XXVIII. 37 (*Cass. Psalm.* V. 2 schema...*metabole*, idest i. u. r. s. u. u.).

metafora, idest translatio cum mutatur nomen aut uerbum ex eo loco in quo proprium est, XXVIII. 76 (*Cass. Psalm.* XXXI. 9 *metaphora* id est tr.c.m.n.a.u.e.e.l. ubi proprium est, in eum in quo aut proprium deest, aut translatum proprio melius est).—**metaforan**, latini per translationem dicunt cum rem aliquam sub breui preconio quę sit ostendimus, XXVIII. 55 (*Cass. Psalm.* XVIII. 7 species definitionis quam Graeci κατὰ μεταφοράν, Latini per t.d.c.r. a.s.b. præconio quæ s.o.). Cf. *metafora*, translatio rerum, Cp. M139; *m.* (*matafora*), t.r. uel uerborum, Ep. 14E39 & Ef.[1] 371, 57.

metafrasin, interpretationem, XXX. 61 (*Cat. Hier.* LXV col. 675[c] scripsit et μετάφρασιν in Ecclesiasten brevem; B: scripsit *metaphrasin* idest *interpretationem* in eccl. b.; C: scripsit et ecclesiastes breuem).—**metafrasin**, interpretatio, XXXV. 36 (*Ruf.* VII. 25 fol. 127[a] *Metaphrasin*... scripsit)=*metafrasin*, interpraetatio, Cp. M124; Ep. 14C11; Ef.[1] 370, 44.

metalla, uincula, IV. 54 (*Eccl. Istor.*)= (*Ruf.* IV. 23 fol. 69[a] per *metalla* fratribus relegatis).—**per metalla**, per diuersas artes ferri uel alias, XXXV. 143 (*De Eus.*)=(*Ruf.* III. 7 fol. 39[a] iuuenum...reliquos...vinctos ad opera Ægypti *per metalla* destinatos; X. 4 fol. 160[b] *per metalla* damnauerat).—**in metallo**, in carcere, XXXV. 205 (*Ruf.* VIII. 14 fol. 142[b] *in metallo* Fanensi; VIII. 14 fol. 142[a] in...*metalla*)=*in metallo*, in carcere, Cp. I87; Ep. 11E23; Ef.[1] 365, 35.

metallo, XXXV. 205, see *in metallo* sub v. *metalla*.

metaphora, see *metafora*.

metaphrasin, see *metafrasin*.

metempschosis [-psychosis], motatio (!) anime [-mae] alię [-ae] in alterum hominem, XXIX. 56 (*Uerb. Interpr.*=*Hier. in Matth.* XI. 14, 15 quosdam hæreticos qui μετεμψύχωσιν introducunt; XIV. 1, 2 μετεμψυχώσις (!), and μετεμψυχώσεως).

metempsychosis, see *metempschosis*.

meticulosi, pauidi, IV. 67 (*Ruf.* VI. 31 fol. 112[b] ad moriendum...*meticulosi* viderentur).

metonymia, transnominatio ut est qui habitat in cęlis inridebit, XXVIII. 28 (*Cass. Psalm.* II. 4 haec figura Graece dicitur *metonymia*, Latine *transnominatio*; [ut est, added by the Glossator, referring to] qui h. in coelis inr. eos [quoted by Cass.]. See also IX. 40)=*metonomia*, transnominatio, Cp. M169; *m-*, grece transnominatio, Ep. 15C15; *m-*, grece transnomina, Ef.[1] 372, 38.

metopoea, XXVIII. 34, see *figura metopoea*.

metreta, mensura una ut quidam dicunt habent sextarios c mensura autem grece metrum dicitur unde et metreta dicitur Notandum uero quod mensura hebraicum nomen est, XXXIII. 13 (*Euch. De pond.* p. 159, 5 *metreta* una, ut quidam d. habet sextarios centum, m. a. Graece METRON d. u. e. m. appellatur, n. u. q. m. Hebraeum n. e.).

metron, see *metreta*.

metropolis, mater ciuitatum, XXXV. 47 (*Ruf.* X. 6 fol. 161[b] *Metropolitani* episcopi).

metropolitani, see *metropolis*.

metrum, modium, XXXV. 133 (*Ruf.* III. 6 fol. 36[a] mercati sunt vnum *metrum*...frumenti)=*metrum*, modium, Cp. M128; Ep. 14E11; Ef.[1] 371, 29. For *metrum* see also (XXXIII. 13) *metreta*.

meus, XXVIII. 52, 53.

micat, XLI. 15, see *topation*.

Micene, nomen ciuitatis et plurale sicut Kalendae, XLIII. 16 (*De div. nominibus*= Donati *Ars grammat.*, p. 374, 2 Agamemnoniaeque *Mycenae* [Virg. *A.* 6, 838]; id., p. 377, 2 quaedam...pluralia...ut Athenae Cumae...*Mycenae*; id., p. 376, 27 pluralia, ut *Kalendae* nundinae...).

micidus, see *preteriola*.

micina, XV. 11, see *preteriola*.

micinos, XV. 43, see *puluillos*.

mifortis, XXXV. 19, see *miherculi*.

migdalum, see *amictalum*.

migma et mixtum, idem est, XIII. 39 (*Isai.* XXX. 24 commistum *migma* comedent). Cf. *migma*, commixtum, Cp. M229.

miherculi, mifortis, XXXV. 19 (*Ruf.* IV. 9 fol. 58[a] *me hercule*).

mila, VIII. 16, see *mala aurea*....

miles, see *pugil*.

milia, XXIII. 2, see *filii faros*; XXXV. 31, see *legio*.

milicie [militiae], XII. 42, see *uasa*.

milis [-les], XLVI. 2, see *pugil*.

milites, XIV. 31, see *tyrones*; XXXVII. 19, see *laurus*; XXXIX. 28, see *qui in numero*...

militiae, see *uasa castrorum*.

militibus, I. 112, see *stipendiis*.

militum, XXXV. 28, see *munerum diebus*, 71, see *calonum*; XXXIX. 28, see *qui in numero*...

milui, xiii. 37, see *malus nauis.*

Milvio, see *ponte moluio.*

mina Grece mina sex uncias, xxxi. 33 (*De ponder.*?).—**mina** habet stateras xxii idest dragmas c scrupulos ccc quod facit libram unam et semiunciam, xxxii. 9 (*De ponder.*?).—**mina** est libra una et semiuncia, xxxiii. 2 (*De pond. Euch.*, p. 158, 9 *mina* e.l.u.e. *semuncia*). For *mina* see also (xxxiii. 3) *talentum.* Cf. Blume, i. 374, 16.

minas, mine, xxxiii. 3, see *talentum.*

mingere, xxxix. 48, see *calculum.*

minime, xliii. 49, see *parcę*, 50, see *lucus.*

minister, xlv. 21, see *adsecla.*

ministeriis [ministris?], iv. 45, see *parethris.*

ministerio, i. 41, see *diaconico.*

ministra, xlv. 22, see *pedissequa.*

ministrabat, x. 24, see *Salamitis.*

ministrante, xix. 52, see *obsetricante.*

ministratio, iii. 46, see *apparabilis.*

ministretur, ii. 159, see *subrogetur.*

ministri, vi. 18, see *nemphe*; xix. 18, see *inquilini.*

ministris, xxxv. 78, see *parethis*; see also *parethris.*

ministros, xxxix. 18, see *paritores.*

minor, xxxi. 14, see *hin*; xxxix. 31, see *carabum*; **minor**, xxxi. 9, see *comor minor.*

minores, xxiii. 4, see *cymentarii.*

MINORIBUS, xvii *tit.*

minus, see *pusilluminus*; **minus**, ii. 158, see *si quo minus.*

minuta, xxix. 9, see *quadrans*; xlv. 10, see *gyt.*

minutae, see *calculus.*

minuti, xlvi. 16, see *liser.*

minutissima, xii. 12, see *calculus.*

minutum, v. 1, see *cyati.*

mirabilis, xxviii. 62, see *tapynosin.*

miraculis, xii. 48, see *pululent.*

mire [for miri?], x. 16, see *crocus.*

miri, x. 10, see *cyprus*; xiii. 57, see *saliuncula*; see also *crocus.*

miricę, arbor est latine tramaritius [for *tamaricius*, the tamarisk] dicitur, xiv. 10 (*Hier.* xvii. 6 erit...quasi *myricae* in deserto; xlviii. 6 *id.*).

miror, xxxiii. 5, see *dedragma.*

mirtę [myrtae], xvii. 20, see *myrteta.*

misalis [=*missalis*, of or belonging to the *missa*], xxxix. 32, see *dalmatica.*

miserere, ii. 98, see *Kyrieleison.*

missa, xi. 11, see *in aqua...*

missae, see *missas.*

missalis, see *dalmatica.*

missas, amissas uel finite [finitae, or finitas?], ii. 110 (*Bened. reg.* 17, 9 [13; see note] recitetur lectio una...et *missas*, 12 [19; see note] *missas*, 17 [36] *missae*; 35, 20 [35] usque ad *missas*; 38, 5 [6] post *missas*; 60, 9 [12] *missas* tenere.—**ad missas**, ad [fi]nitas, ii. 10 (*Bened. reg.* 35, 20 [35] usque *ad missas*).

mitras, haetas, xxvi. 8 (*Isid. Offic.* ii. 5, 2 impones eis *mitras*). Cf. *mitra*, haet, Cp. M227. For *haetas* (accus. plur., headbands, turbans) see Bosw. T. (*hæt, hætt*); cf. Napier, 5242.

mittent, i. 50, see *emancipent.*

mittere, i. 7, see *alligare*; xlv. 10, see *gyt.*

mitterentur, i. 76, see *manumissio.*

mittit, xx. 5, see *extricat*; **mittit**, xxxviii. 18, see *creta comam-*; see also *alligare.*

mittitur, viii. 17, see *nitrum*; xii. 35, see *equus emissarius*; xv. 5, see *paxillus.*

mittunt, xv. 21, see *foramina.*

mittuntur, xlvii. 28, see *saburica.*

mixtum, xiii. 39, see *migma*, 42, see *epocentaurus.*

mna, see *talentum.*

mobilis, xxxiv. 41, see *nutabundus.*

mocum, quasi fabę [fabae] albo colore inueniuntur in conca [concha], xxiv. 5 (*Math.*? not in the Vulgate?). Cf. Papias (Du C.): *mocum*, simile est fabae, legumen est. Ital. *moco* (Tommaseo, *Diz.*); Diez, *Etym. Wörterb.* 385 (*moco*).

moderamine, xliv. 10, see *cardines.*

moderate, temperate, ii. 124 (*Bened. reg.* 22, 15 [26] invicem se *moderate* cohortentur).—moderate [for *moderatae*?] i. 71, see *modeste.*

moderatione, ii. 174, see *temperiem*; xii. 34, see *infrunita.*

modernos, nouos, xxxix. 16 (*Greg. Dial.* iii. 25 col. 280c ad *modernos* Patres) = *modernos*, nouos, Cp. M263; Ep. 15A23; Ef.[1] 372, 20.

modeste, moderate uel recte, i. 71 (*De Canon.* ? *Decret. Gelas.* ii *modestae* conuersationis; cf. Isid. *Etym.* x. 169).

modestia, ii. 83, see *grauitas*; xxxv. 301, see *fruga.*

modi, see *batus*; *chorus.*

modica, xiii. 9, see *olfactoriola*, 40, see *perpendiculum*; xvi. 4, see *ilicus*, 5, see *lentiscus*, 17, see *castrum*; xix. 53, see *gurgitum*; xxiii. 17, see *ciuitas dauid*; xxxv. 117, see *territoria*, 291, see *stipis*; xxxix. 31, see *carabum*, 36, see *sex untias.*

modicae, see *crocus*; *meatus*; *pastoforie.*

modicas, xiv. 8, see *lumbare*; xxxvii. 9, see *tabulas legat.*

modice [-cae], x. 16, see *crocus*; xxxv. 62, see *pastoforie.*

modicę [-cae], XXIX. 22, see *meatus*; see also *ilicus*.
modici, XVI. 4, see *ilicus*; XIX. 21, see *glarea*; XXXIX. 7, see *erucę*.
modicis, XXII. 12, see *urna*; XXXV. 40, see *troclei*.
modico, X. 22, see *areola*.
modicos, XXII. 12, see *urna*.
modicum, XIV. 9, see *in unge*; XXV. 1, see *catinum*; XXXV. 64, see *martyrium*; see also *quippiam*.
modicus autem **gomor** XXII sextarios, XXXI. 2; see *gomor*. For *modicus* see also (XIII. 48) *myrtus*; (XXIII. 10) *ualuas*.
modii, XXXIII. 9, see *chorus*, 10, see *batus*, 12, see *ephi*, 15, see *sata*.
modios, XVI. 22, see *trinte*; XXXI. 1, see *gomor maior*, 10, see *sextarium*, 24, see *choros*, 39, see *chatos*, 40, see *amphora*, 41, see *bathos*; XXXIII. 14, see *artabę*, 19, see *nebel*.
modis [for *modicum*?], II. 143, see *quippiam*.
modium, XXXI. 36, see *sata*; XXXV. 133, see *metrum*.
modo, XXX. 47, see *musica*.
modolabilis, see *musica*.
modolatis, see *modulatis*.
modoli, lateria, VI. 19 (*Breu. exsol.*?).
modulabilis, see *musica*.
modulatio, XXVI. 10, see *melodia*.
modulatis, suauiter cantatis, II. 109 (*Bened. reg.* 11, 4 [5] *modolatis* [*modulatis*]...sex psalmis; cf. 18, 27 modulatione).
modum, XLV. 18, see *pedum*.
moera, XLIV. 16, see *antarticus*; see also *moeris*; *moerorum*; *moerum*; *murorum*; *muris*.
moeris, see *moerorum*, *muris*.
moerorum [neut. gen. plur. of *moerum* (=*moera*, see Lewis & Sh.), a degree], see *murorum*.
moerum, see *moerorum*, *muris*.
Moëzel, see *Mozel*.
molas, intimi dentes, XIX. 56 (*Job* XXIX. 17 conterebam *molas* iniqui).
molata (!), XXVI. 1, see *commolita*.
molestia, I. 133, see *scrupulum*; II. 153, see *scrupolositas*.
molestus, XXXV. 263, see *infestus*.
moliri, XLIV. 29, see *axem*.
molitio, meditatio mali, XXXV. 128 (*Ruf.* II. 26 fol. 33b nouarum rerum *molitionibus*). Cf. *molitionibus*, dispositionibus, Cp. M282, which Schlutter thinks is taken from Orosius, IV. 14, 5, see *Arch. f. Lat. Lexic.* X. 363.
molitionibus, see *molitio*.
mollescere, see *lentiscere*.
molliores, XII. 15, see *cementa*.
molliscere [mollesc-], XXXIV. 18, see *lentiscere*.
moloncolia [melancholia], humor fellis, XXVII. 30 (*Lib. Rot.*=*Isid. Lib. de nat. rer.*?)=*meloncolia*, umor fellis, Cp. M133; Ep. 14C37; Ef.[1] 371, 15: cf. Isid. *Etym.* IV. 5, 5 *melancholia* dicta, eo quod ex nigri sanguinis faece admixta sit abundantia fellis.
molosi, canes, VI. 20 (*Breu. exsol.*?). Cf. *Dracont.* I. 279 Et raucos timuit discurrens dama *molossos*; and Napier, 3641, 4745.
moluerunt, manserunt uel senuerunt, XXXV. 93, see *inoleuit*.
moluio, XXXV. 242, see *ponte moluio*.
momentaneas, cotidianas, XL. 15 (*Uerba*?).
monachi, II. 189, see *monasterium*.
monachus, graece singularis latine, II. 107 (*Bened. reg.* 1, 1 [1] De generibus *monachorum*. *Monachorum*...genera; 7, 112 [180] si...contentus sit *monachus*).
monaptolmon, luscus, XXX. 70 (*Cat. Hier.* XCVIII col. 699A Acacius, quem, quia *luscus* erat, *μονόφθαλμον* nuncupabant; B: Ac. quem q.l.e. *monothalmon* monoculum nunc.; C: Ac. quem q.l.e. [blank] noncupababant). Cf. *monotalmis*, luscis, Cp. M287 (which seems=Napier, 2, 142 and 7, 225). See also *monon*.
monarchia, regiminis culmen uel pugnę, IV. 52 (*Ruf.* IV. 18 fol. 66b; V. 20 fol. 88b). As regards *pugnę*, see monarcha (for monomachia) pugna singularis, Cp. M273.
—**monarchia**, ubi unius, XXX. 5; see *anarchius*.
monasterio, see *monasterium*.
monasterium, unius monachi est habitatio mono enim apud grecos solum est, II. 189 (*Bened. reg.*, Prol. 103 [135] in *monasterio* perseverantes).
monilia, see *redimicula*.
monita, XXII. 15, see *scita*.
mono, II. 189, see *monasterium*.
monocerus, unicornis, XIX. 32 (*Job*?. Cf. Hieron. *Comm. in libr. Job* XXXIX. 9, ap. Migne, *Patr. Lat.* XXVI col. 770D 'Numquid volet rhinoceros servire tibi, aut morabitur ad praesepe tuum?' Sive, ut alii dixerunt: 'Numquid volet *monoceros* servire tibi?' Ex diversa editione transferentium advertimus, quod ipsum sit *rhinoceros* quod et *monoceros*, et Latine intelligatur *unicornis*, sive super nares cornu habens). See further Sabatier, *in loc.*, versio ant., and also below *rinocerus*.
monoculum, see *monaptolmon*; *monon*.
monogamia, XXX. 43, see *de monogamia*.
monon, unius, XXX. 84 (*Cat. Hier.* XCVIII col. 699A quem, quia luscus erat, *μονό-*

φθαλμον nuncupabant; B: q. q. l. e. monothalmon monoculum nunc.; C: q. q. l. e. [blank] nō cupababant). Cf. also *monaptolmon*. For *monon* see also *cinticta*.

monothalmon, see *monaptolmon*; *monon*.

mons, xx. 2, see *Nason*; xlv. 13, see *Massica*.

monsica, see *musica*.

monstra, see *pilosi*.

monstratur, xxviii. 74, see *ironia*.

monstri [for *monstra?*], xiii. 24, see *pilosi*.

monstrum, xxix. 38, see *hyinę*; see also *epocentaurus*.

monstruose, i. 95, see *portentuose*.

montes, x. 14, see *Amana*.

montibus, ix. 5, see *capparis*; xiii. 57, see *saliuncula*.

montis, iv. 36, see *meandrum*.

montium, xxi. 4, see *arge*; xxxv. 277, see *iugum montium*; xxxvi. 2, see *Armenias pilas*.

monumento, vii. 6, see *in mausilio*.

moralium, see *tropicon*.

morare [=morari], i. 63, see *inhibere*.

moras, see *lentiscus*.

morbida, languida, ii. 111 (*Bened. reg.* 28, 17 [31] ovis *morbida*; cf. 2, 17 [24] *morbidis*...actibus).

morbo re[gi]o, leprositas, iv. 89 (*Eccl. Istor.*=*Ruf.* x. 25 fol. 172^b interius exteriusque *morbo regio* corruptus).—**regio morbus**, corpus afficit colore sicut pedes accipitris, xxxv. 181 (*De Eus.*=*Ruf.* vi. 7 fol. 100^a ne *regio morbo* corrumperetur... *morbo regio*...repletur atque consumitur) =*regius morbus*, corporis color efficitur sicut pedes accipitur, Cp. R32; *r.m.*, c. c. e. s. pede accippitris, Ep. 22A16; *r.m.*, c. c. e. s. pedes accipitris, Ef.[1] 386, 35.

morbus, xxxiv. 31, see *tabo*; **morbus**, xxxv. 181, see *morbo regio*.

mordacius, see *mordatius*.

mordatius, clox, xlvii. 21 (*Alia*=?)= *mordacius*, clouae, Cp. M264; *m*-, clofae, Ep. 15A29^a and Ef.[1] 372, 24.—*mordacius*, *mordatius* = O. Fr. *mordant* (Godefroy, Dict.)=*mourdaunt* in Chaucer, *Rom. Rose* (Chaucer's Works, ed. Skeat, i. 139) li. 1094, where the Fr. text (li. 1083) has *mordens* (from the Lat. *mordēre*, to bite, grip); it differed from the *boucle* (Fr. text, li. 1075). Halliwell and others explain it "the tongue of a buckle," but see Skeat's note, ib. p. 425, who says it was "probably the metal chape or tag fixed to the end of a girdle or strap, viz. to the end *remote* from the buckle," and refers to Fairholt, *Costume in England*, Gloss., Vol. ii. p. 288 in ed. 1885. Cf. also *Cent. Dict.* in v. *Clox* is a miswriting for clouae, clofae, in Cp., Ep. and Ef.[1], from A.S. *cleōfan*, to split, and=the mod. E. *clove* (Oxf. Dict. *clove*, sb.[1], one of the small bulbs which make up the compound bulb of garlic, shallot, etc.). The application to the mordant may have been that the slice of metal or gem which composed the mordant somewhat resembled a bit of a clove.

mori, xvii. 3, see *occumbere*.

morosa, diuturna uel longa, ii. 113 (*Bened. reg.* 58, 29 sub tam *morosa* deliberatione [50 *morosam*]; cf. 43, 9 [11] *morose* volumus dici). On this *morosus* (lingering, slow, from *mora*), see Lewis & Sh. (2 *morosus*).

morosam, morose, see *morosa*.

morsus, xvi. 2, see *offa*.

mortali, iv. 29, see *exitiali*; xxxiv. 2, see *letheo*.

mortalium, see *tropicon*.

mortem, i. 39, see *diuus*.

mortiferis, i. 53, see *funestis*.

mortis, xii. 3, see *obductionis*; xix. 48, see *necromantia*.

mortua, iii. 61, see *explosa*; mortui, xxxv. 136, see *efflabant*.

mortuorum, xvi. 27, see *malefici*; xliii. 31, see *manes*; xlvi. 34, see *inferie*.

Mosel, see *Mozel*.

moster [for *monstrum?*], xiii. 42, see *epocentaurus*.

motatio, xxix. 56, see *metempschosis*.

motatores, iv. 101, see *πorsutas*.

motum, xxviii. 42, see *idea*.

motus, xliv. 27, see *dextera*.

mouere, iv. 42, see *quatere*.

moysica, see *musica*.

Mozel, mauritani, xv. 16 (*Ezech.* xxvii. 19 Vulg.: Dan...et *Mosel*; Heyse, in note *Mozel*; Sabat. in note *Moëzel*).

mucronibus, xxxv. 304, see *pugionibus*.

muebri [muliebri], i. 127, see *striones*.

mulcata, uincta, xxxv. 303 (*De Eus.*); **mulcatus**, percussus, iv. 28 (*Eccl. Istor.*); **multata**, percussa, xxxv. 131 (*De Eus.*)= (*Ruf.* iii. 5 fol. 35^b gens...vniuersa *mulctata* sit). Cf. *multata*, percussa, Cp. M330; Ep. 14E34; Ef.[1] 371, 52.

mulcatus, percussus, iv. 28, see *mulcata*.

mulctata, see *mulcata*.

mulctra, see *multhra*.

muliebrem, xxii. 11, see *mundum muliebrem*.

muliebri, see *striones*.

mulierem, xxxvii. 9, see *tabulas legat*.

mulieres, xiii. 6, see *lunulas*, 9, see *olfactoriola*, 28, see *sirene*.

mulieris, xiii. 43, see *lamia*.

mulierum, xxxv. 258, see *lenonibus*.

mulsum, dulce, xxiii. 19 (2 *Esdr.* viii. 10 comeditè pinguia, bibite *mulsum*).

multa, xxviii. 45, 63, 75, 77; xxxix. 49.

multae, see *multę*; *malagma*.

multas, xiii. 36, see *in serris*.

multata, percussa, xxxv. 131, see *mulcata*.

multe [-tae], xi. 12, see *malagma*; xxxix. 50, see *sentina*.

multę [multae], xvii. 20, see *myrteta*.

multhra, celdre, xlviii. 61 (*De Cass.?*). The lemma is not found in Cassianus' works, but seems = *muluctra*, ceoldre, Cp. M314. As hardly any Cassianus glosses appear in Cp., the above is, perhaps, one wrongly arranged among those excerpted from him. *Multhra*, *muluctra* = class. Lat. *mulctra*, a milk-pail, and *celdre*, perhaps a *kettle*, derived from *caldarium*, a caldr(on); see Kluge, *Ang. Leseb.* p. 166[a]; Schlutter, in *Anglia*, xix. 488; Holthausen, ib. xxi. 237; Kluge, *Altg. Dial.*, p. 335; Goetz, vi. 714. If *mulctra* were *the milk in a milk-pail*, *celdre* might = A.S. *cealre* (pressed curds). Cf. Bosw. T.; Grimm, *D. Wört.* (v. *Keller*).

multi, xiii. 43, see *lamia*; xl. 13, see *bachal*.

multis, xxix. 67, see *sumenumerus*; MULTIS, xlv *tit.*

multiuoca, xliii. 11, see *polionima*.

multo, xxii. 11, see *mundum muliebrem*.

multorum, xxx. 6, see *monarchia*.

multos, xxxix. 7, see *erucę*.

multum, xxxvii. 12, see *ore camerato*; xxxix. 19, see *freniticus*; xlvii. 2, see *usquequaque*.

Muluio, see *ponte moluio*.

mundantes, xxiv. 12, see *exolantes*.

mundatam, x. 1, see *osculetur me*.

mundate, xiv. 25, see *polite*.

mundati, xv. 47, see *limati*.

mundi, xlviii. 52, see *inmunes*.

mundiora, xiii. 11, see *mutatoria*.

mundo, xliv. 17, see *cous*.

mundorum, xxx. 64, see *catheron*.

mundos, xxxv. 295, see *cathanos*.

mundum muliebrem, multo tempore debuerunt unguere uariis pigmentis et indui uestibus regalibus illud dicitur mundum muliebrem, xxii. 11 (*Esther* ii. 3 accipiant *mundum muliebrem*; ii. 9 ut acceleraret *mundum muliebrem*). For *mundum* see also (xliv. 10) *cardines*.

munera, iv. 48, see *munerarius*; x. 15, see *emissiones tuę*; xxxv. 253, see *solaria*.

munerario, see *munerarius*.

munerarius, munera accipiens, iv. 48 (*Ruf.* iv. 15 fol. 63[a] acclamabant Philippo *munerario*).

munerum [sine interpret.], iv. 61 (*Eccl. Istor.*); **munerum diebus**, remunerationis militum, xxxv. 28 (*De Eus.*) = (*Ruf.* v. 2 fol. 76[b] Maturus & Sanctus...*munerum diebus*...statuuntur in medio arenae) = *munerum dies*, remunerationes militum, Cp. M331; Ep. 14E35; Ef.[1] 371, 53.

municipalia, i. 58, see *gesta municipalia*.

municipii, tributarii, xxxix. 61 (not in Greg. Dial., but *Decr. Hilar.* praef. p. 251[a] Ecclesia illius *municipii*; *Decr. Leon.* xlix p. 238[b] solitariis *municipiis*).

munieres, xxxvii. 11, see *ambieres*.

munificentia, largitas, xxxv. 221 (*Ruf.* xi. 19 fol. 185[b] religione et *munificentia*) = Cp. M333; Ep. 14E36; Ef.[1] 371, 54.

munitionem, xxvi. 3, see *communitorium*.

munuscula, parua dona, ii. 115 (*Bened. reg.* 54, 5 [5] quaelibet *munuscula* accipere). For *munuscula* see also (iii. 18) *senium*.

muraenulam, see *murenula*.

muras [for *moras*?], xvi. 5, see *lentiscus*.

murem, soricem, xiii. 61 (*Isai.* lxvi. 17 comedebant...abominationem et *murem*).

murena, see *maruca*.

murenula, piscis similis anguile [anguillae] marinus sed grossior, xix. 8 (*Job*; *Praef. Hieron.* p. xiv[b] anguillam vel *murenulam* strictis tenere manibus). Migne, *P. L.* xxviii col. 1081[A] anguillam aut *muræenulam*..., but *murenulam* in note c; Heyse, p. l *muraenulam*, but *murenulam* in note i. The Cambr. MS. has *murenulam*. Piscis marinus similis anguillę.—**murenulas**, catenulas, xiii. 10 (*Isai.* iii. 20 auferet Dominus...*murenulas*). The Cambr. MS. *Murenulas*, catenas de auro mirifice factas.

murex, see *maruca*.

murica, see *mauria*.

muriceps, xxxviii. 4, see *gattas*.

muris, xvi. 17, see *castrum*.

muris [= *moeris*, see *murorum*], xliv. 16, see *antarticus*.

murmur, uastrung, iii. 48 (*De S. Mart. Stor.* = *Sulp. Sev. Dial.* ii. 13, 2 conloquentium *murmur* audimus; & *Vit. S. Mart.* 23, 6 *murmur*...multarum uocum audiebatur). For *uastrung* = *hwāstrung*, *hwæstrung*, a whispering, murmuring, see Bosw. T.

murmurans, xix. 23, see *susurrat*.

murmuretur, ii. 24, see *causetur*.

murorum [? for *moerorum*, neut. gen. plur. of *moerum* = *moera*, a degree], xliv. 16, see *antarticus*.

murra, see *cassia*.

murra et aloe, herbe [-bae] sunt, x. 18 (*Cant.* iv. 14 Vers. ant. Sab. & Vulg.:

myrrha et *aloe*; Heyse, in not. *murra*) = *murra* et *aloe* herbae sunt, Cp. M313.

murratum, amarum, xxv. 2 (*Marc.* xv. 23 dabant ei bibere *myrrhatum* vinum; Wordsw. & White *murratum*) = *murratum*, amarum, Cp. M374.

murtacia, see *mustacra*.

murus, xxiii. 10, see *ualuas*.

mus araneus, see *musiranus*.

musca canina, quę in cane habitat, xxxvi. 11 (*Oros.* i. 10, 11 post *muscas caninas*; id. vii. 27. 7 *muscae caninae*).—For muscas (xxi. 16) see *conopeum*.

muscus, bestia et sanguis eius boni odoris est, xlvii. 8 (*Alia* = ?). Germ. *Moschus*, see Grimm, *D. Wörterb.*; Goetz, vi. p. 721. Cf. *muscus*, genus herbae, Cp. M312.

musica, modo labiis [for *modulabilis*?], xxx. 47; see *dialectica*; = *moysica*, modulabilis, Cp. M233; *moysica*, modolabilis, Ep. 14C12; *monsica*, modo labilis, Ef.[1] 370, 45.

musicam, see *musica* sub v. *dialectica*.

musiranus, scraeua, xlvii. 78 (*Alia* = ?) = *m*-, screauua, Cp. M336; *m*-, screuua, Ep. 15A26; Ef.[1] —. For (*musiranus* leg.) *mus araneus*, a small mouse, *the shrew-mouse*, see Lewis & Sh. (2 *araneus*); Goetz vi. 721 (*musiranus*) and vi. 720 (*mus haraneus*). For *scraeua* &c., a shrew(-mouse), see Bosw. T. (*screāwa*).

mustacia, see *mustacra*.

mustacra, gronae, xlvii. 32 (*Alia* = ?) = *mustacia*, granae, Cp. M335; Ep. 15A20; *murtacia*, granae, Ef.[1] 372, 18. For mustacia, *a moustache*, see Körting, *Wörterb.* no. 6412; for gronae, granae, see Schade, *Altdeutsches Wrtb.* (*grana*); Kluge, *Etym. Wrtb.* (*Granne*).

mustum, facitur de malis granatis idest malis punicis, x. 26 (*Cant.* viii. 2 dabo tibi...*mustum* malorum granatorum meorum).

mutat, xix. 57, see *plumescit*.

mutationes, xxxviii. 29, see *trapezita*.

mutatoria, uestimenta alia meliora et mundiora, xiii. 11 (*Isai.* iii. 22 [auferet Dominus]...*mutatoria*).

mutatur, xxviii. 76, see *metafora*; xliv. 25, see *dextera*.

mutilabo, dubitabo, xxxvii. 10 (*S. Aug.*?). Q^y^ for *mussitabo*? This form of the verb does not seem to occur in Aug., but we find Quid *mussitant* homines inter se, Serm. 72, 4 (Migne xxxviii col. 468); adhuc *mussitat* serpens, et non tacet, Serm. 341, 5 (ibid. xxxix col. 1496).

Mycenae, see *Micene*.

mygale, see *netila*.

myricae, see *miricę*.

myrmicoleon, see *leopardus*.

myrotheca, see *in myrthece*.

myrrha, see *cassia*; *murra*.

myrrhatum, see *murratum*.

myrtae, see *myrteta*.

myrteta, ubi multę sunt mirtę [myrtae] idest arbores fructuosae, xvii. 20 (*Zachar.* i. 8, 10, 11 stabat inter *myrteta*).

myrthece, xxxv. 169, see *in myrthece*.

myrtum, see *myrtus*.

myrtus, modicus arbor boni odoris semper uiride, xiii. 48 (*Isai.* xli. 19 dabo...*myrtum*; lv. 13 pro urtica crescet *myrtus*).

mythopœia, see *figura metopoea*.

n for *l*: u*n*cus (for u*l*cus).—for *m*: ideo*n*ati (idio*m*ati); teraphi*n* (-phi*m*).—for *r*: catha*n*os (-*r*os); communio*n*e (-*o*re). —for *s*: disce*n*sum (discessum).—n *inserted*: coeme*n*taria, coeme*n*teria (coemeteria); inconpe*n*tentibus (-petentibus); simulta*n*tem (-tatem).—n *omitted*: axietas (a*n*x-); elegos (ele*n*gos); uetorosa (ueter*n*osa).—nn for *n*: duce*nn*arium (duce*n*arium); pa*nn*igericis (pa*n*egyricis).

Naasson, see *Nason*.

nablis, xii. 40, see *cyneris*; **nablis**, vii. 1, see *in nablis*.

Nabo, Naboth, see *Del*.

Nabuchodonosor, xvi. 12, see *regina*.

nabulum, xxxviii. 44, see *epibatis*.

nactus, see *nanctus*.

naenias, see *nenias*.

Nahum, see *Naum*.

nam, xii. 40; xxi. 16; xxxiii. 7; xliii. 46.

namque, xix. 31.

nancisci, inueniri, xxxv. 288 (*Ruf.* ix. 2 fol. 147^b^ quicquid...*nancisci* potuit).

nanctus, nuens, xlviii. 62 (*De Cass.*, *Inst.* v. 39, 2 tum ille *nanctus* [*nactus*, in three MSS.] occasionem). *Nuens* for *inueniens* or *inuentus*; see *nanctus*, inuentus, Cp. N4; Goetz, vi. 724, 5 (in vv. *nancisco*: *nanctus sum*, inueni; *nanctus* occasionem).

naphtha, see *nappa*.

nappa, genus fomitis, xvi. 10 (*Dan.* iii. 46 succendere fornacem *naphtha*; Heyse, in note, *napta*). Cf. *napta*, blaec teoru, Cp. N17; Ep. 16A23; Ef.[1] 374, 14; *napta*, tynder, Cp. N33; *napta*, genus fomenti id est tyndir (Ef.[1] ryndir), Ep. 16A38; Ef.[1] 374, 31; *neptam*, tyndre, Cp. N55. For blaec teoru (black-tar, tar, naphtha), see Bosw. T. (*blæc-teru*); for tynder, tyndir, tyndre (tinder, fuel), see Bosw. T. (*tynder*).

napta, see *nappa*.

nardum, arbor, xxix. 34.—**pisticum**, herba rubicunda uel nardum pisticum idest spicatum uel fidelis, XXIX. 35 (*Uerb. Interpr.* = *Hier. in Matth.* XXVI. 7 *nardum pisticam* posuit...hoc est, veram et absque dolo). Cf. *nardus*, arbor, Cp. N19; Ep. 16A37; Ef.[1] 374, 30; *nardum pisticum*, ex XVIIII herbis conficitur, Cp. N49; pisticum nardum, Cp. P405.—**nardum**, spica unde faciunt unguenta, X. 9 (*Cant.* I. 11 Vers. ant. & Vulg.: *nardus* mea dedit odorem suum; IV. 13 Vulg.: Cypri cum *nardo*; IV. 14 ib. *nardus* et crocus).

nardus, see *nardum*.

nari, XIX. 31, see *rinocerus*.

naricornu, XIX. 31, see *rinocerus*.

narratas, XXVIII. 65, see *epiphonima*.

narratio, XXVIII. 26, see *paradigma*.

narratione, see *phraysi*.

narrationum, XXX. 54, see *et procomian*.

nasci, XIII. 25, see *de radice*.

nascitur, IX. 5, see *capparis*; XXV. 8, see *byssus*; XLIII. 13, see *agrippa*; **nascitur**, XIII. 25, see *de radice*.

Nason, mons, XX. 2 (*Tobias* I. 1 supra *Naasson*).

nastologis, mercedes quę dantur nautis propter regimen nauis, XXXVIII. 43 (*Clem. Rom. Epist. ad Jacobum*, in Migne's *Patr. L.* CXXX col. 24D hi qui catechizant *nautologis* conferantur; ibid. col. 25B *Nautologi* de mercedibus commoneant). See Goetz, VI. 728 (s.v. *naustologus*), Forcell. (s.v. *nautologus*).

nati, I. 95, see *portentuose*; XI. 5, see *uitulamina*; XXIII. 2, see *filii faros*.

natura, I. 130, see *sexus*; X. 11, see *tigna*; XXXVIII. 8, see *genesim*; XLIII. 13, see *agrippa*; XLV. 14, see *genium*.

naturale, I. 57, see *genuinum*.

naturalis, XLV. 29, see *uligo*.

naturalium, XXVII. 27, see *genthliatici*.

naue, XIV. 15, see *cacleuma*; XV. 11, see *preteriola*.

nauem, XLVII. 28, see *saburica*.

naues, XVI. 18, see *trieres*.

naui, XXXIX. 50, see *sentina*.

nauibus, XLIII. 21, see *centaurus*; XLVII. 5, see *corimbis*.

nauigatione, XXXVIII. 44, see *epibatis*.

nauis, XV. 9, see *transtra*; XXXVIII. 43, see *nastologis*; XXXIX. 31, see *carabum*; XLIII. 21, see *centaurus*, 22, see *forinnadas*; XLVI. 30, see *celox*; **nauis**, XIII. 37 (bis), see *malus nauis*.

nauiter, ualde, I. 78 (*De Canon.*; *Can. Conc. Carth.* LVI p. 154a necessitates... *gnauiter* peragendas implere).

nauium, see *forinnadas*.

Naum helcesei, pater ipsius, XVII. 8 (*Nahum*, I. 1 liber visionis *Nahum Elcesæi*; Heyse, in note, *Helcesei*).

nausia, XII. 30, see *colera*.

nautis, XXXVIII. 43, see *nastologis*.

nautologi, nautologis, see *nastologis*.

nazannai, XXIII. 6, see *Stabur nazannai*.

ne, VIII. 3 (ter); XXI. 20; XLVIII. 74.

ne, uel, VI. 1 (*Breu. exsol.*?).

nebel, quidam putant modios III in [for *hin*? see *hin*] sextariis [for *sextarius*? see *hin*] est liquide speciei, XXXIII. 19 (*Euch. De pond.*, p. 159, 13 *nebel* q.p.m. tres. sextarius est liquidae speciei).

necessarium, XLVIII. 58, see *opere precium*.

necromantia, diuinatio de mortis infantibus, XIX. 48 (*Job*? not in the Vulg.?). S. Jerome uses the word twice: *Comm. in Esaiam* XXIX [ed. of 1533, vol. V. 54C] significet magorum νεκρομαντείαν, and *Comm. in Ezech.* XIII [ib. V. 184K] per *necromantias*. Cf. *necromantia*, mortuorum diuinatio, Cp. N83; Ep. 16C22; Ef.[1] 374, 52.

Neemias, see *Nemias*.

negandi, XXVIII. 5, see *infitiandi*.

neglegenter, see *dissimulat*.

neglegit, I. 44, II. 49, see *dissimulat*.

negligens, II. 46, see *desidens*.

negotia, I. 91, see *ptochiis*; XXXIX. 63, see *per pragmaticam formam*.—**negotia ecclesiastica**, actum rei alicuius, I. 77 (*De Canon.*; *Can. Apostt.* XXXIX *negotiorum Ecclesiasticorum* curam Episcopus habeat; *Can. Conc. Calch.* IV *Ecclesiastica negotia*; *Can. Con. Antioch.* XCI super...*Ecclesiasticis negotiis*).

negotialis, XXIX. 45, see *pragmaticam*.

negotiationes, XXXV. 172, see *nundinas*.

negotiationum, XXXVII. 1, see *obsoriorum*.

negotiis, XXIX. 42, see *trapezeta*; see also *negotia*.

negotiorum, see *negotia*.

ne innataris, ne incumberis ne considas, VIII. 3 (*Salam.* III. 5 *ne innitaris* prudentiae tuae).

Nemias, alio nomine atersatha, XXIII. 13 (2 *Esdr.* VIII. 9 Dixit...*Nehemias* (ipse est *Athersatha*) et Esdras; Heyse, in note, *Neemias*).

nemphe, ministri nequam, VI. 18 (*Breu. exsol.*?).

nenias, mendatium [-cium], XXVIII. 35 (*Cass. Psalm.* IV. 2 qui adhuc idolorum *nænias* inquirebat...*mendacium* idola significat); **nenias**, mendatium [-cium], XXIX. 7 (*Uerb. Interpr.* = *Hier. in Matth. Prol.* col. 20A omnes apocryphorum *nænias*).

neotericis, see *neotricis*.

neotricis, noua fide, III. 50 (*De Martin. Stor.*); **neutricis**, nouis, XLII. 5 (*Ex diu. libris*) = (*Sulp. Sev. Dial.* I. 6, 2 in libris *neotericis* [*neutericis*, in one MS.]).

nepos, see *nepus*.

nepus, filius filii, XLIII. 7; **nepus**, adulter, XLIII. 8; **nepus**, consumptor substantie, XLIII. 9 (*De diu. nominibus*= Donati *Ars grammat.*, p. 373, 22 *nepos*).

nequam, VI. 18, see *nemphe*.

nequitia, XXXIV. 43, see *rangor*.

Nereus, deus maris, XLIII. 17 (*De diu. nominibus*=Donati *Ars grammat.* p. 373, 27 masculina aut in des exeunt...aut in ion, ut Nerion a *Nereo*).

neruo, see *neruum*.

neruum, uinculum, IV. 60 (*Ruf.* V. 2 fol. 75b septimo ..puncto in *neruo* pedes... distenti). See below, *puncto*.

netila, herma, XLVII. 77 (*Alia*=?)= *netila*, hearma, Cp. N60; Ep. 16A20; Ef.[1] 374, 11.—For *netila* (=*nitela*, *nitella*, a small mouse, a dormouse), see Lewis & Sh.; Körting, 6547. For *herma*, *hearma*, see Bosw. T. (*hearma*, a shrew-mouse?); Kluge, *A. S. Leseb.* p. 183 (*hearma*, Wiesel); *id. Wrtb.* (*Hermelin*); Oxf., and Skeat Dict. (*ermine*); Körting, 4496. This *herma*, *hearma* also glosses *megale* (=mygale, mus araneus, in pure Lat.) Cp. M166, Ep. 15C14, Ef.[1] 372, 37; and the latter is, in its turn, translated by *squiriolus*, a squirrel (Goetz, VI. 693 *meogallus*); see also *nitela*, *δενδροβάτης* (id. VI. 740).

neutericis, see *neotricis*.

neutricis, nouis, XLII. 5 (*Ex diu. libris*), see *neotricis*.

nigerrimum, II. 175, see *teterrimum*.

nigris, XXVII. 26, see *atris*.

nigro, XV. 10, see *ebor*.

nigrum, XLI. 7, see *iaspis*.

nihilo, I. 88, see *paruipendens*.

nihilum, VIII. 17, see *nitrum*.

nimius, superfluus, II. 122 (*Bened. reg.* 41, 8 [12] si aestatis fervor *nimius* fuerit; 64, 30 [50] non sit *nimius* et obstinatus; cf. 30, 6 [7] tales, dum...ieiuniis *nimiis* adfligantur. As to "superfluus" cf. 61, 13 [22] si *superfluus* aut vitiosus inventus fuerit; 36, 6 [8] non *superfluitate* sua contristent fratres; 61, 6 [7] non...*superfluitate* sua perturbat monasterium).

Niniue trium dierum iter inde ubi in terram proiectus est unam diem per ambitum, XVII. 7 (*Jon.* III. 3 *Ninive* erat civitas magna *itinere trium dierum* [of three days' journey]). The gloss "inde... per ambitum" is, perhaps, with reference to vers. 4, to be read "inde...*perambulabat*" (MS. has per amb'), from thence where he was cast on the earth he traversed one day.

nisan, primus mensis idest martius, XXII. 13 (*Esther* III. 7, 12; XI. 2 *Nisan*; see the quotation under *urna*).

nisi, XXII. 16; XXIII. 1; XXXIV. 6.

nisus, see *adnisus*.

nitas [for *finitas*?], II. 10, see *ad missas* s.v. *missas*.

nitela, nitella, see *netila*.

nitidulam [sine interpret.], III. 17 (*De S. Mart. Stor.*=*Sulp. Sev. Dial.* II. 8, 3 quia...uiduam uagam, *nitidulam*...obiurgauerim).

nititur, XXVIII. 70, see *sinchrisis*; XLIV. 7, see *poli*.

nitore, X. 1, see *osculetur me*.

nitro, see *nitrum*.

nitrum, in terra inuenitur instar atramenti pro sapone habetur si in acętum [acet-] mittitur ad nihilum soluitur qui [quod?] atrumque [utrumque?] amarescit, VIII. 17 (*Salam.* XXV. 20 acetum in *nitro*).—**nitrum** in terra inuenitur, XIV. 2 (*Hier.* II. 22 si laveris te *nitro*).

nix, XXXIX. 51, see *byssus*.

nobile, I. 64, see *insigne*.

nobilium, XIII. 59, see *feretri*.

nobis, II. 98, see *kyrieleison*.

nocte, XXXVIII. 5, see *chantari*; XLIV. 9, see *cęlum*; **nocte**, XIX. 50, see *carmina in nocte*. See also *ciconia*.

noctis, XXI. 2, see *lucubraciuncula*; XLIII. 53, see *eumenides*.

noctua, necthtrefn, XLVII. 54 (*Alia*=?) =*n*-, naeht hraefn, Cp. N145; *n*-, naechthraebn ali dicunt nectigalae, Ep. 16A15; *n*-, necthraebn alii dicitur nacthegelae, Ef.[1] 374, 6. *Noctua*, a night-owl; for *necht-refn* &c. (properly a night-raven), see Bosw. T. (*neaht*, *niht-hræfn*).

nocturnaque [for *-nasque*], XXXV. 179, see *horas diurnas*....

nocturnasque, see *horas diurnas*....

nocturnum, XXIX. 38, see *hyinę*.

nodis, III. 10, see *hispida*.

nodo, see *turnodo*.

NOLK or NOTE?, I. 17a, see note § on p. 1.

nomen, I. 111, see *sicera*; III. 16, see *reda*, 20, see *merocem*; IV. 3, see *ilix*, 17, see *fadus*, 36, see *meandrum*, 37, see *trallis*, 93, see *angiportos*; V. 12, see *labris*; X. 23, see *Aminab*; XII. 24, see *Dorix*; XIII. 16, see *tabehel*, 21, see *carcamis*, 29, see *mede*; XIV. 22, see *in fatores*; XV. 12, see *bibli*, 15, see *Dan*, 23, see *syeres*; XVI. 19, see *apethno*; XVII. 15, see *pile*; XXI. 3, see *Subal*, 4, see *arge*; XXIII. 6, see *stabur*; XXIV. 13, see *alabastrum*; XXVIII. 15, see *Laodes*, 76, see *mętafora*; XXX. 7, see *bibliotheca*, 26, see *diatripas*; XXXIII. 13, see *metreta*; XXXV. 70, see *calonum*, 91, see *Mambre*, 147, see *petalum*, 209, see *Galerius*, 256, see *actio*, 298, see *spiridon*; XXXVI. 2, see *Armenias*; XXXVIII. 22, see *deucalionem*; xxxix. 9, see *interorina*, 10, see *ausaret*; xliii. 16, see *micene*, 18, see *carus*, 28, see *bachus*.—nomen [omitted?] see *ponte moluio*; see also *angulinis*.

nomen tuum, xpistianiam a xpisto et chrismam, x. 5 (*Cant.* i. 2 oleum effusum *nomen tuum*; the Cambr. MS. Kk. 4. 6 has *Christianiam* for *Xpianiam*, and *crisma* for *chrismam*).

nomina, xxviii. 31, see *ausesis*; xliii. 10, see *omonima*.

nominantur, ii. 53, see *decani*; xx. 8, see *taermę*.

nominatur, xv. 35, see *teraphin*; xxiv. 13, see *alabastrum*.

nomine, vi. 14, see *Dum*; xxiii. 13, see *nemias*; xxviii. 57, see *figura*; xxxvi. 1, see *Iani*.

nominem, xxx. 31, see *sub nominem*.

NOMINIBUS, XLI *tit.*; XLIII *tit.*

nominum, xxxiv. 20, see *catalogum*.

nomisma, solidus, xxiv. 11 (*Math.* xxii. 19 ostendite...*numisma* census; Words. & White *nomisma*). See below *nummismum*, and cf. nummismum solidum, Cp. N175; nomisma mynit, *ib.* N144 and Ep. 16A9; nomysma, munit, Ef.[1] 373, 49; nummisma, mynet, Napier 61, 32. For mynit, munit (a coin; O.H.G. *muniz, muniza, muneza*; Germ. *Münze*; D. *munt*, from the Lat. *moneta*), see Bosw. T. (*mynet*).

non, ii. 91, 118 (ter), 121 (bis), 123 (bis); iii. 23 (bis); viii. 19, 20; x. 6, 17, 21; xi. 4, 16; xii. 23 (bis), 41; xiv. 12; xix. 28; xxi. 10; xxii. 16 (bis); xxiii. 5; xxiv. 6; xxviii. 33, 83; xxxiv. 6, 19 (bis); xxxv. 124; xxxviii. 22; xxxix. 15, 48; xli. 1; xliii. 43, 51; xlvii. 28.

non conpluta, sine pluuia, xv. 7 (*Ezech.* xxii. 4 tu es terra immunda, et *non compluta* in die furoris). Cf. *conpluta*, plumis [for *pluuiis*] repleta, Cp. C743 and Ef.[1] 354, 27.

non detegere, non publicare non manifestare, ii. 118 (*Bened. reg.* 46, 12 [18] sciant...aliena vulnera *non detegere* et publicare).

non expedit, non conuenit, ii. 123; see *expedit*.

nonnos, patres, ii. 119 (*Bened. reg.* 63, 22 [40] iuniores...priores suos *nonnos* vocent).

nonnumquam, i. 4, see *alias*.

non obsecundare, non obedire, iii. 23 (*De S. Mart. Stor.*=*Sulp. Sev. Dial.* ii. 8, 5 uoluntati uestrae *non obsecundare* mihi non licet).

non officit, non resistit, xxxiv. 19 (*De Cass., Inst.* xi. 8 non solum *non officit*...).

non prodicus, non superfluus, ii. 121; see *prodicus*.

non trices, non tardes, xii. 23 (*Eccles.* xxxii. 15 *non* te *trices*).

norma, regula, ii. 120 (*Bened. reg.* 73, 10 [15] rectissima *norma* vitae humanae) =Cp. N142; Ef.[1] 373, 44; cf. *norma*, mensura aequat forma exemplum, Ef.[2] 314, 21.

nos, xliv. 11, 19.

nostra, xxviii. 51, see *hyperthesis*.

nostratis, hidirrine, xliii. 38; see *cuiatis*.

nota [for *notam*], xxviii. 51, see *hyperthesis*.

notam, see *hyperthesis*.

notandum, xxxiii. 13, see *metreta*.

NOTE or NOLK?, I. 17[a], see note § on p. 1.

notha, adultera eo quod incerti generis, xliii. 6 (*De diu. nominibus*=Donati *Ars gramm.* p. 373, 20 sunt [nomina] inter Graecam Latinamque formam, quae *notha* appellantur).

notio, xxviii. 83, see *ennoematice*.

noua, iii. 50, see *neotricis*.

nouam, xxxv. 56, see *nouellam*.

nouellam, nouam diminitiuum, xxxv. 56 (*Ruf.* xi. 9 fol. 182[a] oliuarum...domini germinauit *nouellam*).

noui, xiv. 31, see *tyrones*.

nouis, xlii. 5, see *neutricis*.

nouissimo, vii. 2, see *pro octaua*.

nouissimus, xxviii. 23, see *Iouis*.

nouitatem, see *deuterosin*.

nouo, xxxv. 254, see *de octoade*.

nouos, xxxix. 16, see *modernos*.

nouum, iv. 10, see *ogdoade*.

noxa, culpa crimen, ii. 117 (*Bened. reg.* 25, 2 [1] frater qui gravioris culpae *noxa* tenetur). Cf. *noxa*, culpa, Cp. N136 and Ef.[2] 314, 11; Ep. —.

nucum, ix. 4, see *amictalum*.

nuens [for *inueniens*, or *inuentus*], xlviii. 62, see *nanctus*.

nuis, xliii. 55, see *sis*; *cestus*.

nullam, xlii. 21, see *basterna*.

nullius, xxx. 4, see *anarchius*.

nullus, xliv. 29, see *axem*.

numeralis, xxx. 46, see *arethimetica*.

numerat, xxiii. 2, see *filii faros*.

numero, x. 7, see *aduliscentulę*.—**numero**, xxxix. 28, see *qui in numero....*

numeros, see *decanorum*.

numerum, xxxix. 68, see *catalocum*.

numerus, xxxix. 28, see *qui in numero....*

numinis, uirtutis, xxxv. 145 (*Ruf.* iii. 8 fol. 40[b] *numinis*...motus).—**numinis**, diuinitatis, xxxv. 232 (*Ruf.* xi. 25 fol. 189[a] tanti *numinis*...alloquio).

numisma, see *nomisma*; *nummismum*.

nummi, xxix. 9, see *quadrans*.

nummis, xxix. 42, see *trapezeta*; xxxi. 38, see *denarius*.

nummismum, solidum, XXIX. 32 (*Uerb. Interpr.*=*Hier. in Matth.* XXII. 19 ostendite mihi *numisma* census)=Cp. N175. See above *nomisma*.

nummorum, XXXVIII. 29, see *trapezita*.

nummos, XXXVII. 2, see *C uolles*; nummos for *numeros*? XXXVIII. 31, see *decanorum*.

nummularius, XXIX. 42, see *trapezeta*.

nummus, XXIX. 3, see *asse*; XXXIII. 6, see *stater*.

nuncupare, XXVIII. 57, see *figura*.

nundinas [sine interpret.], IV. 62 (*Eccl. Istor.*); **nundinas**, negotiationes, XXXV. 172 (*De Eus.*)=(*Ruf.* V. 3 fol. 77[b] *nundinas*...agere solent)=*nundinae*, negotiationes, Cp. N183; Ep. 16A6; Ef.[1] 373, 46.—**nundinis**, mercatis, XV. 17 (*Ezech.* XXVII. 17, 19, and XLVI. 11 in *nundinis*)=*nundinis*, mercatis, Cp. N174.

nuptiis, XXX. 43, see *de monogamia*.

nutabundus, agitatus, III. 28 (*S. Mart. Storia*; but not found in *Sulp. Sev.*, and it is, perhaps, a further explanation of III. 27 *furibundus* q.v.).—**nutabundus**, mobilis, XXXIV. 41 (*De Cass.*, *Inst.* XII. 4, 3 instabilis...ac *nutabundus* effectus).

nutaret, dubitaret, XX. 7 (*Tobias* VII. 11 cum *nutaret*).

nutatione, dubitatione, XXXV. 170 (*Ruf.* V. 2 fol. 76[b] absque...animi *nutatione*).

nutrimenta, II. 75, see *fomenta*.

nuymeyses, consiliarius, XXIX. 72 (*Uerb. Interpr.*=*Hier. in Matth.* XXVII. 57, 58 Joseph iste βουλευτὴς appellatus, id est, *consiliarius*).

o for *a*: fau*o*rum (for fab*a*rum); hermofr*o*ditus (hermaphr-); hierufontis (hierophantis); mol*o*ncolia (mel*a*ncholia); offer (*a*ffer); oll*o* (oll*a*); solaria (sal-).—for *ae*: propositura (praep-).—for *e*: coemet*o*ria (-teria); m*o*loncolia (m*e*lancholia); uetorosa (uet*e*rnosa).—for *oe*: diocesim, diocesium (di*oe*c-); *o*dippo (*oe*dipo).—for *u*: ad*o*latur (ad*u*lator); c*o*cula (c*u*culla); col*o*mellas (col*u*m-); c*o*mulare (c*u*m-); fist*o*la (-t*u*la); fulg*o*rantes (fulg*u*r-); lux*o*ria (lux*u*r-); perm*o*tatio (perm*u*t-); procons*o*laris (-s*u*laris); pr*o*rigo (pr*u*r-); scrup*o*lositas (scrup*u*l-); t*o*nica (t*u*n-).—for *y*: col*o*bista (coll*y*b-).—o *omitted*: myrthece (myrotheca).

ob, XXXIX. 19.

obductionis, dilectiones idest mortis, XII. 3 (*Eccles.* II. 2 ne festines in tempore *obductionis*). For dilectio*n*es the Cambridge MS. has dilectio*n*is, perhaps for d*e*lectionis, a choosing, choice, separation, or for *defectionis*, failing, deficiency, exhaustion, which would agree more with the lemma. See further *Eccles.* v. 1: in tempore vindictae et *obductionis*; v. 10: in die *obductionis*.

obdurat, XXXIX. 48, see *calculum*.

obedire, III. 23, see *non obsecundare*.

obelis, uirgis, XIX. 1 (*Job*; *Praef. Hier.* p. XIV[a], and Migne, *P. L.* XXVIII col. 1079[A] volumina Origenes *obelis*... distinxerit)= *obelis*, uirgis, Cp. O33; Ep. 16E32; Ef.[1] 375, 45.

obfirmantes, obicientes omne presagio uel signo, XLI. 21 (*De diu. nomin.* ?).

obices, resistentes, XXXV. 216 (*Ruf.* X. 19 fol. 171[b] uelut *obicis* ualidissimi obiectione sublata).

obicientes, XLI. 21, see *obfirmantes*.

obicis, see *obices*.

obiecit, XLIV. 27, see *leua*.

obiicieris, see *subregeris*; *subrigeris*.

obiurgans, XXXV. 214, see *obuncans*.

obiurgetur, increpetur culpetur, II. 127 (*Bened. reg.* 23, 7 [10] Si non emendaverit, *obiurgetur* publice).

obligus, obscurus, XIX. 3 (*Job*; *Praef. Hieron.* p. XIV[b], and Migne, *P. L.* XXVIII col. 1081[A] *obliquus*...totus liber fertur).

obliquus, see *obligus*.

oblitus, II. 57, see *excesserit*.

obliuione, XXI. 19, see *in anathema*.

obliuionem, II. 65, see *excussum*.

obolos, see *sicel*.

obolus, XUIIII siliquas, XXXI. 18 (*De ponder.* ?).—**obolus** pensat siliquas III siliquas tres fit f, XXXII. 4 (*De ponder.* ?).—**obolus** III siliquas solidos XXIIII, XXXIII. 29 (*Euch. De pond.* ?).—**obulus** est scrupule dimedium quod facit siliquas III In hiezechielo siclus autem xx obolus habet, XXXIII. 8 (*Euch. De pond.* p. 158, 19 *obolus* e. *scriptulum* [Mus. MS. *scripulum*] dimidium q. f. s. tres i. Ezechiele s. a. xx obolos habet). After habet the Brit. Mus. MS. adds: Quod si ad eam rationem ueniamus quam ipsi aestimant ponderationem sicli Uncia esse pondus quod in libris canonicis non repperis. Ergo obolus habet silicas VII, et partem quintam siliquae. See also Wotke's note, and Blume, I. 373 sqq.—**obolus medicinalis** III siliquas, XXXI. 19 (*De ponder.* ?). For *obolus* see also (XXXIII. 8) *obulus* sub v. *obolus*.

oppositus, XLIV. 7, see *poli*.

obprobria, XXXV. 125, see *probra*.

obrizum, ymaeti gold, XIX. 54 (*Job* XXVIII. 15 non dabitur aurum *obrizum* pro ea; *ib.* XXXI. 24 *obrizo* dixi)=*obrizum*, smaete gold, Cp. O24; (*ymaeti* for) *smǣti*, *smǣte*, beaten, refined, from *smītan*, to beat, strike, see Bosw. T. (*smǣte*); Kluge, *Etym. Wrt.* (*schmeiszen*); Napier's Index (*obryzum*, *obryzus*).

obruit, xxxiv. 38, see *diruit.*

obscene, iv. 58, see *oedipia*, sub v. *thesteas.*

obscurus, xix. 3, see *obligus.*

obsecundare, iii. 23, see *non obsecundare.*

obsequentes, xxii. 9, see *pedisequas.*

obsetricante, ministrante, xix. 52 (*Job* xxvi. 13 *obstetricante* manu ejus).

obsoriorum, negotiationum, xxxvii. 1 (*S. Aug.*?).

obstetricante, see *obsetricante.*

obstinatus, disperabilis [desp-] uel inreuocabilis, ii. 128 (*Bened. reg.* 64, 30 [55] non sit nimius et *obstinatus*). Cf. *obstinatus*, desperatus, Cp. O85; *obstinatus*, desperatus, inreuocabilis, Ep. 17A38; Ef.[1] 376, 39.

obtentu [sine interpret.], i. 79 (*De Canon.*; *Can. Apostt.* vi sub *obtentu* religionis; xl sub *obtentu* religionis; *Can. Conc. Gangr.* lxi tit. Christianitatis *obtentu*). Cf. *obtentu*, intuitu, Cp. O18; id., Napier, 3915.

obtigit, contigit, vii. 8 (1 *Paral.* xxvi. 14 *obtigit* plaga Septentrionalis).

obturat, see *calculum.*

obuiantes, xxxv. 24, see *auspiciis.*

obuius, x. 11, see *tigna.*

obulus est scrupule dimedium &c., xxxiii. 8; see *obolus.*

obuncans, obiurgans, xxxv. 214 (*Ruf.* x. 17 fol. 170[a] illa...*obiurgans* Timotheum) = *obuncans*, obiurgans, Cp. O25; Ep. 16E8; Ef.[1] 375, 21. If *obuncans* be the right lemma, it was, perhaps, another reading not now found in the current texts, or, perhaps, the mark for transposing the two words was forgotten by the scribe.

occasu, xliv. 27, see *leua.*

occasum, xxvii. 4, see *suprima.*

occidentem, xliv. 9, see *cęlum.*

occidere, xliv. 27, see *dextera.*

occidisti, xvii. 13, see *concidisti.*

occiditur, xxiii. 1, see *exedra.*

occulta, xxxv. 26, see *oethepia*, 227, see *aduta.*

occultiorem, i. 128, see *secretalem.*

occultis, xxxv. 26, see *oethepia.*

occumbere, cadere uel mori, xvii. 3 (*Joel* iii. 11 *occumbere*).

occupare, xii. 31, see *auocare.*

ochimo, herba est quę latine catagoga, xxxviii. 16 (*Clem. Recognitt.* viii. 25 de *ocimo*). For *ochimum*, *ocimum*, also written *ocymum*, *ozymum* (=Gr. ὤκιμον, an aromatic plant, basil) and *ocinum* (=Gr. ὤκινον, an herb for fodder, perhaps a kind of clover) see Lewis & Sh.

ocii, see *otii.*

ocilis, uelotius [-cius], xlviii. 67 (*De Cass.*, *Inst.* vi. 3 *ocius* perueniunt ad salutem).

ocimo, see *ochimo.*

ociosus [otiosus], ii. 9, see *acidiosus.*

ocius, see *ocilis.*

octaua, v. 6, see *de octoade.*

octaua, vii. 2, see *pro octaua.*

octoade, v. 6 and xxxv. 254, see *de octoade* sub v. *ogdoade.*

oculis, xxviii. 42, see *idea.*

odaporikon, see *otheporicon*, sub v. *sinphosin.*

odeporicon, see *sinphosin.*

odippo [for *Oedipo*], v. 14, see *Oedippa.*

odon, lineum est in pede, xxxvii. 8; see *odonis uitam.*

odonis uitam, mihes nostlun, xxxvii. 7; **odon**, lineum est in pede, xxxvii. 8 (*S. Aug.*?). Odonis does not seem to occur in Augustine's works; it may = *udo*, a sort of felt or fur, and *uitam* may be for *uittam*, a band, fillet, which two other MSS. have (see Steinm. *A. H. G.* ii. 41. 4). If *mihes* = *odonis*, it would be the gen. of *meo*, a shoe (see Bosw. T.); *nostlun*, dat. pl. of A.S. *nostle*, a fillet, band, see Bosw. T. Cf. O.H.G. *nusta*, Verknüpfung; *nestila*, Bandschleife (Schade). As regards *odon*, lineum, cp. *linisnes* (O.H.G. *linen*; A.S. *linen*) nestilun, and *linifnes* nestilum in the two MSS. quoted by Steinm. l.c. The two glosses are, perhaps, a further explanation of *caligam*, q.v.

odoporicam, see *otheporicon*, sub v. *sinphosin.*

odor, xlvii. 24, see *osma*; see also *odor ungentorum.*

odoratu, odoratum, see *sitatum.*

odore, xiii. 9, see *olfactoriola.*

odoris, x. 1, see *osculetur me*, 10, see *cyprus*, 16, see *crocus*, 17, see *fistola*; xii. 17, see *platanus*; xiii. 48, see *myrtus*, 57, see *saliuncula*; xlvii. 8, see *muscus.*

odor ungentorum, donum quod in baptismate accipimus, x. 3 (*Cant.* i. 2 Vers. ant. Sab.: *odor unguentorum* tuorum; i. 3 Vulg. & Vers. ant.: curremus in *odorem unguentorum*; iv. 10 *odor unguentorum* [Vers. ant. *vestimentorum* tuorum] tuorum).

Odysseus, see *Polideuces.*

oe for *ăĕ*: foetontis for Phaethontis.—for *o*: foedi for fodi.

oedipia, obscene dapes carnium infantium, iv. 58; see *thesteas.*

Oedipo, see *Oedippa.*

Oedippa, de odippo [Oedipo], v. 14; see *thesteas.*

Oepha, see *ephi.*

oephi, see *ephi*; *sata*.

oethepia, coitum matris et sororis sicut manichei [Manichaei] in occultis idest in occulta loca idolorum, xxxv. 26; see *thesteas*.

ofa, xxxiii. 12, see *ephi*.

offa, morsus, xvi. 2 (*Dan.*, *Praef. Hieron.* p. xvi^b, and Migne xxviii, col. 1293^B *offa* picis) = *offa*, mursus [for morsus], Cp. O137; cf. *offa*, pars fructus uel frusti, Ep. 17C14; Ef.[1] 376, 55.

offendunt, see *operiunt*; *opperiunt*.

offensus, see *infensus*.

offer, adduc qui [for *quia*?] non satiantur, viii. 20 (*Salam*. xxx. 15 sanguisugae ...dicentes *Affer*, *affer*. Tria sunt insaturabilia). If *qui* is not for *quia*, "qui non satiantur" may be a gloss to *insaturabilia*.

offerentes, see *idea*.

officina [sine interpret.], ii. 126 (*Bened. reg*. 4, 55 [84] *officina*).

OFFICIORUM, xxvi tit.

officit, xxxiv. 19, see *non officit*.

officium, xvi. 24, see *iuge sacrificium*.

offusio, effusio, xii. 47 (*Eccles*. xxvii. 16 *effusio* sanguinis). There is no record of a reading *offusio*, which *effusio* seems intended to explain.

ogdoade, nouum testamentum, iv. 10 (*Eccl. Istor.*); **de octoade**, de octaua die, v. 6 (*Eccl. Stor.*); **de octoade**, de nouo testamento, xxxv. 254 (*De Eus.*) = (*Ruf.* v. 20 fol. 88^b Scribit...Irenaeus *De Ogdoade* librum).

olearia, xvii. 16, see *infusuria*.

olei, viii. 15, see *flauescit*.

oleo, xiv. 5, see *placentas*; xxi. 18, see *sancta domini*.

oleum, see *unguentum*.

olfactoriola, turibula modica de auro uel argento [Cambr. MS. adds quę] mulieres habent pro odore, xiii. 9 (*Isai*. iii. 20 auferet Dominus...*olfactoriola*).

oligo, see *uligo*.

olla, de terra et de eramento [aer-] fit, xix. 40 (*Job* xli. 11 *ollae* succensae, *ib*. 22 *ollam*). For *olla* see also (xii. 9) *cacabus*; (xxix. 47) *lagonam*.

ollae, ollam, see *olla*.

ollita, de ollitim, vi. 29 (*Breu. exsol.*?). Cf. *ollita*, ueterana, Cp. O143.

ollitani, senes, xl. 16 (*Uerba*?).

ollitim, vi. 29, see *ollita*.

ollo [for *olla*], xxix. 47, see *lagonam*.

olografia [hol-], totum scriptio, xxxix. 72 (neither in *Greg. Dial.*? nor in any of the *Can. Concc.*?). Cf. *holioglapha*, tota scriptura, Cp. H139; *holographia*, propria manu totum conscriptum testamentum, Ef.[2] 301, 4.

olus, xl. 11, see *malua*.

om̄ [? for omnes?], xliv. 11, see *clima*.

oma, corpus, xxix. 66 (*Uerb. Interpr.* = *Hier. in Matth*. xxiv. 28 *corpus*, idest πτῶμα).

omelias, see *ominas*.

ominas, locutiones, xxx. 89 (*Cat. Hier.* cxvi col. 707^C elaboravit...in Hexaemeron *homilias* novem; B : el....in examereon *omelias* ix; C : el....in extameron *homelias* viiii) = *omelias*, locutiones, Cp. O159; Ef.[1] 375, 42; *omelias* [with *i* above the *e*], locutiones, Ep. 16E29.

omne, ii. 106, see *leguminum*; xxxv. 192, see *basis*; xli. 21, see *obfirmantes*.

omnes, xxix. 67, see *sumenumerus*.

omnes dies septimanę **sabbata** dicebantur, xxxix. 52 (*Greg*. [not Dial., but] *Reg. Past*. iii. 28 col. 106^A [quoting Isa. lvi. 4, 5] qui custodierint *sabbata* mea). See *Dial*. iv. 32 col. 372^C sacratissimo paschali *Sabbato*.

omnia, i. 94, see *passim*, 126, see *spectacula*; xxxvii. 9, see *tabulas*, 13, see *passim*.

omnipotens, xxi. 17, see *Adonai*; see also *pantocranto*.

omnis, i. 111, see *sicera*; iii. 56, see *ependiten*.

omnium, xxviii. 51, see *hyperthesis*; xxx. 19, see *pantocranto*; xxxix. 40, see *paralisin*.

omofagiis, see *omofagis*.

omofagis, quę non nisi cocte [-tae], xxxiv. 6 (*De Cassiano*, *Inst*. iv. 22 qui... xerofagiis uel *omofagiis* utuntur; in note *homofagiis*, *homofagis*). Cf. *xerofagia*.

omonima, uaria nomina, xliii. 10; **polionima**, multiuoca, xliii. 11; **cethetica**, possessiua, xliii. 12 (*De div. nominibus* = Donati *Ars grammat*. p. 373, 21, 22, 28 sunt [nomina] alia *homonyma*..., alia synonyma vel *polyonoma*,...sunt etiam *ctetica* [*thetica*, *theiga*, in note], id est *possessiva*). For *omonima*, see Cp. O158; Ep. 16E13; Ef.[1] 375, 26; for *polionima*, Cp. P510; Ep. 19E23.

omousion, graece latine una substantia patris et filii, i. 80 (*De Canon.*; *Can. Conc. Carth.*, praef. p. 144^a *Prof. fidei Nic. Conc.* unius substantiae cum patre, quod Graeci dicunt *omousion*).

onager, asinus siluaticus, xix. 24 (*Job* vi. 5 rugiet *onager*; cf. xi. 12, xxiv. 5 *onagri*, xxxix. 5 *onagrum*).

onauerit [ornauerit], xxxv. 194, see *expolierit*.

onichinos [onych-], vii. 4, see *lapides onichinos*.

onichinus [onych-], xli. 11, see *sardonix*.

onitaltaon [or -talticon, or -taltccon], xxx. 85, see *cinticta onitaltaon*.

onocentaurus, XIII. 42, see *epocentaurus.*

onorauit [honor-], XXXV. 87, see *afficit.*

onores [honores], V. 25, see *solaria.*

onoribus [hon-], IV. 13, see *fascibus.*

onychinos, see *lapides onichinos.*

onychinus, see *sardonix.*

opaco, see *opago.*

opago tempore denso uel ęstiuo, XXVII. 32 (*Lib. Rot.* = *Isid. Lib. de nat. rer.* XV. 3 sol...*opaco tempore* confouet sanos). Cf. *opacum*, aestiuum, Cp. O209; Ep. 16E34; Ef.[1] 375, 47.

opera, XXXVIII. 20 (bis), see *fidiae.* For *opera*, see also *catastrofon.*

operae pretium, see *opere precium.*

operam dare, benigne facere uel conciliare, I. 82 (*De Canon.*; *Can. Conc. Carth.* LXXIV *dare operam*).

opere, II. 125, see *magnopere.*

opere precium, necessarium, XLVIII. 58 (*De Cass.*, *Inst.* V. 38, 1 *Operae pretium* mihi uidetur) = *operepretium*, necessarium, Cp. O182.

operiremur, expectaremur, XXXV. 281 (*Ruf.* VII. 26 fol. 128[a] aduentum illius *operiremur*; *opper-*, Cacciari, p. 441).

operis, XII. 1, see *euergetis*; XXX. 55, see *erladiocten.*

operiunt, conspiciunt, V. 13 (*Eccl. Stor.*).—**opperiunt**, inueniunt repperiunt, XXXV. 18 (*De Eus.*) = (? *Ruf.* IV. 15 fol. 61[b]: Et ingressi ipsum quidem *offendunt* in superioribus quiescentem). Cf. *operiunt*, inueniunt, Cp. O187; Ep. 16E10; *operientes*, inueniunt, Ef.[1] 375, 23; *operiunt*, expectantes, Ef.[1] 375, 24.

o philon, XXX. 17; see *ho platon.*

opifex, XLIV. 10, see *cardines.*

opilauit [obp-, opp-], gigisdae, XLVII. 26 (*Alia* = ?) = *oppilauit*, clausit, gegiscte, Cp. O206; *oppillauit*, gigiscdae, Ep. 16E21; *o-*, ḡ scdae, Ef.[1] 375, 34. For ge-gīscan (with long *i*?), to stop, shut up, see Kluge, *A. S. Les.* p. 180.

opinantur, see *gomor.*

opinione, XXVIII. 51, see *hyperthesis.*

opperiremur, see *operiremur.*

opperiunt, inueniunt repperiunt, XXXV. 18; see *operiunt.*

oppilauit, oppillauit, see *opilauit.*

oppinantur [opin-], XXXIII. 16, see *gomor.*

oppleta, inpleta, XXXIV. 27 (*De Cass.*, *Inst.* XI. 15 anima...his *oppleta* simulacris).

oppositiones, see *ypo* (sub) *tyos* (hoc) &c.

ops, aput antiquos terra dicitur unde inops inhumatus, XLV. 11 (*Uerba de multis* = *Ars Phocae*, p. 412, 3 feminini generis pix *ops* prex...). Cf. *ops*, terra, Cp. O204; Ef.[1] 375, 40; *ops*, terrae, Ep. 16E27.

optio, XXXIX. 28; see *qui in numero optio...*

opus, IV. 96, see *stomatum*; XXXV. 75, see *iugeres.*

oraculum, orationem uel locutionem, XV. 40 (*Ezech.* XXI. 23 erit quasi consulens ...*oraculum*).

oraria, mappas uel linteamina, XXXV. 37 (*Ruf.* VII. 26 fol. 128[b] *oraria* moueri... expectabat) = *oraria*, linteamina, Cp. O226.—**orarium**, mappam uel linteamen, I. 81 (*De Canon.*; *Can. Conc. Laod.* CXXV cum *orariis*; uti *orario*; CXXVI *orariis*, *orario*).

orariis, orario, see *orarium*, sub v. *oraria.*

orarium, mappam uel linteamen, I. 81; see *oraria.*

oratio, XXX. 74, see *aceuan.*

orationem, XV. 40, see *oraculum.*

oratoriam, sapientiam secularíam [-rem], XXXV. 279 (*De Eus.*) = (*Ruf.* VII. 25 fol. 127[b] *oratoriam*...docuerat); **oratorie**, eloquentie, IV. 51 (*Eccl. Istor.*) = (*Ruf.* IV. 16 fol. 65[a] *oratoriam* docens).

oratorie, eloquentie, IV. 51; see *oratoriam.*

oratorium, XXXV. 64, see *martyrium.*

orbem, XLIV. 10, see *cardines*, 29 (bis), see *axem.*

orbi, XLIV. 10, see *cardines.*

orbibus, XLIV. 27, see *dextera.*

ordei, XXXI. 17, see *cercetea*; XXXIII. 25, see *siliqua una.*

ordeo, VIII. 18, see *ptisanas.*

ordinationem, XXXIX. 22, see *presbitera.*

ordinatum, XLI. 18, see *initiatum.*

ordinauimus, II. 47, see *digessimus.*

ordine, XXII. 1, see *themate*; XXVIII. 25, see *scema*, 67, see *anastrophe.*

ordinem, XXVIII. 47, see *parenthesin.*

orditus, XIII. 34, see *telam orditus.*

ordo, II. 100, see *lectisternia*; XXVIII. 78, see *hyperbaton*, XXIX. 21, see *curia*; XLV. 16, see *antes.*

ore, XIV. 14, see *calati.*

ore camerato, multum clamantem a camera tamen dicitur, XXXVII. 12 (*S. Aug.*?). This expression does not seem to occur in Aug. Sermons. Forcellini records non *camerato* eloquio caperis (Cassiod. 1 Hist. Eccl. 1), and explains "hoc est multum elaborato." Cf. Du C. Non aliquem quaeris verbis uti *cameratis* (tectus, involutus), Acta SS. Febr. I. 898 in Mirac. S. Amandi.

Orestes, see *eunuchus.*

oriatur, XXI. 3, see *Subal.*

orichalcum, see *auriculum.*

orientalis, xliv. 4, see *clima*.

oriente, xliv. 9, see *cęlum*, 11, see *clima*.

origo, ii. 116, see *materia*.

Orion, eburdnung, xxvii. 25 (*Lib. Rot.* =*Isid. Lib. de nat. rer.* xxvi. 8 *Orion*, stella est).—**Oriona**, ebirdhring, xix. 17 (*Job* ix: 9 qui facit Arcturum et *Oriona*) =*Orion*, eburðring, Cp. O255. *Orion*, the constellation, according to the myth, a hunter transported to heaven (Lewis & Sh.);—*ebir*, *ebur*=*eofor* (Bosw. T.), a boar; (dnung for) *drung*, *dhring*, *ðring*, a throng, crowd (Bosw. T. *þring*). Cf. Grimm, *D. Mythol.*, 4th ed. pp. 298, 606. For *ebir* cf. *aper*, ebir, in Steinm. *A.H.G.* iii. 447. 26. The Cambr. MS. has *Oriona*, multę stellę cuiusdam signi in cęlo.

Oriona, ebirdhring, xix. 17; see *Orion*.

oriri, xliv. 27, see *dextera*.

ormentum, xii. 25, see *in ormentum*.

ornamenta, x. 8, see *redimicula*; xx. 10, see *infula*.

ornamento, viii. 16, see *mala aurea*....

ornamentum, xii. 25, see *in ormentum*.

ornata, vi. 6, see *meliorata*.

ornatam, x. 1, see *osculetur me*.

ornatis, xxxv. 89, see *preditis*.

ornatum, xxxv. 185, see *expolitum*.

ornauerit, see *expolierit*.

Orosio, xxxvi *tit*.

ortans [hort-], xxviii. 26, see *paradigma*.

orthodoxam, recte gloriantium, xli. 4 (*De nomin. div.* = *Can. Conc. Calch.* xiv p. 136[a] ad *orthodoxam* fidem; cf. *Defin. fid. Conc. Chalc.*, ap. Mansi vii. 753[b] ad *orthodoxorum* dogmatum confirmationem). See below *ortodoxis*.

orthodoxi, see *ortodoxon* sub v. *ortodoxis*.

orthodoxis, see *ortodoxis*.

orthodoxorum, see *orthodoxam*.

ortodoxi, see *ortodoxon* sub v. *ortodoxis*.

ortodoxis [orthodoxis], recte gloriosis, ii. 129 (*Bened. reg.* 9, 18 [28] quae a nominatis doctorum *orthodoxis* catholicis patribus factae sunt).—**ortodoxon**, gloriosi uel perfecti, xxx. 94 (*Cat. Hier.* cxxxv col. 717[A] Altercationem Luciferiani et *Orthodoxi*; B: alterc. luciferani et *ortodoxi*; C: alterc. luciferiani et *ortodoxi*). Cf. *ortodoxi*, gloriosi, Cp. O227; *orthodoxi*, gloriosi siue perfecti, Ep. 16E30; Ef.[1] 375, 43; *ortodoxis*, gloriosis siue perfectis, Ef.[2] 316, 63. See above *orthodoxam*; and cf. Napier, 1357, 2634.

ortu, xliv. 27, see *leua*.

ortum, x. 22, see *areola*.

os, xxii. 4, see *eburneis*.

oscula, x. 1, see *osculetur me*.

osculetur me, ista oscula quę execlesie [ecclesiae] porrexit xpistus quam baptismi nitore mundatam et ornatam per spiritum sanctum odoris sui gratia inuitat ut sponsam, x. 1 (*Cant.* i. 1 *Osculetur me* osculo oris sui).

Ose, xxxi. 1, see *gomor maior*; Ose, xviii *tit*.

osma, odor, xlvii. 24 (*Alia*=?). Cf. *osma*, suice (Bosw. T. *swice*), Cp. O276; *osma*, suicae, Ep. 16E20 and Ef.[1] 375, 33. For *osma* (=Gr. ὀσμή), a smell, odour, see Goetz, vii. 34 (osmum, saporem=Ep. 17D15; and Ef.[1] 376, 57 osmion, saporem).

osmion, osmum, see *osma*.

ospicium [for *hospitium*], xxx. 28; see *de philoxenia*.

ossibus, xxii. 4, see *eburneis*.

ostendere, xxviii. 83, see *ennoematice*.

ostendimus, xxviii. 55, see *metaforan*.

ostendit, xxx. 36, see *prosefanesen*.

ostentationem, xxviii. 57, see *figura*.

ostiarii, xxxv. 99, see *aeditui*.

ostiarius, iv. 6, see *editus*.

otheporicon, itenerarium [itin-], xxx. 72 (*Cat. Hier.* lxxx).—**otheporicon**, iterarium uel uiarum, xxx. 87 (*Cat. Hier.* cxi); see the quotations sub v. *sinphosin*.

otii, quieti, xxxv. 251 (*Ruf.* v. 14 fol. 85[a] nihil usquam *ocij*).

otio, i. 56, see *foro*.

otiosus, xlvi. 20, see *seres*; see also *acidiosus*.

otium, ii. 46, see *desidens*.

oua, xiv. 11, see *perdix*.

ouans, gaudens, xxxv. 173 (*Ruf.* v. 3 fol. 78[b] exultans et *ouans*). Cf. *ouantes*, gaudentes, Cp. O292.

oues, see *soeue*.

p for *b*: diatri*p*as (for -*b*as); *p*landus; *p*oreo; *p*reuiarium; prosti*p*ulum; pu*p*licationis; pu*p*lico; scro*p*is.—for *ph*: *s*pere (s*ph*aerae); s*p*erico (s*ph*aerico); tro*p*ia (tro*ph*aea); ty*p*o (ty*ph*o); ty*p*um (ty*ph*um).—for *pp*: a*p*ulisse (a*pp*-); o*p*eriremur (o*pp*-).—for *pre*: pusti (*pre*usti).—p *doubled*: oedi*pp*a (Oedi*p*ia); odi*pp*o (Oedi*p*o).

pacificas, xli. 2, see *chorepiscopi* in voc. *presbiteri*.

pactum, v. 29, see *simbulion*.

Paenilopis, uxor achilis [for *Ulixis*], xxxviii. 34 (*Clem. Recognitt.* x. 10 videbimur telam texere *Penelopes*).

paganorum, xxx. 35, see *uarietas stromactis*; xxxvi. 1, see *Iani*; xliii. 29, see *Bachus*.

pagere, see *telopagere*.

pagi, prouintię [-ciae], xxiii. 11 (2 *Esdr.* iii. 15 princeps *pagi*).—**in pago**, in uico conpetis [=*compitis*], iii. 31 (*De S. Mart.*

Stor.); **pagus**, possessio magna, XLI. 19 (*De nomin. div.*) = (*Sulp. Sev. Vit. S. Mart.* 15, p. 125, 1 in *pago* Aeduorum). For "in uico" see *Id.* ibid. 13, 1; 14, 1; *Id. Dial.* III. 8, 4. Cf. *pagus* est possessio ampla, Cp. P119; *pagus*, possessio est ampla, sed sine aliquo iure unde et paganos dicimus alienos a iure uel sacris constitutis, Ef.[2] 318, 31.

palaestrarum, palaestris, see *palestrarum.*

palam, I. 85, see *proscribantur.*

palantibus, pendentibus, XL. 6 (*Uerba?*). —**pallantibus**, apparentibus, XL. 20 (*Uerba?*).

palathas, see *labastes.*

palestrarum, luctantium, XXXIX. 45 (*Greg.* [not Dial., but] *Reg. Past.* III. 37 col. 122B *palaestrarum* more).—**palestris**, luctatio, XXXVIII. 30 (*Clem. Recognitt.* IX. 25 Graecos non exerceri *palaestris*).

paliurus, erba [herba] quę crescit in tectis domorum grossa folia habens fullae, XIII. 41 (*Isai.* XXXIV. 13 Orientur spinae... et *paliurus*). For *paliurus* = παλίουρος, a plant, Christ's-thorn, see Lewis & Sh.; *fullae* is, perhaps, the same as *sin-fulle* (cf. *paliurus*, sinfulle, Cp. P130; *palurus*, sinfullae, Ep. 20A29; *palliurus*, sinfullae, Ef.[1] 382, 39 and Bosw. T.), which is explained as *house-leek*, *sempervivum tectorum*, which would agree with the Glossator's description. Cf. Steinm. *A.H.G.* I. 590, 25; Schlutter, in *Anglia* XXVI. 303; Kluge, *A. S. Leseb.* 177.

pallantibus, apparentibus, XL. 20; see *palantibus.*

pallebat, timebat, XXXVII. 18 (*S. Aug.?*).

pallescere, XXXV. 14, see *diriguere.*

pallidus, XXIX. 40, see *ferrugineas*; XXXV. 4, see *luridus.*

palmarum, X. 21 (bis), see *elatę palmarum.*

palpo, see *panpo.*

Pan, deus arcadię [-diae] uel pastorum, XLIII. 3; see *Themisto.*

Pana, XLIII. 4, see *arcades.*

panaeretos, see *panarethos.*

panagericis, laudabilibus, XXXV. 88 (*De Eus.*); **pannigericis**, in laudibus, IV. 1 (*Eccl. Istor.*) = (*Ruf., Ep. ad Chrom.* fol. 1b *Panegyricis* tractatibus).—**panagericon**, laudabilem, XXX. 59; **eucharistias**, gratiarum actiones, XXX. 60 (*Cat. Hier.* LXV col. 675B: Theodorus proficiscens πανηγυρικὸν [Panegyricum, Rich.] εὐχαριστίας scripsit Origeni; B: Theo. prof. *panegiricum* · *Enchariseon* idest graciarum scripsit Origeni; C: Theo. prof. *pane gericum* [blank] scripsit Origeni) = *panagericum ceuairistias*, laudabilem eruditionem, Cp. P23; Ep. 18C27; Ef.[1] 379, 16; *eucharistias*, gratiarum actiones, Cp. E341; Ef.[1] 358, 30.

panarethos, sapientia, VIII. 1 (*Salam.*; Praef. S. Hier. Fertur et *Panaeretos* [πανάρετος, Migne XXVIII col. 1242; *Panerethos*, Heyse, note 10] Jesu filii Sirach liber).

pane, XIV. 7, see *lignum in pane.*

panegericum, panegiricum, panegyricis, see *panagericis.*

panem, see *lignum in pane.*

panerethos, see *panarethos.*

panes, XIV. 3, see *uorith*; XVI. 1, see *pistrinum*; XXXIX. 43, see *duas coronas*; XLV. 10, see *gyt.*

pangebantur, iungebtur, XL. 4 (*Uerba?*).

panguitur, pinguitur, VI. 27 (*Breu. exsol.?*).

panis, XIV. 21 (bis); see *torta panis.*

pannigericis, in laudibus, IV. 1; see *panagericis.*

panos, XXVII. 11, see *lupercal.*

panpo, genus piscis, XLIII. 15 (*De div. nominibus* = Donati *Ars grammat.*, p. 374, 13 *palpo*). *Palpo*, a flatterer (Lewis & Sh.); cf. Steinm. II. 160, 8 sqq.

pantocranto, omnium, XXX. 19; **paturia theo**, de potentia dei continentia eo dicitur, XXX. 20 (*Cat. Hier.* XIII col. 631A liber ejus qui inscribitur περὶ αὐτοκράτορος λογισμοῦ; B: lib. eius q. i. *pericratopos logismoi* idest de potentia loquendi; C: lib. eius qui inscribitur [blank]). Cp. P120 & 121 has: *pantocranto*, omnium—*paturia theo*, de potentia dei; P50: *pantocraton*, omnipotens, and P198 [= Ef.[1] 377, 43]: *pertes cratorias toyty*, de potentia dei. Taking all these readings together it would seem (1) that St Jerome wrote περὶ παντοκράτορος λογισμοῦ; (2) that παντ- was glossed by "omnium potens," or by "omnipotens" (omnium being a misread omps); (3) that *paturia theo* arose from some imagined or really existing παντοκρατορία θεοῦ, or rather περὶ κρατορίας θεοῦ; (4) that continentia eo dicitur is a gloss to some such word as encratia [= ἐγκράτεια].

pantocraton, see *pantocranto.*

papa [sine interpret.], I. 99 (*De Canon.*; *Can. Conc. Carth.* praef. p. 141a Aurelius *Papa*, 142b sancte *Papa* Aureli; cf. also pp. 328a, 331b).

papilio, see *animalus.*

papiri, unde faciunt cartas, XIII. 31 (*Isai.* XVIII. 2 in vasis *papyri*).

papyri, see *papiri.*

parabole, conparatio, XXVIII. 48 (*Cass. Psalm.* XVI. 9 schema quod Graece *parabole*, Latine comparatio dicitur).

paradigma, narratio per exempla ortans

aliquem aut deterrens, XXVIII. 26 (*Cass. Psalm.* I. 6 *paradigma*, n. p. e. hortans a. a. d. See also XIV. 8; XXXIII. 15; XXXVI. 18).

PARALIPOMENON, VII *tit.*

paralisin, desolutio [dissol-] omnium membrorum, XXXIX. 40 (*Greg. Dial.* IV. 15 col. 345A ea quam...*paralysin* vocant molestia...percussa est)=*paralisin*, dissolutio omnium membrorum, Cp. P127; Ep. 20A12; *paralisin*, desolutio omnium membrorum, Ef.[1] 382, 22.

paralysin, see *paralisin*.

paranimphi, dryctguma, XLII. 8 (*Ex div. libris?*) = *paranymphus*, dryhtguma, Cp. P11 & 150. Paranimphus, a bridesman. For *dryctguma*=*dryct*, *dryht*, a company, train+*guma*, a man (=O.H.G. *truhtigomo*, Schade), see Bosw. T. (*dryhtguma*); Kluge, *A. S. Les.* p. 170; Kern, *Notes on Salic Law* § 83.

paraprosdocia [-doxia], latine inopinatus exitus cum aliud proponitur aliud explicatur ut est deus deus mevs inpolluta uia eius, XXVIII. 53 (*Cass. Psalm.* XVII. 32, col. 132C figura...*paraprosdoxia*, Latine inopinatus e. c. a. p. a. e. [ut est, the Glossator's addition, and col. 132B] Deus meus, impolluta uia eius).

parascheue, preparatione, XXX. 63 (*Cat. Hier.* LXIX col. 679B ἑορταστικαὶ de Pascha plurimae). Cf. *parasceuen*, praeparatio cibi, Cp. Int. 247; *parasceue*, praeparatio, Cp. P109. The gloss "preparatione" in the ablat. case seems to show that "par-, prep." are not intended to explain XXX. 75 (*eyaggences*) or XXX. 76 (*euaggences*) of the present Glossary, but points to "parascheue" (παρασκευή) being another reading for "Pascha," though none of the existing texts have any traces of it.

parasueues, XXX. 76, see *euaggences parasueues*.

paratus, XXII. 16, see *ueredarii*.

parcae, see *parcę*; *striga*.

parcant, XLIII. 49, see *parcę*.

parcę, quae minime parcant, XLIII. 49 (*De div. nominibus*=Donati *Ars Grammat.* p. 402, 5 *Parcae* eo quod nulli parcant). Cf. *parcę*, pyrde, Cp. P16; *parcae*, uuyrdae, Ep. 18C17; *parce*, uuyrdae, Ef.[1] 379, 6; Napier, 5480; 8, 413; 8B, 5. For pyrde, uuyrdae, plur. of *wyrd*, E. *weird*, see Bosw. T., the Fates, weird sisters.

parchredis, prestrigiis [praestigiis], v. 18 (*Eccl. Stor.*); **parethis**, ministris, XXXV. 78 (*De Eus.*); **parethris**, ministeriis [ministris?], IV. 45 (*Eccl. Istor.*)=(*Ruf.* IV. 8 fol. 56b de...dęmoniis *Parhedris*)=*parchedris*, ministris, Cp. P78; Ep. 19E7.—**paredum**, prestigium [praest-], v. 17 (*Eccl. Stor.*)=(*Ruf.* II. 13 fol. 25b adminiculo... daemoniacę virtutis quam πάρεδρον vocant).

parcitate, abstinentie [-tia?], II. 90 (*Bened. reg.* 39, 18 [30] servata in omnibus *parcitate*).

parcus, XII. 32, see *frugis* (for *frugi*).

pardo, XIX. 39, see *leopardus*.

paredum, prestigium [praest-], v. 17; see *parchredis*.

parenthesin, idest interpositionem quoniam in sensu medio recipit uerba quedam quedam ordinem sententie uideantur posse diuidere, XXVIII. 47 (*Cass. Psalm.* XVI. 5 Qui versus figuram continet *parenthesin* id est i. q. i. s. m. r. u. quædam quæ ordinem sententiæ u. p. d.).

parethis, ministris, XXXV. 78; see *parchredis*.

parethris, ministeriis [ministris?], IV. 45; see *parethis*.

parhedris, see *parchredis*.

parietem, see *paxillus*.

parietes, XIII. 40, see *perpendiculum*; XVII. 5, see *trulla*.

paritores, ministros, XXXIX. 18 (*Greg. Dial.* III. 31 col. 292A suos *apparitores* misit).

parochia, see *diocesis*; *in diocesi* (sub v. *diocesim*); *parrochia*.

paroecia, see *diocesim*; *parrochia*.

parra, see *parula*.

parrochia (for *paroecia*) [sine interpret.], I. 83 (*De Canon.*; *Can. Apostt.* XIV *parochia* peruadatur...; alienam *parochiam* peruadere; XV relinquens propriam *parochiam*; ...in aliena *parochia*). Cf. *parochia*, loca adiacentia ecclesia, Cp. P24; *parrochia*, loca adiacentia aeclesiae, Ep. 18E6; *porochia* &c., Ef.[1] 379, 33; *parrochia*, statuta loca, Ef.[2] 318, 57. For *parrochia* see also (XXXIX. 54) *in diocesi*, sub v. *diocesim*; and cf. Napier, 886; 2033; 3, 38.

parrochiis, I. 36, see *diocesis*.

parrula, parrus, see *parula*.

pars, XIX. 6, see *comma*, 49, see *lacertos*; XXXI. 9, see *comor*, 21, see *cathos*; XXXIII. 16, see *gomor*; XLIII. 22, see *forinnadas*; XLIV. 4, see *clima*.

parte, XI. 14, see *poderis*; XIV. 20, see *scalpellum*; XXXV. 82, see *sub axe p-*; XLIII. 35, see *hac*, 36, see *illac*; XLIV. 11, see *clima*.

partem, XXVIII. 41, see *sinecdochen*; XXXI. 13, see *sarre*; XXXIX. 36, see *sex untias*.

partes, XIV. 33, see *lacinias*; XXXV. 268, see *agellis*; XXXVIII. 25, see *climacteras*; XLIV. 5, 10, see *cardines*.

partes autem eius cous axis clima cardines conuexa poli hiemisperia, XLIV. 1

(*Alia*; *de cælo*=*Isid. de nat. rerum*, XII. 3 col. 983 Partes autem ejus: *chous*, *axis* [*clima* not in text], *cardines*, *convexa*, *poli*, sidera [*hemisphæria* in note]). Cf. the words, printed in italics, with their explanations, in their respective alphabetical places in the present Index. Cf. the notes in Migne's Vol. LXXXIII, col. 983 sqq.

participeps, XXXV. 48, see *compos*.

parua, II. 115, see *munuscula*.

parue [paruae], V. 10, see *exedre*.

paruipendens, pro nihilo habens uel ducens, I. 88 (*De Canon.*; *Can. Conc. Gangr.* LXIX *paruipendens* quod geritur; cf. *Can. Conc. Antioch.* XC haec *paruipendentes*; *Can. Conc. Calch.* III Dei... ministerium *paruipendentes*).

paruipendentes, see *paruipendens*.

parula, masae, XLVII. 52 (*Alia*= ?)=*p*-, mase, Cp. P128; *parrula*, masae, Ep. 20A13 & Ef.[1] 382, 23. *Parula*, *parrula*, dimin. of *parra* (the *common* or *barn owl*; or, according to others, *the green woodpecker*, or *the lapwing*; see Lewis & Sh.); *masae*, *mase* (=A.S. *māse*, O.H.G. *meisa*, Germ. *Meise*; D. *mees*; E. -mouse, in *tit-mouse*); see Bosw. T. (*māse*); Goetz VII. 50 (*parra*, *parrus*, αἰγίθαλλος); Kluge, *Et. Wört.* (*Meise*).

parum, paruum, XIII. 17 (*Isai.* VII. 13 numquid *parum* vobis est; XXX. 14 hauriatur *parum* aquae; XLIX. 6 *parum* est).—**parum**, paruum, XXXV. 84 (*Ruf.* X. 30 fol. 174[b] *parum* firmauerim; X. 36 fol. 176[a] dicebat se...dolores *parum* sensisse; XI. 28 fol. 190[b] *Parum* dixerim).

paruulorum, XXXV. 53, see *ludus literarum*.

paruulus, see *pungios*.

paruum, XIII. 17, see *parum*; XV. 3, see *uas transmigrationis*; XXXI. 11, see *ephi*; XXXV. 84, see *parum*.

pascant, XXXV. 119, see *coalescant*.

pascha, see *parascheue*.

paschę, XXXV. 20, see *magni sabbati*.

passim, promiscue publice uulgo uel per omnia, I. 94 (*De Canon.*; *Can. Conc. Calch.* XXI Clericos...accusantes Episcopos, aut Clericos *passim*; *Can. Conc. Carth.* XLIV *passim* vagando).—**passim**, huc atque illuc uel leuiter, II. 134 (*Bened. reg.* 70 tit. Ut non praesumat *passim* aliquis caedere).—**passim**, per omnia, XXXVII. 13 (*S. Aug.*?).

passio, passionem, XXIX. 50, see *prathus*.

passus, XXXI. 25, see *pes*.

pastoforia, gazofilatia [gazophylacia], IV. 92 (*Eccl. Ist.*); **pastoforie**, modice [-cae] domus, XXXV. 62 (*De Eus.*)=(*Ruf.* XI. 23 fol. 187[b] *pastophoria*)=*pastoforia*, modica domus, Cp. P79; Ep. 19E8; Ef.[1] 381, 38.

pastoforie, modice [modicae] domus, XXXV. 62, see *pastoforia*.

pastophoria, see *pastoforia*.

pastoralis, XX. 9, see *de cassidie*.

pastores, XLV. 18, see *pedum*.

pastorum, XLIII. 3, see *Pan*; see also *magalia*.

patebant, XXXVI. 1, see *Iani porte*.

patena, XXIII. 7; XXXVIII. 17, see *cratera*.

pater, II. 4, see *abba*, 7, see *alleluia*; XVII. 8, see *Naum*; XXXIV. 21, see *atauus*; XXXVIII. 40, see *Peleum*; XLIII. 28, see *Bachus*.

patera, uas regia, III. 32 (*De S. Mart. Stor.*=*Sulp. Sev. Vit. S. Mart.* 20, 5 *pateram* regi minister obtulit; 6 *pateram* presbytero...tradidit).

patiens, II. 32, see *contentus*.

patres, II. 119, see *nonnos*.

patria, XXXV. 241, see *extorres*.

patricius senator, consiliarius, XXXV. 272 (*Ruf.* VII. 13 fol. 120[b] uir Romanae urbis *senator*, *patricius*).

patris, I. 80, see *omousion*.

patulis, apertis, XXXV. 231 (*Ruf.* XI. 25 fol. 189[a] *patulis* erepebat cauernis).

paturia theo, XXX. 20, see *pantocranto*.

paturum, fctor, XLVI. 42 (*Alia*=*Ars Phocae*?). The Cp. Gloss. (P253) has *pedo* uel paturum feotur=Ep. 19C11 & Ef.[1] 381, 5 pedo uel paturum fetor. This suggests that *fctor* stands for *fetor*, and =A.S. *feoter*, *feotur*, a fetter (see Bosw. T. in v. *feoter*), not the Lat. *fetor* (faet-, foet-), a stench; cf. also *pedica*.—As regards *pedo*, Glogger suggests that it may be connected with **pediola* (Körting, *Wrterb.* 6979); *paturum* seems=*pastorium*, quod Italis *pastoja* dicitur (Du C.); cf. Körting, 6914; Skeat, *Conc. Et. D.* (*pastern*).

pauidi, IV. 67, see *meticulosi*.

pauimentum, XXXV. 171, see *harene*.

paulatim, XXVIII. 56, see *auxesis*.

paulominus, XV. 46, see *pusilluminus*.

paupertate, XXX. 91, see *peri pthocheas*, sub v. *ptocheus*.

paupertatis, see *ptocheus*.

pauperum, I. 91, see *ptochiis*; XXXIX. 58, see *pitoicis*; XLI. 3, see *sidonicis*.

pauxillum minus, see *pusilluminus*.

paxillus, fusticellus qui in stantem [Cambr. MS. adds *parietem*] mittitur negil, XV. 5 (*Ezech.* XV. 3 fabricabitur de ea *paxillus*). Cf. *paxillus*, fusticellus qui in stamen mittitur in pariete, id est nagal, Steinm. *Althochd. Gl.* I. 640, 5; *paxillum*, palum naegl, Cp. P107. For negil=nægel, nægl (=E. *nail*), see Bosw.

T. (*nægel*). Stans = domus, habitatio (Du C.); cf. also Du C. (*stantia*); Körting, *Lat. R. W.* 9023 *stantia, dwelling-place; Ital. stanza, dwelling, room; Fr. étance, prop, support = E. stance, see *Cent. Dict.*, and Skeat, *Conc. Et. Dict.* (*stanza*).

peccando, XXIV. 6, see *publicani.*

pectorali, see *fascia pectoralis.*

pectoralis, XIII. 13, see *fascia pectoralis.*

pectore, II. 152, see *senpectas.*

pectus, IV. 97, see *thoraces*; XIII. 13, see *fascia pectoralis*; XIX. 42, see *torax.*

pecunia, XV. 24, see *pollinctores.*

pecuniam, XXXIX. 24, see *aduocatus.*

pecuniis, XXXV. 206, see *salariis.*

pedalis, mensura in tela quando [for *quam*?] uolunt incidere, XIV. 30 (*Hier.* LI. 13 venit finis tuus *pedalis* praecisionis tuae).

pede, IV. 59, see *puncto*; XXXVII. 8, see *odon.*

pedes, VII. 1, see *in nablis*; XIII. 43, see *lamia*; XIV. 19, see *arugo*; XXII. 9, see *pedisequas*; XXXV. 27, see *puncto*, 181, see *regio morbus*; XXXIX. 7, see *erucę*; XLIII. 13, see *agrippa.*

pedessequa, see *pedissequa.*

pedibus, XI. 14, see *poderis*; XIX. 10, see *ridhmus.*

pedica, tenticula, XIV. 4 (*Hier.* V. 26 ponentes...*pedicas*).—**pedica**, fezra ligamen, XIX. 19 (*Job* XVIII. 10 *pedica*); *fezra* (O.H.G. *feȝȝera*), a fetter, see Bosw. T. (*feoter*, *feotur*, *feter*); a Bern MS. has *fictor*; see *fctor* sub v. *paturum.*

pedicas, see *pedica.*

pediola, see *paturum.*

pedisequa, see *pedissequa*, sub v. *pedisequas.*

pedisequas, pedes sequentes idest obsequentes, XXII. 9 (*Esther* II. 9 *pedissequas* eius ornaret; Heyse, in note, *pedisequas*).—**pedissequa**, ministra, XLV. 22 (*Uerba de multis* = *Ars Phocae*, p. 412, 27 hic et haec *pedisequa*; in note *pedessequa*).—**pedissequis**, conuiator gegenta, XXXV. 54 (*De Eus.*) = (*Ruf.* XI. 4 fol. 179[a] cum duobus *pedissequis*). *gegenta* for gegenca = *gegenga*, going with, from *ge-*, collective, and *genge*, adj. going; see Bosw. T. (*genge*).

pedissequas, see *pedisequas.*

pedissequis, conuiator gegenta, XXXV. 54, see *pedisequas.*

pedo, see *paturum.*

pedules [sine interpret.], II. 140 (*Bened. reg.* 55, 9 [14] sufficere credimus monachis ...indumenta pedum *pedules* et caligas, 18 [31] *pedules*...reddant, 30 [53] *pedules*, caligas).

pedum, V. 16, see *podagra.*

pedum, fustis quem pastores habent in modum Λ, XLV. 18 (*Uerba de multis* = *Ars Phocae*, p. 412, 14, 15 *pedum*).

Peleum, pater achelis [Achillis], XXXVIII. 40 (*Clem. Rom. Recognitt.* X. 41 *Peleum*... et Thetidem nympham...ponunt; X. 20 *Peleo* cuidam dat eam).

pelle, XV. 45, see *iacincto.*

pellexerat, uocauerat, XXXVI. 16 (*Oros.* II. 4, 5 Sabinorum, quos foedere ludisque *pellexerat*; VII. 6, 6 legiones...ad sacramenti mutationem *pellexerat*).

pellis, XIX. 20, see *tympanum.*

peluem (pelvim), XXV. 13, see *in peluem.*

pena, see *catastrofon.*

pendens, III. 56, see *ependiten.*

pendent, X. 21, see *elatę palmarum.*

pendentia, XXVIII. 45, see *zeuma.*

pendentibus, XL. 6, see *palantibus.*

pendere, XXVIII. 61, see *amphibolia.*

pendica (?), XXXI. 7, see *libra.*

pendicum, XXXI. 23, see *siliquas.*

pene, XI. 3, see *lanugo.*

Penelopes, see *Paenilopis.*

penetrabiliorem, I. 128, see *secretalem.*

pennas, XIV. 20, see *scalpellum*; XXII. 16, see *ueredarii.*

pennias, XLII. 27, see *in pennias.*

pensabat, XXXIX. 20, see *in mare adriatico.*

pensant, XXXIII. 31, see *siliquas sex.*

pensat, XXXI. 31, 32, see *sextarius*; XXXII. 1, see *dragma*, 3, see *scripulus*, 4, see *obolus*, 5, see *uncia*; XXXIII. 22, see *semiuncia*, 25, see *siliqua una*, 28, see *libra.*

pensatur, XXXI. 30, see *scripulus.*

penso, censo, II. 138 (*Bened. reg.* 49, 10 augeamus nobis aliquid solito *penso* [16 *pensu*; *pensum*] servitutis nostrae; 50, 8 [11] servitutis *pensum*...reddere).

pensu, see *penso.*

pensum, XXXII. 6, see *ciatos*; see also *penso.*

pentapolim, u ciuitates quę arserunt, XI. 7 (*Sap.* X. 6 descendente igne in *pentapolim*).

pentecoste, see *pentecosten.*

pentecosten [sine interpret.], II. 131 (*Bened. reg.* 15, 2 usque *pentecosten*; pentecoste, in note, [1] pentecostes, 41, 2 [1] usque ad *pentecosten*).

pentecostes, see *pentecosten.*

penuria, XLVIII. 12, see *frugalitas.*

per, I. 94, 109; VII. 1; VIII. 12, 14; X. 1; XXII. 12; XXVIII. 26, 31, 38 (bis), 43 (bis), 50, 55, 72, 80, 83 (bis); XXXI. 38; XXXV. 120 (bis), 143 (bis), 199; XXXVII. 13; XXXVIII. 29, 31; XXXIX. 24, 33, 63 (bis); XLIII. 25, 26, 44 (bis); XLIV. 3, 29 (bis).—See also *periscema.*—per [prep., corrupted to pref. *pre-*], IV. 31, see *prestatio.*

pera, xx. 9, see *de cassidie*.
peragere, see *telopagere*.
per aggerem [sine interpret.], III. 14; see *aggerem*.
peragunt, XVI. 31, see *incantatores*.
per ambitum, XVII. 7, perhaps for *per ambulabat*, see *Nineue*.
percunctatio, XXVIII. 36, see *peusis*.
percussa, XXXV. 131, see *multata*.
percussus, IV. 28, see *mulcatus*.
percutiaris, see *ypo* (sub) *tyos* (hoc).
perdendum, XII. 45, see *caupo*.
perdit, XIV. 11, see *perdix*.
perditi, XXXIX. 38, see *claui perditi*.
perdix, auis in deserto alter perdit aliter [for *alter*?] fouit oua, XIV. 11 (*Hier.* XVII. 11 *perdix* fovit quae non peperit). On Jeremiah's story of the partridge, adopted by the old Lat. Bestiaries, see Skeat's note to Richard the Redeles, passus III. li. 38, in Vol. II. p. 297, of his ed. of Piers Plowman (Oxf. 1886).
perdono, XLIII. 48, see *cedo*.
perduellibus, see *duellis*.
perduellionis, see *duellionis*.
perdulum, hragra, XLVII. 64 (*Alia*= ?) =*ardia*, hraga et die perdulum, Cp. A729; *ardea* et dieperdulum, hragra, Ep. 2A23 & Ef.[1] 340, 10 (id.). For *dieperdulum* see Steinm. IV. 185, 42 sq. *Ardea* (in Virg. *G.* I. 304) a heron; for *hragra*, *hraga* (a heron) see Bosw. T. (*hrāgra*); Kluge, *Etym. Wrtb.* (*Reiher*); Oxf. D. (*heron*).
peregrinorum, XXXIX. 59, see *xenodochiorum*.
perende [for *perendie*], ofer tua nest, XLIII. 41 (*De div. nominibus*=not? Donati *Ars gramm.*?); *ofer*, over, beyond; *tua* =twā, two; *nest* for *nect*, night=over two nights, the day after to-morrow; see Bosw. T. (*ofer*; *twā*; *twā-nihte*; *nihte*).
perendie, see *perende*.
per energiam, quę actum rei incorpore imaginatione representat, XXVIII. 81 (*Cass. Psalm.* XXXVI. 37 *per energiam* quae a. r. *incorporeae* i. repraesentat. See also id. IV. 2; and id. XXXIII. 3 *energia*, id est imaginatio, quae actum rei incorporeis oculis subministrat).
perfecti, XXX. 94, see *ortodoxon*.
perficiantur, XXII. 16, see *ueredarii*.
per figuram yperbolen, per quam solent aliqua in magnitudinem exaggerationis extendi, XXVIII. 38 (*Cass. Psalm.* VI. 7 Sive hoc *per figuram hyperbolen* potest accipi, per quam s. a. i. m. e. e.).
perforantes, XXXV. 187, see *terebrantes*.
per hironiam, per mendatium, XXXV. 120 (*Ruf.* II. 18 fol. 29[a] *per ironiam*). Cf. *per hironiam*, ðorh hosp, Cp. P239; *per hironiam*, per mendacem iocum, Ep. 18E7; *pro hironiam*, pro mendacem iocum, Ef.[1] 379, 34. For ðorh (through), see Bosw. T. (*þurh*); for hosp (reproach, contempt) id. (*hosp*). Cf. Napier, 5201 (*per hironiam*, per allegoriam, hux, *hosp*).
periaois, see *peridion*.
peribolus [sine interpret.], XV. 26 (*Ezech.* XLII. 7 peribolus exterior). Cf. *peribulus*, in circuitu domus, Cp. P249; *peribulus*, id est in c. d., Ep. 19A38 and Ef.[1] 380, 49.
pericratopos, see *pantocranto*.
periddon, see *peridion*.
peridion, contextum idest unius sensus, XXX. 9 (*Cat. Hier.* VII col. 619[B] περιόδους Pauli...inter apocryphas scripturas computamus; B: *periaois* idest responsionem pauli...i. a. s. c.; C: *periodous* pauli...int. scr. ap. conp.). Cf. *periodoias*, contextus, circutus, Cp. P197; *periodoys*, circuitus contextus, Ep. 17E20; Ef.[1] 377, 41; *periddon*, contextum, Cp. P236; Ep. 18C32; *peridon*, contextum, Ef.[1] 379, 20; *peridoyn*, actus pauli, Cp. P199; *periodoyn*, actus pauli uel pitonicum, Ep. 17E25; *peridony*, actus pauli uel pytonicum, Ef.[1] 376, 46.
periens, XXX. 29, see *capun periens*.
perigamini, membrano, VI. 15 (*Breu. exsol.*?).
periodoias, periodous, periodoyn, periodoys, see *peridion*.
perioi, see *peri pthocheas*.
periotession, periotesyon, see *peri tes zoes*...
peripateticus, see *peripatthiens*.
peripatthiens, ambulator, XXX. 1 (*Cat. Hier.*, *Prol.* 603[A] Hermippus *peripateticus*).
peripsema, see *peripsima*.
peripsima, gaesuopę, IV. 71 (*Eccl. Istor.*); **peripsima**, purgamentum uel quisquilea, XXXV. 195 (*De Eus.*)=(*Ruf.* VII. 20 fol. 122[b] effecti sunt eorum...περίψημα). Cf. tamquam purgamenta huius mundi facti sumus, omnium *peripsima* usque adhuc, 1 Cor. IV. 13. For gae-suopę (=O.H.G. *gasopha*, peripsima, quisquiliae, Schade) see Bosw. T. (*ge-swǣpa*, *-swǣpo*, sweepings, dust), and for other forms, Steinm. *A.H.G.* II. 596, 4; Wright W. (Index); Napier, 4155.
peri pthocheas, de paupertate, XXX. 91; see *ptocheus*.
periscelidas, armillas de tibiis, XIII. 8 (*Isai.* III. 20 auferet Dominus...*periscelidas*. Cambr. MS. *periscelides*, armillas *de argento*). Cf. *perscelides*, armillas in pedibus, Cp. P303; Ep. 19E11; Ef.[1] 381, 41.
periscelides, see *periscelidas*.
periscema icon, quę latini dicitur imagi-

natio, XXVIII. 49 (*Cass. Psalm.* XVI. 9 *Per schema icon*, quae Latine d. i.).

perision [for περιούσιον], XXIX. 51, see *epyuision.*

peri tes zoes theoricas, idest de hac uit[a] contemplatiua, XXX. 13 (*Cat. Hier.* XI col. 629A; see *iereticos*) =*peritesyon*, de hac uita, Cp. P237; *periotesyon*, d. h. u., Ep. 18C33; *periotession*, d. h. u., Ef.[1] 379, 21.

peritia, XXX. 29, see *capun periens.*

peritiae, see *instrumenta.*

peritię [-tiae], II. 88, see *instrumenta.*

perlucentia, XXIX. 14, see *lanternis.*

per metalla, per diuersas artes ferri uel alias, XXXV. 143; see *metalla.*

permiscet, XII. 45, see *caupo.*

permixtione, XXVIII. 85, see *figura sardismos.*

permotatio, XXVIII. 29, see *exallege.*

permutatio, XXVIII. 44, see *hypallage*; see also *exallege.*

permutatione, see *trapezita.*

perna, flicci, XLVII. 13 (*Alia*=?)=*perna*, flicci, Cp. P250; Ep. 19C4 & 20A10 (*p*-, flicii); Ef.[1] 380, 54. For *flicci, flicce,* a flitch of bacon, see Bosw. T.

perna, fossa, XXIV. 2 (*Math.*? not in the Vulg.?). If the lemma is the well-known word *perna*, a flitch of bacon (see Wright W.; Cp. P250; Ep. 19C4, 20A10; Ef.[1] 380, 54), it cannot be explained by the equally well-known word *fossa*, a ditch, trench (see Goetz, VI. 465, *fossa*). Nor is it explained by Papias' *pernae* dicuntur vulgo procellae de montibus. Besides that of Leiden only one other MS. has the gloss: *perna* fossa flycci (Steinm. I. 708, 1). Perhaps the two words are two lemmata, without interpretations; *fossa* would not disagree with *umecta* (q.v.).

pernicies, pernicitas, see *pernities.*

pernities, uelocitas, XLVIII. 31 (*De Cass., Inst.* VIII. 18 equi infrenes...acrius ad *perniciem* aurigae...prorumpunt). *Pernicies* does not agree with *uelocitas*, and hence Goetz (VII. 74) inserts this gloss under *pernicitas*. Cf. Ef.[2] (Goetz, V. 319, 33) *pernicies*, malitia uel uelocitas.

pernix, uelox, XLVI. 29 (*Alia*=*Ars Phocae*, p. 421, 10 hic et haec et hoc *pernix*)=*pernix*, uelox, Cp. P216.

perorans, adloquens, XXXV. 109 (*Ruf.* II. 5 fol. 20b *perorans* apud Caium)=*perorans*, adloquens, Cp. P302; Ep. 19E3; Ef.[1] 381, 34.

perossus, abhominatus, VI. 26 (*Breu. exsol.*? Cf. Ut melius fuerit thalamis caruisse *perosis*, Juvencus III. 481).

perpendiculum, modica petra de plumbo qua licant [*quam ligant*, Cambr. MS.] in filo quando edificant [aed-] parietes pundar, XIII. 40 (*Isai.* XXXIV. 11)=perpendiculum, pundur, Cp. P264. For pundar (which is non-Germanic, and merely late Lat. *pondarium* in A.S. spelling), see Bosw. T. (*pundar*, *pundur*, a plumb-line); cf. Steinm. I. 590, 19—24.

perpera, sine causa, XXXV. 217 (*Ruf.* X. 27 fol. 173a *perperam* gesta).—**perpera**, causa uel prauitas, XXIX. 43 (?*Uerb. Interpr.* =*Hier. in Matth.*?).

perperam, see *perpera.*

perpeti, ueloces, XLVIII. 33 (*De Cass., Inst.* V. 17, 2 *praepeti* conscientiae deuotione; *perpeti* in MS.).

perpetuo, II. 28, see *continuanda.*

per pragmati[c]am formam, per principalia imperia uel negotia, XXXIX. 63; see *pragmatica.*

persarum, XVI. 8, see *satrapa.*

personarum, XXVIII. 80, see *diaforesis.*

personas, XXVIII. 58, see *apostropei.*

personis, XXVIII. 34, see *figura m*-.

personisue, XXVIII. 88, see *diatiposis.*

perspicacem, see *perspicem.*

perspicem, ingenium, XXXV. 296 (*Ruf.* X. 9 fol. 164b Frumentio...quem quasi *perspicacem* deprehenderat).

perstringit, XXVIII. 64, see *epitrocasmos.*

per tes, see *pantocranto.*

pertinax, II. 26, see *contempto.*

pertinent, XXXVII. 9, see *tabulas legat.*

pertingens, XI. 14, see *poderis.*

pertussos, XXXIX. 43, see *duas coronas.*

peruadere alienam rem manifeste praesumere, I. 84 (*De Canon.*; *Can. Apostt.* XIV alienam parochiam...*peruadere*; cf. *ibid.* XXXI *tit.* ecclesia...*peruadatur*; *Can. Conc. Antioch.* XCIV sedem *peruadat*).

peruenient, XXXVIII. 44, see *epibatis.*

peruersio, XXVIII. 67, see *anastrophe.*

peruersus, VIII. 5, see *uersipellis.*

peruia, XVI. 3, see *crypta.*

peruicax, continuum, XXXVI. 9 (*Oros.* I. 7, 1 *peruicax* proelium...gesserunt).

pes, XXXI. 24, see *choros*.—**pes** uocatur quando una uice calcat passus idest fetim IIII cubitorum, XXXI. 25 (*De ponder.*?). For *fetim* Glogger suggests to read "*fet* (acc. plur. of fōt) IIII," and "IIII *cubitos*" for IIII cubitorum.

pessimos darent, circumdarent, IV. 41 (*Eccl. Ist.*); **pessum**, interitum, XXXV. 305 (*De Eus.*)=(*Ruf.* IV. 7 fol. 56a fidelium...si quos...deciperent, *pessundarent*).

pessul, leer, XLVII. 25 (*Alia*=?). Cf. *pessul*, haeca, Cp. P311; *p*-, haca, Ep. 20A9 and Ef.[1] 382, 20. *Leer* could hardly be a corruption of, or another word for, *haeca haca*, of Cp., Ep. & Ef.[1]. The *Glossae Nominum* (Goetz, II. 589, 23) have *pessulum*, *lesera*, clauus ligneus paruus. The original gloss may have been *pessulum* [pessu]le, sera &c.; or an O.H.G. *rigil*, or A.S. *reogol* may have become corrupted to *leer*. Cf. Körting, *Wörterb.* No. 7089. *leer* cannot correspond to O.D. *leer* (*leder*, *leeddre*, *laddere*, *ladere*), a *ladder*, and also *an instrument for torturing* (see Verdam, *ladere*), as Engl. does not drop *d* in this way. It is, perhaps, related to prov. E. *lār*, or *larra*, a bar (see Engl. Dial. Dict.), and may be a synon. of *haeca*, *haca* (D. *hek*), which seem to have meant *a hatch*, *grating*, *a gate* of lattice-work; *a hook*, *bolt* or *bar*. Cf. also the Gr. πάσσαλος, *a peg*, and *a gag*.—**pessuli**, quo cluditur cornu [an *oil-cruet*], III. 19 (*De S. Mart. Stor.*=*Sulp. Sev. Dial.* III. 3, 4 obdendi *pessuli*, quo claudi diligentius seruanda consuerunt, in uitro illo spatium non fuisse; cf. Id. *Epist.* I. 12 cum *pessulo*).

pessulo, see *pessul.*

pessum, interitum, XXXV. 305; see *pessimos darent.*

pessundarent, see *pessimos darent.*

petalum, in quo scriptum est nomen dei uel tetragrammaton, XXXV. 147 (*De Eus.*); **petulum**, lumina [for *lamina*] aurea, IV. 34 (*Eccl. Ist.*)=(*Ruf.* III. 31 fol. 49ᵇ pontificale πέταλον gestans; cf. id. V. 24 fol. 90ᵇ pontificale πέταλον gessit)=*petalum*, lamina aurea in fronte in qua scriptum nomen dei (domini, Ep.) tetragrammaton, Cp. P240; Ep. 18E9; Ef.[1] 379, 36.

petierit, II. 70, see *exigerit.*

petigo, tetrafa, XXXV. 74 (*Ruf.*?). According to the order in which this gloss appears in the Glossary, *petigo* might be looked for in Ch. IX., or in the first two Chapters of Rufinus' work. But it does not seem to occur there, nor *im-(in-)petigo*; and as it is written in the MS. with a small *p*, it is perhaps a further explanation of *ignis sacer* (*Ruf.* IX. 8 fol. 150ᵇ), or of *tentigo* or *prurigo* (*Ruf.* I. 8 fol. 12ᵇ). The Corp. Gl. (I 79) has *inpetigo*, teter; Ep. 11E25 *inpetigo*, tetr; Ef.[1] 365, 37 *inpegit*, teg. *Fa* of *tetrafa* is distinctly so in the MS., but the open *a* may be read as *ic*, therefore *fic*, which a St Gallen MS. (Steinm. II. 597, 17 petigo, tetrafic) has, while a Cod. Selest. has *fig* (*id.* II. 598, 36 petigo, tetrafig), which, like the Lat. *ficus*, means a disease of the skin, the piles. *Tetra* would be good Latin and make, with *petigo*, a suitable gloss to *tentigo*; but the various readings above, and petigo...idest *derda* in another MS. (Steinm. II. 607, 9), point to the A.S. tet(e)r, *tetter*, a cutaneous disease.

petra, XII. 12, see *calculus*; XIII. 40, see *perpendiculum*; XIV. 9, see *in unge*, 13, see *sinopide*; XXXIV. 15, see *scopulosus*; XXXV. 219, see *commenta.*

petrae, see *calculus*; *cementa.*

petre [-rae], XII. 15, see *cementa.*

petris, XXXVIII. 19, see *tholus.*

petulum, lumina [for *lam-*] aurea, IV. 34 (*Eccl. Ist.*), see *petalum.*

peusis, percunctatio ubi et interrogatio fit et responsio, XXVIII. 36 (*Cass. Psalm.* IV. 6 figura...*peusis*, Latine...percunctatio u. e. i. f. e. r.; again VIII. 6; cf. also XLVIII. 5).

ph for *f*: pro*ph*ana (pro*f*ana).—for *p*: e*ph*ichirema (e*p*ich-); e*ph*igrapha (e*p*igr-); *ph*itagoras (*P*yth-).

Phaethontis, see *foetontis.*

phaleras, see *falleras.*

Pharos, see *filii faros.*

pharum, see *fares.*

Phatures, see *in fatores.*

phialae, see *fiole.*

Phidiae, see *fidiae opera.*

philacteria, scriptura diuersa quę propter infirmos habentur uel carmina, I. 90 (*De Canon.*); **filacteria**, scriptura diuersa quę propert [for *propter*] infirmos habentur, XXXIX. 62 (*not* Greg. Dial., but)=(*Can. Conc. Laod.* CXXXIX facere *phylacteria*; qui *phylacteriis* vtuntur, *ibid. tit.*). Cf. *philactaria*, carmina uel x praecepta legis, Cp. P385; *philacteria*, carmina, Ep. 19C37 & Ef.[1] 381, 29 & Ef.[2] 321, 11.

philo, XXX. 17, see *ho platon.*

philocain, grece scopon, XLVII. 95 (*Alia*=?). Neither the lemma nor the gloss *scopon* are clear. The nearest approach to *philocain* is the Gr. φιλόκαινον, a love of novelty or innovation. Kluge (*A. S. Leseb.*) takes *scopon* as A.S. *sceop* (*scop*), a poet; see Bosw. T. (*scōp*).

philogenia, see *de philoxenia.*

philologos, see *philuluguis.*

philon, XXX. 17, see *ho platon.*

philona, philonem, XXX. 15, see *ho platon.*

philophie [for *philophiliae*?], IV. 44, see *amatorie.*

philophiliae (?), see *amatorie.*

philosophi, XVI. 27, see *malefici*; XLIV. 10, see *cardines.*

philosophiam, XVI. 26, see *magi.*

philosophos, see *philuluguis.*

philosten, see *pylominos.*

philoxenia, XXX. 28, see *de philoxenia.*

philuluguis, uerbi amatoris [-res], XXX. 24 (*Cat. Hier.* XX col. 639ᴬ apud *philologos*; B: apud *philosophos*; C: apud *philologos*). Cf. *filologos*, rationes uel uerbi amatores, Cp. F160; *filologoys*, rationis uel uerbi amatores, Ep. 9A6 & Ef.[1] 360, 1; *philologus*, rationis amatores, Cp. P381.

phitagoras, uoluptarius mentis, xxxviii. 10 (*Clem. Recognitt.* viii. 15 *Pythagoras*).

phlebotomum, see *fledomum*.

Phoebe, sol, xxvii. 23 (*Lib. Rot.* = *Isid. Lib. de rer. nat.* xxi. 2 Vnde Lucanus [*Phars.* i. 538]: Iam *Phoebe* totum fratri quum redderet orbem...) = *Phebe*, sol, Cp. P388.

phrasi, see *phraysi*.

phraysi, sensus, xxx. 30 (*Cat. Hier.* xxv col. 645A cum...elegantia et *phrasi* non...congruere; B: cum...elogantia et *phrasi* id est narratione non...cong.; C.: cum...elegancia *effrasi* non...cong.; Rich.: cum...el. et φράσει non...cong.) = *frasi*, sensu, Cp. F311; frassi, sensu, Ep. 9A5; Ef.[1] 359, 65.

phreneticum, see *freniticus*.

Phrygia, Phryx, see *genefrix*.

phylacteria, phylacteriis, see *philacteria*.

piaculum, pollutio, iv. 69 (*Ruf.* vii. 9 fol. 119ª per *piaculum*).

piasma [for *plasmate*], xxx. 27, see *de piasma*.

picem, xix. 44, see *tęde*.

pictarum [pyct-], xliii. 54, see *cestus*.

pictatiola, see *pitatiola*.

pictores, xiii. 53, see *circino*.

picus, see *marsopicus*.

picus, higrę, xlvii. 66 (*Alia* = ?) = *p*-, higre, fina, Cp. P424; *p*-, fina uel higrae, Ep. 20A15 and Ef.[1] 382, 25. In class. Dictt. *picus* is (1) *a woodpecker*; (2) *a griffin*; (3) *the hoopoe* (Goetz vii. 87 ἔποψ). For *higrę*, *higre*, *higrae* (a jay, jackdaw, magpie, or woodpecker), see Bosw. T. (*higera*, *higora*); Kluge, *Et. Wrtb.* (*Häher*); *higrae* also glosses *berna* (Cp. B77; Ef.[1] 348, 6), *cicuanus* (Cp. C438) and *traigis* (Cp. T315). For *fina*, a woodpecker, in Cp., Ep. and Ef. see Bosw. T. and above, *marsopicus*.

pidugio, xiii. 50, see *runtina*.

Pigmaei, see *Pigmei*.

Pigmei, homines cubitales idest unius cubiti, xv. 13 (*Ezech.* xxvii. 11 *Pigmaei*, qui erant in turribus).

pigmenta, xix. 46, see *cassia*.

pigmentis, xxii. 11, see *mundum m*-.

pigmento, xxxv. 306, see *fuco*.

pigmentum, xii. 19, see *calbanus*, 21, see *ungula*; xiii. 51, see *calamum*; xxxvi. 21, see *laser*.

pigrus, ii. 41, see *desidiosus*.

Pilae, see *Pile*.

pilam, xliv. 3, see *axis*.

pilas, xxxvi. 2, see *Armenias pilas*.

Pile, proprium nomen ciuitatis, xvii. 15 (*Sophon.* i. 11 habitatores *Pilae*).

pilo [for *pila*?], viii. 18, see *ptisanas*.

pilos, xiii. 56, see *uellentibus*.

pilosi, incubi monstri idest menae, xiii. 24 (*Isai.* xiii. 21 *pilosi* saltabunt ibi; Cambr. MS. *p.* i. *monstra*, but omits id. men.); *menae* for *merae* (= *mære*, mare, mere), a night-mare, a monster; see Bosw. T. (*mære*).

pina [for *fina*], see *marsopicus*.

pincerna, xxxix. 11, see *uini fusor*.

pingent [-gunt], xiv. 13, see *sinopide*.

pingit, pinguedo, see *pinsit*.

pinguiscebant, xix. 27, see *conpingebantur*.

pinguitudo, xix. 47, see *aruina*; see also *pinsit*.

pinguitur, vi. 27, see *panguitur*.

pingunt, see *sinopide*.

pini, xix. 44, see *tęde*.

pinsit, densitudo, xxxiv. 25 (*De Cass.* ?). There seems to be no trace of the lemma in Cassianus's works. If *densitudo* be right, it is, perhaps, formed like *pinguedo*, or *pinguitudo*, of which *pinsit* may be a corruption. Cf. *Cass. Inst.* ii. 13 *pinguedinem* (*pinguidinem*, *pinguitudinem*) cordis exhauriat; v. 34 pro *pinguedine* (*pinguidine*, *pinguitudine*) uel inmunditia sui cordis; xi. 14 tanta expleturum sanctitate ac rigore *depingit*; in note *depinguit*, *pingit*. Cf. *pinso*, tundo, Cp. P395; 19A27; *pinso*, tunso, Ef.[1] 380, 38.

piperatum, x. 25, see *uinum candidum*.

piramides [pyramides], see *piraondes*.

piraondes, domus in similitudinem ignis nam ignis pirus est, xliii. 46 (*De div. nominibus* = [?] Donati *Ars gramm.* ?). *Piraondes* evidently for piramides (pyramides).

pirgos, turris, xxxv. 248 (*Ruf.* ii. 10 fol. 23ª Cæsaream, quae prius Πύργος Στράτωνος vocabatur) = *pyrgras*, turris, Cp. P888; Ep. 19E10; Ef.[1] 381, 40.

pirus, xliii. 46, see *piraondes*.

pisas, xiii. 35, see *uiciam*.

pisces, xxxvi. 8, see *scabros*; xliii. 51, see *piscina*.

piscina, quę pisces non habet, xliii. 51 (*De div. nominibus* = Donati *Ars grammat.* p. 400, 2 *piscinam quae pisces non habet*). For *piscina* see also (xlvii. 11) *uiuarium*.

piscis, iii. 20, see *merocem*; xix. 8, see *murenula*; xliii. 15, see *panpo*; **piscis**, xlvii. 73, see *porco piscis*.

pisticum, adj., xxix. 35, see *pisticum*, sb.

pisticum, herba rubicunda uel nardum pisticum idest spicatum uel fidelis, xxix. 35; see *nardum*.

pistrinum, ubi panes coquuntur, xvi. 1 (*Dan.*, *Praef. Hieron.*, p. xvi[b], and *Migne* xxviii col. 1292[B] cum me in linguae hujus *pistrinum* reclusissem).

pitatiola, membranula, xxix. 30 (*Uerb. Interpr.* = *Hier. in Matth.* xxiii. 6 col. 168[c] *pictatiola* illa Decalogi, phylacteria vocabant).

pitoicis, dispensatio pauperum, xxxix. 58; see *ptochiis*, sub v. *ptocheus*.

pituita, see *sicunia*.

pix, xiv. 6, see *resina*.

placationem, xii. 7, see *placorem*.

placentas, dulces faciunt de simila et oleo uel adipe et melle, xiv. 5 (*Hier.* vii. 18 ut faciant *placentas* reginae; xliv. 19 fecimus ei *placentas*).

placita, xiv. 23, see *rata*.

placorem, placationem, xii. 7 (*Eccles.* iv. 13 qui vigilaverint ad illam, complectentur *placorem* eius; xxxix. 23 *placor*). —**placoris**, uoluntatis, vi. 22 (*Breu. exsol.*?).

plamatio [for *plasmatio*], xxix. 26, see *protoplastrum*.

plandus [for *blandus*?], ii. 23, see *adolatur*.

plane, sane, certe, ii. 132 (*Bened. reg.* 13, 20 [32] *plane* agenda matutina; 44, 12 ita *plane*; in note *sane*; [17, *plane* in note; in text *sane*]). For *plane* see also (i. 86) *prorsus*; (xvii. 9) *asolatis*.

plasma, forma, xxxv. 269 (*Ruf.* vi. 33 fol. 115[a] uelut nouum *plasma*; i. 11 fol. 13[b] confecta *plasmate*).—**de piasma**, fractura [factura?] uel ars, xxx. 27 (*Cat. Hier.* xxiv col. 643 *de plasmate* librum; texts B and C idem).

plasmate, see *de piasma* sub v. *plasma*.

plasmatio, see *protoplastrum*.

plasmatione, xxxv. 164, see *de figmento*.

plastes, figulus, xiii. 49 (*Isai.* xli. 25 *plastes* conculcans humum; xlv. 11, 18 *plastes*; xliv. 9 *plastae* idoli...nihil sunt).

platanus, arbor est boni odoris, xii. 17 (*Eccles.* xxiv. 19).

platessa, platisa, see *platissu*.

platissu, folc, xlvii. 9 (*Alia* = ?) = *platisa*, flooc, Cp. P464 and Ep. 20A8; *platissa*, floc, Ef.[1] 382, 19. Lewis & Sh. *platessa*, a plaice. For *folc* (for *flōc*) see Bosw. T. (*flōc*, a sole, kind of flat fish); Oxf. D. (*fluke*, sb.[1]); Kluge, *Dict.* (*Flach*).

plato, **platon**, xxx. 14; **platona**, xxx. 16; platonem, xxx. 16; see *ho platon*.—**Platonis ideas**, idest species, xlii. 25 (*Ex div. libris* = *Vita S. Eugen.* 3, Migne lxxiii col. 607[c] *Platonis ideas*) = *Platonis ideas*, species, Cp. P466; *Platonis ideas*, idest species, Ep. 20A20; Ef.[1] 382, 30.

plaustrum, in similitudinem arce rotas habens intus et ipse dentes habent quasi rostra dicitur in quibus frangent spicas, xiii. 47 (*Isai.* xli. 15 *plaustrum* triturans) = Pl. in similitudine arcae r.h.i. et ipsae [*idest* rotae] d.h. qui rostra dicuntur in q. frangent [for frangunt] s., Cp. P481. The Cambr. MS. agrees with Cp. but omits all after habent. See further Isai. v. 18 (plaustri); xxv. 10 (plaustro); xxviii. 27, 28 (plaustri).

plausum, xv. 8, see *conplosi*.

plausus, i. 55, see *fauor*.

Pleiades, see *pliadę*.

plenum, xxix. 59.

plestia, abundantia uel indegeries [indig-], xii. 39 (*Eccles.* xxxvii. 33 *aviditas* appropinquabit usque ad choleram). Sab. and Heyse record, in notes, the reading *aplestia* [= ἀπληστία] for *aviditas*. Cambr. MS.: *Plestia*, habundantia siue *indigeries*.

plexi, see *plexus*.

plexus, truncatus, iv. 15 (*Ruf.* ii. 9 fol. 22[b] capite *plexi* sunt; cf. *ib.* vi. 2 fol. 94[b] capite *plexus*).

pliadę, uii sunt stelle [-llae] in cauda tauri, xliv. 22 (*Alia*; *de cælo* = *Isid. de nat. rerum* xxvi. 1 col. 998[A] [quoting from Job xxxviii. 31] *Pleiades*; ibid. 6 col. 998[c] *Pleiades*; ibid. xxxvi. 2 col. 1006[c] *Pleiades*).

plumacios, see *puluillos*.

plumatios [for *plumacios*], xv. 43, see *puluillos*.

plumbeos, xxii. 12, see *urna*.

plumbo, xiii. 40, see *perpendiculum*.

plumescit, mutat, xix. 57 (*Job* xxxix. 26 *plumescit* accipiter). For *mutare*, to moult, see Körting, *Wrtb.* No. 6422.

plurale, xliii. 16, see *micene*.

plures, xxiii. 1, see *exedra*.

plurimorum, ii. 188, see *coenobium*.

pluto, xxxviii. 39, see *Aides*.

pluuia, xi. 11, see *in aqua...*; xv. 7, see *non conpluta*.

pluuie, xix. 53, see *gurgitum*.

podagra, tumor pedum, v. 16 (*Ruf.* i. 15 fol. 17[a] illum...*podagra* laborantem).

poderis, uestis est sacerdotum a pedibus usque ad umbilicum pertingens et ibi stringebatur cingulo in cuius subteriore parte habebantur tintinnabula et mala punica, xi. 14 (*Sap.* xviii. 24 in veste *poderis*).

poetarum, xix. 51, see *fabula*; xliii. 23, see iiii.

polarchia, xxx. 6, see *monarchia*.

polenta, farina subtilissima, xxi. 15 (*Judith* x. 5 imposuit...abrae suae... *polentam*).

polentam, see *polenta*.

poli, xliv. 1, see *partes*, 26, see *a tergo*. —**poli**, ex celestibus [coel-] ciclis cacumina quo maxime spera nititur alter ad aquilonem expectans boreus alter terrę obpositus austronothus dictus est, XLIV. 7 (*Alia*; *de cælo=Isid. de nat. rerum*, XII. 3 col. 983 *Poli*, e. coelestibus *circulis* c. *quibus* m. *sphaera* n. *quorum* alter a. A. *spectans* B. a. *terrae oppositus Austronotus* d. e.). See above *partes*. — **poli summa**, cęlorum [caelorum] cacumina, XLIV. 18 (*Alia*; *de cælo?*) is, perhaps, a further explanation of XLIV. 7. Or the reference may be to *poli* Isid. *de nat. rer.* XII. 6 col. 985; *polis* ib. XXV. 2 col. 997.

Polideuces pollux, **ulixes**, homines fortissimi, XLIII. 5 (*De div. nominibus*=Donati *Ars gramm.* p. 373, 18, 19 sunt [nomina] tota conversa in Latinam regulam, ut *Polydeuces* [pollideuces, in note] *Pollux*, Odysseus *Vlixes*).

polinctores, see *pollinctores*.

polionima [polyonoma], multiuoca, XLIII. 11; see *omonima*.

polita, see *expolita*.

polite, mundate, XIV. 25 (*Hier.* XLVI. 4 *polite* lanceas).

pollinctores, qui sepeliunt homines pro pecunia, XV. 24 (*Ezech.* XXXIX. 15 os... sepeliant...*polinctores*; Heyse *poll-*).

pollis, grot, XLVI. 21 (*Alia*=*Ars Phocae*, p. 418, 10 hic *pollis*, pollinis) =*pollis*, grytt, Cp. P541. For *grot* (E. *groats*; O. H. G. *gruzzi*; Germ. *Grütze*; O. & Mid. D. *gort*, *gorte*; D. *gort*) cf. Bosw. T. *grot*, a particle, an atom; *grytta*, grits, groats, coarse meal; Verdam, *Middeln. Woord.*

pollutio, IV. 69, see *piaculum*.

Pollux, XLIII. 5, see *Polideuces*.

polo, XLIV. 16, see *antarticus*, 27, see *dextera*.

polum, XLIV. 10, see *cardines*, 16, see *antarticus*.

polus, XXXV. 274, see *axe*.

polydeuces, see *polideuces*.

polyonoma, see *polionima*.

poma, VIII. 16, see *mala aurea*.

pomorum, I. 111, see *sicera*.

pompa, fallatia [-cia], IV. 63 (*Eccl. Ist.*); **pompam**, risionem, XXXV. 249 (*De Eus.*)=(*Ruf.* V. 3 fol. 77[b] ad suppliciorum *pompam*).

pondera, XXXII. 10 and XXXIII. 1, see *talentum*; **pondera**, XXXI. 27, see *libra et p-*.

PONDERIBUS, XXXI *tit.*; XXXII *tit.*; XXXIII *tit.*

ponderis, XXXIII. 7, see *sicel*.

pondo, see *talentum*.

pondus, XXXII. 1, see *dragma*; XXXIII. 7, see *sicel*; **pondus**, XXXIII. 23, see *libra*.

pone, post, XLII. 11 (*Ex div. libris?*)= *pone*, post, Cp. P557.

poni sub [for *subponi?*], XXXV. 192, see *basis*.

ponitur, XLVI. 14, see *suber*.

ponte moluio, propter [for proprium?; nomen omitted] pontis iuxta roma, XXXV. 242 (*Ruf.* IX. 9 fol. 152[b] a *ponte Muluio*; *al.* a *ponte Moluio*; Cacciari, p. 525 à *ponte Milvio*).

pontico, XXXV. 82, see *sub axe p-*.

pontis, XXXV. 242, see *ponte moluio*.

pontus, XXXV. 82, see *sub axe pontico*.

ponuntur, I. 49, see *epistilia*; VII. 1, see *in nablis*; XXX. 7, see *bibliotheca*.

popa, tabernarii qui in domo tabernarii sunt, XLV. 31 (*Uerba de multis*=*Ars Phocae*, p. 412, 20 hic *popa*). Cf. *popa*, tabernarius, Cp. P508; Ep. 19C8; Ef.[1] 381, 1. For popa, in Class. Lat., see Lewis and Sh. Cf. Lat. *popina*, a cookshop.

poplite, see *publite*; *puplites*.

poposcerit, II. 70, see *exigerit*.

poptochi, see *peri pthocheas*.

populorum, XXX. 85, see *cinticta*.

porcaster, see *porcastrum*.

porcastrum, foor, XLVII. 92 (*Alia*=?)= *porcaster*, foor, Cp. P520; Ep. 20A17; *porcaster*, for, Ef.[1] 382, 27. *Porcastrum* for *porcaster* (see Du C., porcus junior; from *porcus*, and the termin. *-aster*, like, or no longer, a pig; cf. pueraster, ἀντίπαις, Gloss. Gr. Lat. ap. Lewis & Sh.). The A.S. *foor*, *fōr* (prob. for **fōrh*) may be allied to A.S. *fearh* (which is cognate with the Lat. *porcus*), a little pig (Bosw. T.; cf. *fear-as* for *fearhas*, Wright W. 119, 27), as *a* (or *ea*) and *ō* interchange in gradation (cf. *fōr*, pt. t. of A.S. *faran*, to travel). Cf. *fōr*, porcaster (Napier, *O.E.G.* 20, 4; 21, 3; 22, 3).

porcis, XXV. 6, see *de siliquis*.

porco piscis, styra, XLVII. 73 (*Alia*=?) =*porcopiscis*, styrga, Cp. P519; *p-*, styria, Ep. 20A16; *porco piscis*, styria, Ef.[1] 382, 26. The lemma, which the Cp. and Ep. Glossaries write as one word, means literally a swine- or hog-fish, still known by the same word in the form *porpoise*, for which see the various Eng. Dictt. The fish is closely allied to the dolphin, but it would seem that the *sturgeon* was also called by this name, as in the Glossaries the *porcopiscis* is always glossed by *styria* or *styrga*; see (besides the Cp., Ep. and Ef.[1]) Wright W. 261, 31; 293, 16; 469, 23. On the other hand *styria* is also applied to other fishes: *cragacus* (Cp. C921; Wright W. 366, 20), *rombus* (Wright W. 180, 25). See further Bosw. T. (*styria*).

porcos, XXXV. 72, see *lanionibus*.

porcus, see *porcastrum*.

poreo [boreo], XLIV. 16, see *antarticus*.

porochia, see *parrochia*.
porrectione, xl. 19, see *conpage*.
porrexit, x. 1, see *osculetur me*.
porro, i. 85, see *proscribantur*.
porrus, xli. 16, see *cypressus*.
πorsutas, motatores, iv. 101 (*Ruf*. vii. 28 fol. 131[b]? Haec autem particula, prima ex duodecim, vernale est æquinoctium, et ipsa est initium mensium et caput circuli et absolutio cursus stellarum πλάναι [stellarum, quae πλάναι planetæ, Cacciari, p. 452], id est vagae dicuntur, ac finis duodecimæ particulæ et totius circuli terminus). The gloss *motatores* seems to refer to these stars, and it is possible that some MSS. had πλανας πλανητας.
porta, xxxvi. 1, see *Iani*. — **porta laurenti**, quia per ipsam corpus eius portatum est, xxxix. 33 (*Greg. Dial*. iv. 54 col. 416[B] juxta *portam* sancti *Laurentii*). —**porta stercoris**, ubi stercora pro [for proiciuntur ?], xxiii. 9 (2 *Esdr*. ii. 13 ad *portam stercoris*).—**portarum indumenta**, idest coria quibus portę indute [-tae] sunt, xxxv. 140 (*Ruf*. iii. 6 fol. 37[b] *scutorum* indumenta, in edit. 1548; *Portarum* indumenta, in edit. 1535 and ap. Cacciari, p. 123, who points out that one Vatic. MS. has *scutorum*) =*portarum indumenta*, corie quibus portae sunt indutae, Cp. P495; Ep. 18E8; *portatorum in-*, coria q.p.s.i., Ef.[1] 379, 35. The different readings (*scutorum*; *portarum*) are apparently due to a confusion between the Gr. θυρων and θυρεων.
portam, xxiii. 10, see *ualuas*.
portant, xiv. 36, see *urceos*; xxix. 15, see *batroperite*.
portantem, xvi. 6, see *discoforum*.
portantes, ii. 82, see *gestantes*.
portantur, xiii. 59, see *feretri*.
portari, x. 13, see *ferculum*.
portarum indumenta, idest coria &c., xxxv. 140; see above *porta*.
portati, ii. 17, see *angariati*.
portatorium, xxv. 4, see *loculum*.
portatum, xxxix. 33, see *porta laurenti*.
portatur, xlii. 21, see *basterna*.
porte [-tae], xxxvi. 1 (bis), see *Iani porte*.
portę, xxxv. 140, see *portarum indumenta*, sub v. *porta*; xlviii. 37, see *postere*.
portentosa, portentuosa, see *portentuose*.
portentuose, monstruose exempli causa cum sex digitis nati, i. 95 (*De Canon.*; *Defin. fid. Calch.*, ap. Man. vii. 751[a] confusione *portentuosa*, 752[a] *portentosa*). Cf. Isid. *Etym*. xi. 3, 6 & 7; Id. *Diff*. 457–459; Helmreich, in *Archiv f. L. L.* xii. 311.
porti, iv. 93, see *angiportos*.
porticibus, xiv. 12, see *domatibus*.
porticos, iii. 40, see *conclauia*.
posite, iv. 98, see *comellas*.
positio, xlvi. 24, see *situs*.
posito, xxxv. 41, see *in aculeis*.
posse, xxviii. 47, see *parenthesin*.
possent, xii. 42, see *uasa*.
possessio, xli. 19, see *pagus*.
possessiones, i. 98, see *predia*.
possessiua, xliii. 12, see *cethetica*.
possumus, xxviii. 57, see *figura*.
possunt, xli. 1, see *presbiteri*, 2, see *chorepiscopi*.
post, i. 39; ii. 183; xxviii. 65; xlii. 11; xliii. 42.
postea, ii. 54, see *demum*.
posterae, see *postere*.
postere, portę, xlviii. 37 (*De Cass*., *Inst*. v. 11, 2 urbs...*posterae* unius...proditione uastabitur).
postorum, see *magalia*.
posttridie, post iii dies, xliii. 42 (*De div. nominibus*=not [?] Donati *Ars grammat.*?).
postulatio, ii. 99, see *laetania*.
posuit, xxiii. 12, see *memores salis*.
potentia, xxx. 20, see *pantocranto*.
potest, i. 111; x. 13; xix. 28; xxxv. 192; xxxix. 48.
potestas, xxx. 4, see *anarchius*.
potestate, xvi. 16, see *ditione*.
potestates, ii. 178, see *tirannides*.
potio, i. 111, see *sicera*.
potiones, ii. 15, see *biberes*.
practicen, xxix. 64, see *theoritisen*.
praebetur, see *spectacula*.
praecedentia, see *prolezomena*.
praecipitans, see *leua*.
praecipua, praecipue, praecipuis, see *precipuis*.
praecipuum, see *epyuision*.
praecone, see *curione*.
praeconio, see *metaforan*.
praedator, see *tyrsamus*.
praedia, see *predia*.
praedicant, see *aruspices*.
praedicationis, see *eyaggences*.
praedicentia, see *prolezomena*.
praeditis, see *preditis*.
praefatio, see *proemium*.
praefatione, see *prosa*.
praefationibus, see *proemiis*.
praefecto, see *balneum Ciceronis*.
praeficit, see *afficit*.
praefocatus, see *prefocatus*.
praelatus, see *prelatus*.
praemissae, see *aetilogia*.
praeoccupatio, see *prolemsis*.
praeparatione, see *in expeditione*.
praeparationis, see *eyaggences apod-*.
praepes, see *prepes*.

praepeti, see *perpeti*.

praepositurae, see *editionis* [but here wrongly suggested for *propositure*, which latter is apparently correct; cf. *propositio*, a setting forth for public view, *exhibition*: panes *propositionis* (shewbread), Exod. xxv. 30; Marc. ii. 26]; *uilicationis*.

praeposituram, see *propositus*.

praepositus, see *prelatus*; *qui in numero....*

praerogatiua, see *prerogatiua*.

praesidem, see *ducennarium*.

praesidens, see *presidens*.

praestanda, see *adhibenda*.

praestantur, see *accommodentur*.

praestigiis, praestigium, see *paredum*.

praestita, see *exhibita*.

praesto esse, see *exhibere*.

praestrigiis, see *prestr-*.

praesul, see *presul*.

praesumere, i. 84, see *peruadere*.

praesumpte, see *temere*.

praesumptuose [or *praesumpte*?], ii. 172, see *temere*.

praesunt, see *hierufontis*.

praeterita, see *dissimulat*.

praeteritis, see *prolemsis*.

praetore, praetorio, see *ex pretore*.

praetoriola, see *preteriola*.

praetorium, see *pretorium*.

praeuidere, see *uasa castrorum*.

praeusti, for *pusti* (q.v.).

pragmatiam for *pragmaticam*, xxxix. 63; see *per pragmaticam formam*, sub v. *pragmatica*.

pragmatica forma, principalia imperia [suppl. *uel negotia*, from i. 91; see *ptochiis*], i. 92 (*De Canon.*); **per pragmati[c]am formam**, per principalia imperia uel negotia, xxxix. 63 (*not in* Greg. Dial., but) = *Can. Conc. Calch.* xii p. 135 *per pragmaticam formam* in duo unam prouinciam diuiserunt. — **pragmaticam**, negotialis, xxix. 45 (*Uerb. Interpr.* = *Hier. in Matth.*?). For *pragmaticam*, see also *pragmatica*; cf. *pragmatica*, principalis, Cp. P655; Ep. 18C37; Ef.[1] 379, 25; *pragmatica*, negotiatio, Cp. P658; Ep. 18E2; Ef.[1] 379, 29.

pragmaticam, negotialis, xxix. 45; see *pragmatica*.

prapatheian, xxix. 50, see *prathus*.

prasinum, xli. 10, see *smaragdus*.

pratearum [for *pratorum*?], x. 10, see *cyprus*.

prathus et prapatheian, passio et probatio, xxix. 50 (*Uerb. Interpr.* = *Hier. in Matth.* v. 28 Inter πάθος et προπάθειαν, idest inter *passionem* et *propassionem*, hoc interest...).

pratorum, see *cyprus*.

prauitas, xxix. 43, see *perpera*.

praxeon, actionum, xxx. 8 (*Cat. Hier.* vii col. 619B volumen ... quod titulo Apostolicarum [al. *Apostolicorum*] πράξεων praenotatur; B: vol. quod tit. apostolorum *praxeon* idest actuum praenotatur; C: vol. quod tit. apostolicorum actuum prenotatur; E: πρατνων idest actuum) = *praxeon*, actionum, Cp. P682; Ep. 19C33; Ef.[1] 381, 26.

pre- for *per*; see *prestatio* for *per stationes*.

prebetur [praeb-], i. 126, see *spectacula*.

preces dictare [sine interpret.], i. 97 (*De Canon.*; *Decret. Innoc.* xxv *preces dictantibus*; ibid. tit. *preces dictant*).

precipitans [praec-], xliv. 27, see *leua*.

precipuis [praec-], maximis, ii. 193 (*Bened. reg.*? cf. 3, 2 [1] quotiens aliqua *praecipua* agenda sunt; adv. 33, 3 [1]; 64, 39 [72] *praecipue*).

precipuum [praec-], xxix. 51, see *epyuision*.

prȩcis [precis], xlv. 8, see *prȩx*.

precium [-tium], xxxvii. 9, see *tabulas legat*.

precium [pretium], xlviii. 58, see *opere precium*.

preconio [praec-], xxviii. 55, see *metaforan*.

predator [praed-], xxxiv. 37, see *tyrsamus*.

predia, possessiones, i. 98 (*De Canon.*; *Can. Conc. Calch.* iii *tit. prædia* aliena conducere; *Can. Conc. Sard.* xv idonea *prædia* habere; *Can. Conc. Carth.* xxxii *prædia* comparant, and xxxiii p. 148a vendere *prædia*). Cf. fundus, *possessiones*, *praedia*, Cp. F411.

predicaciones [praedicationis], xxx. 75, see *eyaggences apod*.

predicant [praed-], xvi. 30, see *aruspices*.

predicentia, xxviii. 21, see *prolezomena*.

preditis, ornatis, xxxv. 89 (*Ruf.* i. 1 fol. 2b pietate *praeditis* viris).

prefacionȩ [praefacione], xix. 14, see *prosa*.

prefacionibus, xxxiv. 11, see *proemiis*.

prefatio [praef-], xxix. 6, see *proemium*.

prefecto [praef-], xxxix. 4, see *balneum ciceronis*.

prefocatus, strangulatus, xxxv. 239 (*Ruf.* ix. 8 fol. 151a si quis...constrictus et *præfocatus*).

prelatus, prepositus, ii. 139 (*Bened. reg.* 65, 31 [60] praepositus...quantum *praelatus* est ceteris).

premuntur, xv. 33, see *uinacia*; xviii. 3, see *uinatia*.

prȩoccupatio [praeoc-], xxviii. 75, see *prolemsis*.

preparatione XXI. 1, see *in expeditione*; XXX. 63, see *parascheue*.

preparationis, -onum [praep-], XXX. 76, see *eyaggences apod-*.

prepes, auis, XLVI. 19 (*Alia = Ars Phocae*, p. 417, 23 hic et haec *praepes*).

preposi̇ture [praeposi̇turae], II. 168, see *uilicationis*.

prepositus [praep-], II. 139, see *prelatus*; XXXIX. 28, see *qui in numero...*

prerogatiua, priuilegium, XXXIV. 40; **prerogatiua**, excellentia, XLVIII. 19 (*De Cass., Inst.* VIII. 1, 2 natalium *praerogatiua*; XII. 4, 1 uirtutem, tantae potentiae *praerogatiua* decoratam).

presagio, XLI. 21, see *obfirmantes*.

presbiter [sine interpret.], II. 130 (*Bened. reg.* 62, 2 [1] *presbyterum* ordinare; 63, 12 [20] *presbyteros* iudicauerunt).—**presbiteri** qui sunt in agris epistolas dare non possunt Ad solos tantum uicinos episcopos litteras distinabunt, XLI. 1; **Chorepiscopi** qui sunt inreprehensibiles dare possunt pacificas idest generales epistulas, XLI. 2 (*De nom. diuersis = Can. Conc. Antioch.* XXCVI p. 126ᵃ *Presbyteri*, qui s. i. a. canonicas epistolas d. n. p. a. s. t. u. e. literas destinabunt. *Chorepiscopi* autem q. s. i. d. p. p. i. g. epistolas).—**presbitera**, uxor presbiteri [-byteri] quam habuit ante ordinationem, XXXIX. 22 (*Greg. Dial.* IV. 11 col. 336ᶜ *presbyteram* suam ut sororem diligens).—**presbiteras**, uxores presbiterorum [presbyt-] quas antea (*sic*; *suppl.* habuerunt), I. 104 (*De Canon.*; *Can. Conc. Laod.* CXIV *tit.* Non congruere *presbyteras*...ordinari).

presbitera, uxor presbiteri &c., XXXIX. 22; **presbiteras**, uxores presbiterorum, &c., I. 104; see *presbiter*.

presbiteri [-byteri], XXXIX. 22, see *presbiter*.

presbiterorum [presbyt-], I. 104, see *presbiteras* in v. *presbiter*.

presbyteram, presbyteras, presbyteri, presbyterorum, see *presbiter*.

presbyteros, presbyterum, see *presbiter*.

presidem [praes-], XXXV. 282, see *ducennarium*.

presidens [praes-], I. 87, see *presul*.

presides [praes-], I. 40, see *defensores*.

prestanda [praest-], II. 19, see *adhibenda*.

prestantur [praest-], II. 22, see *accommodentur*.

prestatio, custodia, IV. 31 (*Ruf.* III. 6 fol. 36ᵇ *per stationes* hostium).

prestigium [praest-], V. 17, see *paredum*.

prestita, II. 56, see *exhibita*.

presto [praesto] esse, I. 52, see *exhibere*.

prestrigiis [praestrigiis ?], V. 18, see *parchredis*.

presul, iudex uel presidens [praesidens] uel defensor, I. 87 (*De Canon.*; *Dionys. Praef.*, p. 101 sancti *praesules*...muniantur; *Can. Conc. Ancyr.* XXXVII vim *praesulibus*...inferre).

prȩsunt [praes-], XXXVIII. 42, see *hierufontis*.

preteriola, domuncula micina in naue unius cubiti in quibus abscondunt cibos suos [refers, perhaps, to *remigantes* of XV. 9], XV. 11 (*Ezech.* XXVII. 6 fecerunt... *praetoriola*). For *micina* the Cambr. MS. has *uicina*; but in XV. 43 occurs *micinos*; *micinus* probably = micidus, meaning *small*. Cf. Du C. *micina*, uno vase de nave, Glossar. Lat. Ital. MS.; *praetoriola*, domuncula in naue, Cp. P665; *praetoriala*, d. i. n., Ep. 19A11; *praetoriocla*, d. i. n., Ef.[1] 380, 22.

preterita [praet-], I. 44, see *dissimulat*; II. 49, see *dissimulat*.

preteritis [praet-], XXVIII. 72, see *anaphora*.

pretium, see *tabulas legat*.

pretore, pretorio [praet-], XXXV. 223, see *ex pretore*.

pretorium, domus iudicaturia, XXIV. 18 (*Math.* XXVII. 27 milites...suscipientes Jesum in *prætorium*; Wordsw. & White, in note, in *praetorio* & *pret.*) = *praetorium*, domus iudicaria, Cp. P622. See Goetz, VI. 126 (*praetorium*).

preuiarium [for breu-], XXX. 73, see *epimehne*.

preuidere [praeu-], XII. 42, see *uasa*.

preusti [= praeusti], for *pusti* (q. v.).

prȩx, unde prȩcis, XLV. 8 (*Uerba de multis = Ars Phocae*, p. 412, 3 feminini generis ops *prex* pars...).

prima, XXIX. 26, see *protoplastrum*.

primaeuo, see *a primeuo flore*.

primatem dioceseos [sine interpret.], I. 93 (*De Canon.*; *Can. Conc. Calch.* IX petat *Primatem diœceseos*; XVII apud *Primatem diœceseos*).

primeuo [primaeuo], XXXIX. 1, see *a primeuo flore*.

primicerius, see *primicirius*.

primicirius [sine interpret.], I. 103 (*De Canon.*; *Append. Conc. Calch.* ap. Mans. VII col. 747ᶜ *primicerius*). Cf. Isid. *Epp.* I. 13.

primitias, XXI. 18, see *sancta domini*.

primo, XXII. 12, see *urna*; XXXIX. 1, see *a primeuo flore*.

primus, XXII. 13, see *nisan*; XLIV. 16, see *antarticus*.

princeps, IV. 27, see *ariopagitis*; XVI. 8, see *satrapa*; XXV. 9, see *decurio*; XXIX. 65, see *cuimarsus*; XXXV. 7, see *toparcha*.

principalia, I. 92, see *pragmatica*; XXXIX. 63, see *per pragmaticam formam.*
principatum, XXX. 38, see *archutomam.*
principia, XXVIII. 72, see *anaphora.*
prineose, prino, prinu, prise, XXX. 95; see *ypo* (sub) *tyos* (hoc) &c.
priuatis, alienatis seperatis [separatis], II. 136 (*Bened. reg.* 13, 1, 3 [*tit.* & 1] *priuatis diebus*).
priuato, II. 81, see *gradu.*
priuigna, nift, XLII. 7 (*Ex div. libris*?); =*priuigna*, nift, Cp. P604; *priuigna*, filia sororis, idest nift, Ep. 18A6; Ef.[1] 378, 13; *priuigna*, a step-daughter; *nift*, likewise step-d., but also a niece, granddaughter; see Bosw. T. *nift.*
priuilegium, XXXIV. 40, see *prerogatiua.*
pro, I. 88, 111, 115; III. 21; VIII. 8, 16, 17; XIII. 9; XIV. 3, 34; XV. 24; XVI. 12, 27; XXIII. 12; XXVIII. 18, 72; XXIX. 67 (bis); XXXIII. 6; XXXV. 14, 179, 210; XXXVIII. 44; XLII. 20; XLIV. 11 (ter).
pro, III. 14 (see note † on p. 7).
probamento, II. 72, see *experimento.*
probatio [for *propassio*], XXIX. 50, see *prathus.*
probationes, XXVIII. 79, see *epexergasia.*
probra, obprobria, XXXV. 125 (*Ruf.* II. 24 fol. 33ª Longum est...*probra* eius...describere).
procacia, adrogantia, IV. 46 (*Ruf.* IV. 15 fol. 61ᵇ *procacia*...et temeritate).
procacitas, I. 61 and II. 96, see *inprobitas.*
procaciter, superbe, II. 133 (*Bened. reg.* 3, 9 [12] *procaciter* defendere).
procax, II. 89, see *inprobus.*
procella, XXXVIII. 41, see *totegis.*
proceres, see *processores.*
proceritas, celsitudo, XXXV. 142 (*Ruf.* III. 7 fol. 39ª *proceritas* corporis).
processores, excelsi, XXXV. 92 (*Ruf.* I. 1 fol. 3ª *proceres* magnificantur); cf. *proceres*, geroefan (reeves), Cp. P827.
procomian, XXX. 54, see *et procomian.*
proconsolaris, in uice consulis quia suffecti erunt [erant] consulibus, I. 100 (*De Canon.*; *Can. Conc. Carth.*, praef. p. 142ª prouinciae *Proconsularis*; *ibid.* XXXIII Episcopi *proconsulares*).
proconsulares, proconsularis, see *proconsolaris.*
procul, I. 86, see *prorsus.*
procuratores, quod uice curatoris fungantur, I. 101 (*De Canon.*; *Can. Conc. Carth.* XVI ut episcopi...non sint...*procuratores*).
prodesse, II. 67, see *expedire.*
prodest, II. 59, see *expedit.*
prodicus, dissipator substantię, II. 137 (*Bened. reg.* 31, 17 [34] neque *prodigus* sit)=*prodigus*, dissipator substantiae, Cp. P747.—**non prodicus**, non superfluus, II. 121 (*Bened. reg.* 31, 4 [6] Cellerarius... *non prodigus*).
prodiderit, manifestauerit, II. 191 (*Bened. reg.* 46, 8 [10] *prodiderit* delictum suum).
prodigus, see *prodicus.*
prodis [for *profundis*?], XIV. 14, see *calati.*
proemiis, prefacionibus [praefation-], XXXIV. 11 (*De Cass.*, *Inst.* X. 7, 3 tantis proferre *prooemiis* differebat; in note: *proemiis*, *praemiis*, *proemisis*).
proemio [for *prooemio*], XIX. 14, see *prosa.*
proemium, prefatio [praef-], XXIX. 6 (*Uerb. Interpr.* =*Hier. in Matth.*, *Prol.* col. 18ᴮ ut ipse in *procemio* confitetur; ibid. col. 19ᴬ in illud *procemium*)=*prohemium*, praefatio, Cp. P625 & 745.
profana, see *prophana.*
profano, I. 113, see *sacrilego.*
proficiens, V. 23, see *suppeditans.*
profundis, see *calati.*
profundum, XXXV. 226, see *in chaos*; XXXIX. 20, see *in mare adriatico.*
profusius, habundantius, XXXV. 108 (*Ruf.* II. 3 fol. 20ª *profusius* effunderetur diuina dignatio).
progenies, XXXV. 98, see *prosapia.*
prohibere, XLVIII. 18, see *inhibere.*
proiectus, XVII. 7, see *Niniue.*
pro[iciuntur], XXIII. 9, see *porta stercoris.*
prolegomena, see *prolezomena.*
prolemsis, pręoccupatio crebra sermonis quę multa colligit unius uerbi iteratione decursa, XXVIII. 75 (*Cass. Psalm.* XXVII. 8 *prolepsis*, Latine *praeoccupatio*, quando res secuturae pro praeteritis ponuntur). The above "crebra sermonis...decursa" is wrongly added in the MS. to this lemma; it belongs to XXVIII. 73 (*epimone*, q. v.), whereas "quando—ponuntur" (wrongly *secuntur*) is in the MS. wrongly under *anaphora* (XXVIII. 72).
prolezomena, idest predicentia [prae-], XXVIII. 21 (*Cass. Psalm.* Praef. XVII col. 24ᴮ *prolegomena, idest præcedentia*).
prolixior, see *lacernam.*
prolixor [-xior], III. 8, see *lacernam.*
PROLOGO, XXX *tit.*; see *De Catalogo.*
promaean, see *et procomian.*
promimus, XXVIII. 67, see *anastrophe.*
promiscue, I. 94, see *passim.*
promisse [for *praemissae*], XXVIII. 46, see *aetilogia.*
promissionis, XIV. 24, see *stipulationis.*
promontorium, hog, III. 35 (*S. Mart. Storia*=*Sulp. Sev. Dial.* I. 3, 5 *promuntoria*, and in note *promunctoria*, *promuntaria*, *promontoria*). For *hog*, a heel,

hough; promontory, see Bosw. T. (*hōh*); E. *hoe* (Oxf. D. sb.[1]).—**promontorium**, ubi terra intrat in mare, XXXVI. 3 (*Oros.* I. 2, 13, 14 *promunturium*; in note *promuntorium*; *promontorium*; see ibid. I. 2, 46, 47, 81, 94, 99, 103 &c.).

promulgantes, proponentes, I. 96 (*De Canon.*; *Defin. fid. Calch.*, ap. Mans. VII col. 754ª sententiam *promulgantes*; cf. *Can. Conc. Carth.*, praef. p. 144ª quae... *promulgata* sunt).

promulgata, see *promulgantes*.

promunctoria, promuntaria, promuntoria, promunturium, see *promontorium*.

pronuba, herdusuepe, XXVI. 6 (*Isid. Offic.* II. 20, 5 eisdem virginibus legitime nubentibus vniuirae *pronubae* adhibentur) =*pronuba*, heorðsuaepe, Cp. P701. *Pronuba*, a bride-woman; *herdu*=A. S. *heorð* (Bosw. T. hearth, fire-place; house; O. & Mod. H. G. *herd*, cf. Kluge; D. *haard*); *suepe*=A. S. *swǣpe*, a sweep (A. S. *swāpan*, Bosw. T.). See also Bosw. T. hād-swǣpa (-swāpe), pronuba, bridesmaid.

pro octaua, in nouissimo die azimorum [azym-], VII. 2 (1 *Paral.* XV. 21 in citharis *pro octava* canebant epinicion); the 8th day after Easter; cf. Exod. XII. 18; on other interpretations of the expression "pro octava," see Thalhofer, *Erklär. der Psalmen*, 7th ed. p. 71.

prooemiis, see *proemiis*.

prooemio, see *proemium* sub v. *proemiis*; *prosa*.

prooemium, see *proemium*.

proparaskenes, see *eyaggences apod-*.

propassionem, see *prathus*.

prope, I. 117, see *secus*; XXXIV. 34, see *comminus*.

propert [for *proprium*?], XXXIX. 34, see *angulinis*; [for *propter*?], XXXIX. 62, see *filacteria*.

properter [for *proprium*], XXXVIII. 13, see *Diodorus*.

prophana, deforma, XV. 44 (*Ezech.* XLVIII. 15 Quinque millia...*profana* erunt). For *deforma* see Lew. & Sh. *deformis*. Cf. *profana*, maculata, Cp. P749.

propheta, IV. 5, see *fates*; XXXV. 97, see *uatis*.

prophetae, see *uina*.

prophete, X. 4, see *uina*; PROPHETE, XIII *tit.*

prophetis, XXXVIII. 42, see *hierufontis*; PROPHETIS, XVII *tit.*

propinquitate, XXXIII. 7, see *sicel*.

propitius, XXIX. 63, see *ileusun cyrię*.

propius, XXXV. 162, see *in comminus*.

proponentes, I. 96, see *promulgantes*.

proponitur, XXVIII. 53, see *paraprosdocia*.

propositura [praep-], IV. 105, see *propositus*.

propositure, XXXV. 23, see *editionis*, where *praepos-* is wrongly suggested.

propositus, uestis regie propositura, IV. 105 (*Ruf.* VII. 28 fol. 130ᵇ ei contulerat purpurae *praeposituram*; cf. Gloss. Werth. [Gallée, p. 343]: propositura propositus, idest uestis regiae).

propri [for *propria*], XXVIII. 33, see *tropus*.

propria, XXVIII. 33, see *tropus*; XLIV. 10, see *cardines*.

proprietas, XIX. 7, see *idioma*.

proprietate, XXX. 56, see *aethimologia*.

propriores, proprios, XXVIII. 43, see *caracterismos*.

proprium, X. 23, see *Aminab*; XII. 24, see *Dorix*; XIII. 16, see *tabehel*; XV. 12, see *bibli*, 15, see *Dan*, 23, see *Syeres*; XVI. 19, see *Apethno*; XVII. 15, see *Pile*; XXIV. 13, see *alabastrum*; XXVIII. 76, see *metafora*; XXIX. 39, see *prorusu*; XXX. 26, see *diatripas*; XXXVIII. 11, 12, 14, see *Calistratus*; XXXIX. 10, see *ausaret*, 26, see *emorphium*. See also *actio*; *angulinis*; *Galerius*; *interorina*; *propter*.

propter, I. 90, see *philacteria*; X. 22, see *areola*; XXI. 16, see *conopeum*; XXXVIII. 43, see *nastologis*. See also *filacteria*.—for *proprium*: XXXV. 209, see *Galerius*, 242, see *ponte moluio*, 256, see *Actio*; XXXIX. 9, see *Interorina*.

prorigo, urido [for urigo?] cutis idest gyccae, XXXV. 3, see *pruriginem*.

prorsus, plane procul dubio uere, I. 86 (*De Canon.*; *Can. Apostt.* XVII *prorsus* ex numero eorum).

prorumpit, XXVIII. 65, see *epiphonima*.

prorusu lembo, prorusu insula proprium lembo a quo ibi faciunt illa uestimenta, XXIX. 39 (*Uerb. Interpr.*=*Hier. in Matth.* XXVII. 27 induant chlamyden coccineam *pro rufo* [*russo*, in note] *limbo*, quo reges veteres utebantur)=*Rusulembo*, genus uestimenti, Cp. R259; cf. Du C. *Russolembus*, muliebre vestimentum; Goetz, V. 578, 9, *Russo lembo*, uestimentum rosei coloris quo reges ueteres utebantur.—Goetz, VI. 148, suggests to read "pro rufo limbo pro rufa infula." But perhaps leg.: (pro) *ruso* (russo) *lembo*, (pro) *russo* insulae [name of insula omitted] proprium; *lembo* &c.

prosa, proemio [prooemio] uel prefacionę [praef-], XIX. 14 (*Job*; *Praef. Hieron.* p. XIVᵇ and Migne *P.L.* XXVIII col. 1081ᴬ *prosa* oratio est; p. XIVᵇ and Migne col. 1082ᴬ *prosa* oratione contexitur). Cf. *prosa*, praefatio, Cp. P656; Ep. 18C38; Ef.[1] 379, 26.

prosaomelian, see *et procomian*.

prosapia, progenies, xxxv. 98 (*Ruf.* I. 1 fol. 7[a] de Noë...omnique *prosapia* scribitur).

proscribantur, porro uel palam scribantur, I. 85 (*De Canon.*; *Can. Apostt.* XL nec Episcopi, vel eius propinqui...*proscribantur*). — **proscribendo**, damnando, xxxv. 207 (*Ruf.* VIII. 17 fol. 144[a] alios... *proscribendo*).

proscriptionem (?), see *scriptionem*.

prosefanesen, ostendit, xxx. 36 (*Cat. Hier.* XXXVIII col. 653A liber unus, quem proprie Alexandro, Hierosolymorum episcopo προσεφώνησε [-ησεν, Rich.]; B: liber unus, que p.a. iherosolimorum e. *prosphonesen ostendit*; C: l. u. quem p. a. ier. e. [blank]) =*prosefanesin*, ostendit, Cp. P568; *prosefanescen*, ostendit uel carcteri, Ep. 17E23; *persefanescem*, ostendit uel caracteri, Ef.[1] 377, 44.

prosepion, see *et procomian*.

prosequantur, comitantur, I. 89 (*De Canon.*; *Can. Conc. Antioch.* XXCIX qui... proficiscentem suis *prosequantur* epistolis). —**prosequor**, deducor [for deduco], I. 102 (*De Canon.*; *Can. Conc. Carth.* XXCVI *prosequor* ea quae...gesta sunt; conf. *ibid.* x quae...*prosecutus* est).

prosomean, prosomian, prosonam, see *et procomian*.

prospera, XXVII. 18 & XXXIV. 16, see *secunda*.

prosperitatem, IV. 49, see *furtunatam*.

prosphonesen, see *prosefanesen*.

prostibulo, see *prostipulum*.

prostipulum, locus fornicationis, IV. 72 (*Eccl. Istor.*); **in prostibulo**, in domo fornicaria, xxxv. 116 (*De Euseb.*)=(*Ruf.* II. 13 fol. 24[b] quae...in *prostibulo* steterat) =*in prostibulo*, in domo fornicaria, Cp. I143; Ef.[1] 366, 19; *in pr-*, in domo foricara, Ep. 12A22.

protegere, II. 180, see *tueri*.

protoplastrum, prima plamatio [plasmatio], XXIX. 26 (*Uerb. Interpr.*=*Hier. in Matth.* xx. 13 *protoplastum* intelligi). Cf. *protuplaustum*, primus figuratum, Cp. P588.

protoplastum, see *protoplastrum*.

protulimus, I. 38, see *depromsimus*.

protulit, x. 12, see *ficus protulit....*

prouide, caute iuste, II. 141 (*Bened. reg.* 3, 13 [17] *prouide* et *iuste*).

prouidere, xxxv. 284, see *consulere*.

prouincia, XXXIX. 13, see *Aurelia*. See also *Canisius*; *Cyprius*; *Decapolim*; *Saba*.

prouinciae, see *Ambiensium*; *pagi*.

prouintia [-cia], XIX. 25, see *Saba*; XXIX. 31, see *decapolim*; xxx. 2, see *Canisius*; xxxv. 299, see *Cyprius*.

prouintie [-ciae], III. 2, see *Ambiensium*.

prouintię [-ciae], XIX. 12, see *Theman*; XXIII. 11, see *pagi*.

prouocat, xxxv. 260, see *lacessit*.

pruriginem, bleci, v. 15 (*Eccl. Hist.*); **prorigo**, urido [for *urigo*?] cutis idest gyccae, xxxv. 3 (*De Eus.*)=(*Ruf.* I. 8 fol. 12[b] *prurigo*...intolerabilis). The latter gloss=*prurigo*, gycenis, Cp. P692; *prorigo*, gycinis, Ep. 19E5; *prurigo*, gycinis, Ef.[1] 381, 36. For *bleci*, *blcce*, blotch, see Bosw. T. (*blǣco*, *blæcþa*, paleness, leprosy); Kluge *A. S. Les.* (*blece*, Aussatz); Oxf. D. & Skeat (blight). For *gyccae*, itch, see Bosw. T. (*giccan*); Oxf. D. & Skeat, *D.* (*itch*, sb.).

prurigo, see *pruriginem*.

psalmi, psalmum, XXVIII. 18, see *apo tu-*.

psalmus, cantus, II. 135 (*Bened. reg.* 9, 6 [6] tertius *psalmus*; psalmum, in note; 12, 4 [3] sextus *psalmus*, &c.).

psalterium, XII. 40 (bis), see *cyneris*.

psaltes, castus [for *cantus* or *cantor*?], IV. 53 (*Eccl. Ist.*); **psaltes**, cythara, [cith-], xxxv. 161 (*De Eus.*)=(*Ruf.* IV. 18 fol. 66[b] alius [liber] qui superscribitur *Psaltes*).

pseudo ephigrapha, falso superscribta [-pta], xxx. 33 (*Cat. Hier.* XXXII col. 647B quasi ψευδόγραφα repudiantur; B: quasi *pseudo epigrapha* idest *false superscriptionis* rep.; C: quasi [blank] repudiantur; Rich.: quasi ψευδεπίγραφα repud.)= *pseodoepigrapha* [*pseudo epigraffa*, Ef.[1]], falsa superscripta, Cp. P835; Ef.[1] 377, 39; *pseodoepigrafa*, falso superscriptura, Ep. 17E18.

pseudo epigrapha, see *pseudo ephigrapha*.

pseudoforum, pseudothyrum, see *ad seduforum*.

psiathio, psiathium, psiatium, see *spiathio*.

psichiexodo, anime exitu, xxx. 81 (*Cat. Hier.* LXXXIII col. 691A de Autexusio [Richardson: De αὐτεξουσίῳ; Migne's Gr. text: περὶ Αὐτεξουσίου]; B: *de aotezozoy* idest *anime exitum*; C: [blank]). In a note to Migne's text, it is correctly remarked: pro Autexusio perperam...*de animae exitu*; but there must have been some reading, de ψυχιεξοδο, to account for the lemma in the Leiden Gloss. and for *animae exitu*; cf. *psychi ezodo*, anima exitus, Cp. P838, and *defixiezodo*, de exitu animae, ib. D59.

psychi ezodo, see *psichiexodo*.

pthocheas, xxx. 91, see *peri pthocheas*, sub v. *ptocheus*.

ptisanas, de ordeo fiunt grana que decorticantur in pilo [for pila?] uel uase lapideo, VIII. 18 (*Salam.* XXVII. 22 si contuderis stultum in pila quasi *ptisanas* feriente desuper pilo).

ptocheus, inopie [-piae], XXX. 68 (*Cat. Hier.* LXXVI col. 685[B] Constat hunc mirae *ἀσκήσεως* et appetitorem voluntariae paupertatis fuisse; B: Constat hunc mire *askeseon* idest *inopie* et appetitorem voluntarie paupertatis; C: Constat hunc mire [blank] et app. vol. paup.)=*prexeos*, inopiae, Cp. P662; Ep. 18E15; *praexeos*, inopiae, Ef.[1] 379, 41; *ptoceos*, inopię, Cp. P840; Ep. 17E16; Ef.[1] 377, 37. The Gr. text has: *Ὡμολόγηται δὲ τοῦτον τῆς τε ἀσκήσεως καὶ ἑκουσίου πτωχείας γεγενῆσθαι ἐραστήν.*—**peri pthocheas**, de paupertate, XXX. 91 (*Cat. Hier.* CXVII col. 709[A] *περὶ φιλοπτωχίας*; B: *perioi poptochi* idest de amore inopie; C [blank].—For *ἀσκήσεως* cf. *arcesi*, intellectui, Cp. A775; *archesi*, intellectui, Ep. 3C9 and *ascesu*, intellectui, *ib.* 1A22; *ascetron*, intellectum, Cp. A848; Ep. 3C11; Ef.[1] 342, 33; *ascesi*, ingeni, Cp. A851 & Ep. 3C22; *arcessi*, ingenii, Ef.[1] 342, 45. Cf. also *perifgetosias*, actus quidam, Cp. P234; Ep. 18C28; *perifgetorias*, actus quidam plomonion, Ef.[1] 379, 17.—**ptochiis**, in dispensationibus pauperum uel negotia [*uel negotia*, belongs to I. 92 *pragmatica forma*, q. v.], I. 91 (*De Canon.*); **pitoicis**, dispensatio pauperum, XXXIX. 58 (*not* Greg. Dial., *but*)=(*Can. Conc. Calch.* VIII De clericis, qui sunt in *ptochiis*...Clerici, qui praeficiuntur *ptochiis*).

ptochiis, see *ptocheus*; *sidonicis*.

ptsaum, XXVIII. 18, see *apo tu ptsaum*.

pubertas [sine interpret.], I. 105 (*De Canon.*; *Can. Conc. Carth.* XVI ad annos *pubertatis*). Cf. *pubertas*, iuuentus tenera legitima tamen, Cp. P857.

publica, I. 58, see *gesta*.

publicam, XXIV. 6, see *publicani*.

publicani, qui publicam rem faciunt non a peccando, XXIV. 6 (*Math.* V. 46 *publicani* hoc faciunt; IX. 10 multi *publicani*, &c.).

publicare, II. 118, see *non detegere*.

publicationis, see *editionis*.

publice, I. 94, see *passim*.

publicis, I. 126, see *spectacula*.

publico, XXXV. 180, see *fisco p-*; see also *sumpto puplico*.

publite, hamme, V. 19 (*Eccl. Hist.*); **puplites**, hommę, XXXV. 204 (*De Eus.*)=(*Ruf.* VIII. 13 fol. 142[a] *poplite*...debilitato; cf. *id.* X. 4 fol. 160[b]; X. 17 fol. 170[a] *poplite*). For *hamme*, *hommę* (the ham, the inner or hind part of the knee), see Bosw. T. (*ham*, *hom*, *hamm*).

pudicas, XXXV. 38, see *sinefactas*.

puella, XXXVII. 9, see *tabulas legat*.

pugil, milis [-les], XLVI. 2 (*Alia*=*Ars Phocae*, p. 414, 20 hic *pugil*).

pugionibus, mucronibus, XXXV. 304 (*De Eus.*); **pungios**, pullus [for *paruulus*?] gladius, IV. 20 (*Eccl. Ist.*)=(*Ruf.* II. 20 fol. 29[b] occultatis *pugionibus*). Cf. *pugionibus*, glaunis (for *gladiis*?), Cp. P847; *pugionibus*, gladiis, Ep. 18A13; Ef.[1] 378, 20.

pugne [pugnae], XXXV. 95, see *gigantemachie*.

pugnę, IV. 52, see *monarchia*; XXXV. 94, see *theomachie*.

pulcra, XXXVIII. 6, see *stragula*.

pulcrę, XIII. 43, see *lamia*.

pulcriores, XXXIV. 23, see *lautiores*.

pullulent, see *pululent*.

pullus [for *paruulus*?], IV. 20, see *pungios*.

pullux, XLIII. 44, see *epul.*

pulpito, I. 65 and XXXIX. 53, see *in pulpito*.

pulsasse, IV. 113, see *apulisse*.

puluillos, plumatios micinos duos coniunctos habent in sella, XV. 43 (*Ezech.* XIII. 18 quae consuunt *pulvillos*; 20 ad *pulvillos*). For plumatios (=plumacios) see Du C.; Körting, *Wörterb.* 7263; Wright W. 124, 20 (*plumacius*, bed-bolster).

pululent, crescunt in miraculis, XII. 48 (*Eccles.* XLVI. 14 & XLIX. 12 ossa (eorum) *pullulent* de loco suo).

puncto, pede, IV. 59 (*Eccl. Ist.*); **puncto**, foramine in quo pedes uinctorum in ligno tenentur cubitali spatio interiecto inter uinctos, XXXV. 27 (*De Eus.*)=(*Ruf.* V. 2 fol. 75[b] septimo (ut dicunt) *puncto* in neruo pedes...distenti)=*puncto*, foramine in quo pedes uinctorum tenentur in ligno cubitali spatio interiecto idest cosp, Ep. 19A3; Ef.[1] 380, 15; cf. *puncto*, cosp, Cp. P865. See also above *neruum*. For *cosp*, a fetter, see Bosw. T. in voce.

pundar, in A.S. spelling, for late Lat. *pondarium*; see *perpendiculum*.

pungios, pullus [for *paruulus*?] gladius, IV. 20, see *pugionibus*.

punica, XI. 14, see *poderis*.

punicis, X. 26, see *mustum*.

puplicationis [public-], XXXV. 23, see *editionis*.

puplico [pub-], XXXV. 137, see *sumptu puplico*.

puplites, hommę, XXXV. 204 (*De Eus.*), see *publite*.

purgamentum, XXXV. 195, see *peripsima*.

purior, IV. 109, see *defecatior*.

purpura, uuylocbaso, XXII. 17 (*Esther*, IV. 9, ap. Sabatier=Vulg. XV. 9 ipse erat vestitus *purpurâ*). See Steinm. I. 488, note 18; Bosw. T. in vv. *weoloc* (a kind of shell-fish, a whelk, cockle), *weoloc-basu*, *wealh-basu*; Kluge, *Ang. Leseb.* p. 161 (*basu*, *beasu*), 217 (*weoloc*); Skeat, *Et. D.* (*whelk*); the present index (*coccus*, *rubeum*).

purulenta, fetida, IV. 88 (*Ruf.* VIII. 18 fol. 145[b] fistulis...*purulentis*).—purulentis, XXXV. 45, see *suppuratis*.

purum, extersum, IV. 111 (*Ruf.* VI. 14 fol. 104[a] Christum...hominem *purum* esse; cf. Ruf. in Lommatzsch Origen XI. 73 Christum non *purum* hominem dicimus). Perhaps this gloss is merely a further explanation of the glosses IV. 109 (*defecatior*, purior) and IV. 110 (*defecatum*, liquidam). For *purum* see also (XLI. 12) *sardius*.

puruys, uenę [-nae], XXIX. 61 (*Uerb. Interpr.* = *Hier. in Matth.* XV. 17, 18 per... meatus corporis, quos Graeci πόρους vocant). See also *meatus*.

pusillanimes, inbicilles [inbec-], II. 192 (*Bened. reg.* 48, 17 [30] propter *pusillanimes*).

pusilluminus, paulominus, XV. 46 (*Ezech.* XVI. 47 neque secundum scelera earum fecisti *pauxillum minus*; Sabat. egisti *paulo minus*).

pusti, brandas, IV. 76, see *reusti*.

puta, see *utpute*.

putant, XXXIII. 6, see *stater*, 19, see *nebel*.

putat, snędit, XLVII. 102 (*Alia* = ?). This gloss, which appears among a group of substantive glosses all recorded in the Cp., Ep. and Ef.[1] glossaries, is not found in any of these. It is evidently 3rd p. sing. pres. of putare, to trim, prune or lop, and hence = A. S. *snaedit* (he snathes), from snædan, to slice, prune trees; see Bosw. T. (*snædan*).

puto, XXXV. 210, see *sexcuplum*.

putredo, see *tabo*.

putrescant, XXI. 20, see *labastes*.

putrido, XXXV. 138, see *tabo*.

pyctarum, see *cestus*.

pylas, see *Armenias pilas*.

pylominos, amator, XXX. 10 (*Cat. Hier.* VII col. 619[C] Tertullianus...refert...quemdam in Asia σπουδαστὴν apostoli Pauli; B: Tert....ref. q. in Asia *philosten* idest *amatorem* pauli apostoli conuictum; C: Tert....ref. q. in Asia apostolo paulo coniunctum; E: in Asia πηρισωπη apostoli pauli). In *Cat. Hier.* V col. 617[B] *Philemoni*, but the gloss does not seem to refer to this word. Cf. *philocompos*, amator iactantiae, Cp. P389; *-pus*, a. i., Ep. 21C34; Ef.[1] 385, 31.

pyramides, see *piraondes*.

pyriflegitonta, ignis ebulliens, XXXVIII. 24 (*Clem. Recognitt.* IX. 11 fluvium quem *Pyriphlegethonta* nominant...nunc nolo *Pyriphlegethonta* adducas; I. 4 *Pyriphlegethonti* fluvio).

pyriphlegethonta, see *pyriflegitonta*.

Pythagoras, see *phitagoras*.

pythonissa, see *striga*.

pytisso, sputum deicio, XLIII. 45 (*De div. nominibus* = Donati *Ars grammat.* p. 382, 4 *pitisso*).

q for *c*: Coquiton for Cocyti.

qua, XIII. 52; XXIX. 23.—[for *quam*] XIII. 40.

quadrans, genus nummi est habens duo minuta, XXIX. 9 (*Uerb. Interpr.* = *Hier. in Matth.* V. 25 col. 38[c] *quadrans* genus est nummi, qui habet duo minuta).

quadraplas die, hoc est III horę quę concrescunt in quarto anno quando fit quidem bissextus, IV. 99 (?*Ruf.*? VII. 28 fol. 131[b]: undecimo calendas Aprilis in qua die sol inuenitur non solum conscendisse primam partem, verumetiam quartam iam in ea die [*not.* quartam in ea diem] habere, id est, in prima ex duodecim partibus).

quadriga, a IIII equis dicitur, XXXV. 15 (*Ruf.* III. 7 fol. 40[a] visi sunt currus et *quadrigae*; III. 25 fol. 46[b] *quadriga*).

quadrigae, see *quadriga*.

quadris, XXX. 39, see *tesseroes*.

quae (nom., neut. plur.) I. 49, 112; XXVIII. 44.—(nom., fem., sing.), XI. 16. See further *que*; *quę*.

quaedam, see *ausesis*; *figura*; *parenthesin*; *quedam*.

quaerit, see *querit*; *trapezita*.

quaestio, see *questio*; *sillogismus*.

quaestionibus, see *quest-*; *sicel*.

quaestionum, see *dedragma*; *quest-*; *sofismatum*; *sophismatum*.

quaestu, see *questus*.

quaestuosa, see *quest-*; *liciniosa*.

quaestus, see *questus*.

qualicumque, XLIV. 11, see *clima*.

quam (pron.), VIII. 12, 14; X. 1; XXVIII. 38, 57, 80; XXXIX. 22, 23.—(adv.) X. 6; XII. 40; XXXIX. 31; see also *pedalis*; *perpendiculum*.

quamuis, II. 103; XIV. 9; XXXVII. 9.

quando, IV. 99; XIII. 40; XV. 18, 33; XVII. 12; XVIII. 3; XXIII. 20; XXVII. 4, 20; XXVIII. 24, 32, 43, 45, 67, 72; XXXI. 25; XXXVI. 1; XXXIX. 28; XLIV. 25; XLVII. 28 (*bis*). For quam (?), XIV. 30.

quantitas, mensura, II. 142 (*Bened. reg.* 10, 4 [3] psalmodiae *quantitas* teneatur; 39, 17 [28] servetur *quantitas*; cf. 10, 9 [14] psalmorum *quantitate*).

quantitate, see *quantitas*.

quare, xliii. 43, see *quidni.*

quarta, quartana, quartanae, see *quartane.*

quartane, xiiii lune [-nae], iii. 3 (*De S. Mart. Stor.*).—**quartane**, quę quarta die uenit, xlii. 23 (*Ex div. libris*?) = (*Sulp. Sev.*, *Vit. S. Mart.* 19, 1 cum... *quartanae* febribus ureretur; *quartanis*, in note). Cf. also *Vit. S. Eug.* xi, Migne lxxiii col. 612B *quartana* vexabatur.

quartanis, see *quartane.*

quarto, iv. 99, see *quadraplas.*

quarum, x. 11, see *cyprus.*

quas, i. 104; xiii. 6; xxxv. 184; xxxviii. 15.

quasi, i. 12, 48; viii. 13; xiii. 23; xxiv. 5; xxx. 35; xxxiii. 7; xxxix. 48; xli. 8. For *qui* (?) xiii. 47.

quatere, mouere, iv. 42 (*Ruf.* iv. 7 fol. 56a eam *quatere* nititur). Cf. *quatere*, commouere, Cp. Q5; *quatare*, commouere, Ef.[2] 326, 21.

quattuor, xix. 20, see *tympanum*; xxxviii. 27, see *tetragono.*

que (=quae, nom. fem. sing.), i. 111; x. 24; xviii. 3; xxviii. 34, 62.—(=quae, nom. neut. plur.), viii. 18.—(=et), see *atque*; *fructusque*; *habentque.*

quę (=quae, nom. fem. sing.), i. 68; xiii. 41; xvii. 4; xix. 28; xxviii. 31, 49, 52, 55, 65, 75, 77, 81, 85; xxxii. 5; xxxvi. 11; xxxviii. 16; xlii. 23; xliii. 4, 51; xliv. 3; xlvi. 24.—(=quae, nom. fem. plur.), iv. 99; v. 3; xi. 7; xxxiii. 14; xxxiv. 5, 6; xxxvi. 1; xxxviii. 43; xliii. 49.—(=quae, nom. neut. plur.), i. 90; vii. 1; x. 21; xiv. 12; xv. 9; xxi. 10; xxviii. 44, 64; xxxix. 62.—(=quae, accus. neut. plur.), x. 1; see also *olfactoriola.*—(for qui, m. sing.), xlvi. 24.

quedam [quaedam], xxviii. 31, 47 (bis), 57.

quem, xlv. 18, see *pedum.*

quemadmodum, ii. 184, see *uti.*

querellam, i. 106, see *querimoniam.*

querimoniam, querellam grauem, i. 106 (*De Canon.*; *Can. Conc. Carth.* xi si *querimoniam* iustam ... non habuerit; cxxxv scripta ... habentia *querimoniam*; cf. *Decret. Innoc.* xxxv *querimoniam*; *Decret. Leon.* xiv p. 228b id.). Cf. *quaeremonus*, grauis querella, Cp. Q7; *quaeremonis*, grauis quaerela, id. Q29; Ep. 21E29; Ef.[1] 386, 9; *quaerimonia*, grauis querella uel accusatio, Ef.[2] 326, 31.

querit [quaerit], xxxviii. 29, see *trapezita.*

questio [quaestio], xxxiv. 44, see *sillogismus.*

questionibus [quaest-], xxxiii. 7, see *sicel.*

questionum [quaest-], iii. 60, see *sofismatum*; xxviii. 22, see *sophismatum*; xxx. 66, see *exenteseon*; xxxiii. 5, see *dedragma.*

questiosa [for *quaestuosa*?], iv. 65, see *liciniosa.*

questus, substantia, xlviii. 5 (*De Cass.*, *Inst.* vii. 7, 5 a spe *quaestus* deciderit; iv. 14 de tanto operis sui *quaestu*).

qui (nom. sing.), i. 39; viii. 13; xii. 35, 45; xiii. 25; xiv. 16, 29; xv. 5; xix. 23; xxviii. 28; xxix. 73; xxx. 2; xxxi. 37; xxxiii. 7; xxxv. 22; xxxviii. 29; xxxix. 4, 5, 19, 20, 24, 28 (bis), 48; xli. 11; xlii. 9; xliii. 13, 18, 23–26; xliv. 10, 16; xlvi. 7, 10; xlvii. 15.—(nom. plur.), i. 127; ii. 161; viii. 20; xi. 5; xv. 12, 24; xvi. 7, 25–27, 30–32; xxi. 12; xxii. 16; xxiii. 2, 3, 4; xxiv. 6; xxv. 3; xxix. 15, 42; xxxv. 24, 72; xxxviii. 5, 31, 37, 42, 44; xxxix. 7; xli. 1, 2; xliv. 27; xlv. 31.—(for *quod*?) viii. 17.—(for *quia*, or *quae*?) ii. 149.

quia, i. 100; x. 21; xvii. 19; xxxvii. 9; xxxix. 33.

quibus, xiii. 47, 59; xiv. 36; xv. 9, 11; xxxv. 73, 140; xliv. 10.

quibuscumque, ii. 104, see *libet.*

quibusdam, xxviii. 32, see *climax.*

quibuslibet, see *libet.*

quicumque, xxii. 12, see *urna.*

quidam, xxviii. 18; xxxiii. 6, 13, 16, 19.

quidem, iv. 99, see *quadraplas.*

qui dixerit fratri suo racha reus erit concilio idest reconciliatione, xxix. 73 (*Uerb. Interpr.* = *Hier. in Matth.* v. 22 *qui autem dixerit fratri suo raca, reus erit concilio*).

quidni, quare non, xliii. 43 (*De div. nominibus* = Donati *Ars grammat.* p. 386, 8–10 adverbia ... adfirmandi, ut etiam *quinni*; in note *quidni*).

quieti, xxxv. 251, see *otii.*

qui in numero optio fuit, numerus dicitur quando milites fiunt. Optio, dispensator qui dispensat stipendia militum prepositus [praep-] eorum, xxxix. 28 (*Greg. Dial.* iv. 35 col. 377C quidam Stephanus, *qui in numero Optio fuit*). Cf. *optio*, dispensator in militum stipendis, Cp. O207; Ef.[1] 375, 35; *optio*, dispensatur in militum stipendiis, Ep. 16E22.

quinni, see *quidni.*

quinquaginta, xxxi. 12, see *sata.*

quippiam, modis [for modicum?], ii. 143 (*Bened. reg.* 46, 6 [6] fregerit *quippiam*; 67, 13 [24] *quippiam*...facere). Cf. *quippiam*, modicumque, Cp. Q63; Ef.[1] 386, 25;

quippeam, modicum cumque, Ep. 22A6; *quippiam* modicum, Ef.[2] 326, 62.
quirie eleison, see *kyrieleison*.
quis, XXVIII. 70.
quisquilea [-lia], XXXV. 195, see *peripsima*.—**quisquilia**, inmundicia [-tia] erbarum [herb-], XXIX. 20 (*Uerb. Interpr.* = *Hier. in Matth.* XIII. 45, 46 quasi purgamenta contemnit et *quisquilias*; XXVI. 19 *quisquilias*). For *quisquilia*, see also *peripsima*.
quisquilias, see *quisquilia*.
quo, II. 6, 158; III. 19; XIII. 1; XIX. 44; XXVIII. 33 (bis), 76; XXIX. 39; XXXV. 27, 42, 57, 147; XLIV. 2, 7, 16.
[quo], see *deucalionem*.
quoadquo, adusque [for **quoad**, quoadusque?], VI. 30 (*Breu. exsol.*?).
quocumque, V. 20, see *quorsum*.
quod (pron., nom.), X. 13; XI. 2; XV. 33; XXIV. 8, 9; XXVIII. 74, 83; XXXII. 1; XXXIII. 15; XXXV. 192.—(pron., accus.), X. 3; XIII. 36; XIV. 20; XXVIII. 83; XXXIII. 7, 16; XLIV. 19.—(conj.), I. 76, 101, 109, 111; II. 146; X. 6; XII. 42; XXVIII. 18, 69; XXIX. 67; XXXII. 7–11; XXXIII. 1, 8, 13, 16; XXXIX. 42; XLIII. 6, 50; XLIV. 17, 27, 29.
quodam, I. 2, see *alea*.
quodcumque, XVI. 9, see *malleolis*.
quomodo, XXXIII. 5, see *dedragma*.
quoniam, XXVIII. 47, see *parenthesin*.
quoque, XLIV. 10, see *cardines*; 28, see *extremi*.
quorsum, quocumque, V. 20 (?*Ruf.*?) = *quorsum*, quocumque, Cp. Q76; Ep. 21E21; Ef.[1] 386, 1.
quorum, XLIV. 8.
quos, XIV. 3; XVI. 29; XLIV. 10.
quoties, XXVIII. 40, 44, 46, 58, 62, 63, 72, 74, 79.
quotus, hu ald, XLIII. 39; **totus**, suæ ald, XLIII. 40 (*De div. nominibus* = Donati *Ars grammat.* p. 380, 1 ut *quotus totus*). For *hu* (how); suæ (= *swǣ*, so); *ald* (a Mercian form = A.S. *eald*, old), see Bosw. T. sub vv.

r for *l*: f*r*ora (for f*l*ora).—for *n*: a*r*ge (for a*n*ge); sapo*r*em (for sapo*n*em).—for *rr*: sa*r*ientur (sa*rr*-).—r *omitted*: onauerit (o*r*n-); paredum (-d*r*um).—r *inserted*: lanist*r*a (-ta); p*r*athus (pathos); prest*r*igiis (praestigiis ?); protoplast*r*um (-tum); rub*r*i (rubi); t*r*amaritus (tam-).—r *doubled*: pa*rr*ochia (parochia).
raca; **racha**, XXIX. 73, see *qui dixerit*.
radice, XIII. 25, see *de radice*.
radix, XLVI. 28, see *matrix*.
raeda, raedam, see *reda*.
ramis, XXXV. 86, see *busta*.
ramunculi, XXIX. 48, see *cauliculi*.
rancor, rancorem, see *rangor*.
rangor, nequitia, XXXIV. 43 (*De Cass.*, *Inst.* XII. 27, 5 contra fratrem *rancorem* quendam...conceperit; XII. 27, 6 aduersus fratrem *rancor*; XII. 29, 2 in responsione *rancor*, &c.).
rapitur, XVII. 4, see *torris*.
rata, iusta, XXXV. 101; **rata**, confirmata, XXXV. 300 (*Ruf.* I. 6 fol. 11[a] *rata*...atque integra generatio; Cacciari p. 32, note g says that his MS. adds *idest firma* after *rata*).—**rata**, placita, XIV. 23 (*Hier.* XXXII. 11 accepi... stipulationes et *rata* et signa...).
ratio, II. 147, see *ratiociniis*; XXVIII. 46, see *aetilogia*; XXX. 85, see *cinticta*.
ratiociniis, unde ratio conprobetur, II. 147 (*Bened. reg.* 2, 88 [135] de alienis *ratiociniis*).
rationabile, XXIX. 58, see *lutugisprum*.
raucos, crispantes, VI. 23 (*Breu. exsol.*? = *Dracont.* I. 279? see *molosi*).
rebus, XII. 11, see *inpendiis*; XXVIII. 62, see *tapynosin*, 88, see *diatiposis*; rebus for *res*, XXVIII. 65, see *epiphonima*.
recapitulatio, IX. 6, see *anacefaleos*; XXXVIII. 21, see *anacefaleosin*.
recenserunt, legerunt, XXIII. 8 (1 *Esdr.* IV. 19 *recensuerunt* inveneruntque; VI. 1 *recensuerunt* in bibliotheca librorum; cf. IV. 15 *recenseas* in libris; V. 17 *recenseat* in bibliotheca regis).
recensuerunt, see *recenserunt*.
recipiant, I. 110, see *resipiscant*.
recipit, XXVIII. 47, see *parenthesin*.
reciproca, II. 5, see *antiphona*.
recollicet, recollocet, see *reculicet*.
reconciliatione, XXIX. 73, see *qui dixerit-*.
reconditorium, II. 13, see *biblioteca*.
recreare [sine interpret.], II. 148 (*Bened. reg.* 4, 10 [12] pauperes *recreare*). Cf. *recreare*, nutrire, Cp. R36.
recta, XLIV. 3, see *axis*.
recte, II. 129, see *ortodoxis*, 146, see *regula*; XLI. 4, see *orthodoxam*.—[for *rectae*], I. 71, see *modeste*.
reculcet, II. 145; see *reculicet*.
reculicet, reculcet reu[ertatur?], II. 145 (*Bened. reg.* 43, 17 qui se...*recollocet*; *conlocet* in note [26 *culicet*, *recollocet*, recollicet, collocet]). Cf. Du C. *collocare*, *culcare*.
reda, nomen uehiculi [pro exercitu?], III. 16 (*De S. Mart. Stor.* = *Sulp. Sev. Dial.* II. 3, 2 fiscalis *raeda*, and *reda*, *rheda* in note; ibid. II. 3, 5 *raedam*). Cf. *Fiscalis reda*, ȝebellicum þægnfearu, Cp. F200. For "pro exercitu" see above p. 7 note †, and the quotation sub v. *aggerem*.

reddibitiones, retributiones, XLVIII. 60 (*De Cass. Inst.* v. 39, 1 quodam *redhibitionis* colore; in note *reddibitionis*, *redibitionis*).
redditio, XXVIII. 46, see *aetilogia.*
redditus, see *reditus.*
redegerit, see *redigerit.*
redhibitionis, redibitionis, see *reddibitiones.*
redigerit, reuocauit, I. 108 (*De Canon.*; *Can. Conc. Calch.* II *redegerit* gratiam). Cf. *redigitur*, reuocatur, Cp. R160.
redimicula, sunt ornamenta ceruicis, X. 8 (*Cant.* I. 9 vers. ant. Sab.: cervix tua sicut *redimicula*; Vulg.: collum tuum sicut *monilia*).
reditus, facultates, XXXV. 276 (*Ruf.* VII. 25 fol. 125[b] praediuites *reditus*...praestabantur; Cacciari, p. 433, *redditus*).—**reditus**, substantia, XLVIII. 45 (*De Cass. Inst.* IV. 14 tantos...*reditus* conferat monasterio).
redolens, XII. 20, see *aromatizans.*
refugii, XXXV. 50, see *asillum.*
refutant, II. 161, see *sarabaite.*
regali, XXXV. 137, see *sumptu puplico.*
regalibus, XXII. 11, see *mundum m-.*
regalis, XXXV. 152, see *sceptrum*; XLVI. 3, see *tanaquil.*—**regalis**, XXXUI siliqua, XXXI. 16 (*De ponder.*?).
regia, III. 32, see *patera.*
regie, IV. 105, see *propositus.*
regimen, XXXVIII. 43, see *nastologis.*
regiminis, IV. 52, see *monarchia.*
regina, uxor nabuchodonosor pro reuerentia, XVI. 12 (*Dan.* v. 10). For *regina* see also (XLII. 3) *memphitica.*
reginae, see *regine*; *Laodes.*
regine [for *reginae*], XVI. 14, see *ex latere regni*; XXVIII. 15, see *Laodes.*
re[gi]o, IV. 89, see *morbo regio.*
regio morbus, corpus afficit colore sicut pedes accipitris, XXXV. 181; see *morbo regio.*
regione, IV. 98, see *comellas*; XXXVIII. 35, see *ex diametro.*
regis, XXXVIII. 22, see *deucalionem*; see also *ex latere regni.*
regni, XVI. 14; see *ex latere regni.*
regula, II. 120, see *norma.*—**regula**, dicta eo quod recte ducit, II. 146 (*Bened. reg.* I. 4 [4] militans sub *regula*; 3, 14 [19] sequantur *regulam*, &c.; Edit. Casin. 1 *tit.* textus *regule. regula* appellatur ab hoc quod oboedientum dirigat mores).
regulam, see *regula.*
regulares, II. 37, see *canonicas.*
regularum, XXX. 77, see *cronicon.*
REGULIS, II *tit.*, see *interpretatio.*
regulus, XIII. 25; see *de radice.*
rei, I. 12, see *aemulum*, 77, see *negotia*; XXVIII. 37, see *metabole*, 42, see *idea*, 46, see *aetilogia*, 81, see *per energiam.*
reis, inmundis, XL. 14 (*Uerba*?).
relatio, see *anaphora.*
religamur, I. 109, see *religio.*
religio, quod per eam uni deo religamur, I. 109 (*De Canon.*; *Can. Apostt.* VI sub obtentu *religionis*, XIV in causa *religionis*; *Can. Conc. Carth.* LX *religionis*...accessus).
religionis, see *religio.*
rem, XVI. 31, see *incantatores*; XXIV. 6, see *publicani*; XXVIII. 51, see *hyperthesis*, 55, see *metaforan*, 83, see *ennoematice.*—**rem**, I. 84, see *peruadere.*
rema, for *reuma* (q. v.).
remanet, XV. 33, see *uinacia.*
remansit, XVIII. 3, see *uinatia.*
remigantes, XV. 9, see *transtra.*
remota, ablata, II. 144 (*Bened. reg.* 39, 12 [20] *remota*...crapula). For *remota* see also (II. 84) *heremita*; (XXVIII. 57) *figura.*
remotior, XLIV. 15, see *exemerinus.*
remunerationis, XXXV. 28, see *munerum diebus.*
renes, see *lumbire.*
renitimur, VI. 25, see *defetimur.*
rennuite, II. 161, see *sarabaite.*
renouationes, XXIX. 33, see *deuteres.*
reo, IV. 89, for *re[gi]o* (q. v.).
repagulis, stabulis, XXXIV. 32 (*De Cass. Inst.* VIII. 18 equi...e suis *repagulis*... prorumpunt).
repente, XXIV. 9, see *censum.*
repetens, XXVIII. 30, see *epembabis.*
repetitio, XXVIII. 73, see *epimone.*
repetitur, XXVIII. 72, see *anaphora.*
reponatur, II. 30, see *condatur.*
repperi, XXXIII. 7, see *sicel.*
repperiunt, XXXV. 18, see *opperiunt.*
repraesentat, see *per energiam.*
reprehensione, XII. 38, see *sophistice.*
representat [repraes-], XXVIII. 81, see *per energiam.*
reprobatus, XXXIV. 13, see *confutatus.*
repticius, see *arreptitium.*
reputes, XLVIII. 74.
requies, XXVII. 19, see *feriatus.*
rerum, XXVIII. 31, see *ausesis.*
res, XXVIII. 72, see *anaphora*; XXXIX. 42, see *altare*; see also *epiphonima.*
reses, see *seres.*
resina, de arbore est sicut et pix, XIV. 6 (*Hier.* VIII. 22 *resina* non est...; XLVI. 11 tolle *resinam*; LI. 8 tollite *resinam*).
resipiscant, amissam recipiant sapientiam, I. 110 (*De Canon.*; *Can. Conc. Carth.* LXVI *resipiscant* de diaboli laqueis).
resistentes, XXXV. 216, see *obices.*
resistit, XXXIV. 19, see *non officit.*
resplendit [-det], XLI. 14, see *byrillus.*
responditur, II. 149, see *responsoria.*

responsa, xxii. 16, see *ueredarii*.

responsio, xxviii. 36, see *peusis*.

responsoria, qui ab uno incipitur et ab aliis responditur, ii. 149 (*Bened. reg.* 9, 12 [16] trea *responsoria* cantentur. Duo *responsoria*...dicantur; 20 [30] Post has ...tres lectiones cum *responsoria* sua; *responsoriis* in note); cf. breuis *responsorius*, ibid. 10, 7 [10]; in quarto *responsorio*, ib. 11, 8 [11]; lectiones cum *responsoriis* suis, ib. 11, 12 [19]; post quartum...*responsorium*, ib. 11, 17 [27]; de...*responsoriis*, ib. 11, 26 [43]. The interpretation *qui* &c. refers to the form *responsorius*.

responsoriis, responsorio, responsorium, responsorius, see *responsoria*.

restibus, see *restis*.

restis, funis ex herbis, xxi. 11 (*Judith* vi. 9 vinctum *restibus* dimiserunt eum).

rethorica, eloquentia, xxx. 50, see *dialectica*; cf. *rethorica*, praeclara eloquentia, Cp. R62; *rethorica*, eloquentia, Ep. 22A34 and Ef.[1] 386, 52.

reticetur, xxviii. 54, see *aposiopesis*.

retis, xxi. 16, see *conopeum*.

retributiones, xlviii. 60, see *reddibitiones*.

retrorsum, ii. 8, see *apostatare*.

reu [for *reuertatur*?], ii. 145, see *reculicet*.

reuelatio [for *relatio*], xxviii. 72, see *anaphora*.

reuerentia, xvi. 12, see *regina*.

reu[ertatur], see *reculicet*.

reuma [=rheuma], streum, xlvii. 31 (*Alia*=?)=*rema*, stream, Cp. R51; Ep. 22A25; Ef.[1] 386, 43. For *streum*=strēam, a flow, stream, see Bosw. T. (*strēam*). See also *sicunia*.

reuma (= rheuma, a catarrh), see *sicunia*.

reuocauit, i. 108, see *redigerit*.

reus, xxix. 73, see *qui dixerit* &c.

reusti, iterum usti, xxxv. 200 (*De Euseb.*); **pusti**, brandas, iv. 76 (*Eccl. Istor.*); **uaeri**, uirge ferreę, xxxv. 81 (*De Euseb.*) = (*Ruf.* viii. 13 fol. 141[b], edit. 1548, and ed. 1535, p. 193 Foeminis... *verua* candentia et *reusta*, ardentia...ingerebantur). Cacciari, p. 489 "Foeminis ...*verua* candentia et sudes *praeustae* inardentes ingerebantur," adding, in a note: "In Editis Basiliensibus 1523 legitur: Foeminis quoque *veri*·candentes et *reusti*, ardentes. Notat tamen Rhenanus quosdam sic locum emendasse: *ærei* candentes fustes." Hence, for *pusti*, leg. *preusti* [=*praeusti*], the stroke above the *p*, to make *pre*, having been forgotten. With *aerei* cf. *aerii uirgae*, ferreae, Cp. A298; *aerii uirgae*, uerreae, Ep. 1A249; *a*eri* uirgę, ferreae, Ef.[1] 338, 12; *veru uerba*, uirgae ferrae aelaniorum, Ef.[2] 335, 54; *reustus*, iterum incensus, Cp. R35; Ep. 22A21; Ef.[1] 386, 39. Cf. Wilh. Heraeus, in *Arch. f. L. L.*, x. 522. For *brandas*, see Bosw. T. (*brand*, *brond*, a brand, firebrand).

rex, xxviii. 9, see *Saturnus*.

rheda, see *reda*.

rhetoricam, see *rethorica* sub v. *dialectica*.

rheuma, see *reuma*.

rhinoceros, see *rinocerus*.

rhythmus, see *ridhmus*.

ridhmus, dulcis sermo sine pedibus, xix. 10 (*Job*; *Praef. Hieron.* p. xiv[b], and Migne *P.L.* xxviii col. 1081B *rythmus* [*rhythmus*] ipse dulcis).

rien, lumbis [for lumbus?], xlvi. 5 (*Alia*=*Ars Phocae*, p. 415, 1 hic *rien* rienis).

rigentia, uigentia, xl. 22 (*Uerba*?).

rigor, frigor inflexibilis, xlvii. 3 (*Alia*=?). Cf. *rigor*, a frigore duritia et inflexibilitas, Cp. R197; *rigore*, heardnisse [hardness; see Bosw. T. *heardness*], Cp. R185; *rigore*, heardnissae, Ep. 22C14 & Ef.[1] 387, 14.

rimis, bordremum, xxxix. 21; **rimis**, cinum, xxxix. 39 (*Greg. Dial.* iii. 36 col. 304C *rimis*...patentibus intravit mare). The first gloss occurs also in another MS. (Steinm. *A.H.G.* ii. 246, 45). *Bordremum*, instrum. plur. of *bordrema*, an early spelling of *bordrima* (for *em* changed into *im* cf. A. S. *lempheal*t = *limp*-halt, limping), literally *a board-rim*, from *bord*, a board, plank (Bosw. T.) and *rema*, *rima*, a rim, border, edge, joint (Bosw. T. *rima*). From the same root *rem-* are derived A.S. reōma, and the A.S., Germ. and D. *rand* (cf. Kluge, *Etym. Wrtb.* v. *Rand*). Hence the A.S. *bord-rand* is a variant of *bordrema* (-*rima*). Cf. Steinm. ii. 244, 10. For *cinu*, a chink, fissure, see Bosw. T. (*cīnu*).

rinocerus, naricornu in nari namque cornu habet, xix. 31 (*Job* xxxix. 9 numquid volet *rhinoceros* servire tibi).

risionem, xxxv. 249, see *pompam*.

riui aggerum, congregatio aquarum, xiii. 32; see *aggerem*.

rixa, i. 116, see *seditio*.

rixosa, xii. 29, see *lingua tertia*.

ro' for rae: propositura for praepositura.

rogatio, ii. 99, see *laetania*.

rogus, beel uel aad, xxxv. 158 (*Ruf.* iv. 15 fol. 63[a] extructus est *rogus*). For *beel*=*bǣl*, the fire, flame of a funeral pile, a funeral pile, and *aad*, *ād*, the same, see Bosw. T. (*beel*, *bǣl* and *aad*, *ād*).

roma, xxxv. 242, see *ponte moluio.*

romana, xxxix. 17, see *Sabura*; **romana**, xxxi. 35, see *cimina romana.*

romanis, xxxvi. 1, see *Iani.*

romano, xxxix. 4, see *balneum Ciceronis.*

romanorum, xxxix. 36, see *sex untias.*

romanus, xliii. 20, see *eunuchus.*

rombus, see *porco piscis.*

roscinia, see *ruscinia.*

rostra, xiii. 47, see *plaustrum.*

rotam, xlii. 21, see *basterna.*

rotans, xliv. 29, see *axem.*

rotarum, xxvii *tit.*, see *in libro rotarum.*

rotas, xiii. 47, see *plaustrum.*

rotatio, xxviii. 64, see *epitrocasmos.*

rotis, xxxv. 40, see *troclei.*

rotunditas, xxxv. 220, see *globus.*

rotundum, xxii. 12, see *urna*; xxv. 13, see *in peluem.*

rubea, xiv. 13, see *sinopide.*

rubeum, uuretbaso, xxii. 19 (*Esther* ?not in Vulg., and perhaps merely a further explanation of xxii. 17 and 18 *purpura* and *coccus*, q.v.). uuret-baso literally "ornament-brown," or "artifice-brown," from sb. *wrǣtt* (Bosw. T.), a thing curiously cut, a work of art, jewel, ornament, a derivative of *writan*, to cut, ornament, draw, write + *baso*, brown, purple, scarlet. The colour was artificially produced by the *coccus*, therefore art-brown, or dye-brown; the same colour being also denoted by *weoloc-basu* (q.v.) = whelk-brown (or purple), and *wyrm-basu* (q.v.), worm-brown. Cf. Kluge, *Ang. Les.* 219 (*wrætt*, a trinket, jewel, ornament, and *uuretbaso*, artificial brown); Bosw. T. sub v. *wrætt* (crosswort) wrongly quotes *vermiculum*, warance, wrotte (from Wrt. *Voc.* i. 140. 2), as *vermiculus* in the Vulg. (Exod. xxxv. 25) is the *scarlet worm* (for *coccum*, scarlet colour, Lew. & Sh.).

rubi, see *rubri.*

rubicunda, xxix. 35, see *pisticum.*

rubicundus, xxix. 40, see *ferrugineas.*

rubor, uerecundia, ii. 150 (*Bened. reg.* 73, 17 *rubor* [28 *rubur*] confusionis).

rubras, xvi. 5, see *lentiscus.*

rubri [rubi], xxxv. 90, see *ad ilicem.*

rubro, xi. 13, see *in carcere.*

rubur, see *rubor.*

ruder, mixin, iv. 83 (*Eccl. Ist.*); **ruderibus**, mixinnum, xxxv. 292 (*De Eus.*) = (*Ruf.* x. 7 fol. 163ª purgatis *ruderibus*). For *mixin*, *mixinnum* (instr. plur.), see Bosw. T. (*mixen*, a mixen, dung-heap, also dung); Kluge, *Etym. Wrtb.* (*Mist*).

ruderibus, mixinnum, xxxv. 292, see *ruder.*

rufo, see *prorusu.*

ruinae, ruinas, xlviii. 13, see *cassuae.*

runcina, see *runtina.*

runtina, pidugio uitubil, xiii. 50 (*Isai.* xliv. 13 formavit illud in *runcina*); pidugio for bidugio = bidubium, a bush-hook, see Du C.; cf. Steinm. *A. H. G.* i. 590, 40 ff. (*uidubio*; *bidugio*). For *uitubil* = *uidu-bil*, cf. Bosw. T., *wudubil* (a wood-bill); for *bil* (*bill*) = Germ. *Beil*, D. *bijl*; cf. Kluge, *Et. Wrtb.* (*Beil*).

rupta, xxviii. 20, see *diapsalma.*

ruris, uille, i. 107 (*De Canon.*; *Can. Conc. Neocaes.* lvii Presbyteri *ruris*).

ruscinia, nectigalae, xlvii. 62 (*Alia* = ?) = *roscinia*, naectegale, Cp. R201; *roscinia*, nectaegalae, Ep. 22A27; *roscinia*, necegle, Ef.[1] 386, 45. Cf. *achalantis* uel luscinia uel roscinia nehtęgale, Cp. A121; *a*-, uel luscina uel roscina nctigalae, Ep. 1E6; *a*-, uel luscinia uel roscina nęctęgela Ef.[1] 339, 11. For *ruscinia*, *roscinia* (Fr. *rossignol*), see Körting no. 5751; for *nectigalae* &c. (the nightingale), see Bosw. T. (*nihte-gale*); Skeat, *Conc. Dict.*

rusculum, ruscum, see *auriculum.*

ruscus, cneholen, xlii. 14 (*Ex div. libris*?). **ruscus**, creholegn, xlvii. 103 *Alia* = ?) = *r.*, cnioholen, Cp. R245; *r.*, cnioholaen, Ep. 22C39; *r.*, cniolen, Ef.[1] 387, 38. *Ruscus* (or ruscum) butcher's-broom. For (creholegn, for) *cneholegn* &c. (*knee-holm*, or holly, from *cneōw*, a knee + *holen*, *holegn*, holly, holm), see Bosw. T. (*cneōw-holen*); Oxf. D. (*knee-holly*; *knee-holm*).

russo, see *prorusu.*

rusticatio, cultura terre [-rae], xii. 8 (*Eccles.* vii. 16 non oderis...*rusticationem* creatam ab Altissimo; xxvii. 7 *rusticatio* de ligno ostendit fructum illius).

rusu, see *prorusu.*

rythmus, see *ridhmus.*

s for *x*: asilium (au*x*il-); ausesis (au*x*esis); epizeusis (-xis).—s *dropped* or *omitted*: expectat (ex*s*p-); flore (for flore*s*); plamatio (pla*s*m-); toracina (*sto*racinam).—ss for *st*: suggessionem (for sugges*t*-).

Saba, prouintia [-cia], xix. 25 (*Job* vi. 19 itinera *Saba*).

sabanum, linteum ad balneum, xxxix. 14 (*Greg. Dial.* iii. 17 col. 264ᴬ vestimentis indutum et *sabano* constrictum; iv. 55 col. 417 *sabana* praeberet).

sabbata, xxxix. 52; see *omnes dies*...

sabbati, xxxv. 20, see *magni sabbati.*

sabuli, arene [-nae], xv. 20 (*Ezech.* xlvii. 8 ad tumulos *sabuli* Orientalis).

Sabura, in romana urbe, xxxix. 17 (*Greg. Dial.* iii. 30 col. 288^{A} in regione urbis huius quae *Subura* dicitur).

saburica, dicitur quando mittuntur in nauem quando alia non habent, xlvii. 28 (*Alia*=?) =*saburra*, d. q. lapides et ligna mittunt in n. quae non habent alia honera, Cp. S66 ; Ep. 24A2 ; Ef.[1] 390, 24.

saburra, see *saburica.*

saccelli, correctly for *sacelli* (q.v.).

sacelli, sedes diminitiui, xvii. 6 (*Michaeas*, vi. 11 justificabo...*saccelli* pondera dolosa ; Heyse, in note, also wrongly *sacelli* = [the deceitful weights] of the *bag*). *Sedes* for the A.S. gen. sing. *seádes*, *seódes* from seād, seōd, m., a money-bag, purse, pouch ; cf. Steinm., i. 678. 15 and note 5 ; *id.* iv. 284. 10 and note 5 ; Wright W. *seod*, *seodas*, &c. (in Ind.) ; Bosw. T. (*seād*, *seōd*).

sacerdos, xlvi. 8, see *flamen.*

sacerdotale, xxx. 12, see *iereticos.*

sacerdotes, xxvii. 7, see *luperci.*

sacerdotum, xi. 14, see *poderis.*

sacra, xxvii. 9, see *lupercalia* ; xliii. 29, see *bachus.*

sacrificat, xxxv. 278, see *litat.*

sacrificium, xvi. 24, see *iuge sacrificium.*

sacrilega, sacrilegae, see *sacrilego.*

sacrilego, profano, i. 113 (*De Canon.* ; cf. *Can. Conc. Carth.* xcii *sacrilega* dissensione ; *Decret. Leon.* vi p. 224^{b} *sacrilegae* persuasionis).

sacro tegmini, domini martini, iii. 24 (*De S. Mart. Stor.* = *Sulp. Sev. Dial.* iii. 14, 8 factam *sacro tegmini* sensit iniuriam).

saepe, see *facesso.*

saepius, see *sepius.*

saeuit, see *seuit.*

sagacitas, sagacitate, see *sagatitas.*

sagatitas, inuestigatio uelocitas, ii. 160 (*Bened. reg.* 27, 12 [19] debet...omni *sagacitate*...currere).

saginata, xxiv. 10, see *altilia.*

sago, xv. 18, see *inuoluere.*

sal, xv. 31, see *salinas* ; xxiii. 12, see *memores salis.*

Salamitis, concubina dauid que [quae] ministrabat ei in senectute, x. 24 (*Cant.* vi. 12 Vulg. *Sulamitis* ; Vers. ant. Sab. : *Sunamitis* ; vii. 1 Vulg.: Quid videbis in *Sulamite* ; Vers. ant. Sab. *Solamitide*). The Glossator was evidently thinking of Abisag *Sunamitis*, the concubine of David.

Salamone, viii *tit.*

Salamonis, viii. 9, see *Lamuhel.*

salaria, see *solaria.*

salariis, pecuniis debitis, xxxv. 206 (*Ruf.* viii. 17 fol. 144^{a} *salariis* additis).—**solaria**, onores [hon-], v. 25 (*Eccl. Stor.*) ; **solaria**, munera, xxxv. 253 (*De Eus.*) ; **solaria**, sedes uel loca alta, xxxv. 34 (*De Eus.*), probably all = (*Ruf.* v. 18 fol. 87^{a} qui *salaria* praestat praedicantibus verbum suum), though the latter gloss is apparently explanatory of *solaria* (flat housetops, terraces, balconies), which does not seem to occur in Ruf., though we have rex...in excelso *solario* recubans, ii. 10 fol. 23^{b}. =*salaris* pecunis debitis, Cp. S75 ; Ep. 24C32 ; Ef.[1] 391, 34 (*s.* pecuniis d.). Cf. *simmallis*, salaris pecunis debitis, Cp. S353 ; Ep. 24E36 ; *symmallis*, fallaris pecuniis debitis, Ef.[1] 392, 21.

salice [-ci], x. 10, see *cyprus.*

salices, salhas, xix. 61 (*Job* xl. 17 circumdabunt eum *salices* torrentis). For *salh* = sealh, a willow-tree, E. sallow, sally, see Bosw. T. (*sealh*) ; Kluge, *A. S. Leseb.* 202 ; Steinm. i. 497, 3 ; Skeat, *Dict.* ; cf. *salix*, salh, Cp. S40 ; Ef.[1] 389, 34 ; *salix*, salch, Ep. 23C33.

salici, see *cyprus.*

Salim, ciuitas, xxv. 10 (*Joh.* iii. 23 juxta *Salim*).

salinas, loca ubi sal inuenitur, xv. 31 (*Ezech.* xlvii. 11 in *salinas* dabuntur).

salis, xxiii. 12, see *memores salis.*

saliunca, see *saliuncula.*

saliuncula, erba [herba] medicinalis habens spinas [Cambr. MS. *spicas*] miri odoris crescit in montibus, xiii. 57 (*Isai.* lv. 13 Vulg. & Cambr. MS. *saliunca* ; Migne, *Patr. Lat.* xxix col. 1003^{c}).

salsuginis, xix. 30, see *terra salsuginis.*

saltantium, iv. 81, see *calones.*

salutationes, ii. 58, see *eulogias.*

sancta, xvi. 23, see *agiografa.*—**sancta domini**, primitias uel decimas de oleo et uino, xxi. 18 (*Judith* xi. 12 *sancta Domini* ...quae praecepit Deus non contingi, in frumento, vino et oleo).

Sancti, iii *tit.* ; xxxvii *tit.*

sanctificatus, iv. 86, see *iniciatus.*

sanctiones, iudicationes uel difiniciones [-tiones], i. 122 (*De Canon.* ; *Can. Conc. Carth.* xciii p. 162^{b} quae...frequentibus *sanctionibus* condemnata est).

sanctionibus, see *sanctiones.*

sanctum, iv. 14, see *asitum* ; x. 1, see *osculetur me.*

sanctus, ii. 7, see *alleluia* ; xxvii. 19, see *feriatus* ; xxxv. 50, see *asillum.*

sandalia, calciamenta quę non habent desuper corium, xxi. 10 (*Judith* x. 3 induitque *sandalia* pedibus suis ; xvi. 11 *sandalia* eius) = *sandalia*, calciamenta, Cp. S76 ; *sandalia* (scandalia, Ef., and faintly in Ep.), calciamenta quae non habent desuper corium, Ep. 24C35 ; Ef.[1] 391, 37.

sane, certe, II. 165 (*Bened. reg.* 18, 12 [19] ita *sane*, ut...; cf. 44, 12 note [17]; 48, 30 [53]; 61, 8 [11]). For *sane*, see also (II. 132) *plane*.

sanguessuges, lexas, XLVIII. 51 (*De Cass.*?). *Sanguessuges* [for *sanguisugas* ?] is not found in Cassianus' works, whence it is said to have been extracted. *Lexas* is not marked as A.S. in the Leiden MS., either by the usual v or by a stroke, and Steinm. (*Zeitschr. für d. Alt.* XXXIII p. 248) thinks that it is Med. Lat., not the A.S. *lǣce*, as a Schlettstadt Cassian-Glossary, which, apparently, records the identical gloss, but shows no traces of A.S., has *sanguisuges, lexas egila* (Steinm. *A.H.G.* II. 153, 55). This would, however, be the only instance of *lexas* occurring as Lat. On the other hand, we find *sanguissuga, lœce* (Wright W. 121, 37; 321, 28; 477, 6);' *sanguissuge, lyces* (ibid. 85, 11); *phisillos, leceas* (Cp. P383).

sanguine, VIII. 19, see *si usque ad...*; XVI. 27, see *malefici*.

sanguinis, XXIX. 55, see *emurusem*; XLI. 11, see *sardonix*, 12, see *sardius*.

sanguis, XLVII. 8, see *muscus*.

Sanir, X. 14, see *Amana*.

sannas, see *synicias*.

sanxit, iussit tribuit iudicauit difiniuit [*def-*], I. 125 (*De Canon.*; *Can. Conc. Carth.* v diuina scriptura *sanxit*; *Decret. Caelest.* III *sanxit*) = Ef.[2] 329, 57; cf. *sanxit*, iussit, Cp. S28; *saxit*, tribuit, Cp. S90; Ep. 25E30; Ef.[1] 394, 20.

saphirus, mari similem et quasi aureas stellas habens, XLI. 8 (*De nomin. div.* = *Apoc.* XXI. 19 *saphirus*; see also *Exod.* XXVIII. 18 & XXXIX. 11 *sapphirus*; *Ezek.* XXVIII. 13 id.).

sapiens, IV. 18, see *urbanus*.

sapientes, II. 152, see *senpectas*; XLIV. 9, see *cęlum*.

sapientia, VIII. 1, see *panarethos*; SAPIENTIA, XI *tit.*

sapientiam, I. 110, see *resipiscant*; XXXV. 279, see *oratoriam*.

sapone, VIII. 17, see *nitrum*; see also *uorith*.

saponem, see *herba fullonum*.

sapore [for *sapone*?], XIV. 3, see *uorith*.

saporem [for *saponem*], XVII. 19, see *herba fullonum*.

saporis, X. 17, see *fistola*.

sarabaitarum, see *sarabaite*.

sarabaite, lingua egyptiaca [aeg-] in latinum dicitur rennuite [*renuitae*; see Du C.] qui refutant abbatem habere, II. 161 (*Bened. reg.* 1, 12 [17] genus...*sarabaitarum*, 25 [35] vagi et...deteriores *sarabaitis*).

sarabaitis, see *sarabaite*.

sarabala, see *saraballa*.

saraballa, crura hominum uocant apud caldeos [Chaldaeos], XVI. 11 (*Dan.* III. 94 [27] *sarabala* eorum non fuissent immutata; Sabat., in note, *saraballa*; Heyse, in note, *sarabarae*...inmutatae) = *saraballa*, apud caldeos cura (*crura*) hominum dicuntur, Cp. S74; Ep. 24C34; Ef.[1] 391, 36. The Cambr. MS.: *Sar*, c. h. chaldaice uocantur. Cf. also *sarabare*, braeccę dicitur, Cp. S96; *sarabarę*, braccae lingui persarum, Ep. 25E38; *sarabara*, braccae lingua persarum, Ef.[1] 394, 28. For *saraballa, sarabara, sarabarae* (wide trowsers), cf. Isid. *Etym.* XIX. 23, 2; Lewis & Sh. (*sarabāra*); Gesenius' *Hebr. Lex.* (סַרְבָּלִין); Liddell & Sc. (σαράβᾱρα); Ad. Brüll, *Trachten der Juden*, p. 87 sq., etc. For the Lat. *braeccę, braccae*, trowsers, see Lewis & Sh. (bracae); cf. also Skeat's *Conc. Dict.* (*breeches*).

sarabarae, sarabare, see *saraballa*.

sarculo, see *sarculum*.

sarculum, ferrum fossorium duos dentes habens, XIII. 18 (*Isai.* VII. 25 montes qui in *sarculo* sarrientur).—**sarculum** [sine interpr.], XLVIII. 64 (*De Cass. Inst.* IV. 30, 5 nam *sarculo* deorsum incuruus laxabat holeribus terram).

sardina, see *sardinus*; sardinas, see *giniscula*s.

sardinus, see *sardius*.

sardinus, heringas, XLVII. 74 (*Alia* = ?) = *sardinas*, heringas, Cp. S64 & Ep. 23E32; *sandinas*, heringas, Ef.[1] 390, 15. For (*sardinus*, error for) *sardinas* (acc. pl. of *sardina*) the fish *sardine*, see Lewis & Sh. For *hering* see Bosw. T. (*hæring*).

sardismos, XXVIII. 85, see *figura sardismos*.

sardius, colorem purum sanguinis, XLI. 12 (*De nomin. div.* = *Apoc.* XXI. 20 *sardinus*; for *sardius* see *Exod.* XXVIII. 17, XXXIX. 10, *Ezek.* XXVIII. 13) = *Sardius* colorem purum sanguinis, Cp. S83; Ep. 24E25; Ef.[1] 392, 43.

sardonix, habet colorem sanguinis qui est onichinus [onych-], XLI. 11 (*De nomin. div.* = *Apoc.* XXI. 20 *sardonix*) = *sardonix* habet colorem sanguinis, Cp. S82; Ep. 24E23; Ef.[1] 392, 10. For *onychinus* cf. *Exod.* XXVIII. 20; XXXIX. 13; cf. also *Sper* [Ef.[1] *ser*] qui est onichinus luculentas habet, Cp. S466; Ep. 24E24; Ef.[1] 392, 42.

sarica, see *suricus*.

sarientur, fodientur, XIII. 19 (*Isai.* VII. 25 montes qui in sarculo *sarrientur*; Cambr. MS. *sarcuntur*, fodiuntur).

sarra, see *scina*.

sarre, UII sextarios et u partem, XXXI. 13 (*De ponder.*).

sarrientur, see *sarientur*.

sata idem sunt quod et ephi idest modii III, XXXIII. 15 (*Euch. De pond.*, p. 159, 9 *s.* i. s. quod *oephi &c.*).—**sata** quinquaginta sextarios in liquidis in aridis uero XXUII sata, XXXI. 12 (*De ponder.?*).—**sata** unum et dimedium modium habens, XXXI. 36 (*De ponder.?*). Cf. *sata*, modius et dimedius, Cp. S49; Ep. 23C20; Ef.[1] 389, 21. Cf. Lewis & Sh., in voce *satum*.

satagimus, delibamus [deliberamus] uel cogitamus, I. 132 (*De Canon.*; *Can. Conc. Carth.* LVII p. 155[a] de his, qui infantes baptizati sunt, *satagimus*). Cf. *satagit*, deliberat cogitat uel omnia peragit, Cp. S61.

satiabitur, VIII. 19, see *si usque ad...*

satiantur, VIII. 20, see *offer.*

sationis, seminis, XXXVII. 14 (*S. Aug.?*) =*sationis*, seminis, Cp. S62. Cf. Aug. *Oper. de Gen. ad litt.* (*Summ.* in Zycha's ed. p. 448, 3) ex causali *satione*; Aug. *Quaestt. in Hept.* II. 160 (Exod. 34, 21) *Satione* et messe requiesces? Videtur enim dicere, Tempore *sationis* et messis.

satirum, incubum, XXXVIII. 38 (*Clem. Recognitt.* X. 22 Antiopem Nyctei versus in *satyrum* corrupit).

satrapa, princeps persarum, XVI. 8 (*Dan.* III. 2 ad congregandos *satrapas*; III. 3 congregati sunt *satrapae, &c.*). Cf. *satrapae*, praefecti persarum, Cp. S34.

satrapae, satrapas, see *satrapa*.

satum, see *chatus*.

saturicam [satyr-], XLIII. 26, see *saturicus*.

saturicus [satyr-], qui per saturicam [!] scribsit [scrip-], XLIII. 26 (*De div. nominibus*).

saturnalia, XLIII. 29; see *bachus*.

saturni, XXVIII. 7, see *Tifon*, 23, see *Iouis*.

saturnus, rex grecorum [graec-], XXVIII. 9 (*Lib. Anton.* XLVI col. 159[c] pudeat *Saturni* fugæ). For *saturnus* see also *incuba*.

saturus [for *satyrus*], XLVII. 81, see *incuba*.

satyricam [!], satyricus, see *saturicus*.

satyrum, see *satirum*.

satyrus, see *incuba*.

Saulis, XIII. 26, see *Gabaa*.

sax [A.S. for *six*, or Lat. for *Saxonice?*], XXXI. 6; see *solidos*.

Saxonice?, see *solidos*.

sc for *c*; *scenas*, for cenas (coenas).

scabelli, XXXV. 61, see *exedrę*.

scabros, pisces sunt, XXXVI. 8 (*Oros.* I. 3, 4 lapidum, quos...conchis et ostreis *scabros*).

scafa [scapha], XXXIX. 31, see *carabum*.

scalpantur, XXXVIII. 7, see *columnas uitreas*.

scalpello, see *scalpellum*; *scalpeum*.

scalpellum, see *scalpeum*.

scalpellum, ferrum est quod habent scriptores unde incidunt cartas et pennas acuent [Cambr. MS. *acuunt*] ex altera parte latum sicut graphium, XIV. 20 (*Hier.* XXXVI. 23 scidit illud *scalpello* scribae).—**scalpeum**, boor, XLVIII. 66 (*De Cass. Inst.* VIII. 19, 2 contra calamum...contraue *scalpellum*; id. *Conl.* I. 6, 1 pro *scalpello*).—**scalpellum**, biriis, XLVII. 48 (*Alia* = ?) =*scalpellum*, bor, Cp. S143; *scalpro*, bore, ibid. S136; *scalpellum*, byris, Ep. 23E29; Ef.[1] 390, 12. Cf. *scalprum*, byrs uel þuarm, Cp. S125; *scalprum*, byris uel ut ali thuearm, Ep. 23C21; *scalbrum*, byris uel ut alii duaeram, Ef.[1] 389, 22. Cf. also *scalpellum*, bredisern, Cp. S115; *scalbellum*, br-, Ep. 23A20; *scabellum*, bredisaern, Ef.[1] 388, 33. For *scalpellum* (a small knife, lancet, dim. of *scalprum*), see Körting, 8408; for *biriis* (for biiris, byris?), *byris*, *byrs* (O.H.G. *bursa*), a borer, see Bosw. T. (*byris*); for *boor*, *bor*, *bore* (instr.), a borer, gimlet, id. (*bōr*; so, for short *o*?); Franck, *Woordenb.* (*boren*), for *bred-isern &c.* id. (*brædisen*). Cf. *dasile*, boor, Cp. Int. 89.

scalpeum, boor, XLVIII. 66; see *scalpellum*.

scalpro, scalprum, see *scalpellum*.

scamnis, II. 95, see *in scamnis*.

scandaligeris, scandalizaueris, XII. 2 (*Eccles.* I. 37 non *scandalizeris* in labiis tuis; *ibid.* IX. 5 ne forte *scandalizeris* in decore illius).

scandalizaueris (scandalizeris), XII. 2, see *scandaligeris*.

scandere, ascendere, XLVIII. 43 (*De Cass. Inst.* IV. 8 *scandere*...culmina perfectionis...praeualeat). One MS. has *ascendere* instead of *scandere*; see note 19. Cf. ibid. IV. 43 *scandere* ad perfectionem... praeualeas.

scansio, see *scarpmat*.

scapha, see *carabum*.

scapulare [sine interpret.], II. 154 (*Bened. reg.* 55, 8 [12] sufficere credimus...cucullam...et *scapulare*).

scarpinare, scarpinat, see *scarpmat*.

scarpmat, scribid, XLVII. 39 (*Alia*=?) =*scarpinat*, scripiđ, Cp. S142; *sc-*, scripithaen, Ep. 23E28 and Ef.[1] 390, 11. *Scribid* (*b* perhaps for *p*), *scripiđ*, *scripit*, from A.S. *screpan* (Bosw. T.), to scrape, scratch; *haen* in Ep. & Ef.[1], a hen, points to an omitted *gallina* after the lemma *scarpinat*, which is perhaps corrupt for *scalpurit*, or may be an unrecorded *scarpinare* (to scrape), traces of which Schlutter (*Anglia*, XIX. 474, 5) sees in *scansio* (Cp. S130) for *scarsio* = a roman. *excarptio*; see Körting, *Wörterb.* 3343–3347.

scarsio, see *scarpmat.*

scatentibus, credenti, XXXIV. 48 (*De Cass. Inst.* XII. 27, 3 totum se uel *scatentibus* uermibus uel acutissimis sudibus credat insidere). As none of the words excerpted from Cassianus are glossed by A.S. words in the present Glossary, it would almost seem as if *credenti* were Lat., suggested by *credat insidere*. But we find *scaturirent*, *cridu* (Steinm. *AHG.* I. 298, 30); *scaturit*, *criid* (Cp. S150); *scaturiat*, *criþ* (Napier, OEG. p. 166, 104); *scaturiat* (ebulliat), crið (Napier, 158, 101). Cf. Goetz, VII. 239 (scatens, &c., where Kluge suggests *criendi*, Sievers *stredenti*); Napier, OEG. p. 158 note to 101; Schlutter, in *Anglia* (XXVI. 302), and *Journ. Germ. Phil.* I. 62. The infin. of the A.S. words is *crūdan* (pr. s. *crȳdeþ*, pt. t. *crēad*), to crowd; see Oxf. Dict. (*crowd*, vb.[1]); Skeat, *Conc. D.* (*crowd*).

scedule, carte, XXXIX. 69 (not in Greg. Dial., but, perhaps, *Can. Conc. Afric.* C p. 164 cum lecta fuisset *scheda*).

scelestis, I. 53, see *funestis.*

scema, est figura dictionis in ordine uerborum cum decore conposita, XXVIII. 25 (*Cass. Psalm.* I. 6 *schema* autem est f. d.i.o.u.c.d.c.). See *scema*, figura, Cp. S120; *scema* figura uel parabula, Ep. 23C4 and Ef.[1] 389, 5; *thema*, figura, Cp. T146; Ep. 26E1 and Ef.[1] 395, 49; cf. Schlutter, in *Arch. f. L. L.* X. 198.—**scema**, figura, XXXVIII. 33; see *thema.*

scenas turpes [add *commessationes*], **incesta** coinquinata, XXXV. 166 (*Ruf.* V. 1 fol. 74[a] Thyesteas *coenas* et *incesta* Oedipia perpetrantes).

scenicis, see *scinici.*

scenis, see *scina.*

sceptra, see *sceptrum.*

sceptrum, uirga regalis, XXXV. 152 (*Ruf.* IV. 3 fol. 54[b] in *sceptra* succedit) = *sceptrum*, uirga regalis, Cp. S152.

scheda, see *scedule.*

schema, see *periscema*; *scema.*

schismatici, schismaticis, schismaticorum, see *scismatici.*

schola, see *ludus literarum.*

scholasticus, see *scolasticus.*

scientes, IV. 43, see *gnostici.*

sciiria, see *scina.*

scina, imitatio uel grina [for grima? a mask], XXVII. 5 (*Lib. Rot.*?). *Scina* is an uncertain reading, and may also be read as *sciiria*, or *scuria*. According to the Glossary, the word is excerpted from Isidore's *Liber Rotarum* (= *Lib. de natura rerum*). Steinm. (II. 341, 4) read *Sarra*, and identifies it with *Sirius*, the dog-star (*Lib. de nat. rer.* XXVI. 14 S. stella est, quam vulgo canem appellant. Sirius quippe appellata propter flammae candorem). But another Glossary (Steinm. IV. 335, 2) has *scyna*, imitatio uel grima, and an Ambrosian MS., quoted by Goetz V. 426, 20, has *scina*, imitatio. The gloss appears in Cp. (S137) as *scina*, nititio; Ep. 24E30 & Ef.[1] 392, 15 *scina*, nitatio uel grima; and Ep. 23E26 and Ef.[1] 390, 9 have again *scina*, grima. Glogger adopts the reading *scina*, which he connects with diem...*scenis* et luxuriae sacrauerunt, in Isid. *De Offic.* I. 41, 1. See further Goetz, VII. 241 (*scina*); Heraeus, in *Arch. f. Lat. Lex.* X. 514. For *scina* = *scena*, outward show, see Lew. & Sh. (*scaena*); for *grima*, a mask, spectre, see Bosw. T. in V.

scindaris, scindat, scineoose, XXX. 96, see *ypo* (sub) *tyos* (hoc).

scinici, scinnenas, XXXIX. 55 (not in Greg. Dial., but *Can. Concil. Afr.* XLV p. 150 Vt *scenicis* atque histrionibus... gratia uel reconciliatio non negetur) = *scienices*, scinneras, Cp. S185; *scienicis*, scinneras, Ep. 24E26; *scienicis*, scineras, Ef.[1] 392, 11. *Scinneras* (for *scinnenas*), evil spirits, spectres, magicians, see Bosw. T. (*scīn*, *scinere*, *scinnere*); Kluge, *Altg. Dial.* p. 344; id. *A. S. Leseb.* p. 201 (*scinn*, *scinna*, *scinnere*). Cf. *histriones*, saltatores uel *scenici*, Cp. H95; *emaones*, scinneras, Cp. E170. Lewis & Sh. (*scaena*, *scaenicus*).

scino, scinu, XXX. 96, see *ypo* (sub) *tyos* (hoc) &c.

scira, acurna, XLVII. 88 (*Alia* = ?) = *scirra*, aqueorna, Cp. S170; *scira*, aqueorna, Ep. 23E33; *scira*, aquorna, Ef.[1] 390, 16. *Scira* = *sciurus*, a squirrel; for *ac-urna* &c. see Bosw. T. (*āc-wern*); Kluge, *Wrtb.* (*Eichhorn*).

scirra, see *scira.*

scismatici, dissensatores seperatores [separ-], I. 119 (*De Canon.*; *Can. Conc. Laod.* CXXXVI de *schismaticis*; cum...*schismaticis*; *Can. Conc. Carth.* LXV de...*schismaticorum*...insidiis, LXIX de...*schismaticis*; *Decret. Caelest.* XI ut *schismatici*... accipiant).

scissura, scissuras, XIII. 4, see *fissura.*

scita, idest monita, XXII. 15 (*Esther* III. 8 regis *scita* contemnens).—**scita**, documenta, XLVIII. 42 (*De Cass. Inst.* V. 24 seniorum *scita* discere cupientes).—**scithis**, speciosas, XLII. 15 (*Ex div. libris* = *Sulp.*

Sev. Dial. III. 15, 2 p. 213, 23 puellas *scitis* uultibus coemisse).

scitatum, see *sitatum*.

scithis, speciosas, XLII. 15; see *scita*.

scitis, see *scithis*.

sciurus, see *scira*.

scola [schola], XXXV. 53, see *ludus literarum*.

scolae, see *auditorio*.

scolasticus [sine interpr.], I. 123 (*De Canon.*; *Can. Conc. Sard.* XIII *scholasticus* de foro, aut ex administratione; *Can. Conc. Carth.* XCVII *scholasticos* qui in actu sunt). See *foro*.

scole [-lae], XXXV. 247, see *auditorio*.

scolis, see *sinphosin*.

scopulosus, petra, XXXIV. 15 (*De Cass. Inst.* XI. 3 quidam perniciosissimus *scopulus*).

scopulus, see *scopulosus*.

scorellus, see *scorelus*.

scorelus, emaer, XLVII. 58 (*Alia* = ?) = *s*-, omer, Cp. S166; *s*-, emer, Ep. 23E31 and Ef.[1] 390, 14. Scorelus, also written *scorellus*, is glossed *amore*, Wright W. 260, 27, and clod*hamer*, ib. 287, 17. For *emaer*, *omer*, *emer*, &c. (the yellow bunting or yellow-*hammer*), see Oxf. D. (*hammer*, sb.[2]); Bosw. T. (*omer*); Kluge, *Et. D.* (*Ammer*); Skeat, *Conc. Et. D.* (*yellow-hammer*).

scorpiones, in similitudine cancri cauda longa, XXV. 5 (*Luc.* X. 19 supra serpentes et *scorpiones*).

scribantur, I. 85, see *proscribantur*.

scribitur, XXXIII. 5, see *dedragma*.

scribsit [scripsit], XLIII. 24, see *traicus*, 26, see *saturicus*.

scribta [-pta], XXXVI. 1, see *Iani*.

scribtos [-ptos], XXII. 12, see *urna*.

scribturae [script-], XXX. 37, see *cronographias*.

scribuntur, XXXVII. 9, see *tabulas legat*.

scripsi, XLVIII. 74.

scripsit, XLIII. 23, see *comicus*; see also *scribsit*.

scripta, XXXV. 51, see *gesta*; see also *scribta*; *Iani porte*.

scriptio, XXXIX. 72, see *olografia*.

scriptionem, calcum [=calculum?], IV. 107 (? *Ruf.* VI. 2 fol. 95[b] per *proscriptionem*? Cf. V. 19 fol. 88[b] *subscriptiones*, and VII. 26 fol. 130[a] *subscriptionem*).

scriptis, XXXIII. 7, see *sicel*.

scriptores, XIV. 20, see *scalpellum*; XXVII. 27, see *genthliatici*.

scriptori, XLVIII. 74.

scriptos, see *scribtos*; *urna*.

scriptula, see *dragma*; *sicel*.

scriptulum, see *obulus*.

scriptum, XXXIII. 7, see *sicel*; XXXV. 147, see *petalum*.

scriptura, I. 90, see *philacteria*; XVI. 23, see *agiografa*; XXXIX. 62, see *filacteria*.

scripturae, see *scribturae*.

scripturas, see *caracteries*.

scripturis [for *scripturas*?], XXXIV. 51, see *caracteries*.

scripula, see *dragma*; *sicel*.

scripulum, XXXIII. 27, see *siliquae sex*, 31, see *siliquas sex*; see also *obulus*.

scripulus sex siliquas pensatur, XXXI. 30 (*De ponder.*?).—**scripulus** pensat siliquas sex ab aliquibus fit duo, XXXII. 3 (*De ponder.*?). Cf. Blume, I. 373, 27, and E. *scruple*, a small weight.

scrobis, see *scropis*.

scrofa, see *scrufa*.

scropis, groop, XLVI. 22 (*Alia* = *Ars Phocae*, p. 418, 16 haec *scrobis*). Cf. Kluge, *A. S. Leseb.* p. 181, grōp = groep, grēp; Bosw. T. *grep* [for *grēp*?], a furrow, burrow; O.H.G. *gruoba*, *gruopa*, *cruoba*, *kruopa* (Schade, *Grube*; *Grab*). Schlutter (*Anglia*, XXVI. 302) regards *groop* as a misread or miswritten *groof*, whence he derives E. *groove* (see also Kluge, *Leseb.* p. 181 grōf, *grube*) referring to Steinm. *A.H.G.* I. 449, 3 Latrinas cloacas aqueductus idest *groua*.—But the Glossaries related to the present one all have *p*; see *scrobibus*, groepum, Cp. S181 and Ep. 24C14; *scropibus*, groepum, Ef.[1] 391, 17; *latrina*, genge, *groepe*, [*atque*, for] aquae ductus, cloacas, Cp. L30. *Groop*, dialectically still exists, see Eng. Dial. Dict. (*groop*); Oxf. D. (*groop*); Verdam, *Mid. Woord.* (*groepa*), and differs from E. *groove*, for which see Oxf. D.; Skeat, *Conc. Et. Dict.*; Verdam, *l.c.* (*groeve*).

scrufa, sugu, XLVII. 93 (*Alia* = ?) = *scrofa*, sugu, Cp. S172 & Ep. 23E34; *scrofa*, ruga, Ef.[1] 390, 17. Scrufa = *scrofa*, a breeding-sow; for A.S. *sugu*, a sow, see Bosw. T. (in v.), and Kluge, *Etym. Wrtb.* (*Sau*).

scrupeas, dubitationes, XXXVIII. 23 (*Clem. Recognitt.* VIII. 61 isti per devia incedentes et *scrupeas* verborum difficultates).

scrupolositas, dubietas uel anxietas uel animi molestia, II. 153 (*Bened. reg.* 40, 3 [4] cum aliqua *scrupulositate*). See also *scrupulum*.

scrupula, XXXIII. 7, see *sicel*.

scrupule [scrupulum], XXXIII. 8, see *obulus*.

scrupulos, XXXII. 7, see *acitabulus*, 8, see *cotule*, 9, see *mina*; XXXIII. 4, see *dragma*; see also *libra*.

scrupulositas, scrupulositate, see *scrupolositas.*

scrupulum, axietas [anxietas] angor molestia, I. 133 (*De Canon.*; *Can. Conc. Carth.* LXXII absque ullo *scrupulo*; CXXVI si...aliquo mortis periculoso *scrupulo* compuncta fuerit; CXXXII *scrupulo*...conscientiæ). See also *scrupolositas.* For scrupulum, see also *obulus.*

scrupulus, XXXII. 7, see *acitabulus.* See also *scripulus* (for *scrup-*).

sculpentur, see *columnas uitreas.*

scupulos [*scrupulos*], XXXII. 11, see *libra.*

scuria, see *scina.*

scuriosa, sordida, XXXV. 225 (*Ruf.* XI. 23 fol. 187[a] vetustas *curiosa*; so also Cacciari II. p. 100. *scuriosa* (for *scoriosa*?) may have been another reading) = *scuriora*, sordida, Cp. S118; Ep. 23A34; Ef.[1] 388, 47; see Goetz, VII. 243 (*scoriosa*).

scurra, scurrax, scurrus? see *histrio.*

scutorum, see *portarum.*

scylla, see *uertigo.*

scyna, see *scina.*

se, II. 60; XXI. 19; XLIV. 26, 27.

secel, see *sicel.*

secet, XXX. 95, see *ypo* (sub) *tyos* (hoc) &c.

secretalem, penetrabiliorem occultiorem, I. 128 (*Def. fid. Calch.*, ap. Mans. VII col. 752[b] *secretalem* incarnationem, 754[b] substantiam *secretalem*).

secta, heresis [haeresis] insecutio, I. 121 (*De Canon.*; *Can. Conc. Calch.* XIV uxorem *sectae* alterius accipere; *Can. Conc. Carth.* LVII eiusdem *sectae* clerici) = *secta*, heresis, Cp. S210.

secta, XXVII. 28, see *uia secta.*

sectura [for secutura?], XXXV. 67, see *cissura.*

secularem, see *oratoriam.*

seculares, XXXV. 184, see *liberales litera.*

seculariam [-rem], XXXV. 279, see *oratoriam.*

secularium, XXIX. 12, see *comicus.*

secunda, II. 52, see *deuteronomii*; XXX. 22, see *deuterosin.*—**secunda**, prospera, XXVII. 18 (*Lib. Rot.* = *Isid. Lib. de nat. rer.* XXVI. 13 prout cuique sunt motus, ita *secunda* vel aduersa portendere).—**secunda**, prospera, XXXIV. 16 (*De Cass. Inst.* XI. 3 *secundo* nauigantibus uento; XI. 11 rerum *secundarum*...successus).

secundo, see *secunda.*

secundum, XIII. 25, see *de radice*; XXX. 44, see *cata manthan*; XXXIX. 68, see *catalocum*; XLIV. 11, see *clima*; SECUNDUM, XXXIII *tit.*

secundus, XLIV. 16, see *antarticus.*

secuntur [wrongly for *ponuntur*], XXVIII. 72, see *anaphora.*

securem, XXXV. 60, see *bibennem.*

securis, IV. 120, see *bibennem.*

secus contra difinita, aliter prope, I. 117 (*De Canon.*; *Can. Conc. Antioch.* XCVII si *secus contra definita* factum fuerit). Cf. *secus*, aliter, Cp. S257.

secutura, see *cissura.*

secuturę [-rae], XXVIII. 72, see *anaphora.*

sed, XIX. 8; XXXV. 210; XLIV. 29.

sedecenalem [-cennalem], XXX. 52, see *ex ca.*

sedecim, I. 115, see *sescopla*; XXXV. 210, see *sexcuplum.*

sedem, I. 6, see *absidam*; XXXIX. 56, see *ante absida.*

sedent, XV. 9, see *transtra.*

sedes, XXXV. 34, see *solaria*; for A.S. *seðdes*, XVII. 6; see *sacelli.*

sedet, XV. 29, see *thalamus.*

seditio, rixa tumultus, I. 116 (*De Canon.*; *Can. Conc. Ancyr.* XXXVII *seditiones*...excitando; *Can. Conc. Nic.* XV propter *seditiones*; *Can. Conc. Carth.* LXXIV *seditionibus*). Cf. tumultus, seditio, Cp. T343.

seditiones, seditionibus, see *seditio.*

seduforum [pseudoforum], III. 21, see *ad seduforum.*

seduxit, XII. 4, see *inplanauit.*

sella, XV. 43, see *puluillos.*

semel, XLIV. 9, see *cęlum.*

semeuncias, XXXIII. 5, see *dedragma.*

semi, I. 115 (bis; semi dupla; semi tripla); see *sescopla.*

semiduplum, XXXV. 210, see *sexcuplum.*

seminis, XXXVII. 14, see *sationis*; XLV. 10, see *gyt.*

seminon, honestorum conuenticulum, XXXV. 302 (*Ruf.* II. 17 fol. 27[a] σεμνεῖον...in nostra lingua significare potest *honestorum conuenticulum*).

semis, XXXII. 7, see *acitabulus*; see also *talentum.*

semiuir, eunuchus, XLVI. 17 (*Alia* = *Ars Phocae*, p. 416, 3 hic *semivir*).

semiuncia, III pensat, XXXIII. 22 (*Euch. De pond.*?); see also (XXXIII. 2) *mina.*

semiunciam, XXXII. 9, see *mina.*

semiustae, see *amazones.*

semiuste [-tae], XXXVI. 15, see *amazones.*

sempectas, see *senpectas.*

semper, II. 28; XIII. 48; XXII. 16; XXIV. 8; XXVIII. 32, 34, 85; XLII. 21; XLIV. 10.

semuncia, see *dedragma*; *mina.*

senator, XXXV. 272, see *patricius.*—**senatores**, iudices, XXIII. 16 (*Esdras*? not in the Vulg., but cum *senatoribus* Prov. XXXI. 23, and *senatores* et judices Dan. vi. 7. In 1 Esdras III. 12 and VI. 14 occur *seniores*).

senecias, senecio, see *synicias.*

senectute, X. 24, see *Salamitis.*

senes, xl. 16, see *ollitani*; see also *ypo* (sub) *tyos* (hoc).

senior, xxxix. 35, see *iuuenior*.

seniores, ii. 152, see *senpectas*; see also *senatores*.

seniscatas, v. 27, see *sinisactas*.

senium, munuscula, iii. 18 (*Sulp. Sev. Dial.* ii. 12, 6 *xenium* transmisit...; *xenium*...accepit).

senpectas, sapientes uel seniores pectore, ii. 152 (*Bened. reg.* 27, 6 inmittere *senpectas*, id est seniores sapientes fratres; and, *in note*, four MSS.: *senpectas* id est *sympaectas*; [7] *senpectas*, *sinpectas*, *sempectas*; cf. Woelfflin, in Praef. xi and in *Arch. f. Lat. Lexic.* x. 550).

sensu, xxviii. 47, see *parenthesin*.

sensus, xxix. 2, see *anagogen*; xxx. 9, see *peridion*, 30, see *phraysi*.

sententia, xxviii. 45, see *zeuma*, 51, see *hyperthesis*.

sententiae, see *sententie*.

sententiam, xxviii. 61, see *amphibolia*, 67, see *anastrophe*.

sententie [-tiae], xxviii. 47, see *parenthesin*.

sentina, dicitur ubi multe [-tae] aquę [-uae] fiunt collecte [-tae] in naui, xxxix. 50 (*Greg.* [not *Dial.*, but] *Reg. Past.* iii. 33 col. 116A hoc agit *sentina* latenter excrescens).

senuerunt, xxxv. 93, see *moluerunt*.

separantur, xlii. 1, see *excipiuntur*.

separatio, see *discretio*.

separatione, xxi. 19, see *in anathema*.

separatis, see *priuatis*.

separatores, see *scismatici*.

separetur, ii. 155, see *suspendatur*.

sepe, xvi. 27, see *malefici*.

sepe [saepe], xliii. 52, see *facesso*.

sepeliunt, xv. 24, see *pollinctores*.

sepelleum, see *aspeleo*.

seperatio [separ-], ii. 44, see *discretio*.

seperatis [separ-], ii. 136, see *priuatis*.

seperatores [separ-], i. 119, see *scismatici*.

sepius [saep-], xliv. 11, see *clima*.

seplum, see *sescuplum*.

septem, ii. 69, see *eptaticum*; xxxi. 9, see *comor*.

septemplici, v. 8, see *auo*.

septenarium, ii. 69, see *eptaticum*.

septentrio, xix. 33, see *arcturum*.

septentrionalis, xliv. 12, see *clima*, 28, see *extremi*.

septimanę, xxxix. 52, see *omnes dies*.

sepulcrum, iii. 58, see *memoria*.

sepulture [-rae], i. 24, see *cymiteria*; xxxv. 237, see *coementeria*.

sepultus, viii. 8, see *in aceruo m-*.

sequentes, xxii. 9, see *pedisequas*.

sequitur, xxx. 16, see *ho platon*.

sequor, xxxiii. 16, see *gomor*.

sera, see *pessul*.

seres, otiosus, xlvi. 20 (*Alia* = *Ars Phocae*, p. 417, 27 *reses* residis, *deses* desidis). Cf. *reses*, resides, Cp. R81; Ep. 22C37; Ef.[1] 387, 36.

sericus, see *suricus*.

series, xxxiv. 20, see *catalogum*.

sermo, xvi. 27, see *malefici*; xix. 10, see *ridhmus*.

sermocinatione, see *uerbi gratione*.

sermonem, xxviii. 68, see *anadiplosis*.

sermonis, xvi. 15 (bis), see *ab exitu sermonis*; xxviii. 75, see *prolemsis*.

sermonum, xxviii. 20, see *diapsalma*; SERMONUM, ii *tit.*, see *interpretatio*.

sermotinatione [sermocin-], ii. 171, see *uerbigratione*.

serpens, xxiii. 1, see *exedra*.

serpentem, xi. 10, see *signum*.

serpentes, xxiii. 1, see *exedra*.

serra, serris, xiii. 36, see *in serris*.

seruorum, xxxv. 71, see *calonum*.

seruum [?], xxix. 18, see *flacidium*.

sescopla, semi dupla uel semi tripla uel sedecim (!) pro uno, i. 115 (*De Canon.*; *Can. Conc. Nic.* xvii hemiolia, id est *sescupla* exigens; *Can. Conc. Laod.* cviii quae dicuntur *sescupla*, id est et summam capitis, et dimidium summae percipere).—**sescuplum**, dridehalpf, v. 30 (*Eccl. Stor.*); **sexcuplum**, sedecim pro uno sed semiduplum puto, xxxv. 210 (*De Euseb.*) = (*Ruf.* x. 6 fol. 162b *sesquiplum*, vel...duplum recipi; Cacciari, ii. 16: *sexcuplum*, and in note: *sesquiplum* and *seplum*); dridehalpf = ðriddehalf (here, perhaps, the third half = one and a half); see Bosw. T. (*þridda* and *healf*).

sescupla, see *sescopla*.

sescuplum, dridehalpf, v. 30; see *sescopla*.

sesquiplum, see *sexcuplum*, sub v. *sescopla*.

sessionibus, xvi. 18, see *trieres*.

seuit, glimith, xlii. 10 (*Ex div. libris* = *Sulp. Sev. Dial.* i. 14 p. 167, 5 cui mite est omne quod *saeuit*; ibid. iii. 16, p. 214, 25 *saeuit* in clericos). Schlutter (*Anglia*, xix. p. 465) suggests *grimith* for *glimith*; cf. Bosw. T. *grimman*.

sex, i. 95, see *portentuose*; xxxi. 30, see *scripulus*, 33, see *mina*; xxxii. 3, see *scripulus*; xxxiii. 27, see *siliquae sex*, 31, see *siliquas sex*; xxxv. 31, see *legio*, 250, see *in exameron*; xxxix. 36, see *sex untias*.

sexcuplum, sedecim pro uno sed semiduplum puto, xxxv. 210; see *sescopla*.

sexta, xxxi. 21, see *cathos*.

sextarii, xxxi. 9, see *comor*, 11, see *ephi*, 21, see *cathos*.

sextariis [-rius?], xxxiii. 19, see *nebel*.
sextarios, xxxi. 2, see *modicus*, 9, see *comor*, 11, see *ephi*, 12, see *sata*, 13, see *sarre*, 14, see *hin*; xxxiii. 13, see *metreta*, 16 (bis), see *gomor*, 17, see *hin*; see also *abattidis*.
sextarium, xxxi. 10, see *Aquila* dixit, in voce *sextarius*.
sextarius autem duo libra et dimedium, xxxi. 3 (*De ponder.*?).—**sextarius** iiii libras pensat, xxxi. 31 (*De ponder.*?).—**sextarius** Grece duas libras et dimidium pensat, xxxi. 32 (*De ponder.*?).—**sextarius**, libras iiii, xxxiii. 26 (*Euch.*, *De pond.*?).—Aquila dixit **sextarium** iii modios, xxxi. 10 (*De ponder.*?). On the *sextarius* cf. Blume, i. 375, 5 sq. For *sextarius* see also ii. 86, *himina*; xxxi. 8, *emina*, 35, *cimina*; xxxiii. 24, *urbicus*.
sexum, see *sexus*.
sex untias [uncias] mediam partem unius uille &c., xxxix. 36; see *uncia*.
sexus, natura, i. 30 (*De Canon.*; *Can. Conc. Carth.* lxii nec *sexum* excusandum esse, cxxxviii p. 174[b] propter *sexus*). For *sexus* see also (xlii. 13) *hermofroditus*.
si, ii. 182; viii. 17, 19 (bis); xxiii. 1; xxxix. 15; xliv. 11, 15.
si quo minus, alioquin, ii. 158 (*Bened. reg.*?). This expression (for which see Souter, *Study of Ambrosiaster*, pp. 75, 76), which does not seem to occur in the *Reg. Bened.*, is here, perhaps, a further explanation of (ii. 157) *sin alias* (q.v.).
si usque ad lacum fuerit, idest si stagnum faciat de sanguine non satiabitur, viii. 19 (*Salam.* xxviii. 17 Hominem qui calumniatur animae sanguinem, *si usque ad lacum fugerit* [Heyse *fuerit*, in note] nemo sustinet).
sibi, xxxvii. 19, see *laurus*; xliv. 17, see *cous*, 25, see *dextera*.
sic, x. 12; xi. 4; xv. 35; xx. 8; xxiv. 13; xxxii. 1, 2 (bis), 5.
sicarii, gladiatores, iv. 19 (*Ruf.* ii. 20 fol. 29[b] *sicarii* plebibus admixti). Cf. *sicarius*, gladiator, Cp. S335; Ep. 23E17; Ef.[1] 389, 57.
siccans, xvii. 1, see *area sitiens*.
siccant, xiv. 3, see *uorith*.
siccate [-tae], xxix. 13, see *frixi ciceris*.
sicel qui latine lingue corruptę siclos dicitur in questionibus supra scriptis uncia pondus habet ut alibi scriptum repperi scrupula x quod ipse arbitror Nam siclus ipse uel sicel de propinquitate ponderis quasi siclus sonat, xxxiii. 7 (*De pond.*, *Euch.* p. 158, 15 *secel* q. in *Latina lingua corrupte siclus* [Mus. M. siclos] d. ut in quaestionibus supradictis indicatur unciae p.h., u.a.s.r. *scriptula* [Mus. M. scripula] decem q. et ipse a. [Mus. MS. adds qf sil lx] n.s.i.u. *secel* de p.p.q. *sicilicus* s.). The Brit. Mus. adds after sonat: Habet autem secel xx obolos; see also *siclus*.
sicera, est omnis potio que extra uinum inebriare potest cuius licet nomen hebreum [hebraeum] sit tamen latinum sonat pro eo quod ex suco frumentorum et pomorum conficitur, i. 111 (*De Canon.*; *Can. Apostt.* iii offerat...pro vino *siceram*) = *sicera* (dicitur, Ep. & Ef.), omnis potio quo (que, Ef.) inebriari potest excepto uino, Cp. S351; Ep. 24E27; Ef.[1] 392, 12. Cf. *sicera*, qui (quod, Ep.) fit dactylo (dactyli, Ep., Ef.) sucus, Cp. S350; Ep. 24E21; Ef.[1] 392, 8; Isid. *Etym.* xx. 3. 16; Eucher. *Instr.* p. 121, 12; 148, 16.
siceram, see *sicera*.
sicilicus, see *sicel*.
siclos, xxxiii. 7, see *sicel*.
siclus, xxxiii. 7 (bis), see *sicel*, 8, see *obulus*.
siclus lxxii siliquas, xxxi. 15 (*De ponder.*?). Cf. Lewis & Short, in v., and Isid. *Orig.* xvi. 25, 18; cf. above, *sicel*.
sicunia, gibreci, xlvii. 30 (*Alia* = ?). As *gebrec* interprets *pituita* in Cp. P398; Ep. 19C5 (*p*-, gibrec); Ef.[1] 380, 55 (*p*-, gibreec), also *reuma* in Cp. R58 (*r*-, gebrec); Ep. 22A26 (*r*-, gibrec); Ef.[1] 386, 44 (*r*-, gebrec), and *umecta*, Cp. U246 (*u*-, gibrec; and below xxiv. 3 *u*-, gebyraec), it seems that *sicunia*, of which there is no trace elsewhere, is a misread *reuma* (= rheuma), a flow, catarrh, rheum, *si* being a misread A.S. *r* (ɲ) and *ni* for *m*. The A.S. *gibreci*, *gebrec*, *gibrec*, *gebyraec*, &c., quoted above, are all substt., derived from *brecan*, to break; (1) those which interpret *reuma* (*rheuma*), and *pituita* refer to the *noise* of coughing, and hence the Glossaries also explain the Lat. *fragor* (a crash, noise, from *frangere*, to break) by the same word, see Wright W. 404, 17; 400, 17 (fragore, gebrece, instr.), while (2) those which interpret *umecta* refer to the *broken* (unsafe) state of marshy ground, *brook*-land (= A.S. brōc, E. *brook*, a small stream; Du. *broek*; G. *Bruch*, a marsh); cf. Kluge, *Wrtb.* (*Bruch*[2]); Franck (*Broek*).
sicut, ii. 170; viii. 9; x. 10, 21; xii. 9; xiii. 59; xiv. 6, 9 (bis), 19, 20; xvi. 4; xxii. 12; xxviii. 57; xxxv. 26, 181; xxxviii. 5; xxxix. 51; xliii. 16; xliv. 27; xlviii. 74.
sicuti, ii. 184, see *uti*.
sideralem, xxvii. 10, see *zoziacum*.
sideralis, xliv. 23, see *zodiacus*.
siderum, xxx. 51, see *astronomia*.
Sidon, ciuitas, xxiv. 15 (*Math.* xi. 21, 22 & xv. 21); see *Tyrus*.

sidonicis, hospicia pauperum, XLI. 3 (*De div. nomin.?*). This gloss seems to be the same as Cp. S728 *synodicus* (Ep. 24E33 *synodiciis*; Ef.[1] 392, 18 *synnodicis*) susceptionibus peregrinorum, and to point, as its source, to *Can. Conc. Calch.* VIII p. 135[a] Clerici qui praeficiuntur *ptochiis*; with traces, perhaps, in the first part of the lemma, of *xenodochiorum*, which occurs ibid. *Can.* X. Cf. *xenodociorum*, collectionum, Cp. X1 *xenodochia*, susceptio peregrinorum, & ib. X2, and the present Glossary XXXIX. 58, 59.

Sieres, see *Syeres*.

signa, III. 51, see *stigmata*; XXXV. 126, see *tropia*.

signatore, IV. 119, see *antesignato*.

significans, XXVIII. 39, see *allegoria*.

significantes, XXI. 5, see *cum coronis*.

significantiam, see *silemsis*.

significat, X. 11, see *tigna*.

significationem, XXVIII. 40, see *silemsis*.

signis, XL. 21, see *liniamentis*.

signo, XLI. 21, see *obfirmantes*; XLII. 22, see *typo*.

signum, I. 118, see *simbulum*; VIII. 6, see *fornicem*.—**signum habentes**, serpentem aeneum, XI. 10 (*Sap.* XVI. 6 *signum habentes* salutis. For the gloss cf. *Num.* XXI. 9).

silemsis, quoties casus discrepantes in unam significationem congregamus, XXVIII. 40 (*Cass. Psalm.* VIII. 1 figura...*syllepsis* q. c. d. i. u. significantiam c.).

siler, see *liser*.

siliqua, XXXI. 16, see *regalis*.

siliqua una IIII grana ordei pensat, XXXIII. 25 (*Euch. De Pond.?*).—**siliquae sex**, scripulum unum, XXXIII. 27 (*Euch. De Pond.?*).—**siliquae tres** argenteos solidum faciunt, XXXIII. 30 (*Euch. De Pond.?*).—**siliquas sex**, scripulum unum pensant. finit, XXXIII. 31 (*Euch. De Pond.?*).—**siliquas** argeos idest pendicum, XXXI. 23 (*De Ponder.*).—**de siliquis**, fructus arboris colligitur porcis, XXV. 6 (*Luc.* XV. 16 implere ventrem suum *de siliquis*, quas porci manducant).—For siliquas, see also XXXI. 15 (*siclus*), 18, 19 (*obolus*), 22 (*Epiphanius*), 29 (*solidus*), 30 (*scripulus*), 34 (*statera*); XXXII. 1 (*dragma*), 3 (*scripulus*), 4 (*obolus*, bis), 5 (*uncia*); XXXIII. 8 (*obulus*), 29 (*obolus*).

siliquae, siliquas, see *siliqua*.

siliquis, XXV. 6, see *de siliquis*, sub v. *siliqua*.

Silla, consul, XLIII. 33 (*De div. nominibus* = Donati *Ars grammat.* p. 378, 1 *Sylla*).

sillogismus, questio [quaestio] ineuitabilis, XXXIV. 44 (*De Cass. Inst.* XII. 19 *syllogismis* dialecticis; in note *sillogismis*). Cf. *sillogismo*, inebitabile, Cp. Int. 309. For *sillogismus* [syll-], see also (XXVIII. 84) *hypotheticus*.

siloam, stagnum, XXIX. 36 (*Uerb. Interpr.* = *Hier. in Matth.* XXIII. 35, 36 col. 174[A] Siloam ducunt).

siluae, see *Armenias*.

siluaticus, XIX. 24, see *onager*.

silue [-uae], XXXVI. 2, see *Armenias*.

siluę, XIII. 43, see *lamia*.

simbolum, see *simbulis*.

simbulion, pactum, V. 29; see *simbulis*.

simbulis, consiliis conpactis, V. 28 (*Ruf.* VIII. 17 fol. 144[a] diuinationibus ac *symbolis* adquiesceret).—**simbulion**, pactum, V. 29 (? *Ruf.* ?). This seems a further explanation of V. 28. According to Glogger a Bern MS. has *simbulon*, compactum.—**simbulum**, graece latine signum uel cognitio, I. 118 (*De Canon.*; *Can. Conc. Laod.* CX hi...nostrae doceantur fidei *symbolum*; *Can. Conc. Carth.* CXXXVII Huic *symbolo* fidei). Cf. *simbulum*, herebenc, Cp. S373; *symbulum*, herebæcun, id. S721; *simbulum*, herebaecon, Ep. 24A8; *symbulum*, herebecon, Ef.[1] 390, 30; *simbolum*, conlatum uel confessio, Ef.[2] 332, 29. For A.S. *herebenc* (for *herebecn*) &c., a military ensign, standard, see Bosw. T. (*herebēacen*; from *here*, an army + *bēacen*, a beacon, sign).

simcosion [for *symposium*], XXX. 80; see *et simcosion*.

simila, smetuma, XXVI. 7 (*Isid. Offic.* I. 18, 5 nec corpus Domini potest esse *simila* sola). For *simila*, see also (XIV. 5) *placentas*. For *smetuma* = *smeoduma*, *smedema*, *smeodema* &c. (fine flour, meal), see Bosw. T. (*smedema*).

similaginem, genus tritici, XII. 36 (*Eccles.* XXXV. 4 qui offert *similaginem*) = Cp. S363. Cf. Steinm. *A. H. G.* I. 561 note 2.

simile, XXXVII. 5, see *capsaces*.

similem, XLI. 8, see *saphirus*.

similes, XIII. 43, see *lamia*; XXXIX. 43, see *duas coronas*.

simili, XXXVIII. 7, see *columnas uitreas*.

similis, X. 10, see *cyprus*, 20, see *cassia*; XIX. 8, see *murenula*; XXI. 13, see *ascopa*; XXIX. 38, see *hyinę*; XLII. 21, see *basterna*; XLVII. 89, see *bulinus*.

similiter, XIII. 22, see *calanan*.

similitudine, XIII. 3, see *uermiculus*, 6, see *lunulas*, 37, see *malus nauis*, 58, see *in lecticis*; XXI. 16, see *conopeum*, 20, see *labastes*; XXV. 5, see *scorpiones*; XXVII. 16, see *hyadas*.

similitudinem, III. 21, see *ad seduforum*; XIII. 47, see *plaustrum*; XXIV. 1, see *fiole*; XXV. 15, see *hysopo*; XXX. 80, see *et simco-*

sion; XLIII. 46, see *piraondes*; see also *sinphosin*.

simphosium, see *sinphosin*.

simplex, aenli, XLVI. 39 (*Alia = Ars Phocae*, p. 421, 2 *simplex*). Cf. *bilex*. For *aenli* (simple, 'singular, only) see Bosw. T. (*ǣnlīc*, *ānlīc*).

simposium, see *et simcosion*, sub v. *sinphosin*.

simul, XXXV. 193, see *contribulibus*.

simultantem, contentionem, XXXV. 182 (*Ruf.* VI. 10 fol. 101[b] inimicitiam *simultatemque* uidetur inferre).

simultatem, see *simultantem*.

sin, II. 157 (bis).

sinagogae [syn-], IV. 27, see *ariopagitis*.

sin alias, sin aliter, II. 157 (*Bened. reg.* 2, 41 [60] *sin alias*; 60, 9 [13] id.).

sinastrismus, quę uno tractu atque circuitu cremina multa concludit, XXVIII. 77 (*Cass. Psalm.* XXXV. 4 *synathroismos*, quae uno t. a. c. crimina m. c.—Cf. XXX. 27 *synatroesmos*, Latine congregatio, ubi in unum, aut multa crimina, aut multa beneficia colliguntur).—**sinatrismos**, congregatio quoties multa in unum colliguntur, XXVIII. 63 (*Cass. Psalm.* XXII. 1 *synathroismos*...c. q. m. i. u. c. See also XI. 1 per figuram *synathroesmos*).

sinaxis, solemnitas uespertinorum uel collectio coadunatio, II. 151 (*Bened. reg.* 17, 14 [22] Vespertina *synaxis* quattuor psalmis...terminetur).—**sinaxeos**, celebrationes, XLVIII. 68 (*De Cass.*).—**synaxeos cura** [sine interpret.], XLVIII. 41 (*De Cass.*) = (*De Cass. Inst.* II. 17 cui...*synaxeos cura* committitur; II. 11, 2 ad finem *synaxeos*...; fastidium *synaxeos*). According to a St Gallen MS. the interpretation, which is wanting here, is: curae uel celebrationes, for which see also the preceding gloss. Cf. *Inst.* II. 10, 1 sollemnitates quas illi *synaxis* (al. *sinaxes*) uocant; III. 5, 1 *synaxin*; IV. 16, 1 in *synaxi*; IV. 16, 2 dimissa *synaxi*.

sincera, integra, II. 166 (*Bened. reg.* 72, 11 [18] abbatem...*sincera*...caritate diligant).

sinceritas, integritas, I. 131 (*De Canon.*; *Can. Conc. Carth.* LVI p. 154[a] cum approbauerit vestra *sinceritas*; XCIII p. 162[a] *sinceritas* Catholica).

sinchrisis, est cum causam suam quis aduersariis nititur efficere meliorem, XXVIII. 70; see *syncrisis*.

sinchronon, unius temporis, XV. 32 (*S. Hier. in* XII *Prophetas Praef.* Osee *synchronon* Isaiae). The Cambr. MS. has: *Syncronon* unius t. vel contemporaneus.

sincopin, defectio stomachi, XXXIX. 47 (*Greg. Dial.* III. 33 col. 297[B] quam... molestiam...*syncopin* vocant).

sindetus, ligaturas, XXXVIII. 36 (*Clem. Recognitt.* X. 11 quia in his omnibus aliquis aut *asyndetus* fuit cum malo, aut invisibilis; Migne, in note col. 1426, *syndetus*). Glogger would read *ligatus* for *ligaturas*, as two MSS. have *ligaturus*.

sine, II. 172; VIII. 7; XI. 4, 13; XII. 13, 34; XV. 7; XVI. 5 (with accus.); XIX. 10; XXXV. 189, 217; XXXVIII. 19.

sinecdochen, a toto partem, XXVIII. 41 (*Cass. Psalm.* IX. 1 Usus Scripturarum est per *synecdochen* figuram, quae significat a toto partem, dicere omnia; see also XXI praef.).

sinefactas, pudicas uel abstinentes, XXXV. 38; see *sinisactas*.

singula, XXVIII. 31, see *ausesis*.

singularibus, XXX. 43, see *de monogamia*.

singularis, II. 107, see *monachus*; XXXIX. 44, see *glebum*.

singulis, XXVIII. 24, see *ypozeuxis*.

sinisactas, sociatrices, XXXV. 283 (*De Euseb.*).—**sinefactas**, pudicas uel abstinentes, XXXV. 38 (*De Euseb.*) = *synefactas*, puplicas, Cp. S710; Ep. 23A32; *synefactas*, publicas, Ef.[1] 388, 45; *synesactas*, pudicas, Cp. S711; *synesactas*, pudicas uel abstinentes, Ep. 23A36; *synefactas*, p. u. a., Ef.[1] 388, 49, 50; *sonisactas*, sociatrices, Cp. S395, Ep. 23A31; Ef.[1] 388, 44.—**sinisascas**, sociatrices, IV. 103 (*Eccl. Istor.*).—**siniscas** uel **seniscatas** [sine interpret., but a St Gallen MS. has as gloss *sociatrices*], V. 27 (*Eccl. Storia*) all = (*Ruf.* VII. 26 fol. 128[b] De mulieribus...quas συνεισάκτους appellant).

sinisascas, sociatrices, IV. 103, see *sinisactas*.

siniscas uel **seniscatas**, V. 27, see *sinisactas*.

sinoktezetnyaton, see *cinticta*.

sinopide, petra rubea unde pingent [-gunt], XIV. 13 (*Hier.* XXII. 14 pingitque *sinopide*). Cf. *sinopede*, redestan, Cp. S365.

sinpectas, see *senpectas*.

sinphosin, iterarium [itiner-] uel uiarum [uiaticum?], XXX. 71; **otheporicon**, itenerarium, XXX. 72 (*Cat. Hier.* LXXX col. 687[B] Habemus ejus *Symposium*, quod adolescentulus scripsit; ὁδοιπορικὸν de Africa usque Nicomediam; B: Hab. e. *simphosium* idest *similitudinem* quem adol. scripsit *in scolis Affrice* et *odeporicon* idest *viaticum*, vel itinera de affrica vsque in nicomediam; C: Hab. e. *symposium* quod ad. scripsit africe et *hodiporitum* de af. usque in conmediam). From these readings it seems clear that the gloss to *symposium* is omitted in the present Glossary, but the reading of text B shows that it had been glossed in some text by *similitudinem*, therefore = *synfosion*, similitudinem, Cp. S722; *synfosio*, similitudinem, Ep. 24E11; *symfosion*, similitudinem, Ef.[1] 391, 52, and also in the present Glossary **et simcosion**, similitudinem, xxx. 80 (= *Cat. Hier.* lxxxiii col. 691A confecit = *et symposium* [Gr. text καὶ συμπόσιον] decem virginum; B: confecit...*et simphosium* idest similitudinem decem virginum; C: conf. *et simposium* x virginum).—There is no record of *symposium* meaning *similitudo*, and it would seem that the Glossator was thinking of *symphonia*.—The gloss that follows the word *sinphosin* belongs to ὁδοιπορικὸν (hodoeporicon) which follows in the same Ch. of St Jerome's Cat., and is here glossed twice, while it occurs once more in the Glossary **otheporicon**, iterarium uel uiarum, xxx. 87, which refers to *Cat. Hier.* cxi col. 705B (composuit volumen, quasi ὁδοιπορικὸν; B: *odaporikon* idest itinerarium; C: *odoporicam*) = *caeporicon*, itararium uel uiarum, Cp. C71; *caeporicon*, iterarium uel uiarum, Ep. 8C5; Ef.[1] 352, 15; *etodeporicon*, uiaticum iterarium, Cp. E320; Ep.—; *etodiforicon*, iterarium uel uiaticum, Ef.[1] 358, 33.—On the different readings in Ch. lxxx of the *Catal.* see Migne's note [i].

sintagmata [synt-], xxx. 31; see *sintagmaton*.

sintagmaton, documentorum, xxx. 69 (*Cat. Hier.* lxxv col. 686A ὥστε αὐτὸν μέγιστον μέρος τῶν Ὠριγένους συνταγμάτων ἰδίᾳ χειρὶ καταγράψαι; the Lat. text of Migne, Richardson, and B and C has *voluminum* instead of συντ-).—**sub nominem consintagmata**, documenta, xxx. 31; **syntagma**, documentum, xxx. 32 = (*Cat. Hier.* xxxii col. 647B Feruntur sub nomine eius et alia syntagmata [συντάγματα, Rich.]; B: Fer. s. n. e. e. a. *sintagmata*; C: Fer. s. n. e. e. alia [blank]) = *Syntasma*, documentum, Cp. S723; Ep. 24E12; Ef.[1] 391, 53; *syntasmata*, documenta, Cp. S724; Ep. 24E13. For *sub nominem con-* see the present Glossary, p. 27, note **.—xxx. 32 (*synt. doc.*) is evidently a gloss to xxx. 31, though σύνταγμα occurs in Cat. Hier. xxxv in some MSS., for which others have commentarium; Text B: *sintagma* idest *documentum*; Text C: commentarium.

Sion, see *ciuitas dauid*.

sinthema, spica conpositio, xxix. 69 (*Uerb. Interpr.* = *Hier. in Matth.* xxvi. 73 Ephrathæi in Judicum libro (cap. xii) non possunt σύνθημα dicere, to give the *watchword*). Here *conpositio* also means *a watchword*. *Spica* is explained by a reference to Jud. xii. 6, quoted by Jer., Dic ergo Scibboleth (שִׁבֹּלֶת), quod interpretatur *Spica*.

sinum, ubi mare intrat in terram, xxxvi. 4 (*Oros.* i. 2, 18 habent...a meridie...*sinum* Persicum; i. 2, 21 inter *sinum* Persicum; see also i. 2, 23, 25, 34 (*sinus*), 56, 58, 59, 72 (*sinu*), &c.).

sirenae, see *sirene*.

sirene, mulieres marine, xiii. 28 (*Isai.* xiii. 22 respondebunt...*sirenes* in delubris. Heyse *sirenae* in note).

sirenes, see *sirene*.

Siriis [Syriis], xxv. 3, see *sirofenissa*.

Sirius, see *scina*.

sirofenissa, de siriis [Syriis] qui in cananea [-naea] sunt, xxv. 3 (*Marc.* vii. 26 mulier...*Syrophænissa* genere; Wordsw. & White, in note, *sirofenisse* &c.).

sirte, harena, xlii. 17 (*Ex div. libris*).—**in sirtim**, mare arenosa [!], iii. 33 (*De S. Mart. Stor.* = *Sulp. Sev. Dial.* i. 3, 2, p. 154, 27 in *Syrten* inlati sumus; in note *syrtim, syrtes*). Cf. *in sirtim*, in sondgepearp [= *sandgeweorp*, a sandbank, quicksand, Bosw. T.], Cp. I414.

sirtim, iii. 33; see *in sirtim* sub v. *sirte*.

siser, see *liser*.

sis, nuis [together for A. S. sīma?], xliii. 55; see *cestus*.

sit, i. 111; xiv. 9; xxviii. 55; xxxiii. 16; xxxix. 36.

sitatum, malleum duratum, xxxviii. 45 (*Clem.* ?). *Sitatum* does not seem to occur in Clemens Romanus. Two other MSS. read *scitatum*, male odoratu (-tum). It follows in the Glossary after two words extracted from Clemens' *Epist. ad Jacobum* (Migne, *Patr. Lat.* cxxx col. 2119 sqq.), and Glogger suggests that it may be a corruption for *Bithalassum*, glossing *Bithalassa*...loca (*ibid.* col. 25), mare undatum. Cf. Goetz, vi. 144 (bithalassum), where other suggestive interpretations are given. The Corp. Gloss. (B231) has *bythalasma* ubi duo maria conueniunt. For *bythalasma* the Ep. Gl. (6A16) has *bythalass.*; Ef.[1] 347, 30 *bathalasa*.

sitiens, xvii. 1, see *area sitiens*.

situs, lana quę [quae] crescit in loco quę [qui] caret sole uel positio, xlvi. 24 (*Alia* = *Ars Phocae*, p. 420, 6 *situs*). Cf. *situs*, positio, Cp. S366; *situs*, antiquitas uel positio, Ep. 25E18; Ef.[1] 394, 8; *scitus*, positio, Cp. S132.

siue, ii. 7, 173; xiii. 1; xvi. 26; xxiii. 7; xxxiii. 12; xxxix. 36 (bis).

smaragdus, uiridem colorem habet hoc est prasinum, XLI. 10 (*De nomin. div.* = Apoc. XXI. 19 *smaragdus*; see also *Exod.* XXVIII. 17, XXXIX. 10; *Ezek.* XXVIII. 13) = *smaragdus* uiridem habet colorem, Cp. S378; Ep. 24E22; Ef.[1] 392, 9.—For "hoc est prasinum" in Cp., Ep. & Ef.[1] see above *calcidon.*

smigmata, unguenta, XVI. 20 (*Dan.* XIII. 17 Afferte mihi...*smigmata*).

Sobal, see *Subal.*

sociatrices, IV. 103 and XXXV. 283, see *sinisactas.*

socibus, XXXV. 286, see *sodalibus.*

socius, I. 28, see *coetus.*

sodales, XXXVI. 18, see *conmanipulares.*

sodalibus, socibus, XXXV. 286 (*Ruf.* VII. 29 fol. 132b mel Atticum a *sodalibus* uocaretur; VIII. 6 fol. 135b ex Dorothei *sodalibus*). Cf. above *factionibus*, and *sodales*, socii, Cp. S383.

soeue, su, III. 44 (*De S. Mart. Stor.* = *Sulp. Sev. Dial.* II. 10, 3 *sues* pascit; one MS. has *oues* pascit; cf. *ibid.* III. 10, 4 captiuumque *suem*). For A.S. *su*, a sow, female pig, also written *sugu*, see Bosw. T. in vv.; Skeat, *Conc. Dict.*

sofismatum, questionum [quaest-], III. 60; see *sophismatum.*

sol, XXVII. 4, see *suprima*, 23, see *Phoebe*; XXXVI. 12, see *foetontis.*

Solamitide, see *Salamitis.*

solaria, XXVII. 29, see *titania.*—**solaria**, onores [hon-], V. 25.—**solaria**, munera, XXXV. 253.—**solaria**, sedes uel loca alta, XXXV. 34; all for *salaria?* see *salariis.*

solario, XXIII. 14, see *in domate suo*; see also *solaria*, sub v. *salariis.*

sole, XI. 16, see *bonam escam*; XII. 42, see *uasa*; XXIX. 13, see *frixi ciceris*; XLVI. 24, see *situs.*

solem, XVII. 12, see *fulgorantes*; XLIV. 27, see *dextera.*

solemnes, XXX. 62, see *eortatica.*

solemnitas, II. 151, see *sinaxis.*

solempnis, see *eortatica.*

solent, XXVIII. 38, see *per figuram y-.*

solide, fortiter, XII. 28 (*Eccles.* XXIX. 7 si...potuerit reddere, adversabitur, *solidi* vix reddet dimidium, et computabit illud quasi inventionem). Sab. and Heyse record, in notes, the reading *solide* and Sab. also *solidum.* On this passage see Wace, *Apocr.* II. 148.

solidi, XXXIII. 21, see *uncia*; see also *solide.*—solidorum, XXXII. 6, see *ciatos.*—solidos, XXIV. 7, see *stater*; XXXI. 5, see *uncia*, 7 (bis), see *libra*; XXXII. 5, see *uncia*; XXXIII. 28, see *libra*, 29, see *obolus.*

solidos tres trymisas sax, XXXI. 6 (*De ponder.* ?). It is not clear whether *tres* belongs to the lemma (*solidos*) or to *trymisas* (plur. of *trymis*, a coin); see Bosworth T. *trimes.* Above *sax* the MS. has **v**, which it usually uses to mark A. S. words. It is doubtful whether it could be a Teutonic form for *six*? or for *Saxonice*?—**solidum**, XXIX. 32, see *nummismum*; XXXI. 28, see *tres argenteos*; XXXIII. 30, see *siliquae tres*; see also *solide.*—solidus, XXIV. 11, see *nomisma.*—**solidus** XXIIII siliquas, XXXI. 29 (*De ponder.?*). Cf. Blume, I. 374. 1 sqq.

solis, XXI. 12, see *filii titan.*

sollicitationibus [for sollitat- II. 93], see *inlecebris.*

sollicitum, XV. 39, see *exertum.*

sollitationibus, for sollicitat-, q.v.

solos, XLI. 1, see *presbiteri.*

soluebatur, XI. 16, see *bonam escam.*

soluit, XXVII. 22, see *fatescit.*

soluitur, VIII. 17, see *nitrum.*

solum, II. 189, see *monasterium*; XLIV. 2, see *cous.*

sonans, XIX. 4, see *tinnulus.*

sonare, V. 26, see *subsaltare.*

sonat, I. 111, see *sicera*; XXXIII. 7, see *sicel.*

sonitum, XXXVIII. 37, see *coribantas.*

sonitus, XXXV. 215, see *fragor.*

sophismatum, questionum [quaest-], XXVIII. 22. — **sofismatum**, questionum [quaest-], III. 60 = (*Lib. Anton.* XLVI col. 158D arguta *sophismatum* interrogatione; cf. also XLVIII *sophismatum*...conclusio, and XLIX *sophismatum*...versutiae) = *sophismatum*, quaestionum, Cp. S420; *s.* quaestionem, Ep. 24E28; *s.* questionum, Ef.[1] 392, 13.

sophistice, conclusione uel reprehensione, XII. 38 (*Eccles.* XXXVII. 23 qui *sophistice* loquitur).

sordida, XXXV. 225, see *scuriosa.*

sordidam, XXVIII. 10, see *luridam.*

soricem, XIII. 61, see *murem.*

sororis, XXXV. 26, see *oethepia.*

sors, see *fors.*

sortiuntur, XXII. 12, see *urna.*

spatiis, XLIV. 16 (ter), see *antarticus.*

spatio, XXXV. 27, see *puncto.*

specialiter, see *spetialiter.*

speciei, XXXIII. 19, see *nebel.*

speciem, XXVIII. 42, see *idea.*

species, XLII. 25, see *Platonis ideas*; see also *speties ęris.*

speciosas, XLII. 15, see *scithis.*

spectacula, ubi omnia publicis uisibus prebetur [praeb-] inspectio, I. 126 [*De Canon.*; *Can. Apostt.* XVIII quae publicis *spectaculis* mancipantur; *Can. Conc. Laod.* CLVII ludicris *spectaculis* interesse; *Can. Conc. Carth.* XV *spectacula* saecularia;

LXI de *spectaculis*; ad haec *spectacula*]; cf. Isid. *Etym.* XVIII. 16. 1.
spectaculis, see *spectacula*.
spectaculum (circum), XXX. 21, see *amphitheatrum*.
spectandi, see *uectandi*.
spectans, see *expectans*.
spectat, see *allectat*.
spelaeo, speleo, speleum, see *aspeleo*.
spelunca, XVI. 3, see *crypta*.
spera [sphaera], XLIV. 7, see *poli*.
spere [sphaerae], XLIV. 3, see *axis*.
speri [for sphaerae ?], XLIV. 29, see *axem*.
sperico [sphaer-], XLIV. 10, see *cardines*.
spernendo, despiciendo, II. 163 (*Bened. reg.* 31, 8 [15] non *spernendo* eum contristet).
spetialiter [spec-], XVIII *tit*.
speties ęris, de eramento [aer-] dicitur, XV. 22 (*Ezech.* XL. 3 *species aeris*).
sphaera, see *poli*.
sphaerae, see *axis*.
sphaerico, see *sperico*.
spiathiis, spiatium, spiato, see *spiathio*.
spiathio, mattae, XXXIV. 3 (*De Cassiano, Inst.* V. 35 incubantem *psiathio* repperisset; cf. ib. IV. 13 *psiathium* [in note *phiathium, psiatium, spiatium*], and *Conl.* XV. 1 li. 2 *psiathiis* [in note *psiathis, psiatiis, spiathiis*]; cf. *spiato*, matte, Cp. S487. MS. has v above *mattae*, which would indicate that the word was regarded as A. S. But as there are no A. S. glosses in the Cassianus Chapter, it seems that *mattae* is the dat. of Lat. matta, corresponding to dat. case of *spiathio*).
spica, X. 9, see *nardum*; XXIX. 69, see *sinthema*.
spicas, XIII. 47, see *plaustrum*; see also *saliuncula*.
spicatum, XXIX. 35, see *pisticum*.
spinarum, VIII. 7, see *domatis*.
spinas, XIII. 57, see *saliuncula*.
spinosis, XXXVIII. 2, see *dumosis*.
Spiridion, see *Spiridon*.
Spiridon, nomen hominis, XXXV. 298 (*Ruf.* X. 5 fol. 160[b] *Spiridion* Cyprius episcopus).
spiritum, X. 1, see *osculetur me*.
spiritus, II. 7, see *alleluia*.
[splendidissime], splendissime [for splendidiss-], XXXV. 163, see *luculentissime*.
splendor, XLVIII. 15, see *iubar*.
spodasten, amatorem, XXIX. 70 (*Uerb. Interpr.* = *Hier. de Vir. illustr.* VII. refert presbyterum quemdam in Asia σπουδαστὴν apostoli Pauli).
spolia, XXIX. 25, see *exuuia*.
sponsa, XV. 29, see *thalamus*.
sponsam, X. 1, see *osculetur me*.
spurca, inmunda, IV. 80.—**spurca**, inmunda, XXXV. 246 (*Ruf.* IX. 5 fol. 148[b] *spurca* quaedam...committerentur).
sputaculum, see *sputacum*.
sputacum, sputum, XXVIII. 8 (*Lib. Anton.* XX col. 144[c] *sputaculum*...in os ejus ingeminans; see note on the word ibid. col. 179) = *sputaculum*, sputum, Cp. S468; *sputacum*, sputum, Ep. 24E29 and Ef.[1] 392, 14.
sputum, XXVIII. 8, see *sputacum*; XLIII. 45, see *pytisso*.
squalor, XI. 3, see *lanugo*.
squiriolus, see *netila*.
stabulis, XXXIV. 32, see *repagulis*.
stabur nazannai, nomen fluminis, XXIII. 6 (1 *Esdr.* V. 3 venit...Thathanai, qui erat dux trans flumen, et *Stharbuzanai*, et consiliarii eorum; id. V. 6 & VI. 13 Thathanai dux regionis trans Flumen, et *Stharbuzanai*, et consiliatores eius; VI. 6 Thathanai dux regionis, quæ est trans Flumen, *Stharbuzanai* et consiliarii vestri. Heyse, in notes, *Stharbuzannai, Starbuzannai*). As Stharbuzanai was one of the counsellors of Darius, it seems that the Codex used by the Glossator had not the word *et* between *flumen* and the proper name.
stadio, see *stadium*.
stadium, ubi iocus agitur, IV. 47 (*Eccl. Ist.*).—**ad stadium**, ad locum certaminis, XXXV. 156 (*De Eus.*) = (*Ruf.* IV. 15 fol. 62[a] pergebat *ad stadium*...; in *stadio*).
stagnello, X. 22, see *areola*.
stagnum, VIII. 19, see *si usque ad*...; XXIX. 36, see *Siloam*; XXXV. 252, see *Meandrum*.
stantem, XV. 5, see *paxillus*.
stat, X. 22, see *areola*.
stater, III solidos, XXIV. 7 (*Math.* XVII. 26 invenies *staterem*).—**stater** nummus est habens ut quidam adfirmaut unciam unam idest aureos VI ut alii putant III in euangelio enim pro duobus dragmis stater datur, XXXIII. 6 (*De pond. Euch.* p. 158, 12 *stater* n. e. h., u. q. a., u. u., i. a. sex, u. a. p. tres; i. e. e. p. duobus *didragmis* s. datur; *datum*, in Brit. Mus. MS., which adds: NOMICMA, denarius est qui pro decim inputatur nummis). See also *statera*.
statera, Grece LXXII siliquas, XXXI. 34.—**Hieronimus** dicit **statera** dicitur qui duo didragma habet, XXXI. 37 (*De ponder.* ?). Cf. Blume, I. 373. 29, and see also *stater*.
stateras, XXXII. 9, see *mina*.
staterem, see *stater*.
statim, VI. 8, see *ast*; XXVIII. 4, see *extimplo*; XXXV. 58, see *uix*.

statione, uigilatione, xxxiv. 39 (*De Cass. Inst.* xii. 4, 1 ex...angelorum *statione*).

stationes, see *prestatio* [for *per stationes*].

statuunt, xxxv. 179, see *horas diurnas*.

stellas, xli. 8, see *saphirus*, 13, see *crisolitus*, 16, see *cypressus*.

stelle [-llae], xliv. 22, see *pliadę*.

stellis, xix. 2, see *asteriscis*.

Stephanus, coronatus, xxxv. 106 (*Ruf.* ii. 1 fol. 18ª Stephanus...lapidatur ab his, qui et dominum occiderunt, per quod et nominis sui στεφάνω [for στεφάνῳ] donatur a Christo). Cf. *stefanus*, coronatus, Cp. Int. 294 (= Euch. 92).

stercora, **stercoris**, xxiii. 9, see *porta stercoris*.

sterelis [sterilis], xix. 30, see *terra salsuginis*.

sternatione, xxx. 35, see *uarietas stromactis*.

sternent, see *stratores*.

sternentem [for *sternent eum*; see the quot. sub v. *stratores*], allidentem, xiv. 28.

sternutatio, nor, xix. 65 (*Job* xli. 9 *sternutatio* eius splendor ignis) = sternutatio, fnora, Cp. S521; Ep. 23C13; *sternutatio*, huora [for *hnora*], Ef.[1] 389, 14; for *nor* (for *hnor*), see Kluge, *Et. Wört. der d. Sprache* (*Niesen*); id. *Ang. Leseb.* (*hnor*); Steinm. *Alth. Gl.* i. 497, 17 & 26 sternutatio, nor, nur, hynona; Wright W. (index, sub vv.) *sternutatio*, *fnora*, *fneosung*; Bosw. T. (*fnora*, *fneōsung*). *hnor, *hnora, are from an unrecorded A.S. strong verb **hnēosan* (equivalent to Norse *hnjōsa*), a parallel imitative form of *fnēosan* (whence *fnora* &c.), Mod. E. *snore*; see Skeat, *Conc. Dict.* (*neese*, *neeze*).

Stharbuzanai, Stharbuzannai, see *Staburnazannai*.

stibia, xxxv. 42, see *stibiis*.

stibiis, coloribus stibia erba de quo faciunt, xxxv. 42 (*Ruf.* v. 18 fol. 88ª *stibiis* tingitur).

stibulationem (ad), xl. 8, for *adstipulationem* (?), see *ad infirmationem* (for *adfirmationem* ?).

sticulus, gaeuo, xlvii. 65 (*Alia* = ?). There is nothing resembling this gloss in the Cp. Glossary, nor in Ep., Ef.[1] The lemma looks like a dim. of *sticus* recorded by Du C. But this means *a fish*, perh. the *tinca*, whereas *sticulus* appears in the present Glossary among a group of *birds*. Perhaps *sti-* is a corruption for *cu-* the cuckoo, cf. *cuculus*, gaec, Cp. C948; Ep. —; *cuculus*, gęc, Ef.[1] 353, 50, but *gǣc*, *geāc* (cuckoo, gawk, see Bosw. T.) has no final *o* like *gaeuo*, which latter, for the same reason, could not be another form for *giw* (Wright W. 258, 7), or *giu* (ib. 413, 21, 22), or *giow* (ib. 284, 5), all meaning a *griffin*.

sticus, see *sticulus*.

stigmata, signa, iii. 51 (*De S. Mart. Stor.* = *Sulp. Sev. Vit. S. Mart.* 24, 7 crucis *stigmata* praeferentem). Cf. *stigmata*, ignea, Cp. S495.

stilo, xxx. 92, see *cataracteras*.

stipantur, conplentur, xxviii. 12 (*Lib. Anton.* xx col. 145ᴮ solitudines...monachorum *stipantur* choris).

stipendia, xxxix. 28, see *qui in numero....*

stipendiis, quae militibus dantur, i. 112 (*De Canon.*; *Can. Apostt.* xli nec miles *stipendiis* propriis contra hostes arma sustulit; *Decret. Zosimi* i, p. 211ª diuinis *stipendiis* eruditus). Cf. *stipendia*, munera, Cp. S491.

stipis, esca modica, xxxv. 291 (*Ruf.* ix. 8 fol. 150ᵇ *stipis* petendae gratia).

stipulas (?), see *dapulas*.

stipulatio, testatio, i. 124 (*De Canon.*; cf. *Can. Conc. Carth.*, praef., pp. 142ᵇ, 144ª sub *adstipulatione* literarum; *id.* cxxxvi p. 173ª sub fidei *adstipulatione*; cf. Steinm. *A.H.G.* ii. 117, 44).—**stipulationis**, promissionis, xiv. 24 (*Hierem.* xxxii. 11 accepi...*stipulationes*; the *gen. sing.* represents, perhaps, another reading).—**adstipulatio**, confirmatio, xxxv. 11 (*De Eus.*); **adstipulatio**, adfirmatio, xxxv. 129 (*De Eus.* = Cp. A174; Ep. 1A19); **adstipulatione**, adiutorio, iv. 26 (*Eccl. Ist.*) = (*Ruf.* iii. 3 fol. 34ᵇ veterum *adstipulatione* firmabimus; *id.* iii. 24 fol. 45ᵇ *adstipulatione* diuinę virtutis indigeat).—**adstipulatione**, congregatione, xxxix. 70 (*not* Greg. Dial., but *Can. Conc. Carth.*, praef., pp. 142ᵇ, 144ª, see above *stipulatio*). See further *ad infirmationem* (for *adfirmationem* ?). Cf. Isid. *Etym.* v. 24, 30; x. 258; id. *Diff.* 162.

stipulationes, see *stipulatio*.

stipulationis, promissionis, xiv. 24 (*Hierem.* xxxii. 11), see *stipulatio*.

stirpator, desertator, ii. 156 (*Bened. reg.* 31, 18 [35] *stirpator* substantiae monasterii).

stiuam, manubrium, xxxvi. 19 (*Oros.* ii. 12, 8 quasi *stiuam* tenens).

stomachi, xxxix. 47, see *sincopin*.

stomacho, see *bulinus*.

stomatum, opus uariatum, iv. 96; see *stromatum*.

storacinam, see *toracina*.

storax, incensum, xii. 22 (*Eccles.* xxiv. 21 quasi *storax*).

storia, iii *tit.*; v *tit.*

stragula, curtina pulcra uarietate depicta, XXXVIII. 6 (*Clem. Recognitt.* VII. 6 *stragula* pulcra componere).

stranguillato [-gulato], v. 31, see *sugillato*.

strangulatus, XXXV. 239, see *prefocatus*.

stratores, compositores, XIV. 27; **sternentem**, allidentem, XIV. 28 (*Hier.* XLVIII. 12 mittam ei...*stratores* laguncularum, et *sternent* eum).

striga, haegtis, XLVII. 80 (*Alia*=?)=*st-*, haegtis, Cp. S528; *strigia*, haegtis, Ep. 23E35; *striga*, hegtis, Ef.[1] 390, 18. *Striga*, a hag, witch; for haegtis, hegtis (a witch, hag) see Bosw. T. (*hægtesse*); Kluge, *Wrtb.* (*hexe*). The A.S. word also glosses (Erenis=) *Erynnis*, hægtes (Wright W. 392, 18; Cp. E283 *Erenis*, haegtis, furia); *Eumenides*, hægtesse (ib. 392, 19; Cp. E354); *Furia*, hægtesse (ib. 404, 33, 34; 533, 21; Cp. F434); *Pythonissa*..., hægtesse (ib. 188, 33); *Parcae*, hægtesse (ib. 189, 12).

stringebatur, XI. 14, see *poderis*.

striones, qui muebri [muliebri] indumento &c., I. 127; see *histrio*.

strofa, fraus, XXIX. 28 (*Uerb. Interpr.*= *Hier. in Matth.* XXI. 12, 13 col. 150[B] Hanc *stropham* eorum crebra venientium inopia dissipabat).

stromactis, stromateicos, XXX. 35, see *uarietas stromactis*, sub v. *stromatum*.

stromatum, lectorum, XXXV. 16 (*De Euseb.*).—**stomatum**, opus uariatum, IV. 96 (*Eccl. Istor.*)=(*Ruf.* III. 29 fol. 48[b] in tertio libro στροματῶν (!); cf. VI. 3 fol. 97[a] in opere στρωματέων; VI. 11 fol. 101[b] στρωματέων libri octo=*stromatum*, opus uarie contextum, Cp. S516; *stromatum*, opus uariae textum, Ep. 23A19; Ef.[1] 388, 32).—**uarietas** [gloss, not lemma] **stromactis**, de sternatione ubi paganorum et xpistianorum colleguntur (collig-) quasi ex lectulo uarietatis, XXX. 35 (*Cat. Hier.* XXXVIII col. 653[A] E quibus illa sunt στρωματεῖς, libri octo; B: E.q.i.s. *stromateicos* idest *varietatum*; C: Ex q.i.s. [blank]). Cf. *stramete*, istos huius uarietatis, Cp. S544; *straomate*, istos huius uarietatis, Ep. 24E16; Ef.[1] 392, 2.

stropham, see *strofa*.

strues, see *struices*.

struices, congregationes, XV. 6 (*Ezech.* XXIV. 5 Vulg. compone...*strues* ossium; Heyse, in note: *struices* òssuum).

studio, XXVIII. 30, see *epembabis*.

studiorum [for *studiosorum*?], XLVIII. 26, see *effeborum*.

studiosorum, see *effeborum*.

studiosum, I. 12, see *aemulum*.

stulta, XI. 1, see *fascinatio*.

stulti, XXXV. 160, see *idiotae*.

stupore, XXXV. 14, see *diriguere*.

sturfus, see *marsopicus*.

sturnus, stęr, XLVII. 53 (*Alia*=?)=*s-*, staer, Cp. S526 and Ep. 23E30; *s-*, sterm, Ef.[1] 390, 13. For *sturnus* (a starling or stare) see Lewis & Sh.; for *stęr*, *staer* (with short *æ*, and hence E. *stare*, see also Engl. Dial. D.) see Bosw. T. (*stær*); Kluge, *Ags. Leseb.*, prints long *æ* (*stǣr*), id. *Etym. Wrtb.* (*Star*), and refers to O.H.G. *stâra*, which Schade prints with short *a*.

sua, XXII. 16, see *ueredarii*.

suadeatur, suademus, see *suaderi*.

suaderi, censeri hortari, II. 164 (*Bened. reg.*; cf. 49, 4[5] ideo *suademus*; 61, 18 [32] *suadeatur* ut stet). As suaderi is an alteration in the MS. from an original suadere (see note ‖ on p. 6), the scribe perhaps meant to equalise suaderi and censeri to hortari.

suam, XXVIII. 70; XXXVI. 1.

suauiter [see note ‖ on p. 5], II. 109, see *modulatis*.

sub, XIX. 51; XXVIII. 37, 55, 74; XXX. 31, 95, 96; XXXV. 82 (bis); XXXVIII. 22; XLIV. 8.

sub [for *subponi*?], XXXV. 192; see *basis*.

sub axe pontico, sub illa parte ubi pontus est, XXXV. 82 (*Ruf.* X. 10 fol. 165[a] gens, quae *sub axe Pontico* iacet).

Subal, nomen uiri unde oriatur illa gens, XXI. 3 (*Judith* III. 1, 14 *Sobal*; Heyse, in notes, *Subal*).

subditione, II. 162, see *subiectione*.

subdolibus, XXXV. 267, see *factionibus*.

suber, genus ligni ex hoc cortix [-tex] in calcimenta [calciam-] ponitur, XLVI. 14 (*Alia*=*Ars Phocae*, p. 415, 15 hoc *suber*). Cf. *suber*, lignum, Cp. S639; Ep. 24A11; Ef.[1] 390, 33.

subieceris, XXXV. 21, see *subregeris*.

subiecte [-tae], I. 120, see *subnixe*.

subigens, confice macera, XVII. 14 (*Nahum* III. 14 intra in lutum, et calca, *subigens* tene laterem). See below *tene laterem*.

subiectione, subditione, II. 162 (*Bened. reg.* 3, 9 [11] cum omni humilitatis *subiectione*; 6, 16 [22] cum...*subiectione*).

subiectis, XXVIII. 88, see *diatiposis*.

subigeris, see *subregeris*; *subrigeris*.

subitanea, see *aporia*.

subitania [-nea], XII. 26, see *aporia*.

subitatione, see *subtatio*.

subito, II. 76, see *fortuitu*; XI. 2, see *subtatio*.

subiunctis, XXXV. 77, see *subnixis*.

subiungitur, XXVIII. 46, see *aetilogia*.

sublata, I. 51, see *exempta*.

sublectilem, xxxiv. 4, see *enticam*.
subleuans, xliv. 27, see *leua*.
sublime, viii. 13, see *in sublime*.
sublimi, xliv. 26, see *a tergo*.
submittatur, see *submittitur*.
submittitur [-atur], ii. 159, see *subrogetur*.
subnixae, subnixis, see *subnixe*.
subnixe, subposite [-tae], subiecte [-tae], i. 120 (*De Canon.*; *Can. Conc. Calch.* xii ciuitates...*subnixae* sunt; cf. *Ep. S. Cyr. Alex.* p. 179^b confessionibus veritate *subnixis*).—**subnixis**, subiunctis, xxxv. 77 (*Ruf.* iv. 8 fol. 56^b assertionibus vera ratione *subnixis*).
subpellectilem, xlviii. 70, see *enthetam*.
subponi, see *basis*.
subposite [-tae], i. 120, see *subnixe*.
subprimitur, xxvii. 4, see *suprima*.
subregeris, subieceris, xxxv. 21; see *subrigeris*.
subregit, xliv. 25, see *dextera*.
subrigeris, eleuaris, v. 24 (*Eccl. Stor.*); **subregeris**, subieceris, xxxv. 21 (*De Euseb.*) = (*Ruf.* iv. 15 fol. 62^b Bestias habeo paratas, quibus *obiicieris*; Cacciari, p. 210 quibus *subrigeris*, and in note: *subrogaueris* & *subigeris*. Cf. bestiis *subriguntur*, ibid. ix. 6 fol. 148^b) = *subregeres*, subieceris, Cp. S588; *subregeris*, subieceris, Ep. 23A37; Ef.[1] 388, 51.
subrogaueris, see *subrigeris*.
subrogetur, submittitur [submittatur] uel ministretur, ii. 159 (*Bened. reg.* 21, 12 [20] qui dignus est *succedat*; in note *subrogetur*; 65, 38 [74] qui dignus est in loco eius *subrogetur*).
subsaltare, sonare, v. 26; **subsaltare**, intrepetan, xxxv. 197 (*Ruf.* vii. 26 fol. 128^b pede...*subsaltare*). For (*in-*)*trepetan*, to tread, dance, see Bosw. T. (*treppan*, *betræppan*); Steinm., *A.H.G.* ii. 597, 37 who refers to O.H.G. *trepizan* (*Zeitschr. f. d. A.* xv p. 99 No. 68); id. ii. 674, 14.
subscriptionem (?), see *scriptionem*.
subselli, xxxv. 61, see *exedrę*.
subselliis, ii. 95, see *in scamnis*.
substantia, i. 46, see *essentia*, 80, see *omousion*; xlviii. 5, see *questus*, 45, see *reditus*.
substantiae, see *nepus*; *prodicus*.
substantiam, xxxix. 36, see *sex untias*.
substantias, xxxvii. 9, see *tabulas legat*.
substantie [-tiae], xliii. 9, see *nepus*.
substantię [-tiae], ii. 137, see *prodicus*.
subtalare, xxxvii. 6, see *caligam*.
subtatio, quod subito fit, xi. 2 (*Sap.* v. 2 in *subitatione* insperatae salutis).
subter, see *hiemisperia*.
subteriore, xi. 14, see *poderis*.
subtilis, xxii. 12, see *urna*; xxxv. 230, see *exesum*.
subtilissima, xiii. 12, see *teristra*; xxi. 15, see *polenta*.
Subura, see *Sabura*.
succidi, interfici [-feci], xvii. 17 (*Zachar.* xi. 8 *succidi* tres pastores).
succincte, xxviii. 64, see *epitrocasmos*.
suco, i. 111, see *sicera*.
sucus, x. 11, see *tigna*.
suem, sues, see *soeue*.
suffecti, i. 100, see *proconsolaris*.
sufficiens, ii. 32, see *contentus*.
suffragationem, ii. 167, see *suggessionem*.
suffusione, circumfusione, xlviii. 50 (*De Cass. Inst.* v. 34 si...fuerint a *suffusione* uel caligine caecitatis inmunes).
suggerere, i. 66, see *intimare*.
suggessionem, supplicationem indicationem suffragationem, ii. 167 (*Bened. reg.* 68, 7 [14] post *suggestionem* suam).
suggestionem, see *suggessionem*.
suggillationem, see *sugillationem*.
suggillato, inclinato, xxxv. 234, see *sugillato*.
sugillationem, iniuriam, xxxiv. 47 (*De Cass. Inst.* xii. 27, 3 ob suam *suggillationem*; in note *sugillationem*).
sugillato, stranguillato [-gulato], v. 31 (*Eccl. Stor.*); **suggillato**, inclinato, xxxv. 234 (*De Euseb.*) = (*Ruf.* xi. 26 fol. 190^a attracto collo et quasi *sugillato*). Cf. *sugillatum*, inclinatum, Cp. S586; Ep. 23A33; Ef.[1] 388, 46.
sui, x. 1; xxviii. 18.
Sulamitis, see *salamitis*.
sumenumerus, quod pro uno omnes et pro multis unus, xxix. 67 (*Uerb. Interpr.* = *Hier. in Matth.* xxvi. 8, 9 nescientes tropum, qui vocatur σύλληψις, vel synecdoche, quo et *pro uno omnes et pro multis unus* appellari soleat). Cf. also xxvii. 44 per tropum, qui appellatur σύλληψις, pro uno latrone uterque inducitur blasphemasse. Migne, ibid. note ^b, records the readings σύμμιξις, σύμΗΚτις, or συμέωξις.
summa, xliv. 18, see *poli*.
summum, xliv. 26, see *a tergo*.
sumptu puplico, adiutorium [-torio?] regali, xxxv. 137 (*Ruf.* iii. 6 fol. 37^b *sumptu publico* sepelire mortuos iusserant).
Sunamitis, see *Salamitis*.
sunt, viii. 2; x. 8, 14, 18; xiii. 55; xvi. 29, 31; xvii. 20; xxi. 12; xxiii. 2; xxv. 3; xxviii. 44, 64; xxix. 42; xxxi. 27; xxxiii. 5, 15, 23; xxxiv. 52 (bis); xxxv. 69, 136, 140; xxxvi. 8; xli. 1, 2; xliv. 5, 8, 10 (bis), 16, 22, 27 (bis); xlv. 31.

suo, xxiii. 14 (bis); xliv. 10.—**suo**, ii. 81, see *gradu suo*; xxix. 73, see *qui dixerit....*

suos, xv. 11, see *preteriola*; **suos**, x. 12, see *ficus protulit....*

super, i. 49; x. 6; xiii. 59; xxii. 16; xxv. 9; xxxvi. 1; xliv. 8; xlvii. 15.

superbe, ii. 133, see *procaciter.*

superbia, ii. 179, see *typo*; xlviii. 36, see *faustus.*

superbus, ii. 26, see *contempto*; xii. 10, see *ceruicatus.*

superfluitas, see *nimius.*

superfluus, ii. 121, see *non prodicus*, 122, see *nimius.*

superhumerale, see *ephod.*

superior, xxix. 2, see *anagogen.*

superiora, xxviii. 56, see *auxesis.*

superioris, xxviii. 82, see *efexegresis.*

superlatio, xxviii. 51, see *hyperthesis.*

superna, xliv. 11, see *clima.*

supernus, xxxiv. 29, see *theorice.*

supersanus, xxix. 53, see *epiasis.*

superscribta [-pta], xxx. 33, see *pseudo ephigrapha.*

superscriptionis, see *pseudo epigrapha.*

superumerale, v. 9, see *ephod.*

suppeditans, proficiens, v. 23 (*Ruf.* ii. 13 fol. 24[a] adminicula...*suppeditans*).

supplicationem, ii. 167, see *suggessionem.*

suppuratis, turgidis, iv. 78 (*Eccl. Istor.*); **suppuratis**, insania fluentis uel purulentis, xxxv. 45 (*De Euseb.*)=(*Ruf.* viii. 18 fol. 145[b] ille...inflatis...visceribus, *suppuratis*que distenditur).

supra, xxxiii. 7.

suprema, see *suprima.*

supremum, extremum, xi. 6 (*Sap.* iv. 19 usque ad *supremum* desolabuntur).

suprima, quando sol ad occasum subprimitur, xxvii. 4 (*Lib. Rot.*=*Isid. de nat. rer.* i. 2 partes...diei tres sunt, mane, meridies et *suprema*)=*Suprema*, quando sol supp̄, Cp. S654; *supprema*, quando sol suppremit, Ep. 24E31; Ef.[1] 392, 16.

sura, see *suricus.*

surgens, xliv. 27, see *leua.*

surgent, xxiii. 1, see *exedra.*

surgentes [for *urgentes*], iv. 112, see *adigent.*

surgit, i. 45, see *emergit.*

suricus, brooc, xlviii. 55 (*De Cass.*?). The lemma does not seem to occur in Cassianus' works, and its meaning is not known. Some suggest *sericus*, and *brooc* as=the A. S. *broc*, breech, D. *broek* (cf. Goetz, vii. 322). Glogger suggests that *suricus* may be a graphic mistake for *alueus* (which occurs in Cassian. in the same line as *citra*, q.v.), which in the Glossary precedes *suricus*, because *alveus* is glossed by *torrens* (Goetz, vi. 57), and *torrens* by *brōc* (Bosw. T.). If *suricus* is right and not a mistake for *sarica* (a kind of tunic, Du Cange), perhaps the Glossator regarded *suricus* as a derivative of *sura*, calf of the leg, and thinking it meant a legging, leg-covering, explained it by *brook* =A.S. *brōc*, breeches.

sursum, x. 21, see *elatę palmarum*; **sursum**, xliv. 27, see *dextera.*

susceptio, xxxix. 59, see *xenodochiorum.*

suscitata, xxxiv. 26, see *inlecta.*

suscitationem, xl. 8, see *ad infirmationem.*

suscitator, xxxiv. 14, see *incentor.*

suspectum, iv. 119, see *antesignato.*

suspendatur, separetur, ii. 155 (*Bened. reg.* 25, 3 [2] *suspendatur* a mensa).

suspensus, xxviii. 78, see *hyperbaton.*

suspicio, coniectura uel argumentum, i. 129 (*De Canon.*; *Can. Conc. Nic.* iii ap. Maassen, p. 925 *suspicio*; cf. *Can. Apostt.* ix & *Can. Conc. Sard.* xv *suspicionem*).

suspicionem, see *suspicio.*

sustentare, xix. 51, see *fabula.*

sustinuisset, iv. 32, see *dependisset.*

susurrat, qui in aurem murmurans loquitur, xix. 23 (*Job* iv. 12 suscepit auris mea venas *susurri* eius; Heyse, in note, *susurrii.* Perhaps *susurrat* represents another reading). Cf. *susurrat*, murmurat, Cp. S604.

susurrii, see *susurrat.*

sutrinator, scoehere, xlii. 6 (*Ex div. libris*?)=*sutrinator*, scoere, Cp. S696. For *scoehere*, a shoemaker, see Bosw. T. (*scōhere*, scōere).

suum, xliv. 10, see *cardines.*

Syenes, see *Syeres.*

Syeres, proprium nomen loci, xv. 23 (*Ezech.* xxix. 10 and xxx. 6 a turre *Syenes*; the Cambr. MS. *Sieres*, p.n.l.).

Sylla, see *Silla.*

syllepsis, see *silemsis.*

syllogismis, see *sillogismus.*

syllogismus, see *hypotheticus.*

symbolis, symbolo, symbolum, symbulum, see *simbulis.*

symfosion, see *sinphosin.*

sympaectas, see *senpectas.*

symphonia, de tibiis et cornu, xxv. 7 (*Luc.* xv. 25 audivit *symphoniam*). For *symphonia*, see also *sinphosin.*

symphoniam, see *symphonia.*

symposium, see *sinphosin.*

sympsalma, uocum adunata copulatio, xxviii. 19 (*Cass. Psalm.* Praef. xi *sympsalma* quippe dicitur Graeco vocabulo *vocum adunata copulatio*)=Cp. S715. Ep. 23C31 and Ef.[1] 389, 31 *sympsalma*, diapsalma, which are two lemmata without the interpretations; see *diapsalma.*

synagogae, see *ariopagitis.*

synathroismos, synatroesmos, see *sinastrismus*; *sinatrismos.*

synaxeos cura [sine interpret.], XLVIII. 41; see *sinaxis.*

synaxis, see *sinaxis.*

synchronon, see *sinchronon* and ϹΥΝ-ΧΡΟΝΟΝ.

syncopin, see *sincopin.*

syncrisis, conparatio, XXVIII. 59 (*Cass. Psalm.* XIX. 8 *syncrisis*, Latine comparatio; cf. XXXIV. 8).—**sinchrisis**, est cum causam suam quis aduersariis nititur efficere meliorem, XXVIII. 70 (*Cass. Psalm.* XXV. 11 schema *syncrisis* est c.c.s. quis ab adversariis suis nititur e.m.).

synecdochen, see *sinecdochen.*

synfosio, synfosion, see *sinphosin.*

synicias, uituperans, XV. 2 (*Ezech.*; Praef. S. Hier., ap. Migne, *Patr. L.* XXVIII col. 940: Vereor ne illud eis eueniat quod Graece significantius dicitur, ut uocentur *φαγολοίδοροι*, quod est *manducantes sannas*; Heyse, p. LXII note i: *φαγολυδοροι* hoc est *manducantes senecias.* The Cambr. MS. Kk. 4. 6: Fagolydoros hoc est manducans *senecias*). Migne, *l.c.* records another reading *senedas.* The gloss *uituperans* gives *the sense* of what is given here as St Jerome's expression; as regards the lemma *synicias* or *senecias* cf. Forcellini, in v. *senecia, senicia, senitia*; Du C. in vv. *fagolidori, senecia,* where there is a confusion between it and *senecio*, groundsel, whence Fr. *seneçon*, groundsel (Cotgrave), prov. E. *sencion, simpson* (Eng. Dial. D.). The Gr. name of the plant was *ἠριγέρων* (Lidd. & Sc.), of which Lat. *senecio* (from *senex*) was a sort of translation. Cf. Steinm. I. 641, 41.

synnodicis, see *sidonicis.*

synodi, see *synodus.*

synodiciis, synodicus, see *sidonicis.*

synodum, see *synodus.*

synodus, graece latine comitatus uel coetus, I. 114 (*De Canon.*; *Can. Conc. Ancyr.* XXV ante hanc *synodum*; XXXVI praecepit sancta *synodus*; *Can. Conc. Nic.* III & XVII *synodus*; *Dion. praef.* p. 101 synodi, synodum).

syntagma (XXX. 32); syntagmata, see *sintagmaton.*

Syriis, see *Sirofenissa.*

Syrophoenissa, see *Sirofenissa.*

Syrten, Syrtes, Syrtim, see *Sirte.*

Syrum, II. 4, see *abba.*

t for *c*: enthetam (for enthecam); fallatia; gazofilatia; iuditium; mendatium; plumatios; prouintia, prouintie; runtina; sagatitas; sermotinatione; spetialiter; speties; uelotius; uinatia; untialibus; untias; untinos.—for *ch*: brantie (branchiae).—for *ct*: artofilax (arctophylax).—for *d*: amictalum (amygdalum); octoade (ogd-); parethris (parhedris); tenticulam (tend-).—for *l*: asitum (asyl-).—for *th*: apotecas (apoth-); baratrum (-thrum); calati (-thi); cyati (-thi); enticam (-thecam); foetontis (Phaeth-); iacincto, iacinctino (hyacintho, -thino); phitagoras (Pythag-); pyriflegitonta (-thonta); terinos (therinus); tesbites (Thesb-).—t *dropped*: labefacare (-factare); mulcatus (mulct-).

tabanus, brimisa, XLVII. 82 (*Alia*=?)= *tabunus*, briosa, Cp. T20; Ep. 27A17; *tabanus*, briosa, Ef.[1] 396, 46. *Tabanus*, a gad-fly, horse-fly, ox-fly, breese, called also *asilus* (Lewis & Sh.). *Brimisa* is a correction of an original *priusa*, corrected into *briusa* (see note §§§, p. 49 above). This original form, together with *briosa* of Cp., Ep. and Ef.[1], points to the Engl. *breese, breeze* (see Oxf. D. *breeze*, sb.[1]), while *brimisa* points to E. *brimse* (see Oxf. D.; Kluge, *Wrtb. breme, bremse*). Observe that *briosa* explains also *asilus* or *asilo* (Cp. A832; Ep. 1E7; Ef.[1] 339, 12 asilo, briosa); see also *asilus*, a drane (Wright W. 767, 18); *tabanus*, a humbyl bee (ib. 767, 20); *crestrum*, a brese (ib. 767, 24).

tabe, see *tabo.*

Tabeel, see *Tabehel.*

tabefactus, XLVIII. 44, see *distabui.*

Tabehel, proprium nomen uiri, XIII. 16 (*Isai.* VII. 6 filium *Tabeel*; Heyse records *Tabehel* in note).

tabernarii, XLV. 31 (bis), see *popa.*

tabo, morbus, XXXIV. 31 (*De Cass. Inst.* X. 7, 8 ne...sanas membrorum partes *tabo* serpente corrumpat)=*tabo*, morbo, Cp. T39.—**tabo**, putrido [putredo], XXXV. 138 (*Ruf.* III. 6 fol. 37[b] cum...peruidisset... humani corporis *tabe* patriam terram rigari; Cacciari p. 122 *tabo*)=*tabo*, putrido, Cp. T7; Ep. 26E20; Ef.[1] 396, 10.

tabula [for *tabulae*], XV. 9, see *transtra.*

tabulas, XXXVII. 9 (bis), see *tabulas legat.*

tabulas legat, idest tabulas matronales [matrimoniales] quia omnia scribuntur in curia et substantias disponunt in XII uncias quamuis magnas uel modicas et ad maritum pertinent VIII ad mulierem IIII Unde in dialogo gregorii [see the present Glossary, XXXIX. 36] VI untias idest medium precium accipit puella, XXXVII. 9 (*S. Aug.*). *Tabulas legat*, which seems to be the lemma, appears not to be found in S. Aug. Opera. But he speaks of *tabulae* (matrimoniales) in Serm. 9, 18 (Migne, XXXVIII col. 88) nam id etiam *tabulae* indicant, ubi scribitur Liberorum procreandorum causa....—Serm. 37, 7 (ibid. col. 225) *tabulas* matrimoniales instrumenta emptionis suae deputat.—Serm. 51, 22 (ibid. col. 345) contra ipsas *tabulas* facit, quibus eam duxit uxorem. Recitantur *tabulae*...et vocantur *tabulae* matrimoniales &c.—183, 11 (ibid. col. 991) imple *tabulas* matrimoniales...(col. 992) *tabulas legamus*...ego *tabulas lego*.—238, 1 (ibid. col. 1125) matrimoniales...*tabulas* audiamus.—268, 4 (ibid. col. 1233) matrimoniales *tabulas lege*.—Append. Serm. 292, 3 (ibid. XXXIX col. 2298) *tabulae* matrimoniales hoc continent.—Aug. *Confess.* VIIII. 19 *tabulas* quae matrimoniales uocantur.—id. *De genes. ad litt.* XI. 41 conscriptio *tabularum*; id. *Enarr. in Psalm.* LXXXI. 21 (Migne XXXVII col. 1045) modum non ibi teneat praescriptum *tabulis*, liberorum procreandorum causa.

tabulę, I. 2, see *alea*.

tabulis, XXV. 4, see *loculum*.

tabunus, see *tabanus*.

taermę [thermae], aque calide et balnea lapidea sic nominantur, XX. 8 (*Tobias*?; not? in the Vulg.).

taeterrimum, see *teterrimum*.

talentum habet pondera LX quod facit libras LXXII, XXXII. 10 (*De ponder.*?).—**talentum** habet pondera LXII quod faciunt LXXX librę attice, XXXIII. 1 (*De pond. Euch.*, p. 158, 8 *talentum* est pondo LXII semis q. f. &c.); **talentum** habet LX [minas] mina grece latine mine dicitur, XXXIII. 3 (*De pond. Euch.* p. 158, 9 *tal-* minas habet LX mna Graece, Latine mina d.).—**taletum** [for *talentum*], centum XXV libras, XXXI. 20 (*De ponder.*). Cf. Lewis & Sh.; Blume, I. 374, 18.

tales, XXI. 20, see *labastes*.

talpa, uoond, XLVII. 79 (*Alia*=?)=*t-*, pond, Cp. T16; *t-*, pand, Ep. 27A15[a]; *t-*, uuond, Ef.[1] 396, 44. *Talpa*, a mole; for *uoond*, *pond* &c. (id.), see Bosw. T. (*wand*, *wande-weorpe*); Eng. Dial. D. (prov. E. *want*); cf. Kluge, *Wrtb.* (*Maulwurf*).

taltaon [or *talticon*, or *taltccon*], see *cinticta*.

tamaricius, see *miricę*.

tamen, I. 111; XIV. 9; XXXVII. 12; XLI. 14.

Tanaquil, uirga [-go] regalis, XLVI. 3 (*Alia*=*Ars Phocae*, p. 414, 21 haec *Tanaquil*).

tangendo, XXVIII. 18, see *apotu*.

tantum, XXIV. 10; XXVIII. 18; XLI. 1.

tapetas, see *bibli*.

tapetia, see *abctape*.

tapetibus, rihum, XLII. 2 (*Ex div. libris*?). For *rihum* (instr. plur., with rugs, blankets), see Bosw. T. (*rȳhe, rȳe*).

tapinosin, see *tapynosin*.

tappula, uermis qui currit super aquas, XLVII. 15 (*Alia*=?)=*tippula* [the water-spider], uermis aquaticus, Cp. T181; Ep. 27C31; Ef.[1] 397, 44.

tapynosin, que latine humiliatio dicitur quoties magnitudo mirabilis rebus humilissimus conparatur, XXVIII. 62 (*Cass. Psalm.* XXI. 6 per figuram dicitur *tapinosin*, quae Latine h. nuncupatur q.m.m.r. humillimis c.).

tardes, XII. 23, see *non trices*.

tardiores, XLIV. 27, see *dextera*.

tauri, XXVII. 16, see *hyadas*; XLIV. 22, see *pliadę*.

taxatio, deputatio, XXXVII. 16 (*S. Aug.* Serm. 166 Append. Migne XXXIX col. 2069, Salutis humanae...et mundi rediviva libertas non modica *taxatione* requiritur; Julian. ap. Aug. *op. imperf. contra Julian.* II. 141, Migne XLV col. 1200 etsi æqualis esset gratiæ peccatique *taxatio*), cf. Forcellini, in v.

taxauimus, designauimus, II. 177 (*Bened. reg.* 18, 41 [74] sicut supra *taxavimus* impleatur).

te, XXX. 95, 96; see *ypo* (sub) *tyos* (hoc) &c.

Tebeth, see *Tebetht*.

tebetht, idest december, XXII. 14 (*Esther* II. 16 mense decimo qui vocatur *Tebeth*).

technam, see *tecnam*.

tecnam, artem, XXIX. 29 (*Uerb. Interpr.*=*Hier. in Matth.* XXI. 12, 13 col. 150[c] excogitauerunt et aliam *technam*).

tecta, X. 11, see *tigna*.

tectio, IX. 3, see *contegnatio*.

tectis, XIII. 41, see *paliurus*.

tecto, VIII. 7, see *domatis*.

tectum, IV. 50, see *camerum*; XXXVIII. 19, see *tholus*.

tectura, XXII. 2, see *tentoria*.

tedae, see *tęde*.

tęde, facule [-lae] de ligno pini de quo picem faciunt, XIX. 44 (*Job* XLI. 10 sicut *tedae* ignis accensae).

tegent, XIV. 12, see *domatibus*.

tegmini [roof, house], III. 24, see *sacro tegmini*.

tela, XIV. 30, see *pedalis*.

telam orditus, inuuerpan uuep, XIII. 34 (*Isai.* XXV. 7 praecipitabit...*telam*, quam *orditus* est super omnes nationes); *inuuerpan*, to begin a web (cf. *wearp*, a warp, Bosw. T.); for *uuep*, a web, see Bosw. T. (*web*, *webb*); Napier (Index of

Engl. words); for the *p* of uuep, see Sievers, *Gr.* § 190.

telo, see *telopagere.*

telopagere, bibere, xlviii. 59 (*De Cass.*?). These words are, perhaps, corruptions. For *pagere* and *bibere* Glogger suggests to read *peragere* and *vivere*, referring to Cass. *Conl.* xxi. 1, 2 cum...hic unius lustri tempus cum coniuge *peregisset*. And *telo* may refer to Cass. *Inst.* xii. 4, 1 angelum illum...*telo* superbiae uulneratum; id. *Nest.* iii. 10, 2 persequeris opinionis impiae *telo*; id. *Conl.* i. 2, 1 *telos* hoc est fin̨em.

telos, see *telopagere.*

temere, sine consilio uel praesumptuose, ii. 172 (*Bened. reg.* 3, 15 [20] neque ab [regula] *temere* declinetur).

temoys, libros, xxx. 86 (*Cat. Hier.* cix col. 705A in Isaiam *tomos* decem et octo; B: in ysayam *thomos* octodecim; C: in ysaiam *thomos* x & viii).

temperamento, ii. 176, see *temperius.*

temperate, ii. 124, see *moderate.*

temperie, see *temperiem.*

temperiem, moderatione, ii. 174 (*Bened. reg.* 55, 3 secundum...aerum *temperiem*, [4 *temperiem*, corr. from *temperie*]. Edm. Schmidt, *Regula*: temperiem; temperie; temperies). Cf. *temperiem*, uueder [see Bosw. T. *weder*, weather], Cp. T121.

temperies, see *temperiem.*

temperius, temperamento [?], ii. 176 (*Bened. reg.* 11, 3 Dominicis diebus *temporius* surgatur, [1 *temperius*; *temporius*; *temporibus*]; 48, 11 Agatur nona *temperius* [19 *temperius*, *temporius*]).

tempestate, xxxv. 178, see *ea tempestate.*

templa, xxxv. 224, see *delubra.*

templi, xxxvi. 1, see *Iani.*

templum, iv. 6, see *editus*; xxi. 19, see *in anathema*; xxvii. 11, see *lupercal.*

temporalis, xxx. 37, see *cronographias.*

temporalium, xxx. 77, see *cronicon.*

tempore, xxii. 11, see *mundum m-*; xxxv. 178, see *ea tempestate*; **tempore**, xxvii. 32, see *opago tempore.*

temporis, xv. 32, see *sinchronon*; xviii. 1, see *sinchronon.*

temporius, see *temperius.*

tempus [temple of the head], xxxix. 19, see *freniticus.*

tenacitas, xxxv. 6, see *tentigo.*

tenda, trabus [*trabis* or *trabes*?] gezelt, xxii. 5 (*Esther*? not in the Vulg.). These three words would seem to be a further explanation to xxii. 2: *tentoria* tectura; cf. *tentorium*, geteld, Cp. T76; *tentorium*, papilionem, Ep. 26C11; Ef.[1] 395, 22. For *tenda* (a variant of *tenta*, a tent) cf. Du C., who also, quoting from Papias' Glossary, has "Tenda quae rustice *trabis* dicitur. Cod. alius *trabea* praefert. Gloss. Sax. Aelfrici: Tenda, tyldsyle, i.e. domus limen." See further Diefenbach (trabea); Goetz, v. 250, 3 (trabea, porticus tecta dicitur) and A.S. *traef* (from trabs?) in Bosw. T.—*gezelt* is O.H.G. for tent (cf. Schade, 280; Steinm. i. 488, 5); A.S. (Bosw. T.) *geteald*, *geteld.*

tendiculam, see *decipulam.*

tendit, xliv. 3, see *axis.*

tene laterem, fac laterem, xvii. 18 (*Nahum* iii. 14 subigens *tene laterem*). See above *subigens.*

tenentur, xxxv. 27, see *puncto.*

tensam, xxxv. 122, see *callos.*

tenta, see *tenda.*

tenticula, xiv. 4, see *pedica.*

tenticulam, xxix. 23, see *decipulam.*

tentigo, tenacitas uentris idest ebind, xxxv. 6 (*Ruf.* i. 8 fol. 12b *tentigo* obscoena ...et execranda). The gloss points to a meaning of *tentigo* different from the class. tension of the privy member; perhaps hardness, stiffness of the bowels, costiveness is meant; see W. W. 232, 32: extentio, i. tenacitas uentris, *tentigo*, gebind; *id.* 615, 47; cf. Steinm. ii. 597 n. 2 who refers to O. N. abbindi. See Schlutter, *Jour. Germ. Phil.*, i. 330. For *e-bind*, *ge-bind* see Bosw. T. (*ge-bind*, a binding, fastening).

tentoria, tectura, xxii. 2 (*Esther* i. 6 et pendebant ex omni parte *tentoria* aerij coloris). For *tentoria* see also above *tenda.*

teraphim, see *teraphin.*

teraphin, idolum sic nominatur, xv. 35 (*Osee*, iii. 4 sine *teraphim*). The Cambr. MS. has: *therafin*, idolum sic nominatum.

terebellus, nębugaar, xlvii. 46 (*Alia*=?) =*t-*, nabogaar, Cp. T87; *terrebellus*, nabfogar, Ep. 27A12; *terebellus*, naboger, Ef.[1] 396, 41. For *terebellus*, -um (dimin. of *terebrum*), a small borer, auger, gimlet, see Körting, 9460. For *nębugaar*, *nabogaar* &c. (literally, nave-borer, from *næbu*, *nafu*, the *nave*, of a wheel + *gār*, a spear, shaft, borer), see Bosw. T. (*nafu*, *nafugar*, *gār*); Kluge, *Et. Wört.* (*Nabe*); Oxf. D. (*auger*); Skeat, *Conc. Dict.* (*auger*); Kluge & Lutz, *E. Etym.* (*auger*).

terebrantes, borgenti, iv. 66 (*Eccl. Istor.*); **terebrantes**, perforantes, xxxv. 187 (*De Euseb.*) = (*Ruf.* vi. 31 fol. 112a oculos acutis calamis *terebrantes*).

tergo, xliv. 26, see *a tergo.*

Terinos [for therinus = θερινός], idest bestialis, xliv. 13; see *arcticos.*

teristra, subtilissima curtina, xiii. 12 (*Isai.* iii. 23 auferet Dominus...*theristra*. Cambr. MS. *theristra*, subtilissima *corona*).

termae, see *angulinis*.
termę [-mae], xxxix. 34, see *angulinis*.
terra, viii. 17; xiv. 2, see *nitrum*; xiv. 18, see *arua*; xix. 30 (bis), 40, see *olla*; xxxv. 41, see *in aculeis*; xxxvi. 3, see *promontorium*; xxxix. 13, see *Aurelia*, 51, see *byssus*; xliv. 8, see *hiemisperia*; xlv. 11, see *ops*.
terra salsuginis, terra sterelis [sterilis, as in the Cambr. MS.], xix. 30 (*Job* xxxix. 6 in *terra salsuginis*).
terrae, see *agellis*: *rusticatio*.
terram, xvii. 7, see *Niniue*; xix. 51, see *fabula*; xxix. 46, see *arue*; xxxvi. 4, see *sinum*; xliv. 8, see *hiemisperia*.
terre [-rae], xii. 8, see *rusticatio*; xxx. 48, see *geometrica*; xxxv. 117, see *territoria*, 268, see *agellis*.
terrę [-rae], xliv. 7, see *poli*, 29, see *axem*; xlv. 29, see *uligo*.
terrebellus, see *terebellus*.
terris, i. 48, see *extorris*.
territoria, loca modica terrę, xxxv. 117 (*Ruf.* ii. 17 fol. 27[a] per singula quaeque *territoria*) = *territoria*, loca modica, Cp. T72; Ep. 26A37; Ef.[1] 395, 10.
terroribus, xliv. 2, see *cous*.
tertia, xii. 29; see *lingua tertia*.
tes, xxx. 13, see *iereticos*.
Tesbites, castella, xlviii. 27 (*De Cass. Inst.* i. 1, 3 [from iiii Reg. i. 8] Helias *Thesbites* est).
tessella, see *tesseras*.
tesseras, tesulas, xxxv. 35 (*Ruf.* v. 18 fol. 88[a] ad *tesseras* ludit). Cf. *tessera*, tasul, Cp. T84; *tessera*, tasol quadrangulum, Ep. 26E33; *t.*, tasul q., Ef.[1] 396, 23. As regards *tesulas*, Steinm. (ii. 597 note 2) thinks it is Lat.; if so, it might be a corruption for *tessellas* or *tesserulas*. But the word is marked in the MS. by v, and it may be acc. pl. of A.S. *tasul* (or *tesul*, borrowed from Lat. *tessella*; see Bosw. T. sub voce *teosol*), m., a die; cf. Bülbring, *Altengl. Elementarbuch* § 417; Kluge, *Angels. Leseb.*, p. 209 *tasol*.
tesseris, see *tesseroes*.
tesseroes, quadris, xxx. 39 (*Cat. Hier.* xl col. 655[B] ludit et *tesseris*; B & C: l. e. *tesseris*) = *teserois*, quadris, Cp. T78; *tesserois*, quadris, Ep. 26C36; *theserois*, quadris, Ef.[1] 395, 47.
tesserula, see *tesseras*.
testa, xii. 9, see *cacabus*.
testamento, xxxv. 254, see *de octoade*.
testamentum, iv. 10, see *ogdoade*.
testatio, i. 124, see *stipulatio*.
teterrimum, nigerrimum, ii. 175 (*Bened. reg.* 1, 12 [17] Tertium...monachorum *teterrimum* genus est).
Tethis, aquis, xxvii. 31 (*Lib. Rot.* = *Isid. Lib. de nat. rer.* xl. 3 [quoting *Lucan.*] quum litora *Tethys*) = *Thedis*, aquis, Cp. T75; *thethis*, aquis, Ep. 26C18; *Thetis*, aquis, Ef.[1] 395, 29.
Tethys, see *tethis*.
tetrafa, xxxv. 74, see *petigo*.
tetragono, quattuor angulos, xxxviii. 27 (*Clem. Recognitt.* ix. 17 ex *tetragono* respexerit...; schema *tetragonum* habens).
tetragrammaton, xxxv. 147, see *petalum*.
tetris, xxvii. 26, see *atris*.
th for *d*: oe*th*epia for oe*d*ipia.
thalami, xxviii. 86, see *epithalamium*.
thalamus, altior locus ubi sedet sponsa, xv. 29 (*Ezech.* xl. 7 [mensus est] *thalamum* ...et inter *thalamos* quinque cubitos; 10 *thalami* portae; 12 marginem ante *thalamos* &c.).
theatri, xxxv. 171, see *harene*.
theatrii [for *theatri*], xxxv. 29, see *harene*.
thecis, custodiis, iv. 85 (*Eccl. Istor.*); **thecis**, custodiis fabricam [for *fabricatis*?] de argento, xxxv. 294 (*De Euseb.*) = (*Ruf.* x. 8 fol. 163[b] partem...*thecis* argenteis conditam).
thema, doctrina, xxxviii. 32; **scema**, figura, xxxviii. 33 (*Clem. Recognitt.* ix. 32 audi conjugis meae *thema*, et invenies *schema* cujus exitus accidit). Cf. *thema*, figura, Cp. T146; Ep. 26E1; Ef.[1] 395, 49.—**themate**, conpositione uel ordine, xxii. 1 (*Esther*; *Hieron. Praef.* p. xiv[a] & Migne, *Patr. Lat.* xxviii col. 1433[B] sumpto *themate*). For *Thema*, see also *Theman*.
Theman, idest prouintię, xix. 12 (*Job* vi. 19 considerate semitas *Thema*; Migne, *P. L.* xxviii col. 1089, and Heyse, in notes, *Theman*).
themate, conpositione uel ordine, xxii. 1; see *thema*.
Themisto, insula; **Calipso**, insula; **Pan** deus arcadię [-diae; cf. Verg. *ecl.* x. 26] uel pastorum; **Arcades**, gens dicitur quę colebat pana, xliii. 1–4 (*De div. nominibus* = Donati *Ars gramm.* p. 373, 17, 18 sunt nomina tota Graecae declinationis, ut *Themisto Calypso Pan*). *Arcades* seems to be a gloss to *arcadię*.
theo, xxx. 20, see *pantocranto*.
Theodorus, xii. 40, see *cyneris*.
theologia, iv. 114 and xxxv. 17, see *a theologia*.
theomachiae, see *theomachie*.
theomachie, deorum pugnę, xxxv. 94 (*Ruf.* i. 1 fol. 3[b] *Theomachiae*...exortae sunt).
theoretica, theoreticam, theorica, see *theorice*.
theoreticen, see *theoritisen*.
theoriae, see *theorice*.

theoricas, xxx. 13, see *iereticos*.

theorice, supernus intellectus, xxxiv. 29 (*De Cass. Inst.* xi. 18 diuinae *theoriae*... inhaerere; cf. *Conl.* i. 8, 2 in *theoria* sola; i. 12 huic *theoriae*...adfixus; &c. &c.). See also *Conl.* i. 1 *theoretica* uirtute; id. xiv. 8, 3 *theoreticam* disciplinam; id. xiv. 1 θεωρητική; id. xix. 5 *theoretica* (theorica, in note) sublimitate.

theoritisen et **practicen** contemplatiuum et actiuum, xxix. 64 (*Uerb. Interpr.* = *Hier. in Matth.* xxi. 1 misit duos discipulos suos, θεωρητικὸν καὶ ἐργαστικόν). Other MSS. θεωρητικὴν καὶ πρακτικὴν, and one MS. in Latin characters *theoreticen* et *practicen*, Migne, in note [d].

therinus, see *terinos*.

theristra, see *teristra*.

thermae, see *taermę*.

Thesbites, see *tesbites*.

thesteas, indiscretas concubitas, iv. 57 & **oedipia**, obscene Dapes carnium infantium, iv. 58 (*Eccl. Istor.*) [leg. **Thyesteas**, obscene Dapes carnium infantium—**Oedipia**, indiscretas concubitas]; **thiesteas**, commessationes, xxxv. 25 (*De Eus.*).—**Oedippa**, de odippo [Oedipo], v. 14 (*Eccl. Stor.*);—**Oethepia**, coitum matris et sororis sicut manichei [Manichaei] in occultis idest in occulta loca idolorum, xxxv. 26 (*De Eus.*) all = (*Ruf.* v. 1 fol. 74[a] *Thyesteas* cœnas et incesta *Oedipia* perpetrantes). Cf. *Thyesteas*, comesationes, Cp. T150; *Oethippia*, coitum matris, Cp. O130.

thestisuir [Q[y] Latin or A.S.?], v. 21, see *editiones*.

thia, matertera, xxxv. 46 (*Ruf.* x. 6 fol. 161[b] vel sorore, vel θεία).

thiarati, diuini, xl. 18 (*Uerba* ?).

thiesteas, commessationes, xxxv. 25; see *thesteas*.

thimiamateria, turibula, xiv. 35 (*Hier.* lii. 19 tulerunt et hydrias et *thymiamateria*).

thimisiun, xxix. 59, see *tu thimisiun*.

thiticum, marinam, vi. 9 (*Breu. exsol.* ?).

tholos, see *tholus*.

tholus, tectum de petris sine ligno, xxxviii. 19 (*Clem. Recognitt.* viii. 18 qui ædificiorum *tholos*...instruunt).

thomos, see *temoys*.

thorace, see *torax* sub v. *thoraces*.

thoraces, capud [caput] et pectus, iv. 97 (*Eccl. Istor.*); **thoraces**, imagines, v. 32 (*Eccl. Stor.*) = (*Ruf.* xi. 29 fol. 190[b] *thoraces* [busts] Serapis...abscissi sunt).—**toraca**, lurica [lor-], xlv. 17 (*Uerba de multis* = *Ars Phocae*, p. 425, 22 ut *thorax* thoracis).—**torax**, lurica [lor-] manicas non habens et tunica sine manicis sic dicitur, xi. 4 (*Sap.* v. 19 Induet pro *thorace* justitiam). Cf. *torax*, lurica, Cp. T196.—**torax**, pectus, xix. 42 (*Job* xli. 17 subsistere non poterit neque hasta, neque *thorax*; see Sabat. vers. ant.: hastae elevatio et *thoracis*; and in note: hastam et *thoracem*) = *thorax*, pectus, Cp. T138; Ep. 26A38; *torax*, pectus, Ef.[1] 395, 11.

thorax, see *thoraces*.

thyesteas, see *editiones*; *scenas turpes*; *thesteas*.

tibia, xlvi. 7, see *tybicen*.

tibicen, see *tybicen*.

tibiis, xiii. 8, see *periscelidas*; xxv. 7, see *symphonia*.

Tifon, filius saturni, xxviii. 7 (*Lib. Anton.* xlvi col. 159[c] Pudeat...vos insidiarum *Typhonis*).

tigna, tecta cedri natura arborum cedri inputribili uigore consistunt quarum sucus uermibus est obuius significat apostolos, x. 11 (*Cant.* i. 16 *Vulg.*: *tigna* domorum nostrarum *cedrina*; *Vers. ant. Sab.*: trabes domorum nostrarum *cedri*). It is clear that *tecta* is a gloss to *tigna*; *cedri natura* may be a corruption for *cedrina*, and *arborum* perhaps for *arbores*. But the Cambridge MS. Kk. 4. 6, omitting "significat apostolos," has: "*Cedrus* arbor natura cuius inputribili uigore consistit. Cuius etiam sucus uermibus obuius est," which seems to give the sense of the gloss (Roofs of cedar, owing to the nature of cedar trees, are of incorruptible force).

tigris, genus leonis uario colore et uelocissimus, xix. 15 (*Job* iv. 11 *tigris* periit). For *tigris* see also *leopardus*.

tilaris, laurice, xlvii. 61 (*Alia* = ?) = *tilares*, lauricae, Cp. T179; *tilaris*, lauuercae, Ep. 27A14; *itilaris*, lauuercae, Ef.[1] 396, 42. For *laurice* &c. (a lark; which also glosses *alauda*, *caradrion*, *laudae* &c.) see Bosw. T. (*lāwerce*); Oxf. D. & Skeat Dict. (*lark*); Kluge, *Et. Wrtb.* (*Lerche*).

tilia, see *tilio*.

tilio, lind, xlvii. 100 (*Alia* = ?) = *tilia*, lind, Cp. T161; *tilio*, lind uel baest, Ep. 27A18; *tilio*, lind uel best, Ef.[1] 396, 47. Tilio (= tilia, as in Cp.) *the linden* or *lime-tree* = A. S. *lind*, see Bosw. T. (*lind*). For *baest*, *best*, E. bast, the inner bark (of the linden, a second meaning of tilia), of the Ep. and Ef.[1] Gloss. see Bosw. T. (*bæst*); Oxf. D. (*bast*); Skeat, D. (*bast*).

timebat, xxxvii. 18, see *pallebat*.

timor [for *tumor* ?], xlviii. 14, see *fastus*.

tinca, see *tinct*.

tinct, slii, xlvii. 71 (*Alia* = ?) = *tincti*, sli, Cp. T169; Ep. 27A16; Ef.[1] 396, 45. *Tinct* seems an error for *tinca*, a small fish, perh. the *tench*. For *slii*, *sli* (Germ. *Schleie*) see Bosw. T. (*slīw*).

tincti, see *tinct.*

tinguitur, see *malleolis.*

tinnulus, sonans, xix. 4 (*Job*; *Praef. Hieron.* p. xiv[b], and Migne, *P. L.* col. 1081[B] rhythmus ipse dulcis et *tinnulus* fertur).

tintinnabula, xi. 14, see *poderis.*

tipho, tipo, see *typo.*

tippula, see *tappula.*

tipu, see *typo.*

tirannidem, crudelem siue duriter [the latter two words belong, perhaps, to ii. 172; see *temere*], ii. 173 (*Bened. reg.* 27, 15 Noverit...se...suscepisse...non *tyrannidem* [24 *tyrannidem*, corr. *tyrannides*]; 65, 5 [8] adsumentes sibi *tyrannidem*).

tirannides [tyr-], iniquas potestates, ii. 178 (*Bened. reg.*; cf. *tyrannides* in 27, 15 [24] quoted above sub v. *tirannidem*).

titan, xxi. 12, see *filii titan.*

titania, solaria, xxvii. 29 (*Lib. Rot.* = *Isid. Lib. de nat. rer.* xxvii. 2 *titania*que astra). Cf. *titania*, sideralia, Cp. T157; Ep. 26C19; Ef.[1] 395, 30.

Tobia, xx *tit.*

toga, dignitas, xxxvii. 20 (*S. Aug.*?). For *toga*, see also *lena.*

tollentibus, xiii. 56, see *uellentibus.*

tolli, i. 15, see *aboleri.*

tomos, see *temoys.*

ton, xxx. 16, see *ho platon.*

tonica [tunica], iii. 56, see *ependiten*; xxix. 11, see *mauria*; xxxix. 32, see *dalmatica*; see further *tunica.*

ton philona, xxx. 15; see *ho platon.*

topadius, see *topation.*

toparcha, loci princeps topus locus, xxxv. 7 (*Ruf.* i. 15 fol. 16[a] *Toparcha*) = *toparca*, loci princeps, Cp. T203; Ep. 26C23; Ef.[1] 395, 34.

topation, ut aurum micat, xli. 15 (*De nomin. div.*? = *Apoc.* xxi. 20 *topadius*; *Exod.* xxviii. 17, xxxix. 10; *Ezek.* xxviii. 13 *topazius*; cf. *Psa.* cxviii. 127 dilexi mandata tua super aurum et *topazion*) = *topazion* ut aqua micat ut est porrus, Cp. T210; Ep. 26E2; Ef.[1] 395, 50. For *ut est porrus* in the present Glossary see above *cypressus.*

topazion, topazius, see *topation.*

topicon, see *tropicon.*

topus, xxxv. 7, see *toparcha.*

toraca, lurica [lor-], xlv. 17; see *thoraces.*

toracina, haeslin, iii. 38 (*De S. Mart. Stor.* = *Sulp. Sev. Dial.* i. 19, 1 *storacinam* uirgam). Cf. Werden fragm. *toracia*, haeslin (Gallée, *O. Sax. Texts*, 344, 239). For *haeslin* (of hazel), cf. Bosw. T. (*hæslen*).—For *toracina*, see also *toronicum.*

torax, lurica [lor-] manicas non habens &c. xi. 4; **torax**, pectus, xix. 42; see *thoraces.*

toreuma, tormina, see *uertigo.*

toronicam, see *toronicum.*

toronicum, genus ligni, iii. 6 (*De S. Mart. Stor.*?). Cf. Sulp. Sev. *Dial.* i. 27, 2 audietis me...ut *Gurdonicum* [in note: *gorthonicum*, *gortonicum*, *gurtonicum*, *gorgonicum*] hominem, nihil cum fuco aut cothurno loquentem). With this word, however, the interpretation (genus ligni) does not agree, which was, perhaps, intended for *toracina* q. v. If this be the case, the interpretation to *toronicum* is wanting. Cf. the Werd. Gloss. *toronicam*, genis ligni (Gallée, *O. Sax. texts* 344, 238).

torquemina, xii. 27, see *tortura.*

torqueri, xliv. 10, see *cardines.*

torrens, see *suricus.*

torris, arrura quę de igne rapitur, xvii. 4 (*Amos* iv. 11 facti estis quasi *torris* raptus ab incendio). Cf. *torris*, prant (A.S. and M. E. *brand*), Steinm. i. 672, 61; for *arrura* perhaps leg. *arsura* (Du C.), or **assura.*

torta panis, incisus panis, xiv. 21 (*Hier.* xxxviii. 20 daretur ei *torta panis*).

tortura, torquemina, xii. 27 (*Eccles.* xxxi. 23 Vigilia, cholera et *tortura* viro infrunito).

tos (hoc), xxx. 96; see *ypo* (sub) *tos* (hoc) &c.

toscia [= *toxa* = *toga*], ii. 101, see *lena.*

tota, xlii. 21, see *basterna.*

totam, xxxix. 36, see *sex untias.*

totegis, procella, xxxviii. 41 (*Clem. Rom. Recognitt.* x. 32 Hanc *procellam*, quae καταιγὶς Graece appellatur).

toto, xxviii. 41, see *sinecdochen.*

totum, xiii. 43, see *lamia*; xxxix. 72, see *olografia.*

totus, suæ ald, xliii. 40; see *quotus.*

toxa, see *lena.*

toyty, see *pantocranto.*

trabea, trabes, trabis, see *tenda.*

trabus, xxii. 5, see *tenda.*

tractatores, xlviii. 48, see *commectarum.*

tractatus, iv. 8, see *commentatus.*

tractu, xxviii. 77, see *sinastrismus.*

tradiderunt, xx. 1, see *manciparunt.*

tradito, ii. 21, see *adsignato.*

tragica, tragicus, see *traicus.*

trago, xxxv. 1, see *tragoedia.*

tragoedia, luctus ac cladis, iv. 11; **tragoedia**, bellica cantica uel fabulatio uel hircania Trago Hircus, xxxv. 1 (*Ruf.* i. 8 fol. 12[a] *Tragœdia* magis quam historia texi uidebitur; iii. 6 fol. 36[a] omnis...luctuosa *Tragoedia*). Cf. *tragoedia*, bebbi cantio, Cp. T263; *tragoedia*, belli cantia uel fabulatio, Ep. 26E18; *tragoedia*, belli c.

u. f., Ef.[1] 396, 8. On the H (of Hircus) see note § on p. 33. For *tragoedia* see also *eunuchus*.

trahent, XIII. 36, see *in serris*.

traica [tragica], XLIII. 24, see *traicus*.

traicus [tragicus], qui traica [tragica] scribsit [scrip-], XLIII. 24, see *comicus*.

traiectione, XII. 33, see *de traiectione*.

traigis, see *picus*.

trallis, nomen ecclesię, IV. 37 (*Ruf.* III. 36 fol. 51[a] ecclesiæ quæ est *Trallis* scribit).

tramaritius [for *tamaricius*], XIV. 10, see *miricę*.

transcensio, XXVIII. 87, see *yperbaton*.

transferuntur, XXVIII. 44, see *hypallage*.

translata, XXVIII. 33, see *tropus*.

translatio, IV. 98, see *comellas*; XXVIII. 76, see *metafora*.

translationem, XXVIII. 55, see *metaforan*.

transmigrationis, XV. 3, see *uas transmigrationis*.

transnominatio, XXVIII. 28, see *metonymia*.

transportare, XLIII. 18, see *carus*.

transtra, tabula [Cambr. MS. *tabulę*] quę iacent in transuersu [Cambr. MS. *transuersum*] nauis in quibus sedent remigantes, XV. 9 (*Ezech.* XXVII. 6 *transtra* tua fecerunt). Cf. E. *thwart* (a seat across the boat on which an oarsman sits, Cent. Dict.) and *transom* (Skeat, *Conc. Dict.*).

transuersu, transuersum, XV. 9, see *transtra*.

trapezeta et **nummularius** et **colobista** idem sunt qui nummis fenerantur et uilis negotiis, XXIX. 42 (*Uerb. Interpr.*=*Hier. in Matth.* XXV. 26–28 col. 188[B] qui dari debuit *nummulariis* et *trapezitis*; ibid. XXI. 12, 13 col. 150[C] pro *nummulariis collybistas* facerent...usuras accipere non poterant *collybistæ*). Cf. *trapizeta*, mensularius, Cp. T275; Ep. 27C39; Ef.[1] 397, 52.—**trapezita**, qui in mensa nummorum per mutationes uictum querit [quaerit], XXXVIII. 29 (*Clem. Recognitt.* IX. 24 vel sculptores vel *trapezitas* efficiat...nunquam invenitur *trapezita*). Goetz (VII. 363) suggests to read *permutatione* for *per mutationes*.

trapezitas [for *trapetias*?], XV. 12, see *bibli*.

trapezitis, see *trapezeta*.

trea (=tria), see *responsoria*.

tres, XXXI. 6, see *solidos*; 11, see *ephi*, 39, see *chatos*; XXXII. 4, see *obolus*; **tres**, XXXIII. 30, see *siliquae tres*.—**tres argenteos** solidum faciunt, XXXI. 28 (*De ponder.*?).

triangulum, XII. 40, see *cyneris*.

tribuit, I. 125, see *sanxit*.

tribulatione, XIX. 50, see *carmina in nocte*.

tribus, IV. 79, see *de triuio*; XIII. 30, see *in triuiis*; XVI. 18, see *trieres*; XXXV. 238, see *de triuio*.

tributarii, XXXIX. 61, see *municipii*.

tributum, quod semper fit, XXIV. 8 (*Math.* XVII. 24 accipiunt *tributum*). For *tributum* see also (IV. 64) *fiscum*.

trices, XII. 23, see *non trices*.

trie, see *trinte artabę*.

trieres, idest naues a tribus sessionibus, XVI. 18 (*Dan.* XI. 30 venient super eum *trieres*). Cf. *trieris*, magna nauis tribus, Cp. T253; *t.*, m. n. t. remigis, Ep. 26C26; *t.*, m. n. t. remit, Ef.[1] 395, 37.

trifulus, see *truffulus*.

trilex, see *bilex*.

trinte artabę, XI modios faciunt, XVI. 22 (*Dan.* XIV. 2 impendebantur...similae *artabae* duodecim). For XI the Glossary had XIII, but the last two numerals are marked for erasure. The Cambr. MS. has *Trie artabę* Decem modios faciunt. Cf. *tres artabae* X modios faciunt, Cp. T248; Ep. 26C2; Ef.[1] 395, 14.

tripla, I. 115, see *sescopla*.

triplex, drili, XLVI. 41, see *bilex*.

tripudiaret, uinceret, XXXV. 174 (*Ruf.* V. 3 fol. 78[b] fiebat, ut in uerberibus *tripudiaret*). Cf. *tripudiare*, uincere, Cp. T265; Ep. 26E23; Ef.[1] 396, 13.

triste, XII. 6, see *acide*.

tristis, II. 9, see *acidiosus*.

tritici, XII. 36, see *similaginem*; XXXVII. 3, 4, see *fidelia farris*.

tritura, XVII. 1, see *area sitiens*.

[triuium] in triuiis, in tribus uiis, XIII. 30 (*Isai.* XV. 3 *in triviis* eius)=*in triuis*, in tribus uis, Cp. I145; *in triuiis*, in tribus uiis, Ep. 12A25; *in triuis*, in tribus uiis, Ef.[1] 366, 22.—**de triuio**, de tribus uiis, IV. 79 (*Eccl. Istor.*) and XXXV. 238 (*De Eus.*) =(*Ruf.* IX. 5 fol. 148[b] mulierculas *de triuio* conquisitas).

trium, XVII. 7, see *Niniue*.

trochleis, see *troclei*; *trogleis*.

troclei, rotis modicis, XXXV. 40 (*De Euseb.*); **trogleis**, hlędrę, IV. 74 (*Eccl. Istor.*)=(*Ruf.* VIII. 10 fol. 139[b] alii...*trochleis* distenti). The first gloss seems to mean "pulleys with small wheels." *Trochlea*, *troclea*, is explained (by Lewis and Sh.) as "a mechanical contrivance for raising weights, a case or sheaf containing one or more pulleys, a block." The Gr. τροχιλέα, the sheaf of a pulley, roller of a windlass (Liddell & Sc.), and this from τροχός (1) a wheel; (2) a course, place for running. Some Glossators may have understood it to mean "a thing to run up, with small *rounds*," i.e. "a ladder," and hence *hlędrę* (= *hlædræ*), which may = A.S. *hlæder*, *hlædder*, a ladder, flight of steps. Glogger suggests A.S. *hlædel* (Bosw. T.), a ladle, an instrument for drawing water. Cf. *trocleis*, stricilum, Cp. T266; *trocleis*, rotis modicis uel stricilum, Ep. 26E25; Ef.[1] 396, 15. For *stricilum* (instr. pl. of *stricel*), see Bosw. T. (*stricel*, a strickle).

trofon, see *catastrofon*.

trogleis, hlędrę, IV. 74, see *troclei*.

trophaea, see *tropia*.

tropia, signa, XXXV. 126 (*Ruf.* II. 25 fol. 33ª habeo *trophaea* apostolorum; ibid. fol. 33ᵇ inuenies *trophaea*).

tropicon, maralium [mor-], XXX. 78 (*Cat. Hier.* LXXXI col. 689ᴮ τοπικῶν liber; B: *topicon* idest mortalium librum; C: [blank]) = *tropicon*, moralium, Cp. T255.

tropus est dictio ab eo loco in quo propria est translata in eum locum in quo propri (!) non est ut est exsurge domine, XXVIII. 33 (*Cass. Psalm.* III. 6 col. 46ᴬ *Tropus* autem est d. a. e. l. i. q. p. e. t. i. e. l. i. q. propria n. e. [ut est added by Glossator] exsurge domine [quoted from col. 45ᴰ]).

trudit, XLVIII. 8, see *inpegit*.

truffulus, felospric, XLVII. 18 (*Alia* = ?) = *trufulus*, feluspreci, Cp. T288; *trifulus*, felospraeci, Ep. 27A10; *trufulus*, feluspraeici, Ef.[1] 396, 39. *Felospric* &c., much talking (Germ. *vielgesprächig*) from *felo*, *felu*, much; and *spraeci* &c. speech, talking. For *trifulus*, *truffulus*, Goetz (VII. 370) unnecessarily suggests to read *friuolus*. Glogger connects it with Ital. *truffa* (Körting, *Wört.* 9794), deceit, boasting, and regards *truffulus* as a subst., meaning a braggart (Ital. *truffaldino*).—It really = E. "trifler"; see Skeat, *Conc. Etym. Dict.* (*trifle*). Cf. John Florio *Dict.* (1598), "*Truffarello*, a craftie, cosening, cheating, conicatching, filching knave." The double spelling *trifulus*, *trufulus* still appears in M. E. *trifle*, *trufle*.

trufulus, see *truffulus*.

trulla, ferrum latum unde parietes liment, XVII. 5 (*Amos*, VII. 7 in manu eius *trulla* caementarii; VII. 8 *trullam*). E. *trowel*.

truncatis, see *busta*.

truncatus, IV. 15, see *plexus*.

trungatis [trunc-], XXXV. 86, see *busta*.

tu, XXVIII. 18, see *apo tu-*.

tuae, see *emissiones*.

tuba, XLVIII. 57, see *classica*.

tuber, in dorso cameli, XLVI. 13 (*Alia* = *Ars Phocae*, p. 415, 15 hoc *tuber*). Cf. *tuber*, tumor, asuollen, Cp. T326; *t.*, t. uel suollaen, Ep. 27A19; *t.*, t. uel assuollam, Ef.[1] 396, 48.

tubolo, fala, XLVII. 41 (*Alia* = ?) = *tubolo*, fala, Cp. T321; *tabula*, fala, Ep. 27A11; *tabulo*, fala, Ef.[1] 396, 40. For *tubolo* Glogger suggests *tubulus*, a small pipe or tube; and Schlutter (*Journ. Germ. Phil.* I p. 314) would read *stabula*, *fald*. But this gloss, which was discussed in my Preface (p. XLIII) to the Corpus Glossary, seems to need no alteration except *tabula* (a plank) for *tubolo*. From the A. S. *fala* (a plank) was derived *falod*, a fold, (sheep-)pen, lit. "a thing made of wooden bars" (= L. *tabulatum*, planking). It is not recorded in Bosw. T., but see Bobellum (for *bovellum* = *bovillum*, a cattle-stall), *falod*, Wright W. 358, 21; bofellum (for *bovillum*), *falud*, Cp. B148; bobellum, *falaed*, Ep. 6A1 and Ef.[1] 347, 12; stabulum, *falaed*, Cp. S549; Ep. 25A13; Ef.[1] 392, 37. See further Skeat, *Conc. Et. Dict.* (*fold*); Oxf. D. (fold); Franck, *Woordenb.* (*vaalt*).

tuę, X. 15, see *emissiones tuę*.

tu epitimitisun, concupiscibili, XXIX. 60 (*Uerb. Interpr.* = *Hier. in Matth.* XIII. 33 τὸ ἐπιθυμητικὸν quod appellamus *concupiscibile*).

tueri, protegere uel custodire, II. 180 (*Bened. reg.* 69, 4 [4] ne...praesumat alter alium...*tueri*).

tugurium, domuncula, XIII. 2 (*Isai.* I. 8 *tugurium* in cucumerario).

tumor, V. 16, see *podagra*; see also *fastus*.

tumultuosam, XXIII. 18, see *contionem*.

tumultus, I. 116, see *seditio*.

tumulum, IV. 100, see *bustus*.

tunguitur [for *tinguitur*?], XVI. 9, see *malleolis*.

tunica, XI. 4, see *torax*; also written *tonica* (q. v.).

turba, IV. 81, see *calones*; XLVIII. 16, see *manus*.

turbam, XXXV. 121, see *manum*.

turdela, see *turdella*.

turdella, drostlae, XLVII. 55 (*Alia* = ?) = *t.*, ðrostle, Cp. T323; *t-*, throstlae, Ep. 27A13 and Ef.[1] 396, 42. For *turdella* (dim. of *turdus*, a thrush, fieldfare), see Forcellini-De-Vit (*turdela*); Isid. *Etym.* XII. 7, 71 (*turdela*); Georg. *Lat. D. Wrt.* (*turdela*, *turdella*, eine kleine Drossel). For *drostlae*, *throstlae*, *ðrostle*, a throstle, see Bosw. T. (*þrostle*); Kluge, *Et. Wrtb.* (*Drossel*); Skeat, *Conc. Dict.* (*throstle*).

turdus, scruc, XLVII. 63 (*Alia* = ?) = *t-*, scric, Cp. T324; *t-*, scric, Ep. 27A15; *t-*, screc, Ef.[1] 396, 43. *turdus*, a thrush, fieldfare. For (*scruc*, in the MS., read) *scriic*, *scric*, *screc* (a shrike; skrike, screech), see Bosw. T. (*scric*). For *turdus*, see also *turdella*.

turgidis, IV. 78, see *suppuratis*.

turibula, XIII. 9, see *olfactoriola*; XIV. 35, see *thimia materia*.

turno-, see *turnodo*.

turnodo [sine interpret.], III. 9 (*De S. Martyni Storia?*). Glogger suggests as lemma *cothurno* [elevated style] in *Sulp. Sev. Dial.* I. 27, 2: audietis me...ut Gurdonicum hominem, nihil cum fuco aut *cothurno* [*coturno*, in some MSS.] loquentem. He regards -do as a corrupted A. S. word, referring to Corpus C840: Coturno, podhae (instr. of poþ, eloquence), which has been misunderstood by Wülcker (*Vocab.* 15, 33), where coturno is taken as=coturnix, and a wood-hen made of it; see Schlutter in *Anglia*, XXVI. 308, and cf. Werden *Gloss.* turno .i. nodo (Gallée, *O. Sax. texts* 345, 266); and Münst. *Gloss* cuturno crincę (ibid. 336, 7).

turpem, II. 11, see *absurdum*.

turpes, XXXV. 166, see *scenas turpes*.

turpiter, XXXV. 33, see *bachantes*.

turres, XXXVI. 5, see *fares*.

turris, XXXV. 248, see *pirgos*.

tu thimisiun, plenum irę, XXIX. 59 (*Uerb. Interpr.*=*Hier. in Matth.* XIII. 33 τὸ θυμικὸν quod dicamus *plenum iræ*).

tuum, X. 5, see *nomen tuum*.

tybicen, qui tibia cantat, XLVI. 7 (*Alia*= *Ars Phocae*, p. 415, 3 hic *tibicen*). Cf. *tibicen*, qui cum tibia canit, Cp. T176; Ep. 27C24; Ef.[1] 396, 50.

tyfo, see *typo*.

tympanum, in quattuor lignis extensa pellis, XIX. 20 (*Job* XXI. 12 tenent *tympanum*).

tyos (hoc), XXX. 95; see *ypo* (sub) *tyos* &c.

typho [the correct form for] *typo*, q.v.

Typhonis, see *tifon*.

typhum, see *typum*.

typo [for *typho*], inflatio cordis uel superbia, II. 179 (*Bened. reg.* 31, 25 constitutam annonam sine aliquo *typho*... offerat [*typo*, *tipu*, in note]; 50 *tyfo*, *tipho*, *typo*, *tipo*). Cf. *tipo*, draca uel inflatio, Cp. T182; *tipo*, droco, Ep. 27E23; *tipo*, draco, Ef.[1] 398, 20.—**typum**, inflationem, XXXIX. 71 (not in Greg. Dial., but *Can. Conc. Carth.* CXXXIV p. 172ᵃ non sumus iam istum *typhum* passuri; id. CXXXVIII p. 174ᵇ ne fumosum *typhum* seculi... videamur inducere).

typo, signo, XLII. 22 (*Ex div. libris?*). Cf. Isid. *contra Judaeos*, in Napier's *Old Engl. Glosses*, p. 206, 17 (*tipo*, hiwe).

typum [for *typhum*], inflationem, XXXIX. 71, see *typo* (for *typho*).

tyrannidem, see *tirannidem*.

tyrannides, see *tirannidem*, *tirannides*.

tyrannus, see *tyrsamus*.

tyrones, noui milites, XIV. 31 (*Hier.* LII. 25 probabat *tyrones*).

tyrsamus, predator [praed-], XXXIV. 37 (*De Cass. Inst.* XII. 3, 2 *tyrannus*...ciuitatem diruit).

Tyrus, insula, XXIV. 14 (*Math.* XI. 21 Si in *Tyro* et Sidone factae essent virtutes; XI. 22 *Tyro* et Sidoni remissius erit; XV. 21 Jesus secessit in partes *Tyri* et Sidonis).

u for *a*: lucunar (for lac-); lumina (lam-); petulum (petalum); platissu (platissa).—for *b*: Ceruerus (Cerb-); fauę (fabae); fauorum (fabarum); uorith (borith).—for *f*: inuastum (infausti); uolles (folles).—for *i*: tunguitur (tinguitur).—for *o*: adolatur (? for adulator); adsentatur (? for adsentator); aduliscentulę (adolescentulae); emulumentum (emol-); furtunam (fort-); furtunatam (fortunam); hierufontis (hierophantis); infusuria (-soria); lurica (lor-); philuluguis (philologos); publite (poplite); puplites (poplite); simbulis (symbolis); simbulum (symbolum).—for *y*: saturicus (satyr-); saturus (satyrus).—u (v) *omitted*: expolierit (-liuerit); u *omitted*: inuastum (infausti); sectura (secutura); ungentorum (unguent-).

uacasse, see *uaruassi*.

uacca, III. 26, see *bacula*.

uacillantem, fugantem, XLVIII. 4 (*De Cass., Inst.* V. 6 mentem...escarum nimietas *uacillantem*...reddit).

uacua, IX. 2, see *cassa*.

uacuasse, see *uaruassi*.

uaena, dicitur per quam aqua currit, VIII. 12; **blena**, dicitur per quam aqua currit, VIII. 14 (*Salam.* V. 18 Sit *vena* tua benedicta; X. 11 *vena* vitae; XXV. 26 *vena* corrupta).

uaene [uenae], XXIX. 22, see *meatus*.

uaeri, uirge ferreę, XXXV. 81; see the explanation in v. *reusti*.

uagus, II. 9, see *acidiosus*.

ualde, I. 78, see *nauiter*.

ualebat, XI. 11, see *in aqua ualebat*.

ualens, XLIII. 19, see *cruda*.

ualuas, modicus murus ante portam, XXIII. 10 (2 *Esdra* III. 1 statuerunt *valvas* ejus; see also *ibid.* III. 3, 6, 13 &c.).

uana [uano?], XXVI. 13, see *uaruassi*.

uangas, spaedun, XXXIX. 12 (*Greg. Dial.* III. 14 col. 245ᴮ ferramenta quae usitato nos nomine *vangas* vocamus...; Tot *vangas* in hortum projicite, &c. *four times*)= *uangas*, spadan, Cp. U13; Ep. 28C25;

Ef.[1] 399, 43. *vanga*, a kind of mattock, or a spade with a cross-bar (Lew. and Sh.); for *spaedun*, *spadan*, see Bosw. T. (*spadu*, *spædu*, a spade); Skeat, *Conc. D.* (*spade*[1]).

uano, see *uaruassi.*

uaporat, exurit, xxvii. 12 (*Isid. Lib. Rot.*=*Lib. de nat. rer.* vii. 3 aerem ipsum *vaporat*)=Cp. U10; Ep. 28C5; Ef.[1] 399, 24 *uaporat*, inurit.

uaria, xliii. 10, see *omonima.*

uariatum, iv. 96, see *stomatum.*

uaricat [he straddles, strides], stritęd, xlvii. 43 (*Alia*=?)=*u*-, stridit, Cp. U12; Ep. 28C24; Ef.[1] 399, 41. For *stritęd*, *stridit*, he strides, see Bosw. T. (*strīdan*); Skeat, *Conc. D.* (*stride*).

uarietas stromactis, de sternatione ubi paganorum et xpistianorum colleguntur quasi ex lectulo uarietatis, xxx. 35; see *stromatum.*

uarietate, xxviii. 37, see *metabole*; xxxviii. 6, see *stragula.*

uarietatis, xxx. 35, see *uarietas stromactis.*

uarietatum, see *uarietas stromactis.*

uariis, xxii. 11, see *mundum m-.*

uario, xix. 15, see *tigris.*

uarix, omprę in cruribus hominum, xlvi. 27 (*Alia*=*Ars Phocae*, p. 421, 6 hic *varix* varicis)=*uarix*, ampre, Cp. U8; *uarix*, amprae, Ep. 28A40; *uarix*, omprae, Ef.[1] 399, 19. For *omprę*, *ampre*, cf. the Oxf. Dict. *amper* (a tumour or swelling), *anbury*; Schlutter (in *Anglia* xix. 493 sq.).

uaruassi, de uana [uano?] dictum, xxvi. 13 (*Isid. Offic.*?). Glogger suggests vac[u]asse; see Isid. *Offic.* i. 18, 9 *vacasse* ab opere, and Steinm. ii. 342, 47 *uacasse.*

uas, vi. 12, see *albri*; xv. 1, see *atramentarium*, 3 (bis), see *uas transmigrationis*; xxii. 12, see *urna*; xxiv. 13, see *alabastrum*; xxv. 13, see *in peluem*; xxix. 47, see *lagonam*; xxxv. 57, see *cunabulum*; xxxvii. 3–5, see *fidelia farris.*—[fem., *uas regia*], iii. 32, see *patera.*—**uas transmigrationis**, aut carrum aut uas alterum paruum, xv. 3 (*Ezech.* xii. 3 fac tibi *vasa transmigrationis*; xii. 4 *vasa transmigrationis*).—uasa, xiv. 36, see *urceos*; xvii. 16, see *infusuria*; xxix. 14, see *lanternis.*—**uasa castrorum**, arma exercitum [-tuum] idest milicie [militiae] cęli [caeli] dicitur enim quod bella futura possent preuidere [praeu-] in sole et luna, xii. 42 (*Eccles.* xliii. 9 *vas castrorum*; Camb. MS. *Vasa c.*, a. exercituum Militie cęli dicuntur q. b. f. possint prouideri i. s. e. l.)=*uasa castrorum*, arma exercituum, idest militiae caeli dicuntur, Cp. U51. On this phrase see Wace's *Apocr.* ii. 207.

uasa castrorum, arma exercitum &c., see above, sub v. *uas.*

uase, viii. 18, see *ptisanas*; xxii. 12, see *urna*; xxxv. 49, see *loculo.*

uates, see *uatis.*

uatis, propheta, xxxv. 97 (*De Euseb.*); **fates**, propheta, iv. 5 (*Eccl. Istor.*)=(*Ruf.* i. 1 fol. 5[a] Dauid magnificus *vates*; i. 1 fol. 5[b] *vates* Esaias).

ubera, apostoli, x. 2 (*Cant.* i. 1 meliora sunt *ubera* tua vino; i. 3 memores *uberum* tuorum; i. 12 inter *ubera* mea).

ubi, i. 65, 126; ii. 169 (bis); iv. 47; viii. 8, 10; x. 22 (bis); xv. 21, 29, 31; xvi. 1; xvii. 7, 20; xxiii. 9; xxvii. 28; xxviii. 36, 88; xxix. 21; xxx. 4–7, 26, 35; xxxv. 82, 235; xxxvi. 3, 4; xxxix. 50, 53; xlv. 1.

ubicumque, ii. 169, see *ubi et ubi.*

ubi et ubi, ubicumque, ii. 169 (*Bened. reg.* 46, 6 *ibi*; note *ubi et*, *ubiubi*; [7 *ubi*; note *ubi ubi*, *ubi uel ubi*]); Edm. Schmidt *Regula*, ubiubi, and ubi et ubi; 63, 33 *ubique*; in MS. T *ubiubi*; in MS. S *ubi et ubi*; [60 *ubiubi*, *ubi et ubi* note]. See further Traube, *Textgeschichte*, p. 695.

ubique, ubiubi, see *ubi et ubi.*

udo, see *odonis uittam.*

-ue, xxviii. 88, see *personisue.*

uecordiae, see *uecors.*

uecors, malo corde, xxxv. 114 (*Ruf.* ii. 11 fol. 24[a] *vecordiae* eius indulsit).

uectandi gratia, exercendi, xlii. 24 (*Ex div. libris*=? *Vita S. Eugen.* 3, Migne lxxiii col. 607[B] ut *spectandi gratia* permitteretur praedia sua... circuire)=*uectandi gratia*, exercendi, Cp. U91; *uectandi gratia*, idest exercendi, Ep. 28A36; Ef.[1] 399, 16. *Uectandi* seems to be a different reading.

uectical [-gal], xlvi. 11, see *lucar.*

uectigal, see *lucar.*

uectis, v. 4, see *canto.*

ueemoth, bestia ignota, xix. 37 (*Job* xl. 10 Ecce *Behemoth*; Heyse, in note, *vehemoth*).

ueendo [uehendo], xxii. 16, see *ueredarii.*

vehemoth, see *ueemoth.*

uehendo, see *ueredarii.*

uehiculi, iii. 16, see *reda.*

uel, i. 4 (bis), 19, 22, 27, 28 (bis), 30, 35, 36, 45, 47, 52–54, 57, 58, 71, 81, 82, 85, 87 (bis), 88, 90, 91, 94, 114, 115 (bis), 118, 122, 129, 132; ii. 3, 21, 27, 46, 65, 67, 69, 70, 88, 100, 110, 113, 116, 125, 128, 134, 151, 152, 153 (bis), 159, 172, 179, 180, 182; iii. 56 (bis), 59; iv. 4, 52, 100; v. 27; vi. 1; vii. 3; viii. 7, 10, 18; x. 7, 25; xii. 1, 29, 34, 38, 39; xiii. 6, 7 (bis), 9, 15, 21; xiv. 5, 12; xv. 4, 12, 14,

18, 40; xvi. 21; xvii. *tit.*, 3; xix. 14, 59; xxi. 5, 17–19; xxii. 1; xxiii. 12; xxv. 1; xxvi. 9; xxvii. 3, 5, 19, 20, 27, 32; xxviii. 6, 17, 71; xxix. 12, 35 (bis), 40, 43, 71; xxx. 27, 29, 38, 65, 71, 73, 87, 92, 94; xxxiii. 7; xxxv. 1 (bis), 24, 34, 37, 38, 45, 59, 61, 71, 72, 80, 87, 93, 96, 107, 110, 141, 143, 146–148, 158, 171, 176, 186, 194, 195, 211, 215, 226, 243, 252, 260; xxxvi. 2 (ter); xxxvii. 9; xxxviii. 42; xxxix. 13, 24, 63; xli. 21; xlii. 3, 21; xliii. 3, 29, 48, 52, 56; xliv. 4 (bis); xlvi. 23–25, 28; xlvii. 81; xlviii. 14, 15, 38.

uellentibus, tollentibus pilos de genis, xiii. 56 (*Isai.* l. 6 dedi...genas meas *vellentibus*).

vellere, see *lanugo*.

ueloces, xlviii. 33, see *perpeti*.

uelocissimus, xix. 15, see *tigris*.

uelocitas, ii. 160, see *sagatitas*; xlviii. 31, see *pernities*.

uelociter, xxxv. 8, see *age*; see also *uelotiter*; *efficaciter*.

uelocius, see *ocilis*.

uelotiter [ueloc-], ii. 63, see *efficaciter*, 77, see *facile*.

uelotius [-cius], xlviii. 67, see *ocilis*.

uelox, xlvi. 29, see *pernix*.

uelut, xxviii. 42, see *idea*.

uena, see *blena*; *uaena*.

uenae, see *meatus*.

uenas, xxxv. 190, see *fibras*.

uendentur, xlviii. 47, see *distrauntur*.

uendunt, xxxv. 72, see *lanionibus*.

uenę [-nae], xxix. 61, see *puruys*.

uenit, xlii. 23, see *quartane*.

uentis, v. 12, see *labris*.

uentris, xxxiv. 36, see *gastrimargia*; xxxv. 2, see *coli*, 6, see *tentigo*.

uerba, xxviii. 24, see *ypozeuxis*, 30, see *epembabis*, 44, see *hypallage*, 47, see *parenthesin*, 58, see *apostropei*; xl *tit.*—uerba de multis, xlv *tit.*—uerba de sancti martyni storia, iii *tit.*

uerbera, flagella, ii. 185 (*Bened. reg.* 2, 61 [91] *uerberum* vel corporis castigatione; 28, 5 [6] *uerberum* vindictae; 30, 7 [9] acris *uerberibus* coerceantur).

uerberibus, uerberum, see *uerbera*.

uerbi, ii. 182 (bis), see *uerbi gratia*; xxviii. 75, see *prolemsis*; xxx. 24, see *philuluguis*.

uerbi geratione, see *uerbigratione*.

uerbi gratia, ut si forte uel uerbi causa, ii. 182 (*Bened. reg.* 24, 10 [16] si *verbi gratia*; 63, 15 [26] ut *verbi gratia*). Cf. *uerbi gratia*, uuordes intinga (for the sake of a word; Bosw. T. *word*; *intinga*), Cp. U149.

uerbigratione, sermotinatione [sermocin-], ii. 171 (*Bened. reg.*? Goetz in his Index prints *verbigeratione*, and on this word cf. G. Landgraf in *Archiv f. Lat. Lex.* ix. 440).

uerbis, iv. 68, see *elogis*; xvi. 31, see *incantatores*; xix. 28, see *iubilo*; xxxv. 270, see *elogiis*.

uerbo, xxviii. 45, see *zeuma*.

uerborum, i *tit.*, see *glosae*; xxviii. 25, see *scema*, 37, see *metabole*, 78, see *hyperbaton*; xxix *tit.*

uerbositate, ii. 105, see *loquacitate*.

uerbotenus, sicut dico, ii. 70 (*Bened. reg.*?).

uerbum, xxviii. 72, see *anaphora*, 76, see *metafora*.

uere, i. 86, see *prorsus*.

uerecundia, ii. 150, see *rubor*.

ueredarii, dicuntur a ueendo [uehendo] qui festinanter in equis currunt non descendentes de equis antequam liberant responsa sua habent pennas in capite ut inde intellegatur festinatio itineris daturque eis semper equus paratus non manducant nisi super equos antequam perficiantur, xxii. 16 (*Esther* viii. 10 epistolæ...missæ per *veredarios*; viii. 14 egressi sunt *veredarii*). See Steinm. i. 488, note 17; Skeat, *Conc. Et. Dict.* (*palfrey*).

uermes, xxxviii. 5, see *chantari*; xxxix. 7, see *erucę*.

uermibus, x. 11, see *tigna*; xiv. 34, see *uitulam...*

uermiculus, a similitudine uermis, xiii. 3 (*Isai.* i. 18 si fuerint peccata vestra... rubra quasi *vermiculus*). Cambr. MS. *vermiculus*. Tinctura ad similitudinem vermis. For *vermiculus* see also *rubeum*.

uermis, xiii. 3, see *uermiculus*; xlvii. 15, see *tappula*, 89, see *bulinus*.

uerna, mancipium, xlv. 23 (*Uerba de multis*=*Ars Phocae*, p. 412, 27 auriga conviva *verna*).

uero, xvi. 27; xxviii. 18, 20; xxxi. 12; xxxiii. 13.

uerres, uerris, see *bęrrus*.

uerruca, see *berruca*.

uerrus, see *bęrrus*.

uersę, viii. 2, see *coacuerint*.

uersipellis, peruersus, viii. 5 (*Salam.* xiv. 25 profert mendacia *versipellis*).

uersum, contra, xlviii. 49 (*De Cass.*, *Inst.* iv. 21 *uersus* mare...tenditur).—**uersus**, contra, vi. 4 (*Breu. exsol.*?).

uertente, xxii. 12, see *urna*.

uertex, see *uertix*.

uerti, xliv. 9, see *cęlum*.

uerticem, xxxv. 277, see *iugum montium*; xliv. 16, see *antarticus*, 19, see *hiemisperium*.

uertigo, eduallę, xlvii. 16 (*Alia* = ?) =

uertigo, eduuelle, Cp. U89; *u*-, edwalla? Ep. 28A33; *u*-, edualla, Ef.[1] 399, 13. It would seem that the A. S. interpretation may mean *giddiness, dizziness*, as perhaps here, or *a whirlpool, eddy, vortex*, as Cp. A490 (alueum, eduaell), F300 (uortex, edpelle), S129 (scylla, eduuelle), T214 (toreuma for tormina? eduuaelle); see *ed-wielle*, a whirlpool, dizziness (Bosw. T.). Kluge (*A. S. Leseb.* p. 172) gives only *strudel* (whirlpool). Cf. Goetz, vii. 407 (*uertigo*).
uertix [-tex], xliv. 25, see *dextera*, 26, see *a tergo*, 27, see *leua*.
ueru, snaas, xlvi. 1 (*Alia*=*Ars Phocae*, p. 414, 13 *veru*). For *snaas*, a spit, skewer, see Bosw. T. (*snās, snǣs*).
verua, see *uaeri*.
uesani, insani, xxxv. 177 (*Ruf.* v. 16 fol. 85[b] *uesani* et...bacchantes).
uespertinorum, ii. 151, see *sinaxis*.
ueste, xii. 41, see *lino crudo*.
uestibus, iii. 56, see *ependiten*; xxii. 11, see *mundum m*-.
uestigia, xxxi. 24, see *choros*.
uestimenta, xiii. 11, see *mutatoria*; xxix. 39, see *prorusu*; see also *lectisternia*.
uestimentum, xv. 18, see *inuoluere*; xxv. 8, see *byssus*.
uestis, iii. 56, see *ependiten*; iv. 105, see *propositus*; xi. 14, see *poderis*; xiii. 13, see *fascia pectoralis*; xxvi. 5, see *folligantes*, 12, see *follicantes*.
uestium, xiv. 33, see *lacinias*.
uestmenta [uestim-], ii. 100; see *lectisternia*.
uetellus, see *uitelios*.
ueteranorum, see *ueternorum*.
ueterem, ii. 187, see *uetustam*.
ueternorum, ueterum, iii. 1 (*De S. Mart. Stor.*=*Sulp. Sev. Vit. S. Mart.* 1, 2, 5 *ueteranorum* filii).
ueternosa, see *decrepita*.
ueterum, iii. 1, see *ueternorum*.
uetorosa [ueternosa], xxvi. 9, see *decrepita*.
uetustam, ueterem, ii. 187 (*Bened. reg.* 55, 8 [12] sufficere credimus...cucullam... *vetustam*).
ui for *y*: Coquiton for Cocyti.
ui, i. 48, see *extorris*; xliv. 10, see *cardines*.
uia, viii. 8, see *in aceruo m*-; xxviii. 53, see *paraprosdocia*; xxxix. 44, see *glebum*. —**uia secta**, iringesuuec, xxvii. 28; see *in georgicis*.
uiarum, xxx. 87, see *otheporicon*; [for *uiaticum*?] xxx. 71, see *sinphosin*.
uiaticum, see *sinphosin*.
uice, i. 100, see *proconsolaris*, 101, see *procuratores*; xxxi. 25, see *pes*.
uicia, see *uicias*.
uiciam, pisas agrestes idest fugles beane, xiii. 35 (*Isai.* xxviii. 25 ponet... *viciam* in finibus suis); **uicias**, fuglues benae, xlvii. 33 (*Alia*=?)=*uicium*, fugles bean, Cp. U182; *u*-, fuglaes bean, Ep. 28C23; *u*-, flugles bean, Ef.[1] 399, 40. *uicia*, a vetch; *pisas agrestes*, wild peas; for *fugles* (gen. of *fugel*, a bird) *bēane* &c. (vetch; lit. bird-beans), see Bosw. T. (*fugles beán*; *fugel*); on the form *flugles* see Skeat, *Conc. Et. Dict.* (*fowl*).
uiciati [uit-], xxxv. 280, see *infecti*.
uicibus, unum post unum, ii. 183 (*Bened. reg.* 38, 13 sic sibi *uicibus* ministrent fratres [20 *uicissim*; Edm. Schmidt, *Regula* uicissim; uicibus]; 32, 8 *uicissim* succedunt [11 uicissim, uicibus, *note*; Edm. Schmidt, *Reg.* uicissim, uicibus]).
uicina, see *preteriola*.
uicinos, xli. 1, see *presbiteri*.
uicissim, see *uicibus*.
uicium, see *uicias*.
uico, iii. 31, see *in pago*.
uictimis, xvi. 27, see *malefici*.
uictoria, xxxvii. 19, see *laurus*.
uictoriam, xxi. 5, see *cum coronis*.
uictorię, viii. 6, see *fornicem*.
uictum, xxxviii. 29, see *trapezita*.
uideantur, xxviii. 47, see *parenthesin*.
uiderunt, xiii. 43, see *lamia*.
uigentia, xl. 22, see *rigentia*.
uigilantia, xxi. 2, see *lucubraciuncula*.
uigilat, xxxix. 19, see *freniticus*.
uigilatione, xxxiv. 39, see *statione*.
uigore, x. 11, see *tigna*.
uiis, iv. 79, see *de triuio*; xiii. 30, see *in triuiis*; xxxv. 238, see *de triuio*.
uilicationis, prepositure [praepositurae], ii. 168 (*Bened. reg.* 64, 17 [30] redditurus est rationem *uilicationis* suae; also *uillicationis*). Cf. Luke xvi. 2 redde rationem *uilicationis* (*uill*-) *tuae*.
uilis, xxix. 42, see *trapezeta*.
uillae, see *sex untias*.
uille [uillae], i. 107, see *ruris*; xxix. 65, see *cuimarsus*; xxxix. 36, see *sex untias*.
uillicationis, see *uilicationis*.
uina, prophete, x. 4; see *uinum*.
uinacia, quod remanet in uuis quando premuntur, xv. 33; **uinatia**, que remansit in uuis quando premuntur, xviii. 3 (*Osee*, iii. 1 diligunt *vinacia* uvarum).
uinatia, see *uinacia*.
uinceret, xxxv. 174, see *tripudiaret*.
uincta, xxxv. 303, see *mulcata*.
uinctorum, uinctos, xxxv. 27, see *puncto*.
uincula, iv. 54, see *metalla*.
uinculum, iv. 60, see *neruum*.
uindicatur, defenditur, xxxvii. 15 (*S. Aug.* ?). Cf. Serm. 57, 8 (Migne, *P. L.*

xxxviii. 8 col. 390) incipiatis vos velle *vindicare* de inimicis vestris.

uindictis, xxxv. 104, see *gladibus*.

uinearum, xiii. 15, see *decem iugera uinearum*; xlv. 16, see *antes*.

uini fusor, pincerna, xxxix. 11 (*Greg. Dial.* iii. 5 col. 225 *vini fusoris*...animum corrupisset).

uino, xxi. 18, see *sancta domini*; see also *uinum candidum* and *uina* sub v. *uinum*.

uinum, i. 111, see *sicera*; xii. 45, see *caupo*. —**uinum candidum**, piperatum uel mellatum, x. 25 (*Cant.* viii. 2 Vulg. dabo tibi poculum ex *vino condito*) = *uinum conditum*, piperatum et melleatum, Cp. U155.—**uina**, prophete, x. 4 (*Cant.* i. 1 meliora sunt ubera tua *vino*; i. 3 super *vinum*).

uiola, herba iacinctina [hyacinthina], xxix. 10 (*Uerb. Interpr.* = *Hier. in Matth.* vii. 28–30 col. 46A *Violae* vero purpuram, nullo superari murice).

uiolenter, i. 51, see *exempta*.

uiolentia, fortia, ii. 181 (*Bened. reg.* 48, 44 [79] nec *violentia* laboris opprimantur).

uirga, xxxv. 152, see *sceptrum*; for *uirgo* (?) xlvi. 3, see *Tanaquil*.

uirgae, see *uaeri*; *pusti*.

uirge [uirgae], xxxv. 81, see *uaeri*.

uirginis, xxi. 7, see *femur uirginis*.

uirgis, xiv. 14, see *calati*; xix. 1, see *obelis*.

uiri, x. 23, see *Aminab*; xiii. 16, see *Tabehel*; xxi. 3, see *Subal*; xxxviii. 11–14, see *Calistratus*.—**uiri cordati**, bono corde, xix. 62 (*Job* xxxiv. 10 *uiri cordati* audite me) = *uiri cordati*, bono corde, Cp. U194; Ep. 28E15; Ef.[1] 400, 11.

uiridario, xlii. 20, see *in uiridario domus*, sub v. *uiridarium*.

uiridarium, a uirido dicitur, iii. 62 (*Vit. S. Anton.* ?).—**in uiridario domus**, in atrio pro uiriditate herbarum, xlii. 20 (*Ex div. libris* ?).

uiride, xii. 41, see *lino crudo*; xiii. 48, see *myrtus*.

uiridem, xli. 7, see *iaspis*, 10, see *smaragdus*, 16, see *cypressus*.

uiridis, xxii. 7, see *carbasini*.

uiriditate, xlii. 20, see *in uiridario domus*, sub v. *uiridarium*.

uirido, iii. 62, see *uiridarium*.

uirilia, xxxix. 48, see *calculum*.

uirtus, xliv. 29, see *axem*.

uirtutis, xxxv. 145, see *numinis*.

uiscera, iii. 36, see *uitaha*, for *uitalia*.

uiscerade, vi. 2, see *uiscide*.

uiscide, uiscerade, vi. 2 (*Breu. exsol.* ?); **uiscide**, ineluctabile idest maius luctu, xl. 1 (*Uerba* ?). See *Addenda*.

uisibus, i. 126, see *spectacula*.

visionis, see *epimehne*.

uit[a], xxx. 13, see *iereticos*.

uitaha, uiscera, iii. 36 (*De S. Mart. Stor.* = *Sulp. Sev. Dial.* i. 16, 2 doloribus *uitalia* uniuersa quaterentur) = *uitalia*, uiscera, Cp. U209.

uitalia, see *uitaha* (for *uitalia*).

uitam [for *uittam* ?], xxxvii. 7, see *odonis uitam*.

uiteas, see *columnas uitreas*.

uiteleos, iuuenes, xxxvi. 22 (*Oros.* ii. 5. 1 Brutus...uxoris suae fratres, *Vitellios iuuenes*...in contionem protraxit; in note *uitelios*). Cf. *uitelli*, sueoras, Cp. U177 and Ef.[1] 399, 3; *uitelli*, suehoras, Ep. 28A24. The quotation from Oros. shows that *uiteleos iuuenes* in the present Glossary is *a lemma* without an interpretation. The first word (altered to a *nom. plur.*) has crept into the Cp., Ep. and Ef. Gloss., supplemented by an apparent interpretation (*sueoras*, *suehoras*, nom. plur. of *suēor*, from *sweohor*, see Bosw. T. *sweór*, *swehor* = G. *Schwäher*, *Schwager*, *Schwieger*, Du. *zwager*, a term which, according to Kluge, originally meant a wife's brother). The first word appears again (as a *nom. sing.*, with the same interpretation, also in the sing.) in Ef.[1] 400, 43 (*vetellus*, sueor). But the A. S. words do not interpret a *word* (*Vitellios*), but explain the *fact* that the Vitellii were "the brothers of the wife of Brutus," that is, "his brothers-in-law (*sueoras*)." This *vetellus*, *vitellus*, should, therefore, not be altered to *vitricus*, as is suggested by Diefenbach and Goetz; nor find a place in any Lat. Dict.

uitelios, see *uiteleos*.

uitelli, Vitellios, see *uiteleos*.

uitiati, see *infecti*.

uitiginem, bleci, xxxvi. 10 (*Oros.* i. 8, 5 Aegyptii cum...*uitiliginem* paterentur; i. 10, 11 scabiem ac *uitiliginem*) = *uitiginem*, bleci, Cp. U168; *uitiligo*, blectha, Ep. 28A34; *uitiligo*, blectha, Ef.[1] 399, 14. For *bleci*, *blectha*, leprosy (also E. blight ?), see Bosw. T. (*blæcþa*).

uitiliginem, see *uitiginem*.

uitis, xxxviii. 7, see *columnas uitreas*.

uitreas [for *uiteas*], xxxviii. 7, see *columnas uitreas*.

uitreum, xxxvii. 5, see *capsaces*.

uitricum, steuffeder, xxxvi. 14 (*Oros.* i. 12, 9 omitto Oedipum...*uitricum* suum). Cf. *uitricius*, steopfaeder, Cp. U181; *u.*, steupfaedaer, Ep. 28A35; *u.*, staupfotar, Ef.[1] 399, 15. Cf. Bosw. T. (*steópfæder*); Skeat, *Conc. Dict.* (*stepchild*); *steuf-* = O. H. G. *stiof-*

uittam, see *odonis uitam.*

uitula, see *uitulam consternantem.*

uitulam consternantem, lasciuiantem aut aeste pro uermibus, xiv. 34 (*Hierem.* xlviii. 34 *vitula conternante*; [*vitulam*] *consternantem*, ap. Migne, *Patr. L.* xxix col. 1010D). Cf. *Isai.* xv. 5 *vitulam conternantem*; Cp. C527 (*consternantem*, indomitam); *aut aeste* (which begins a new line in the MS., but with no capital A) perh. for *aut aestuantem*? Glogger, however, makes a separate lemma of it, referring it to *Hierem.* xxxvi. 30 cadaver eius proicietur *ad aestum* per diem.

uitulamina, idest filii a uitulis dicuntur qui de adulterio nati, xi. 5 (*Sap.* iv. 3 spuria *vitulamina* non dabunt radices altas).

uitulis, xi. 5, see *uitulamina.*

uituperans, xv. 2, see *synicias.*

uituperationis, xxviii. 74, see *ironia.*

uiuarium, piscina, xlvii. 11 (*Alia*=?)= *bifarius*, piscina, Cp. B112; Ep. 6C9; Ef.[1] 347, 52.

uiuens, ii. 33, see *cenobita.*

uiuere, see *telopagere.*

uix, statim, xxxv. 58 (*Ruf.* xi. 12 fol. 184a *vixdum* coepto bello; Cacciari p. 90 *vix dum* c. b.; cf. v. 1 fol. 75b *vix* credi... potest; vii. 8 fol. 118b *vix* a nobis cohortatus; vii. 18 fol. 122a &c.). For *uix* (xliv. 2) see *cous.*

uixdum, see *uix.*

uixilla et **labrum** idem sunt, idest segin, xxxv. 69 (*Ruf.* ix. 9 fol. 152a in militaria *vexilla* transformat, ac *labarum*...exaptat). Cf. *uexilla*, seign, Cp. U85. For *segin*, *seign* (from Lat. *signum*), a sign, token, see Bosw. T. (*segn*, *segen*).

ulcanalia [uulcan-], xliii. 29, see *bachus.*

ulcus, lepra uel uulnus, xxxv. 107 (*De Euseb.*); **uncus**, lepra, iv. 12 (*Eccl. Istor.*) =(*Ruf.* ii. 1 fol. 19a serpit...sermo...sicut *ulcus* in gregibus).

uligo, terrę naturalis, xlv. 29 (*Uerba de multis*=*Ars Phocae*, p. 413, 20 haec caligo *fuligo*; in note *oligo*). Cf. *uligo*, humor terrae, Cp. U236; Ep. 28A19; Ef.[1] 398, 52.

ulixes, xliii. 5; see *polideuces.*—Ulixis, see *Paenilopis.*

ullo, xliv. 10, see *cardines.*

ulteriorem, xxxv. 32, see *ceteriorem.*

ultro, citro, hidirandidir, iii. 64 (*Vit. S. Anton.* xlvi col. 159B *ultro citro*que). Cf. *ultroque citroque*, hider ond hider, Cp. U229.

-um omitted, by the omission of a stroke over r: *lor* for *lorum.*

umbellas, see *umbrellas.*

umbilicum, xi. 14, see *poderis.*

umbonem, see *labrum.*

umbrellas, stalo to fuglam, xlvii. 14 (*Alia*=?)=*unibrellas* (for umbr-), stalu to fuglum, Cp. U252; Ep. 28A32b; Ef.[1] 399, 12. Umbrellas=*umbellas*, sun-shades (Lewis & Sh.). *Stalo*, *stalu*, pl. of *stæl*, a place, stead, stall; see Kluge, *Etym. Wörterb.* (*Stall*).

umecta, gebyraec, xxiv. 3 (*Math.*? not in the Vulg.?)=*umecta*, gibrec, Cp. U246. The *y* in *gebyraec* is, perhaps, a misreading of a mark written above the word in the MS. which the scribe followed. For *ge-braec*, *gebrec* &c. see Bosw. T. (*bræc*, a breaking, flowing, rheum); Kluge, *Wrtb.* (*brach*; *Brackwasser*, *Bruch*[2] &c.).—For *umecta*, see also *sicunia.*

una, i. 80; xi. 12; xxviii. 45; xxix. 31; xxxi. 25; xxxii. 7; xxxiii. 2, 10, 13, 21, 25 (*siliqua una*).

unam, xvii. 7; xxviii. 40; xxxii. 9; xxxiii. 6.

unamquamque, xxviii. 83, see *ennoematice.*

unaquaeque, see *Iani porte.*

unaqueque [unaquaeque] xxxvi. 1, see *Iani porte.*

uncia, xxxii. 5, see *uncia*, 7, see *acitabulus*; xxxiii. 7, see *sicel.*—**uncia** ui solidos, xxxi. 5 (*De ponder.*?). **uncia** fit sic : \ quę uncia pensat siliquas cxliiii hoc est solidos ui, xxxii. 5 (*De ponder.*?). **uncia una**, solidi ui, xxxiii. 21 (*Euch. De pond.*?). Cf. Blume, i. 373. 30, 374. 2 &c. —**sex untias** [uncias] mediam partem unius uille [-lae] consuetudo est romanorum totam substantiam xii untias [uncias] dicere siue magna sit siue modica, xxxix. 36 (*Greg. Dial.* iii. 21 col. 272c nihil...ei aliud nisi *sex uncias* unius possessiunculae largiretur...ex eodem fundo, quem in *sex unciis* a patre perceperat). For *sex unciae* cf. the present Glossary (xxxvii. 9) *tabulas legat.*

uncialibus, see *untialibus.*

unciam, xxxiii. 6, see *stater.*

uncias, xxxi. 4, see *libra*, 26, see *conurbicus*, 33, see *mina*; xxxvii. 9 (bis), see *tabulas legat*; see also *sex untias*, sub v. *uncia.*

uncinos, see *ancones.*

uncis, xli. 17, see *mastigia.*

unctus, xxvi. 4, see *delibutus.*

uncus, lepra, iv. 12; see *ulcus.*

unde, ii. 147; x. 9; xiii. 7, 31, 53; xiv. 13, 20; xvii. 5, 16; xxi. 3; xxii. 12; xxxiii. 5, 13; xxxvii. 9, 19; xliv. 2; xlv. 7, 8, 11; xlvi. 33.

undique, xxii. 12, see *urna*; xliv. 11, see *clima.*

unge [ungue], XIV. 9, see *in unge*.

ungentorum [unguentorum], X. 3, see *odor ungentorum*.

ungue, see *in unge adamantino*.

unguenta, X. 9, see *nardum*; XVI. 20, see *smigmata*.—unguentorum, XXXV. 169, see *in myrthece*. **unguentum exinanitum**, Chrisme uocabulum dedictum [for dedicatum? as in a Bern MS.] est quod non ante dicitur chrisma quam super hominem fuerit fusum, X. 6 (*Cant.* I. 2 vers. ant. Sab. *unguentum exinanitum* [*oleum effusum*, Vulg.] est nomen tuum); see also *odor ungentorum*.

unguere, XXII. 11, see *mundum m-*.

ungula, XIV. 9, see *in unge*.—**ungula et gutta**, pigmentum de arboribus, XII. 21 (*Eccles.* XXIV. 21 quasi storax et galbanus et *ungula et gutta*).—**ungulam**, ferrum curuum ut digiti, XXXV. 39 (*Ruf.* VIII. 3 fol. 135a *vngulis* fodiebantur; VIII. 10 fol. 139b *vngulis* exarari; fol. 140a ad vngues *vngula* perueniebat) = *ungula*, ferrum curbunt (sic) digiti, Cp. U255; Ep. 28C7; Ef.[1] 399, 26.

ungulis, see *ungulam*.

uni, I. 109; XXVIII. 79.

unibrellas, for *umbrellas* (q.v.).

unicornis, XIX. 32, see *monocerus*.

uniuersalis, I. 31; II. 34, see *catholicus*.

unius, II. 189; XV. 11, 13, 32; XVIII. 1; XXI. 2; XXVIII. 37, 75; XXX. 5, 9, 84; XXXV. 75; XXXIX. 36; XLIII. 28.

uniuscuiusque, IV. 98, see *comellas*.

uno, I. 115; II. 149; XXVIII. 45, 77; XXIX. 67; XXXV. 210.

untialibus, longis, XIX. 9 (*Job*; *Praef. Hieron.* p. XIVb, and Migne, *P. L.* XXVIII col. 1083A *uncialibus*, ut vulgo aiunt, litteris) = *uncialibus*, longos, Cp. U254; *uncialibus*, longis, Ep. 28C4; Ef.[1] 399, 23.

untias [unc-], XXXVII. 9, see *tabulas legat*; **untias** [unc-], XXXIX. 36, see *sex untias*, sub v. *uncia*.

untinos [for *uncinos*], XLVII. 4, see *anconos*.

unum, II. 183 (bis); IV. 98; XXVIII. 63, 72; XXXI. 36; XXXIII. 27, 31; XXXIX. 49.

unus, XIII. 60; XXIX. 67; XLIII. 21.

unusquisque, VIII. 8, see *in aceruo m-*.

uocabulum, X. 6, see *unguentum exinanitum*.

uocamus, XLIV. 11, see *clima*, 19, see *hiemisperium*.

uocant, V. 3, see *conolas*; XVI. 11, see *saraballa*; **uocant**, XXXVIII. 15, see *hygę*.

uocare, XXVIII. 71, see *ephichirema*.

uocat, XVI. 29, see *chaldei*.

uocationes, II. 97, see *kalende*.

uocato, XX. 4, see *accito*.

uocatur, XXX. 2, see *Canisius*; XXXI. 25, see *pes*; XXXIX. 24, see *aduocatus*.

uocauerat, XXXVI. 16, see *pellexerat*.

uocum, XXVIII. 19, see *sympsalma*.

uolles [for *folles*], XXXVII. 2, see *c. uolles*.

uoluitur, XIII. 13, see *fascia pectoralis*.

voluminum, see *sintagmaton*.

uolunt, XIV. 30, see *pedalis*; XXVIII. 18, see *apo tu-*; XLVIII. 11, see *gestiunt*.

uoluntatis, VI. 22, see *placoris*.

uoluptarius, XXXVIII. 9, see *epicurius*, 10, see *phitagoras*.

uomitum, II. 27, see *crapula*.

uorith, erba [herba] est de ipsa panes faciunt quos erbaticas (Cambr. MS. *berbaticas*) appellant et siccant illos habentque pro sapore [sapone?], XIV. 3 (*Hier.* II. 22 multiplicaveris tibi herbam *borith*).

uortex, see *uertigo*.

uoti compos, xpistiana, IV. 84; **uoti copos** [!], xpistiana [christiana], XXXV. 293; see *compos*.

uox, II. 5, see *antiphona*; XXXV. 215, see *fragor*.

upipa, see *cucuzata*.

urbana, see *urbanus*.

urbanus, sapiens, IV. 18 (*Ruf.* II. 18 fol. 29a uita *urbana*).

urbe, XXXIX. 17, see *Sabura*.

urbicus et **sextarius** ęquali mensura, XXXIII. 24 (*Euch. de pond.*?). Cf. *conurbicus*, XXXI. 26.

urceos, uasa erea [aer-] in quibus aquam portant, XIV. 36 (*Hier.* LII. 19 tulerunt et *urceos*).

urgentes [to be read for *surgentes*], see *adigent*.

urido [for *urigo*?], XXXV. 3, see *prorigo*.

urigo, see *prorigo*.

urna, idest uas aureum rotundum longum aliquid subtilis in duobus finibus clusum undique exceptis foraminibus modicis in lateribus habens intus XII ciatos [cyathos] modicos plumbeos habentes XII menses scribtos [scriptos] in eis unde sortiuntur quicumque primo exiit per foramen uertente uase sicut ante condixerunt, XXII. 12 (*Esther* III. 7 Mense primo, cujus vocabulum est Nisan,.. missa est sors in *urnam*...quo die et quo mense gens Judæorum deberet interfici: et exivit mensis duodecimus). Cf. Steinm. I. 489, 28.

urnam, see *urna*.

urnas, XXXIII. 11, see *chatus*.

ursi [?] XVI. 5, see *lentiscus*.

usque, VIII. 19, see *si usque ad...*; XI. 14, see *poderis*; XXXV. 262, see *illo usque*.

usque quaque, multum, XLVII. 2 (*Alia* =?).

usti, xxxv. 200, see *reusti*.

ustum, iv. 100 (*ab ustum*, for *ambustum*?).

usura, i. 54, see *foenus*.

ut, i. 39; ii. 182; x. 1; xxii. 16; xxviii. 28, 33, 52, 53; xxxiii. 6, 7, 13, 16; xxxv. 39; xli. 9, 14–16; xliv. 4, 10, 16.

utatur, fruatur, ii. 186 (*Bened. reg.* 3, 24 [32] seniorum...*utatur* consilio; 28, 15 [26] *utatur* abbas ferro abscisionis).

utensilia, ii. 88, see *instrumenta*.

uterem, see *catastrofon*.

uterus, xlvi. 28, see *matrix*.

utest, xxxiv. 8, see *utpute*.

utj, v. 8, see *auo*.

uti, quemadmodum sicuti, ii. 184 (cf. *Bened. reg.* 27, 5 ideo *uti* debet omni modo ut sapiens medicus).

utilis, i. 62, see *idonea*.

utpote, see *utpute*.

utpute, utest, xxxiv. 8 (*De Cassiano, Inst.* vi. 3 *ut puta* irae, tristitiae; vii. 3 *ut puta* carnis simplices motus nonne uidemus...; viii. 4, 2 *ut puta*.—*Praef.* p. 6 li. 6 *utpote* [*utpute*, in note] qui; v. 30, 2 *utpote* [*utpute*, in note] iudicans; x. 2, 1 *utpote* [*utpute*, in note]).

utri, xxi. 13, see *ascopa*.

utris, xxix. 15, see *batroperite*.

utriusque, xlii. 13, see *hermofroditus*.

utrumque, see *nitrum*.

uuas, xiii. 14, see *lambruscas*.

uuis, xv. 33, see *uinacia*; xviii. 3, see *uinatia*.

uulcanalia, see *bachus*.

uulcani, xxviii. 13, see *Ionan*.

uulgari, huni, xxxix. 25 (*Greg. Dial.* iv. 26 col. 361D spatharius *Bulgar*...Bulgarica lingua locutus est). *Huni* may be for the Lat. *Hunni*, or be correct as it stands, an earlier form (see Sievers, *A. S. Gramm.* § 133a) of A.S. *Hūne*, a Hun (Bosw. T.); cf. O. H. G. *Huni* (Graff, iv. 960; Schade, 429). Cf. Steinm. ii. 244, 19, where one MS. has *hun*.

uulgo, i. 94, see *passim*.

uulgus, xvi. 29, see *Chaldei*.

uulnerum, xi. 12, see *malagma*.

uulnus, xxxv. 107, see *ulcus*.

uulnusculum [sine interpret.], iii. 13 (*De S. Mart. Stor.*=*Sulp. Sev. Dial.* 2, 2, 5 prope ipsum *uulnusculum*).

vultur, see *arpa*.

uxor, xvi. 12, see *regina*; xxxviii. 34, see *paenilopis*; xxxix. 22, see *presbitera*.

uxores, i. 104, see *presbiteras*.

x for *ch*: xenodo*x*iorum (for xenodo*ch*iorum).

xenia, see *exenia*.

xenium, see *senium*.

xenodochiorum, susceptio peregrinorum, xxxix. 59 (not in Greg. Dial., but *Can. Conc. Calched.* x. p. 135 aut ptochiorum, aut *xenodochiorum* rebus) = *xenodochia*, susceptio peregrinorum, Cp. X2; Ep.—; Ef.[1] 401, 4.

xenodoxiorum [-dochiorum], collectionum, xxix. 44 (*Uerb. Interpr.*=*Hier. in Matth.* ?) = *xenodociorum*, collectionum, Cp. X1. See also *sidonicis*.

xerofagia, herbe [-bae] quę comeduntur incocte [-tae], xxxiv. 5 (*De Cassiano, Inst.* iv. 21 ut *xerofagia* contenti essent; in note *exerofagia*, *xerofagiis*; ibid. iv. 22 qui maxime *xerofagiis*...utuntur).

xerophagia, see *xerofagia*.

xp for *chr*: xpistiana, xpistianiam, xpistianorum; xpisto; xpistus (for *Christ-*).

xpistiana [christ-], iv. 84, see *uoti compos*; xxxv. 293, see *uoti copos*.

xpistianiam [for Christiani?], x. 5, see *nomen tuum*.

xpistianorum, xxx. 35, see *uarietas stromactis*.

xpisto [Christo], x. 5, see *nomen tuum*.

xpistus [Christus], x. 1, see *osculetur me*.

y for *ae*: c*y*mentarii (for c*æ*m-).—for *i*: byrrum (b*i*rrum); cyneris (c*i*nyris); cythara (c*i*th-); dyaleticam (d*i*alect-); gyt (g*i*t); iacyntini (hyac*i*nthini); tapynosin (tap*i*n-); tybicen (t*i*b-).—for *oe*: cymiteria (c*oe*meteria).

ylex [for *ilex*], see *ilicus*.

ymnum, see *hymnum*.

yperbaton, idest transcensio, xxviii. 87; see *hyperbaton*.

yperberetheus, i. 73, see *mensis yperberetheus*.

yperbolen, xxviii. 38, see *per figuram y-*.

ypo (sub) **tos** (hoc) **scino** (scinu), scineoose scindat te, xxx. 96 (*Cat. Hier.* lxiii), for which see **ypo** (sub) **tyos** (hoc) (**prino**).

ypo (sub) **tyos** (hoc) **prino prineose**, secet te, xxx. 95; **ypo** (sub) **tos** (hoc) **scino** (scinu) **scineoose**, scindat te, xxx. 96 (*Cat. Hier.* lxiii col. 675A Hujus [Julii Africani] est epistola ad Origenem super quaestione Susannae; eo quod dicat in Hebraeo hanc fabulam non haberi nec convenire cum Hebraica etymologia *ἀπὸ τοῦ σχίνου σχίσαι, καὶ ἀπὸ τοῦ πρίνου πρίσαι*; *Rich.*: Hujus e. e. a. O. s. q. S. eo q. d. in H. h. f. n. h. nec conv. c. H. et. *ἀπὸ τοῦ πρίνου πρίσαι καὶ ἀπὸ τοῦ σχίνου σχίσαι*; B: ...nec conv. c. h. eth. apotu prinu prise kai apotu chinou chisau idest origine prino percutiaris: et a scino scindaris; C: ...nec conu. cum hebraica [here follows a whole blank line, after which this Augsb. ed. has the following five words] *oppositiones Danihelis ad conuincendos senes*, which are not in any of the edd. that I have seen).—The meaning of the above is "this story of Susannah cannot have been in the Hebrew, because only in Greek you can derive πρίζειν (πρίσαι), to saw, from the name of the tree called πρῖνος (prinus, Lew. & Sh.), and the verb σχίζειν (σχίσαι), to cleave, from the name of the tree called σχῖνος (schinus, Lew. & Sh.)."—These etymologies are wrong, but not the argument, especially if the author had said "it can't be Hebrew because both the tree-names are *Greek*."—The five words in the Augsb. ed. are correct, and in the blank line it may have been said "for we find these tree-names when we read" *oppositiones* Danihelis (i.e. Daniel's questions) tending to convict the elders.

ypoteseon, see *de entoetromito.*

ypotheseon, see *ypophesion.*

ypocheseon, see *ypophesion.*

ypophesion [for *hypotheseon*], instructionum, xxx. 93 (*Cat. Hier.* cxviii col. 709B variarum *hypotheseon* libelli; *Richardson*: Variarum ὑποθέσεων libelli; B: variarum *ypocheseon* idest expositionum libelli; C: variarum libelli [blank]; conf. cxxv col. 713A diuersarum *hypotheseon* tractatus; B: diuersarum *ypotheseon* idest expositionum tractatus; C: diu. [blank] tractatus). Cf. *ytiafesion*, structionum, Cp. Y4; Ef.[1] 401, 12 and Cp. Y1.

ypotheseon [for *hypotyposeon*], dispositionum, xxx. 3 (*Cat. Hier.* ii. 611A: Clemens in septimo ὑποτυπώσεων; B: clemens in septimo *ypotyposeon* id est disputationum vel informationum; C: clemens in vii [blank] Hoc est informacionum; E: ιπωθησηον idest disputationum) = *ypoteseon*, dispositionum, Cp. Y1; *ypotesseon*, dispositionum, Ef.[1] 401, 5.

ypotyposeon, see *ypotheseon.*

ypozeuxis, quando diuersa uerba singulis apta clausulis apponuntur, xxviii. 24 (*Cass. Psalm.* i. 1 col. 29A Quae figura dicitur *hypozeuxis*, q. d. u. s. a. c. a.).

z for *ch*: cate*z*izatur (cate*ch*iz-).—for *d*: zo*z*iacum (zo*d*-).—for *g*: prole*z*omena (prole*g*-).

zeli, ii. 73, see *emulatione.*

zeugma, see *zeuma.*

zeuma, idest coniunctio quando multa pendentia aut uno uerbo aut una sententia concluduntur, xxviii. 45 (*Cass. Psalm.* xiv. 12 *zeugma*, id est c. q. m. p. a. u. u. a. u. s. c.).

zodiacum, see *zoziacum*, sub v. *zodiacus.*

zodiacus, sideralis, xliv. 23 (*Alia*; *de cælo*); **zoziacum**, sideralem, xxvii. 10 (*Lib. Rot.*) = (Isid. *de nat. rerum* iv. 1 col. 969 luna *Zodiacum* circulum perducitur) = *zotiacum*, sideralem, Cp. Z6; zociacum, sideralem, Ef.[1] 401, 18.

zoes, xxx. 13, see *iereticos.*

zona, ii. 14, see *bracile.*

zoziacum, sideralem, xxvii. 10, see *zodiacus.*

END OF I. INDEX (*LATIN*).

II. INDEX (*Latin Numerals* expressed by Roman Signs).

N.B. The references are to the (I.) Index (*Latin*, pp. 51—217).

ii (duo), xxxi. 11, see *ephi*; xxxiii. 17, see *hin*; xxxix. 43, see *duas coronas.*

iii (tres), ii. 86, see *himina*; iv. 99, see *quadraplas*; xxiv. 7, see *stater*; xxxi. 10, see *Aquila*, 19, see *obolus*, 40, see *amphora*, 41, see *bathos*; xxxii. 4, see *obolus*; xxxiii. 4, see *dragma*, 6, see *stater*, 8, see *obulus*, 10, see *batus*, 11, see *chatus*, 12, see *ephi*, 14, see *artabę*, 15, see *sata*, 16, see *gomor*, 19, see *nebel*, 22, see *semiuncia*, 29, see *obolus*; xliii. 42, see *posttridie.*

iii (tertius), xliv. 16, see *antarticus.*

iiii (quatuor), xiii. 59, see *feretri*; xxxi. 17, see *Grece*, 25, see *pes*, 31, see *sextarius*; xxxiii. 25, see *siliqua una*, 26, see *sextarius*; xxxv. 15, see *quadriga*; xxxvii. 9, see *tabulas legat*; xliv. 16 ter, see *antarticus*, 17, see *cous.* — *IIII GENERA POETARUM* [heading to xliii. 22—27; see *comicus*].

iiii (quartus), xxxiv. 21, see *atauus*; xliv. 16, see *antarticus.*

U, and V (quinque), XI. 7, see *pentapolim*; XXXIII. 16, see *gomor*, 18, see *abattidis*; XLIV. 16 bis, see *antarticus*.—(quinta), XXXI. 9, see *comor*; (quintam), XXXI. 13, see *sarre*; V (quintus), XLIV. 16, see *antarticus*.

UI, and VI (sex), XIX. 11, see *in exaplois*; XXX. 52, see *ex ca*; XXXI. 5, see *uncia*; XXXII. 5, 6, see *uncia*; XXXIII. 6, see *stater*, 21, see *uncia*; XXXVII. 9, see *tabulas legat*; XLIV. 16 bis, see *antarticus*.

VII (septem), XXXI. 13, see *sarre*; XLIV. 22, see *pliadę*, 27, see *dextera*.

VIII (octo), XXXI. 14, see *hin*; XXXVII. 9, see *tabulas legat*.

VIIII (nouem), XXXII. 7, see *acitabulus*; XXXII. 8, see *cotule*.

X (decem), XIII. 15, see *decem iugera...*; XXV. 9, see *decurio*; XXIX. 31, see *decapolim*; XXXI. 38, see *denarius*; XXXIII. 7, see *sicel*, 14, see *artabę*; XXXVIII. 31, see *decanorum*.

XI (undecim), XVI. 22, see *trinte*.

XII (duodecim), XXII. 12 bis, see *urna*; XXXI. 4, see *libra*; XXXIII. 16, see *gomor*; XXXVII. 9, see *tabulas legat*; XXXIX. 36, see *sex untias*.

XIIII (quattuordecim), III. 3, see *quartane*.

XV (quindecim), XXXI. 1, see *gomor maior*, XXXII. 7, see *acitabulus*.

XVIII (octodecim), XXXI. 14, see *hin*; XXXII. 1, see *dragma*.

XVIIII (novemdecim), XXXI. 18, see *obolus*.

XX (viginti), XXXIII. 8, see *obulus*; XXXV. 179, see *horas diurnas*.

XXII (duo et viginti), XXXI. 2, see *modicus*; XXXII. 9, see *mina*.

XXIIII (viginti quattuor), XXXI. 29, see *solidus*; XXXIII. 29, see *obolus*.

XXV (viginti quinque), XXXI. 20, see *taletum*.

XXVI (viginti sex), XXXI. 26, see *conurbicus*.

XXVII (viginti septem), XXXI. 12, see *sata*.

XXVIII (duodetriginta), XXXI. 22, see *Epiphanius*.

XXX (triginta), XXXI. 24, see *choros*; XXXIII. 9, see *chorus*.

XXXVI (triginta sex), XXXI. 16, see *regalis*.

XL (quadraginta), XXXV. 179, see *horas diurnas*.

XLII (quadraginta duo), XXXII. 7, see *acitabulus*.

LX (sexaginta), XXXII. 10; XXXIII. 3, see *talentum*.

LXII (sexaginta duo), XXXIII. 1, see *talentum*.

LXXII (septuaginta duo), XXXI. 7, see *libra*, 15, see *siclus*, 34, see *statera*; XXXII. 8, see *cotule*, 10, see *talentum*; XXXIII. 28, see *libra*.

LXXX (octoginta), XXXIII. 1, see *talentum*.

LXXXIIII (octoginta quattuor), XXXI. 7, see *libra*.

XCVI (nonaginta sex), XXXII. 11, see *libra*.

C (centum), XXXII. 9, see *mina*; XXXIII. 13, see *metreta*.

CXLIIII (centum quadraginta quattuor), XXXII. 5, see *uncia*.

CCXVI (ducenti sedecim), XXXII. 8, see *cotule*.

CCLXXVIII (ducenti septuaginta octo), XXXII. 11, see *libra*.

CCC (trecenti), XXXII. 9, see *mina*.

III. INDEX (*Greek*).

N.B. The Greek words occurring in the Glossary are all (except CYNXPONON, and the initial of *πorsutas*) written in *Latin* characters, and appear, therefore, in their alphabetical order in the (I.) *Latin* Index (pp. 51—217). But the Greek words *quoted* in that Index are all alphabetized (unaltered) here, with references to the Latin Index.

ἀβρός; Ἅβρων; Ἅβρωνος βίος; see *ambrones*.

Ἁγιόγραφα, see *agiografa*.

ἁγνὸν, see *ason*.

ἀγορᾷ, see *agora*.

ἀγών, see *diatribas*.

ἄδυτα, see *aduta*.

αἰγίθαλλος, see *parula*.

αἱμοῤῥοοῦσα, see *emurusem*.

ἀκέφαλον, see *aceuan*.

ἀκεφάλῳ, see *aceuan*; *epitomen*.

ἀκοήν, see *aceuan*.

ἀκολουθεῖ, see *ho platon*.

αναρκιας, ἀναρχίας, see *anarchius*.

ἀντίφρασιν, see *cataantis*.

ἀπληστία, see *plestia*.

ἀπὸ, see *apo tu-*; *ypo* (sub) *tyos*.
ἀποδείξεως, see *eyaggences apod-*.
ἀπολογίας, see *apologus*, sub v. *apologis*.
ἀριθμητικὴν, see *dialectica*.
ἅρπη, see *arpa*.
ἀρχαιογονίαν, see *archutomam*.
Ἀρχαιότητος, αρχηωρηθος, see *archeretoys*.
ἀρωμάτων, see *aspaltum*.
ἀσκήσει, see *ascesi*.
ἀσκήσεως, see *ptocheus*.
ἀσκητικὸν, see *ascetron*, sub v. *ascesi*.
ἀσπάλαθος, see *aspaltum*.
αὐτεξουσίου, αὐτεξουσίῳ, see *psichiexodo*.
αὐτήν, see *ecacusen* (where wrongly *aut in* aut in).
αὐτοκράτορος, see *pantocranto*.
αὐτὸν, see *ancillis*; *sintagmaton*.
βίου, see *iereticos*.
βουλευτὴς, see *nuymeyses*.
βυρσεύς, see *byrseus*.
γεγενῆσθαι, see *ptocheus*.
γένους, see *iereticos*.
γεωμετρικὴν, see *dialectica*.
γραμματεύς, see *grammateos*.
γραμματικὴν, see *dialectica*.
γυμνικὸς, see *diatribas*.
γῦπα, see *arpa*.
γύψ, see *arpa*.
δὲ, see *enrusa*; *ptocheus*.
δενδροβάτης, see *netila*.
δευτερώσεις, see *deuteres*.
δευτέρωσιν, see *deuterosin*.
δήσεις, see *ancillis*.
διαλεκτικὴν, see *dialectica*.
διατριβάς, διατριβή, see *diatribas*.
διαφωνίᾳ, διαφωνίαν, see *diaphonian*.
διῶρυξ, see *dorix*.
ἐγγαστριμύθου [and -θῳ], see *de entoetromito*.
ἐγκράτεια, see *pantocranto*.
ἐκάκωσεν αὐτήν, see *ecacusen*.
ἑκκαιδεκαετηρίδα, see *ex ca*.
ἑκουσίου, see *ptocheus*.
ἐκστάσει, ἐκστάσεως, see *extasei*.
ΕΚωωΙC, see *ho platon*.
ἔλεγχος, see *elegos*.
ἐν ἀγορᾷ, see *agora*.
ἐννεακαιδεκαετηρίδα, see *ex ca*.
ἐννοηματικὴ, see *ennoematice*.
ἐνσωμάτου, see *capun periens*.
ἐξαίρετον, see *epyuision*; *exiareton*.
ἐξάλειπτρον, ἐξαλείφω, see *enrusa*.
ἐξαπλᾶ, see *auo*.
Ἑξαπλοῖς, see *in exaplois*.
ἐξηγήσεων, see *exenteseon*.
ἑορταστικαὶ, see *elegos*; *eortatica*; *parascheue*.
ἔπαινον, see *catepenon*.
ἐπαίνων, see *et procomian*.
ἐπεπληρώκει, see *editiones*.
ἐπιθυμητικὸν, see *tu epitimitisun*.
ἐπιούσιον, see *epyuision*.
ἐπίτασις, XXIX. 53, see *epiasis*.
ἐπιτομὴν, see *epitomen*.
ἔποψ, see *picus*.
ἐραστήν, see *ptocheus*.
ἐργαστικόν, see *theoritisen*.
ἐργοδιώκτην, see *erladiocten*.
ἐσχηματισμένος, see *eschematismenos*.
εὐαγγελικῆς, see *eyaggences apod-*.
εὐνοῶν, see *eynum*.
εὐχαριστίας, see *panagericon*.
εὐχήν, see *aceuan*.
ζητημάτων, see *cinticta*.
ζοης, see *iereticos*.
ζωης, see *iereticos*.
ἤ, see *ancillis*; *h*; *ho platon* (HO, for H O).
ἥγηται, see *enrusa*.
ἡμῶν, see *et procomian*.
ἠριγέρων, see *synicias*.
θάλασσαν, see *enrusa*.
θεία, see *thia*.
θεοσηκας, see *iereticos*.
θεοῦ, see *capun periens*; *pantocranto*.
θερινός, see *Terinos*.
θεωρητικὴν, θεωρητικὸν, see *theoritisen*.
θεωρητικοῦ, see *iereticos*.
θυμικὸν, see *tu thimisiun*.
θυρεων, θυρων, see *portarum*.
ἰδίᾳ, see *sintagmaton*.
ἱερατικοῦ, see *iereticos*.
ἱερέων, see *iereticos*.
Ἰησοῦ, see *et procomian*.
ἱκετῶν, see *iereticos*.
ἵλεώς σοι, Κύριε, see *ileusun cyrię*.
ἵππουρος ἰχθύς, see *glis*.
ιπωθησηον, see *ypotheseon*.
ἰσημερινός, see *Isemerinus*.
ἱστορίας, see *cronicon*.
ἰχθύς, see *glis*.
καθαροὺς, see *cathanos*.
καθαρῶν, see *catheron*.
καὶ, see *capun periens*; *dialectica*; *malleolis*; *ptocheus*; *sinphosin*; *theoritisen*; *ypo* (sub) *tyos*.
καίοντες, see *malleolis*.
ΚΑΙΤΟΙΤΕΡΙΕΝCΩΜΑΤΟΥ, see *capun periens*.
κακομήχανος, see *cacomicanus*.
καλυμαύκιον (late Gr.), see *calomaucus*.
καλυμμάτιον, see *calomaucus*.
καμηλαύκι, καμηλαύκιον, see *calomaucus*.
κάμινον, see *malleolis*.
κανθαρίς, see *chantari*.
κανόνων, see *cronicon canuon*.
κατὰ, see *cataantis*; *catha manthan*; *metafora*.
καταγράψαι, see *sintagmaton*.
καταιγίς, see *totegis*.

καταστροφὴν, see *catastrofon.*
κατ' ἔπαινον, see *catepenon.*
κατηχήσεις, κατηχήσεων, κατηχήσεως, see *cataceeos.*
καψάκης, see *capsaces.*
κενοδοξίας, see *cenodoxia.*
κέφαλος, see *caefalus.*
κληματίδα, see *malleolis.*
κρατορίας, see *pantocranto.*
κυλλοῖς, κυλλὸς, κυλλοὺς, see *de citiuis.*
κυνηγέσια, see *editiones.*
Κύριε, see above ἵλεώς σοι, Κύριε.
κυρίου, see *et procomian.*
κωμάρχης, see *cuimarsus.*
κώνωψ, see *conopeum.*
ΛΑΩRΗΤΟΝ, see *cinticta.*
λογικὸν, see *lutugisprum.*
λογισμοῦ, see *pantocranto.*
λογιστικὸν, see *lutugisprum.*
λορδὸς, see *lurdus.*
Ματθαῖον, see *catha manthan.*
μαυλιστής, see *maulistis.*
μαχόμενος, see *machomenus.*
μέγιστον, see *sintagmaton.*
μέρος, see *sintagmaton.*
μεταφοράν, see *metaforan.*
μετάφρασιν, see *metafrasin.*
μετεμψυχώσεως, μετεμψύχωσιν, -σις, see *metempschosis.*
μῆλα, see *mala aurea.*
μονόφθαλμον; see *cinticta*; *monaptolmon*; *monon.*
μουσικὴν, see *dialectica.*
νάφθαν, see *malleolis.*
νεκρομαντείαν, see *necromantia.*
ΝΟΜΙϹΜΑ, see *stater.*
ὁ; Ο, see *ho platon.*
ὁδοιπορικὸν, see *otheporicon*, sub v. *sinphosin.*
ὁμιλιῶν, see *et procomian.*
ὀσμή, see *osma.*
π changed into c; see *simcosion.*
πάθος, see *prathus.*
παιδίῳ, see *ancillis.*
παλάθης, see *labastes.*
παλίουρος, see *paliurus.*
πανάρετος, see *panarethos.*
πανηγυρικὸν, see *panagericon.*
παντοκρατορία, παντοκράτορος, see *pantocranto.*
πάντων, see *dialectica.*
παρασκευή, see *parascheue.*
παρασκευῆς, see *eyaggences apod-.*
πάρεδρον, see *paredum.*
πάσσαλος, see *pessul.*
πεῖραν, see *catastrofon.*
περὶ, see *capun periens*; *de entoetromito*; *et procomian*; *iereticos*; *pantocranto*; *peri pthocheas*; *ptocheus.*
περιόδους, see *peridion.*
περιούσιον, see *epyuision.*
περίψημα, see *peripsima.*
πέταλον, see *petulum*, sub v. *petalum.*
πηρι, see *iereticos.*
πηρισωπη, see *pylominos.*
ΠΙΛΘΟΝΑ, see *ho platon.*
πλάναι (planetae); πλανας; πλανητας, see *πorsutas.*
ΠΛΑΤΟΝ; Πλάτων; Πλάτωνα; πλατωνίζει, see *ho platon.*
πομφόλυξ, see *famfelucas.*
πόρους, see *puruys.*
πorsutas (? Gr. ?), see *πorsutas.*
πρακτικὴν, see *theoritisen.*
πράξεων, see *praxeon.*
πρατνων, see *praxeon.*
πρίζειν; πρῖνος; πρίνου; πρίσαι, see *ypo* (sub) *tyos.*
προδείξεως, see *eyaggences apod-.*
προπάθειαν, see *prathus.*
προπαρασκευῆς, see *eyaggences.*
πρὸς, see *et procomian.*
προσεφώνησε[ν], see *prosefanesen.*
προσομιλίαν, προσομιλιῶν, see *et procomian.*
πτῶμα, see *oma.*
πτωχείας, see *ptocheus.*
Πύργος, see *pirgos.*
ῥητορικὴν, see *dialectica.*
σαράβαρα, see *saraballa.*
σεμνεῖον, see *seminon.*
σοι, see above ἵλεώς σοι.
σπουδαστὴν, see *pylominos*; *spodasten.*
στεφάνω, for στεφάνῳ, see *Stephanus.*
Στράτωνος, see *pirgos.*
στροματῶν (!), see *stromatum.*
στρουθίον, see *ancillis.*
στρωματέας, see *laciniosa.*
στρωματεῖς, στρωματέων, see *stromatum.*
σύγχρονον, see ϹΥΝΧΡΟΝΟΝ.
σύλληψις, see *sumenumerus.*
συμέωξις, see *sumenumerus.*
σύμΗΚτις, see *sumenumerus.*
συμμίκτων, see *cinticta.*
σύμμιξις, see *sumenumerus.*
συμπόσιον, see *sinphosin.*
συνεισάκτους, see *sinisactas.*
σύνθημα, see *sinthema.*
σύνταγμα; συντάγματα; συνταγμάτων, see *sintagmaton.*
σχίζειν; σχῖνος; σχίνου; σχίσαι, see *ypo* (sub) *tyos* (hoc), &c.
τὰ, see *editiones.*
τε, see *ptocheus.*
ΤΗΙѠΙϹ, see *ho platon.*
τὴν, see *malleolis.*
τῆς, see *ptocheus.*
ΤΗϹΗΤѠΝ, see *ho platon.*
τὸ, see *lutugisprum.*
τὸ ἐπιθυμητικὸν, see *tu epitimitisun.*
τὸ θυμικὸν, see *tu thimisiun.*
τὸν, see *capun periens*; *ho platon.*

τοπικῶν, see *tropicon.*
τοῦ, see *apo tu-*; *et procomian*; *ypo* (sub) *tyos.*
τοῦτον, see *ptocheus.*
τροχιλέα,-τροχός, see *troclei.*
ΤωΗΤω, see *ho platon.*
τῶν, see *et procomian*; *sintagmaton.*
ὑποθέσεων, see *de entoetromito*; *ypophesion.*
ὑποτυπώσεων, see *ypotheseon.*
φαγολοίδοροι, φαγολυδοροι, see *synicias.*
φιλόκαινον, see *philocain.*
ΦΙΛΟΝ, see *ho platon.*
φιλοξενίᾳ, see *de philoxenia.*
φιλοπτωχίας, see *ptocheus.*
Φίλων; Φίλωνα; ΦΙΛωΝΑ; φιλωνίζει, see *ho platon.*
φλάσκων, see *flasconi.*
φράσει, see *phraysi.*
χαρακτῆρα, see *cataracteras.*
χειμερινός, see *exemerinus.*
χειρί, see *sintagmaton.*
χοῦς, see *cous.*
χριστοῦ, see *et procomian.*
χρονικῶν, see *cronicon.*
χρονογραφεῖον, see *chri fiscus.*
χρονογραφίας, see *cronographias.*
ψαύειν, see *apo tu ptsaum.*
ψευδεπίγραφα; ψευδόγραφα, see *pseudo ephigrapha.*
ψυχάριον, see *animalus.*
ψυχή, see *animalus.*
ψυχιεξοδο, see *psichiexodo.*
ὤκιμον, see *ochimo.*
ὤκινον, see *ochimo.*
ὡμολόγηται, see *ptocheus.*
Ὠριγένους, see *sintagmaton.*
ὥσπερ, see *ancillis*; *enrusa.*
ὥστε, see *sintagmaton.*

IV. INDEX (*Hebrew*)

records the Hebrew words quoted in the I. Index (*Latin*).

אֲרִי, see *Arihellio.*
אֲרִיאֵל, see *Arihellio.*
בֹּרִית, see *borit*; *herba fullonum.*
חָשַׂף (חֲשׂוּפָה), see *exertum.*
מֶרְקָחָה, see *enrusa.*
נֵבֶל ; נֶבֶל, see *in nablis.*
נַעֲרָה (לְנַעֲרוֹתֶיךָ), see *ancillis.*
סגולה, see *epyuision.*
סַרְבָּלִין, see *saraballa.*
קָשַׁר (וְתִקְשְׁרֶנּוּ)*, see *ancillis.*
שִׁבֹּלֶת, see *sinthema.*

* Read so instead of the word printed in the I. Index (*Latin*).

V. INDEX (*Germanic*, but chiefly *A.Sax.*).

N.B. All the Germanic words that appear in the Glossary itself are treated in this Index as *chief entries*, therefore printed in *black* or *Clarendon* type (ex. gr. **aad**), with references to the *text* (pp. 1 to 50). But all entries printed in ordinary type (ex. gr. aam) are *quotations* either from the Corpus, Epinal and Erfurt Glossaries, or from other sources.

The references in *black* type are to the I. or *Latin Index* (pp. 51 to 217); those in *italics* to this present V. Index (ex. gr. under **adexa**, reference is made to **lacerta** in the I. *Latin* Index, and to *aðexa* and *haegtis* in this V. Index).

ā- (pref., intens.), see *a-fyrhte*; *a-gleddęgo*; *an-a-treten*; *a-suollen*; *a-swellan*; *a-tredan*.

aad (*ād*), XXXV. 158, *the fire, flame* of a funeral pile; *a funeral pile*; see **rogus**.

aam, Cp.; haam, Ep.; fam, Ef. The first word is supposed to be for *ām*, which Bosw. T. explain *the reed or slay of a weaver's loom*. If so, then *haam* and *fam* are corruptions. They are a gloss to **cautere** (q.v.), ablat. of *cauter*, a branding-iron, and both Ep. and Ef. give also "ferrum" as gloss. But in the present Glossary *cautere* is glossed in one place by *tunderi*, in another by "*ferrum melius tindre*."

acus, ęcus for æcus, aesc, *an ax*; see *brad-acus*.

ād, see *aad*.

adexa (for aðexa; aðexe, Cp.), XXXV. 55, *a lizard, newt*; see **lacerta**, and below *aðexa*; *haegtis*.

aei (ib-), *ivy*; see *ib-aei*.

aen-li (=ǣn-lic, ān-lic), XLVI. 39, *simple, singular*; see **simplex**.

æren, *an eagle*, see *arngeus*.

æren-geat, or two words *æren* (an eagle) and *geat* (a vulture); see *arngeus*.

ærn, *house*; see *ern*.

aern, *an eagle*; see *arngeus*.

aern-geup, or two words *aern* (an eagle) and *geup* (a vulture); see *arngeus*.

aer-uuica, *an earwig*, see *ęr-uigga*.

aesc, *an ax*; see *brad-acus*.

aesil, see *hel*.

a-fyrhte, Cp. (pp. of *ā-fyrhtan*, from *ā-*, intensive, and *fyrhtan*, to terrify) *affrighted*; see **adtonitis**.

a-gleddęgo (infin. for agleddęgon, for which see Sievers, *Gramm.* § 363) =**ā-gleddian*, to overthrow, from *ā-*, intens. + *gleddian*, to throw; or from a causat. of *ā-glīdan*, to cause to glide, or totter?), III. 63; see **labefacare**.

ā-gleddian, see *a-gleddęgo*.

ā-glīdan, see *a-gleddęgo*.

ahga (tyrf-), see *tyrf-ahga*.

ail(s), E., *the awn of barley* or other corn, see *glis*.

alaer (id. Ep.; *aler*, Cp. & Ef.), XLVII. 99, *an alder*; see **alnus**, and below *aler-holt*.

ald (a Mercian form=A.S. *eald*), *old*; see *hu ald*.

aler, see *alaer*.

aler-holt (id. Cp. & Ef.; *alter-holt*, Ep.) XLVII. 101, *an alder wood*; see **almenta** (for *alneta*).

alter-holt, see *aler-holt*.

ambihtes sciir, see *thestisuir*.

ambras, Cp., Ep. & Ef. (plur. of *amber*, a measure); see **cathos**.

amore, see *emaer*.

amprae, ampre, *a tumor*; see *omprę*.

an (=A.S. *and*), *and*; see *hidir-an-didir*.

ana, for hana (holt-); see *holt-hona*.

ana-boz (O.H.G.); see *osifelti*.

an-a-treten for *un-a-treden*, pp. of *un-a-tredan* (from *un-*, verb. pref. for which see Skeat, *Conc. Et. Dict.* *un-*[2] + *ā-*, pref. intens., and *tredan*, to tread), unpassed, untrodden, XLVIII. 3; see **inextricabiles**.

and-, see *an-sceat*.

an-feld, an-filte, see *osi-felti*.

anga, see *onga*.

an-sceat, Cp. for *an-scēat*; an-seot, Ef. for *an-s[c]ēot*, *the bowels*, from *an-* (perh. for *and-* or *on-*), and the verb *scēotan* (pt. t. *scēat*) to shoot; perh., therefore, a 'channel' or 'conduit' through which food is conducted or 'shot'; see **extentera**.

an-wald, *sole power* (Bosw. T.); see *monarchia*, sub v. **anarchius**.

aq-ueorna; aq-uorna, *a squirrel*; see *ac-urna*.

arn, *an eagle*, see *arngeus*.

arngeus (*earngeot*, Cp.; *earngeat*, Ep.; *aerngeup*, Ef.; *ærengeat*, *eargeat*, *earngeap*, Wright W.), XLVII. 57, Q^y compounds? or two different, alternative words, the first (*arn*, *earn*, *aern*, *æren*, *ear*) meaning *an eagle* (E. erne); the second (*geus*, *geup*, *geap*, *geot*, *geat*) *a vulture*, which latter seems to be the Gr. *γύψ*, Latinized as *geus*, or *γῦπα*, Latinized as *geup*, this being Anglicized as *geop*, and this corrupted to *geot*, and finally to *geat*; see **arpa.**

as-suollam, see *a-suollen.*

a-suollen, Cp.; pt. of *ā-swellan*, to swell; suollaen, Ep.; pt. of *swellan*, to swell; as-suollam, Ef. for *a-suollan*; pt. of *ā-swellan*, to swell; as a subst., *a tumor*, *swelling*; see **tuber**.

a-swellan, *to swell*; see *a-suollen.*

aðexa, aðexe; see *adexa.*

áðexe, see *hegi-tissę.*

a-tredan, see *an-a-treten.*

a-treten, for a-treden (an-, for un-), see *an-a-treten.*

b for p? see *scribid.*

baan (elpend-), see *elpend-baan.*

baar (id. Cp., Ep. & Ef.), XLVII. 94, a male swine, *a boar*; see **bęrrus**.

baecon, bæcun (here-), see *here-benc.*

baeg (nord-, for rond, =rand-); see *nord-baeg.*

bǣl, see *beel.*

baers, *a perch*; see *breuis.*

baest, Ep.; *best*, Ef., the inner bark of the linden, *bast*; see **tilio**.

baeues, beoþes, beouuas (gen. of *baew*, *beow*, grain), see *hond-ful.*

baew, beow, *grain*; see *hond-ful.*

baso, *brown*, or *purple*, *crimson*, *scarlet*; (wrætt-, uuret-), *ornament-brown*; see *uuret-baso.*—(uuyloc-), *whelk-brown*, or *purple*; see *uuyloc-baso.*—(uuyrm-), *worm-brown*, or *purple*; see *uuyrm-baso.*

basu (wealh-, weoloc-), see *uuyloc-baso.*

batne (=bēatne) stāne (un-ge-); see *un-ge-batne stane.*

beag, beah (rand-), see *nord-baeg* (for *rond-baeg*).

bean, beane, see *fugles beane.*

bearug, see *bęrg.*

bēatne stāne (un-ge-), see *batne stāne.*

beber, bebir, *a beaver*; see *bebor.*

bebor (*beber*, Cp.; *bebir*, Ef.), XLVII. 87, *a beaver*; see **castorius.**

becn, becon (here-), see *here-benc.*

bee (humbyl-), see *humbyl-bee.*

beed (berian); see *berian beed.*

beel (=*bǣl*), XXXV. 158, *the fire*, *flame* of a funeral pile; *a funeral pile*; see **rogus.**

beer, Cp., Ep. & Ef., *a bier*, *bed* (Bosw. T.); see **basterna.**

be-heonan, see *bihina.*

benae, see *fugles beane.*

benc for becn (here-), see *here-benc.*

beost, *biest*; see *beust.*

beow, beouuas, beoþes, see *baeues*; *baew.*

bęrg (bearug, Cp. & Ep.), XLVII. 91, *a castrated boar*, *barrow-pig*; see **maialis.**

berian beed, XXII. 8, *a bearable bed*; see **lecti aurei.**

best, see *baest.*

be-swīc, see *bi-suic-falle.*

betst=E. *best*, see **cos.**

beust (*beost*, Cp. & Ef.), XLVII. 27, *biest*, *biestings*, *beestings*; see **colostrum.**

bi-heonan, see *bi-hina.*

bi-hina (=A.S. *bi-heonan*, *be-heonan*), XLVIII. 54, *on this side*; see **citra.**

biiris; see *biriis.*

bil, *a bill* (uidu-, uitu-, wudu-), see *uitu-bil.*

bind (e-, ge-), see *e-bind.*

biriis for *biiris* (*byrs*, Cp., *byris*, Ep.), XLVII. 48, *a borer*; see **scalpellum.**

bi-suic-falle, Cp. (=*be-swīc*, a falling thing, trap+*falle*=*fealle*, a fall, snare, see *Zeitschr. f. d. Alt.* IX. 502, 520; Bosw. T. *feall*), a falling thing that beguiles, see **decipulam.**

blǣco, see *bleci.*

blaec teoru (in Cp., Ep. & Ef.), *black-tar*, *naphtha*; see **nappa.**

blæcþa, see *bleci.*

bleci (so also in Cp.; *blectha*, Ep. & Ef. = *blǣco*, *blæcþa*), V. 15; XXXVI. 10, *paleness*, *leprosy*, *blotch*, *blight*; see **pruriginem**; **uitiginem.**

blectha, see *bleci.*

blod-saex (so also in Cp.), XXXIX. 6, *a blood-knife*, *lancet*, *fleam*; see **fledomum.**

boeg (erm-), see *erm-boeg.*

bolla, *a cup*, *bowl*; droh-, throt-, ðrot-bolla, *the gullet*; see *droh-bolla.*

bonan (seolf-), *a suicide*; see **biothanti.**

boor (*bor*, Cp.; *bore*, instrum., Cp.), XLVIII. 66, *a borer*, *gimlet*; see **scalpellum.**

bor, see *boor.*

bord-rand, *a board-rim*, see **rimis.**

bore (instr. of *bor*), see *boor.*

bord-remum (instr. plur. of *bord-rema*= *bord-rima*, from *bord*, a board, plank+ *rema*, *rima*, a rim), XXXIX. 21, lit. *with board-rims*; see **rimis.**

borg, in Cp., *a pledge*, *loan*; see **foenus.**

borgende, see *borgenti.*

borgenti, old form for A.S. *borgende*= **borjenti*, pr. pt. plur. of *borjan*, older form of *borian*, to bore, perforate, IV. 66; see **terebrantes.**

borian, borjan, borjenti, see *borgenti.*
braad-last ęcus, see *brad-acus.*
brad-acus (*braad-last-ęcus*, Cp.; *braed-laestu aesc*, Ef.; from *brād*, broad + *acus*, *ęcus* for *æcus*, *aesc* = *æx*, an ax; *last*, *laestu*, a foot-track, last), XLVII. 47, *a broad-ax* (ax with a broad head); see **dolabella.**
bræd-, see *bred-isern.*
braed-laestu aesc, see *brad-acus.*
brand, see *brandas.*
brandas (plur. of *brand*, *a brand*, *fire-brand*), IV. 76; see **reusti.**
brand-rad, brand-rod, see *brond-ra.*
brec, breci, breec (ge-, gi-); see *gi-breci.*
brecan, see *gi-breci.*
bred-isern, Cp. & Ep.; *bred-isaern*, Ef. (= *brǣd*, part. of *brēdan* (= *bregdan*), to draw, pluck + *isen*, *isern*, iron, an implement made of iron), *a scraping* or *graving tool*, *file*; see **scalpellum.**
brēoþan, see *briudid.*
brers, see *breuis.*
brese, see *brimisa.*
breuis, XLVII. 72 (error for A.S. *brers* or *brems*; *brers*, Cp.; *baers*, Ep. & Ef.) = *baers*, a perch; see **lupus.**
brimisa = Engl. *brimse* (so altered from an orig. *priusa*, corrected into *briusa* = *briosa*, Cp., Ep., & Ef.; *brese*, WW. = Engl. breese, breeze, *a gadfly*, *breese*), XLVII. 82, *a breese*, *gadfly*; see **tabanus.**
briosa, see *brimisa.*
briudid (3rd sing., from A.S. *brēoþan*, to ruin, destroy), III. 34, *goes to ruin*, *comes to grief*; see **fatescit.**
briusa, see *brimisa.*
brōc, *breeches*; see *brooc.*
brōc, *a small stream*, *brook*; see *gi-breci.*
brocco (O.H.G.), see **labastes.**
brôdi (O.H.G.), *crippled*, *weak*; see **fatescit.**
brond-ra (*brand-rod*, *brand-rad*, Ep.; *brond-rad*, Ef.), XLVII. 42, *a branding-rod*, *gridiron*; see **andeda**; cf. Bosw. T. (*brand-rād*).
brond-rad, see *brond-ra.*
brooc (? = A.S. brōc?), *breeches*, XLVIII. 55; see **suricus.**
broðor-sunu, Cp., *a brother's son*, *a nephew*; see **fratruelis.**
byrae (byre, Cp.), XLVI. 37, *cottages*, *dwellings*; see **magalia.**
byraec, for braec? (ge-); see *ge-byraec.*
byris, byrs, see *biriis.*

c for r: uuac for uuar.
cade (E.), see **cathos.**
caelor (O.H.G.), see *chelor.*
cealre, see *celdre.*
celdre (*ceoldre*, Cp.), XLVIII. 61, *a kettle*; or perhaps (= A.S. *cealre*) *pressed curds*; see **multhra.**
celor, celur (O.H.G.); see *chelor.*
ceol, *a keel*; see **celox.**
ceoldre, see *celdre.*
ceoler, see *chelor.*
ceosel, see *cisil-stan.*
cetel, cetil, *a kettle*; see *cacabus.*
chelor (O.H.G., also *celur*, *celor*, *caelor*, *cilor* = A.S. *ceolor*), XIX. 38, *a hovel*, *hut*; see **gurgustium.**
cheuon, cheuun, see *chyun.*
chrustula, O.H.G., see **cartillago.**
chyun, XX. 3 (*cian*, Cp., Ep., & Ef.; *cyan*, *kio*, *cheuon*, *cheuun*, in Steinm.), *the gills of fish*; see **brantie.**
cian, see *chyun.*
cil, for *cild*, a child; see *cil-trog.*
cild-trog, see *cil-trog.*
cilor (O.H.G.), see *chelor.*
cil-trog (= *cild-trog*; from *cild*, a child + *trog*, a trough, basin), XLVI. 33, *a child's cradle*; see **cune.**
cinum (instr. plur. of *cinu*, a chink, fissure), XXXIX. 39, lit. *with chinks*, *fissures*; see **rimis.**
cisal, cisil, see *cisil-stan.*
cisil-stan, Cp. (*cisil*, Ep.; *cisal*, Ef. = ceosel, cisil + stan), *gravel*, *sand*; see **glarea.**
clam, XV. 4, *cloam*, *clay*; see **litura.**
clate, XVIII. 2; **clitę**, XV. 36 (*clibe*, Cp.; *cliþae*, Ep.; *clifae*, Ef.), the herb *clote-bur*; see **lappa.**
-clað, -claþ, see *flycti-clað.*
clibe, see *clate.*
clifae, see *clate.*
clitę, see *clate.*
cliþae, see *clate.*
clofae, clouae, see *clox.*
clox (a miswriting; = *clouae*, Cp.; *clofae*, Ep. & Ef.), XLVII. 21, *a clove*; see **mordatius.**
clustor-loc, Cp.; clustor-locae, Ep.; cluster-locae, Ef., from *clustor*, an enclosure, prison + *loc*, a fastening, lock, hence *a prison-lock*, *lock*, *bar*; see **clustello**; cf. Bosw. T. in voce and Skeat, *Conc. Dict.* (*cloister* and *lock*).
cluster-locae, see *clustor-loc.*
cneholegn, see *cne-holen.*
cne-holen, XLII. 14; **cre-holegn** (for cne-h.), XLVII. 103 (*cnio-holen*, Cp.; *cnio-holaen*, Ep.; *cni-olen*, Ef.), *knee-holm*, or *holly*; see **ruscus.**
cnio-holaen, holen, see *cne-holen.*
cni-olen, see *cne-holen.*
cōp, Cp. & Ef., *a cope*; see **ependiten.**
cosp, Cp., Ep., Ef., *a fetter*; see **puncto.**
cottuc, cotuc, *mallow*; see *malua.*

credenti, instr. plur. (also *cridu*, Steinm.; *criid*, Cp.; *criþ*, Napier; *crið*, id., from *crūdan*, to crowd, pr. s. *crȳdeþ*, pt. t. *crēad*), xxxiv. 48; see **scatentibus**.

cre-holegn (for *cne-holegn*), xlvii. 103; see *cne-holen*.

cridu, see *credenti*.

criid, see *credenti*.

crinçe, see *turnodo*.

criþ, crið, see *credenti*.

crog (so also in Cp.; *croog*, Ep. & Ef.), xxix. 47, *a large earthen vessel, a crock*; see **lagonam**; see also below *croog*.

croog, xix. 60, *a crock*; see **lagunculas**; see also *crog*.

crūdan, see *credenti*.

cyan, see *chyun*.

cyline, in Cp., a loan-word from the Lat. *culina, a kiln*; see **fornacula**.

cyll, kylle, Cp. (=Lat. culleus, culeus), *a leather bottle, flagon*; see **ascopa**.

cymin, *the herb cummin*; see **cinamum**.

-da, -dae, -ðe, a suffix found in *egi-da* (q.v.), *eg-dae, ege-ðe, eg-ðe*.

dæl, *a dale, vale, valley*; see *dal*.

daerm (snedil-), see *snedil-daerm*.

dal (O.H.G.), xxxv. 176=A.S. *dæl*, in Cp. *a dale, vale, valley, pit, gulf*; see **baratrum**.

darmana (gen. pl. of A.S. *þearm*, O.H.G. *darm*, a gut, intestine), v. 22, *of the intestines*; see **fibrarum**.

degn, see *þegn*.

derda, O.H.G., see *tetrafa*.

dhring (ebir-), see *ebur-dnung*.

didir = ðider, *thither*; see *hidir-andidir*.

dingere (=þingere), xxxix. 24, *an advocate, intercessor*; see **aduocatus**.

distyl-tige (*þistel-tuige*, Cp.; *thistil*, Ef.), xlvii. 70, *the thistle-finch, goldfinch*; see **cardella**.

dnung, for drung (ebur-), see *ebur-dnung*.

dobend (*dobgendi*, Cp.; *dobendi*, Ef.), xxxix. 30, *doting*; see **decrepita**.

dobgendi, *doting*; see *dobend*.

dorsos, see *dros*.

dox, see *pox*.

draca, Cp.; draco, Ef.; *droco*, Ep. (Angl. Sax. forms of Lat. *draco*), *a serpent, devil*; see **typo**.

drane, *a drone*; see **tabanus**.

dredum (instr. plur. of *ðrēd, ðrǣd*, a thread), xxxv. 233, *with threads*; see **lineolis**.

drep (perhaps = Lat. *trabs*, a beam, a timber, roof; A. S. *træf*, borrowed from Lat. *trabem*. E. *thrave* suits neither in sense nor in form, as it should be *thrape* or *threp*. Perhaps *drep* is meant to be *þrep*), xxxv. 59; see **fornice** and cf. Körting, *Lat. Wrtb.* (*treffa*).

dride-halpf (for ðriddehalf), v. 30, *two and a half* (?); see **sescopla**.

drili (ðrili, Cp. = þrili), xlvi. 41, *triple*; see **triplex**, sub v. **bilex**.

dritung (ymb-), see *ymb-ðriodung*.

droccerum, a misreading for *oroccerum* (q.v.).

droco, see *draca*.

droh-bolla (*ðrot-bolla*, Cp. & Ef.; *throt-bolla*, Ep., from *ðrotu*, the throat + *bolla*, a cup, bowl), xlv. 27, *the gullet, windpipe*; see **gurgullio**.

dros (id. Ep. & Ef.; *dorsos*, Cp.; *drosna, drosne, dross*), xlvii. 50, *grounds, dregs, dross, scum*; see **auriculum**.

drosna, drosne, dross, see *dros*.

drostlae (*ðrostle*, Cp.; *throstlae*, Ep. & Ef.), xlvii. 55, *a thrush, throstle*; see **turdella**.

drung (ebur-), see *ebur-dnung*.

dryct-guma (*dryht-guma*, Cp.), xlii. 8, lit. *a company-*, or *train-man*; see **paranimphi**.

dryht-guma, see *dryct-guma*.

duaeram, see *þuarm*.

dunnę (= *dunnae*, scil. stānas), vii. 4, *dun, swarthy, dusky*; see **lapides onichinos**.

-dur, -durt, unstressed forms of *treów*, a tree, see *mapal-durt*.

ear, for earn, *an eagle*, see *arngeus*.

ear, *an ear*; see *ęr-uigga*.

earfed-lice, Cp.; erabed-licae, Ef., *with difficulty*; see **egre**.

ear-geat, or two words *ear*, for *earn* (an eagle), and *geat* (a vulture); see *arngeus*.

earn, *an eagle*, see *arn-geus*.

earn-geap, earn-geat, earn-geot, or two words *earn* (an eagle) and *geap, geat, geot* (a vulture), see *arngeus*.

ear-uuigga, ear-picga, *an earwig*; see *ęr-uigga*.

e-bind (*ge-bind*, Wright W.), xxxv. 6, *a binding, fastening*; see **tentigo**.

ebir-dhring; see *ebur-dnung*.

ebur-dnung, **ebir-dhring** (*eburðring*, Cp.), xxvii. 25 and xix. 17, literally *boar-thringer*, or *thronger*, i.e. *boar-hunter*, from *ebir, ebur*=A. S. *eofor*, a boar + *dnung* for *drung, dhring*=*þring*, a thringer, thronger. The old form would be **ebur-dring-a* (-*a* = E. -*er*); see **Orion**.

ebur-ðring, see *ebur-dnung*.

ęcus, for æcus, *an ax*; see *bradacus*.

eddy, E., see *ed-uallę*.

ed-uaell, see *ed-uallę*.

ed-ualla, see *ed-uallę*.

ed-uallę (*ed-uuelle*, Cp.; *ed-walla*, Ep.; *ed-ualla*, Ef.; *ed-uaell*; *ed-pelle*; *ed-uuelle*; *ed-uuaelle*, Cp.; probably all from the A. S. prefix *ed-* backwards, again = Lat. re-, found in E. ed-dy + *ualle*, *uuelle*, *uualla* &c. = A. S. wæl, a pool, gulf, from *weallan*, G. *wallen*, to boil; hence *ed-walla* 'that which boils over again' or 'to & fro,' or 'round and round' = whirlpool), XLVII. 16; where it means *giddiness*, *dizziness*; see **uertigo**, where other applications of the word are given. Another form has the mutation of *ea* to *ie*: *ed-walla*, *ed-weallę*, and by mutation *ed-wielle* (see Bosw. T. in v.). Mod. E. dialects have *weel*; cf. mod. E. *well*. Cf. Skeat, *Conc. Dict.* (*eddy*).

ed-uuaelle, ed-walla, ed-weallę, see *ed-uallę*.

ed-uuelle, ed-pelle, ed-wielle, see *ed-uallę*.

eg (if-), *ivy*; see *ib-aei*.

eg-dae, see *egida*.

ege-ðe, ege-þe, *a mattock*, *hoe*, see *egida*.

egge (G. & Du.), *a hoe*; see *tyrf-ahga*.

egi-da (O. H. G. altered from an original *egldae*, for *egidae*? *eg-ðe*, Cp.; *eg-dae*, Ef. = A. S. *ege-ðe*), XLVII. 22, *a harrow*, *hoe*, *rake*, *mattock* = Du. & G. *egge*, with an additional suffix; see **erpica**; **ligones**, and below *tyrf-ahga*.

egilae, egla, eglae, see *egle*.

egle (id. Cp.; *eglae*, Ep.; *egilae*, Ef.; *egla*, Wright W.), XLV. 6, *a dormouse*?; or *the awn of barley*?; see **glis**.

egn (if-), *ivy*; see *ib-aei*.

eg-ðe, see *egida*.

ē-gylt, Cp. (= ǣ-gylt), *a fault*, *trespass* (against the law); see **excessus**.

elha (*eola*, Cp. & Ef.), XLV. 20, a fallow deer, buck, doe, *elk*; see **damma**.

elin, XVI. 28, *an ell*; see **cubitum**.

elothr, see *elotr*.

elotr, Cp.; elothr, Ef. (A. S. spelling of *electrum* q.v.), *a mixed metal* resembling amber in colour. (In *elotr* the *c* is dropped; in *eloþr* not only is the *c* dropped, but the *t* has become þ by 'Lautverschiebung' which proves a *very early* borrowing.)

elpend-baan, Cp., *an elephant's bone*, *ivory*; see **ebor**.

emaer (*omer*, Cp.; *emer*, Ep. & Ef.; *amore*, Wright W.; clod*hamer*, ib.), XLVII. 58, a song-bird, the yellow-*hammer*, yellow-*ammer*; see **scorelus**.

emer, see *emaer*.

eola, see *elha*.

ęr-, ear-, *an ear*; see *ęr-uigga*.

erabed-licae, see *earfed-lice*.

erm-boeg, XIX. 43, *an armring*, *bracelet*; see **armilla**.

ernum (abl. plur. of *ern* = ærn, house); see *heb-ernum*.

ęr-uigga (*ear-picga*, Cp.; *ear-uuigga*, Ep.; *aer-uuica*, Ef.), XLVII. 86, *an earwig*; see **auricula**, **auriculum**.

f for *p*, see *fi-faldae*.

-fa?; see *tetrafa*.

faam, Cp., Ep., Ef., *foam*, *a water-bubble*, see *famfelucas*.

fācen, see *facni*.

facni, Cp., Ep. & Ef. (instrum. of *fācn*, also written *fācne*, *fācen*, deceit, guile), *with deceit*, *guile*; see *astu*.

faedaer (steup-), see *steuf-feder*.

faeder (steop-), see *steuf-feder*.

fala (id. Cp., Ep., Ef.; whence *falod*, WW.; *falud*, Cp.; *falaed*, Cp., Ep., Ef. a fold, pen), XLVII. 41, *a plank*; see **tubolo**. Cf. Wright W. 279. 10, and Schlutter, *Journ. Germ. Phil.* v. 141.

falaed, falod, falud, *a fold*, *pen*; see *fala*.

faldae (fi-, fif-), see *fi-faldae*.

falle (bi-suīc-), see *bi-suic-falle*.

fam, see *aam*.

fctor, for *fetor*? (*feotur*, Cp.; *fetor*, Ep. & Ef.; perh. = A. S. *feoter*, *feotur*, a fetter), XLVI. 42; see **paturum**; see also below *fezza*.

f[e]alde (fif-), see *fi-faldae*.

feall, fealle, see *bi-suic-falle*.

fearh, see *foor*.

fearu (þægn-), *waggon-journey*; see *ge-bellicum*.

feder (steuf-), see *steuf-feder*.

feld (an-), see *osi-felti*.

felo-spraeci, see *felo-spric*.

felo-spric (*felu-spreci*, Cp.; *felo-spraeci*, Ep.; *felu-spraeici*, Ef.; from *felo*, *felu*, much + *spric*, *spraeci*, speech, talking), XLVII. 18, *much talking*; see **truffulus**.

felti (osi-), *an anvil*; see *osi-felti*.

felu-spraeici, felu-spreci, see *felo-spric*.

feol, see *fiil*.

feoter, feotur; see *fctor*.

fet, acc. pl. of fōt, *a foot*, see *fetim*.

fetim, XXXI. 25, for *fethim* = fæthm (Bosw. T.), *a fathom*? Cf. Schlutter, *Journ. E. Phil.* v. 468; see **pes**.

fetor, see *fctor*.

fezra (= O. H. G. *feȝȝera*; cf. above *fctor*), XIX. 19, *a fetter*; see **pedica**.

feȝȝera, O. H. G., *a fetter*; see *fezra*.

fi-faldae (in later A. S. *fīf-f*[*e*]*alde*, as in Bosw. T., lit. 'five-fold,' a popular etymology, which makes nonsense, but gives the word a sort of sense; and it may be a Teut. form corresponding to Lat.

papilio; *p* being older than *f*), XLIII. 47, *a butterfly*; see **animalus.**
fif-f[e]alde, see *fi-faldae.*
figel (?), see *figl.*
figl, with stroke over the *g*, XIX. 63; Qʸ for A. S. figel, or fugel, fugul, *a bird*? or is it a Latin word (figuraliter?)? see **ancillis.**
fiil (id. Cp.), fil = feol, XIII. 52, *a file*; see **lima.**
fil, see *fiil.*
filte (an-, on-), see *osi-felti.*
filti (on-), see *osi-felti.*
fina, Cp., Ep. & Ef., *a woodpecker*; see *uinu.*
finc, *a finch*; see *uinc.*
firgen, see *firgin-gata.*
firgin-gata (gen. plur. of *firgin-gāt* = of mountain-goats; sing. *firgen-gaet*, Cp., Ep. & Ef.; from *firgin*, *firgen*, a mountain + *gāt*, *gaet*, a goat), XIX. 29; see **hibicum.**
flicci (id. Cp., Ep., Ef.; *flicii*, Ep.; flycci, Steinm.), XLVII. 13, *a flitch* of bacon; see **perna.**
flicii, see *flicci.*
flōc, see *folc.*
floda (*flode*, Cp.; *flodae*, Ep. and Ef.), III. 53, *a channel*, *sink*, *gutter*; see **lacuna.**
flodae, flode, see *floda.*
flooc, see *folc.*
flugles, see *fugles beane.*
flycci, see *flicci.*
flycti-clað, Cp. (= *flyht-claþ*, Bosw. T., from *flycti*, old form of A. S. *flyht* = E. 'flight' + *clāð*, cloth; therefore 'flight-cloth,' as it were fugitive, i.e. foreign, bit of cloth, a patch from another bit of stuff); see Kluge, *Et. Wrtb.* (Fleck, flicken); Du. *vlikken.*
flyht-claþ, see *flycti-clað.*
fnēosan, see *nor.*
fnora, see *nor.*
fodor (*fothr*, Cp. & Ef. = Germ. *futter*, a case), XLIII. 30, *a case, cover, sheath*; see **emblema** (= ἔμβλημα, that which is put in or on, a thing that is fitted on; and hence = *fodor*, a case, cover &c.).
foedils, Cp., *fowls*, see **altilia.**
folc, for *flōc* (*flooc*, Cp. & Ep.; *floc*, Ef.), XLVII. 9, *a sole, kind of flat fish, plaice, fluke*; see **platissu.**
foor (id. Cp. & Ep.; *for*, Ef., perh. for **fōrh*, which may be allied to A. S. *fearh*), XLVII. 92, *a little pig*; see **porcastrum.**
for, *forh, see *foor.*
fōt, *a foot*; see *fetim.*
fotar (staup-), see *steuf-feder.*
fothr, see *fodor.*
fraefeli, Cp. (instrum. of *fraefel*, D. *wrevel*), *with sauciness*; see **astu.**
frio-letan, see *friu-lactum.*
friu-lactum, XLVI. 32 (for *friu-lǣtum*, instr. plur. fem., from *frīu-lǣte*? a freedwoman, from *frēo*, *frīo*, free + *lǣte*, a woman of a class above that of the slave; *frio-letan*, Cp.); see *libertabus.*
friu-læte, see *friu-lactum.*
frīu-lǣtum, see *friu-lactum.*
from-lice, Cp., *strongly*, *speedily*; see **efficaciter.**
fugel (?), see *figl.*
fugel, see *fugles beane.*
fuglaes, see *fugles beane.*
fuglam for *fuglum*: see *stalo.*
fugles beane, XIII. 35; **fuglues benae**, XLVII. 33 (*fugles bean*, Cp.; *fuglaes bean*, Ep.; *flugles bean*, Ef., all for *fugles*, gen. of *fugel*, a bird + *bēan*, sing. and *bēane*, plur. of *bēan*, vetch), XIII. 35, lit. *bird-beans*; see **uiciam.**
fuglues, see *fugles beane.*
fuglum, see *stalo.*
fugul (?), see *figl.*
ful (hand-, hond-), see *hond-ful baeues.*
fullae (? = sin-*fulle*, Cp.; sin-*fullae*, Ep. & Ef., *ever entire*, from *sin-*, ever + *full*, entire, complete = sempervivum), XIII. 41; see **paliurus.**
fyrhte (ā-), see *a-fyrhte.*

gaar (nabo-, nębu-), see *nębu-gaar.*
gabar, perh. not A. S., but corrupted Lat., on which see G. F. Hildebrand, *Gloss. Lat.* p. 42, who suggests to read *galearii*, a kind of soldiers' servants; *Arch. f. Lat. Lex.* IX. 368; X. 205. See **calones.**
gabel-rend, see *gabo-rind.*
gabol; gabol-rind, see *gabo-rind.*
gabo-rind (*gabul-rond*, Cp.; *gabel-rend*, Ef.; *gabul-roid*, for *-rond*; *gafol-rand*, Bosw. T.; Irish *ogabul-rind*), borrowed from A. S. (from A. S. *gabol*, later *gafol*, still later *geafel*, for which see Bosw. T., a fork, G. *gabel* + *rind*, *rond*, *rand*, a rim, outer circle; hence *gabol-rind*, &c. 'rim made by a two-legged instrument,' a pair of compasses), XIII. 53; see **circino.**
gabul-roid, for *gabul-rond*; see *gabo-rind.*
gabul-rond, see *gabul-roid.*
gaebles, gen. of *gaebel*, *a tribute, tax*; see *monung gaebles.*
gaec, gǣc, see *gaeuo.*
gæde-ling, see *geadu-ling.*
gae-suopę (= *ge-swæpa*, *-swæpo*), IV. 71, *sweepings, dust*; see **peripsima.**
gaet (firgen-), see *firgin-gata.*
gaeuo, perhaps *a cuckoo*, XLVII. 65; see **sticulus** (cf. *gaec*, Cp.; *gęc*, Ef., = *gǣc*, *geāc*, a cuckoo, gawk, which cannot = *gaeuo*; nor can *giw*, *giu*, *giow*, a griffin).

gafol, *a fork*, see *gabo-rind*.
gafol-lic, *fiscal*, see *gebel-licum*.
gafol-rand, A. S., see *gabo-rind*.
galae, gale (necti-, naecte-), see *necti-galae*.
gar (nabfo-), see *nębu-gaar*.
gasram, gāsran, see *raed-gasram*.
gata (firgin-), gen. plur.; see *firgin-gata*.
geabules, gen. of *geabul, a tribute, tax*; see *monung gaebles*.
geāc, see *gaeuo*.
geadu-ling, *a relation, kinsman* (in Cp. =*fratruelis*)=A. S. *gæde-ling*; Goth. *ga-diliggs*; O. H. G. *gatuling*; see Diefenb. *Wrtb. goth. Spr.* II. 373; Grimm, *Wrtb.* (*Gätling*); Schade (*gatuling*); see **fratruelis.**
geafel, *a fork*, see *gabo-rind*.
geap, *a vulture*, see *arngeus*.
gēap, *spacious, lofty*; see *gipparre*.
geappre (? comp. of *gēap, spacious, lofty*); see *gipparre*.
gearpan leaf, *yarrow*; see **malua.**
geat, *a vulture*, see *arngeus*.
ge-batne (=ge-bēatne) stāne (un-), see *un-ge-batne stane*.
gebel-licum (=A. S. *gafol-lic*, fiscal, lit. suitable for tax or tribute) pægn-fearu (=*pægn*, a waggon+*fearu*, journey), lit. *fiscal waggon-journey*; see **reda.**
ge-bind, see *e-bind*.
gebles, gen. of *gebel, a tribute, tax*; see *monung gaebles*.
ge-brec, see *gi-breci*.
ge-byraec (for ge-braec?), XXIV. 3; see **umecta,** and **sicunia.**
gęc, see *gaeuo*.
ge-genca, ge-genga, see *ge-genta*.
ge-genta (for *ge-genca*=*ge-genga*), XXXV. 54, (one) *going with*; see *pedissequis* sub v. *pedisequas*.
ge-giscan, see *gi-gisdae*.
ge-giscte, see *gi-gisdae*.
gela (nęctę-), see *necti-galae*.
gelae (nacthe-), see *necti-galae*.
geleod, see *geloed*.
ge-loed, Cp.; gloed, Ep.; ge-leod, Ef. (as A. S. *oe* becomes *ē*, umlaut of *ō*, the stem is *lōd-*, and every *ō* being due to *a*, the root is *lad-*, which may=Goth. *lap-, for which see Kluge, sub v. *Laden*, a stall, shop; hence *gelēd*, G. *Laden*, perh. =Lat. *catasta*, a stage, scaffold, stall); see **catastam,** and, for another interpretation of *ge-loed*, see Schlutter, in *Journ. of Engl. and Germ. Philol.* v. 466.
genca, genga, genta (ge-), see *ge-genta*.
genge (naect-), *a night-goer*, see *naect-genge*.
geonath, *yawneth*; see *ginat*.
geot, *a vulture*, see *arngeus*.
ger (nabo-), see *nębu-gaar*.
gēr, *a year*; see *gere*.
gere, geri, instr. of *gēr*, a year; see *þys gere*.
ge-rēfa; see *ge-roefan*.
ge-roefan, Cp. (plur. of *ge-rēfa*, an officer); see **processores,** and cf. Skeat, *Conc. Dict.* (reeve[2]).
ge-span (=Ep.; *gespon*, Cp. & Ef.), XXIX. 11, *a clasp*; see **mauria.**
ge-spon, see *ge-span*.
ge-swæpa, -swæpo; see *gae-suopę*.
ge-tæld (-teald, -teld), *a tent*; see *ge-zelt*.
ge-þuxsað, see **lurida.**
ge-uiif, for *ge-uuif*, XXXV. 157, *a web; fate, fortune*; see **furtunam.**
geup, *a vulture*, see *arngeus*.
geus (arn-), see *arngeus*.
ge-wald-leðrum, Cp. (instr. plur., from *ge-weald*, power, and *leðer*, leather), *with power-leathers, reins*; see **abenis.**
ge-weald, see *ge-wald-leðrum*.
ge-pearp (sond-), see *in sond-ge-pearp*.
ge-weorp (sand-), see *in sond-ge-pearp*.
ge-zelt, O.H.G. (=*ge-teld*, Cp.=*ge-teald, ge-tæld*, Bosw. T.), XXII. 5, *a tent*; see **tenda.**
gi-brec, see *gi-breci*.
gi-breci (*ge-brec*, Cp.; *gi-brec*, Ep.; *gi-breec*, Ef., from *brecan*, to break), XLVII. 30, *a catarrh, rheum*; see **sicunia.**
gi-breec, see *gi-breci*.
gi-giscdae, see *gi-gisdae*.
gi-gisdae (*gegiscte*, Cp.; *gigiscdae*, Ep. & Ef., 3rd pret. sing. of *ge-gīscan*, to stop, shut up), XLVII. 26, *he has stopped*, or *shut up*; see **opilauit.**
ginat (*geonath*, Cp.; *ginath*, Ep. & Ef.), XLVII. 44, *yawneth*; see **battat.**
giow, see *gaeuo*.
gipparre (? for A.S. *gīeppre=Lat. *callidior*, comp. of *gēap*, spacious, lofty?), XLVIII. 40, *more skilful, adroit*; see **excellentiores.**
giscdae, gisdae (gi-), see *gi-gisdae*.
giu, giw, see *gaeuo*.
gle (nece-), see *necti-galae*.
gleddęgo, gleddian (ā-), see *a-gleddęgo*.
glīdan (ā-), see *a-gleddęgo*.
glimith (for *grimith*, he rages, roars, pr. s., of *grimman*?, to rage, roar), XLII. 10; see **seuit** (for *saeuit*).
glitinat, see *glitinot*.
glitinot (*glitinat*, Cp.; from *glitinian*, to glitter), VIII. 15, *glitters*; see **flauescit.**
gloed, see *geloed*.
gluttina, IV. 91=**cementa,** q. v. This is, perhaps, an A.S. spelling of a Lat. word. The Lat. *glū-ten* is allied to A.S.

clā-m, loam, clay; the *g* being older than *c*.

gold, see *ymaeti gold*.

grǣdig, see *gredge*.

grǣg, see *greig*.

granae, *a moustache*, see *gronae*.

gredge, Cp. (plur. of *grēdig*=*grǣdig*, greedy; see Skeat, *Conc. Dict.* sub v. *greedy*), *greedy persons*; see **ambrones**.

grēdig, see *gredge*.

greig, Cp. (=grǣg), *gray*, *grey*; see **ferrugineas**.

grep, grēp, see **scropis**.

grima, see *grina*.

grimith (pr. s. of *grimman*?), see *glimith*.

grina (for *grima*?), XXVII. 5, *a mask*, *spectre*; see **scina**.

grist, see *grost*.

gristlae, gristle (naes-), see *naes-gristle*.

gristle, see *grost*.

groepe, see *groop*.

groepum, instr. plur., see *groop*.

gronae (*granae*, Cp., Ep., & Ef.), XLVII. 32, *a moustache*; see **mustacra**.

groop (*groepe*, Cp.; *groepum*, Cp., Ep., & Ef., instr. plur.), XLVI. 22, *a furrow*, *burrow*; see **scropis**.

groove (E.), see **scropis**.

grōp, see **scropis**.

grost (also written *grist*=A.S. *grystle*, *gristle*; O.H.G. *g. ostila*, *chrustula*), XIX. 59, *gristle*; see **cartillago**, and below *naes-gristle*.

grostila, O.H.G., see *grost*.

grot (*grytt*, Cp.), XLVI. 21, coarse meal, *groats*, *grits*; see **pollis**.

grystle, see *grost*.

grytt, see *grot*.

guma (dryct-, dryht-), see *dryct-guma*.

gyccae (*gycenis*, Cp.; *gycinis*, Ep. & Ef.), XXXV. 3, *itch*; see **prorigo**, sub v. **pruriginem**.

gycenis, *itch*, see *gyccae*.

gycer (A.S.?), *a juger* or *acre of land*, XXXV. 75; see **iugeres**.

gycinis, see *gyccae*.

gylt (ē-), see *ē-gylt*.

h missing, see *ueo-stun*.

haam, *weaver's reed* (?); see *aam*.

haam (=ham, hama, hom, homa, Bosw. T.), *a covering*, *shirt*; see **camisa**.

habuc (palch-), see *ualc-hefuc*.

haca, see *haeca*.

haebuc (uualh-), see *ualc-hefuc*.

haeca, Cp.; *haca*, Ep. & Ef., perhaps *a hatch*, *grating*; *a hook*, or *bar*; see **pessul**.

hæf, *sea*, see *heb*.

haefuc, XIX. 36, *a hawk*; see **accipitres**.

hæg-tes, hæg-tesse, see *haegtis*.

haeg-tis (id. Cp. & Ep.; *heg-tis*, Ef.; *hæg-tes*, WW.; *hæg-tesse*, ib.), XLVII. 80.—**hegi-tissę** (*haeh-tisse*, Cp.), XLIII. 53, *a witch*, *fury*, *hag*; see **eumenides**; **striga**. Cf. also Erenis, *haegtis*, furia, Cp. E283; Striga, *haegtis*, Cp. S528; Strigia, *haegtis*, Ep. 23E35; Striga, *hegtis*, Ef.[1] 390. 18; furia, *haehtis*, Cp. F434. Haeg-tis &c. from *haeg*, hedge, field+*tis* &c.=O.H.G. *hagazussa*, for which see Schade, who suggests that the deriv. of *-tis* &c. is from A.S. *teosu*, *tesu*, see Bosw. T.=harm, injury, whence the verb *teswian*, to harm. Thus **hagi-teswe*, and *hęgi-tesse*, i.e. hedge-harmer, destroyer of hedges. See Kluge, *Wrtb.* (*Eidechse*); Franck, *Woordenb.* (*Hagedis*); Bosw. T. (*āđexe*, a lizard).

haeh-tis, haeh-tisse, *a hag*; see *haeg-tis*.

haen, *a hen*, see *scribid*.

haerd-haeu (*heard-heau*, Cp.; *heard-heui*, Ef.), XLVII. 49, *a hardy hewer*, or *hoe*; see **ciscillus**.

haerd-hera (*heard-hara*, Cp. & Ef.), XLVII. 12, the name of *a fish* (*hard hare*); see **caefalus**.

haerg=*hearh*, *a temple*, *an idol*; see **Luperci**.

hæring, see *heringas*.

haesel, haesl (*hazel*), see *hel*.

haesel-hnutu, *a hazel-nut*, see *hel*.

haesl-in (adj. of haesl), III. 38, *hazel-*, *of hazel*; see **toracina**.

haet (*hæt*), *a hood*, *hat*, or *a head-band*, *coif*, V. 11; see **labrum**.—**haetas** (accus. pl. of *hæt*), XXVI. 8, *head-bands*, *turbans*, *coifs*; see **mitras**.—**het** (*haet*, Cp.; *haeth*, Ef.), XLVII. 7, *a hat*; see **calomaucus**.

haetas, accus. pl. of *hæt* (q.v.).

haeth, *a hat*; see *haet*.

haeu (haerd-), *a hardy hewer*, *hoe*; see *haerd-haeu*.

hæwen, *blue*, *azure*; see *heuuin*.

hald (lemp-), see *lemp-hald*.

half (ðridde-), see *dride-halpf*.

halpf (dride-), see *dride-halpf*.

hals=A.S. heals, *neck*; see *hals-ledir*.

hals-ledir (hals = A.S. heals, *neck* + ledir=leðer, *leather*), III. 37, *neck-leather*, *a rein*; see **abenis**.

halt (lemp-, laempi-, lemphi-), see *lemp-hald*.

ham, hama, see *haam*.

hamer (clod-), see *emaer*.

hamme, V. 19; **hommę**, XXXV. 204, the inner or hind part of the knee, *the ham* (see Skeat, *Conc. Dict.*; Oxf. D. *ham*, sb[1] No. 1); see **publite**.

hana (holt-), see *holt-hona*.

hand-ful beouuas, beouaes; see *hond-ful baeues*.

hara, *a hare*; heard-, *a fish*; see *haerd-hera*.

harperi (=*hearpere*), XLVI. 9, *a harper*; see **fidicen**.

haubit-loh (=O.H.G. *houbit-loh*), XIX. 26, *a head-opening*; see **capitio**, and below *loh*.

haue, XXII. 3, *blue, azure*; see **aeri**, and below *hæwen*, *heuuin*.

heard-hara, the name of *a fish* (hard hare); see *haerd-hera*.

heard-heau, heard-heui, *a hardy hewer, hoe*; see *haerd-haeu*.

heard-n-isse, heard-n-issae, *hardness*; see **rigor** (on the suffixes see Skeat, *Princ. of Engl. Etym.*, 1st Ser. 2nd ed. p. 253).

heardra, see *haerd-hera*.

hearh, see *haerg*.

hearma, *a shrew-mouse?*, see *herma*.

hearpere, see *harperi*.

hearst, hearste; see *herst*.

heau (heard-), *a hardy hewer, hoe*; see *haerd-haeu*.

heaw, heawa, *a hewer, hoe*; see *haerd-haeu*.

heb (=hæf, sea), see *heb-ernum*.

heb-ernum (abl. plur., from *heb*=*hæf*, sea, and *ern*=*ærn*, house), XXXVI. 7, literally, *with sea-houses*, here, *with crabs, mussels*; see **choncis**.

hebuc (uualh-), see *ualc-hefuc*.

hefuc (ualc-), see *ualc-hefuc*.

hegi-tissę, see **haeg-tis**.

heg-tis, see *haeg-tis*.

hel (*haesl*, Cp. & Ef.; *aesil*, Ep.; *haesel-hnutu*, Cp.; *hnutu*, Ef.; *hrutu*, Ep.), XLVII. 1, *hazel(-nut)*; see **abellana**.

heonan (be-, bi-), see *bi-hina*.

heorþ, heorðe, Cp., *a hearth*; see *herth* and *herdu-suepe*.

heorð-suaepe, see *herdu-suepe*.

hera, *a hare*; (haerd-), *a fish*, see *haerd-hera*.

herdu-suepe (*heorð-suaepe*, Cp.; from *herdu*=A.S. *heorð*, a hearth+suepe=A.S. swǣpe, a sweep), XXVI. 6, lit. *a hearth-sweep*, i.e. a bride-woman; see **pronuba**.

here, *a hearth*; see *herth*.

here-benc, for *here-becn*, Cp. (also *here-bæcun*, Cp.; *here-baecon*, Ep.; *here-becon*, Ef.), *an army-beacon*, or *sign*; see **simbulis**.

heringas (acc. plur. of *hering*=*hæring*), XLVII. 74, *herrings, sardines*; see **sardinus** and **giniscula**s.

herma (*hearma*, Cp., Ep. & Ef.), XLVII. 77, *a kind of mouse, a shrew-mouse?* see **netila**.

herst (=*hearst, hearste, hierst*), *a grid-iron*, IV. 75; see **latriuncula** (for *craticula*); XXXV. 175; see **graticulis** (for *crat-*).

herth (*heorðe, here*, in Cp.=*heorþ*), XLII. 12, *a hearth, fire-place*; see **fornacula**, and above *herdu-suepe*.

hestiuis (?), see *editiones*.

het, XLVII. 7, *a hat*; see *haet*.

heui (heard-), *a hardy hewer* or *hoe*; see *haerd-haeu*.

heuuin=hæwen (q.v.), *blue, azure*; see *haue*; *syitor heuuin*.

hider, *hither*; see *hidir-an-didir*, and *hidir-rinę*.

hidir-an-didir (*hider ond hider*, Cp.= A.S. *hider, hither + and, ond + ðider*, thither), III. 64, *hither and thither*; see **ultro**.

hidir-rinę (=*hider*, hither+*rinę*=*rynę*, a run, running), XLIII. 38, *hither-running* (*from our country*); see **nostratis**, sub v. **cuiatis**.

hierst, see *herst*.

hiʒ (if-), *ivy*; see *ib-aei*.

higera, higora=*higrę* (q.v.).

higrae, higre, see *higrę*.

higrę (*higre*, Cp.; *higrae*, Ep. & Ef.), XLVII. 66, *a jay, jackdaw, magpie* or *wood-pecker*; see **picus**.

hina (bi-), see *bihina*.

hinana (O.H.G.), see *bihina*.

hlædder, hlæder, hlædræ, see *hlędrę*.

hlædel, *a ladle*; see **troclei**.

hlędrę=hlædræ, perh.=A.S. *hlǣder, hlædder*, a ladder, flight of steps, IV. 74; see **troclei**.

hlēo(w) ?, *protection, shelter*; see **ari-hellio**; **lio**. With respect to this word *hlēow*, Schlutter (*Journ. of Engl. and Germ. Philol.* v. 468) points out that *lio* is more likely *leo*, a lion, as in Steinmeyer IV. 240 (note 2) one MS. has 'Arihel interpretatur leo dei.'

hlosnian, see *hlysnende*.

hlysnende, Cp. (pres. pt. of **hlysnian*, to listen, which has *hlosnian* as a by-form. Bosw. T. record *hlystan*; cf. mod. E. *listen*, for which see Skeat, *Conc. Dict.*), *listening*; see **adtonitis**.

*hlysnian, see *hlysnende*.

*hnēosan, see *nor*.

hnitu (id. Cp., Ep. & Ef.), XLVII. 84, *a louse's egg, nit*; see **lendina**.

hnor, hnora, see *nor*.

hnutu (haesel-), see *hel* and *hrutu*.

hocc (hoc), Cp., *hock, mallow*; see **malua**.

hog, III. 35, *a heel, hough, how, promontory*; see **promontorium**.

holaen (cnio-), see *cne-holen*.

holegn, holen, Cp., *holly*; see **acri-folium**.—holegn (cre-, for cne-), see *cne-holen*.—holen (cne-, cnio-), see *cne-holen*.

holt (aler-, alter-), see *alerholt*.

holt-hona (id. Cp.; *holt-hana*, Ep.; *holt-ana*, Ef.), XLVII. 59, *a woodcock*; see **acega**.

hom, homa, see *haam*.

hommę, *the ham*; see *hamme*.

hona, for hana (holt-), see *holt-hona*.

hond-ful baeues (*hond-ful beopes*, Cp.; *hand-ful beouuas*, Ep.; *hand-ful beouaes*, Ef.), XLVII. 34, *a handful of corn* or *barley*; see **manticum**.

horn, for *hron* (q.v.).

hosp, see *ðorh hosp*.

houbit-loh (O.H.G.); see *haubit-loh*.

hraebn (naecht-, nect-), *a night-raven*, see *necth̄t-refn*.

hraecli, *a robe*, *rail*; see *hręgli*.

hraefn (naeht-), see *necth̄t-refn*.

hraegl, *a robe*, *rail*; see *hręgli*.

hraga, see *hragra*.

hragra (id. Ep. & Ef.; *hraga*, Cp. = A.S. hrāgra), XLVII. 64, *a heron*; see **perdulum**.

hran, *a whale*; see *hron*.

hręgli, Cp.; hraecli, Ep.; hraegl, Ef. *a garment*, *rail*; see **amiculo**.

hreod, XIX. 16, *a reed*; see **carectum**.

hroc (*hrooc*, Cp., Ep. & Ef.), XLVII. 51, *a rook*, *raven*; see **garallus**.

hron (id. Ef.; *horn*, Cp.; *hran*, Ep.), XLVII. 10, *a whale*; see **balera**.

hrooc, *a rook*; see *hroc*.

hrutu (for *hnutu*), see *hel*.

hryste, Cp. = *hyrst*, *an ornament*, *trapping*; see **falleras**.

hu ald (*how old*), XLIII. 39; **suæ ald** (*so old*), XLIII. 40; see **quotus**.

huete-stan, hueti-stan, see *ueo-stun*.

huidir-rynę (= *hwider*, whither + *rynę*, a run, running), XLIII. 37, *whither-running*, *whither-derived* or *originating*; see **cuiatis**.

humbyl-bee; see **tabanus**.

Hūne, see *huni*.

Huni, O.H.G.; see *huni*.

huni (perh. = A.S. *Hune*), XXXIX. 25, *a Hun*; see **uulgari**.

huora for *hnora*; see **nor**.

husc, see *hux*.

huses, gen. of hūs, *a house*; see **domatis**, in v. **domate**.

hux = *husc*, *scorn*, *scoffing*; see **per hironiam**.

hwæstrung, hwāstrung, see *uastrung*.

hwet-stān, see *ueo-stun*.

hwider, *whither*; see *huidir-rynę*.

hynona, O.H.G.; see *nor*.

hyrst, see *hryste*.

ib-aei (*if-egn*, Cp.; *if-eg*, Ef. = A.S. *if-iȝ*, short for *if-hīȝ*), XVII. 11, *ivy*; see **hederam** (to the references there given add Oxf. D.; Skeat, *Conc. Dict.*, *ivy*).

iesen, Cp. (*iesend*, *iesende*, *iesendne*, Wright W. 396, 22; 521, 33; *isen*, ib. 393, 11), *entrails*; see **exta**.

iesend, iesende, iesendne, see *iesen*.

if-eg, if-egn, *ivy*; see *ib-aei*.

iȝ, for hiȝ (if-), *ivy*; see *ib-aei*.

ile, see *ill*.

ill, Cp. = ile, *a piece of hard skin*; see **callos**.

in sond-ge-pearp, Cp. (= *sand-ge-weorp*), *on a sand-bank*, *quicksand*; see **in sirte**.

in-tinga, *for the sake*, *cause of*; see *uuordes intinga*.

in-trepetan (from *in-*, pref. in, upon + *trepetan*, frequent. of *treppan*, to dance, trip. In this case the pref. may mean 'upon,' to keep on dancing upon, or it may mean little, and have been merely suggested by *sub-* of *sub-saltare*), XXXV. 197, *to tread*, *dance*; see **subsaltare**.

in-uuerpan (= *in-weorpan*, cast, throw, begin a wearp) **uuep** (a web), XIII. 34; see **telam orditus**.

Iringis-uuec, XXVII. 28, *milky way*; see *in georgicis*.

isaern (bred-), see *bred-isern*.

isen (for *isern*), see *bred-isern*.

isen, see *iesen*.

isern (bræd-), see *bred-isern*.

kio, see *chyun*.

kylle, see *cyll*.

laad, see *luad*.

laam (id. Cp. & Ep.; *sram*, Ef.; *lam*, Aldh.), XLVII. 37, *loam*; see **argella**.

laath = lād, see *luad*.

lactum, lǣtum (friu-), see *friu-lactum*.

lad-, see *ge-loed*.

Laden (G.), see *ge-loed*.

lǣce, *a leech*, see **lexas**.

laempi-halt, see *lemp-hald*.

laepae-uincae, see *laepi-uincę*.

laepi-uincę (*lepe-uuince*, Cp.; *laepae-uincae*, Ef.), XLVII. 60, *a lapwing*; see **cucuzata**.

laestu (braed-), see *brad-acus*.

laesung, see *laesungae*.

laesungae (*lēasung*, Cp. & Ep.; *laesung*, Ef.), XLVII. 19, *falsehood*, *leasing*; see **famfelucas**, and cf. Skeat, *Conc. Dict.* (*leasing*).

lǣte, lǣtum (friu-), see *friu-lactum*.

lagu (ober-), see *ober-lagu*.

lam, see *laam*.

lār or *larra*, Prov. E.; see *leer*.

last (braad-), see *brad-acus*.

*laþ- (Goth.), see *ge-loed*.

lād, see *luad*.

lath = lād, see *luad*.

laurice (*lauricae*, Cp.; *lauuercae*, Ep.

& Ef.; perhaps compounded of *la-*, or *lǣ-* + *wrecæ*, *urice*, *uricæ*, *uuercæ*, treason-wreaker), XLVII. 61, *a lark*; see **tilaris**.

lauuercae, see *laurice*.

leac trogas, Cp.; leac trocas, Ep. & Ef. (*lēac*, a garden herb + *trog*, a trough, vessel), *vegetable baskets*; see **corimbis**.

leaf (gearpan), see *gearpan leaf*.

leas, see *lees*.

lēasung, *falsehood*, *leasing*; see *laesungae*.

leceas, see **lexas**.

lēd (ge-), see *ge-loed*.

ledir = leðer, *leather* (hals-); see *hals-ledir*.

ledir-uuyrcta, *a leather-wright*; see *ledir-uyrcta*.

ledir-uyrcta (*leđer-uyrhta*, Cp.; *ledir-uuyrcta*, Ep.; *ledir-uyrhta*, Ef.), XLVII. 40, *a leather-wright*; see **byrseus**.

ledir-uyrhta, *a leather-wright*; see *ledir-uyrcta*.

leer, also *lesera* (perhaps related to prov. E. *lār*, or *larra*, a bar), XLVII. 25, *a bar* (?); see **pessul**.

lees (? = A.S. *lēas*, loose, false, deceitful, as subst.), *a deceiver* (?), XLV. 26; see **histrio**; cf. *scurra*, leuuis, Cp. S146; Ep. 25A36; Ef.[1] 393, 7; Schlutter, *Journ. E. Phil.* v. 143.

lema, see *lomum*.

lemp-hald (*lemp-halt*, Cp.; *laempi-halt*, Ep.; *lemphi-halt*, Ef.), XLVII. 45, *limp-halting*; see **lurdus**.

lemphi-halt, see *lemp-hald*.

leoma, *a ray of light*, and *a branch*; see *lomum*.

lepe-uuince, see *laepi-uincę*.

lesera, see *leer*.

letan (frio-), see *friu-lactum*.

leđer-uyrhta, *a leather-wright*; see *ledir-uyrcta*.

leðrum, see *ge-wald-leðrum*.

leuuis, see *lees*.

lexas, XLVIII. 51 (if A.S., it would be the plur. of *lǣce*, a leech; cf. *lyces*, Wright W.; *leceas*, Cp.); see **sanguessuges**.

li (aen-), see *aen-li*.

licae, lice (earfed-); see *earfed-lice*.

lice (from-), see *from-lice*.

liim, Cp.; lim, Ef., *cement*, *mortar*, *lime*, see **cementa**; **lim**, XV. 4, see **litura**.

lim, *lime*; see *liim*.

lim (*a joint*), limum; see *lomum*.

limp-halt, see *lemp-halt*.

lind (id. Cp., Ep., & Ef.), XLVII. 100, *the linden* or *lime-tree*; see **tilio**.

-ling, see *gæde-ling*, *geadu-ling*.

loc, *a hole*, *abyss*, *lock*; see *loh*.

loc (clustor-), locae (cluster-, clustor-), *a prison-lock*, *lock*, *bar*; see *clustor-loc*.

locc, locca, loccum, *lock*, *locks of hair*; see **crinicuł**.

lōd, see *ge-loed*.

logdor (id. Ef.; *logđor*, Cp.), XLVII. 83, *plotting mischief*, *crafty*; see **cacomicanus**.

logđor, see *logdor*.

loh (O.H.G.), XXXV. 176 = A.S. *loc*, *an enclosure*, *hole*, *abyss*, *lock*; see **baratrum**.

—loh (haubit-, houbit-), see *haubit-loh*.

loma, *a tool*; see *lomum*.

lomum (instr. pl., not of *loma*, a tool; nor of *leoma*, a ray of light; nor for *lonum*, from *lone*; nor for *limum*, from *lim*, but) = *lomum* for *leomum*, from *leoma*, also written *lema*, from A.S. *lim*, a limb, joint, especially *a branch*, v. 2; see **colomellas**.

lone, lonum; see *lomum*.

luad, for laad (lath, Cp. & Ef.; laath, Ep. = lāđ), XXXV. 289, *hateful*, *hated*; see **inuisum**.

lyces, see *lexas*.

madmas (plur.), III. 66, *precious things*, *ornaments*; see **exenia**.

maeful-dur, for *maepul-dur*; see *mapal-durt*.

maerae (*maere*, Cp.; *mera*, Ep.; *merae*, Ef.), XLVII. 81, *an incubus*, (night)-*mare*; see **incuba**.

maere, see *maerae*.

mære, see *menae*.

maerth (*mearð*, Cp.; *mearth*, Ep.; *meard*, Ef.), XLVII. 76, *a marten*, *kind of weasel*; see **furunculas**.

maest, XXXIX. 37, *a pole*, *mast*; see **arbor**.

manung, see *monung*.

mapal-durt (*mapuldur*, Cp. & Ep.; *maeful-dur*, Ef.), XLVII. 97, *the maple-tree* (māpal, māpul, the maple + durt, dur, unstressed forms of A.S. *trēow*, a tree; see Skeat, *Dict.* v. *maple*); see **acerafulus**.

mapul-dur, see *mapal-durt*.

mare, see *menae*.

masae (so also in Ep. & Ef.; *mase*, Cp. = A.S. *māse*), XLVII. 52, (a tit-)*mouse*; see **parula**.

mase, māse, see *masae*.

mattae, not A.S., but dat. of Lat. *matta*, XXXIV. 3, see **spiathio**.

meard, *a marten*; see *maerth*.

mearth, mearð, *a marten*; see *maerth*.

menae, for *merae* (= *mære*, mare, mere), XIII. 24, *a night-mare*, *a monster*; see **pilosi**.

meo, *a shoe*; see *mihes*.

meottucas (Cp.); mettocas (Ep.); metocas (Ef.), *mattocks*, *hoes*; see **ligones**.

mera, merae, see *maerae*.

merae, mere, see *menae*.

metocas, **mettocas**, see *meottucas*.

mihes (? gen. of *mēo*, a shoe), XXXVII. 7; see **odonis uitam**.

miltę (*milte*, Cp. & Ef.; *multi*, Ep.), XLVI. 6, *the milt, spleen*; see **lien**.

mit, *with*; see **arguta**.

miđiδ, Cp., *he dissembles* (from *miđan*, to conceal, dissemble), see **dissimulat**.

mixen, see *mixin*.

mixin (=mixen, *a mixen, dung-heap*), IV. 83; **mixinnum** (instr. pl.), XXXV. 292; see **ruder**.

mixinnum, see *mixin*.

monung gaebles (*geabules monung*, Cp.; *gebles-monung*, Ef.), XXXIX. 27, *a claiming* or *exaction of debt*, or *tribute*, or *tax*; see **exactio**.

mucxle, see *muscellas*.

multi, see *miltę*.

muscellas, Cp. & Ep.; muscellae, Ef., plur. of *muscelle* = muxle, mucxle, *a muscle* or *mussel, a shell-fish*; see **ginisculas**.

muxle, see *muscellas*.

mynit, Cp. & Ep. (*munit*, Ef.; *mynet*, Napier, *Gl.*), *a coin*; see **nomisma**.

n for r; scinnenas (q.v.) for scinneras.

nabfo-gar, nabo-gaar, nabo-ger, see *nębu-gaar*.

nacthe-gelae, see *necti-galae*.

næbu, see *nębu-gaar*.

naecht-hraebn, see *necth t-refn*.

naecte-gale, see *necti-galae*.

naect-genge, Cp., *a night-goer*; see **hyinę**.

nægel, naegl, nægl; see *negil*.

naeht-hraefn, see *necth t-refn*.

naes-gristle, Cp.; naes-gristlae, Ep. & Ef., *nose-gristle*; see **cartillago**, and above, *grost*.

nafu, see *nębu-gaar*.

ncti-galae, see *necti-galae*.

nębu-gaar (*nabo-gaar*, Cp.; *nabfo-gar*, Ep.; *nabo-ger*, Ef.; from A.S. *næbu, nafu*, a nave + *gār*, a spear, borer), XLVII. 46, *a nave-borer, auger, gimlet*; see **terebellus**.

nece-gle, see *necti-galae*.

nect, *night*; see *ofer tua nest*.

nectae-galae, see *necti-galae*.

nęctę-gela, see *necti-galae*.

nect-hraebn, see *necth t-refn*.

necth t-refn (*naeht-hraefn*, Cp.; *naecht-hraebn*, Ep.; *nect-hraebn*, Ef.), XLVII. 54, *a night-raven*; see **noctua**; see also *nectigalae*.

necti-galae (*naecte-gale, nehtę-gale*, Cp.; *nectae-galae, ncti-galae, necti-galae*, Ep.; *nece-gle, nacthe-gelae, nęctę-gela*, Ef.; see Skeat, *Conc. Dict.*). XLVII. 62, *a night singer, a nightingale*; see **ruscinia** and **noctua**.

negil (*naegl*, Cp. = A.S. *nægel, nægl*), XV. 5, *a nail*; see **paxillus**.

nehtę-gale, see *necti-galae*.

nest for *nect*, night; see *ofer tua nest*.

nift (id. Cp., Ep. & Ef.), *a step-daughter*, or *a niece, grand-daughter*, XLII. 7; see **priuigna**.

niht-hræfn, see *necth t-refn*.

-n-issae, -n-isse (heard-), *hardness*; see *heard-n-isse* (and on this suffix, cf. Skeat, *Princ. of Engl. Etym.*, first Ser., 2nd ed., p. 253).

nor, for *hnor*; *huora*, for *hnora*, Ef. from an unrecorded A. S. strong verb **hnēosan*; and *fnora* (Cp. & Ep.); from A. S. *fnēosan*; (O. H. G. forms *nur*; *hynona*), XIX. 65, *a snore, neese, neeze*; see **sternutatio**.

nord-baeg, for *rond-baeg* (*rond-baeg*, Cp. & Ef., *rand-beag*, Ep.), XLVII. 17, *the boss of a shield*, or *a shield*; see **buculus**.

nostle, *a fillet, band*; see *nostlun*.

nostlun (dat. plur. of A. S. *nostle*), *a fillet, band*, XXXVII. 7; see **odonis uitam**.

nur, O. H. G.; see *nor*.

ober-lagu, III. 11, *an over* (upper) cloak (see Bosw. T. *ofer-læg*); see **anfibula**, sub v. **amphibalum**.

ober-scoeiddo, XLII. 27, for *ofer-scaeþþu*? over, exceeding scathe, insolence, mischief; see **in pennias** (for *impunitas*?).

ofer-scaeþþu (?), see *ober-scoeiddo*.

ofer tua nest (*ofer*, over, beyond; *tua* = *twā*, two; *nest* for *nect*, night), XLIII. 41, *over two nights, the day after tomorrow*; see **perende**.

ogabul-rind (Ir.), see *gabo-rind*.

olen (cni-), see *cne-holen*.

oma (oman, Cp.), XXXV. 66, *erysipelas*; see **ignis sacer**.

oman, see *oma*.

omer, see *emaer*.

omprae, see *omprę*.

omprę (*ampre*, Cp.; *amprae*, Ep.; *omprae*), XLVI. 27, *a tumor* or *swelling*; see **uarix**.

on-, see *an-sceat*.

ond (= A. S. *and*, and); see *hidir-andidir*.

on-felti, on-filte, on-filti, see *osi-felti*.

onga (id. Cp.; *anga*, Ep. & Ef.), XLVII. 85, *a sting*; see **aquilius**.

orc, see *oroccerum*.

ordancas (for *orþance*?), III. 65, *with cunning, skilful*; see **arguta**.

oroccerum (dat. plur.; also misread *droccerum*, perh. from *orc*, a stage-player, or monster = Lat. *orcus*, the infernal regions), xxxix. 57; see **histrio**.

orþancas, orþance, see *ordancas*.

osi-felti, perhaps for on-felti (*on-filti*, Cp.; *an-filte*, WW.; *on-filte*, id.; *an-feld*, id.; O. H. G. *ueliti*, *ana-boz*, *ana-poz*, *ana-bolz*; but cf. O. H. G. *ysi-folto*, Steinm. i. 497, 18), xix. 41, *an anvil*; see **incus** (on the etymology of the word cf. Skeat, *Conc. Dict.* sub v. *anvil*).

pina, for *fina*; see *uinu*.

poccas (plur. of *pocc*), v. 5, *pocks*, *pustules*; see **carbunculi**.

pox, for *þox? (= A. S. *dox*), iii. 57, *dusk*; see **lurida**.

prant, O. H. G. = A. S. & M. E. *brand*; see **torris**.

priusa, see *brimisa*.

pundar (*pundur*, Cp.; A. S. spelling of late Lat. *pondarium*), xiii. 40, *a plumb-line*; see **perpendiculum**.

pundur, see *pundar*.

pung (Cp. & Ef.), *a small bag*, *purse*; see **de cassidie**.

r for n: *c*reholegn for *c*neholegn.

ra (brond-), see *brond-ra*.

rad (brand-, brond-), see *brond-ra*.

raed-gasram, Cp. (perh. for *rǽd-gāsran*, of which the real sense is not known); see **hyadas**.

rand (bord-), see *bord-rand*.

rand (gafol-), see *gabo-rind*.

rand-beag, *the boss of a shield*, or *a shield*; see *nord-baeg* (for *rond-baeg*).

read (uuiloc-, pioloc-), see *pioloc-read*.

rede-stan, Cp., *red-stone*; see **sinopide**.

rēfa (ge-), see *ge-roefan*.

refn (necctht-), *a night-raven*, see *hraebn*.

rema, remum (bord-); see *bord-remum*.

rend (gabel-); rind (gabo-); rond (gabul-); *a pair of compasses*; see *gabo-rind*.

reogol, see **pessul**.

reud (uusluc-), see *pioloc-read*.

rigil, O. H. G., see **pessul**.

rihe, see *rihum*.

rihum (instr. plur. of *rihe* = *rӯhe*, *a rug*, *blanket*), xlii. 2, *with rugs*, *blankets*; see **tapetibus**.

rima (bord-), see *bord-remum*.

rind (gabo-, gabol-), see *gabo-rind*.

rinę (hidir-), see *hidir-rinę* and *huidir-rynę*.

risel, Cp. (= rysel, D. *reuzel*, lard, suet), *grease*, *fat*; see **aruina**.

rod (brand-), see *brond-ra*.

roefan (ge-), see *ge-roefan*.

rond (gabul-), see *gabo-rind*.

rond-baeg = *rand-beag* (q. v.).

ruga for *sugu* (q. v.).

rӯhe, *a rug*; see *rihum*.

ryndir, wrongly for *tyndir*; see *tynder*.

rynę (huidir-), see *huidir-rynę* and *hidir-rinę*.

rysel, see *risel*.

saex = seax, *a knife*; see *blod-saex*.

salch, salh, see *salhas*.

salhas, plur. of *salh* = *sealh*, a willow-tree, a sallow, sally (*salh*, Cp. & Ef.; *salch*, Ep.), xix. 61; see **salices**.

sand-ge-weorp, see *in sond-ge-pearp*.

sax (?), if A.S., for *six*? or abbrev. Lat. for *Saxonice*?; see **solidos**, sub v. **solidi**.

scaeþþu (ofer-), see *ober-scoeiddo*.

sceat (an-), see *an-sceat*.

sceaþa, sceaþan, see **in pennias**.

scelb (also O.H.G. *scelf*, *scelp*, *scelb*); perhaps the same as A.S. *scylf* (Bosw. T.), a peak, crag, turret, or *scilfe*, a shelf, ledge, floor, xxxv. 59; see **fornice**.

scelf, scelp (O.H.G.), see *scelb*.

sceop, *a poet*; see *scopon*.

sceot (an-), see *an-sceat*.

scēotan, *to shoot*, see *an-sceat*.

sceþþu, see **in pennias**.

sciir, *a charge*, see *thestisuir*.

scilfe, see *scelb*.

scineras, see *scinnenas*.

scinnenas, for scinneras (*scinneras*, Cp. & Ep.; *scineras*, Ef., plur. of scīn, scinn, scinna, scinere), xxxix. 55, *evil spirits*, *spectres*, *magicians*; see **scinici**.

scinneras, see *scinnenas*.

scoehere (*scoere*, Cp.), xlii. 6, *a shoemaker*; see **sutrinator**.

scoere, see *scoehere*.

scoh, *a shoe*; see **caligam**.

scop, *a poet*; see *scopon*.

scopon? A.S. for *sceop*, *scop*? *a poet*, xlvii. 95; see **philocain**.

scraeua (*screauua*, Cp.; *screuua*, Ep.), xlvii. 78, *a shrew*(-mouse); see **musiranus**.

screauua, see *scraeua*.

screc, see *scruc*.

screuua, see *scraeua*.

scribid (*scripid*, Cp.; *scripit haen*, Ep. & Ef. from A.S. *screpan*), *he scrapes*, *scratches*, xlvii. 39; see **scarpmat**.

scric, see *scruc*.

scrid, *a chariot*, *litter* (Bosw. T.); see **basterna**.

scriic, see *scruc*.

scripit, scripid, see *scribid*.

scruc, for *scriic* (*scric*, Cp. & Ep.; *screc*, Ef.), xlvii. 63, *a shrike*, *skrike*, *screech*; see **turdus**.

sculdre, sculdrę, xxi. 20, *shoulder*; see **labastes**.

scyan, see *scyhend*.

scyend, see *scyhend*.

scyhan, see *scyhend*.

scyhend (=Ep.; *scyend*, Cp., part. sb. of *scȳhan*, *scȳan*), XLVII. 35, *a seducer, corrupter*; see **maulistis**.

scylf, see *scelb*.

seād, see *sedes*.

sealh, see *salhas*.

seax, see *saex*.

secg, sech, *sedge*; see *seic*.

sedes (for A.S. gen. sing. *seādes*, *seōdes*, from *seād*, *seōd*), XVII. 6, of *a money-bag, purse* or *pouch*; see **sacelli**.

segin (*seign*, Cp., a loan-word, from the Lat. *signum*), XXXV. 69, *a sign, token*; see **uixilla**; see also *segn*, Cp. & Ef.; *seng*, Ep., sub v. *labrum*.

segn, see *segin*.

seic (*secg*, Cp.; *sech*, Ef.), XLVI. 26, *sedge*; see **carex**.

seign, see *segin*.

sele (teld-), *a tent*; see *tyld-syle*.

seng, see *segin*.

seōd, see *sedes*.

seolf-bonan, Cp., *a suicide*; see **biothanti**.

seot, for sceot (an-), see *an-sceat*.

sīma (siima), *a cord, rope*; see **cestus**.

sin-fullae, -fulle; see *fullae*.

sli, see *slii*.

slii (*sli*, Cp.; Ep.; Ef.=A.S. *slīw*), XLVII. 71, *a fish*, perh. *the tench*, or *mullet*; see **tinct**.

slitendę (part. of *slītan*, to slit, tear), XXXV. 183, *patched*; see **laciniosa**.

slīw, see *slii*.

smæti (*smaete*, Cp.) **gold**, *beaten, refined gold*, see *ymaeti gold*.

smedema, see *smetuma*.

smeodema, smeoduma, see *smetuma*.

smetuma (=*smeoduma*, *smedema*, *smeodema*), XXVI. 7, *fine flour, meal*; see **simila**.

snaas (=*snās*, *snǣs*), XLVI. 1, *a spit, skewer*; see **ueru**.

snædan, see *snędit*.

snaedil, snaedil-þearm; see *snedil-daerm*.

snædit, see *snędit*.

snægl (*snegl*, Cp. & Ep.), XLVII. 90, *a snail*; see **maruca**.

snearh, snearu, see *sner*.

snedil-daerm (*snaedil-þearm*, Cp.; *snaedil* uel *thearm*, Ef.), XXXV. 203, *the great gut*; see **extale**.

snędit (=snaedit, 3rd pers. sing. of *snǣdan*, to slice, prune trees), XLVII. 102, *he snathes, prunes trees*; see **putat**.

snegl, see *snægl*.

sner (=*snearu*, *snearh*), XLVI. 18, *the string* of a musical instrument; see **fidis**.

snīte, Cp. *a snite, snipe*; and uudu-, *a wood-snite*, see **acega**.

sond-ge-pearp, see *in sond-ge-pearp*.

sorgendi, Cp., Ep., Ef., *being anxious*; see **anxius**.

spadan, see *spaedun*.

spaedun (*spadan*, Cp., Ep. & Ef., accus. plur. of *spadu*, *spædu*, a spade, *mattock*), XXXIX. 12; see **uangas**.

spaldr, see *spaldur*.

spaldur (id. Cp. & Ef.; *spaldr*, Ep.; *spalor*, *sypaldor*; ?A.S.), XII. 18, *asphalt*; see **aspaltum**.

spalor, see *spaldur*.

span, spon (**ge-**), *a clasp*; see *ge-span*.

spraeci (felo-), see *felo-spric*.

spraeici, spreci (felu-), see *felo-spric*.

spric (felo-), see *felo-spric*.

sram, for lam=*laam* (q.v.).

stæl, see *stalo*.

staer, see *stęr*.

stalo to fuglam (*stalu to fuglum*, Cp., Ep., Ef.; *stalo*, *stalu*, pl. of *stæl*, a place, stall; *fuglam* for *fuglum*, instr. pl. of *fugel*, better form *fugol*, a fowl), XLVII. 14, *a place, stall for fowls*; see **umbrellas**.

stalu, see *stalo*.

stan (cisil-), see *cisil-stan*; (huete-, hueti-), see *ueo-stan*; (rede-), see *rede-stan*.

stanas, see *dunnę*.

stane (un-ge-batne), see *un-ge-batne stane*.

staup-fotar, see *steuf-feder*.

steeli, see *stel*.

stegn, see *steng*.

stel (or *stele*, *steli*, Cp. & Ef.; *steeli*, Ep.), XLVII. 38, *steel*; see **accearium**.

stele, steli, see *stel*.

steng, Cp.; stegn, Ep.; stęng, Ef., *a stang* (Prov. E.); see **claua**.

steop-faeder, see *steuf-feder*.

stęr (*staer*, Cp. & Ep.; *sterm*, Ef.), XLVII. 53, *a starling* or *stare* (with short *æ*: stǣr means a history); see **sturnus**.

sterm, see *stęr*.

steuf-feder (*steop-faeder*, Cp.; *steup-faedaer*, Ep.; *staup-fotar*, Ef.), XXXVI. 14, *a stepfather*; see **uitricum**.

steup-faedaer, see *steuf-feder*.

stilith, Cp., *steals*; see **conpellare**.

stillit (un-), see *un-stillit*.

stilnis (un-), see *un-stilnis*.

stofn, see *stofun*.

stofun (=*stofn*; Prov. E. *stoven*, *stovin*, *stoving*, *stowan*), XXXV. 73, *a stem, stump of a tree*; see **codicibus**.

storc, *a stork*; see *storhc*.

storhc (*storc*, Cp. & Ef.), XLVII. 56, *a stork*; see **ciconia**.

stoven, stovin, stoving, stowan (Prov. E., stump of a tree), see *stofun*.
stream, see *streum*.
streum (*stream*, Cp., Ep. & Ef. = *strēam*, *a flow, stream*), XLVII. 31; see **reuma.**
stricilum, Cp., Ep. & Ef. (instr. pl. of *stricel*, a strickle); see **troclei.**
strīdan, stridid, see *striteͅd*.
striteͅd (*stridit*, Cp., Ep. & Ef., 3rd pr. of *strīdan*), XLVII. 43, *he straddles, strides*; see **uaricat.**
stun, for *stan* (ueo-, for hueot-), see *ueo-stun*.
styra (*styrga*, Cp.; *styria*, Ep. & Ef.), XLVII. 73, *a sturgeon*; see **porco piscis.**
styrga, see *styra*.
styria, see *styra*.
su (for *sū*), III. 44, *a sow, female pig*; see **soeue**; also written **sugu** = *sŭgŭ* (id. Cp. & Ep.; *ruga*, Ef.), XLVII. 93 (O. H. G. *su*; Germ. *Sau*; Du. *zeug*); see **scrufa.**
suæ (= *swǣ*), *so*; see *hu ald*.
suaepe (heorð-), see *herdu-suepe*.
suca (*sugga*, Cp. & Ep.; *sucga*), XLVII. 68, the name of a bird, *the fig-pecker?*; see **ficetula.**
sucga, see *suca*.
suedilas, see *suithelon*.
suehoras, see *sueoras*.
suenceth, Cp., *he distresses*; see **deficiet.**
suēor, see *sueoras*.
sueoras, Cp. & Ef.; *suehoras*, Ep. (nom. plur. of *suēor*, from *sweohor* = G. *Schwäher*, *Schwager*, *Schwieger*; Du. *zwager*, *a brother in law*); see **uiteleos iuuenes** [where it is pointed out that the A. S. words explain *the fact* that the *Vitelei* were *the brothers in law* of Brutus and, therefore, do not interpret *a word*].
suepe (herdu-), see *herdu-suepe*.
sueðelas, see *suithelon*.
sugga, see *suca*.
sugu, *a sow*; see above, *su*.
suh-ter-ga, Cp., also written *suh-ter-iga* (from *suh-* allied to *sweh-* in A. S. *sweh-or*, older form of *swēor*, for which see Bosw. T., + the suff. *-ter*, the same as in E. daugh-*ter*, sis-*ter*, and *-iga*. The A. S. *sweh-* becomes *sweg-* (by Verner's law) in A. S. *sweg-er*. As to *suh-*, cf. Lat. *soc-* in *soc-er*), *a brother's son, a nephew*; see **fratruelis,** and cf. Schade (*suhtrja*).
suice, Cp.; suicae, Ep. & Ef., *a smell, odour*, see **osma.**
suīc-falle (bi-), see *bi-suic-falle*.
suiopum, Cp. (instr. plur. of *swiopu* = *swipu*, a whip; D. *zweep*), *with scourges, with whips*; see **flagris.**
suithelon (instr. plur., from *suithel* = A. S. *sweþel*, *sweoþol*, with swaddling-bands; *sueðelas*, *suedilas*, nom., or acc. plur.), XXV. 12; see **institis.**
suole, Cp. (instr. of *swōl*, *heat, burning*); see **caumate.**
suollaen; suollen (a-), suollam (as-), see *a-suollen*.
suopeͅ (gae-), *sweepings, dust*; see *gae-suopeͅ*.
swæpa, swæpo (ge-), see *gae-suopeͅ*.
swāpan, *to sweep*; see **pronuba.**
sweohor, see *sueoras*.
sweoþel, sweþel, see *suithelon*.
swīc (be-), see *bi-suic-falle*.
swiopu, see *suiopum*.
swipu, see *suiopum*.
swīðe, see *syitor*.
swīðor, comp. of *swīðe*; see *syitor*.
swōl, see *suole*.
syitor (for *swīðor*, comp. of *swīðe*, very much) **heuuin** (= *hǣwen*, blue, azure), XXII. 6, *very much blue, azure*; see **iacyntini.**
syl, Cp., *a pillar, column*; see **basis.**
syle (tyld-), *a tent*; see *tyld-syle*.
sypaldor, see *spaldur*.

t missing, see *ueo-stun*.
tæfl, see *alea*.
tæflere, see *teblheri*.
tæld (ge-), *a tent*; see *ge-zelt*.
tasol, tasul, *a die*; see *tesulas*.
teald (ge-), *a tent*; see *ge-zelt*.
tebl (id. Cp.; *teblae*, Ep.; *tefil*, Ef.; A.S. form for Lat. *tabula*), XLV. 25, *a board* for the playing of a game, and *a game* played on such a board; see **alea.**
teblae, see *tebl*.
teblere, see *teblheri*.
teblheri (*teblere*, Cp., Ep. & Ef. = tæflere), XLV. 24, *a gamester, dicer*; see **aleo.**
tefil, see *tebl*.
teg, see *tetrafa*.
teld (ge-), *a tent*; see *ge-zelt*.
teld-sele, *a tent*; see *tyld-syle*.
teoru (blaec), *black-tar*, see *blaec teoru*.
tesul, see *tesulas*.
tesulas (perh. acc. pl. of A.S. *tasul*, in Cp. & Ef.; or *tesul*; *tasol*, in Ep., all borrowed from Lat. *tessella*, a die), XXXV. 35, *dies*; see **tesseras.**
teter, tetr, see *tetrafa*.
tetrafa (? *teter*, Cp.; *tetr*, Ep.; *teg*, Ef.; *derda*, Steinm.; *fa* seems a corruption of some word; *tetra*, &c. perh. = A.S. *teter*, tetter, a cutaneous disease + *fa*), XXXV. 74; see **petigo.**
-ðe (suffix), see *-da*, *-dae* and *egi-da*.
thearm, see *snedil-daerm*; þearm, see *darmana*; þearm (snaedil-), see *snedil-daerm*.
thegn, see *þegn*.

þegn, Cp.; thegn, Ep.; degn, Ef., *a servant*, *officer*; see **adsecla.**

thestisuir (? if A.S. perhaps for *ambihtes sciir*, charge of office; if Lat., perh. for *thyestaeas*), v. 21; see **editiones.**

ðider, *thither*; see *hidir-an-didir.*

þingere, see *dingere.*

þistel, see *cardella.*

þistel-tuige, see *distyl-tige.*

thistil, see *distyl-tige.*

þoden, *a violent wind*; see **alcianus.**

ðorh (= þurh, through) hosp (reproach, contempt), Cp.; see **per hironiam.**

*þox, see *pox.*

ðrǣd, ðrēd, see *dredum.*

ðridde-half, see *dride-halpf.*

ðrili, þrili, *triple*; see *drili.*

ðring (ebur-), see *ebur-dnung.*

ðriodung (ymb-), see *ymb-ðriodung.*

throstlae, ðrostle, *a throstle*; see *drostlae.*

throt-bolla, ðrot-bolla, see *droh-bolla.*

ðrotu, *the throat*; see *droh-bolla.*

þuarm, Cp. (*thuearm*, Ep.; *duaeram*, Ef.; orig. form properly *þwar-m*, whence A.S. *þwearm*, Bosw. T., by the breaking of *ar* to *ear*. It is very likely allied to Lat. *tor-q-uēre*, and to the E. *thwar-t*; see Goth. *þwairhs* in Uhlenbeck's *Etym. Goth. Wörterb.*), *a cutting instrument*, *a borer* (*scalprum*); see **scalpellum.**

thuearm, see *þuarm.*

þurh, *through*; see *ðorh.*

þuxsað (ge-), see **lurida.**

þwairhs (Goth.), see *þuarm.*

þwarm, see *þuarm.*

thwart, E., see *þuarm.*

þwearm, see *þuarm.*

þys gere, Cp.; thys geri, Ep. & Ef. (þys, thys, *this* + gere, geri, instr. of gēr, *a year*), in *this year*; see **horno.**

tige, tuige [for *twige*, from *twiccian*, to pluck, twitch?] (distyl-, þistel-); see *distyl-tige.*

tili (for *twili*), xlvi. 40, *double*, *twill*; see **bilex.**

tindre, *tinder*; see *tunderi.*

tinga (in-), see *in-tinga.*

tionan, Cp., *annoyances*; see **infestionibus.**

tis, tisse, tissę (haeg-, heg-; haeh-; hegi-); see *haeg-tis.*

to, *to*, *for*, see *stalo.*

traef, see **tenda**, and above *drep.*

tredan, treden, treten (a-), see *an-a-treten.*

trepetan (in-), see *in-trepetan.*

treppan, see *in-trepetan.*

treten, for treden (an-a-, for un-a), see *an-a-treten.*

trimes, see *trymisas.*

trocas, see *leac trogas.*

trog, *a trough*, see *leac trogas*; (cil-, for cild-), see *cil-trog.*

trogas, *baskets*; see *leac trogas.*

trymis, see *trymisas.*

trymisas (plur. of *trymis* = *trimes*), xxxi. 6, *a coin*; see **solidos**, sub v. **solidi.**

tua = twā, *two*; see *ofer tua nest.*

tuige (for twige?), see *tige.*

tuigin, see *tuin.*

tuin, Cp.; tuum, Ep.; tuigin, Ef., *linen* (twyne, twine; D. *twijn*; see Bosw. T. *twīn*; Skeat, *twine*); see **byssus.**

tunder, see *tunderi.*

tunderi, tindre (instrum.? of *tunder*, or = *tundre*), iv. 77, *tinder*, *fuel*; see **cautere.**

tundre, see *tunderi.*

tusc, Cp., *a tusk*; see **genuinum decus.**

tuum (for twin?), see *tuin.*

twige, see *tige.*

twīli, see *tili.*

tychtingum, Cp.; tyctinnum, Ep. & Ef. (instr. pl. of *tyhtenn*, an allurement, bait), see **inlecebris.**

tyctinnum, see *tychtingum.*

tyhtenn, see *tychtingum.*

tyld-syle, = *teld-sele*, *a tent-house* or *dwelling*; see *tenda.*

tynder (Cp., also *tyndre*; *tyndir*, Ep.; *ryndir*, Ef.), *tinder*, *fuel*; see **nappa.**—**tyndri** (tyndrin, Cp. & Ef.; tyndirm, Ep.), xlvii. 29, see **isica.**

tyndirm, see *tynder.*

tyndri, tyndrin, see *tynder.*

tyrf-ahga, xvii. 2, *a turf* (sod)-*mattock* or *hoe*; see **ligones.**

tysce, *mantel*, see **lena.**

tysse, xlvi. 43, *coverlet*, *blanket*, *counterpane* [? = O. H. G. *zussa* which glosses Lat. *lodix*]; see **abctape.**

u for f: see *u*inu for fina; *u*inc, and *f*inc.

uaar, see *uuac.*

uaell(ed-), see *ed-uallę.*

uaertae, *a wart*; see *uaertę.*

uaertę (*uearte*, Cp.; *uueartae*, Ep.; *uaertae*, Ef.), xlvii. 36, *a wart*; see **berruca.**

ualc-hefuc (*palch habuc*, Cp.; *uualh hebuc*, Ep.; *uualh haebuc*, Ef.), xix. 35, *foreign hawk*; see **herodion.**

ualla, uallę (ed-), see *ed-uallę.*

ual-uyrt (*pal-uyrt*, Cp. & Ef.; *wæl-wyrt*, Aldh.; from *wealh*, foreign + *wyrt*, a root), xlii. 4, *wallwort*; see **elleus.**

uar, see *uuac.*

uarras (pl.; also *peorras*, Cp.; *paar*, sing., Cp.), iv. 24 and xxxv. 122 = A. S. wearr, *a piece of hard skin*; see **callos.**

uastrung (=*hwǣstrung, hwæstrung*), III. 48, *a whispering, murmuring*; see **murmur.**
uearte, *a wart*; see *uaertę.*
ueliti (O. H. G.), see *osi-felti.*
ueorna (aq-), *a squirrel*; see *ac-urna.*
ueo-stun, for *hueot-stan*=*hwet-stān* (*huete-stan*, Cp.; *hueti-stan*, Ef.), XLVI. 4, *a whetstone*; see **cos.**
uidu-bil, see *uitu-bil.*
-uigga, -uuica, -ƿicga, -uuigga, *a wig, worm*; see *ęr-uigga.*
uiif, for *uuif* (ge-), *fate, fortune*; see *ge-uiif.*
uina, see *uinu.*
uinc (*finc*, Cp.; Ep. & Ef.), XLVII. 69, *a finch*; see **fringella.**
uincae (laepae-), see *laepi-uincę.*
uincę (laepi-), see *laepi-uincę.*
uinu (for *uina*; *fina*, Cp. & Ep.; *pina*, Ef.), XLVII. 67, *a woodpecker*; see **marsopicus.**
uitu-bil (=*uidu-bil, wudu-bil*), XIII. 50, *a wood-bill*; see **runtina.**
un-a-treden, see *an-a-treten.*
un-ge-batne stane (=un-ge-bēatne stāne, instrum.), XXIII. 5, *unbeaten stone*; see **lapide inpolito.**
un-stillit (3rd sing. from *unstillan*, to be restless), XLVIII. 28, (he) *is not still, restless*; see **insolescit.**
un-stilnis (Bosw. T. *un-stillness*), *restlessness*; see **insolescit.**
unza, O. H. G., see *libra.*
uoond (*ƿond*, Cp.; *ƿand*, Ep.; *uuond*, Ef. from *wandian*, from the strong verb *windan*, to turn), XLVII. 79, *a mole*; Prov. E. *want*; see **talpa.**
uorna (aq-), *a squirrel*; see *ac-urna.*
uricae, urice (la-), see *laurice.*
urna (ac-), *a squirrel*; see *ac-urna.*

ƿaar, *a piece of hard skin*; see *uarras.*
ƿaar, *sea-weed, waur, wore*; see *uuac.*
uuac, wrongly for uuar (*ƿaar*, Cp.; ƿaar corr. into *uaar*, Ep.; *uar*, Ef.), XLVII. 23, *sea-weed, waur, wore*; see **alga.**
ƿægn-fearu, *waggon-journey*; see *gebellicum.*
wǣl, *a pool, gulf*; see *ed-uallę.*
uuaelle (ed-), see *ed-uallę.*
wæl-wyrt, *foreign root, wallwort*; see *ual-uyrt.*
ƿalch habuc, *foreign hawk*; see *ualc-hefuc.*
wald (an-), see *an-wald.*
uualh haebuc (hebuc), *foreign hawk*; see *ualc-hefuc.*
walla (ed-), see *ed-uallę.*
waltowahso (O. H. G.), see *cartillago.*
pal-uyrt, *foreign root, wallwort*; see *ual-uyrt.*
ƿand, see *uoond.*
wandian, see *uoond.*
uuar, see *uuac.*
ƿase, Cp., *ooze, mud, slime*; see **ceno.**
uudu-binde, see *uudu-bindlae.*
uudubindlae (uudubinde, Cp.; uuidubindlae, Ep; uuydublindae, Ef.), XLVII. 98, *woodbine*; see **inuoluco.** On the etym. cf. Skeat, *Dict.* (*Wood*[1]); Cent. Dict. (*Woodbine*); Oxf. Dict. (*bind*, sb.[3]; *bine*[2]).
uudu-snite, Cp., *a wood-snite* (or snipe), see **acega,** and above *snite.*
weald-weax, see *uuldpaexhsue.*
wealh-basu, see *uuyloc-baso.*
weallan, see *ed-uallę.*
weallę (ed-), see *ed-uallę.*
pearp (sond-ge-), see *in sond-ge-ƿearp.*
uueartae, *a wart*; see *uaertę.*
uuec (Iringis-), see *Iringis-uuec.*
uueder, Cp., *weather*; see *temperiem.*
weel (E. Dial.), see *ed-uallę.*
well (E.), see *ed-uallę.*
uuelle, ƿelle (ed-), see *ed-uallę.*
weoloc, see *uuiolocas*; *uuluc.*
weoloc-basu, see *uuyloc-baso.*
weoloc-read, see *ƿioloc-read.*
weoluc, see *uuluc.*
weorp (sand-ge-), see *in sond-ge-ƿearp.*
ƿeorras, *pieces of hard skin*; see *uarras.*
uuep, *a web*; see *in-uuerpan uuep.*
uuercae (la-), see *laurice.*
uuerpan (in-), see *in-uuerpan.*
-uuica, -ƿicga, *a wig, worm*; see *ęr-uigga.*
uuidu-bindlae, see *uudu-bindlae.*
wielle (ed-), see *ed-uallę.*
uuif (ge-), see *ge-uiif.*
-uuigga, see *ęr-uigga.*
wilk, Prov. E., *a whelk*; see **inuolucrus.**
wiluc, see **inuolucrus.**
uuince (lepe-), see *laepi-uincę.*
windan, see *uoond.*
uuiolocas, uuylocas (whelks, plur. of *weoloc*, a kind of shell-fish, a whelk); see **conolas.**
ƿioloc-read, uuiloc-read, uusluc-reud (=weoloc-read, lit. *whelk-red*), *scarlet, purple*; see **coccus.**
wir, *myrtle*; see **lentiscus.**
uuld-paexhsue (in one MS. *yulpa exhsaey*, for *wuld-waexhsae*=A.S. weald-weax?), XIX. 59, *a nerve, sinew, tendon*=E. *paxwax*; see **cartillago.**
uulluc, see *uuluc.*
vulluch (O.H.G.), see *inuolucrus.*
uuluc (*uulluc*, Cp. & Ef.; *uuluc*, Ep.; *weoluc*, W.; *vulluch* and *uuolloch*, O.H.G.; probably all=*weoluc*=*weoloc*), XLVII. 20; see **inuolucrus.**
ƿodhae (instr. of ƿoþ, eloquence), see **turnodo.**

uuoedende (pt. plur. of wēdan), *the raving ones*; see **bachantes.**
uuolloch (O.H.G.), see *uuluc.*
pond, uuond, see *uoond.*
uuordes in-tinga, *for the sake of a word*; see *uerbi gratia.*
poþ, see *podhae.*
wræcca, wrecca; see *praeccan.*
praeccan, Cp., plur. of wræcca, wrecca (see Bosw. T.), *an exile*; see **extorris.**
wrǣtt-baso, see *uuret-baso.*
uuret-baso (=*wrǣtt-baso*, lit. ornament-brown, from *wrǣtt*, ornament + *baso*, brown, purple), XXII. 19; see **rubeum.**
uusluc-reud, see *pioloc-read.*
wudu-bil, see *uitu-bil.*
wuld-waexhsae, see *uuld-paexhsue.*
uuydu-blindae, see *uudu-bindlae.*
uuylocas, see *uuiolocas.*
uüyloc-baso (=*weoloc-basu, wealh-basu*), XXII. 17, lit. *whelk-brown, crimson, purple*; see **purpura.**
uuyrcta (ledir-), see *ledir-uyrcta.*
wyrd, pyrd, *fate*; see *uyrd.*
uuyrdae, see *pyrde.*
pyrde, Cp.; *uuyrdae*, Ep. and Ef. (plur. of *wyrd*, q.v., fate, destiny, weird), *the Fates, weird sisters*; see **parcę.**
uuyrm-baso (literally worm-purple), XXII. 18, *purple, carmoisin*; see **coccus.**
wyrt (wæl-), see *ual-uyrt.*
uyrcta (ledir-), see *ledir-uyrcta.*
uyrd (=*wyrd*, pyrd, Cp.), XXXV. 165 and XLV. 4, *fate, fortune*; see **fatum, fors,** and above (the plur.) *pyrde.*
uyrhta (ledir-, leđer-), see *ledir-uyrcta.*
uyrt (ual-, pal-), *foreign root, wallwort*; see *ual-uyrt.*

y inserted (by misreading the mark above A. S. words): ge-byraec for ge-braec.
ymaeti (for *smǣti*) **gold** (*smaete gold*, Cp.), XIX. 54, *beaten, refined gold*; see **obrizum.**
ymb-ðriodung, Cp.; ymb-dritung, Ef. (=*ymb-þreodung*; from *ymb*, about, round +*þreodung*, deliberation, from *þreodian*, to deliberate), *deliberation*: see **deliberatio.**
ynce, *an inch*; see **libra.**
ysi-folto (O.H.G.), see *osi-felti.*
yulpa exhsaey, for *wuld-waexhsae*; see *uuld-paexhsue.*

zelt (ge-), O.H.G., *a tent*; see *ge-zelt.*
zussa (O.H.G.), see *tysse.*

CORRIGENDA, ADDENDA, &c.

p. 4 (gloss 29), the third *e* in conferentes should be *ę*.
p. 11ª (gloss 17), for atrumque, it is possible to read *ce*trumque.
p. 13ᵇ (gloss 43), MS. has really cestare (not ce*r*tare).
p. 13ᵇ (gloss 7 of Ch. XIII.), MS. has really disce*n*nuntur.
p. 43ª lance; cf. Aldh. 24, 12 justa discretionis *lance.*
p. 53ᵇ line 4, for (*theoritisen*), read, see *theoritisen.*
p. 53ᵇ, article *adfecit*, add: cf. Schlutter in *Journ. of Engl. and Germ. Phil.* v. 469.
p. 67ª, after li. 14 add: attoniti, attonitos, attonitus, see *adtonitis.*
p. 69ª, article *baratrum*, add: see Schlutter in *Journ. of Engl. and Germ. Philol.* v. 469.
p. 70ª, after li. 29 add: bidubium, bidugio, see *runtina.*
p. 71ᵇ l. 27, after cicius add: concionaretur (cont-).
p. 73ª li. 8, after peorras add: paar.
p. 74ª li. 31, for χαρακ: read χαρακ-
p. 75ᵇ li. 2, for perdi read perdi-
p. 88ª li. 8, before *For* insert "=*cox*, huetestan, Cp. C746; Ep.—; *cox*, huetistan, Ef.[2] 354, 37."
p. 88ª, after li. 42 add: cox, see above *cos.*
p. 91ᵇ li. 3, for auguriantur Souter suggests to read *angariantur.*
p. 92ª, article *de entoetromito*, for *deflicto* Souter suggests to read *de afflicto.*
p. 97ᵇ, article *dissimulat*, for "neglegiter [neglegenter]" read, as in text, "neglegit."
p. 101ª, article *editiones*, li. 2 and 3, read "[publ-], propositure [for *propositurae*], XXXV." &c.—li. 10 read "*publicationis* and *propositurae*"; propositur[a]e of the Glossator is quite right, and an alternative to "puplicationis"; cf. *propositio*, πρόθεσις, used of the shewbread; it=*exhibitio.*
p. 110ª li. 4, "commodare" perhaps for *adcommodare.*

p. 111[a] li. 5, after Bosw. T.) add: , Cp. E411.
p. 113[a] li. 22, read: For *briudið*, 3 pers. sing. pres., goes to ruin, comes.
p. 113[a] li. 31, after fatiscebat, insert fatiscente.
p. 117[b] l. 14, after finc insert , a finch.
p. 121[b], article *gurgustium*, li. 6, for ceolor read ceoler.
p. 124[a] li. 7 from foot, read: H O, not HO.
p. 124[a], after li. 21 add the line: hospitium, see *de philoxenia*.
p. 132[a] li. 2, 3, for insolence, mischief, read: "or presumption."
p. 139[b], after lexas insert (q[y] A.S.).
p. 145[a] li. 8, after 414 insert; Corp. Inscr. Lat. VII. 1345.
p. 162[a] (art. *parchredis*) on *prestrigiis* see Souter, in *Sitzungsber. der Wiener Akad.*, Philos. hist. Kl. Bd. 149, p. 6.
p. 167[b], article philocain; cf. Schlutter, in *Journ. of Engl. and Germ. Philol.* v. 470, who points out that *philocain*=φιλοκαλιν (of Goetz' *Corpus G.L.* III. 321, 50), late Greek for φιλοκάλιον, and glossed by *scopa*; and that *scopan* may, therefore= scopam.
p. 180[a], under *r* for *n* add , perhaps, obsoriorum (q.v.) for obso*n*-.
p. 189[a] li. 22, after scurrax, add: scurres.
p. 191[b] li. 3, after Mus. add: MS.
p. 191[b] li. 36, before *and* insert "*c* for *e*."
p. 194[b], article *sitatum* li. 7, for 2119 read 19, and li. 10, for 25 read 25A.
p. 203, article *tenda*, to the references add: Schlutter, in *Journ. of Engl. and Germ. Philol.* v. 468.
p. 208, article *tubolo*, to the references add: Wright-W. 279, 10.

The following remarks and references relate to Chapter VI. (ent. *Breuis exsolutio*) of the Glossary, the lemmata of which have, with one or two exceptions, all been traced to *Gildas* (see above, p. xxxviii), after the whole First or Latin Index had been printed. The references are to Gildas' text in Migne's *Patr. Lat.* Vol. LXIX (P.), and Mommsen's text (M.) in *Monum. German. Histor.* (Chronica Minora, Vol. III.).

1. ne (P. col. 330D, 340B, 341B; M. I. 1; XVII. 6).—2. uiscide (Schlutter, *Journ. of Engl. and Germ. Phil.* v. 466 refers this to Aldhelm 109, 31 Germanitatis *uscidae*; and uiscerade to Aldh. 253 No. 10, 1 viscere terrae). Cf. Corp. Gl. U294 *uscide*, tohlice (toughly); Epin. 28A25 *uscidae*, tholicae (?).—3. eatenus (P. 332C, M. I. p. 27, li. 15). —4. uersus (P. 333B; M. III. 6).—5. boriali (P. 333B; M. III. 7).—6. meliorata (P. 333C; M. III. 13).—7. ambrones (P. 340A; M. XVI. 1, 2).—8. ast (P. 340C; M. XVII. 15).—9. Thiticum (P. 341B; M. XIX. 9 *Tithicam* vallem).

10. crusticis (P. 341B de *curicis*; M. XIX. 8 de *curucis*; in notes *carruchis*.—This word, which means a kind of *skiff*, or boat, seems to be the one excerpted by the Glossator. If so, the interpretation *bucellis* should, perhaps, be read *butellis*, see DuC. butta[3]). If *crustis* (which occurs P. 346B, M. XXIV. 21) were meant, bucellis would be a dimin. of *buca* (*bucca*).

11. catastam (P. 345B; M. XXIII. 2 mittit satellitum canumque prolixiorem *catastam*). Gildas uses the word *catastam* again (P. 390C; M. p. 84 li. 29); "rectius erat, ut ad carcerem vel *catastam* poenalem quam ad sacerdotium traheremini," and here it clearly means *a scaffold*, just as in the authors quoted by Lewis and Short, and elsewhere. But this interpretation is unsuitable to the first quotation, in regard to which Hugh Williams points out (p. 54), that Beda uses the words *classis prolixior* instead, and that DuC. quotes from a MS. treatise on military tactics "accensis *catastis* lignorum," where *catastis* must mean "*heaps* of *felled* wood," a meaning which would easily afford "the signification of *a raft*, in which sense Gildas employs the word here as a contemptuous expression with *ratibus*." Either of these meanings would suit Gildas' text in the first instance, but here the difficulty is that our Glossator interprets *catastam* by *lupam* (which cannot be the well-known classical *lupa*), in which Schlutter (*Journ. of Engl. and Germ. Philol.* v. 466) sees an A.S. *lūpe*, and from which he derives Engl. *loop*. But as every E. *oo* comes from A.S. *ō*, we require an A.S. **lōp*. The only known exception to this rule is A.S. *rūm*=E. *room*, but here the old sound has been preserved by the *r* preceding, and A.S. *lūs*=E. *louse*. There is also some phonetic difficulty in accepting Schlutter's interpretation (p. 467 ibid.) of *geloed*, *gloed*, *geleod*, which glosses *catastam* in Cp., Ep. and Ef. (see above v. Index, p. 228[a]).

12. albri (P. 347A; M. XXV. 10 apes *alvearii*; in notes *alveariis*; *alveario*).—

INCIP IN IOB;

Obelis; uirgis; Asteris; stellis;

Obliquus; obscurus; Tinnulus; sonans;

Ecdemonarius monos; id est duo cuius latera aequalia

Commate; breuis pars; Lagn

Rhomae; pprie lacus; Murenulae; pisces

similes congule maioris sed grossior;

Unicalibus; longis;

Rithmus; dulcis sermo sine pedibus;

Inexplebilis; Ut edomoneris gregatio;

Themen; regionalis;

Lumbare; praecinctorium; praecinctio

Tigris; genus leonis uaria colore & uelocitas

Coccinum; read; Lsim

Orionae; ebirdhring

Ingluuiem; ministh

Pedica; fetor ligaturae; pal

Tympanum; in quo tecta ligno; extenso

Clasto; lapides modici

Tede; faculae de ligno pini de quo pice faciunt;

Adamantes; electos; cassitae; pigmentae;

Aruina; pinguitudo; lb;

Hieromantiae; diuinatio demortuis infernis

Lacertos; pars bracchii;

Carmina in nocte; laudem in tribulatione;

Fabulae; poetarum & gigantes tres sufferentes

terrae sub aquis;

Obsequium; cente; ministrante;

Gurgitum; modica congregatio aquae pluuiae;

Obrizum; ymaeti gold

Concentum; contum; Moles; molendinum;

Plumarii; mirum; iuniper arbor;

Castillago; uuldpaeschisue; t grost;

Lagunculas; lagina domin; cibos;

Sedes; sadlbas; uuisbordum; bonocordo;

Anallecta; connmalibus; fircl;

Apostata; discessus a fide;

Sternutatio; nor; INCIP IN TOBIA;

MS. BIBL. LUGD. BAT. (Voss. Q°. Lat. N°. 69), fol. 26, cum parte fol. 27.

13. for (forte, by chance, P. 347A; M. XXV. 12; or more likely) *sors*, P. 349A; M. XXVII. 23.—14. Dum (leaenae *Damnoniae*...catulus, P. 349A; M. XXVIII. 28; other readings *Damnone*, *Dannoniae*, *Domnanie*).—15. Perigamini (?).—16. leonine (P. 350A; M. XXX. 3 catule *leonine*).—17. lanio (P. 351A; M. XXXII. 5 lanio fulve; laniobibus, P. 342A; M. XIX. 21).—18. Nemphe (P. 351B; M. XXXII. 9 hebetudine nympharum).—19. Modoli (P. 352C; M. XXXIV. 19 pingues tauri *moduli* tui; P. 378D; M. LXXXIV. 8 *moduli* tui).—20. Molosi (P. 353A; M. XXXIV. 7 more *molossi* aegri).—21. conueniens (P. 357C; M. XLII. 24 principes...*conveniens*; P. 369A; M. LXVI. 6 *convenientes*).—22. placoris (P. 358A; M. XLII. 1 *placoris* vicissitudinem).—23. raucos (P. 368C; M. LXVI. 23 taurorum more *raucos*).—24. intentos (P. 368C; M. LXVI. 23 strenuos et *intentos*; P. 372A; M. LXXI. 21 *intenti*).—25. defetimur (P. 370A; M. LXIX. 19 nos *diffitemur*).—26. perossus (P. 370B; M. LXIX. 24 quis *perosus* est; from Psa. xxv. 5).—27. panguitur (P. 371C; M. LXXI. 9 *pangitur*).—28. clustello (P. 372A; M. LXXI. 23 penurii *clustello*).—29. ollita (? cf. P. 332B *inolitorum* scelerum funem).—30. quoad (?).—31. inequiperabilis (P. 369C; M. LXVII. 2 *inaequiparabilis* pulchritudo).

The following remarks and references relate to Chapter XL., the lemmata of which I have likewise traced, with a few exceptions, to *Gildas* (see above). Here the references are to Mommsen's pages.

1. Uiscide (?); ineluctabile (*P. L.* vol. LXIX, col. 332b; M. p. 27, li. 3).—2. fatere (P. 332c dixisse pedi, Speculare; et manui, *Fatere*; M. p. 25, 6 d. p. sp. et m. *fare*; in note *fatere*).—3. deuotatum (P. 332c; M. 27, 16 and in note *deuotaturi* magi *de. uoturi* populum).—4. pangebantur (P. 334B; M. 28, 15).—5. alternandis (P. 334B; M. 28, 17 *alternandis* animalium pastibus).—6. palantibus (P. 334C; M. 28, 20 undis veluti glareas *pellentibus*, and in note one MS. *pallantibus*, another *palantibus* forte *perluentibus*).—7. crinicul (P. 357A; M. 51, 4 scelerum...*criniculis*).—8. ad infirmationem (?).—9. inperagrata (P. 353B; M. 46, 17 amoena quaeque *inperagrata*).—10. cicima (?).—11. malua (P. 365A; M. 59, 3 *malva* in aestu, from Job 27, 14).—12. fulmentatur (P. 371C; M. 66, 9 pangitur ac *fulcimentatur*).—13. Bachal (P. 372A; M. 66, 20 *Baal*).—14. reis (?).—15. momentaneas (P. 372D; M. 67, 8 *momentaneas* mortes).—16. ollitani (cf. P. 332B; M. 27, 5 *inolitorum* scelerum? or perhaps *veterani*, P. 389D; M. 83, 35, and in note *verterani*).—17. insigniri (?).—18. thiarati (P. 332C; M. 27, 16 *tiarati* magi).—19. conpage (P. 334B; M. 28, 15 in edito forti *compage*).—20. pallantibus (see above No. 6).—21. liniamentis (P. 335A; M. 29, 11 *liniamentis* adhuc deformibus).—22. rigentia (P. 335B; M. 29, 12 moenia...*rigentia*).

CAMBRIDGE: PRINTED BY JOHN CLAY, M.A. AT THE UNIVERSITY PRESS.

For EU product safety concerns, contact us at Calle de José Abascal, 56–1°, 28003 Madrid, Spain or eugpsr@cambridge.org.

www.ingramcontent.com/pod-product-compliance
Ingram Content Group UK Ltd.
Pitfield, Milton Keynes, MK11 3LW, UK
UKHW010348140625
459647UK00010B/919

* 9 7 8 1 1 0 8 0 2 9 0 9 4 *